HOW TO LOSE A KINGDOM IN 400 YEARS

Books by Michael Whitworth

The Epic of God

The Derision of Heaven

Living & Longing for the Lord

Esau's Doom

Bethlehem Road

The Pouting Preacher

The Son's Supremacy

Splinters of the Cross

Life in the Shadow of Death

HOW TO LOSE A KINGDOM IN 400 YEARS

A GUIDE TO 1-2 KINGS

MICHAEL WHITWORTH

START2FINISH

ISBN 978-1-941972-03-8 (softcover)
ISBN 978-1-941972-08-3 (hardcover)
ISBN 978-1-941972-04-5 (ebook)

Library of Congress Control Number 2014920894

Published by Start2Finish
Bend, Oregon 97702
start2finish.org

Printed in the United States of America

Cover Design by Evangela

For my son
2013–2015

"*Unless you change and become like little children,
you will never enter the kingdom of heaven.*"

MATTHEW 18:3 NIV

CONTENTS

FOREWORD

I have known Michael Whitworth since he was a teenager and visited the Christian Chapel congregation in Hatley, Mississippi, with his father, Daniel, nearly twenty years ago. I was preaching at Christian Chapel at the time and was immediately struck with his poise when he led a public prayer that night. Our friendship has only grown over the years. We have worked in at least three different future minister training camps together.

As I began to read his manuscript, my mind went back to the summer of 2003 and the Future Preachers Training Camp at the Pennington Bend church of Christ in Nashville, Tennessee. I was a staff member at the camp, and Michael was a counselor. I had studied 1–2 Kings in a graduate course with Dr. Rodney Cloud in the Fall 2002 and was so struck by their power and relevance, that I decided we would use them as the basis of our sermons for the camp. The movie *How to Lose a Guy in 10 Days* had been released earlier that year, and we used it as a springboard for our study of the wonderful Books of Kings. Every boy at the camp prepared a sermon based on a portion of these books. I am excited to see the work Michael has done to bring these intriguing and applicable books to life. They are just as relevant for sermons and classes today as they were in A.D. 2003 or A.D. 33.

Michael has had a gift for communicating as long as I have known him. I first witnessed it in his preaching and then later in his writing. He has a passion for God and his Word and an understanding of how to use language to relay meaning, promote thinking, and enliven the emotions. He recognizes the importance of context as we interpret Scripture, and he puts great effort into understanding the historical, literary, and biblical setting of the books of which he writes. He also has a gift for bringing the stories to life and applying them to our lives. I have benefited from several of his books and currently use one of his books in a course I teach at Freed-Hardeman University. I look forward to using this present work in years to come, and I am confident it will be a blessing and asset to all who read it.

As you read this work, may it become a window through time into the tumultuous and history-changing events in ancient Israel. My greatest desire, however, is that you will bring what you have learned back to the present and live it out. It does not matter if we learn how Israel lost a kingdom in four hundred years if it does not compel us to learn from their mistakes and live our lives committed to the eternal kingdom of our Lord, Savior, and King—Jesus Christ.

— Dr. W. Kirk Brothers
Freed-Hardeman University

INTRODUCTION

n 2003, Paramount Pictures released the romantic comedy *How to Lose a Guy in 10 Days*, starring Kate Hudson and Matthew McConaughey. In the film, a writer (Hudson) for a national women's magazine begins a relationship "undercover," but intentionally attempts to hijack it by committing typical relationship faux pas. McConaughey, meanwhile, plays a New York playboy seemingly incapable of nurturing a long-term relationship. He begins dating Hudson on a dare from two female coworkers.

Of course, the guy and girl fall in love in the end, and everyone lives happily ever after. But with the girl driving the guy crazy so that he will break up with her, and the guy struggling to ditch his commitment-phobe reputation, the film prompts reflection of the myriad ways in which people sabotage their most meaningful relationships. It reminded me that, as a teenager/young adult, I had exhibited a hysterically low dating IQ.

In fact, if you're reading this book and you and I ever went out on a date, I am sooooo sorry...

On the other hand, the film also led me to think of how Christians often sabotage their relationship with the Lord. I'm not saying we scare God away with roses on the first date or by calling too soon, but Scripture is replete with examples of how our foolish decisions destroy intimate fellowship with our Father. As a written history of God's covenant people, the Old Testament is particularly saturated with such stories. Paul wrote that "For whatever was written in former days was written for our instruction" (Rom 15:4).

The history of Israel, from the beginning of Solomon's reign to the destruction of Jerusalem and the Babylonian Exile, is preserved in 1–2 Kings. More than just a dry history book, the narrator takes great pains to educate his readers as to why covenant Israel went from a revered international superpower under Solomon to a laughingstock on the world stage a mere four centuries later. Kings gives us insight into how you lose a kingdom in four hundred years.

Since Americans are fast approaching the four hundredth anniversary of the Pilgrims landing at Plymouth, it might do us a boatload of good to take Kings seriously. Is the American dream becoming a nightmare? Is our democratic experiment about to fail? When scholars one day write the definitive history of America from beginning to end—the good, the bad, and the ugly—what will they say? What moral lessons will there be for future generations to learn, lest they repeat the same mistakes?

Before we dive into the text of Kings, we would do well to notice three themes that feature prominently in its pages.

First, though the books are named *Kings*, it's the prophets that occupy center stage. For every Solomon and Ahab and Hezekiah, there is an Ahijah, Elijah, and Isaiah. The cycle of 1) God speaking through his prophets and 2) the dramatic (often unlikely) fulfillment of that word becomes a familiar refrain. For every age, Kings is a powerful reminder that God intends for his Word to be taken seriously—"For as the rain and the snow come down from heaven and do not return there but water the earth, making it bring forth and sprout, giving seed to the sower and bread to the eater, so shall my word be that goes out from my mouth; it shall not return to me empty, but it shall accomplish that which I purpose, and shall succeed in the thing for which I sent it" (Isa 55:10–11).

That the narrator is as interested in Israel's prophets as he is her kings should give us pause. In his commentary, Olley offers this excellent insight: "The book may be called Kings, but throughout prophets often take the lead. That in itself may challenge our own perceptions as to who are the 'history makers'. Is it those with political power, commonly associated with military and economic might, or people who are open to the word of God and understand his purposes?"[1]

Second, from the early days of Solomon's reign, Israel wrestled with the seductive influence of false gods and illicit worship locales. Whether it was the high places around Jerusalem, or the alternative worship sites established at Dan and Bethel by Jeroboam, or the introduction of Baal worship by Ahab, failure to eliminate these illegitimate, idolatrous shrines often brought religious reforms to a screeching halt. Christians still worship one God, and though the *place* of

---

1. John W. Olley, *The Message of Kings* (Downers Grove, IL: InterVarsity Press, 2011), 43.

worship no longer matters in the age of Christ (John 4:21; Acts 17:21), *how* we worship remains important.

Finally, God's grace is never so amazing than when it is immediately juxtaposed with his fierce wrath. There is an uncomfortable fierceness and gravity to God's righteous indignation in Kings. Nations experience plague, war, and famine. Because of God's sin-triggered wrath, people are struck with physical ailments and their families wiped out in bloodshed. But lest we consider God to be little more than a cosmic traffic cop with a bad attitude, we must consider the multitude of times he spared his people from disaster because of his love for them. God is righteous, so he must punish sin, but he is also gracious, and his four-hundred-year forbearance is beyond our ability to fathom, much less emulate. Indeed, in Kings, "The possibility of repentance is held out virtually to the end."[2]

When once-vibrant churches close their doors forever, it's natural to ask, "What went wrong?" When once-passionate marriages end tragically in divorce, it's natural to ask, "What went wrong?" When once devout Christ-followers go the way of Judas, Demas, and Diotrephes, it's natural to ask, "What went wrong?" Kings was written to Jews exiled in Babylon to answer a lingering question: "What went wrong?" Why had the glory of Israel departed? Why was David's dynasty no more? Why had the lamp been extinguished? How had Israel gone from power and prestige to despair and disgrace in four hundred years?

As you read the stories of Kings, you'll come to love and hate the narrator. He ushers you to heights of glory and peaks of hope—only to expose that same glory as a façade—and then he proceeds to take that hope and shove it off onto the jagged rocks below. As I read and meditated on Kings, I found myself demoralized by Israel's unfaithfulness, thrilled by her reforms, and then broken-hearted when I realized any hope that Israel would finally "turn things around" would never materialize. It wasn't until the end of this project that I realized that roller coaster of despair, hope, and broken-heartedness was familiar. Every sports fan knows what I'm talking about:

The team's big slugger comes to the plate with two outs, bottom of the ninth in Game 7, down by two, and runners at the corners. But instead of a walk-off home run, fireworks, being mobbed by teammates at home plate, and an elated post-game interview on ESPN, he grounds out with a slow roller to first.

Down by four, the quarterback drives the offense down the field for a go-ahead touchdown. In front of the home crowd, your team is about to pull off

---

2. McConville, "Kings, Books of," *DOTHB* 630.

an impossible upset. With 0:00 on the clock, the quarterback sidearms a pass to a receiver in the end zone, and the fans go ecstatic. But instead of a Gatorade shower and jubilation in the locker room, the home team will go to the showers despondent. Flag on the play. Holding on the offense. The touchdown is waved off, and the game is over.

The nagging frustration of mistakes and poor play—

The adrenaline-fueled elation of hopes resurrected, of pulling off the impossible—

The despair and finality of defeat snatched from the jaws of victory—

These are the emotions of anyone brave enough to read Kings.

In some ways, reading Kings is like glancing through a playbook on how to take something wonderful and ruin it, on how to lose a kingdom in four hundred years. But in other ways, Kings is about relationships. Instead of "4 Tips for Deeper Intimacy" or "21 Ways to Say 'I Love You,'" however, Kings is about God's relationship with his people—three thousand years ago and now. A few cultural details in the text will seem very foreign to us, but I think you will also be struck by how modern some of these stories really are.

Kings illustrates how God desperately desires our success, yet jealously warns that such success comes only on his terms, not ours. Kings gives hope to God's people—whether in exile in Babylon or in America—that ordinary people and anonymous prophets are the real "movers and shakers" of the world. Kings cries out like a herald with the message that if God's people worship him and serve him alone, he will make them prosperous and give them every spiritual success.

More importantly, Kings is a somber warning that God means what he says. His Word will not return to him void; rather, it stands forever. Like historical Israel, the church might ascend the mountaintop of spiritual greatness, but we will not remain there long if we do not learn from Israel's failures. Judgment will certainly come on all the disobedient, but it begins with "the household of God; and if it begins with us, what will be the outcome for those who do not obey the gospel of God?" (1 Pet 4:17).

This subject should be one of supreme interest to all of us. Failure to heed history's cautionary tales resigns us to yesteryear's fate. Whether you are a prophet, priest, shepherd, king, or commoner among God's people, I pray we will consider Israel's foolish sins and repent of, not repeat, them.

How do you lose a kingdom in four hundred years? You start by...

KINGS Q&A

n a recent interview with myself, I asked a few questions about this guide to
Kings—once one book, now two. I hope the answers orient you both to 1–2
Kings and to this guide.

Q: Who wrote 1–2 Kings?

A: The text doesn't say, so we can't be sure. The Talmud claimed, "Jeremiah
wrote the book that is called by his name, the book of Kings, and and Lamentations."[1] Such a claim isn't implausible; there is, in fact, a good deal of
overlap between the latter chapters of 2 Kings and portions of Jeremiah (cf.
2 Kgs 24:18–25:30; Jer 52).[2] Archer reasonably argued that the only way
to account for Jeremiah's conspicuous absence from the pages of 2 Kings
is that he was the author and humbly chose not to mention himself.[3] But
the prophet died in Egypt (Jer 43:1–8) and would not have been alive for
the events of 2 Kings 25:27–30, so Jeremiah could not have been the sole
author of the book. Plus, portions of 2 Kings 18–20 are repeated nearly
verbatim in Isaiah 36–39, suggesting Isaiah authored parts of the book.
In his own work, the Chronicler refers to the scrolls of several different
prophets (1 Chr 29:29; 2 Chr 9:29; 12:15; 20:34; 26:22; 32:32) that might
have together made up what we now know as 1–2 Kings. Perhaps an editor

---

1. *Baba Bathra* 15a.

2. However, though these passages are quite similar, verbal differences do exist (R. K.
Harrison, *Introduction to the Old Testament* [Grand Rapids: Eerdmans, 1969], 720).

3. Gleason L. Archer, Jr., *A Survey of Old Testament Introduction*, rev. ed. (Chicago: Moody,
1974), 289.

came along in the latter years of the Exile and compiled Kings into its final form. If you want to get technical, God authored Kings because his Spirit inspired its composition (2 Pet 1:21).

Q: When was Kings compiled?

A: Likely during the latter years of Israel's Exile in Babylon (c. 560–536). Kings opens with Solomon's accession in 970 and ends with Jehoiachin's release about 560 after a thirty-seven-year incarceration. The recurring phrase "to this day" may indicate that much of the book was written before the Exile.[4] But its final form cannot be dated any earlier than Jehoiachin's release. As a side note, about half-way through this project, I got tired of typing "B.C." all the time. So it will help to know that all years in the book are B.C. unless otherwise noted.

Q: What can you tell us about the sources used to compile Kings?

A: There seem to be four main sources used by the author of Kings to compile his work, though he mentions only three explicitly. The first is called "the Book of the Acts of Solomon" (1 Kgs 11:41). The second is "the Book of the Chronicles of the Kings of Israel" and is cited some seventeen times (e.g., 1 Kgs 14:19). Harrison explains that "Book of the Chronicles" was a technical term in ancient times "for official records of significant political happenings that were kept for safety in the state archives."[5] The third source explicitly cited is "the Book of the Chronicles of the Kings of Judah," mentioned about fifteen times (e.g., 1 Kgs 14:29). A fourth source, Isaiah 36–39, is of course the origin for some of the material in 2 Kings 18–20.[6]

Q: Has Kings always been a two-volume work?

A: No. It was originally one book and wasn't divided until the Old Testament was translated into Greek, what became known as the Septuagint (LXX). The books of Samuel and Chronicles were also split in two at that time. It wasn't until A.D. 1517 that Kings was divided into two books in a Hebrew

---

4. Ibid. cf. 1 Kings 8:8, 61; 9:13, 21; 10:12; 12:19; 2 Kings 2:22; 8:22; 10:27; 14:7; 16:6; 17:34, 41.

5. Harrison, *Introduction*, 726.

6. Archer, *Survey*, 288–89. For more on sources, see Ball, "Kings, Books of," *ISBE* 3:30–33.

version of the Old Testament. Upon inspection, the division of Kings is rather arbitrary, occurring right in the middle of Ahaziah's reign.

Q: Why was Kings written?
A: I explained that in the Introduction.

Q: So I should read the Introduction if I haven't already?
A: Yes.

Q: You really want me to read the Introduction, don't you?
A: Yes.

Q: What will happen if I don't?
A: God will strike your goldfish with a devastating disease.

Q: Seriously?
A: No.

Q: Are you always like this?
A: Only if the Dallas Cowboys haven't won the Super Bowl in a *really* long time.

Q: What advice do you have for reading Kings?
A: First, know that Kings is as much about prophets as it is monarchs. The title *Kings* is a bit misleading. In actuality, it is written from the perspective of the *prophets*: Nathan, Ahijah, Jehu, Micaiah, Isaiah, Huldah, Elijah, and Elisha are all mentioned, as are several anonymous prophets. Second, don't expect every narrative to have a clear-cut resolution; sometimes the stories just end abruptly (e.g., 2 Kgs 3). Finally, don't lose sight of Kings' ultimate question: "Who is on the Lord's side?" Yahweh demanded—and demands still!—total loyalty from his people. The obedient were blessed, while the rebellious suffered under God's curse.

Q: Is there a book in the Old Testament that has any close ties to Kings?
A: Actually, yes. The books of Joshua, Judges, Ruth, Samuel, and Kings are known in scholarly circles as the Deuteronomistic Histories. Essentially, the theology represented in those books is originally found in Deuterono-

my; put another way, those books must be read through the lens of Deuter-onomy. Scholars claim other things about Deuteronomy that I don't agree with, but it's certainly true that passages and themes in Deuteronomy have a lot of bearing on Kings (e.g., David's farewell address to Solomon, Solomon's prayer at the Temple's dedication), and we will note those connections as we go along.

Q: What can you tell us about Kings' chronological problems?

A: Anyone who has ever attempted to add up the years of each king's reign has eventually discovered that the math doesn't work out. The chronology of Kings was a hopelessly tangled knot until Edwin Thiele's *Mysterious Numbers of the Hebrew Kings*. Simply put, Thiele explained the numbers didn't add up unless one took into account certain details like co-regencies (two kings reigning at the same time) and accession year versus non-accession year reckoning (a king's first year counted as "year 1" versus "year 0"). Thiele's theories didn't solve every chronological issue, but they did shed light on many of them.[7] This all may seem hopelessly confusing right now, but in this guide, we will note chronological issues and their solutions as they arise. At the end of this book, you can find charts for the kings of Israel and Judah.

Q: What would be the best way to use this guide?

A: If you ever needed something to elevate a table lamp...

Q: Seriously?

A: Well, if you were desperate, I guess so. My mom tried to do that with some of my books once. But I think the answer you are looking for is this: I recommend a four-pass system of reading Scripture. Let's take 1 Kings 18 as an example. It always helps to read the broader context of a passage first; 1 Kings 17–19 comprises the early years of Elijah's ministry. If you wanted to study the showdown at Carmel, then I would recommend you read 1.) 1 Kings 17–19, 2.) 1 Kings 18, 3.) that passage's section in this guide, and 4.) 1 Kings 18 again. Reading through the passage several times, plus studying it in this guide, will hopefully cement it in your mind.

---

7. See also Leslie McFall, "Has the Chronology of the Hebrew Kings Been Finally Settled?" *Themelios* 17/1 (1991): 6–11.

Q: Similar to how driving the same road time after time helps familiarize us with the route?

A: Exactly!

Q: What can you tell us about how this guide came together?

A: As always, I wrestled with what to include versus omit. Some scholarly debates are much ado about nothing, and sharing everything a commentator said can be more of a hindrance than a help. I wanted the reader to understand God's Word, so I tried to anticipate and answer common questions that arise from the text. Don't expect me to deal with every issue, because that would exhaust us all. Besides, I don't expect you always to agree with my conclusions. I do, however, expect you to study and reflect on your own; then, and only then, make an informed decision. I want this guide to resemble a friendly conversation about Kings. Pretend you and I are just sitting in a coffee shop somewhere, sipping a cup of joe, and talking about Kings. Each chapter ends with Talking Points, points of application I hope will provide useful material for lessons or sermons and spark positive discussion in a class or small-group setting. In the end, I want everyone who reads this guide to have a better grasp on what Kings is saying, and consequently to be closer to the heart of the King of kings. Ultimately, only the reader can judge for himself whether I have succeeded.

Q: Do you recommend a particular Bible translation?

A: No. This guide primarily uses the English Standard Version (ESV), but it always helps to read the Bible in more than one translation. I definitely recommend a good Study Bible.

Q: Would you like to add anything else before we wrap up?

A: Did you read the Introduction?

Q: Yes.

A: Then the only other thing I would add is an encouragement to meditate on what God has to say in Kings. Again, I hope that the study of Kings draws you closer to the heart of the King of kings.

In 970, Solomon, son of David, ascended his father's throne. During his reign, Israel became an unrivaled international power.

In 586, the nation was exiled in humiliation far away to Babylon.

This is the story of how to lose a kingdom in four hundred years.

1

LOOSE ENDS

The opening narrative of 1 Kings is one I never heard as a child in Sunday school or VBS—or in any sermon, for that matter. It's ripe with all the things we try to keep away from our children: sleazy back-room politics, royal family intrigue, threats of murder and assassination, and a national beauty pageant, the winner of which gets to sleep in the old king's bed. Most shocking of all? That last sentence had to do with a story in Holy Scripture, not an episode of *Game of Thrones*.

This story depicts David in a pathetic state. Winters in Israel turned stone palaces into chilly refrigerators, and the king's once-vigorous, battle-tested body could no longer keep him warm. But there seems to have been a second motive for finding a young virgin to keep David warm. In the thinking of the day, if a king was no longer sexually virile, he wasn't fit to serve. And lest you recoil at this primitive barbarity, I'd remind you Western civilization hasn't evolved that much.[1]

When Adonijah learned that the young virgin, Abishag, had failed to arouse his father sexually, he set about seizing the kingdom himself, thinking it was his right as David's oldest living son. What follows is a sordid tale of political intrigue that has a happy ending: Solomon is made king, rather than the scheming Adonijah. Solomon went on to lead Israel into her glory years as a nation, and we are left to wonder what would have happened had Adonijah's coup been successful.

---

1. Even if it is not a sex scandal, Americans like their leaders fit, energetic, and full of life. Voters are accustomed to images of Jimmy Carter and Bill Clinton jogging, Ronald Reagan chopping wood, George W. Bush working on his ranch, or Barak Obama shooting basketball (cf. Walter Brueggemann, *1 & 2 Kings* [Macon, GA: Smyth & Helwys, 2000], 40–41).

Modern readers will understandably be suspicious of the events of these opening chapters. On the one hand, Solomon appears pious and moral in 1 Kings 1. On the other hand, how are we to interpret the events of 1 Kings 2 as anything more than a cold-blooded political hatchet job?

Admittedly, these chapters have the feel of a *Godfather* film. I'd forgive you if, halfway through, you thought this was a story about the house of Corleone and not the house of David—a man whom Scripture remembers as being after God's own heart. However, we must bear in mind that the divine narrator approvingly relates these events to establish Solomon as the wise and legitimate heir to David's throne. Enemies of God and his people have always existed, and they must be eliminated judiciously (and violently, if necessary) if God's people are to have rest—something David's predecessors (e.g., Moses, Joshua, Samuel) knew full well. There were loose ends to tie up.

For the Jews living in Exile, this story affirmed that Israel's throne, and even Israel herself, fell under the sovereign rule of God. He would neutralize her enemies, establish her in regal splendor, and give her every success—if she would only trust and obey.

For Christians, the opening narrative of Kings, for all its bloody politics, points the way to the Lord Jesus Christ, the King of kings, whom God has established on his throne to rule in majesty and power forever; a Chosen Son under whose feet God has sworn to place all his enemies, and "the last enemy to be destroyed is death" (1 Cor 15:26).

Long live the King!

1 KINGS 1:1–4

Veteran Bible readers aren't accustomed to a book opening with someone's death. More common is for books to begin with birth (e.g., Exodus, 1 Samuel) or ascendancy (Joshua, 2 Samuel). Death belongs at the end (Genesis, Deuteronomy). But Kings opens with David on his deathbed. Sadly, the scene carries over from the end of 2 Samuel, where the former giant-slayer had appeared more like "an exhausted and impotent lame duck."[2] There's no question that David's sins (2 Sam 11) had cost him both credibility and control in the kingdom, not to mention his own household (2 Sam 12:11). The courageous warrior now appears cowardly and decrepit on his deathbed.

---

2. Peter J. Leithart, *1 & 2 Kings* (Grand Rapids: Brazos, 2006), 29.

David was about seventy years old (cf. 2 Sam 5:4; 1 Kgs 2:11), which was remarkable in an age when most people, even royalty, did not live beyond their forties.[3] But he was now unable to keep warm[4] in his bed. The damp cold of Jerusalem winters would have made pneumonia a real concern. To "keep his body temperature up,"[5] David's aides led a nation-wide search[6] and brought him a young and very attractive woman. The king's advanced age is underscored by the detail that David "had no sexual relations with her" (v. 4 NIV).

That note shouldn't surprise us, because the aides intended for Abishag to be more than a warm blanket for David. She became in every sense a concubine of the king. For one thing, polygamy (principally among the wealthy and powerful) was an accepted practice at that time. For another, when Adonijah later requested permission to marry Abishag, Solomon interpreted it as an act of treason (2:21–22). Finally, though David's aides at first claim that Abishag will "wait on the king and be in his service," it is their last suggestion that gives their plan away. "Let her lie in your arms" (v. 3) is sexually suggestive (cf. Gen 16:5; 2 Sam 12:3, 8; Mic 7:5).

Bizarre as it may sound to us, the king's sexual impotence was considered politically scandalous in that time.[7] Though he once had no trouble wooing

---

3. Philip J. King and Lawrence E. Stager, *Life in Biblical Israel* (Louisville: Westminster John Knox, 2001), 58; David Noel Freedman, "Kingly Chronologies: Then and Later," *Eretz Israel* 24 (1993): 41–65.

4. "The verb in the imperfect indicates repeated attempts that failed," (Mordechai Cogan, *I Kings* [New York: Doubleday, 2001], 156).

5. "We might take the phrase as a hint of poor circulation, except the antidote to his problem is a 'very beautiful' young virgin. Her presence in the narrative (and in the king's bed) is not simply as a hot water bottle. Her role rather is to arouse the king sexually. Because of the last phrase of v. 4, 'did not know her sexually,' it is probable that 'not get warm' means not to have an erection," (Brueggemann, *1 & 2 Kings*, 12).

6. The village of Shunem was in northern Israel, located southeast of Carmel (cf. Josh 19:18; 1 Sam 28:4; 2 Kgs 4:8). The selection of Abishag from a northern village "may have been a way to maintain strong ties between the Judean monarch and the rival northern tribes," (John Monson, "1 Kings," in *Zondervan Illustrated Bible Backgrounds Commentary*, vol. 3, ed. John H. Walton [Grand Rapids: Zondervan, 2009], 12).

7. "Loss of virility was in many cultures considered to be grounds for bringing in a younger king," (Richard D. Patterson and Hermann J. Austel, "1, 2 Kings," in *The Expositor's Bible Commentary*, rev. ed., vol. 3, eds. Tremper Longman III and David E. Garland [Grand Rapids: Zondervan, 2009], 641; cf. John Gray, *I & II Kings* [Philadelphia: Westminster, 1963], 76).

women, David now had "lost it," and I don't mean mentally. The text makes no mention that David's mind was slipping; in fact, he has a very sensible conversation with Solomon in the next chapter. But for the sole reason that he couldn't "conquer" the beautiful young Abishag in the bedroom, the king was now considered by some to be unfit for rule. Once David's "weakness" became evident, "one senses the vultures around the court, circling for the kill."[8]

1 KINGS 1:5-10

With David no longer buying green bananas, his oldest living son, Adonijah, prepared to seize the throne. On the one hand, it was almost unprecedented for anyone but the oldest surviving son to inherit the throne when the king died. His was a position of birthright and privilege. David's oldest, Amnon, had been assassinated by Absalom, and Absalom (third-oldest) had been killed while attempting a coup. The second-oldest, Chileab, is never mentioned after his birth in 2 Samuel 3:3, so it's safe to assume he had died also, leaving Adonijah next in line. And since there was no other precedent in Israel to dictate the events of this chapter (cf. 1 Sam 20:31; 1 Kgs 2:22), Adonijah may have only been doing what was expected.

"But what kind of man cannot wait for his father to die before seeking power?" asks House,[9] and I agree—what kind of person does such a thing? The narrator may be tipping us off to Adonijah's disturbingly ambitious character by telling us that he "exalted himself." As House puts it, "He acts like a king before being made king."[10] In what was a very ego-maniacal move, Adonijah secured an entourage (v. 5; cf. 1 Sam 8:11), even though his father had never had much use for chariots (cf. 2 Sam 8:4). And if any of this seems too archaic to be relevant, bear in mind that three thousand years later, a limo, motorcade, and entourage still scream, "I'm important!" to onlookers. St. John of the Cross once said, "God hates to see men ready to accept dignities, even when it is His will that they should accept them, but it is not His will that they should do so eagerly and

8. Brueggemann, 1 & 2 Kings, 12.

9. Paul R. House, 1, 2 Kings (Nashville: Broadman, 1995), 88.

10. Ibid. "His claim 'I will be king' (v. 5) contains an emphatic pronoun in Hebrew. (Such emphasis is often lost in English because our language requires pronouns where Hebrew does not. Its force here is 'I, and no one else, shall be king.')," (Jerome T. Walsh, 1 Kings [Collegeville, MN: Liturgical Press, 1996], 7).

promptly." In every way, Adonijah comes across as a spoiled brat who was all too eager to seize power that wasn't rightfully his.

As the picture of Adonijah is developed in these verses, we can see his older brother, Absalom, reflected in this fourth son of David.[11]

- Like Absalom, Adonijah got "himself chariots and horsemen, and fifty men to run before him" (v. 5; cf. 2 Sam 15:1).

- Like Absalom, Adonijah was handsome[12] (v. 6; cf. 2 Sam 14:25).

- Like Absalom and Amnon (2 Sam 18:5; 13:21), sadly, Adonijah enjoyed a little too much of his father's favor—"[David] had never crossed him at any time" (v. 6 NASU).

Not only did Adonijah enjoy handsome features and a royal entourage, but he also had a lot of powerful supporters on his side. There was Joab, David's nephew (1 Chr 2:16) and chairman of the Joint Chiefs of Staff (2 Sam 8:16; 19:13). "Joab is decisive, powerful, and politically dangerous."[13] There was also Abiathar, the co-high priest who had been with David since the massacre at Nob (1 Sam 22:20). He had also been entrusted with possession of the ephod which David used to discern the Lord's will (1 Sam 23:6–12; 30:7–8). With a military leader and a religious leader on his side, Adonijah posed a formidable threat.

Based on every conceivable metric, Adonijah was a shoo-in for the throne. Adonijah had it all—at least from a worldly perspective. And therein lies the crucial message of Kings. What the world often considers to be so critical to seizing and maintaining power—good looks, money, fame, charisma, power—mean not a thing to God. The ideal king in the eyes of Yahweh is one whose heart seeks first the kingdom of God. And the Lord not only looks at the heart of a man; his

---

11. "The subtle invocation of Absalom's ghost constrains us to see Adonijah's moves in the worst possible light," (Richard D. Nelson, *First and Second Kings* [Louisville: John Knox, 1987], 19). There are also some allusions here to Saul (cf. 1 Sam 9:2; 10:23–24) and Eliab (1 Sam 16:6–7). "All these royal or potentially royal persons were physically impressive and either disastrous or rejected. Adonijah, our writer implies, belongs to that class," (Dale Ralph Davis, *1 Kings* [Ross-shire, Scotland: Christian Focus, 2002], 17).

12. "The Israelites praised physical beauty not so much out of a fleshly orientation as for the fact that it was taken as a token of Yahweh's spirit, driving its possessor to uncommon deeds, whether of good or of evil," (Simon J. DeVries, *1 Kings*, 2nd ed. [Nashville: Nelson, 2003], 13).

13. House, *1, 2 Kings*, 89.

Spirit also rests mightily on his anointed ones as well so that not even unbeatable giants can stand against them. When God chooses people, he protects them, equips them, and exalts them in due time (1 Pet 5:6).

So it was that Adonijah, despite his perfect pedigree and solid résumé, was not Yahweh's chosen to inherit the throne of David. The Lord's primeval preference for the younger over the older—Abel, not Cain; Isaac, not Ishmael; Jacob, not Esau; Perez, not Zerah; Joseph, not his brothers—shows itself again. Yahweh had sworn to establish David's throne forever (2 Sam 7:13–14); thus it was Yahweh's prerogative to handpick David's successor.

As had Absalom (2 Sam 15:7–12), Adonijah vainly attempted to forge his coalition with a kick-off barbecue at a place called the "Serpent's Stone" or "Sliding Stone,"[14] a recognizable landmark (a rockslide?) in the narrator's time near En-rogel, which was a spring located southeast of Jerusalem where the Hinnom and Kidron valleys converge, and just a half-mile from David's palace. En-rogel "was somewhat secluded and was thus ideally suited for Adonijah's clandestine gathering,"[15] (cf. 2 Sam 17:17). To this spot Adonijah's powerful allies were invited, along with all of David's sons and "the royal officials of Judah."

But those *not* on Adonijah's guest list are more conspicuous than those who made it. Zadok had been appointed high priest by Saul after the slaughter at Nob (1 Chr 16:39), and David had retained both Zadok and Abiathar as co-high priests when he became king. Benaiah was the commander of the Cherethites and the Pelethites, the palace guards who functioned as David's Secret Service (2 Sam 8:18; 23:22–23). Nathan the prophet had been David's faithful spiritual counselor, and he was joined in his resistance to Adonijah by all of David's mighty men. In this way, there arose a rift in David's administration.

Also absent was another son of David: Solomon. A family meeting had been called, but like his father (1 Sam 16:11), he had not been invited.

1 KINGS 1:11-27

As he witnessed Adonijah's actions unfold, Nathan the prophet was understandably concerned. He felt a close, personal connection to Solomon (2 Sam 12:24–25). So Nathan advised Bathsheba to act quickly, or her life and Solo-

---

14. Patterson, "1, 2 Kings," 644.

15. Ibid., 643.

mon's would both be in extreme jeopardy if Adonijah were to establish himself as David's successor[16] (cf. Judg 9:5; 1 Kgs 15:29; 2 Kgs 10:6–14; 11:1).

A lot of scholarly ink has been spilled over whether David had indeed made a prior promise to make Solomon his successor. The reality, some commentators claim, is that Bathsheba and Nathan only make it *seem* as if David had sworn such an oath, playing on the king's senility. "As we read the next scenes in David's bedchamber, we have to make up our own minds whether Nathan and Bathsheba are reminding the king of a promise once made concerning Solomon, or whether they are 'pulling a fast one' over an old man with neither the wit to spot their strategy nor the energy to do anything about it."[17]

For those who believe this prior oath to be pure fiction, the sole argument seems to be that the narrator of 2 Samuel nowhere records such a promise—"No other record of the oath is found in the biblical narrative, and this is most remarkable in view of its importance."[18] That's it; that's the only reason for doubting the veracity of Bathsheba's claim. From this point, some scholars' interpretation descends into a nasty quagmire of anti-Solomon rhetoric, depicting him as a dirty schemer who plays last-minute, back-room, political hard-ball and wins the throne with all the integrity of a Chicago politician.

In his book, *The Poetics of Biblical Narrative*, Meir Sternberg observes how biblical narrators often foment skepticism in the reader when details of an event are first reported by a character in the story (e.g., Gen 50:15–17; Exod 14:12). "With the understandable exception of prophetic messages, it rarely happens that the utterance of a forecast or the occurrence of an event emerges only from a later scene of report. So much so that when the reader finds the natural order subverted, he is entitled to take it as a question mark about the reliability of the report or the reporting character."[19]

---

16. "The omission of Solomon from the 'guest list' was a sure sign that he was marked for death if Adonijah succeeded. The normal practice was for the successful claimant to the throne to execute any unsuccessful rival," (Ibid., 646). For a parallel of the Assyrian king Esarhaddon eliminating his rivals, see Monson, "1 Kings," 13.

17. A. Graeme Auld, *I & II Kings* (Philadelphia: Westminster, 1986), 9.

18. Gwilym H. Jones, *1 and 2 Kings* (Grand Rapids: Eerdmans, 1984), 1:93. Wray Beal counters that the oath's "absence does not require its non-existence," (Lissa M. Wray Beal, *1 & 2 Kings* [Downers Grove, IL: InterVarsity Press, 2014], 80).

19. Meir Sternberg, *The Poetics of Biblical Narrative: Ideological Literature and the Drama of Reading* (Bloomington: Indiana Univ. Press, 1987), 379.

For those who aren't so quick to consider this scene to be a last-minute political coup, they point out that:

- In his promise to establish David's throne forever, God had explicitly said, "When your days are fulfilled and you lie down with your fathers, I will raise up your offspring after you, who *shall* come from your body, and I will establish his kingdom" (2 Sam 7:12; emphasis mine). Based on this, Keil argues that God "did not ensure the establishment of the throne to any one of his existing sons, but to him that would come out of his loins (i.e., to Solomon, who was not yet born)."[20]

- Following the death of their first child, David may have promised Bathsheba that their next child would inherit the throne. While we can't know this for sure, it does seem "to have been the kind of thing that a king would say to his favourite wife."[21]

- Though no place in 2 Samuel contains David's promise, the author of Chronicles claims that God swore to make Solomon the next king (1 Chr 22:9–10, 28:5), and that David appointed Solomon to be his successor (1 Chr 23:1; 29:22).

For what it's worth, I believe David had indeed made such a prior promise, and even if he technically had not, it was God's will that Solomon be king and not Adonijah.[22] David may be sexually impotent, but he's far from senile and forgetful. As already mentioned, his mind is still sharp.

What is more, so far in the story of David, the prophet Nathan has been known as a person of unimpeachable integrity—why would he go along with this last-minute attempt to dupe the king? After all, he had delivered a message to David and Bathsheba when Solomon had been born (2 Sam 12:25), so I think the prophet connected the dots and concluded it was God's will that Solomon be king (cf. 1 Kgs 2:15). And I think the narrator makes it *seem* as if Nathan

20. C. F. Keil and F. Delitzsch, *Biblical Commentary on the Old Testament*, vol. 6 (Grand Rapids: Eerdmans, 1950), 18.

21. J. Robinson, *The First Book of Kings* (Cambridge: Cambridge Univ. Press, 1972), 28.

22. That Solomon is designated as the "ruler" (Hebrew *nagid*) in v. 35 is significant since this term in Samuel–Kings (e.g., 1 Sam 9:16; 10:1; 13:14; 2 Sam 7:8; 1 Kgs 14:7; 2 Kgs 20:5) always referred to one anointed by Yahweh to lead his people (Aitken, "נָגִיד," *NIDOTTE* 3:20).

is calling the shots in order to "stress the divine choice of Solomon"—in other words, the narrator wants the initiative to be taken by a prophet.[23] Nathan will not be the last prophet to play a major role in Israel's history as told in Kings. What is more, remember that Sternberg's exception above was in the case of "prophetic messages." If Nathan has done little more than serve as God's mouthpiece throughout the Davidic narrative, why are we to assume he isn't merely fulfilling that role here? Olley is right: "While Adonijah had key priestly and military support, only for Solomon was a *prophet* involved."[24]

Finally, Adonijah's behavior throughout the entire narrative betrays the fact that he knew Solomon was the hand-picked successor. His use of the chariot and runners, as well as his currying favor by throwing a big barbecue and inviting most everyone except Solomon, smacks of someone who knows he's the dark horse and is desperately over-reaching for legitimacy. In the next chapter, he will concede to Bathsheba that it was God's will that Solomon be king.

When this passage is read with an open mind, it is Adonijah who comes across as the dirty, back-room politician—not Solomon. Indeed, for Solomon truly to be the sleazy opportunist in this story, we must allege that 1 Chronicles 22–23 is not inspired Scripture, but rather the editorial notes of someone conducting a propaganda campaign five centuries after the fact.

Bathsheba agreed with Nathan's plan and approached the king in his bedroom. How awkward it must have been for Bathsheba to entreat the king concerning Solomon while Abishag, Bathsheba's much younger replacement, lay in bed with the king! The queen informed David of Adonijah's deeds, of the feast he was hosting for all his allies and the sons of David, and of Solomon's lack of an invitation. She didn't need to connect many of the dots for David—he knew what Adonijah was up to and that Bathsheba was right when she said, "If you fail to act, the moment you're buried my son Solomon and I are as good as dead" (v. 21 Msg).

According to the plan, Nathan entered the room to confirm all that Bathsheba had said and needled David into taking action. It is not an overstatement to say that this man of God stood in the gap at a pivotal moment in Israel's history and fearlessly ministered God's word to the throne as he had always done.

23. Robinson, *First Book*, 28.

24. Olley, *Message of Kings*, 46; emphasis his.

It was Nathan who had conveyed God's promise to establish David's dynasty forever (2 Sam 7:1–17); it was also Nathan who had confronted the tyrant over his adultery with Bathsheba and the murder of Uriah (2 Sam 12:1–15). Nathan shrewdly knew which buttons needed pushing within David.[25] Notice how the prophet passive-aggressively interrogated the king:

- "Have you said, 'Adonijah shall reign after me, and he shall sit on my throne'?" (v. 24).

- "Has this thing been brought about by my lord the king and you have not told your servants who should sit on the throne of my lord the king after him?" (v. 27).

Brueggemann correctly detects what Nathan is doing: "The questions suggest a reprimand to the king, not a reprimand about what the king ostensibly has done, but a scolding that David allegedly has acted without telling Nathan. The prophet subtly shames the king for acting without his counsel; Nathan's tone is as if the prophet believes David has indeed authorized Adonijah, even though Nathan knows better."[26]

1 KINGS 1:28-53

Nathan's subtle scolding had the intended effect; for the first time in Kings, David is aroused from out of his lethargy and prompted to action. He announced his intent to keep his promise and make Solomon king. There remained only three VIPs in David's administration that had not sided with Adonijah: Zadok the priest, Nathan the prophet, and Benaiah, who was head of David's bodyguards. David instructed these three men to take Solomon to Gihon and anoint him king. "David's shrewdness in assembling such a well-chosen party of supporters contrasts with the picture of a fumbling, senile old man given in the previous verses."[27]

---

25. "His strategy for kindling the wrath of David is to draw him into the narrative account of this *injustice*, forcing the king to make a judgment. The same tactics are used in [2 Sam 12:1–15] with the story of the 'two men in one city,'" (Keith Bodner, "Nathan: Prophet, Politician and Novelist?" *JSOT* 95 [2001]: 53; emphasis his).

26. Brueggemann, *1 & 2 Kings*, 15.

27. Jones, *1 and 2 Kings*, 1:98.

The narrator identifies David's bodyguards as Cherethites and Pelethites (v. 38; cf. 2 Sam 8:18; 15:18; 20:7, 23). It is thought that these two groups shared a common origin. Bizarre as it may seem to us today, it was not uncommon in the ancient Near East for kings to hire foreign mercenaries as palace guards, which "ensured that [the king's] personal security was not dependent on Israelites who could become involved with persons or causes opposed to the king."[28] It is believed that the Cherethites and Pelethites originated somewhere in the Aegean and were closely related to the Philistines.[29]

David may have been in decline, but he was still a shrewd tactician and an expert in political theater. His instructions were carefully orchestrated to ensure that Adonijah's coup was stopped dead in its tracks and the nation's heart did not swing to him as it had to Absalom. The sight of Solomon on David's mule would have had a strong psychological impact on the public, serving as "dramatic and visual evidence that royal authority has been turned over to the rightful heir,"[30] (cf. Esth 6:6–11; Zech 9:9; Matt 21:1–11); Brueggemann likens David lending Solomon his mule to the president allowing his successor use of the presidential limo or to fly on Air Force One. "David knows how to make a king!"[31] Unlike donkeys, which were simple beasts of burden (e.g., 1 Sam 25:42; 2 Sam 16:2; 1 Kgs 13:13), the mule seems to have been a favored animal among the upper echelon of society (cf. 2 Sam 13:29; 18:9),[32] likely because crossbreeding was illegal in Israel (Lev 19:19), making the mule an expensive import.

The place where Solomon was anointed was also special. Solomon was proclaimed king at a conspicuous landmark in Jerusalem. Like En-rogel (where Adonijah had gathered his allies), Gihon was a spring just outside of Jerusalem. Since it was the source of the city's water, Gihon was a perfect place to coronate a new sovereign; the route from the palace to the spring would have been one

---

28. Monson, "1 Kings," 14–15.

29. Ehrlich, "Pelethites," *ABD* 5:219; Cogan, *I Kings*, 162; Greenfield, "Cherethites and Pelethites," *IDB* 1:557.

30. August H. Konkel, *1 & 2 Kings* (Grand Rapids: Zondervan, 2006), 55. "Ancient convention disallowed casual use of royal property. David's provision of his own animal confirms that Solomon's accession to the throne is indeed supported by David and is not a partisan act," (Ziony Zevit, "1 Kings," in *The Jewish Study Bible*, eds. Adele Berlin and Marc Zvi Brettler [Oxford: Oxford Univ. Press, 2004], 673).

31. Brueggemann, *1 & 2 Kings*, 16–17.

32. Cogan, *I Kings*, 161.

of Jerusalem's busiest streets, and the spring itself would have been like a city square, a natural public gathering place.[33]

So great was the celebration over Solomon's anointing that the roar of the approving crowd could be heard about 650 yards south at En-rogel where Adonijah was still dining with his guests. Abiathar's son, Jonathan, enters the scene and explains to Adonijah and his guests what has transpired. For the third time in the narrative, the reader is told what has happened, drawing conspicuous attention to the significance of Solomon's anointing. David had stopped the coup in its tracks; Bathsheba's son was now the bona fide king; Adonijah's dream boat has been torpedoed; all of Adonijah's friends scattered like mice before the cat.

The way in which Solomon was proclaimed king stands in stark contrast to Adonijah's manipulative scheme. Solomon was led out on a humble mule; Adonijah had insisted on a gaudy entourage. Solomon was proclaimed king in front of all the people; Adonijah had thrown a fancy dinner and invited only an elite few. Solomon was anointed with oil, proclaiming him Israel's new messiah and affirming him as Yahweh's choice. There is music and raucous celebration and exceedingly great joy.[34] In a New York minute, Adonijah went from being the front-runner to a traitor and enemy of the state.

So Adonijah did what any persona non grata must do; he fled to the altar of God and begged for mercy by clinging to its horns.[35] When Adonijah gave his word to Solomon that he would not engage in any seditious activities, he was allowed[36] to return home, meaning he was being forced to retire from public life, at least until he returned to Solomon's good graces.

---

33. Robinson further adds, "The source of the city's water supply may have been thought to be the right place for king making since the king was thought to guarantee life and prosperity to the city as water did to the earth," (*First Book*, 31). Even after the royal inauguration ceremony was relocated to the Temple, it seems some sort of purification rite was performed at Gihon (cf. Ps 110:7) in which the king drank holy water from the spring (S. Mowinckel, *He That Cometh*, trans. G. W. Anderson [Oxford: Blackwell, 1956], 63–64).

34. The phrase "the earth was split by their noise" (v. 40) is likely a hyperbolic metaphor meaning, "the very earth reverberat[ed] to the sound" (Msg).

35. "To seek refuge in a sanctuary, protected from summary execution, was widely practiced in the ancient world, so much so that the Romans had to abolish it," (DeVries, *1 Kings*, 19; cf. Tacitus, *Annals* 3.60–63).

36. "The expression, 'Not one of his hairs shall fall from his head' in reference to Adonijah is chilling. [...] It was by the very hairs of his own head (2 Sam 18:9) that Absalom met his death. In several ways, then, this exchange between Solomon and Adonijah is worrisome. The resolu-

A few hundred years prior, the legislation of Exodus 21:12–14 allowed for someone to claim sanctuary on the horns of the altar. The practice of seeking asylum at holy places was not limited to Israel, but was in fact a custom throughout the ancient Near East. "Two monumental stone altars some six feet square, with horns at the corners large enough for one to cling to and thus be immovable" have now been discovered by archaeologists at Dan and Beersheba.[37] The horns of these altars would have been smeared with blood by the priests during sacrifices (cf. Exod 27:2; 30:2; Lev 16:18; Ezek 43:20; Amos 3:14). Adonijah was in effect saying, "You should leave me alone; only Yahweh can judge me."

Yahweh would do exactly that.

1 KINGS 2:1–12

His chosen son properly anointed, David called Solomon to his side to express his last will and testament. It is not by accident that this scene resembles other occasions when a major transfer of leadership took place (e.g., Moses to Joshua, Deut 31:1–8; Joshua to Israel, Josh 23; Samuel to Saul, 1 Sam 12). David's final charge also echoes Jacob's (Gen 48–49) and foreshadows that of Jesus (John 13–17) and Paul (Acts 20:18–35).

In his deathbed charge, David's comments frequently derive from Deuteronomy[38] (cf. 8:6, 10–12). In Deuteronomy 17, the ideal king is devoted to God and his Law, and Kings will go on to evaluate every monarch by this standard. Particularly noteworthy is the command that the king write out by hand a copy of the Law for his personal use (Deut 17:18–19), a task that apparently couldn't be delegated to the king's scribe. Such an obligation would have reminded the king that he was not above the Law (Deut 17:20). Solomon's fidelity to the Law was a concern for David for another reason. Though God had established

---

tion of the story's conflict has not ended the strife between brothers," (Gina Hens-Piazza, *1–2 Kings* [Nashville: Abingdon, 2006], 20–21). "Solomon's response is shrewd. He apparently accedes to Adonijah's request, but in fact he holds back on two important counts: he does not swear an oath, and the amnesty he grants is conditional rather than absolute," (Walsh, *1 Kings*, 32).

37. William G. Dever, "Archaeology and the Question of Sources in Kings," in *The Books of Kings: Sources, Composition, Historiography and Reception*, eds., André Lemaire and Baruch Halpern (Leiden: Brill, 2010), 535; cf. Herzog, "Beersheba," *NEAEHL* 1:171–72; Avraham Biran, *Biblical Dan* (Jerusalem: Israelite Exploration Society, 1994), 202–3.

38. Volkmar Fritz, *1 & 2 Kings*, trans. Anselm Hagedorn (Minneapolis: Fortress, 2003), 24; Jones, *1 and 2 Kings*, 1:107.

David's throne forever (2 Sam 7:13), this man after God's own heart knew the success and longevity of the Davidic dynasty depended on his sons' obedience to the Law. "Being 'a man' means following God's ways—and that means close attention to the written legacy of Moses."[39]

A fter extolling Torah fidelity, David's charge takes a violent turn. Indeed, it is difficult for some to square such pious speak with so violent an order as David gives here. First, he says, Joab must be executed. The dying king recalls what his right-hand man and former general had done by murdering Abner and Amasa. The former had been murdered in cold blood under a flag of truce (2 Sam 3:26–30). The latter had replaced Joab as David's chairman of the Joint Chiefs (2 Sam 19:13); furious, Joab lured Amasa into a trap, stabbing him in the stomach while pretending to kiss him in friendly greeting (2 Sam 20:4–10). In this way, Joab had retained his position as head of the military (2 Sam 20:23).

The king's wish for Joab was clear: "Do not let his gray head go down to Sheol in peace" (v. 6), which not only precluded the widely preferred natural death at a ripe old age, but also expressed the wish that Joab die outside of "covenant accord with God and man."[40] David desperately wanted to enjoy the afterlife far away from Joab.

But why? It is hard to believe that Joab had done anything personally injurious to David; indeed, most of Joab's crimes had been committed *in defense of* David. For one thing, he had arranged Uriah's death at David's order (2 Sam 11:14–15). The king doesn't even mention perhaps Joab's gravest sin—the execution of Absalom, which the king had forbidden—perhaps because he was never told. Why was David insistent that Joab be eliminated once David had passed?

Simply stated, Joab represented the greatest threat to Solomon's control of Israel's throne, the most dangerous "loose end." David knew how powerful and crafty Joab was. What would prevent him from raising up another rival claimant to the throne after David's death? Let's face it; Joab was nothing more than a thug, a political hatchet-man in the most literal sense.

---

39.   Auld, *I & II Kings*, 11–12. "There can be no doubt that much of Solomon's early spiritual vitality and dedication to God may be attributed to David's deep personal relationship to the Lord and desire to honor him," (Patterson, "1, 2 Kings," 649).

40.   Donald J. Wiseman, *1 and 2 Kings* (Downers Grove, IL: InterVarsity Press, 2008), 83.

David was also fearful that Joab's blood-guilt would continue to haunt the royal family if not properly avenged (cf. 2 Sam 21:1–14). The king said that Joab, in murdering rivals in cold blood, had accessorized himself with blood-guilt as if it were a belt and shoes (v. 5).[41] In that light, it was not enough simply to condemn Joab to life in prison; he had to be executed. Unlike Adonijah and Shimei, Joab met his untimely end in this chapter through no additional provocation, meaning his fate was a greater foregone conclusion than the others. David had never shied away from eliminating his enemies in a messy way. But for whatever reason, he had never had the guts to punish Joab himself. Now at the end of his life, he didn't want his son to make the same spineless mistake.

Another troublemaker had to be dealt with. As with Joab, we wonder why Shimei deserved the death penalty instead of life in prison. What real threat did this former estate manager of the old regime pose?

Shimei had cursed David while on the run from Absalom (2 Sam 16:5–12), and in ancient Israel, cursing the Lord's anointed earned the perpetrator a "Go to Sheol, go directly to Sheol. Do not pass Go. Do not collect $200" card (Exod 22:28; 1 Kgs 21:10). After being restored to the throne, the king had sworn not to execute Shimei for his crime, perhaps in a magnanimous plea for bipartisanship.[42]

But the oath did not in any way prohibit *Solomon* from doing the deed. "Ancient thought regarded the entire family—even succeeding generations—as a single unit. Shimei's curse could still afflict Solomon and his successors."[43] As a member of the tribe of Benjamin—Saul's tribe—Shimei would continue to pose a threat. David anticipated that Shimei's elimination would require more skill and shrewdness than Joab's, but he had confidence in Solomon's wisdom (v. 9).

In stark contrast to the fates of Joab and Shimei, David wished for Solomon to reward the loyalty of Barzillai, a wealthy landowner in Gilead who had provided David with badly-needed food and support during Absalom's insurrection (2 Sam 17:27–29). Though the aged Barzillai had initially declined David's invitation to join his court in Jerusalem (2 Sam 19:31–40), it was commanded that Barzillai's family be invited to the king's table, effectively placing them on a royal

---

41. The waist and feet were ancient symbols for one's center of being and lifestyle, respectively (Robert L. Hubbard, Jr., *First and Second Kings* [Chicago: Moody, 1991], 27).

42. "Many think that David's generous promise of pardon given at the moment of his return may have been a tactical move on his part, considering that Shimei showed up with a thousand Benjaminites in tow (cf. 2 Sam 19:16–24)," (Cogan, *I Kings*, 174).

43. Hubbard, *First and Second Kings*, 28; cf. Gray, *I & II Kings*, 100–01.

pension of sorts (cf. 2 Sam 9:7; 19:28; 1 Kgs 18:19; Neh 5:17). For what it's worth, we never read of Solomon fulfilling this command, unlike David's other instructions. Make of that what you will.

His final wishes communicated, the death of David is accounted in a fashion that will become somewhat standard throughout Kings. His grave is noted (cf. Neh 3:16; Acts 2:29),[44] as is the length of his reign and his successor. The "City of David" refers to the walled fortress of the old city Jebus which David had conquered earlier in his reign (2 Sam 5:6–9).

I t would be impossible to overstate David's legacy in Israel. For the rest of Kings, he will be the standard by which other kings are judged (1 Kgs 14:8; 15:11; 2 Kgs 14:3; 16:20). So faithful was he to God and the Law that only his adultery with Bathsheba and subsequent murder of Uriah are remembered against him (1 Kgs 15:5). "Indeed, David defends Jerusalem long after his death, since God spares the city for centuries simply for the sake of the promises made to David (2 Kgs 20:6)."[45]

Moving into the New Testament, David became the embodiment of all Israel hoped for in a deliverer—the archetype messiah figure. But Peter at Pentecost made it a point to observe that David's grave was still occupied, while Jesus' was empty (Acts 2:29). In doing so, Peter affirmed that, through Jesus, God had kept all his promises to David and established a kingdom that would never fail (Dan 2:44). Now seated on the throne of God's kingdom is a Sovereign who has died and yet is now alive forevermore (Rev 1:18).

After David's death, Israel often looked back on his reign with longing and yearned again for the good old days. Christians, however, look forward to the return of their King, to the day when all his enemies will be placed under his feet—to the day when the kingdom will be the Lord's.

---

44. The tombs of David and his successors were located on the southern slope of the Ophel or Citadel of David (DeVries, *1 Kings*, 36–37). A millennium later, Josephus claimed the royal tombs had been looted during the days of Hyrcanus and Herod (*Antiquities* 7.392–94; 13.249; 16.179).

45. House, *1, 2 Kings*, 98.

1 KINGS 2:13-27

After David's death, Bathsheba was approached by a humiliated Adonijah. He begrudgingly acknowledged that Solomon was the legitimate king of Israel—"for it was his from the LORD"—but could not give up the idea that it was still somehow rightfully his—"the kingdom was mine, and [...] all Israel fully expected me to reign" (v. 15). So I guess as a consolation prize for losing the crown, Adonijah requested that Bathsheba ask Solomon to give Abishag, David's final concubine, to Adonijah as a wife—only his request betrayed the fact that it was the throne he really sought.[46]

Bathsheba consented to carrying Adonijah's request to the king. Solomon's reception of his mother underscores the place of honor held by Bathsheba in the kingdom. Not only did the king leave his throne and bow before her, but she was seated on a throne at her son's right hand (v. 19), a special place of honor in ancient times (Ps 110:1; Heb 1:3; 10:12; 1 Pet 3:22).

So far, the narrator has painted a sweet and serene portrait of Solomon, but here, that image is shredded by a volcanic eruption of righteous indignation. The king immediately ordered the execution of his brother. Why? "Because Abishag was David's last concubine, and whoever possessed the harem controlled the kingdom" (cf. 2 Sam 3:6–7; 12:8; 16:21–22).[47] It was clear to Solomon that his older brother had not totally surrendered his claim to the throne or dream of being king—notice Solomon's words to Bathsheba: "You might as well request the kingdom for him" (v. 22 NIV).

What motive does Bathsheba have for bringing Adonijah's request to her son? Does she naïvely not understand the implications of the request? "Or is she shrewd, calculating that onward transmission of the request is likely to lead

---

46. Wray Beal, *1 & 2 Kings*, 76. As to the outside chance that Adonijah was just a helpless romantic and didn't deserve his demise, I offer up Cross' point: "If Adonijah did in fact behave as claimed, he deserved to be executed—for stupidity," (Frank Moore Cross, *Canaanite Myth and Hebrew Epic* [Cambridge: Harvard Univ. Press, 1973], 237).

47. House, *1, 2 Kings*, 99; cf. Matitiahu Tsevat, "Marriage and Monarchial Legitimacy in Ugarit and Israel," *JSS* 3 (1958): 241–42. "The loss of the harem to another monarch, as described in the Assyrian annals of Sennacherib, was a sign of submission or being deposed," (John H. Walton, Victor H. Matthews, and Mark W. Chavalas, *The IVP Bible Background Commentary: Old Testament* [Downers Grove, IL: InterVarsity Press, 2000], 358; cf. Roland de Vaux, *Ancient Israel* [New York: McGraw-Hill, 1961], 1:116–17).

to Adonijah's death, and thus greater safety for both herself and Solomon?"[48] For my money, I think Bathsheba knew exactly what she was doing. She knew sleeping with the king's concubine was an act of treason and rebellion. She also knew her son's temperament.

Layered within Solomon's emotional reaction is the narrator's justification for Adonijah's execution, as well as its aftermath. It was Solomon's conviction that Yahweh had established him on Israel's throne as part of his promise to David in 2 Samuel 7:12–16. In other words, I don't consider Solomon's reaction to be one solely of personal offense, but rather an act of righteous indignation since, as king, he was now God's minister of justice (Rom 13:4). The key term of 1 Kings 2 is *establish* (vv. 4, 12, 24, 45–46), and for Solomon's throne to be securely established by God, extreme and violent measures had to be taken by the divinely-ordained king.

After signing Adonijah's execution warrant, Solomon also sent the high priest Abiathar into exile. It could be argued that the aged priest did not pose a real threat to Solomon; the king's stated reason for sparing Abiathar was that he had held the distinction of carrying the Ark of the Covenant and had served David faithfully during the latter's outlaw existence in the wilderness before Saul's death (2:26; cf. 1 Sam 23:6–12; 2 Sam 15:24–29, 35–36; 20:25). But Abiathar had nonetheless been a part of the pro-Adonijah party, and thus could enjoy no place of honor or privilege in Solomon's administration.

Abiathar lived out his years at his estate in Anathoth, a town about three miles northeast of Jerusalem overlooking the Jordan Valley and the Dead Sea's north shore. This community was a city of refuge and the place where priests lived when not serving in the Lord's house (Josh 21:1–3, 18). It was also the home of Jeremiah (Jer 1:1; 29:27), who may have been descended from Abiathar. Since Abiathar's name is still listed as a priest along with Zadok in 1 Kings 4:4, it's possible that he still held some sort of emeritus position, though he had certainly been forced into early retirement.[49]

Finally, the narrator takes this opportunity to stress a prominent theme in Kings—the word of the Lord always comes to pass. The demotion of Abiathar fulfilled the prophecy made in 1 Samuel 2:27–36 and 3:11–14 concerning Eli's family—Abiathar was the grandson of Ahitub, the grandson of Eli (cf. 1 Sam

---

48. Iain W. Provan, *1 & 2 Kings* (Peabody, MA: Hendrickson, 1995), 38.

49. The descendants of Zadok held the priesthood until 171 when Antiochus IV Epiphanes scandalously installed Menelaus (of the tribe of Benjamin) as the new high priest.

14:2–3; 22:20). Such a detail is more than a cutesy "Now you know the rest of the story" type comment; it's a not-so-subtle reminder that God fulfills his word and works his plan for Israel in the midst of dirty politics.

1 KINGS 2:28-35

When Joab learned that Adonijah was swimming with the fishes, he panicked and fled to claim sanctuary on the horns of the altar (just as Adonijah himself had done at the end of 1 Kings 1). Joab isn't a dummy; he knows he doesn't stand a chance out on his own, but he underestimates Solomon. Joab likely wagers that Solomon won't have the cojones to off him on holy ground, but it's a bad bet, and the hit is put out. Joab's response to Benaiah, "I will die here," was meant in the same way as our sarcastic, "You can have it when you pry it from my cold dead fingers." Learning of Joab's response, Solomon says, "Have it your way."

Lest we have pity on Joab and make Solomon out to be the bad guy (which some scholars do), the king reminds everyone that Joab was a war criminal worthy of death: "Strike him down and bury him, and thus take away from me and from my father's house the guilt for the blood that Joab shed without cause. The LORD will bring back his bloody deeds on his own head, because, without the knowledge of my father David, he attacked and killed with the sword two men more righteous and better than himself" (vv. 31–32).

Joab deserved a violent death—those who live by the sword die by the sword (Matt 26:52). And because of his bloody past, Joab's claim of asylum in the house of God was illegitimate, since it applied only to those guilty of accidental manslaughter, not premeditated murder (cf. Exod 21:13–14; Deut 27:24). But though he deserved to die for his crimes, Joab was not dishonored in death. He was allowed to be buried on his family's estate "in the wilderness" or "out in the country" (v. 34 NIV).[50]

1 KINGS 2:36-46

Eradicating the final threat to Solomon's throne took greater patience and ingenuity, demonstrating some of the wisdom and savvy for which he would become legendary. Shimei, the former caretaker of Saul's estate, was summoned before the king. Solomon effectively convicted Shimei of manslaughter for his

---

50. "The family grave was in Bethlehem (cf. 2 Sam 2:32), which is located at the edge of the Judean steppe," (Cogan, *I Kings*, 179).

curse on David and appropriately sentenced him to house arrest in Jerusalem as if it were a city of refuge (Num 35:9–34).[51] The sentence was not to cross the Kidron, which would have been necessary for Shimei to visit his hometown of Bahurim and have contact with his kin. "But the point of Solomon's order was that Shimei was under house arrest within Jerusalem and all exits were closed to him, east as well as west (to Gath)."[52] It should be noted that Shimei consented to this restriction (v. 38).

But since Shimei's business interests were elsewhere, this presented a problem. Modern readers should know that Jerusalem wasn't a large place at this point—just 4,500 feet (not quite a mile) in circumference, about 11 acres in size, and with a population of no more than 2,500.[53] I mention this because I've always read this story and concluded that this wasn't a bad punishment at all, somehow equating Jerusalem in 970 with modern-day New York, Chicago, or Dallas. But for a businessman with holdings scattered throughout ancient Israel, being confined to eleven acres of real estate must have been maddening, especially when his absence inevitably meant poor management for his estates.

Sure enough, it didn't take long for Shimei to crack. After three years, two of his servants escaped to the Philistine city of Gath, about twenty-five miles southwest of Jerusalem. Shimei ventured out to fetch them back to service, but Solomon was waiting for Shimei when he returned.[54] For breaking his oath to the king, to say nothing of his cursing David so many years before, Shimei was eliminated by Benaiah.

And lest we be tempted to think Shimei's punishment was a mortifying act of injustice or gross abuse of power, we must remember his crimes, Solomon's

---

51. Leithart, 1 & 2 Kings, 39.

52. Cogan, I Kings, 179; cf. LaSor, "Kidron, Brook; Kidron Valley," ISBE 3:14. Nelson conjectures, "The narrator may intend the reader to realize that Solomon had a political motive for keeping Shimei on the Jerusalem side of the Kidron (v. 37), away from his pro-Saul kinfolk in nearby Bahurim (v. 8)," (First and Second Kings, 28).

53. George Adam Smith, Jerusalem: The Topography, Economics and History from the Earliest Times to A.D. 70, vol. 1 (London: Hodder, 1907), 142; Tomoo Ishida, The Royal Dynasties in Ancient Israel (Berlin: de Gruyter, 1977), 134; John Wilkinson, "Ancient Jerusalem: Its Water Supply and Population," PEQ 106 (1974): 50.

54. Gray astutely points out that Shimei "did not actually cross the Kidron" to fetch his servants, meaning "he did not violate the letter but the spirit of Solomon's ban," (I & II Kings, 109), to which House further speculates, "Perhaps Shimei thinks he is more clever than Solomon," (1, 2 Kings, 103).

original leniency, and Shimei's own oath not to break the terms of his parole. "Had Shimei taken the conditions of his confinement seriously and been an honest man, he would have gone to Solomon and requested either that the latter regain his slaves for him or else allow him to make the trip."[55] The narrator's final words of the chapter, "So the kingdom was established in the hand of Solomon" (v. 46), effectively gives divine sanction to the king's punitive measures and fixes Solomon as a shrewd and sound sovereign possessing extraordinary wisdom.

As you read this sordid political tale of Adonijah's downfall and Solomon's ascendancy, you could be excused for asking, "Where is God in this?" Though this may appear to be a textbook case of biblical *deus absconditus*, God was at work behind the scenes of this narrative, manipulating human sinfulness to achieve his far-reaching purposes. It was not necessarily his will that Adonijah and others behave the way they did, but God worked through them, nonetheless. Amidst all the turmoil and uncertainty of the chapter, an Israelite could still trust that Yahweh was in control.

This is a principle relevant in every time. The people of God believe—absurdly, at times—that God is at work in the complicated nuances of international diplomacy, the glacial quagmire of national politics, and the daily grind of everyday life in the flyover states. The apostle Paul assures the church that God works all things for our good (Rom 8:28), that he works everything out "in agreement with the decision of His will" (Eph 1:11 HCSB).

How do you react when the president announces a policy or signs an executive order you know to be contrary to biblical values? How do you react when Congress votes or the Supreme Court decides in a way contradictory to God's worldview? I can name a few inappropriate responses: fear, anger, doubt, anxiety. If there is one thing I've learned over the last few years, it's that God has no greater commitment to anything other than the glory and exaltation of his own Name. And if God's glory is God's #1 priority, I can rest secure in the knowledge that everything that happens will end up bringing God glory.

---

55. Patterson, "1, 2 Kings," 656–57. Robinson adds, "The editors may have used him as an example of the fate of those who rebel against a reigning king. [...] The editors saw this as purposely willed by God to punish Shimei without bringing any reproach upon Solomon. God was showing through events whom he blesses and whom he cursed," (*First Book*, 46).

More specifically for Christians, it is disturbing that Solomon established his throne through such violent means. For whatever reason, we give David a pass for his bloody ethos; we expect more, however, out of Solomon. For one thing, God denied David the opportunity to build the Temple for the very reason that he had too much blood on his hands (5:3–4; 1 Chr 28:3), while David's son was given this privilege because he did not. How do we reconcile such a violent beginning for a king whose name means *peace*?

In the first chapter of his book, *The Jesus I Never Knew*, author Philip Yancey observes how many equate Christ with a Mister Rogers or Captain Kangaroo-type character, and then are confused when they read the crucifixion narrative.[56] Who would ever want to kill Mister Rogers?

At the heart of the gospel, however, is the claim that Jesus is King, to the exclusion of all the pretend, wannabe regents of earth. Indeed, all those who have ever rejected Jesus as Lord and Savior have done so because Christ was a threat to their personal sovereignty. The kingdom of heaven was established violently with Jesus' death and resurrection—"[Jesus] disarmed the spiritual rulers and authorities. He shamed them publicly by his victory over them on the cross" (Col 2:15 NLT). Such rhetoric from the apostle Paul smacks of a humiliating military beatdown as if the Pentagon declared war on Martha's Vineyard.

But it isn't so much the reality of Jesus' victory, but *how* Jesus gained victory, that is noteworthy. In spite of Jewish expectations, Jesus did not lead a violent revolt in order to triumph. Rather, "The violent establishment of Solomon is but a faint shadow of the greater Solomon, who establishes a new creation first of all by suffering violence rather than deploying it."[57] Though many of them no doubt began to follow Jesus with visions of political cabinet positions dancing in their heads, as the Lord's ministry progressed, the apostles heard their Rabbi talk more and more about crosses and less and less about thrones.

Yet, the New Testament also speaks of a day when Christ will return with a vengeful agenda and establish his kingdom in violence (e.g., Matt 13:40–43; 2 Thess 1:7–8; 2 Pet 3:10). In his Apocalypse, John saw Jesus astride a white war horse, with sword drawn, and riding point for the army of heaven, furiously stomping on his enemies as if they were grapes in God's winepress (Rev 19:11–15). In the next scene, an angel summons the buzzards to feast on the corpses of those foolish enough to resist the King of kings. The great enemies of Christ are

---

56. Philip Yancey, *The Jesus I Never Knew* (Grand Rapids: Zondervan, 1995), 14–15.

57. Leithart, *1 & 2 Kings*, 41.

scornfully tossed into the lake of fire, "And the rest were slain by the sword that came from the mouth of him who was sitting on the horse, and all the birds were gorged with their flesh" (Rev 19:21).

Jesus is a lot of things, but Captain Kangaroo he is not.

There is one final tie between 1 Kings 1–2 and the final scenes of Revelation. In 1 Kings 1, we behold a presumptuously arrogant Adonijah hosting a feast for the Who's Who of Israel. But the party grows quite lame when the raucous celebration of Solomon's coronation spills over into the countryside. Having realized that they had gotten the chariot before the stallion, all of Adonijah's "friends" fled in dreadful panic, and the premature victory feast grew cold.

Jesus, too, has promised to share a feast with us. When the Lord instituted his Supper, he told the apostles that he would not eat and drink with them again until he did so in his Father's kingdom (Matt 26:29). What's ironic is that Christ, like Adonijah, hosts this victory feast before the kingdom has been established and the battle is won. In Revelation 19:6–9, John sees a vision of the Lamb's victorious wedding feast, though the last battle has not yet been waged!

But unlike Adonijah, this is no presumptuous pep rally. Instead, so assured is Christ's final triumph that he throws a victory feast before the last trumpet has sounded. We serve a commander-in-chief who divides the spoils of war before dawn's *Reveille*; a ball coach who dons his Super Bowl ring before the start of training camp. He who created all and redeemed all will conquer all.

And just as Barzillai was seated at the king's table because of his faithfulness, we too will be given a seat at our Lord's banquet feast if we are found faithful. Even in this life, as we gather around the Lord's table to commemorate his death and anticipate his return, we sing with one voice the victory song of the saints: "The Lord our God the Almighty reigns. Let us rejoice and exult and give him the glory" (Rev 19:6–7).

Long live the King!

TALKING POINTS

Sin makes cowards of us all." I'm not sure where I first heard that. It's not original to me, but whoever said it was right. Beginning with his sin with Bathsheba in 2 Samuel 11, David's strong leadership slowly erodes, both in his family and in Israel.[58] The once charismatic warrior-poet is no longer a loving shepherd of his people, but a borderline tyrant. In 1 Kings 1, David is indecisive at best.[59] As with Amnon (2 Sam 13:21) and Absalom (2 Sam 18:5), he had been unable to discipline Adonijah. Only at the behest of Bathsheba and Nathan does he finally hit the Go button and proclaim Solomon his co-regent and successor. Sin makes cowards of us all, and that is never truer than for leaders. The moral courage required to make necessary, tough decisions evaporates as we cede more of our souls to Satan. I believe with all my heart that any sin can be forgiven, and that people deserve second chances. But there's a reason persistent sin gives cause for concern about a leader's character. A leader who wishes to remain effective over the long haul must petition God daily to root out sin in his heart, or persistent moral failure will make him a coward like the aged David.

It requires an exceptionally strong leader to extend grace and forgiveness to enemies. The end of 1 Kings 1 finds Adonijah clinging to the horns of the altar, seeking asylum or sanctuary, and begging his half-brother for clemency for his treason. No one in that age would have faulted Solomon for having Adonijah executed. Adonijah was a rival to the throne, and such rivals had to be exterminated—so the thinking went. If this had been a *Godfather* movie, Adonijah should have awoken to a horse head in his bed. But Solomon extended grace, so long as Adonijah promised to behave himself. Some leaders, even ecclesiastical ones, seem to think that strong leadership is exemplified by being punitive and harsh when dispensing punishment. But if God's discipline is always meant

---

58. "From this time [David's sin with Bathsheba] on, though God's love never lets him go, he appears to have lost some of the joy and strength that once characterised him. His feelings of guilt impaired his ability to witness to truth and righteousness, and he was unable to become a decisive influence within his own family whom he tended to neglect," (Ronald S. Wallace, *Readings in 1 Kings* [Grand Rapids: Eerdmans, 1996], 1).

59. Walsh makes the grammatical note that, in the opening scene, David "is the subject of no active verbs; things are done *to* him, not *by* him," (*1 Kings*, 5; emphasis his).

to correct and restore, what good do leaders achieve by simply being cruel? Extending grace and forgiveness to our enemies, as well as to the wayward, is the most difficult thing a leader must do. Grace and forgiveness are not signs of weakness, but of extraordinary strength.

There is an ironic contrast between Adonijah's actions and Nathan's. The first was obviously driven by his own will and inconsiderate of God's or his father's. Nathan, meanwhile, was determined to allow God to have his way. One would then think that Adonijah would be the most industrious character in this story, but it is Nathan who merits that distinction. Adonijah begins to act as king before he is king, counting chickens and celebrating victories before they materialize. Meanwhile, Nathan and Bathsheba were not lulled into inaction by God's sovereignty, but were prompted by it. "Their belief animated their action. They knew what God willed, and therefore they worked strenuously to effect that will. We may bewilder our brains with speculations about the relation between God's sovereignty and man's freedom, but, when it comes to practical work, we have to put out the best and most that is in us to prevent God's will from being thwarted by rebellious men, and to ensure its being carried into effect through our efforts, 'for we are God's fellow-workers,'"[60] (1 Cor 3:9).

---

60. Alexander Maclaren, *Expositions of Holy Scripture* (Grand Rapids: Baker, 1984), 4:154.

2

GLORY DAYS

On January 31, 1993, something magical happened: I watched my first Dallas Cowboys game. I vividly remember how excited Dad was leading up to Super Bowl XXVII. Dallas had been his boyhood team, and after many years of excruciating mediocrity (including an embarrassing 1-15 season in 1989), the Cowboys had returned to football's promised land. As I watched the game with my dad, my seven-year-old mind became helplessly hooked, and I don't need all ten fingers to count the number of games I've missed since then.

With their victory over the Buffalo Bills, Dallas began a dynasty that would see them win a total of three Lombardi trophies in four years. But then the dynasty ended. The Green Bay Packers won the championship in January 1997, only to give way to the Denver Broncos a year later, who gave way to the St. Louis Rams after that, who gave way to the New England Patriots, who gave way to the Pittsburgh Steelers, who gave way to the…

In politics, we still speak of "dynasties"—families that hold tremendous sway in American affairs of state. In the twentieth century, it was the Roosevelts and then the Kennedys. Now it is the Bushes and Clintons. But none of these families have held power for more than a couple of decades, which is scarcely a dynasty in comparison to the empires of history. And that's the problem with dynasties—they never last very long. Camelot collapses, the glory days fade into hazy nostalgia, and it is left to historians to figure out what went wrong.

With forty years on the throne, David had unequivocally established a dynasty. Now Solomon receives an unprecedented blessing from God as he begins his reign in 1 Kings 3. In 1 Kings 4, the details of Solomon's reign, though tedious, underscore just how successful he was. Since Israel's benefactor existed beyond the heavens, not even the sky was her limit. To an Israelite in exile in Babylon, this passage was a painful reminder of what had once been.

But the seeds of our destruction are often sown in the soil of our success. Solomon was wise, wealthy, and powerful; the narrator is in awe of his other-worldly wisdom, administrative acumen, and political savvy. Indeed, Solomon gets a lot of love from the narrator all the way through 1 Kings 10, peaking with the visit by the Queen of Sheba. There is no denying that Solomon was God's choice to rule the chosen people, and the narrator goes to extravagant lengths to illustrate that.

Even the narrator, however, cannot help but note trends that seemed innocent at the time, but would prove to be significant problems for Solomon in the future. Attempting to forge a formidable international alliance with Egypt, Solomon marries "outside the faith," and his faithfulness to the Lord was compromised. Needing funding for his ambitious building programs and general royal excess, he taxed the nation and mandated forced labor, proving to be more of a hedonistic despot and less of a shepherd of the flock. The glory of Solomon came at a cost. As you read these chapters, you'll be tempted to think nothing could go wrong for Solomon. But all is not exactly well in Camelot.

Dynasties never last very long.

1 KINGS 3:1-15

There is much about Solomon's reign that is admittedly ambiguous, and the first detail of the king's incumbency is a perfect example. How are we to take his political marriage to Pharaoh's daughter? Is it proof of Solomon's international influence, or was it Egypt's way of reestablishing its power in Palestine?

In light of the bloodshed of 1 Kings 2, Provan calls the king's nuptials "another dubious act!"[1] In the Old Testament, Egypt was often symbolic of oppression and temptation. And just as Deuteronomy cautioned against returning there (Deut 17:16), it also warned against intermarriage with the nations, lest Israel be seduced into apostasy (Deut 7:3–4).[2] This is exactly what Solomon's

---

1. Provan, *1 & 2 Kings*, 44.

2. Jewish tradition did not frown on Solomon's marriage since Egypt is not listed among the verboten nations in Deuteronomy 7. But though that passage does not explicitly forbid Israel from intermarrying with Egypt, many scholars agree that the spirit of the Law would have pro-

foreign wives would accomplish (cf. 11:1–8; Neh 13:23–27). Provan concludes, "First Kings 3:1a cannot, therefore, represent anything other than a criticism of Solomon, particularly in view of what David has said in 2:1–4 about keeping the law of Moses."[3]

Dissenting from Provan, Leithart argues, "The author is hardly an uncritical admirer of Solomon, but he does not criticize the king for his marriage to Pharaoh's daughter (3:[1]). Solomon's marriage to Pharaoh's daughter instead fulfills the Abrahamic promise to bless the nations."[4] And he has a point. If anything, Pharaoh giving his daughter in marriage to a foreigner (something Egypt rarely did) is indicative of Egypt's weakness at this time. Add to this the fact that Solomon acquired the site of Gezer, an important crossroads for trade near the Mediterranean coast, as a part of his wife's dowry (9:16),[5] and it seems Solomon got the better end of this deal.

It's no accident that the narrator mentions Solomon's marriage to Pharaoh's daughter before moving on to the more well-known aspects of Solomon's reign, such as his world-renowned wisdom and massive building projects. Though the marriage is quickly noted before the narrative moves forward, "its primary position in this passage alerts us that it will play an important role as the tale of Sol-

---

hibited such unless the Gentile spouse converted to faith in Yahweh.

3. Provan, *1 & 2 Kings*, 44. Walsh adds that the same Hebrew verb translated "made a marriage alliance with" (v. 1) "also carries negative connotations in all its other occurrences in the Hebrew Bible. In every case the man who 'becomes son-in-law' to another man makes himself subservient to his father-in-law or vulnerable to the harmful influence of his wife. [...] To use the term here of Solomon's alliance with Pharaoh can imply that Solomon is in some measure subordinate to Pharaoh; it can also suggest that Pharaoh's daughter will adversely affect Solomon's behavior. Both possibilities will be borne out in later passages" (*1 Kings*, 70). It should also be noted that Solomon already had a wife at this point, Naamah the Ammonite, the mother of Rehoboam (cf. 11:42–43; 14:21).

4. Leithart, *1 & 2 Kings*, 43.

5. "This arrangement secured Solomon's main access route to the coast and to Phoenicia beyond, a critical component for his alliance with Phoenicia and the building projects it entailed," (Monson, "1 Kings," 99, n. 59). Walsh counters that Gezer "lies only twenty miles from Jerusalem, deep within Solomon's own territory. Apparently Pharaoh's might is greater than Solomon's and can achieve decisively even inside Solomon's own kingdom what Solomon himself cannot," (*1 Kings*, 70).

omon's reign unfolds."[6] On the one hand, this marriage lent Solomon significant international prestige. But on the other, it led him "away from old Mosaic roots."[7]

Long-term, Israel suffered spiritually from this wedding, but she (primarily Solomon) benefitted immediately in the short-term. We're assured that Solomon loved the Lord, but short-term blessings can become long-term headaches and kingdoms can slip away when we sacrifice radical obedience for political expediency. For what it's worth, Pharaoh's daughter was barred from the palace until a new one had been constructed just for her (7:8; 9:24). She was not allowed in Solomon's palace, which had been David's palace, for—as Solomon himself put it—"the places to which the ark of the LORD has come are holy" (2 Chr 8:11). Make of that what you will.

Equally ambiguous is the note that Israel was worshiping at the "high places" (v. 2), since there was no house of the Lord. Mentioned over one hundred times in the Bible, these open-air sites were often very ornate and entailed a raised, stepped platform of some kind (natural or constructed) with an altar on which sacrifices were offered to deity. Several of these high places have been unearthed in Israel by archaeologists. Upon entering Canaan, Israel had been commanded to destroy all non-Israelite high places (Num 33:52; Deut 7:5; 12:3), "whereas Israelite ones would be tolerated until such time that the temple was completed."[8] Pagan sites housed idols, Asherah poles, monoliths, and altars. The Israelite high places were used for sacrifices, festivals, and worship to Yahweh (1 Sam 9:12; 10:5; 2 Chr 33:17). But once the Temple was built, these high places became illegitimate (cf. Deut 12). In Kings, therefore, they "soon emerge in the narrative as a troubling issue associated with apostasy,"[9] (1 Kgs 11:7; 12:31; 14:23; 15:14; 22:43; 2 Kgs

---

6. Ibid., 71.

7. Brueggemann, *1 & 2 Kings*, 43. Later, he adds, "'Egypt' is a term in Israelite memory and tradition that bespeaks brutality, exploitation, and bondage, the demeaning of the human spirit, and the suppression of covenantal relations. Indeed, Israelite memory concerning Yahweh is that the taproot of faith and life is emancipation from Pharaoh. Notably the Pharaoh is not identified. Historical calculations suggest that the Pharaoh of the moment is perhaps Siamun. It is, however, crucial that he is not named, for in his anonymity he is emotionally connected to the ancient pharaoh of the Exodus narrative, also left unnamed (Exod 1:8). All Pharaohs are the same in Israelite imagination, and they are all a threat to Israel. But now, through the wedding, they have become 'family,'" (Ibid., 45).

8. Monson, "1 Kings," 20.

9. Terence E. Fretheim, *First and Second Kings* (Louisville: Westminster John Knox, 1999), 31. "Kings are measured by their attitude towards them, with full approval granted only

12:3; 14:4; 15:4, 35; 16:4; 17:9; 21:3). At this point, Gibeon was one such high place, and it housed the Tabernacle (2 Chr 1:3; cf. 1 Chr 16:39–40).

W hile at Gibeon,[10] Solomon had a dream in which God offered to grant him a wish. In the dream,[11] Solomon responded by praising Yahweh's faithfulness to David. If God came to you in a dream and promised you anything you wanted, what would you request? All the money in the world? All the power in the world? Would you ask for your health to be made perfect? Would you wish for a spouse? Children? A new job?

In November 2015, the news ran a tragic, heart-warming story of Daniel Fleetwood, a thirty-two-year-old Houston resident dying of spindle cell sarcoma. Fleetwood was a life-long *Star Wars* fan, and as the result of an intensive social media campaign, director J. J. Abrams arranged for Fleetwood to receive a private screening of Episode VII: *The Force Awakens*, which was not slated to debut in theaters until December. A few days after viewing the film, Fleetwood died.

Fleetwood's experience reminds us that our greatest wish or desire changes based on our circumstances. When I was eleven years old, I so desperately wanted to go to a live Dallas Cowboys football game. When I was seventeen, I wanted my own car. When I was twenty, I wanted my dad to come back to life. Now? I only want one more opportunity to hug my son and tell him how much I love

---

to those who removed them (2 Kgs 18:4; 23:8)," (Wray Beal, *1 & 2 Kings*, 85). For more on high places, see King, *Life in Biblical Israel*, 319–22; Beth Alpert Nakhai, "What's a Bamah? How Sacred Space Functioned in Ancient Israel," *BAR* 20/3 (1994): 18–29.

10. Gibeon lay about four miles north of Jerusalem atop a plateau. It was a city of Levites (Josh 21:17) and a crossroads of sorts for Palestine since its roads led to the four compass points: west to the Mediterranean, north to Shechem, east to Jericho and beyond the Jordan, and south to Jerusalem.

11. Though dreams in which the gods communicated with the king were a common phenomenon in the ancient world, it seems they carried a different significance for the righteous in Israel. Whereas for the pagans it reinforced the notion that certain gods approved or disapproved of the king (and were thus manipulated for political purposes), in Israel, the Lord revealing himself through dreams reinforced the notion "that important decisions are made by God [and are] well beyond the control or even understanding of the royal person. That is, the dream subverts the certainty of royal control," (Brueggemann, *1 & 2 Kings*, 47). "It is noteworthy that the two recorded communications between God and Solomon take place not, as usual with the kings of Israel, through prophet or priest, but through dreams in a sacred place," (Wallace, *1 Kings*, 31).

him. Our greatest wish at any given moment is dictated by the circumstances of our lives at that moment.

We can't divorce Solomon's answer to God's magnanimous offer from the timing and location of the event. He had just become king. He had subdued enemies of his throne. He had brokered peaceful relations with Egypt to the south and secured access to grander economic opportunities to the north. But the immensity or enormity of the responsibility before Solomon weighed on his heart. From the nearby hilltop known as Nebi-Samwil, Solomon could see much of Israel. In Gibeon itself was the Tabernacle, placed there by David, and one wonders how many times Solomon had accompanied his father to offer sacrifices to Yahweh. As he thought of his God and his people, Solomon knew he had big shoes to fill.

The king then confessed to God that he felt as "but a little child" (the same term is used in Exod 2:6 and 1 Sam 1:22) and did "not know how to go out or come in" (v. 7). This latter phrase "is a general expression for the duties of leadership, with military leadership especially in mind"[12] (cf. Num 27:17; Deut 28:6; 31:2–3; Josh 14:11; 1 Sam 18:13, 16; 29:6; 2 Kgs 11:8). From a pragmatic, political perspective, Solomon was on to something. It had been only about seventy years since Israel had switched from a loose confederacy of tribes to a monarchy, and that transition had been rocky. The first king, Saul, had started well, but then turned into an unbalanced, narcissistic megalomaniac. Even David's reign had been handicapped with revolt and family dysfunction. Meanwhile, Israel's population had continued to explode, and Solomon sensed "that perhaps old ways of governing may not meet the current needs of his subjects."[13] Solomon knew he was not the warrior his father had been, and that wasn't what Israel needed at that point anyway. They needed a leader who would excel in administration (cf. v. 9).

More importantly, and from a spiritual perspective, Solomon recognized a king's ability to become stubborn and hard-hearted versus discerning. Rather than becoming deaf to the divine word and blind to his need for divine aid, Solomon wanted to remain sensitive to God's guidance and direction.[14] Power

---

12. Nelson, *First and Second Kings*, 33; cf. Anton van der Lingen, "BW'-YS' ('To Go Out and to Come In') as a Military Term," *VT* 42 (1992): 59–66.

13. House, *1, 2 Kings*, 110.

14. "In the petition itself, the king asks for an 'understanding mind.' This conventional translation is scarcely adequate; it would be better to render 'a hearing heart,' or even 'an obedient heart,'" (Brueggemann, *1 & 2 Kings*, 47). This request for a "hearing heart" reminds us of David's

corrupts; absolute power corrupts absolutely; and the first thing to go is often a self-awareness of one's own inadequacies. It's noteworthy what Solomon did *not* ask for: long life (Ps 72:15), riches (Pss 21:3, 5; 72:15–16), or the death of his enemies (Ps 21:8–12)—all of which fit the "pattern for kingship that Deuteronomy warned against (Deut. 17:16–17), as had Samuel (I Sam. 8:11–18)."[15]

The king's humility is remarkable.[16] He understood the enormous responsibility before him; what is more, he knew discharging his duty faithfully and successfully required divine help. It's not hard to imagine that the *Fisherman's Prayer* might have enjoyed a place in Solomon's Oval Office as it did in Kennedy's—"O, God, thy sea is so great and my boat is so small."

Yahweh was pleased with Solomon's humble request. In addition to extraordinary, unprecedented wisdom, the Lord gave the king unprecedented "riches and honor, so that no other king shall compare with you" (v. 13). In addition, Solomon would receive lengthened days (i.e., a long life) if he were faithful to the covenant. The note at the end of the section—that he returned to the Ark in Jerusalem and sacrificed there—reaffirms his faithfulness to the covenant and Law of Moses. Solomon also threw a sumptuous feast for his ministers and aides, a celebration of God's blessing on the new king. For now, Yahweh is unequivocally Solomon's choice of gods, and Solomon is unequivocally God's choice of king.

SOLOMON'S WISDOM

It's a bit of an understatement to say that, with this passage, Solomon's name becomes inextricably synonymous with wisdom.[17] It was the mark of God's election and approval of Solomon as king over Israel. More than Israel's wisest king, however, Solomon becomes the wisest man to ever live until the advent of Christ. And remnants of that wisdom are not just limited to anecdotes such as the one about the two prostitutes (vv. 16–28); they are also preserved in Proverbs.

---

relationship with the Lord (1 Sam 13:14; cf. 1 Kgs 2:4).

15. Nelson, *First and Second Kings*, 31.

16. "Rather than wisdom in general, he asked for wisdom to rule wisely. The very choice itself revealed a humble, sensitive, tender heart," (Hubbard, *First and Second Kings*, 33).

17. "In the whole narrative from Joshua to Kings the Hebrew root *hkm* ('wise', etc.) occurs once in Judges (5:29), six times in 2 Samuel 13–24, but twenty-one times in 1 Kings 2–11 and nowhere else in those books," (Olley, *Message of Kings*, 73).

But what exactly is meant by "Solomon's wisdom"? What precisely did he desire when he requested that Yahweh give him "an understanding mind [...] to discern what is right" (vv. 9, 11)? Gray believes the idea of *wisdom* in Scripture "is so pregnant of meaning as to defy translation."[18] This wisdom certainly has to do with what is prudent or consistent with "common sense." In our day, we would consider a wise person to possess discernment; wisdom is not book-smarts, but the ability to use knowledge to discern the right choice or direction.

Yet, there is more to wisdom than that—much more. Biblical wisdom is not something one is born with, nor is it something gained by self-discipline or careful observance.[19] Rather, Brueggemann observes that "to be wise is to understand what Yahweh wills and to practice it."[20] Put another way, "Wisdom is not primarily a matter of the head; it is a matter of the heart."[21] Wisdom, then, in a biblical sense has to do with one's orientation to God. A wise man is one who seeks God and thus wisdom. A fool seeks something else other than the Lord, and thus does not understand wisdom at all. This is why Solomon claims, "The fear of the LORD is the beginning of wisdom" (Prov 9:10).

However, there is another aspect of biblical wisdom that is often ignored. It cannot be true that Solomon was the only Israelite of his day who was correctly oriented with Yahweh and the covenant. In other words, there is more to biblical wisdom than being in a right relationship with God; the apostle James addressed his letter to Christian brethren who nonetheless lacked wisdom (1:2, 5). The Hebrew term for *wisdom* often means "artistic skill." In Exodus, it is used of those skilled craftsmen who constructed the Tabernacle under the inspiration and empowerment of God's Spirit (Exod 28:3; 31:3; 35:31; cf. 1 Kgs 7:14).

Biblical wisdom, then, is not just a desire to please God. It also entails knowing what is pleasing to God in a given situation and how to do it skillfully and for his glory. Solomon "wanted something more than mere worldly prudence, or the shrewdness and tact that come from long human experience. He prays for the divine power to identify the good and evil in every human situation however

---

18. Gray, *I & II Kings*, 100.

19. Provan, *1 & 2 Kings*, 49.

20. Brueggemann, *1 & 2 Kings*, 52. "Thus the picture of 'Solomon in all his glory' is set in perspective by an insistence that the king must be God's faithful servant," (Nelson, *First and Second Kings*, 36).

21. Gary Inrig, *I & II Kings* (Nashville: Holman, 2003), 31.

complex and confused."[22] As the rest of Kings will bear out, really smart people can do really dumb things because they never seek God's direction or God's skill.

Finally, the wisdom God gave to Solomon was not automatic in nature, nor was it irrevocable. Instead, this wisdom was a product of God's divine presence in Solomon's heart as long as the king sought the Lord through his word. Deuteronomy mandated that the king become fluent in the Law (17:19; cf. 1 Kgs 2:3), and 1 Kings 3:28 will claim that "the wisdom of God was in" Solomon (cf. 4:29; 5:12). The king was thus free to heed or ignore the word of God at any time, which he did.[23] But ignoring the divine word and abusing a divine privilege are two ways one can lose a kingdom in four hundred years.

1 KINGS 3:16-28

Without question, this is the most famous story from Solomon's reign (though the fact that it involved two prostitutes, instead of two ordinary women, was mysteriously omitted from the Sunday school curriculum of my childhood). We've just learned that Solomon's wisdom has a divine source; this episode is presented as an anecdote of such wisdom. More specifically, this story is representative not only of how Solomon shrewdly adjudicated cases brought before him, but also how he did so without bias concerning the social standing of the contestants. It paints him as a compassionate shepherd concerned with the everyday issues of his people (cf. Ps 72:4, 12, 14), as opposed to an out-of-touch, couldn't-care-less bureaucrat (which David became late in life, as did Solomon).[24] In other words, the story proved Solomon was as compassionate as he was smart.

---

22. Wallace, *1 Kings*, 25.

23. "There are moments and events of great wisdom in Solomon's reign, but it is the state of his heart – whether he listens or not – that determines the extent of wisdom's display in his reign. Ultimately, it is the state of his heart that directs his reign and sets the direction for the remainder of the book of Kings (1 Kgs 11:1–13; 26–40)," (Wray Beal, *1 & 2 Kings*, 91).

24. "It was affirmed throughout the ancient Near East that a king's central role was to do justice. For example, around 1700 BC Hammurabi, king of Babylon, wrote that the supreme gods 'named me to promote the welfare of the people … to cause justice to prevail in the land, to destroy the wicked and the evil, that the strong might not oppress the weak'. It is said of David that he 'reigned over all Israel, doing what was just and right for all his people' (2 Sam. 8:15), while 'doing what is just and right' is consistently given elsewhere as the king's major responsibility (e.g., 1 Kgs 10:9; Ps. 72:1–3; Jer. 22:3, 15; Ezek. 45:9)," (Olley, *Message of Kings*, 67).

No matter how moral a society may be, prostitution will always have its customers, and this was certainly true of ancient Israel, despite it being outlawed (Lev 19:29; Deut 23:18). The profession of these two women is meant to arouse more sympathy than shame—prostitutes became such by being sold into the lifestyle by their parents or themselves because they had no other means of financial support.[25] These two women were at the bottom of their social hierarchy, the least likely to receive (let alone deserve) justice. Whatever your politics, the recent advent of #BlackLivesMatter demonstrates that a segment of American society considers themselves less likely to receive justice in given situations, and the plight of prostitutes in ancient Israel was not much different. In both cases, it was perceived that the system had failed—or worse, was against—them. Though "human justice has always been available to the well heeled or the well connected," God takes notice of the poor and disenfranchised (1 Sam 2:8; Luke 1:52–53).[26]

The first woman relates to the king a tragic story of two births, a midnight accident while the women were alone (i.e., without "customers," but also making this a "she said, she said" issue), a swapping of infants, and ambiguity as to which woman is the birth mother of the surviving child. Not even the narrator means for us to know who is telling the truth—we merely assume that the first woman speaks the truth (cf. NIV), but on what basis?[27] Indeed, Proverbs reminds us, "The person who tells one side of a story seems right, until someone else comes and asks questions" (18:17 NCV). If there had been a second witness who could corroborate one side or the other, the legal process could have played out (Deut 19:15).[28] But of course, there wasn't, and it couldn't.

---

25. "The normal expectation for a woman was to be married and live in her husband's house, bearing his children. Women who had to support themselves by yielding to the lust of strangers, and whose children were destined to grow up as bastards and paupers, were wretched and altogether to be pitied," (DeVries, *1 Kings*, 59).

26. Nelson, *First and Second Kings*, 39.

27. Leithart admits the women's testimony "quite literally goes in circles," (*1 & 2 Kings*, 45). Rendsburg believes the first woman is the liar and mother of the dead infant (Gary A. Rendsburg, "The Guilty Party in 1 Kings III 16–28," *VT* 48 [1998]: 534–41). See also Stuart Lasine, "The Riddle of Solomon's Judgment and the Riddle of Human Nature in the Hebrew Bible," *JSOT* 45 (1989): 61–86.

28. Provan, *1 & 2 Kings*, 51.

Solomon's famous solution[29] was to cut the Gordian knot by splitting the child in two with a sword—a solution that abhorred the actual mother, instantly giving the king the answer to the question.[30] Nelson points out that, in the past, such a quandary as this one could have been solved by the casting of lots, use of the Urim and Thummim (1 Sam 28:6), or an ordeal like the one described in Numbers 5:11–31. "In this case, however, the 'wisdom of God' is available directly from the king,"[31] (cf. Prov 8:15; 16:10–11). Later, Solomon would speak of how "a king who sits on the throne of judgment winnows all evil with his eyes" (Prov 20:8), and that though God conceals certain things, "the glory of kings is to search things out" (Prov 25:2). Indeed, while David had been Yahweh's mighty man of war on the throne, Solomon would be his all-wise and discerning administrator of Israel.

1 KINGS 4

David was arguably Israel's greatest king—the narrator of Kings will go on to bear that out, as he is the standard by which all his successors are judged. But it doesn't seem as if David had had much of a domestic agenda. Rather, he was always off fighting wars with one enemy or another.[32] And as the last few American presidents can testify, war always distracts everyone from having to tackle thorny domestic issues such as recession, civil rights, moral bankruptcy, and the sound governance of a nation.

But Solomon had successfully secured his kingdom in peace, to say nothing of having received a remarkable endowment of divine wisdom. Thus, this chapter goes on to demonstrate how Solomon went about establishing a sound

---

29. "Godly leadership sometimes requires discretion, sometimes radical decisiveness," (William H. Barnes, *1–2 Kings* [Carol Stream, IL: Tyndale, 2012], 55).

30. Threatened with the execution of her child, the real mother's love welled up into an emphatic outburst "because she felt great compassion for her son" (v. 26 HCSB). Wray Beal notes that the Hebrew word translated "compassion" (*raḥămîm*) shares the same root with "womb" (*rehem*), "thus emphasizing her compassion arises out of her mother-love," (*1 & 2 Kings*, 88).

31. Nelson, *First and Second Kings*, 38.

32. "Biblical sources only hint at the administrative structure set up by David in the conquered territories; governors were appointed in several lands adjacent to Israelite holdings (cf. 2 Sam 8:6, 14)," (Cogan, *I Kings*, 219).

government so that the affairs of the nation were adequately addressed.[33] In the early verses of the chapter, we are introduced to his cabinet:

- Zadok's grandson, Azariah (2 Sam 15:29, 36; 1 Chr 6:9), was the high priest.[34] His father was presumably still alive and likely serving in an emeritus position since he is mentioned in v. 4.[35]

- Solomon's two secretaries, Elihoreph and Ahijah, enjoyed very high positions in the government,[36] second only to the master of the palace. One may have been a secretary or minister of international relations, while the other was over internal or domestic affairs,[37] as was done in Assyria.

- The recorder, Jehoshaphat, had served David (2 Sam 8:16; 20:24) and now functioned as a "royal herald." He brought public needs to the king's attention and then turned around and served as the king's spokesman or press secretary[38] (cf. 2 Kgs 18:18). It's possible that his duties also included that of a state prosecutor or attorney general.[39]

- As we have already discovered, Benaiah was Solomon's top military commander.

- Azariah, the son of Nathan the prophet,[40] "was over the officers,"

---

33. Solomon's roster of officials is very similar to his father's, but with one conspicuous exception. "In David's roster of officials, the army commander-in-chief came first (2 Sam. 8:16; 20:23). Here the priest and other officials preceded the military leader (v. 4), implying that Solomon's reign was one of peace, not war," (Hubbard, *First and Second Kings*, 34–35).

34. de Vaux, *Ancient Israel*, 2:378.

35. Abiathar is also mentioned as priest, though Solomon had sent him into retirement in 1 Kings 2. Either he had returned to Solomon's favor (Provan, *1 & 2 Kings*, 54), or the king graciously allowed him to retain an emeritus position alongside Zadok because of his ancestry (as suggested by Theodoret in the sixth century A.D.).

36. A. D. Crown, "Messengers and Scribes: The ספר and מלאך in the Old Testament," *VT* 24 (1974): 366–70.

37. Wiseman, *1 and 2 Kings*, 96–97.

38. de Vaux, *Ancient Israel*, 1:132.

39. Provan, *1 & 2 Kings*, 54.

40. Contra Barnes, who believes this Nathan to be David's son (2 Sam 5:14), "or possibly someone else entirely (the name was quite common)," (*1–2 Kings*, 58).

meaning the governors set over the administrative districts in
Israel (vv. 7–19).

- Nathan's other son, Zabud, "was priest and king's friend." This
  last position was likely that of chief personal advisor to Solomon, not unlike a combination of the White House's chief of
  staff and the president's personal chaplain.[41] In David's administration, Hushai had held this position (2 Sam 15:37; 16:16).

- Next is Ahishar, the palace overseer or head servant (cf. 16:9;
  18:3),[42] and Adoniram, chief of corvée or forced labor[43] (cf.
  5:13–18; 9:15–22). Over the course of time, Ahishar's position
  gained considerable influence (cf. Isa 22:15–24), perhaps as
  high as Joseph's had been in Egypt (Gen 41:40–45).

We also learn that Solomon divided Israel into a dozen administrative districts, with officers or governors in charge of each. For one month each year, a
district was responsible for feeding the royal household.[44] Beyond this, the exact
nature of this position is ambiguous. Were they district administrators, such as
a state governor? Or something more narrow, such as a local tax enforcer? We
can't know. But noteworthy in this list are Ben-abinadab (v. 11) and Ahimaaz
(v. 15), sons-in-law of Solomon who would have aided the king in neutralizing
enemies of the royal family.[45]

Solomon's twelve districts were somewhat based on old tribal territories,
but not rigidly. Solomon again demonstrates his administrative acumen by re-
drawing district lines in his favor.[46] Conspicuously absent from the list is any

---

41. Patterson, "1, 2 Kings," 667.

42. de Vaux, *Ancient Israel*, 1:129–31.

43. Cogan notes that this title appears in a seal from the seventh century, indicating the
position (as well as the phenomenon of corvée labor) existed for much of Judah's existence as
a nation (*I Kings*, 204; cf. Nahman Avigad, "The Chief of the Corvée," *IEJ* 30 [1980]: 170–73.).

44. "Samuel had warned the people that having a king would have costs in terms of people and provisions (1 Sam. 8:11–18); now they were experiencing the reality," (Olley, *Message
of Kings*, 70).

45. House, *1, 2 Kings*, 116.

46. "The northern tribes under Sheba had already attempted to secede from the united
kingdom (2 Sam 20:1–2). If new political boundaries could be redrawn so that tribal populations and the new Canaanite cities added to the nation were mixed together, then the king might

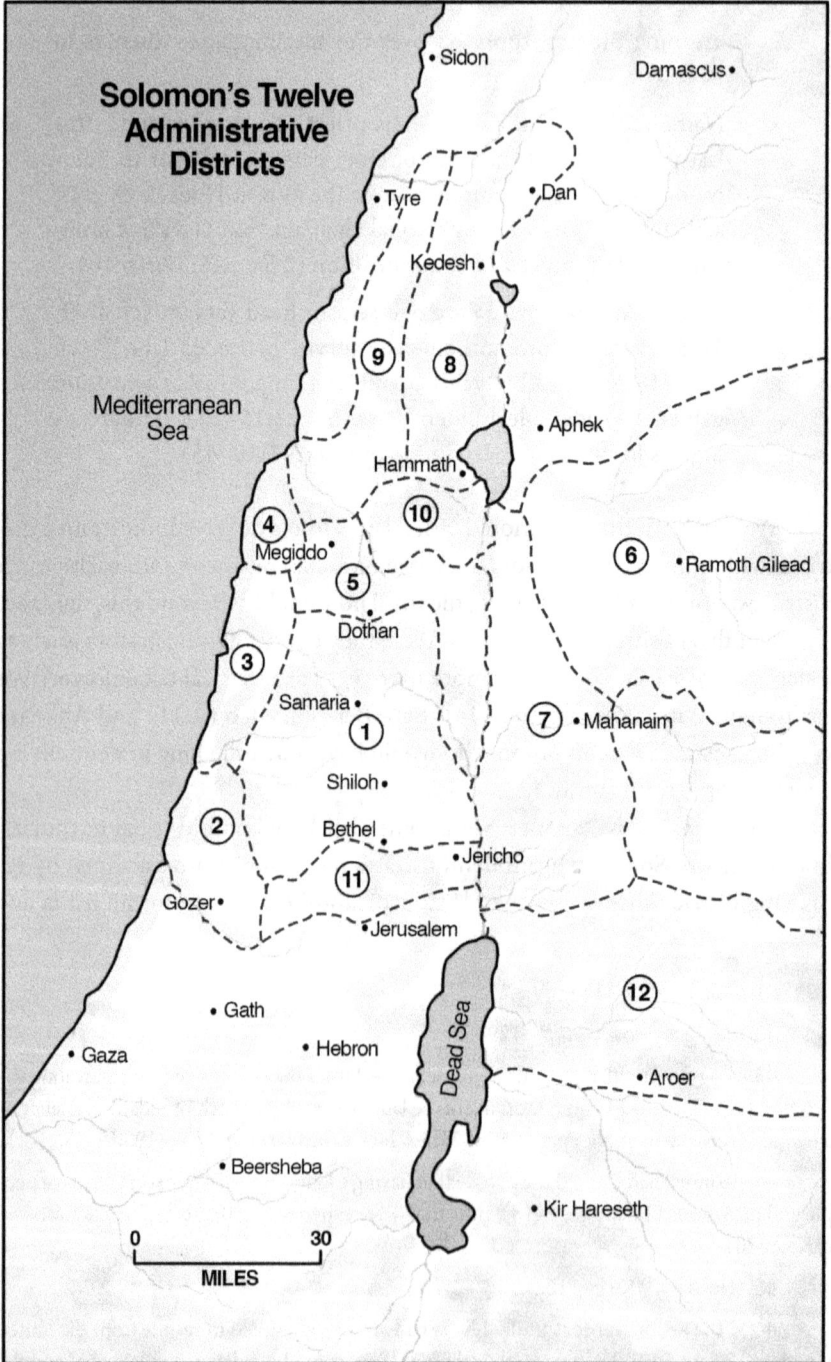

Solomon's Twelve
Administrative
Districts

Mediterranean
Sea

• Sidon

Damascus •

• Tyre

• Dan

Kedesh •

⑨   ⑧

• Aphek

Hammath •

⑩

④

Megiddo •

⑤

Dothan •

③

Samaria •

①

Shiloh •

②

Bethel •

⑪

Gozer •

• Jericho

• Jerusalem

⑥   • Ramoth Gilead

⑦ • Mahanaim

⑫

• Gath

• Hebron

Dead Sea

• Gaza

• Aroer

• Beersheba

• Kir Hareseth

0   30
MILES

mention of the tribe or territory of Judah, which may have been exempted from taxation—"Whereas [Solomon] apparently ruled Judah directly as his home tribe, he ruled Israel through administrators much as one would rule a foreign or subject state."[47] In a nutshell:

- District 1 contained most of the hill country of Ephraim.

- District 2 was on the Mediterranean coast just north of the Philistines and south of Joppa, formerly the territory of Dan before they migrated north (Judg 17–18).

- District 3 was the forested, swampy, sparsely-populated area north of Joppa on the coast.

- District 4 was the coastal area south of the Carmel range.

- District 5 included Megiddo in northern Israel, southwest of Galilee.

- District 6 was the Transjordan region of Gilead and Bashan.

- District 7 was the Transjordan region south of Jabbok, including the territories of Manasseh and Gad.

- District 8 included the territory of Naphtali in northern Israel, northwest of Galilee.

- District 9 included the territory of Asher, west of Galilee.

- District 10 included the territory of Issachar (and possibly Zebulun), the Jezreel Valley, and the area south of Galilee.

- District 11 was the tribe of Benjamin.

- District 12 included the ancient kingdoms of Sihon and Og, south of Gad in Transjordan and east of the Dead Sea.

Brueggemann sums up the main point of this passage: "That regime must have been enormously successful and deeply impressive to Israelites who were only two generations removed from hill-country subsistence living."[48]

---

forestall future political problems," (Walton, *Bible Background*, 359).

47. Marvin A. Sweeney, *I & II Kings* (Louisville: Westminster John Knox, 2007), 89.

48. Brueggemann, *1 & 2 Kings*, 57.

The narrator succinctly expresses the point of the second half of 1 Kings 4 with "Judah and Israel were as many as the sand by the sea. They ate and drank and were happy" (v. 19). Surprising as it might be, this is the first time in the Old Testament that this statement is made about Israel as a present reality. Only now was God's promise to Abraham fulfilled—"I will surely bless you, and I will surely multiply your offspring as the stars of heaven and as the sand that is on the seashore" (Gen 22:17). Not even under David's leadership did Israel realize the Abrahamic promise to this degree.

It was also under Solomon's watch that Israel's territory finally expanded to encompass all that God had promised the patriarch. "Solomon ruled over all the kingdoms from the Euphrates to the land of the Philistines and to the border of Egypt" (v. 21; cf. Gen 12:1–9; 15:18; Exod 23:31; Deut 11:24; Josh 1:4).

The remainder of the passage expresses the narrator's gushing admiration for the glory days of Solomon. On any given day, the king's table required 180 bushels[49] of flour, 360 bushels of meal, 10 oxen, 20 cattle, 100 sheep, and assorted deer, gazelles, roebucks, and birds (Wiseman identifies the latter as geese, guineas, and hens[50]). Surely, Solomon's daily dining table redefined the phrase "a meal fit for a king.[51]

And his stables full of horses and horsemen weren't too shabby, either (vv. 26–28). Though this passage numbers Solomon's stalls at forty thousand, the parallel passage in 2 Chronicles 9:25 claims it was four thousand, which scholars take as a much more plausible number and claim that "forty thousand" in 1 Kings 4:26 is a scribal error. In ancient Palestine, three horses made up a chariot team—two to pull the chariot, and one in reserve. This would give Solomon twelve thousand horses (the same number as his horsemen) and four thousand chariots. In comparison, Ahab would have two thousand chariots at his disposal at the battle of Qarqar a century later.[52]

---

49. A "cor" (ESV) was equal to about six bushels (Wiseman, *1 and 2 Kings*, 102).

50. Ibid.

51. For those who believe this to be too much for one table, Patterson reminds us, "It may well be that the food supported those stationed in the various garrisons as well as those connected with the palace itself," ("1, 2 Kings," 670). "Estimates of the number of persons Solomon sustained vary from fourteen thousand to thirty-two thousand," (House, *1, 2 Kings*, 117).

52. "The archaeological remains of chariot cities such as Megiddo and the consistently large numbers of chariots recorded in ancient Near Eastern and biblical battles do allow for the possibility that these numbers are indeed accurate," (Monson, "1 Kings," 24; cf. Alan R. Millard,

To the king's personal largesse is added a statement about the dominion he enjoyed over so expansive a territory and the peace he oversaw. The vassals he had inherited from his father continued to honor him with lavish tribute.[53] "From Dan even to Beersheba" (v. 25; cf. "from sea to shining sea"), Israel was safe and secure. Surely this peace was due to the other-worldly wisdom God had bestowed on his royal servant. Solomon was the author of 3,000 proverbs, of which the book of Proverbs contains about 582 by one count.[54] He is said to have been wiser than the Egyptians (cf. Gen 41:8; Isa 19:11), even wiser than the Einsteins of his day—Ethan, Heman, Calcol, and Darda (cf. 1 Chr 2:6; 6:33; Pss 88–89). Solomon also had an interest in and drew insight from his observations of botany and zoology.[55] Similar to Nebuchadnezzar's Hanging Gardens some four centuries later, Solomon might have cultivated a large, impressive botanical garden near his palace[56] (Eccl 2:5; cf. Song 1:14; 2:3; 6:2). Josephus claims Solomon had such a garden five to six miles south of Jerusalem outside of Bethlehem.[57] All in all, "the land Moses desired, Joshua conquered, and David subdued now lay in the hands of a man of unsurpassed wisdom."[58]

"The inauguration of Solomon's reign is Israel's cultural zenith. This view of the first part of Solomon's reign as unmitigated blessing not only demonstrates

---

"Large Numbers in the Assyrian Royal Inscriptions," in *Ah, Assyria...: Studies in Assyrian History and Ancient Near Eastern Historiography Presented to Hayim Tadmor*, eds. Mordechai Cogan and Israel Eph'al [Jerusalem: Magnes, 1991], 213–22).

53. "The usual experience of ancient empire builders was that when the old king died, the subject nations would withhold tribute and challenge the new king in mounting a rebellion, thus necessitating repeated punitive expeditions by the new king to reinforce the former king's terms and to prove the ability of the new king to enforce his will. Solomon did not have this problem. God granted him a peaceful reign in which he could focus his energies on the temple and other building projects, as well as on administrative matters and on the building up of extensive and expanding foreign trade," (Patterson, "1, 2 Kings," 670).

54. Wiseman, *1 and 2 Kings*, 104. Cogan claims, "Both 'three thousand' and 'a thousand and five' are meant to convey the idea of very large numbers and then some, like 'a thousand and one nights,'" (*I Kings*, 222).

55. cf. Judges 9:8–15; 2 Kings 14:9; Proverbs 6:6–8; 11:22; 17:12; 19:12; 22:13; 26:13; 26:2, 11; 30:15, 17, 19, 25–28, 30–31.

56. Walled royal gardens were a common fixture for Assyrian kings; the garden of Ashurnasirpal II (c. 883–859) contained eighty-five different species (Wiseman, *1 and 2 Kings*, 104–5).

57. Josephus, *Antiquities* 8.186.

58. House, *1, 2 Kings*, 116.

the ideal of the monarchy, but the fulfillment of the divine promise to David,"[59] (cf. 2 Sam 7:10–11). Indeed, this passage gushes with praise to God for keeping his promises. In both Deuteronomy and in the Prophets, living in safety under a vine and fig tree (v. 25) indicated a long life pregnant with the covenant blessings (cf. Deut 12:10; Joel 2:22; Mic 4:4; Zech 3:10)—the idea evoked roughly the same emotions that white sandy beaches or cozy wilderness cabins do for Americans. In virtually every conceivable way, Israel under Solomon enjoyed all the blessings promised to them in the Sinai covenant.

To be honest, I'm not sure what to think about Solomon. Marrying a foreigner (or worse, an Egyptian!) does not square with Deuteronomy. Mention of multiple wives, a large stable of horses and chariots, and unparalleled wealth is meant to trigger remembrance of the admonition in Deuteronomy 17:14–20 that the king should not put his trust in such things (cf. 1 Sam 8:10–18). Yet the rest of this section goes on to describe with sincere admiration the glory of Solomon's giftedness and empire.

As we continue to read Kings through the lens of Deuteronomy, we can appreciate Konkel's observation: "The problem for the Deuteronomist [i.e., the narrator of Kings] is that the success of the kingdom is the very thing that makes it vulnerable to demise. [...] While the statements about wealth and power may demonstrate the success of Solomon, they are also the point of his vulnerability."[60] Jeremiah will attest that these issues only worsened (Jer 22:13–17), and the annals of human history abound with anecdotes of what happens when absolute power meets unsurpassed wealth. Solomon is a cautionary tale of how the seeds of our destruction are often sown in the soil of our success.

Like Solomon, our Lord found in the natural world insight and divine wisdom. It was on a hillside, one perhaps carpeted with wildflowers, that Jesus once preached a rather famous sermon. In it, he urged us to "consider the lilies of the field, how they grow: they neither toil nor spin, yet I tell you, even Solomon in all his glory was not arrayed like one of these" (Matt 6:28–29). Worried as we often are about making ends meet, Jesus deliberately invoked Solomon's largesse when he said, "Do not be anxious, saying, 'What shall we eat?' or 'What shall

59. Konkel, *1 & 2 Kings*, 103.
60. Ibid.

we drink?'" (6:31). Indeed, whatever our concerns might be, they are mitigated when we seek first the kingdom of God (6:33).

Christians can rejoice that one greater than Solomon has come (Matt 12:42). In him, Paul says, "are hidden all the treasures of wisdom and knowledge" (Col 2:3; cf. 1 Cor 1:24). As the King of kings, he rules with a wisdom that far surpasses Solomon's; unlike mortal judges, his judgments are not limited by what he sees and hears, but emanate from the righteousness inherent in his character (Isa 11:3–4). "And if such a King already has begun to reign (Eph. 1:20-22), must we not assume, as his subjects, that he will never ordain or order anything in our circumstances, except what is in line with wisdom at its highest and best?"[61]

Solomon was wise and skilled at so many things, yet he ultimately failed to discover the end of all wisdom—uninterrupted fellowship with Yahweh. In reality, Solomon had just enough wisdom to make it to the top of the totem pole in his world, but not enough to teach him to rely on the Lord for all things.

This, then, is the standard by which we consider Christ's glory to be far greater than Solomon's. Though humiliated with a torn robe and crown of thorns, the Lord Jesus Christ has now been exalted to God's right hand. Though Solomon was honored by "all the kings west of the Euphrates" (v. 24), Christ has been given a "name that is above every name," and he will witness every knee "in heaven and on earth and under the earth" acknowledge his splendor and glory (Phil 2:9–11). And our Lord will receive such because he glorified the Father on earth with his obedience (John 17:4–5).

From a worldly standpoint, the peace and prosperity of Solomon's time seem unattainable and almost unbelievable. Whether recession, war, or plague, something always seems to ruin our glory days and steal our shalom. Isn't it impressive (and just a bit outlandish?) that God offers members of his kingdom a glory greater than Solomon ever had? If God cares so much about the flora and fauna of earth—of which Solomon knew so much—how will he also not provide for our every need in Christ? Seek first God's kingdom, and you'll discover something of which Solomon could only dream.

---

61. Davis, *1 Kings,* 41.

TALKING POINTS

T here is much in this section concerning Solomon that will never be attainable by simple people like myself (e.g., the promise of extraordinary wisdom, riches, power). But the same God who so generously gave to Solomon when he prayed remains the God who hears the prayers of all his people and answers generously. In prayer, Jesus taught us to ask, seek, and knock in order to receive good gifts from our Father (Matt 7:7, 11; 21:22; John 14:13–14). God gives above and beyond our wildest imaginations (Eph 3:20). But some people never experience the fullness of their Father's generosity, either because they are unwilling to work for it, or because they never ask (Jas 4:2). In Solomon's prayer at Gibeon, he models for us how we ought to approach God. He acknowledged God's past action, he asked for God's continued blessing, he expressed humility, and, finally, he asked for the strength to do God's will.[62] As the rest of Kings will prove, prayer isn't a religious good luck charm or "Get Out of Jail Free" card; what matters to God is whether we walk before him in faith and obedience. For my sake alone, the words of my prayers should remind me 1) of what God has done for me in the past, 2) that God is the source of all good things, 3) that he's God, and I'm not, but 4) that I need to put legs on my prayers, putting God's power to work in my life.

T here is arguably no greater trait so essential to effective leadership than wisdom (cf. Acts 6:3). By this, I do not mean heightened intellect, strong secular education, common sense, or even having a commanding knowledge of Scripture. The sort of wisdom necessary for effective leadership encompasses a right relationship with God and knowing in one moment to the next what will be pleasing to God. Solomon began his reign well; he exemplified wisdom in so many critical areas (e.g., judicial reasoning, domestic administration, international politics). But despite all the sage advice he left behind in Proverbs, he proved a failure at following much of his own counsel. Some leaders may be "book smart," have impressive credentials, possess business sav-

---

62. Wiseman, *1 and 2 Kings*, 92. Davis notes that Solomon, above all, desires the welfare of his people above his own personal enhancement. "The king is a model here. We should not worry over how to succeed but over how we may most profit the people of God. Anxiety over the people of God controls Solomon's petition," (*1 Kings*, 37).

vy, talk a good game, or even be fluent in Scripture. But none of these things can prevent them from proving to be fools when and where it matters most. As we attempt to discern wisdom in potential leaders, we ought to ask, "Does this person seek wisdom for wisdom's sake, or to draw nearer to God and bless the lives of others?" Put another way, biblically-wise leaders will use their wisdom authentically, not to elevate themselves above the crowd, but to seek ways to fulfill the two greatest commandments: love God and love people.

For anyone who knows the rest of the story, the note that Solomon married an Egyptian sounds an ominous tone at the beginning of his reign. Since Solomon was already married, it seems this union was politically motivated, which was hardly uncommon in ancient times. But intermarrying with the Gentiles proved to be the beginning of the end of Solomon's reign and Israel's decline. Less than a century after returning from Babylonian Exile, Nehemiah lividly expelled a Jew from the Jerusalem community for marrying a foreigner, citing Solomon as the reason and essentially lamenting, "Haven't we learned anything from our past mistakes?" (Neh 13:23–27). Nehemiah understood that kingdoms enter decline when what is pragmatic or politically expedient takes precedence over what God has commanded. Sadly, our success often blinds us to our spiritual blunders until it's too late. It's not unlike taking on a curve on a windy road at a high rate of speed. Most of the time, one can enter a curve in the road and safely leave unheeded the warning sign to slow down. But it only takes one ignored caution and one curve taken too fast to lead to our death, and our folly will be realized too late. Better to obey and leave the consequences to God than to consider his laws as "no big deal" and see our kingdom slip away.

3

IN THIS HOUSE

Throughout human history, a civilization's priorities could be determined in part by its buildings. As the archaeologist's spade has uncovered the remains of societies in the Fertile Crescent, Europe, and the Americas, each site has given clues as to what these peoples prized above all else. Temples. Palaces. Extravagant wonders of the world that defy even a twenty-first-century, Western imagination. Five thousand years from now, what will archaeologists conclude concerning our priorities?

It's little secret that I'm a huge football fan. College, pro, paper—it doesn't matter. But even I am concerned with the skyrocketing public cost of America's favorite sport. In the last twenty years, $7 billion of taxpayers' money has been spent on constructing or renovating NFL stadiums, accounting for 46% of the total cost of these projects.

- In 2017, the Atlanta Falcons will move into their new home in Mercedes-Benz Stadium, a gorgeous facility with a $1.4 billion price tag, $600 million of which came from public funds.

- In 2016, the Minnesota Vikings opened US Bank Stadium in Minneapolis, a $1.1 billion facility that cost taxpayers just under $500 million.

- My beloved Dallas Cowboys cut the ribbon on AT&T Stadium in 2009, a gorgeous $1.3 billion temple to the football gods that cost Arlington, Texas residents $300 million.

- The worst offender seems to have been the Indianapolis Colts, a franchise worth $1 billion, who built Lucas Oil Stadium in 2008 for $719 million, $619 million of which came from the public.[1]

Americans have always demanded the biggest and best money could buy. Whereas we once marveled at the size of the Astrodome or the Sears Tower, they were eventually surpassed by even grander stadiums and skyscrapers. Societies have always demonstrated their priorities in their buildings, and one could argue that being bigger, larger, or better is crucial to our identity as Americans—our funding of buildings, public and private, proves this.

For ancient civilizations, temples and palaces were almost always at the center of a developed society, and the construction and maintenance of them was always the purview of the king. In 1 Kings 5–8, we read of Solomon's construction of the Temple and his palace. We have already been witness to the king's judicial (3:16–28), administrative (4:1–28), and intellectual (4:29–34) wisdom;[2] in these chapters, we see his political and architectural acumen come alive. Surely, God's blessing rests on Solomon.

Once built, the importance of the Temple to Israel's self-identity can hardly be overstated. Wray Beal considers these chapters in Kings to be the high point of Israel's covenant history,[3] while Monson observes, "The temple, like Jerusalem, is mentioned throughout the Bible as a reminder of God's sovereignty, the setting of his worship, and a barometer of Israel's spiritual health. [...] Through the frequent fluctuations of Israel's faith, the temple serves as the witness to judgment and renewal alike (Ps. 79:1; Jer. 7:1-7)."[4]

---

1. To be fair, municipal governments often fund these projects by increasing taxes on hotels, car rentals, and the like. And there is a persuasive argument to be made that such funding is an investment in the local economy. New stadiums are contracted in hopes of landing a Super Bowl (Arlington hosted one in 2011; Indianapolis, in 2012; and Minneapolis will host in 2018) and other major sporting events (NBA All-Star Game, NCAA Final Four, etc.). In the case of Arlington, they now expect to pay back their $300 million bond for AT&T Stadium ten years early, due to a larger-than-expected windfall the stadium has brought the city.

2. House, *1, 2 Kings*, 123.

3. Wray Beal, *1 & 2 Kings*, 140.

4. John M. Monson, "The Temple of Solomon: Heart of Jerusalem," in *Zion, City of our God*, eds. Richard S. Hess and Gordon J. Wenham (Grand Rapids: Eerdmans, 1999), 1. Later, he adds, "In sum, the triad of God, monarch, and people intersected in the temple of Zion. Nowhere are the physical and emotional impact of this theology better expressed than in Psalms 68, 84,

I'll admit these chapters will at times be as exciting as watching grass grow. But just as we are often impressed with stadiums and skyscrapers enough to want to visit (I've toured AT&T Stadium three times), the narrator insists on giving us a tour of Solomon's Temple and palace, noting their origin and history. As stadiums/skyscrapers shape our identity, the Temple was critical to Israel's. Later in Kings, the narrator will increasingly become more concerned with the Temple and its fate. Though it was worthy of care as God's house, Israel eventually put too much emphasis on the physical structure at the expense of its Owner, providing a cautionary tale for God's people today.

1 KINGS 5

The narrative of the Temple's construction commences with a scene-shift to the coastal city-state of Tyre, some fifty miles north of Jerusalem. David had been allied with Hiram (c. 980–950), the king of Tyre, and had previously contracted with him to supply Israel with the necessary materials for building the Temple (1 Chr 22:4). Recall that David had not been allowed to build the Temple himself because he was a man of war, not peace (1 Chr 28:3).

Since Hiram constructed no less than three impressive temples of his own,[5] he naturally would have known how to help. Hiram's affection and gratitude for David (v. 1) likely was based on the latter's success in putting the Philistines, Tyre's rival in maritime commerce, in their place (2 Sam 8:1). This had allowed Tyre to trade more freely. Under Hiram, "trade arrangements expanded and colonies b[e]gan to be established in the western Mediterranean, perhaps as far as Cadiz [Spain]."[6]

Having secured his kingdom, Solomon sent a request to Hiram for the building materials David had first solicited. Solomon proposed that both Solomon's and Hiram's servants be used in the venture, with Solomon footing the

---

and 122," (Ibid., 8).

5. Josephus, *Antiquities* 8.146–47.

6. Lowell K. Handy, "Phoenicians in the Tenth Century BCE: A Sketch of an Outline," in *The Age of Solomon: Scholarship at the Turn of the Millennium*, ed. Lowell K. Handy (Leiden: Brill, 1997), 163. For more on the mutual benefit of the Israel/Tyre trade agreement, see Brian Peckham, "Israel and Phoenecia," in *Magnalia Dei, The Mighty Acts of God: Essays on the Bible and Archaeology in Memory of G. Ernest Wright*, eds. Frank Moore Cross, Werner E. Lemke, and Patrick D. Miller, Jr. (Garden City, NY: Doubleday, 1976), 231–33.

bill. Thus began the process of erecting a permanent place for God in Israel, a prophecy made by Moses several times in Deuteronomy.[7]

The cedars of Lebanon were famous in antiquity for their grandeur and beauty (Ps 92:12; Ezek 31:3; 2 Kgs 14:9; 19:23; Isa 2:13; 10:34). The wood "was durable, resistant to rot and worms, closely-grained, and could be polished to a fine shine."[8] A typical cedar would grow to around one hundred feet; by comparison, an average oak is just fifty feet, while the coastal redwoods of California grow to more than two hundred feet. The cedars' length made them valuable in shipbuilding and "a symbol of luxury in architecture."[9] Though he sent his own workmen to aid Hiram's and was even willing to pay everyone out of his own pocket, Solomon seemed to insist that Hiram's workers do the actual felling of the trees. He conceded, "There is no one among us who knows how to cut timber like the Sidonians" (v. 6). Indeed, no one in the ancient Near East matched the men of Sidon in this talent.[10]

Hiram had the cedar logs floated down to Joppa (cf. 2 Chr 2:16) as rafts, then broken apart and shipped inland to Jerusalem. In return, Solomon paid Hiram an annual stipend in agricultural produce: over 50,000 bushels (800 tons) of grain and more than 100,000 gallons of pure olive oil,[11] neither of which were "found in abundance in mountainous Phoenicia, whose economy was primarily based on an extensive shipping trade and export of timber."[12] From all appear-

---

7. Deuteronomy 12:5, 11, 14, 18, 21, 26; 12:11; 14:23–25; 15:20; 16:2, 6–7, 11, 15–16; 17:8, 10; 18:6; 26:2; 31:11; cf. 1 Kings 8:16, 44, 48; 11:13, 32, 36; 14:21; 2 Kings 21:7; 23:27.

8. Hubbard, *First and Second Kings*, 40. He adds, "For centuries Tyre did a brisk export business in cedarwood. A popular Egyptian tale, 'The Journey of Wen-Amon to Phoenicia' (11th cent. B.C.), told how Wen-Amon traded a host of Egyptian goods for cedar lumber from Gebal, a major seaport north of Tyre," (Ibid.).

9. Monson, "1 Kings," 26.

10. Cogan, *I Kings*, 227. Tyre and Sidon were sister cities and often existed under the same rule.

11. Pure olive oil was made from beating olives by hand with a pestle and mortar. Plain olive oil, however, was a less-pure form made from cylindrical stone presses (Gray, *I & II Kings*, 146). While the LXX lists "twenty thousand" cors of oil, the Hebrew reads only "twenty," equaling a little more than seventeen hundred gallons.

12. Patterson, "1, 2 Kings," 675. "Since the coastal strip near the Phoenician towns has always been fairly narrow, it was difficult to meet the agricultural needs of the population," (Fritz, *1 & 2 Kings*, 61).

ances, no expense was spared in securing materials for the Temple, and such a fact highlights the building's importance to Solomon.

To assist with the logging, Solomon drafted thirty thousand Canaanites[13] (cf. 9:15–23) to work in Lebanon in one-month-on/two-months-off shifts. To prepare the raw materials for the Temple's construction, Solomon conscripted an additional 150,000 workers in Israel, all overseen by 3,300 officials. Stone-cutters were especially valuable in this enterprise—away from the Temple site, they had to prepare[14] the stones (some of them seven feet in size) and fit them together without mortar like an intricate puzzle. Singled out among all the work-men were "the men of Gebal." Gebal was located on the northern boundary of Canaan (Josh 13:5). Later in the Old Testament, these same craftsmen were identified as partly responsible for Tyre's success in maritime commerce (Ezek 27:9), indicating they were exceptionally skilled at masonry and carpentry.

In this way, Solomon procured the supplies necessary to build the Temple. He proved himself to be a master negotiator; I imagine our narrator would have thought Solomon could teach President Trump much about "the art of a deal." For the moment, Solomon is also a trusted ally. God's blessing was indeed great on Solomon's administration (v. 12). Soon, Yahweh would have a house of his own in the Promised Land.

1 KINGS 6–7

In his opening comments on 1 Kings 6, Provan writes, "Much is obscure to us as readers who stand at such a distance from the authors of the text, and we shall not pause at any length to puzzle over the architectural detail or marvel at

---

13. In the present passage, the use of forced or corvée labor by Solomon (a common practice among Israel's neighbors) seems to be evidence of God's wisdom resting on him (cf. v. 12). Note that this was not slavery; the workers only labored four months out of the year. "Such conscripted labor was common for temple building or maintenance projects. Solomon was, af-ter all, running a monarchy, not a ballot-box democracy," (Davis, *1 Kings*, 56–57). However, as with many blessings, selfish abuse of corvée labor eventually led to trouble in Solomon's para-dise (cf. 9:15; 12:4, 14–16). For the alleged discrepancy in numbers of workers and foremen between Kings and Chronicles, see House, *1, 2 Kings*, 125.

14. "The use of dressed stones for the foundation emphasizes the precious character of the building, since the foundations were normally made from undressed stones," (Fritz, *1 & 2 Kings*, 64). Several ancient stone quarries have been discovered in Palestine dating to the tenth and ninth centuries (Yigal Shiloh and Aharon Horowitz, "Ashlar Quarries of the Iron Age In the Hill Country of Israel," *BASOR* 217 [1975]: 37–48).

all the glitter and the gold. Little that is important for interpreting the book of Kings hangs on any such detail,"[15] and I agree. But there are a few juicy nuggets of interest in this passage, and those I intend to explore.

It wasn't uncommon in ancient times for kings to mark the foundation of an important building by dating it in relation to a momentous event in the nation's history.[16] Thus, this chapter opens with the note that the Temple groundbreaking occurred in the 480th year[17] of the Exodus. Such a date-stamp is of major significance for several reasons. For one, it "reminds readers that the permanent worship center is one more proof that God has given Israel the promised land."[18] The Temple celebrated Yahweh as Israel's God, a monument of gratitude for his covenant and his faithfulness to it. The Ark of the Covenant's presence in the Temple's Most Holy Place was the capstone on this concept.

But going deeper, mention of the Exodus also points to the impending Exile. Throughout the Temple narrative, there are several references to the great deliverance from Egypt that God had wrought on Israel's behalf (6:11–13; 8:9, 16, 21, 51, 53, 56–58). The account, however, will also be punctuated with a forecast of the Exile, a reversal of the Exodus (8:48–53). This is an important point for the original audience of Kings to understand. The narrator wants to drive home the truth that God had been powerfully present with and had poured out favor on his people *before* the Temple; there was thus no reason to believe he wouldn't do so *after* the Temple was gone. In other words, even as the narrator celebrates the Temple, he subtly encourages Israel to see beyond it, not to place false hope in it, to see it as an icon and not an idol.

The capital city of Jerusalem Solomon inherited from his father was rather small by today's standards, occupying just eleven acres. It thus did not have room for a larger royal residence or the Temple, so the entire complex was constructed to the north of the old city upon Mount Moriah, on what had been Araunah's threshing floor[19] (2 Sam 24:16; 1 Chr 22:1; 2 Chr 3:1; Ezek 41:8, 13–14). To-

---

15. Provan, *1 & 2 Kings*, 66.

16. Wiseman, *1 and 2 Kings*, 111–13.

17. It is unclear if this number is meant to be literal or symbolic, *480* possibly representing twelve periods (representing Israel's tribes) of forty years (or twelve generations).

18. House, *1, 2 Kings*, 126.

19. See illustrations of Jerusalem during David's versus Solomon's reign in *Crossway ESV Bible Atlas*, eds. John D. Currid and David P. Barrett (Wheaton, IL: Crossway, 2010), 127, 131.

day, the Dome of the Rock sits on the site of the Temple, preventing any archaeological exploration.

The measurements of the Temple are given as sixty cubits[20] long, twenty cubits wide, and forty cubits high (v. 2). Compare this to the Tabernacle (see chart below), which was a hundred cubits long, fifty cubits wide, and more than eight cubits high—the dimensions of the Tabernacle, though larger, included the courtyard. Take away the Tabernacle's courtyard, and the Temple was nearly double its size (cf. Exod 26:15–25; 36:24). Also, the Temple was more than three times the height of the Tabernacle (about fourteen feet), towering five stories (v. 6) or nearly sixty feet above the surrounding landscape.

	Tabernacle	Temple
Length	100 cubits	60 cubits
Width	50 cubits	20 cubits
Height	8 cubits	40 cubits

Tabernacle and Temple by Comparison

As I just mentioned, the Dome of the Rock currently sits on the site of the Temple. Thus, the archaeologist's spade is incapable of illuminating this passage for us. But elsewhere in the ancient Near East, they have unearthed other temples with very similar blueprints,[21] meaning Solomon's Temple followed a pattern common throughout the region. This would make sense, given that craftsmen from the same area of the world worked on Solomon's Temple also. Most significant has been the discovery of the temple at 'Ain Dara (forty miles northwest of Aleppo), which is quite similar to the biblical description of Solomon's Temple.[22]

---

20. When the Temple was constructed, a cubit was about 17½ inches. "Toward the end of the monarchic period, a larger cubit measure was adopted, 'a cubit plus one handbreadth,' about 20 inches (cf. Ezek 40:5; 43:13); cf. 2 Chr 3:3 for the notation that the dimensions were given according to 'the former measure,'" (Cogan, *I Kings*, 237). On the other hand, the measurement of a cubit at the construction of the Tabernacle had been the Egyptian royal cubit, roughly equal to 20.625 inches (Unger, "Tabernacle of Israel," *NUBD* 1240).

21. Monson, "Temple of Solomon," 10–22; Volkmar Fritz, "Temple Architecture: What Can Archaeology Tell Us About Solomon's Temple?" *BAR* 13/4 (1987): 38–49; Christopher J. Davey, "Temples of the Levant and the Buildings of Solomon," *TynBul* 31 (1980): 107–46.

22. John Monson, "The New 'Ain Dara Temple: Closest Solomonic Parallel," *BAR* 26/3

The Temple's basic design was long and narrow and included:

- a vestibule or entry hall
- a main hall measuring approximately 1,700 square feet
- an inner sanctuary (the Most Holy Place) measuring 850 square feet[23]
- side rooms (for storage, presumably) off the main hall
- windows with "recessed frames"[24] (v. 4)
- frame and beams of Lebanon cedars provided by Hiram (v. 9)

If you and I had been able to tour the Temple upon its completion, we would have surely drawn the same conclusion as DeVries: "All in all, this was a dark and mysterious structure, conducive to a sense of awe."[25]

The ancient Israelites were very sensitive to maintaining holiness in a particular place. Thus, the note that no hammers, axes, or other iron tools were used on the construction site (v. 7) speaks to the sacredness of the Temple grounds[26] (cf. Exod 20:25; Deut 27:5–6; Josh 8:31)—there was none of the typical cacophony one would be accustomed to hearing in such a place. Instead, it seems

---

(2000): 20–35; Victor Horowitz, "Solomon's Temple in Context," *BAR* 37/2 (2011): 46–57, 77–78. "The only significant difference between the two is the inclusion of the antechamber in the 'Ain Dara plan. With this exception the two plans are almost identical," (Monson, "New 'Ain Dara Temple," 30).

23. The height of the Most Holy Place was ten cubits less than the rest of the Temple, meaning the Temple had a sloping roof, or the Most Holy Place sat on a platform and was accessed by a flight of stairs (Davey, "Temples of the Levant," 109).

24. "Because the architectural terms found in the Hebrew are technical terms, their exact meaning is uncertain. Some suggest that the windows were constructed with a narrow opening on the outside and a wider opening on the inside (see Ezek 40:16). It is also possible that latticed windows are meant here. The lack of windows in Mesopotamian temples, however, argues against natural light entering Solomon's temple (see 1 Kings 8:12). The 'Ain Dara temple had false windows carved into the stone with a lattice-work design," (Walton, *Bible Background*, 362). If the Temple indeed was devoid of natural light, "This would accord with the impression the Bible gives of the temple as a dark, mysterious place," (Monson, "1 Kings," 28).

25. DeVries, *1 Kings*, 94.

26. Josephus also interpreted this as a sign of the builders' skill (*Antiquities* 8.69).

Solomon's Temple

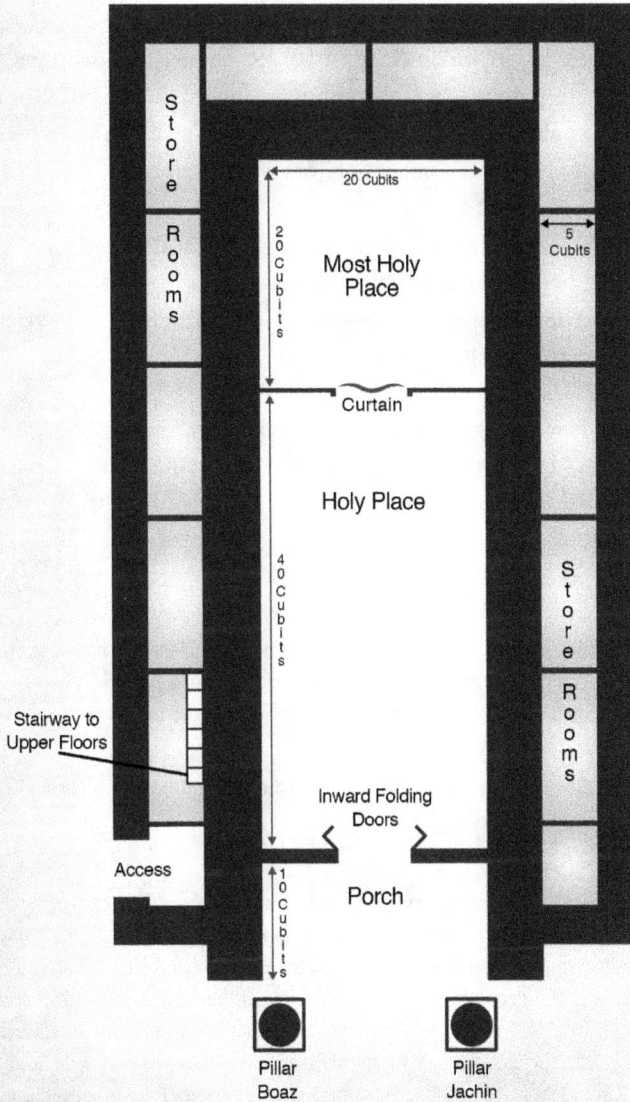

Store Rooms

20 Cubits

20 Cubits

5 Cubits

Most Holy Place

Curtain

Holy Place

40 Cubits

Store Rooms

Stairway to Upper Floors

Inward Folding Doors

Access

10 Cubits

Porch

Pillar Boaz

Pillar Jachin

the work was done at the original location, and the finished product was only then brought onto the site.[27]

To highlight the uniqueness of this building, we should also note that "the predominant word is gold[28] (vv. 20–22, 28, 30, 32, 35), and there is reference to carvings of more cherubim (vv. 29, 32, 35) and to carvings of gourds (vv. 18, a wild fruit; cf. 2 Kgs. 4:39), open flowers (vv. 18, 29, 32, 35), and palm trees (vv. 29, 32, 35)—symbols, perhaps, of God's gift of fertility."[29] In ancient Near Eastern symbology, the palm tree particularly represented fertility and the tree of life, and the totality of the carved images of flora was meant to conjure an image of paradise.

The cherubim were particularly prominent in the Most Holy Place, where they rose to half the height of the actual room and their wings towered over the space. In Scripture, cherubs always represented God's presence; they were part of the divine entourage in ancient thinking.[30]

- Yahweh was thought to be enthroned upon and among the cherubim (1 Sam 4:4; 2 Kgs 19:15; Pss 18:11; 80:2; 99:1; Ezek 10:18–19).

- A cherub was placed to guard the way back to Eden (Gen 3:24;

---

27. "The stone that was quarried was white limestone and famous for its beauty (called the 'royal stone' by the Arabs). It is reduced to lime when exposed to a hot fire. Thus when the temple burned (2Ki 25:9), it was not only the wood that burned; the stones themselves were reduced to powdered lime," (Patterson, "1, 2 Kings," 683).

28. The word translated "overlaid" can also indicate gold gilding or plating (Konkel, "צָפָה," NIDOTTE 3:832–33).

29. Provan, 1 & 2 Kings, 67.

30. "Several of the north Syrian temples yielded stone cherubim that are reminiscent of the ones described in this passage. They crouch at the entrance of the temples in order, it would seem, to reinforce the fearful power of the deity and to demarcate the perimeter of his presence," (Monson, "1 Kings," 31; cf. Elizabeth Bloch-Smith, "'Who Is the King of Glory?' Solomon's Temple and Its Symbolism," in Scripture and Other Artifacts: Essays on the Bible and Archaeology in Honor of Philip J. King, eds. Michael Coogan, J. Cheryl Exum, and Lawrence E. Stager [Louisville: Westminster John Knox, 1994], 18–31). Barnes intriguingly notes that the preferred image in Yahweh's Temple was the cherub, rather than the bull—the latter being common in the pagan mythology of Egypt and Canaan. "Yahweh, apparently from the very beginning, preferred cherub imagery—mysterious, Mesopotamian, but less likely to be connected with fertility religion," (1–2 Kings, 74).

Ezek 28:13–14).

• Cherubs were part of the artwork of Phoenician throne rooms.[31]

Ezekiel's description of cherubim (Ezek 1:4–14)—if that's what they were, and I believe so—in his first vision is particularly helpful in giving us an idea of what cherubs look like. In fact, if the Ezekiel passage affirms anything, it's that cherubs in both the Old Testament and the ancient Near East were "large, fearsome creatures and nothing like the cute, angelic baby 'cherubs' found in Renaissance art and on modern valentines!"[32]

All total, the Temple's construction took 7½ years—the month of Ziv (v. 1) being roughly equal to our May, and the month of Bul (v. 38) being equal to our November. The names of these months actually come from the old Phoenician, not Israelite, calendar, and thus may suggest "that the building report stems from an old Israelite record of the project influenced by the contacts with the Phoenicians responsible for the construction."[33]

Though the Temple took over seven years to build, the narrator seems to be a bit offended that Solomon took twice as long to build a new royal residence (7:1). Of course, the differences in time-tables could be due to the Temple's smaller size and the king's urgency to build it—of the discrepancy, Leithart reminds us, "Solomon is nowhere criticized for this."[34] But when the grandeur of both houses is considered, it's harder to give Solomon the benefit of the doubt. Indeed, in reading 1 Kings 6–7 as a whole, it's clear that "there are two 'houses' in view, and an emphatic contrast is made between them."[35] Wray Beal explains further:

---

31. Cogan, *I Kings*, 244. "Artistic representations of cherubim have been recovered from several Near Eastern sites including Taanach, Carchemish, Tell Halâf, and Aleppo. Particularly fine examples came from Nimrûd, where an ivory panel depicted two winged, sphinx-like creatures standing back to back, and also from Samaria, where cherubim were represented in considerable detail on ivory panels. These showed a figure with a human face, a four-legged animal body, and two large wings," (Harrison, "Cherubim," *ISBE* 1:642).

32. Barnes, *1–2 Kings*, 73.

33. Cogan, *I Kings*, 236–37.

34. Leithart, *1 & 2 Kings*, 60.

35. Provan, *1 & 2 Kings*, 69.

Whether in reality the temple is built concurrently with the palace, vv. 1–12 are placed here to suggest Solomon delays work on the temple furnishing (vv. 13–50) until his own home is complete. That delay means that the people continue to worship on the high places rather than at the Deuterono-mistically sanctioned temple. [...] Nor is the contrast simply a reflection on the size of each project. Instead, the grammar shows it is a negative contrast by placing the object ('his own house') before the subject-verb. Thus while he is 'seven years in building [the temple], *his own house* Solomon took thirteen years to build'. Even more, while he finishes the temple (and, by this passage's placement, the completion is only partial), he finished 'all' his house. Grand though his project is, Solomon is once again presented in an ambiguous light.[36]

The palace complex was known as "the House of the Forest of Lebanon," both because of the abundance of cedar that adorned the residence (much more than the Temple, cf. 6:9–10, 15–16, 18, 20, 36; 7:2–3, 7, 11–12), and because of the four rows of cedar columns that made the palace resemble an actual cedar forest in Lebanon. This first house measured a hundred cubits long, fifty cubits wide, and thirty cubits high—the same height as (but occupying a much larger footprint than) the Temple. This building at times served as both a large assembly or reception hall and also an armory (cf. 10:17; Isa 22:8). Like the Temple, Solomon's palace resembled other palaces unearthed in the ancient Near East by archaeologists.

Included in the palace was the Hall of Pillars, which measured fifty cubits by thirty cubits, but its use is not stated. There was also the Hall of the Throne, where Solomon sat enthroned and adjudicated cases brought before him. Next came his dwelling and that of his Egyptian wife—the fact "that special quarters were built for Pharaoh's daughter points to her privileged position among the king's other wives."[37] The narrator makes no mention as to whether Mrs. Solo-

---

36. Wray Beal, *1 & 2 Kings*, 122; emphasis hers. Olley is even more skeptical of Solomon's piety: "The positioning of the description of the palace complex in the middle of the temple account is one way the writer points to the seeds of destruction being present at the very beginning of the temple worship, seeds that were to bear their poisonous fruit in injustice, oppression and apostasy," (*Message of Kings*, 87).

37. Cogan, *I Kings*, 256.

mon was pleased with the size of her powder room or walk-in closet. The entire complex was decorated with expensive stonework and ornamented in cedar.

But our tour guide does not linger long here. "The descriptions of the porches and halls of the palace complex are considerably less detailed than the descriptions given for the Temple. Except for the House of the Forest of Lebanon (vv. 2–5), which was apparently a most impressive building, the others are dismissed with a single verse—the king's private quarters with even less, a simple 'ditto' (cf. v. 8)—leaving the reader uncertain as to their configuration. For [the narrator of Kings], it was not important to expand on these secular buildings, and so he returned in vv. 13–51 to matters of the Temple."[38]

Returning to the Temple, we learn that Solomon brought in a gifted sculptor of bronze, an Israelite of Naphtali (vv. 13–14). This Hiram of Tyre is not to be confused with King Hiram, whom Solomon solicited for help with the Temple's raw materials (the Israelite Hiram is called "Huram" by the Chronicler, 2 Chr 2:13; 4:16). Though he was from Tyre, Hiram is clearly an Israelite through his mother.[39] Like Bezalel and Oholiab, who worked on the Tabernacle (Exod 31:2–11; 35:31), Hiram is said to have been divinely gifted in wisdom and skill for his craft.

It was he who designed and cast the two free-standing[40] pillars of Solomon's Temple, Jachin and Boaz. Both were nearly three stories in height (thirty-four feet, including the capitals), eighteen feet in circumference, and, though hollow inside, the metal was four fingers thick (v. 15; cf. Jer 52:21). Of all the theories submitted for the origin of *Jachin* and *Boaz*, the names of the twin pillars, the most sensible one is that each is the first word in two separate inscriptions often reflected in the Psalms, meaning Jachin bore the phrase, "He will establish the throne of David" (cf. Pss 89:4; 132:11), and Boaz, "In the strength of Yahweh

---

38. Ibid., 257.

39. "It ought also to be noted that Hiram was the son of a widow—a considerable handicap in the ancient world. That he should achieve such renown in his craftsmanship attests not only to his diligence but also to the grace of God," (Patterson, "1, 2 Kings," 690).

40. It is assumed that these pillars were free-standing, since they are not described in the Temple's architecture in 1 Kings 6. Temples in Phoenicia and Assyria also had free-standing pillars in front.

shall the king rejoice" (cf. Pss 21:1; 61:11)—affirming God's presence and blessing on the king, and, by extension, all Israel.[41]

The large bronze sea, or water tank, in the Temple courtyard was over fourteen feet in diameter and seven feet high; it sat upon a stand of a dozen oxen
(possibly reflecting the twelve tribes), three pointing in each direction. Used as
draft animals, oxen were a natural symbol of strength in ancient times. The sea
could hold twelve thousand gallons[42] of water. To put that in perspective, the
average backyard, in-ground pool holds eighteen to twenty thousand gallons.

Other such basins set upon bulls are known to have been present at other
temple sites in the ancient Near East.[43] In the abstract, such a large basin of water
invoked the primeval sea, which itself represented the unknown or the forces
of chaos in ancient thought (cf. Ps 74:12–14). Thus, this massive basin of water
represented God's sovereignty over all chaos (cf. Gen 1:2, 9–10; Pss 18:15–17;
29:10; 74:12–15; Isa 27:1; Nah 1:4), most plainly demonstrated in Israel's history in their miraculous crossing of the Red Sea (cf. Exod 15:4–10; Pss 77:17–21;
89:11–12). In heaven, the sea of glass that stretches out from the throne of God
(Rev 4:6) serves the same symbolic function.[44] In our own worship of the Lord,
it's important that we remind ourselves often of God's utter sovereignty over all
things, even the "chaotic" forces of evil that seem to overwhelm at times. The constant confession of the church's worship must be that God is large and in charge;
anything short of that declaration will create a breeding ground for idolatry.

Hiram made ten mobile stands of bronze,[45] richly ornamented, and upon
these stands rested ten bronze basins, each holding 240 gallons of water (by
comparison, the average household hot water heater holds 60-80 gallons). These
stands and their basins were placed on either side of the Temple and used for

---

41. Auld, *I & II Kings*, 52–53; cf. R. B. Y. Scott, "The Pillars Jachin and Boaz," *JBL* 58
(1939): 143–49.

42. The measurement given in the text is a *bath*. At Lachish, archaeologists uncovered a
jar dating to the eighth century with the inscription "royal bath." The jar held 5.8 gallons (Konkel,
1 & 2 Kings, 132, n. 49).

43. Othmar Keel, *The Symbolism of the Biblical World*, trans. Timothy J. Hallet (Winona
Lake, IN: Eisenbrauns, 1997), 136.

44. Leithart, *1 & 2 Kings*, 57.

45. At Cyprus, two bronze stands similar to the ones in the Temple have been discovered
(C. F. Burney, *Notes on the Hebrew Text of the Book of Kings* [Oxford: Clarendon, 1903], 91).

rinsing/washing purposes (2 Chr 4:6)—with all the blood and gore involved with animal sacrifices, I'm sure they saw a lot of use!

All of the bronze work was done, the narrator tells us, between Succoth and Zarethan (v. 46), at the junction of the Jordan and Jabbok. The area contained clay suitable for creating molds, and the forests on the western shore of the Jordan would have provided fuel for heat. The precise site of Zarethan is unknown, but at Succoth, traces of metal smelting have been uncovered.[46] The immense amount of copper necessary for the bronze was likely obtained and stockpiled by David (cf. 2 Sam 8:8).

Hiram also cast in bronze the various pots and utensils used in Temple service by the priests. But note that Solomon is given credit for the sacred vessels made of gold, including the altar, table, and ten golden lampstands. Upon completion, into the Temple's storerooms Solomon brought immense treasures first collected and dedicated to the Lord by David (2 Sam 8:7–12), an act that "affirmed that God's promise to David had indeed been fulfilled."[47]

1 KINGS 8

The Temple now completed,[48] Solomon instructed that the Ark be brought to its new home. In 2 Samuel 6, David had brought the Ark from Kiriath-jearim into the city, and since then, it had been in a tent somewhere in Jerusalem (2 Sam 6:17; 7:2; 1 Kgs 3:15). Now, with great fanfare and innumerable sacrifices (v. 5; cf. 2 Sam 6:1–19), the Ark and the holy vessels were placed in the Temple, with the Ark specifically in the Most Holy Place, its poles so long that they stuck out. The outstretched cherubim "cover the ark, thus protecting it and approximating God's 'throne room' in heaven."[49]

---

46. Nelson Glueck, "Three Israelite Towns in the Jordan Valley: Zarethan, Succoth, Zaphon," *BASOR* 90 (1943): 2–23.

47. Hubbard, *First and Second Kings*, 52.

48. "The chronology of Kings delays the dedication eleven months after the completion of the temple (6:38), perhaps in order to set it in the four hundred forty-eighth year (divisible by seven) after Moses gave the command to read the law every seven years (Deut. 31:10–12; cf. 6:1, 38 with Deut. 1:3)," (Nelson, *First and Second Kings*, 51). The month of Ethanim (v. 2) in the Canaanite calendar corresponded to the Israelite month Tishri or our late-September/early-October. The feast mentioned would have been the Feast of Booths, a time when Israel reflected on their ancestors' forty years of wandering in the wilderness (Lev 23:33–43; Deut 16:13–17).

49. House, *1, 2 Kings*, 139.

Whereas the Ark in the Tabernacle had once housed Aaron's rod, a container of manna, and the Commandments (Exod 16:33; Num 17:10; Heb 9:4), by the time it was placed in the Temple, the Ark housed only the Commandments (v. 9).[50] Significantly, the narrator would have us realize that no idol or image of God existed. "The ark is witness to his covenant and symbol of his real presence. It cannot capture or define him."[51]

In the history of the Ark, God's presence had always been associated with it in a very powerful, very tangible way (e.g., Num 10:35–36; 1 Sam 4:21–22). So when the Ark had arrived at the Temple, a cloud—symbolic of the Lord's glory (Exod 13:21–22; 16:10; 19:9)—filled the Temple to the point that the priests could not perform their duties (cf. Exod 40:35; Acts 2:1–4). Such was affirmation of divine approval for what Solomon had accomplished.

Solomon's blessing on the people assembled (vv. 13–21) invoked three important ideas. *First, God's covenant with his father, David, was an outgrowth of his covenant with Israel at Sinai* (vv. 16–17). In other words, God's favor to the house of David was only a part of his grander favor to the children of Abraham, Isaac, and Jacob. Indeed, God's covenant with David (2 Sam 7:1–17) is a prominent theme of this passage. It was important for Solomon to underscore this continuity.

Second, Solomon explained why there had been a delay in building the Temple in the Promised Land (vv. 18–19). David had desired to build it, and God had commended him for the desire, but had reserved such an honor for David's son. In ancient times, it was quite common for kings to lay claim to divine favor by building a temple as Solomon did; the gods' sanction of a king's rule could be seen in allowing him to build such an impressive building. By noting God's allowing Solomon to build the Temple, the king is reminding the people that he is God's anointed. Solomon, however, knows that God owes the king (or Israel) nothing. God does not operate on quid pro quo, so the king and the people rely instead on God's faithfulness to his covenant with Israel and David.[52]

Finally, the king celebrated how the Temple would house both the Ark and God's Name (vv. 20–21). "The temple—in spite of the statement of verse 13—is not to be thought of as a place where *God* is but only as a place where God's

---

50. Boyd speculates that the rod and pot of manna were pilfered by the Philistines in 1 Samuel 5 and destroyed, but that the stone tablets were not touched due to superstition (J. Oscar Boyd, "What Was in the Ark?" *EvQ* 11 [1939]: 165–68).

51. Provan, *1 & 2 Kings*, 76.

52. Cogan, *I Kings*, 292.

Name is, a place towards which God's eyes are open (v. 29; cf. Isa. 66:1–3)."[53]
Solomon is not under the impression that God will dwell in the Temple (v. 27),
but that the building exists to glorify the Lord's greatness. But because the Temple houses both God's Ark and God's Name (cf. 3:2; 9:3), it is unique and to be
venerated. "From this point on, every king of Israel or Judah will be judged on
whether he permitted sacrifice anywhere else but in this temple."[54]

Solomon's subsequent prayer (vv. 22–53) is important to our understanding of the rest of Kings; Nelson encourages the reader to "mark this chapter, at
least mentally, and return to it repeatedly at critical points,"[55] and I agree. In addition, much of Solomon's prayer in turn is rooted in the covenant blessings/
curses found in Leviticus 26 and Deuteronomy 27–28. "Leviticus 26 particularly describes an escalating intensity or seriousness of difficulties, an ever-wors-
ening series of events that will come on a disobedient people. Each calamity is
designed to bring them to repentance; but if they still will not repent, then worse
will come. In both passages the final blow is exile from the Promised Land."[56]

In his opening remarks of this prayer, Solomon confessed that the God
of Israel was unique and beyond comparison to any other god (vv. 23–24). He
asked that God be faithful to his covenant with David and, barring disobedience,
see to it that a son of David occupied Israel's throne forever (vv. 25–26). He also
requested that the prayers of many offered in and toward the Temple might be
answered by Israel's God (vv. 27–53).

Concerning this last request, Solomon went on to make seven more specific requests concerning prayers in the Temple. He asked that Yahweh would:

---

53. Provan, *1 & 2 Kings*, 79; emphasis his. "One important feature of this speech (vv.
16–20), and also of the prayer that follows in verses 22–53, is the way in which the word Name
is used as a way of avoiding saying that God actually dwells in the temple (cf. also 3:2; 5:3, 5).
God's presence in the temple is real enough, and people will get God's attention by calling the
name, but God is not to be thought of as 'living' there in any sense that detracts from the reality
of God's transcendence. This is one way of overcoming the problem language presents us with
when we want to talk of a God who is both immanent (with us) and transcendent (beyond us;
cf. further Matt. 23:21–22)," (Ibid., 76–77).

54. Nelson, *First and Second Kings*, 48.

55. Ibid., 49.

56. Patterson, "1, 2 Kings," 706.

1. *Hear the prayer of one who is falsely accused*[57] (vv. 31–32; cf. Exod 22:7–12; Deut 25:1). "Solomon recognizes that the Lord, the heavenly King, must decide cases that he, the earthly king, cannot possibly solve. This is quite an admission from the man who settled the prostitute case."[58]

2. *Hear the prayer of Israel when she is defeated and repents* (vv. 33–34; cf. Josh 7:1–12; 1 Sam 4:1–11). Recall that military defeat as punishment for sin was among the covenant curses (Lev 26:33; Deut 28:36–37).

3. *Hear the prayer of Israel when she suffers drought*[59] (vv. 35–36), which was also among the covenant curses (Lev 26:19; Deut 11:13–17; 28:23–24). Note specifically that Solomon asked God not simply to restore rain to the land when Israel repented, but to also "teach them the good way in which they should walk" (v. 36).[60] The king understood that repenting of sin is only part of a right relationship with God; we must also learn what he expects of us. Contrition and instruction go hand in hand.[61]

4. *Hear the prayer of Israel when she suffers famine or plague* (vv. 37–40). "Solomon listed specific examples: famines, epidemics, mildew or blight of crops, invasions of locusts or grasshoppers,

---

57. "These cases have to do with damage or loss of property entrusted to another person, dispute over lost and found property, or the perpetration of fraud of some sort. Solomon prays that when an oath is brought before the Lord in such a case, he will judge the guilty party and establish the innocence of the other," (Ibid., 708).

58. House, *1, 2 Kings*, 144.

59. "As with the defeats in 8:33–34, the droughts he mentions are not normal, uncaused events. Rather, they are direct natural punishment from the Creator of heaven and earth for the people's rebellion," (Ibid., 145).

60. "Israel's crops depended on good and well-timed fall and spring rains. The Canaanites thought to ensure for themselves fertility for their land and abundant rains by worshiping Baal, the supposed god of the storm. The Israelites were prone to emulate their neighbors in the licentious worship of this idol. As a consequence God withheld the rain [cf. 1 Kgs 17–18] so that they might realize the Lord alone is the provider of all blessings," (Patterson, "1, 2 Kings," 708).

61. "Once Israel turns from its sin, forgiveness will come in the form of rain. Solomon hopes that such obvious correlation between human prayer and divine response will 'teach them the right way to live.' Thus, punishment will have a positive, not negative, function. God corrects in order to effect needed changes, not to vent personal anger," (House, *1, 2 Kings*, 145).

blockades by armies,"[62] (cf. Deut 28:21–22, 27, 35, 38–39, 42, 59–61).

5. *Hear the prayer of a foreigner in order to glorify yourself to the ends of the earth* (vv. 41–43; cf. Num 15:14; Josh 2:9–11; Ruth 1:16). It is in this request that Solomon's prayer takes on a more international tone. Of all Solomon's requests, this might be the most Christological in nature, since "the temple as a place of assembly for prayer points to the future incorporation of Gentiles and Jews into one new body."[63]

6. *Hear the prayer of Israel when she goes to war* (vv. 44–45), specifically that God would "maintain their cause." In ancient warfare, people believed a battle between two nations was merely a physical parallel to war in the divine realm between the nation's two patron deities (cf. Num 27:21; 1 Sam 5). Thus, Solomon is asking that God vindicate his people by vindicating himself whenever Israel took up the sword.

7. *Hear the prayer of Israel in exile and restore her to the Promised Land* (vv. 46–51; cf. Deut 28:36–37, 58–68). This final request is striking because it seems to presuppose that the people will *not* be faithful, that exile is inevitable. Put another way, Solomon is acknowledging that this magnificent Temple he had constructed would not "secure a trouble-free future for the people of God."[64]

Leithart points out that "the seven petitions at the center of the passage offer a rough preview of the trials that Israel will face in the subsequent centuries."[65] Indeed, these seven prayer requests double as a preview or outline of the rest of Kings. The first request parallels the entire reign of Solomon, while the second, military disaster, corresponds to the division of Israel under Rehoboam. The warning of drought foreshadows Elijah versus the house of Ahab. Further mention of famine, siege, and plagues point to the many sieges and famines that would

---

62. Hubbard, *First and Second Kings*, 56.

63. Leithart, *1 & 2 Kings*, 68.

64. Fretheim, *First and Second Kings*, 50. For more on the tie between this final request by Solomon and Deuteronomy 30, see J. G. McConville, "1 Kings VIII 46-53 and the Deuteronomic Hope," *VT* 42 (1992): 67–79.

65. Leithart, *1 & 2 Kings*, 70.

afflict Jerusalem and Samaria. Just as we see a foreigner pray towards the Temple, we will witness foreigners like Hiram, Sheba, and Naaman seek Israel's God. The desire of God to uphold Israel's cause in battle will be seen in the many battles of Kings, especially the final battle of Josiah and Judah's struggle against Babylon. Finally, again, Israel will be sent into exile, just as Solomon claims in prayer.[66]

After Solomon's prayer, he stood[67] and blessed the people again (vv. 56–61). The massive number of animals slaughtered (v. 63; cf. 2 Chr 5:6) seems less remarkable[68] when we remember that this was essentially a fellowship offering (Lev 3:1–17; 7:11–38), meaning the crowd partook of the offered meat in what might easily be envisioned as a church potluck. The final verse of the chapter, "[the people] went to their homes joyful and glad of heart for all the goodness that the LORD had shown to David his servant and to Israel his people" (v. 66), is a perfect summary of God's enormous blessing on Israel.[69]

I once preached for a church that, for the first ten years of its life, had met in a rented space in an area strip mall. For a decade, they had no permanent place to call their own. Each Lord's Day required members to arrive early to set up chairs and stay late to take them down. For a decade, they prayed and saved for their own building; to great joy, they reached their goal about a year before I was hired. They were very proud of the facility they had purchased, and they had every right to be.

But the realization of their dream had an unhealthy side effect. Instead of moving on to the next stage of God's plan for them, they seemed a little too

---

66. Ibid.

67. "The reader remembers that the prayer began with him standing (v. 22) and can only conclude that under the weight of his petitions Solomon had sunk to a kneeling position, an act of submission (19:18; II Kings 1:13; Isa. 45:23)," (Nelson, *First and Second Kings*, 55).

68. Keil, *Commentary*, 135–37. The numbers given seem unbelievable. "Taken literally, [the animals] would have required the abandonment of all activity by the entire people for two weeks, and the rate of sacrifice (even assuming non-stop activity) would have been one oxen and six sheep every minute," (Zevit, "1 Kings," 693). An Assyrian inscription, however, mentions a banquet with nearly seventy thousand guests (D. J. Wiseman, "A New Stela of Aššur-nasir-pal II," *Iraq* 14 [1952]: 24–44.), making the quantity of animals for Solomon's sacrifice quite plausible.

69. "It will not be so very long now, however, before Israelites will be found going 'to their tents' for a very different reason and in a very different mood (12:16). The days of joy are strictly numbered—as 9:1–9 will now suggest," (Provan, *1 & 2 Kings*, 83).

content. As a church, they had finally "arrived." Owning (as opposed to renting) their own building was a mark of legitimacy, that they had "grown up" as a congregation. In what I found to be a bitter irony, they believed they were no longer "playing church." Yet, having arrived at such a significant milestone, they began to go through the motions of church life—which in my book is another way of "playing church," as opposed to aggressively fulfilling the Great Commission.

My intent is not to denigrate these brethren, but to draw attention to a disturbing reality in modern American church life. Despite our affirmation to our children that the church is people, not a building, there is nonetheless often an unhealthy emphasis on the building. I'm in no way opposed to having a beautiful facility; if anything, the narrative of Solomon's Temple endorses the idea that nice buildings are entirely legitimate if meant to bring glory to God.[70]

But therein lies the problem. An honest examination of our hearts might expose the reality that sometimes we are more concerned about the physical appearance of our church's building than the spiritual health of the church's members. I've sat in enough church business meetings to know that facilities often comprise a larger part of the agenda than anything else. And few things are more exciting in the life of a congregation than a new building or a new addition to a building.

At the beginning of the chapter, I noted the modern trend of building bigger and better sports stadiums in an effort to land a Super Bowl or other major sporting event. There is a tremendous amount of prestige in a city being billed as the home of the Super Bowl, the Final Four, or the like. Bigger and better is crucial to our identity as Americans, and as far as municipalities are concerned, you haven't "arrived" until you've landed one of these major sporting events. If you don't have a state-of-the-art arena, you might as well be a West Texas town without a Dairy Queen.

Do not be deceived—churches, too, can fall victim to this thinking. But bigger and better facilities are in no way crucial to our identity as God's people. In fact, the church historically has been at its best when it has been mobile and adaptable rather than "established" and institutionalized. Mark my words; it will not be long before the church in America loses its tax-exempt status, and such a change will place an insufferable burden on congregations whose ministry philosophies and missional paradigms are facility-centric (instead of people-centric).

---

70. "There is no place for mediocrity in the mind of God or in any efforts to bring honor to his name. Famously, God himself evaluated carefully his own work of creation: 'Then God looked over all he had made, and he saw that it was very good!' (Gen 1:31a)," (Barnes, *1–2 Kings*, 80).

Though Solomon's Temple was intended to be an icon, a symbol and reminder of God's covenant faithfulness to his people, it eventually became an idol, a grotesque caricature of covenant fidelity. Israel tied God's presence with his people to the Temple (Ps 46; Jer 7:4, 14); they foolishly believed that a great building was a stand-in for faithfulness. They forgot that "the covenant, not the temple, is the means to divine presence."[71]

The reality is that God has always been more concerned with his people's beliefs and behavior than their buildings. If the church loses her tax-exempt status in America, perhaps it will be God's way of teaching us that buildings were never to be the measure of legitimacy, but an icon of his faithfulness and an instrument in fulfilling the Great Commission in our communities.

---

71. Konkel, *1 & 2 Kings*, 125.

TALKING POINTS

Though this section of Kings focuses intently on the Temple as a dwelling place for God and his glory, the narrator's focus is not exclusively on this. Embedded in Solomon's prayer is a reminder that God is glorified when there is harmony with one another (8:31–32). "Worship that is not linked with justice and reconciliation on the human level is abhorrent to God, and loving behaviour is more important than correct ritual and magnificent buildings."[72] Throughout the remainder of Israel's history as a nation, however, she lost sight of this. Social justice and loving one's neighbor took a back seat—to the point that God spurned Israel's sacrifices. "I hate all your show and pretense— the hypocrisy of your religious festivals and solemn assemblies. I will not accept your burnt offerings and grain offerings. I won't even notice all your choice peace offerings. Away with your noisy hymns of praise! I will not listen to the music of your harps. Instead, I want to see a mighty flood of justice, an endless river of righteous living" (Amos 5:21–24 NLT). In the New Testament, we are reminded again that worship is rejected when it comes from a heart that is not at peace with one's fellow man (Matt 5:23–24). This is why Jesus considered the two greatest commandments—love God and love your neighbor—to be of equal importance.

I have often heard it claimed that there was no forgiveness of sins in the Old Testament. A key theme of Solomon's prayer, however, is Israel's repentance (vv. 31–53). The king views the Temple as a place to which the people of God must turn their focus when they seek forgiveness, healing, and restoration. The notion that God would willfully withhold reconciliation from his people is entirely foreign from this text; Solomon depicts the Lord as a heavenly Father eager and willing to forgive his people when they seek his face. In the New Testament, our prayer for forgiveness is also addressed to God via the new "temple," the person of Christ. In both Testaments, then, we can clearly see that the God of creation, the God of Israel, the God of the church, is "not wishing for any to perish but for all to come to repentance" (2 Pet 3:9 NASU).

---

72. Olley, *Message of Kings*, 82.

A fter the Babylonian Exile, Israel was never plagued with idolatry as she had been before. But the Jews did continue to invest too much in the Temple, seeing it as a magic talisman or lucky rabbit's foot. In John 11:48, this very idea is given expression on the lips of members of the Sanhedrin. "If we let him go on like this, everyone will believe in him, and then the Romans will come and take away both our temple and our nation" (NIV).[73] But Jesus warned elsewhere that to reject him as Messiah was to reject the Temple also (Matt 23:38). God had removed his glory from the Temple (Ezek 10–11); he would do so again. Today, buildings are no more integral to the church's survival and success than the type of copier in the office or the brand of grape juice in our communion cups. Rather, it is Jesus—he who "tabernacled" among us (John 1:14); he who likened his body to a temple (John 2:18–21)—who is integral to our survival and success. More than a temple, Jesus is now our great high priest and our great sacrifice (Heb 9–10).[74] There is nothing wrong with beautiful church buildings; I believe it important that we care for our places of worship since it demonstrates a level of honor and reverence for God. But "in the Bible the beauty of temples is never any guarantee that God will not leave them or bring judgment upon them."[75] Temples and buildings are a means to an end; Christ is the end. Let's not lose sight of that.

---

73. "Right in the middle of the description of the temple is a word from God to Solomon, interruptive both literarily and theologically (6:11–13). This placement suggests that, for all the splendor of the temple being described, the temple itself is not to be the focus of attention nor is it to be conceived in such a way as to 'contain' God, or as a vehicle by which God can be controlled. The key concern for Solomon and Israel is faithfulness to God. This commitment must be basic to any talk about the temple as the divine dwelling place. Everything else is of secondary import," (Fretheim, *First and Second Kings*, 42).

74. "By this new and living way a new covenant is forged that depends solely on Christ. In him as new tabernacle, priest and sacrifice all the hopes of the Solomonic temple are for ever realized," (Wray Beal, *1 & 2 Kings*, 128).

75. Provan, *1 & 2 Kings*, 74. "The God of the Bible does make guarantees, but they do not involve structures, systems, or human institutions. God's guarantees involve the person and presence of Jesus Christ (Matt. 18:20; 28:20) and the trustworthiness of God's own promises (for example, Matt. 16:18–19). In Revelation's picture of God's coming new world, there is no temple in New Jerusalem. The direct presence of God and the Lamb takes its place," (Nelson, *First and Second Kings*, 49).

4

SLOW FADE

B ased on a 1992 novel by the same name, the 1998 film *Primary Colors* follows a young, idealistic political operative named Henry Burton as he campaigns for Governor Jack Stanton (a fictionalized version of President Clinton) in the Democratic presidential primary. Burton is at first enamored with the hope and promise Stanton embodies. But the impressive façade quickly gives way to a discouraging mosaic revealing a very flawed man. Waist deep in sordid accusations flying between Stanton and his political rivals, Burton struggles with the cognitive dissonance of campaigning for ideals while also backing such a despicable human being.

I imagine the author of Kings, though divinely inspired, couldn't help but feel similarly about Solomon. Without question, he is deeply impressed with all that David's son managed to achieve. The building projects, the wisdom, the wealth, the territorial expansion, the international prestige—it was all unprecedented. But not even our starstruck narrator can ignore the cracks in the golden veneer. He too struggles with the cognitive dissonance of praising Solomon's many accomplishments in Israel while also acknowledging the king's multitude of spiritual failures.

Carl DeVries makes the excellent observation that Solomon's "gradual apostasy had more disastrous results than the infamous scandal of his father, who sincerely repented."[1] The key phrase in that statement is "gradual apostasy," versus the momentary failure of David. In all the annals of following the Lord and spiritual living, it has been the slow fade—not the sudden fall—that

---

1. Carl E. DeVries, "Solomon," in *The New International Dictionary of the Bible: Pictorial Edition*, eds. J. D. Douglas and Merrill C. Tenney (Grand Rapids: Zondervan, 1987), 954.

has proven most devastating. "People never crumble in a day," claims a Casting Crowns song.

Though Solomon was in many ways Israel's ideal king, he also established minor (albeit unfaithful) precedents that led to her demise—the seeds of our destruction are often sown in the soil of our success. These final three chapters of Solomon's reign return to a few themes already mentioned. The negotiations with Hiram and procurement of laborers in 1 Kings 5 appear in 1 Kings 9. International commerce (4:21, 24) is also revisited (9:26–28), as is public acclaim of his rule (4:21, 34; cf. 10:1–13, 23–25). Running throughout is a strange obsession with Solomon's Egyptian wife.

But if the earlier anecdotes highlighted Solomon's glory, that same glory in 1 Kings 9–11 is slowly fading. Solomon is no longer a business partner beyond reproach. If only in small and never scandalous ways, he is unfaithful to the Torah. He procures horses, marries foreign wives, and hoards gold—which Moses had said should not be done. Whereas he had once been faithful in worshiping Yahweh at Gibeon and the Temple, he now worships other gods at high places he built for his wives. Where there formerly had been no adversaries to stand against him (5:4), Solomon becomes beset with opposition from without and within (11:9–40). The decline of Solomon's glory was a slow fade, but it was most definitely a fade, and for the sole reason that he opted for a paradigm of power fundamentally at odds with the one enshrined in the Covenant of Moses.[2]

Like political idealists whose hope is in a candidate, our hope in Solomon as the ideal king never pays off. He is as imperfect as all the rest, and as we study the end of his life, as well as the lives of all the monarchs who follow him in Kings, we are left to wonder: "Will any king come who does fulfil the righteous requirements of kingship?"[3] Hope in earthly leaders will always disappoint (Jer 17:5), which is why our faith ought to be in the King of kings, one who was infinitely greater than Solomon (Matt 12:42). It will not be on this earth that we find an unshakeable kingdom (Heb 12:28).

1 KINGS 9:1–9

Following the completion of Solomon's building projects (including the palace and the Temple), "the LORD appeared to Solomon a second time, as he

---

2. Olley, *Message of Kings*, 113–14.

3. Wray Beal, *1 & 2 Kings*, 81.

had appeared to him at Gibeon" (v. 2).[4] At this stage, Solomon has been on the throne for twenty-four years (cf. 6:1; 9:10). We have not yet read any explicit condemnation of Solomon—it seems his abject apostasy did not come until later in life.

Add to this fact the note, "all that Solomon desired to build" (v. 1). This phrase informs us that Solomon's building projects were near and dear to his heart, his life's passion, and at their completion, God saw fit to come to him as an intervention of sorts. The king was at a crossroads. The Hebrew term translated "desired" (*ḥēpes*) primarily refers to a physical attachment, but can also refer to a man desiring a woman (Gen 34:8; Deut 21:11), God's love for his people (Deut 7:17; 10:15), and our reciprocal love for God (Ps 91:14). That it is used here of Solomon's construction projects should give us pause. "Solomon's 'desire' is not towards God and his ways but on increasing material wealth, evidenced in buildings. Solomon needs the warning."[5]

The Lord reaffirmed the covenant he had made previously with David (2 Sam 7:14; cf. 1 Kgs 2:4; 8:25), including the reminder that judgment and wrath awaited if Solomon turned away from following Yahweh (vv. 6–7). Despite this warning, Israel would learn the hard way that it was futile to rely on the Temple to provide an unconditional, supernatural force field of protection from abject disaster (Isa 1:10–15; Jer 7:1–15; cf. Mic 3:12). Nothing made the Temple holy or special except God's sovereign election to invest it with his Name, and he could choose at any time to remove his Name from that place if his conditions were not met (cf. Ezek 10).

Notably, God warned that, should Solomon and his sons (all occurrences of *you* in v. 6 are plural) be unfaithful to the covenant, he would turn Solomon's Temple into "a heap of ruins" and the people of Israel would become "a proverb and a byword" among the nations (cf. Deut 28:37; Jer 24:9). In other words, God's people would be "the example par excellence of disaster" and "the international butt of jokes, the laughingstock of nations."[6] Passersby would whistle ("hiss," v.

---

4. "Normally a prophet served as an intermediary between Yahweh and the king [...]. Sadly, Solomon's experience of two theophanies only renders him even more guilty and deserving of punishment for his heinous sins of syncretism," (Barnes, *1–2 Kings*, 93).

5. Olley, *Message of Kings*, 105.

6. Hubbard, *First and Second Kings*, 58. In the Old Testament, Sodom and Gomorrah became a proverb/byword of utter divine destruction (Amos 4:11). A *proverb* in this sense is what we call a "cautionary tale." Likewise, a *byword* in the Old Testament was technically a taunt or

8) in amazement[7] at what Yahweh had done. The irony is that, though Solomon knew many proverbs (4:20), "this proverb regarding the future destruction of his people he does not learn to heed (11:1–11)." And although foreigners like Hiram and the Queen of Sheba praise Solomon and his glory, foreigners would eventually scorn his Temple as a testimony to Israel's final bankruptcy.[8]

That God would renounce or disown his own Temple (let alone his people) is a disturbing idea. Patterson explains that the word translated "cast out" in reference to the Temple (v. 7) "is the word used of a man divorcing his wife. As such it speaks of a far more serious matter than the terminating of a business arrangement. Strong emotions and grief are involved. This figure is also used frequently by the prophets in speaking of God as the husband who will put Israel, the unfaithful wife, away,"[9] and the separation would not be amicable.

In some ways, the reaffirmation God gives to Solomon in these nine verses is intended to remind us of the special arrangement Yahweh had with the Davidic dynasty. But with its emphasis on the consequences should Solomon and the people prove unfaithful, this reaffirmation becomes an introduction to all that is about to transpire—a prelude to the rest of Kings—for God's house will be reduced to ruins at the end of the story.

For now, we are left to ponder how far-reaching the consequences of disobedience can be. "As kings, Solomon and his successors were responsible for the whole nation. Failure on the king's part affected all the people. Israel's subsequent history amply illustrates this principle. As the king went, so went the people."[10] As the exiles in Babylon read the book of Kings for the first time, and though they knew they had no one to blame but themselves for the mess they found themselves in, it was also true that the spiritual failure of their leaders had led to their destruction.

---

cutting remark. The verb form of the word had to do with sharpening weapons (Deut 32:41; Isa 5:28) and so gained the metaphorical meaning of "malicious speech" (Southwell and VanGemeren, "שָׁנַן," *NIDOTTE* 4:195–96).

7. "The horrific wounds inflicted on Jerusalem will appal [*sic*] those who see them, and a sharp expelling of the breath, indicative of the terror which the sight inspires, will issue as a kind of whistling," (William McKane, *A Critical and Exegetical Commentary on Jeremiah*, vol. 1 [Edinburgh: T&T Clark, 1986], 453).

8. Wray Beal, *1 & 2 Kings*, 149.

9. Patterson, "1, 2 Kings," 715.

10. Ibid.

1 KINGS 9:10-28

The remainder of this chapter will remind us of 1 Kings 4–5. In v. 11, we are told Solomon gave[11] twenty Galilean cities to Hiram. Generous indeed, we are intended to think, especially when we realize this area (more or less Solomon's ninth administrative district, 4:16) contained a lot of fertile agricultural land.[12] Upon inspection, however, Hiram discovered they were little more than West Texas towns without a Dairy Queen; the name *Cabul* (v. 14) probably means "worthless."[13]

Actually, the text suggests that once Hiram saw the towns for himself, he wasn't so much put off by their quality as by the realization that he should have gotten more for his money[14]—nearly 4½ tons of gold (cf. v. 14 NIV). "This episode shows a conniving side of Solomon. Readers may wonder whether he is completely trustworthy. Still, Hiram continues to work with Solomon (cf. 9:26–28)."[15]

Much more problematic than whether Solomon gave Hiram a lemon (or whether Hiram overpaid) is the notion that an Israelite king, Yahweh's anointed, effectively deeded some of the Promised Land back to a Canaanite king! The Chronicler reports that Hiram returned the twenty towns to Solomon (2 Chr 8:2), but the damage has already been done to Solomon's reputation—if not in Hiram's eyes, at least in ours. Solomon's action makes him the anti-Joshua and

---

11. It may be that Solomon went into considerable debt with his many building projects and that this anecdote about the twenty Galilean cities is meant to inform us "that things seemed to go downhill rather rapidly," (Barnes, *1–2 Kings*, 96; cf. Wiseman, *1 and 2 Kings*, 125; Abraham Malamat, "A Political Look at the Kingdom of David and Solomon and Its Relations with Egypt," in *Studies in the Period of David and Solomon and Other Essays*, ed. Tomoo Ishida [Winona Lake, IN: Eisenbrauns, 1982], 203–4).

12. Cogan, *I Kings*, 307.

13. Barnes suggests that the portrayal of this land as "no good" was possibly "meant to downplay for later Judean generations the seriousness of Solomon's giving away portions of Israel's Promised Land to non-Israelites," (*1–2 Kings*, 95–96).

14. Konkel, *1 & 2 Kings*, 198.

15. House, *1, 2 Kings*, 157. Westbrook argues persuasively that this episode "is neither a sign of Solomon's stinginess nor of Hiram's greed," but rather a typical example "of veiled bargaining between monarchs" in ancient times (Raymond Westbrook, "Law in Kings," in *The Books of Kings: Sources, Composition, Historiography and Reception*, eds., André Lemaire and Baruch Halpern [Leiden: Brill, 2010], 463).

demonstrates contempt for the Promised Land.[16] The ultimate irony is this proverb attributed to Solomon himself: "Do not move an ancient boundary stone set
up by your ancestors" (Prov 22:28 NIV).

Provan sets the tone for this section with this reminder: "First Kings 9:10–
10:29 brings us back to consider the glory of this empire. It is glory that must
now be seen with respect to 8:22–53 and 9:1–9. It is therefore glory under a
cloud, destined to fade away."[17] Indeed, apparent to a careful reader, several ominous tones are sounded in this section. We've already seen Solomon give away
a part of the Promised Land (of which God was the divine Landlord). Consider
also the mention of:

- *Canaanites still in the land* (v. 21). Yahweh had intended for the
  Amorites, Hittites, Perizzites, Hivites, and Jebusites to be exterminated (Deut 7:2; 20:17) for the express reason that their continued presence would inevitably corrupt Israel's faith. But Solomon, always the pragmatist, "now finds a use for them, and does
  not seek to 'complete' the national task!"[18] Those from outside
  the Promised Land could be pressed into service, but the natives
  were to be devoted to "complete destruction" (Deut 20:10–18).
  Disobedience to the divine command, no matter the reason, is
  still disobedience.

- *Pharaoh's daughter* (vv. 16, 24; cf. 3:1; 7:8; 11:1). The narrator's continued fascination with Pharaoh's daughter reminds
  me of a film director's obsession with something that ends up
  being a major plot point (e.g., glasses of water in M. Night Shyamalan's *Signs*; "If you build it, he will come" in *Field of Dreams*).
  In 1 Kings 11, we will discover that this foreign wife was just the
  "gateway drug" for Solomon's immoral addiction.

- *Accumulation of gold* (vv. 11, 14, 28). The amount of gold seems
  to increase rapidly (120 talents in v. 14; 420 talents in v. 28; 666

---

16. Sweeney, *I & II Kings*, 143–44.

17. Provan, *1 & 2 Kings*, 84. "The arrangement of this material points to an editorial interest in portraying Solomon in a very negative light. The topical arrangement, beginning with notices concerning Solomon's use of forced labor and the strategic placement of otherwise unnec-
essary statements concerning Pharaoh and Pharaoh's daughter, highlights an interest in drawing
an analogy between Solomon and the pharaoh of the exodus," (Sweeney, *I & II Kings*, 141).

18. Auld, *I & II Kings*, 72.

talents in 10:14), and Solomon continues to seek it out in more exotic locations (v. 28; 10:28). Whereas Solomon's prosperity had been couched in terms of an abundance of food (4:20–23), it now seems to be illustrated with the abundance of gold, which is cause for alarm (cf. Deut 17:17; Prov 30:8). Echoing Jesus' statement concerning camels and needles (Matt 19:24), Provan reminds us, "Excessive wealth brings with it the danger of apostasy."[19]

- *Slave labor* (vv. 15–22). The issue of slavery is a rather sensitive one in our own time, but an ancient might very well have asked, "How is a king supposed to build an empire without slave labor?" Using his force of conscripted labor, Solomon engaged in several building projects besides that of the Temple and a new royal palace. The workmen of 5:13–18 are not the same as those invoked here; Solomon's slave labor did not include Israelites (vv. 20–22).

With so many slaves at his disposal, Solomon became increasingly ambitious in his building projects. The identification of the Millo (vv. 15, 24) isn't absolutely certain, but three proposals have been suggested: a terraced architectural structure in the old City of David;[20] a fill bridging the depression between the City of David and the Temple mount;[21] a tower or bastion filling a vulnerable place in Jerusalem's wall[22] (most likely). Whatever the nature of the Millo, Cogan points out that it apparently needed maintenance on a regular basis[23] (11:27; 2 Sam 5:9). Other places in Israel received Solomon's attention:

- *Hazor* was located three miles north of the Sea of Galilee at the intersection of two major trade routes. Excavations by Yigael Yadin have demonstrated that, in Solomon's day, Hazor was a fortified city about 6½ acres in size. "It became Israel's chief bulwark

---

19. Provan, *1 & 2 Kings*, 85.

20. *HALOT* 587; Mitchell, "Millo," *NBD* 766; Kathleen M. Kenyon, *Digging up Jerusalem* (New York: Praeger, 1974), 100; Richard C. Steiner, "New Light on the Biblical *Millo* from Hatran Inscriptions," *BASOR* 276 (1989): 15–23.

21. Barrois, "Millo," *IDB* 3:382–83.

22. Leon J. Wood, *Israel's United Monarchy* (Grand Rapids: Baker, 1979), 230–31.

23. Cogan, *I Kings*, 301.

against northern invaders until it was destroyed in the eighth century by Tiglath-Pileser III."[24]

- *Megiddo's* importance can be seen in that it "guarded a crucial pass in the Carmel Mountains, which linked the Valley of Jezreel and the international coastal highway to Egypt."[25] In fact, Megiddo (and other cities) had been a garrison as far back as Egypt's domination of Canaan during the mid-second millennium. It would later be the sight of Josiah's ill-advised battle with Neco (2 Kgs 23:29). Archaeological investigation has confirmed that it was an important administrative center in Solomon's day.[26]

- *Gezer* was some twenty miles west of Jerusalem on the coastal plain at the intersection of two major trade routes—the international trade route that skirted the Mediterranean coast and the road that led from Jerusalem to Joppa. "From this major city in the northern Shephelah just west of the Aijalon Valley, all inland traffic from the sea coast to the hill country could be controlled."[27] Though located in the territory of Ephraim, it obviously was not inhabited by Israel until Pharaoh razed[28] it and gave it to Solomon, his son-in-law, as a wedding present. Given Gezer's critical location, "it often came under the attack of international powers such as Egypt."[29]

- *Lower Beth-horon* and upper Beth-horon were located a mile and a half apart in the mountain pass between the plain of Ai-

---

24. Patterson, "1, 2 Kings," 718.

25. Hubbard, *First and Second Kings*, 61.

26. William G. Dever, "Monumental Architecture in Ancient Israel in the Period of the United Monarchy," in *Studies in the Period of David and Solomon and Other Essays*, ed. Tomoo Ishida (Winona Lake, IN: Eisenbrauns, 1982), 275.

27. Cogan, *I Kings*, 301.

28. A scene from the Temple of Amun in Tanis may provide extrabiblical confirmation of this battle. It depicts Pharaoh Siamun "smiting an enemy with a doubleheaded axe having crescent-shaped blades. Since the depiction of an axe of this type is unique in Egyptian reliefs, Kitchen argues that this one must depict a specific battle. This type of axe comes from the Aegean or the Balkans, so that it most likely shows a battle with a Philistine," (Patterson, "1, 2 Kings," 719; cf. Kenneth A. Kitchen, "How We Know When Solomon Ruled," *BAR* 27/5 [2001]: 32–37, 58).

29. Monson, "1 Kings," 43; cf. *COS* 2.6. For common archaeological discoveries at Hazor, Megiddo, and Gezer, see Patterson, "1, 2 Kings," 717–19.

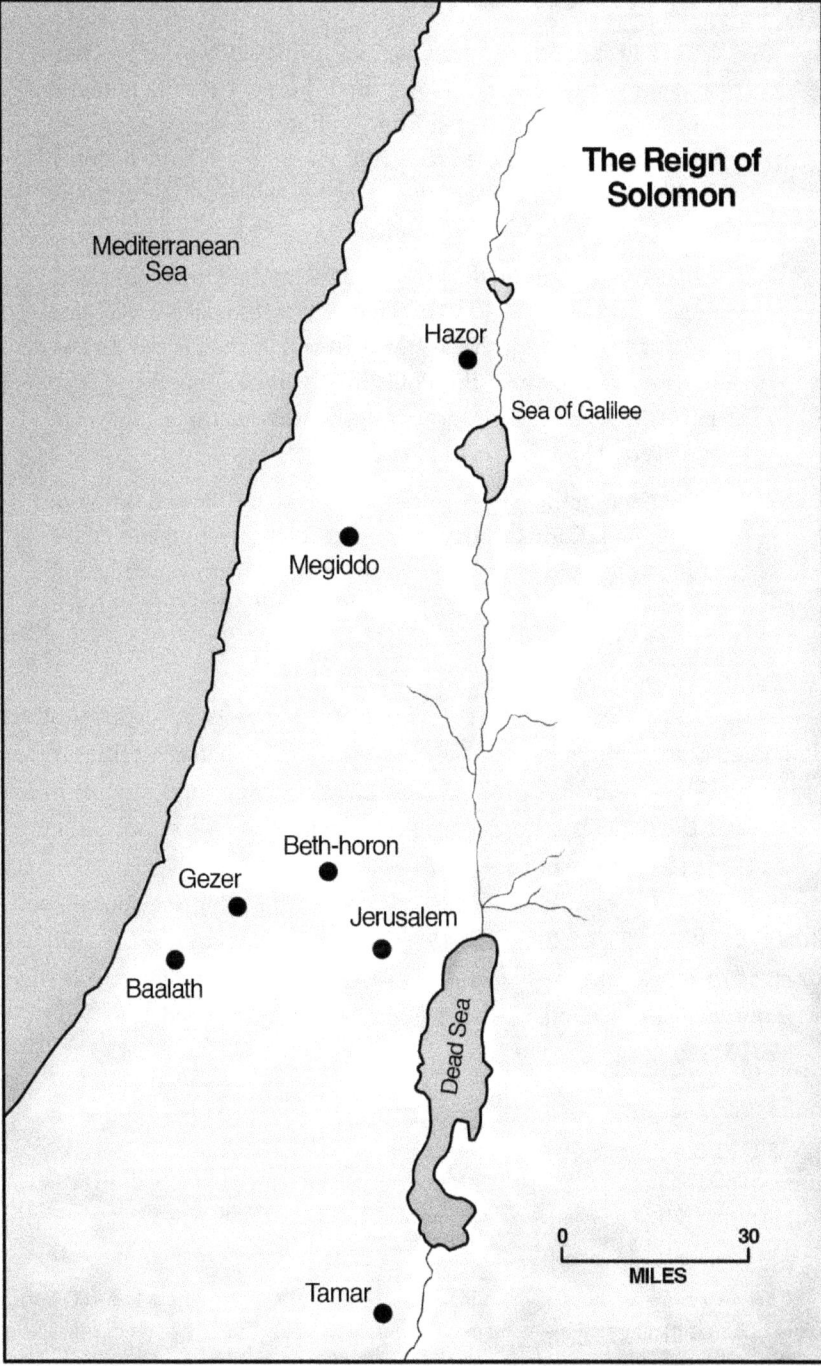

The Reign of Solomon

Mediterranean
Sea

Hazor

Sea of Galilee

Megiddo

Beth-horon

Gezer

Jerusalem

Baalath

Dead Sea

Tamar

0   30
MILES

jalon and the plateau near Gibeon (Josh 10:10; 16:3, 5). Consequently, the elevation of lower Beth-horon was eight hundred feet beneath upper Beth-horon. "Whereas Gezer, Hazor, and Megiddo controlled the main trunk route through the country, Beth Horon was a crucial link between Gezer and Gibeon on the ascent into the Judean highlands."[30]

- Concerning **Baalath**, there are two mentioned in the Old Testament (e.g., Josh 19:8, 44). The one in v. 18 is likely the same as Kiriath-jearim (Josh 15:9), which was located in the former territory of Dan, near the Philistine town of Gibbethon (Josh 19:44; cf. Judg 1:34). It served as "a fortress guarding another of the western approaches to Jerusalem."[31]

- **Tamar** was in the Negev and southwest of the Dead Sea on the border with Edom. Both Solomon's economic opportunities at Ezion-geber and Israel's soured relationship with Edom late in Solomon's reign (11:14–22) made the fortification of this town a wise move.[32]

Despite some unpleasantness over the twenty Galilean cities, it seems Hiram and Solomon did very well as partners in accumulating wealth for their respective kingdoms. Since Solomon controlled the important port city of Ezion-geber on the Red Sea, he ordered a fleet of trading ships be built and Hiram contributed veteran seaman (cf. Ezek 27:3).

Ophir (v. 28) was a location synonymous with gold in the ancient world (10:11; 22:48; Job 22:24; 28:16; Ps 45:9; Isa 13:12) and is thought to be in East Africa, perhaps Somalia, on the western coast of the Arabian Peninsula in modern-day Yemen, or even India.[33] From Ophir, Solomon obtained 420 talents (16

---

30. Monson, "1 Kings," 44–45. "The importance of this pass as the main approach to the interior of the country explains the frequent enlargement and fortification of these two towns through many centuries," (Masterman and Prewitt, "Beth-Horon," *ISBE* 1:469).

31. Patterson, "1, 2 Kings," 718.

32. Regarding all the cities mentioned, "The effect of all this effort is to fortify strong points, establish trading stations along major commercial routes and make it clear that Solomon's jurisdiction is recognized along his borders," (Walton, *Bible Background*, 429).

33. Jones, *1 and 2 Kings*, 1:220; Monson, "1 Kings," 46.

tons[34]) of gold. More than the sheer amount of gold, the bigger point here is that Israelites in Babylon would have had little to no experience at sea. Far-flung places like Ophir might as well have been Timbuktu or the dark side of the moon. In no uncertain terms, Solomon was a master at foreign trade.

1 KINGS 10:1-13

At the outset of Solomon's reign, God had promised the king "both riches and honor, so that no other king shall compare with you" (3:13; cf. 4:29–34). Now, to illustrate the level of fame and notoriety Solomon had achieved, the narrator tells us that the queen of Sheba came for a visit to behold for herself the glory and splendor of Solomon and his God.[35]

The area of Sheba was in what is Yemen today, located in the southwestern portion of the Arabian Peninsula, roughly fourteen hundred miles from Jerusalem. Sheba had been a grandson of Abraham (Gen 27:5). In Solomon's day, the kingdom of Sheba was likely made up of various Arabian tribes, and the Assyrian annals of both Tiglath-pileser III and Sargon II confirm that queens still ruled this area in their time.[36] Its location (positioned between Africa and India, and with terrific access to the Red Sea and Fertile Crescent) made it a natural center of maritime commerce.[37]

With her impressive entourage—one including camels bearing spices,[38] gold, jewels, and gems[39]—the queen came to test Solomon with questions (cf. Judg 14:12–14; Dan 8:23) such as, "What is the square root of π?" "Can God

---

34. Barnes, *1–2 Kings*, 99.

35. "In other words, she recognizes that only a great God could produce such a great king," (House, *1, 2 Kings*, 161).

36. *ANET* 283–86.

37. Gray, *I & II Kings*, 240–41.

38. "Recent archaeological research has uncovered evidence of sedentary populations organized as kingdoms in southern Arabia at the beginning of the first millennium B.C., suggesting that the spice trade operated from there at that time," (Israel Eph'al, *The Ancient Arabs: Nomads on the Borders of the Fertile Crescent, 9th-5th Centuries B.C.* [Jerusalem: Magnes, 1982], 64).

39. Elsewhere in the Old Testament, Sheba is considered a lavish source of gold and spices (Isa 60:6; Jer 6:20; Ezek 27:22). For an example of jewels and gems known in biblical times, see Exodus 28:17–20. "Solomon's wealth is indicated by the enormous gifts the queen needs to give in order to be significant (v. 10); the gold alone is equivalent to what Solomon has received from Hiram (cf. 9:14)," (Konkel, *1 & 2 Kings*, 201).

create a rock too large for him to pick up?" and "What is the airspeed velocity of a coconut-laden swallow?"[40] To all these and more, Solomon answered in a way that blew her away; "there was nothing hidden from the king that he could not explain to her" (v. 3). Add to that the king's palace, his dining table and officials and servants, his wardrobe, to say nothing of the Temple itself—all of the wining and dining stole the queen's breath away (v. 5).[41] Even today, the number, nature, and variety of dishes on a person's dining table is often indicative of their economic status. If you're in college and invite me to dinner, I expect to be fed Ramen noodles. If I'm invited to Warren Buffett's house, I had better be served filet mignon from a cow that was sent to boarding school and owned a yacht, as well as exotic side dishes, the names of which I can't possibly pronounce correctly.

In response, the queen blessed Solomon's God[42] for giving the king such wealth, wisdom, and success (cf. 5:21; Deut 4:37; 7:8, 13; 10:15; 23:6). She then left behind an unprecedented gift of 120 gold talents—the same amount received from Hiram (9:14)—as well as spices, jewels, and gems. The cumulative effect of these gifts was that the queen was expressing her inferiority to Israel's king (cf. Gen 14:20). "Never again came such an abundance of spices as these that the queen of Sheba gave to King Solomon" (v. 10). To reciprocate, Solomon gave her whatever she asked, in addition to the diplomatic gifts she had already received from the royal storehouses (v. 13). If the moon had been his to give, I'm sure the queen would have received that too.

To buttress the glory and splendor of the Solomonic age—lest we think he was in need of Sheba's gifts or that his generosity to her had bankrupted his portfolio (v. 13)—we are also told that the king received from Hiram's trading ships "a very great amount of almug wood [...] No such almug wood has come or been seen to this day" (vv. 11–12), wood which Solomon used to accent the

---

40. Wiseman claims that these were not just riddles, but difficult diplomatic and ethical questions (*1 and 2 Kings*, 139). "Such tests of practical sagacity and poetic susceptibility were part of the diplomatic encounters of the day," (Gray, *I & II Kings*, 241).

41. "The variety of officials in attendance and the extent of his temple offerings are reflective of a large kingdom or even an empire," (Monson, "1 Kings," 47).

42. "Between the confession of Solomon's greatness and the offering of the gifts, the queen makes an important statement about the Lord. She claims that God deserves praise for choosing him to rule Israel. [...] Quite ironically, Solomon and future kings of Israel choose to ignore what even noncovenant rulers seem to know is true: God rules Israel, and God blesses obedient Israelite kings," (House, *1, 2 Kings*, 162).

Temple and the royal palace. Though it is often mentioned in ancient writings, it's proven difficult to identify for certain what exactly almug wood was. It has traditionally been identified (with some uncertainty) with sandalwood, meaning it came from Ceylon (modern Sri Lanka) or India. Both biblical and ancient secular sources note that almug was used in both buildings and musical instruments[43] (cf. 2 Chr 9:11).

When I was young, I could always count on my dad to take my sister and me to the video rental store on Friday afternoon on our way home from school (those of you born after Y2K should ask your parents what video rental stores were). I was always infatuated by live-action Bible epics (e.g., *The Ten Commandments*, *The Greatest Story Ever Told*, *Life of Brian*) so one weekend, I brought home King Vidor's 1959 film, *Solomon and Sheba*, which featured Yul Brynner and Gina Lollobrigida in the lead roles.

Imagine my preadolescent wonder (and my mom's disgust) when, right around the one-hour mark, Solomon walks up to the queen and starts making out with her while everyone belly dances to idolatry around them. Granted, in the age of *The Bachelor* and *Grey's Anatomy*, the scene is pretty PG. But Mom made me turn off the VCR right away and forbade me to watch anymore of the film (which I did anyway when she later went out shopping and Dad was occupied with something else; sorry, Mom!). On that occasion, I remember thinking at the time, "That's not the version of Solomon and Sheba I was told in Bible class!"

Though the biblical text makes no mention of any romance between Solomon and Sheba—"for both sides, these conversations all have dollar signs, not Cupid's arrows, floating over them"[44]—other traditions exist, based mostly on the phrase, "Solomon gave to the queen of Sheba all that she desired, whatever she asked" (v. 13). The Ethiopians believed Solomon seduced her and fathered a child, Menelik, who became the founder of the Ethiopian dynasty. (Another Ethiopian tradition claims Sheba snuck home the Ark of the Covenant). In Jewish tradition, she and Solomon were married.[45] But none of these spurious traditions have any historical corroboration.

---

43. Trever, "Almug," *IDB* 1:88.

44. John Goldingay, *1 and 2 Kings for Everyone* (Louisville: Westminster John Knox, 2011), 51.

45. Fritz, *1 & 2 Kings*, 121.

Jesus, however, tapped into the example of the Queen of Sheba to illustrate the lengths one should go to hear the gospel (Matt 12:42). While she traveled over a thousand miles, the Jews of Jesus' own day often refused to heed his words,[46] and someone greater than Solomon was before them (cf. Luke 11:31). Such is confirmation of the old adage that familiarity breeds contempt. How can we lose a kingdom in four hundred years? Partially by taking for granted the extraordinary spiritual blessings right in front of us.

1 KINGS 10:14-29

A final time, we are told anecdotes stressing Solomon's splendor (cf. Matt 6:29). The amount of gold listed in v. 14 (likely a total from 9:14, 9:28, and 10:10) did not include that gained from tolls and tariffs on maritime exploration and trade and from tax revenues from kings and governors under Solomon (v. 15). Given such a sheer amount of gold—666 talents, representing 25 tons— "no doubt reflects Solomon's control of most trade routes on the eastern Mediterranean seaboard."[47]

With this gold, Solomon had decorative shields[48] made—two hundred large[49] shields (over seven pounds each) and three hundred smaller[50] shields (almost four pounds each)—and hung them in the royal reception hall, the House of the Forest of Lebanon. Together totaling almost two tons of gold, they were likely used only for ceremonial purposes (cf. 14:26). The king's cups and vessels were all of gold. So great was Solomon's accumulation of gold that "silver was not

---

46. House, *1, 2 Kings*, 163.

47. Monson, "1 Kings," 48. Doubt that anyone could accumulate this much gold in ancient times is unfounded. There are known parallels of such wealth among other ancient kings (Alan R. Millard, "Does the Bible Exaggerate King Solomon's Golden Wealth?" *BAR* 15/3 [1989]: 20–34).

48. Alan Millard, "King Solomon's Shields," in *Scripture and Other Artifacts: Essays on the Bible and Archaeology in Honor of Philip J. King*, eds. Michael Coogan, J. Cheryl Exum, and Lawrence E. Stager (Louisville: Westminster John Knox, 1994), 286–95.

49. "A shield of body length to protect the entire person, perhaps on three sides," (Cogan, *I Kings*, 317; cf. 1 Sam 17:7; Ps 5:12). "Sargon II lists six gold shields in his booty list from Urartu, each said to weigh over fifty pounds," (Walton, *Bible Background*, 431).

50. This smaller shield was carried by archers (2 Chr 14:8) "on the left arm, and protected only the upper body. Both shields served as protection against attacks by sword, arrow, or spear," (Fritz, *1 & 2 Kings*, 123).

considered as anything in the days of Solomon" (v. 21). Later, we learn silver was as common as rocks in Solomon's day (v. 27). He simply had more gold than he knew what to do with.[51]

Solomon sat atop an ornate throne of ivory, covered in gold and placed at the top of six steps, with lions on both sides of each step[52] (cf. Gen 49:9). And if we aren't in awe already, the narrator says, "The like of it was never made in any kingdom" (v. 20). All of this was made possible by his fleet of ships commissioned by Solomon and guided by Hiram's men (9:26–28). The "ships of Tarshish" (v. 22; Isa 2:16) is a reference to a type of ship (similar to how "china cabinet" refers to what the cabinet holds, not its origin), and a large oceangoing vessel at that, one that could sustain multi-year voyages[53] (compared to smaller ships that could only successfully navigate the Mediterranean).

Though similar statements as to the sheer wealth of the kingdom appear elsewhere in the ancient Near East (particularly Assyria), the remarkable contrast between those claims and the claims of Solomon is that the Assyrians collected their loot through war and pillaging; Solomon obtained his through more peaceful means.[54] He continued to receive visitors to his kingdom, those wishing to hear and see for themselves the king's wisdom and glory. From these visitors, he received even *more* gifts and tribute—precious metals, clothing, spices, and livestock. He also increased his military hardware with chariots[55] and horsemen

---

51. A similar boast is made by Osorkon I of Egypt (c. 924–920), who claimed that "gold is like dust in the land," (Wiseman, *1 and 2 Kings*, 141).

52. "The tomb of King Tutankhamun, who was buried about 1331 B.C., contained a carved wooden chair covered almost completely with gold. It still retains inlays of glass and colored stones. Gold was beaten into animal heads on the front of the armrests and claw feet on the chair legs. It gleams today much like the great throne of Solomon once did," (Konkel, *1 & 2 Kings*, 204).

53. Herodotus refers to a three-year circumnavigation of Africa by the Phoenicians (*Histories* 4.42). "Given the realities of such a journey, its length was due as much to the rigors of ancient seafaring as it was to the distance to the final port of call. Navigating the Red Sea down to Aden and then through the Straights of Mandab into the Indian Ocean required great skill, with particular attention given to seasonal winds and currents. Long layover periods likely account for much of the 'three years' mentioned," (Cogan, *I Kings*, 319–20).

54. Konkel, *1 & 2 Kings*, 203. "Today, when national dignitaries call on other leaders, they bring gifts as an act of respect, courtesy, and appreciation. Year after year, Solomon's visitors did the same," (Hubbard, *First and Second Kings*, 65).

55. "The royal riches allowed the crown to develop something of a first in Israel—a chari-

(v. 26). He imported horses from Egypt and Kue[56] (or Cilicia, a kingdom be-tween the Amanus and Taurus mountains in what is now southern Turkey); the details of this last transaction (v. 29) depict Solomon as a master at horse trad-ing/international commerce.[57]

Should Solomon be faulted for dealing in horses? Not everyone believes so. As the argument goes, the prohibition in the Law of Moses (Deut 17:16) had to do with looking to Egypt for horses (as opposed to anywhere else). In addition, the narrator of Kings never explicitly condemns Solomon over this.[58]

However, Craigie notes that the spirit of the law was warning against diplo-matic or trade relations, one on which Israel becomes dependent on Egypt[59] (as opposed to the Lord), and that will indeed occur in Kings (cf. Isa 31:1–3). And as to the lack of censure by the narrator for Solomon's horse trading, Sweeney notes, "Although these verses emphasize his wisdom, shrewdness, and wealth, they also point to the fact that Solomon is engaged in trade with Egypt, which is strictly forbidden to the Israelite king in Deut 17:14–20. Placement of this notice deliberately raises questions about the king immediately prior to the ac-count in 1 Kgs 11 of his love of foreign women and his apostasy."[60]

1 KINGS 11

Finally, the narrator explicitly informs us of what we have come to sus-pect[61]—that Solomon has not been as faithful to Yahweh as he should have been.

---

otry branch in the army (vv. 26–29; cf. 1 Kings 4:26, 28). Chariots were the most potent military weapon of that day. The advantage of enemy chariots plagued Israel on different occasions (Josh. 11:6, 9; Judg. 1:19; 4:3; 1 Sam. 31; cf. 1 Sam. 13:5; 14:20)," (Hubbard, *First and Second Kings*, 65).

56. "The Cilicians had been known for some time as breeders of fine horses. Solomon's agents were active in seeking out the best horses and values available," (Patterson, "1, 2 Kings," 727).

57. Soggin explains, "Solomon functioned as a middleman in the Near Eastern trade. Solomon's power and the strategic location of Palestine gave him control over the trade routes between Egypt and southern Syria, and his friendly relations with Egypt no doubt made him an important figure in the international trade of his day," (J. Alberto Soggin, "The Davidic-Solo-monic Kingdom," in *Israelite and Judaean History*, eds. John H. Hayes and J. Maxwell Miller [Phil-adelphia: Westminster, 1977], 374–75).

58. Hubbard, *First and Second Kings*, 66.

59. Peter C. Craigie, *The Book of Deuteronomy* (Grand Rapids: Eerdmans, 1976), 255–56.

60. Sweeney, *I & II Kings*, 152.

61. "While stopping short of questioning his basic commitment, and certainly allowing

The king's downfall began with his passion for "foreign women."[62] Besides his wife from Egypt, he also had wives from Moab, Ammon, Edom, Sidon,[63] and the Hittites—all neighbors of Israel and each marriage likely a calculated political move. But whatever these unions did for Israel's national security or prestige, the narrator considers them to have been a violation of Deuteronomy 7:3–4 (cf. Exod 34:11–16; Josh 23:7, 12). That Solomon loved these foreign women (v. 1) contrasts harshly with his love for Yahweh (3:3).[64]

Just as Moses warned (Deut 17:17), Solomon's foreign wives led him into idolatry,[65] particularly worship of Ashtoreth, Chemosh, and Molech[66] (vv. 5, 7). On the Mount of Olives east of Jerusalem, a traditional worship site (cf. 2 Sam 15:32; 2 Kgs 23:13), Solomon built shrines to these false gods to please the women in his life, and the narrator appropriately calls these an "abomination" (vv. 5, 7). House notes the absurdity of this: "In the ancient world polytheists tended to worship the gods of nations who had conquered their armies or at least the gods of countries more powerful than their own. Ironically, Solomon

---

that he was blessed by God in a tremendous way, our authors have hinted throughout 1 Kings 1–10 that all is not well with Solomon's heart (e.g., 3:1–3; 4:26, 28; 5:14; 6:38–7:1)," (Provan, *1 & 2 Kings*, 91).

62. Solomon is famous for his seven hundred wives and three hundred concubines (cf. David's fifteen wives, 1 Chr 3:1–9, and Rehoboam's eighteen wives and sixty concubines, 2 Chr 11:21), these numbers likely representing "the total for Solomon's entire lifetime, not the number in the royal harem at any one time," (Hubbard, *First and Second Kings*, 67). Wives would have come from a higher social rank than concubines, and the children of concubines would not have been in the line of succession for the throne (Walton, *Bible Background*, 365).

63. One legend claims Solomon married Hiram's daughter (Gray, *I & II Kings*, 254).

64. Brueggemann, *1 & 2 Kings*, 141. "The Israelite was to love the LORD wholeheartedly (Deut. 6:5). But Solomon's heart was divided (v. 4); he was a man unable to practice his own advice to his subjects (8:61)," (Provan, *1 & 2 Kings*, 91).

65. "Just as the construction of the temple is presented as the acme of his piety, so these high places are sufficient evidence that 'his heart was not wholly true to Yahweh his God' (v. 4)," (Nelson, *First and Second Kings*, 70).

66. Ashtoreth, also known as *Ishtar* and *Astarte* in the ancient world, was a goddess of love and fertility and frequently Baal's consort in Canaanite theology (Judg 2:13); later she was identified with the Greek goddess Aphrodite. Molech, also known as *Milcom*, was the same as Baal to the Canaanites, but the Ammonite iteration was big on child sacrifice (2 Kgs 23:10; Jer 32:35). Chemosh, the national deity of Moab, was also a fan of child sacrifice (2 Kgs 3:27).

worships the gods of people he has conquered and already controls. What could he possibly gain from such activity?"[67]

In both the warnings of Deuteronomy and the promises of the Davidic covenant (2 Sam 7:14), God had sworn to discipline the king and his people when they became unfaithful. Sure enough, because of Solomon's apostasy, "the LORD was angry" (v. 9; cf. Deut 1:37; 9:8, 20)—the word translated "angry" (*ānap*) carries an image of snorting breath through the nostrils (cf. Exod 15:8; Job 4:9; Ps 18:7–8, 15; Ezek 38:18). Our idea of steam coming out of the ears would be close. Simply put, Yahweh was outraged.

And lest we think the divine narrator is being too hard on Solomon, we must note that he has not violated some itty bitty, legal minutia in the Law of Moses, but rather the first two commandments of Sinai (Exod 20:3–6). We are also reminded that Yahweh had appeared to the king *twice* (v. 9) and warned him about idolatry—no excuses remained.[68] "Of all the sins recorded in Scripture, God takes idolatry the most seriously, for no other sin has the capability of wrecking the entire covenant by itself. When this sin is committed, God acts swiftly, justly, and redemptively, as Israel discovers in Exodus 32–34; Numbers 20; and the entire Book of Judges."[69]

As punishment, God[70] swore to tear a majority of the kingdom away from the house of David, but not during Solomon's lifetime (cf. 1 Sam 13:13–14). And it would not be the entire kingdom; a tribe would be left "for the sake of David my servant and for the sake of Jerusalem that I have chosen" (v. 13). "Despite these concessions to David's memory, however, the punishment is clear, irrevocable, and stunning. Solomon's sin will soon cause the nation to crash from the heights it has achieved. His idolatry will lead to idolatry among the people.

---

67. House, *1, 2 Kings*, 167.

68. "Solomon lacked neither proof nor evidence of God's love and power. He had abundantly tasted God's love (1) by being chosen, contrary to what might have been expected, as David's successor; (2) in being given the special, personal name 'Jedidiah' (i.e., 'loved by the Lord'); (3) in receiving every benefit imaginable; and (4) in being visited by God twice for encouragement and admonition. He was given success in his endeavors beyond every expectation. These privileges should have created in Solomon a lifelong love and devotion of the deepest kind," (Patterson, "1, 2 Kings," 730).

69. House, *1, 2 Kings*, 168.

70. "This is the last time that God will speak directly to a king; from this point on, God will speak through the prophets," (Fretheim, *First and Second Kings*, 64).

Israel has begun the long road to exile, though they do not know yet that their actions entail such consequences."[71]

To discipline Solomon, Yahweh raised up three adversaries (Hebrew *satan*[72]) against him. Whereas we had previously been told about the extraordinary peace that existed in Solomon's day (5:4; cf. Prov 16:7), now we are to see violence and unrest plaguing his reign. The first of these was Hadad of Edom (vv. 14–22). David had subjugated Edom (2 Sam 8:13–14; 1 Chr 18:11–13; cf. Ps 60), and Joab had remained behind to purge the nation of every male survivor. But Hadad, a prince of Edom and only a small child, had escaped with members of his father's administration. Pharaoh[73] (either Amenemope or Osorkon) offered him political asylum,[74] allowed him to marry into the royal family of Egypt, and nurtured his hatred toward Israel. When Solomon ascended his father's throne, Hadad returned to Edom and eventually became a thorn in Solomon's side.[75] Again, recall the fortification of the town of Tamar in the Negev (9:18);

---

71. House, *1, 2 Kings*, 168.

72. "A *śātān* can be a celestial figure (Num. 22:22, 32; 1 Chr. 21:1; Job 1:6, 9, 12) or, as here, human military and political opponents (1 Sam. 29:4; 1 Kgs 5:[4])," (Wray Beal, *1 & 2 Kings*, 171).

73. "Solomon's first adversary is thus, ironically, set upon him by an old enemy of Israel whom he had unwisely treated as a friend (1 Kgs. 3:1)," (Provan, *1 & 2 Kings*, 94–95). "For its part, Egypt desired to regain its hegemony over the southern Levant at the first available opportunity, as Pharaoh Shishak's invasion would confirm immediately upon Solomon's death (14:25). Egypt had a long tradition of harboring foreigners during times of famine or strife in the Levant, but in this instance the purpose was to cultivate allies for a return to military and economic exploitation of its northern neighbors," (Monson, "1 Kings," 52).

74. "It is an interesting fact of political life in the ancient Near East that political dissidents and royal refugees were often taken in by kings (Egypt, Babylon, Persia and even petty chiefs of Palestine, according to the Tale of Sinuhe). These persons were part of a larger game played by rival monarchs, and what was at stake was the economic and political control of the entire region. The refugees were housed, tied to their patron by marriage and then let loose with some financial or military support to cause as much trouble as they could on a rival king's borders. In this way one power could drain the resources of its rival and eventually set it up for conquest," (Walton, *Bible Background*, 366).

75. Yeivin speculates that Pharaoh sent Hadad back to Edom to invade Israel from the southeast while Egypt invaded from the southwest (S. Yeivin, "Did the Kingdoms of Israel Have a Maritime Policy?" *JQR* 50 [1959–60]: 203). "There is little information to suggest that Edom was a national entity at this time. Hadad more likely represented one of the more powerful tribes in the region. His opposition may have taken the shape of raids on caravans rather than wars of

this was likely done to address the Edomite threat.[76]

The second adversary was Rezon of Damascus (vv. 23–25). Nursing a bitter hatred against David (cf. 2 Sam 8:3–9), he had fled from the land of "Zobah," the region of the Beqaa Valley in modern-day Lebanon, northwest of Damascus, and the dominant Aramean[77] kingdom in the region before Rezon's rise.[78] After gathering a band of guerrillas, he overthrew Israel's garrison in Damascus (2 Sam 8:6) and became the city's king. From Rezon and his people would rise the Arameans, a nation that would continually harass Israel for the next two centuries until finally subdued by the Assyrians. Rezon's unmitigated animosity for God's elect is expressed in that he "loathed Israel" (v. 25). "Rezon opposes the king from the north, Hadad from the south. Where there was peace on all sides, now there are only enemies."[79] And if we consider that one of the reasons for Solomon's many marriages was international peace, the fact that two international enemies rose against him becomes painfully ironic.[80]

The third adversary will become a greater character in the next chapter of Kings—Jeroboam of Ephraim[81] (vv. 26–40). When Solomon began work on the Millo (9:15), it seems he chose Jeroboam as his lead foreman, eventually making

---

independence. There are no references to him in contemporary extrabiblical sources," (Walton, *Bible Background*, 365).

76. Though, as Gray notes, Hadad's success against Solomon must have been limited, since the latter was able to take advantage of Edomite mines and build a factory at the north end of the Gulf of Aqaba (*I & II Kings*, 266).

77. Many translations, including the ESV, use the term "Syria" (the modern name) instead of "Aram" (the ancient name). Since I consider it to be anachronistic to refer to Hadad, Naaman, and others as "Syrians," I chose to retain the use of *Aram* and *Aramean* throughout.

78. Pitard, "Zobah (Place)," *ABD* 6:1108.

79. Provan, *1 & 2 Kings*, 95. For the supposed contradiction between 11:25 and 5:4, see Ibid., 96–97. "The fortification of Hazor in the Upper Galilee (1 Kgs 9:15) can be understood as a response to this new threat to Israel's northern border," (Cogan, *I Kings*, 335).

80. "If God wills otherwise, peace cannot be guaranteed, whether by diplomatic alliances or by military activity," (Barnes, *1–2 Kings*, 110–11).

81. Jeroboam's hometown of Zeredah was located northwest of Bethel and fifteen miles southwest of Shechem "in the center of Ephraim's territory," (Thompson, "Zeredah [Place]," *ABD* 6:1082). The tribe of Ephraim often caused problems for the power structures of Israel (Judg 8:1–3; 12:1–7).

him head[82] of all the laborers of Ephraim and Manasseh (5:13)—meaning he would have gained a reputation among the tribes of the North. That his mother was a widow (v. 26) likely means Jeroboam did not come from any prominent family, hence his rise to power was Yahweh's doing.[83]

One day, as Jeroboam was leaving Jerusalem, he was approached by Ahijah of Shiloh[84]—and for the first time since Nathan's appearance in David's bedroom (1:22), we witness the intervention of a prophet.[85] Ahijah took the new (a fact stressed twice, vv. 29–30, meaning it was costly) garment he wore and tore it into twelve pieces, symbolizing the tribes of Israel. He informed Jeroboam that God was giving him ten of the tribes (cf. 1 Sam 15:27–28; 24:1–7), retaining "one" for the house of David.[86] The twelfth tribe unaccounted for here was either Benjamin (which eventually went with Judah), Simeon (already assimilated into Judah[87]), or Levi (always without territory[88]); but we shouldn't become so

---

82. "His position might be compared to the *rabi Amurrim* (head of the Amorites) in the Mari texts, whose tasks included both military commands as well as being a local labor organizer, supervising construction projects on dams and the renovation of temples," (Walton, *Bible Background*, 366; emphasis his).

83. "A similar expression appears in Akkadian omen literature in which an unfit person who seizes the throne is called 'a widow's son.' In this case, the note on Jeroboam's lineage turns out to be a literary expression bereft of biographical significance," (Cogan, *I Kings*, 337–38).

84. Shiloh was located about ten miles north of Bethel, "just east of the main north-south road between Bethel and Shechem in the hill country of Ephraim," (Barnes, *1–2 Kings*, 128). "Although Shiloh had been previously destroyed by the Philistines (cf. Ps 78:60–64), apparently a small community had grown up there. Jeremiah indicates that the site was desolate again in his day (Jer 7:12, 14; 26:6, 9)," (Patterson, "1, 2 Kings," 751).

85. "Ahijah's prominence in this story begins the prophets' role as major players in the history of Israel. Of course, earlier prophets impact Israel's story, such as Samuel and Nathan, but the prophetic movement now becomes even more significant. In the rest of 1, 2 Kings the prophets act as God's spokespersons, as anointers of new kings, as miracle workers, and as Israel's overall covenant conscience," (House, *1, 2 Kings*, 172).

86. "This mitigation is not due to anything Solomon does, in contrast to the stories told about Ahab (21:27–29) and Jehu (II Kings 10:30). It is solely the result of God's covenant loyalty to David based on David's unparalleled past obedience (cf. 3:6; 8:16, 23)," (Nelson, *First and Second Kings*, 70–71).

87. Barnes, *1–2 Kings*, 112; Cogan, *I Kings*, 340; contra Leon J. Wood, "Simeon, the Tenth Tribe of Israel," *JETS* 14 (1971): 221–25.

88. Jones, *1 and 2 Kings*, 1:244; Sweeney, *I & II Kings*, 160.

focused on making the math work that we miss the point: the Lord is "wresting the bulk of the kingdom from David's son."[89]

Eventually, Solomon put a bounty on Jeroboam's head, forcing the latter to flee to Egypt and seek asylum under Shishak, implying "that at some point Jeroboam was ringleader of a rebellion against [Solomon's] oppressive policy."[90] If this is true, we should also note that Jeroboam, unlike David, took matters into his own hands instead of waiting on the Lord. He will not be the last king in Israel to accept Yahweh's anointing, but reject his timing.

Mention of Shishak (c. 935–914) is likely meant to tip us off that the political scene in Egypt has changed. This new pharaoh, known in extrabiblical literature as Shoshenq I, was the founder of the twenty-second dynasty and passionate about making Egypt great again. "Shishak is not as friendly to Solomon as Siamun was in the past. Perhaps the new Pharaoh resents paying Solomon's tolls, or perhaps he attempts to build a new power base that will serve his own interests. Either way, the Davidic lineage is in trouble. Jeroboam has a constituency in Israel, a significant foreign ally, and God's promise to place him in power. Without question, then, he will soon be the major force in Israelite politics."[91]

T he reign of Solomon is brought to a close by the narrator in a form that will become standard for many of the kings that follow him. The narrator refers us to the royal archives for more information,[92] his total years of service are given, and we are informed of his burial.

---

89. Wray Beal, *1 & 2 Kings*, 173.

90. Hubbard, *First and Second Kings*, 70. He later adds, "The author briefly noted that Solomon unsuccessfully tried to kill Jeroboam (v. 40). It is unlikely that the king moved because of Ahijah's prophecy since it was given in private. More probably the oracle emboldened Jeroboam to lead the acts of insurrection to which v. 26 alludes. He obviously emerged as the ringleader of northern resistance (1 Kings 12:3)," (Ibid., 71–72).

91. House, *1, 2 Kings*, 172. "Intimidated by his power, Egypt once sought Solomon's friendship (1 Kings 3:1; 9:16; cf. 1 Kings 10:28–29). Sensing his weakness, now she sheltered his foes (1 Kings 11:14–22)," (Hubbard, *First and Second Kings*, 72).

92. "The author of this book makes frequent reference to the 'book of annals.' This was likely part of a robust court record of the type discovered in ancient Mesopotamia, Anatolia, and Egypt. Vast archives from these empires and regional kingdoms such as Ebla and Mari provide a glimpse of the size and range of topics that likely characterized the lost court records of ancient Israel. These archives include letters from and to the king, court documents, and records of mil-

To a secular reader of Israel's history, Solomon was the nation's greatest king bar none and the one by whom all subsequent kings should be measured. Still, the standard would prove to be his father. Solomon will not be the last king in Jerusalem to fail to live up to the standard of David (v. 4). Indeed, only Hezekiah and Josiah are considered to have been equals with the famed giant killer.

Auld notes, "After all this talk in chapter 11 of troubles in his realms, the formal notice at the end of our passage concerning Solomon's death and burial seems rather an anti-climax. This king of so great promise seems almost a spent force before his time is finished."[93] I agree; there is something depressingly anti-climactic about Solomon's death, not unlike your favorite sports team crushing opponents and leading the league during the regular season, only to lose in the first round of the playoffs to an inferior opponent.[94]

To be sure, Solomon excelled in many areas. "First, he is an organizational genius. He is able to order, tax, and govern a fairly extensive political and financial empire. Solomon's cognitive abilities make this success possible. Second, he implements an effective foreign policy, which demonstrates his adaptability and willingness to compromise and improvise. Third, Solomon is humble enough to ask for God's help and thoughtful enough to pray for Israel, both in his time and in the future, and for other nations as well. Despite his failings in later years these good traits should not be forgotten."[95] But for all the glory and gold and glitter of the Solomonic age, was Israel better off?

Solomon's legacy reminds us that it takes more than political savvy, diplomatic aplomb, or a robust treasury to establish a kingdom. Indeed, all of these are more easily attainable if a person simply seeks the Lord first (Matt 6:33). In what is arguably the worst irony of his life, Solomon's pursuit of peace and wisdom did not pay the dividends we would expect, and it was because he did not pursue the Lord above all else. And for all the wisdom that was embodied in this son of David, Solomon ended up living out precious little of it.

---

itary campaigns. A fine illustration is the court archival material from the capital of the Hittite empire, dating to the middle of the second millennium B.C. It describes a range of activities that took place in the court," (Monson, "1 Kings," 63).

93. Auld, *I & II Kings*, 83.

94. I hate you, Aaron Rodgers. I hate you. Also, Dez caught it.

95. House, *1, 2 Kings*, 174.

TALKING POINTS

The extent to which Solomon went to increase the riches of his kingdom offers a warning to us. While Solomon's glory was a result of God's gracious provision, and though we see Gentiles praising God because of Solomon, it is also evident that Solomon's riches went to his head. Olley warns, "There is a thin line between 'giving the best to God' and self-centred pride in what *we* are doing."[96] Although perhaps not to Solomon's degree, we are nonetheless an incredibly blessed people. We live in one of the wealthiest nations on earth. Many of us own successful businesses, have enjoyed prosperous careers, live in beautiful homes, drive nice cars, and have closets full of attractive clothes. I grew up in a church culture that emphasized what Olley mentions, that we are to give our best to God. But too often, I have seen this prudent maxim manipulated into an excuse to show off before others. "Give my best to God" is really "dress to impress." "Look at how God has blessed me" is an acceptable way of saying, "Look at how much I have achieved." Our false piety may fool others, but it will not fool God, who knows our hearts.

It is with tremendous sadness that we witness Solomon's slide into apostasy. This son of David will not be the last king in Jerusalem to begin well, yet fail to finish strong (e.g., Asa, Joash, Azariah). Though it is certainly true that many walk away from the Lord in their youth, it's also true that we can lose our faithful fervor as we age (Eccl 12:1). For the young, Solomon's life is a warning that following Jesus becomes more difficult as we age, not less. In high school, college, or our young adult years, we are prone to put off faithfulness until a more convenient season. But I have always found "the next season of life" to be more demanding and less hospitable to faith than the one before it. Obedience to the Lord Jesus Christ becomes harder, not easier, as we age. For the old, Solomon's

---

96. Olley, *Message of Kings*, 112; emphasis his. "One can read the enumeration of Solomon's wealth with a sense of wonder at the magnificent superabundant blessings God gave, in the same way that tourists may marvel at the grandeur of a palace. It can also be read as an expression of Solomon's self-centred acquisition for his own glory, suggesting power and control over his kingdom with religious faith being a formality. The temptations are real in a world where, globally and personally, economic measures and scientific and technological advances are seen to provide solutions," (Ibid., 114).

life should prompt a moment's pause before criticizing the younger generation at the risk of ignoring a plank in one's own eye (Matt 7:3–5). It is easier to trust the Lord when you have nothing; faith is an altogether different proposition when you are old, have accomplished much, are secure in your career or retirement, and are in need of nothing (cf. Deut 8:10–14). Like Jimmy Stewart's character in the film *Shenandoah*, many an older Christian has forgotten what it is to walk by faith and put God first until an "adversary" (e.g., terminal illness, loneliness, financial hardship) is raised against them. Let us take care that Solomon's spiritual slide late in life does not become our own.

S olomon's many wives and concubines offer a warning not to be yoked with unbelievers (2 Cor 6:14). I do not consider it a sin to marry a non-Christian, but just because something isn't sinful doesn't mean it's not unwise. My grandmother, a strong woman with a strong faith in God, married a non-Christian. Even to his death, my grandfather (though a good man) never obeyed the gospel. My grandmother often preached to her daughters (my mom and my aunt) that they should marry Christians. My dad joked that they both ignored her and married preachers! Solomon will not be the last king we meet in this study to suffer spiritually because of his ill-advised nuptials. His great-great-grandson, Jehoshaphat, established an alliance with Ahab and gave his son, Joram, in marriage to Ahab's daughter, Athaliah, and her reign of terror will be documented in 2 Kings 11.[97] Barnes observes, "Marry the unbeliever, get the unbelief (thrown in for free, as it were). This is especially true when the marriage partner is vigorous in personality or from a home with parents of vigorous personalities. [...] As is generally the case, the history here is written with a clear contemporary agenda. And in this case it is that thou shalt not marry unbelievers."[98]

---

97. Omer Sergi, "Foreign Women and the Early Kings of Judah," *ZAW* 126 (2014): 193–207.

98. Barnes, *1–2 Kings*, 252–53. Earlier, he notes the greater choice people have today in whom they marry. "Solomon, ironically, had less freedom in this regard than we do today, since his wives often represented the result of ongoing diplomatic alliances (especially the daughter of the pharaoh); but still, his clear choices and priorities in this area, while understandable to ancient Near Eastern culture, were far from what the Torah had commanded," (Ibid., 108).

T hough Solomon's apostasy leaves us depressed and dubious as to Israel's future, the narrator of 1 Kings 11 would not have us lose hope. The same God whom Solomon rejected was still large and in charge. He raised up adversaries against Solomon, just as he had promised David he would do (2 Sam 7:14). This should hearten us as readers, for we see exemplified God's sovereignty and love. His sovereignty is seen in the fact that the rise and fall of leaders is by his will and affected by his word. But his sovereign judgment on Solomon's reign was also proof of his love. He could have abandoned the Lamp of David to the ash heap of history. But he did not.[99] God disciplines those he loves (Heb 12:5–6). I would recommend you get used to feelings of frustration and despondency as you read through Kings. The outlook will seldom be bright; it often goes from bad to worse. But throughout, God's sovereignty and love show up in the worst of times. And as long as God is sovereign and loving (Rev 11:15; 1 John 4:8), Christians have a lot of reasons to have hope for the future.[100]

99. "By the word of Yahweh dynasties rise and fall; by the word of Yahweh barren widows become fruitful and their stores of food are not exhausted; by the word of Yahweh arrows find chinks in armor; by the word of Yahweh the price of grain tumbles overnight; by the word of Yahweh Jerusalem and the temple are destroyed. If the word of Yahweh is so effective in bringing destruction, the same word will preserve the house of David forever. Even death cannot triumph over the word of Yahweh. He promises that he will not destroy David's house (11:12–13, 34–36), but instead will leave a lamp burning," (Leithart, *1 & 2 Kings*, 89).

100. "Chapter 11 launches four theological themes: royal apostasy, the prophetic word, God's control of international affairs, and the eternal promise to David. These thematic trajectories will cut through the rest of Kings, and they will finally deliver their payloads on Jerusalem and Judah in the last chapters of the book. All four of these theological claims have an impact on today's reader as well," (Nelson, *First and Second Kings*, 73).

5

THE COLD WAR

With Solomon asleep with his fathers, his son, Rehoboam, was poised to inherit all of his father's glory. But Junior quickly proved himself to be the know-nothing grandson intent on running the family business into the ground by doing things his way. At first glance, it seems Rehoboam's coronation at Shechem was as much a foregone conclusion as is the U.S. electoral college's selection of a president and vice-president—a formalized and very symbolic ratification of what everyone had already accepted. But at least for Rehoboam, such was not the case. Challenged by dissidents intent on reform, Solomon's son crudely and caustically spurned their request, inciting schism and ill will that would last decades. Despite virulent efforts at forced unification, Israel remained divided because such was God's will.

To a greater extent, Jeroboam, Rehoboam's Northern rival, was set up for unprecedented success. Much like Saul, God had given Jeroboam the throne and the unequivocal support of his people. But also like Saul, Jeroboam squandered this incredible blessing, inciting the wrath of Yahweh. As soon as he was crowned, Jeroboam bit the divine hand that fed him. For the entire history of the Northern Kingdom, her kings will be remembered for walking in the sin of Jeroboam, son of Nebat; his unfaithfulness becomes the recipe for disaster followed by every monarch to succeed him.

Putting these events in historical perspective is important. Saul, David, and Solomon had reigned for forty years each; for more than a century, only three men had led Israel. But because of division and disobedience, at least for the Northern Kingdom, rulers came and went with astonishing speed. In one of history's bitter ironies, "the kingdom that was to relieve Israel from oppression staggered through seas of blood, and four kings, or would-be kings, died by violence."[1]

An unsettling theme begins to develop in these chapters, one that will not culminate until the end of Kings. With the rise of Rehoboam to his father's throne, we will begin to see a reversal of the Conquest of Canaan and Exodus from Egypt. Indeed, themes from Exodus are prevalent in this section. God hardened Pharaoh's heart to achieve his purposes, and it's apparent that he does something similar with Rehoboam's. Moses led Israel out of slavery in Egypt, and the narrator here presents Jeroboam as Israel's hero of the hour, emerging from Egypt to lead the Northern Kingdom out of Solomon's/Rehoboam's slavery. But you can put that anointing oil away—Jeroboam isn't the new Moses as much as the new Aaron, commissioning golden calves and ushering the people into idolatry. And instead of leading the people on to freedom and promise, he establishes a pattern for losing a kingdom in just two hundred years.

1 KINGS 12:1-24

If 20/20 vision is one of the benefits of hindsight, the common drawback is looking at episodes in history too narrowly. Rather than isolated moments, significant events are often the climaxes of trends that have been going on for decades, if not centuries.

Take, for example, the March on Selma in March 1965 or Martin Luther King's "I Have a Dream" speech in August 1963—where do we begin? With the courageous Rosa Parks on a bus in Montgomery? The South's Jim Crow laws? Reconstruction? The Civil War? Antebellum slavery? The slave-owning Thomas Jefferson's radical assertion in the Declaration of Independence that all men are created equal? Caribbean sugar cane growers' greedy desire for cheap labor? Every event has a context and a backstory, one that can span decades or centuries.

As Israel's post-Solomonic history unfolds, it's easy to conclude that the nation shifted from an international power to a bumbling, divided state in almost no time. But Solomon's empire had been a house of cards in many ways—godless power, prestige, and prosperity can have that effect. His magnificent building programs, which had brought Israel so much acclaim and pride, had been built on the backs of forced laborers and financed by heavy taxes.

---

1. Maclaren, *Expositions*, 4:230.

Even before Solomon, there had been a lot of jealousy and infighting be-tween the tribes of Israel. At the outset, David had reigned for 7½ years over only Judah (2 Sam 5:5), and during his reign, he was often pacifying various factions—so much so that Flanagan concludes, "The underlying tensions that would eventually separate the kingdoms of Judah and Israel after Solomon's reign posed a threat to the dual monarchy even during the time of David."[2] Throughout the story of Judges, Ephraim was especially hot-headed, often walking around with a chip on its collective shoulder (Judg 7:24; 8:1; 12:1; cf. Ps 78:67–68).

That said, Rehoboam certainly did himself no favors. He went to Shechem to be made king, but the inauguration turned into an interrogation. A contin-gent, led by the just-returned-from-exile Jeroboam, beseeched the king to light-en up on the forced labor and high taxes. Rehoboam responded with something amounting to, "Let me check with my people and get back to you in three days."

One wonders why Rehoboam went to Shechem for his coronation and not the Gihon Spring (as had Solomon) or Hebron (David). In ancient Israel, Shechem was centrally-located, but it also was a traditional holy site (cf. Gen 12:6; 33:18–20) that represented a place of covenant renewal[3] (Deut 11:29–32; 27; Josh 24:1–27). It was "a place where the Israelites, having entered the land, first took stock of themselves and reflected upon their identity and direction. [...] Shechem is an ideal place, therefore, to which a prospective king might be invited if you wished to ask him (as the Israelites do) how his kingship was going to be exercised so as to be consonant with the nature of the covenant people of God—if you wished to ask him to reflect on the identity of Israel and her future direction."[4]

From another perspective, the fact that Rehoboam had to go to Shechem to meet with Israel's elders, as opposed to their coming to meet with him, as they had David (2 Sam 5:1), is an early suggestion to the reader that this new king is politically weak. "The dual identity of Israel and Judah that was supposedly

---

2. James W. Flanagan, "Court History or Succession Document? A Study of 2 Samuel 9-20 and 1 Kings 1-2," *JBL* 91 (1972): 181. Jacob Myers suggests that during the days of a unit-ed monarchy, the "structure of a double crown, one of Judah and the other of Israel, was main-tained," (*II Chronicles* [Garden City, NY: Doubleday, 1965], 65).

3. Fritz calls it "the most important town in the north before the foundation of Samaria," (*1 & 2 Kings*, 142).

4. Provan, *1 & 2 Kings*, 103–4. It's possible that "Israel regularly observed a covenant re-newal ceremony at Shechem (Deut. 11:26-32; 27:1-26)," (Hubbard, *First and Second Kings*, 74).

merged under David and cemented under Solomon may not have been quite as unified as it seemed. Rehoboam's kingship cannot be presumed."[5]

When Rehoboam consulted his father's advisors, they unanimously counseled him to rule as a servant-leader (v. 7). This, they said, was the only way to forge national unity among the disparate tribes. But the advice of the king's younger advisors was decidedly worse. "Thus you should say to them, 'My little finger is thicker than my father's loins'" (v. 10 NRSV).

It must be remembered that "young" here is relative. Rehoboam was forty-one years old, and his friends were presumably about the same age. The older advisors almost certainly had served under Solomon and witnessed the burden the king's largesse had placed on the people, hence their urging Rehoboam to be a more compassionate ruler. The younger advisors—having grown up with silver spoons in their mouths—thought only of protecting their cushy lifestyle without thinking of those who provided it.[6] What is telling is how closely Rehoboam identified with the younger versus older advisors; note the use of *we* versus *I* in v. 9, suggesting "a pre-commitment to their advice."[7]

Scholars aren't sure exactly what is meant by "finger" (v. 10), and the confusion isn't helped by the fact that the Hebrew term (*qātōn*) is used only here and in the parallel passage of 2 Chronicles 10:10. But it's thought that what Rehoboam's young friends were advising him to say was, "My penis is bigger than my father's waist."[8] To the king's credit, he omitted this locker room reference from his official statement, but the meaning was still clear: Rehoboam had chosen "slogans over wisdom, machismo over servanthood."[9] In the thinking of these young ad-

---

5. Hens-Piazza, *1–2 Kings*, 122. Shechem is where Abimelech had crowned himself king about two hundred years prior (Judg 9:6); the narrator may intentionally be drawing subtle parallels between Abimelech's and Rehoboam's oppressive leadership styles (Leithart, *1 & 2 Kings*, 90).

6. Halpern speculates, "At Shechem, the young officers, untried and untested, wished to advance themselves by war with Egypt, a war which could be made possible only through an increase in taxation and corvee. As opposed to the established advisors of Solomon's court, these sought a swift promotion through the ranks of favor; no quicker path was available than war," (Baruch Halpern, "Sectionalism and the Schism," *JBL* 93 [1974]: 527).

7. Wray Beal, *1 & 2 Kings*, 182.

8. *HALOT* 1093; Jones, *1 and 2 Kings*, 1:251–52. "Whatever is the case, the claim is that Rehoboam is a bigger man than his father—a power to be reckoned with," (Provan, *1 & 2 Kings*, 107).

9. Nelson, *First and Second Kings*, 79.

visors, the only way to forge national unity was by being a bully.[10] The double mention of "scorpions" (vv. 11, 14) was a reference to a particularly harsh type of whip "that produced wounds so painful as to be compared to a scorpion's sting. Perhaps, as often maintained, it was made with spiked barbs or nails."[11]

It's important to note that Israel was not asking for the unreasonable. Their request was not for the *removal* of the yoke—a common metaphor for service to a superior (cf. Gen 27:40; Deut 28:48; Isa 14:25; 47:6; Jer 27:8; Ezek 34:27)— but that it be *lightened*. The taxes and forced labor Solomon had placed upon his people had become increasingly unbearable. In the ancient Near East, it was not uncommon for a new ruler to curry favor with his subjects by freeing slaves and lowering taxes.[12] Thus, in exchange for their acknowledgment and consent to be ruled by the house of David, the other tribes needed some things in return.

Whenever I have heard this story retold, the emphasis is almost always placed on Rehoboam's foolishness in listening to his younger versus older advisors. Unlike his father (3:16–28), Rehoboam was unable to discern wisely between two parties giving him conflicting arguments.[13] But Rehoboam's political fumble is only one of many threads in this tapestry of regal stupidity. He should have listened to the older advisors, but not because they were older. It was the throne's leadership dynamic—one of self-serving bullies instead of self-sacrificing shepherds (cf. 1 Sam 8:10–17)—that proved to be the reason for the split. What had begun with David in the latter years of his reign and been perpetuated by Solomon, now continued with Rehoboam. And the people of Israel had had enough.

How do you lose a kingdom in four hundred years? By ignoring the wise counsel of those who have learned from the mistakes of the past—either their

---

10. "If Israel feels 'raped' by Solomon, Rehoboam plans to give them more of the same. Rehoboam's advisors are 'boys' who identify cruelty with leadership, who are flexing their political muscles for the first time, who think that the main thing that people need is a good dose of discipline," (Leithart, *1 & 2 Kings*, 92).

11. Patterson, "1, 2 Kings," 740.

12. Robert Alter, *Ancient Israel: The Former Prophets: Joshua, Judges, Samuel, and Kings* (New York: Norton, 2013), 668.

13. "It is ironic that the epitome of foolish leadership in the Book of 1 Kings is the son of the king whose reign began with a prayer for wisdom, whose early years showed so much of it, and whose proverbs, given to his son, speak so much about wisdom and foolishness," (Inrig, *I & II Kings*, 92).

own, or others', or both. More specifically, you lose it by reigning with force versus grace, by leveraging your power to protect yourself instead of blessing others.

I n 1972, social psychologist Irving Janis coined the term *groupthink*, "a psychological phenomenon in which people strive for consensus within a group. In many cases, people will set aside their own personal beliefs or adopt the opinion of the rest of the group."[14] On the other hand, group members with alternative views often remain silent so as not to rock the boat.

You're likely unwittingly familiar with a few textbook examples of groupthink. In April 1961, newly-minted President Kennedy authorized the Bay of Pigs invasion in an attempt to unseat Fidel Castro from power in Cuba. The mission met with colossal failure, and though Kennedy admirably accepted blame with a "the buck stops here" attitude, the CIA was widely criticized as having been predisposed to a certain way of doing things without giving ear to dissent. Their plan had too many "best-case scenario" assumptions; they were counting on too many things going their way without planning appropriate contingencies. Everyone expected the Cuban people would instantly join the coup d'état; they didn't. Everyone assumed the rebels would successfully melt away into the mountains if they encountered resistance; no one mentioned the seventy miles of swamps the guerrillas would have to get past to make it to the mountains. Kennedy's aides knew the president wanted to get rid of Castro, so they were more interested in pleasing their boss with a consensus than in giving him the best possible counsel.

The 1957 film *12 Angry Men* demonstrates groupthink at its best (or worst, depending on your perspective). In the movie, a room full of jurors argue the guilt/innocence of a young boy accused of murdering his father. One is struck early in the film with just how easy it is to agree blindly with the group. In fact, the film serves up an excellent model of how groupthink can be challenged successfully.

There is an important leadership lesson to be learned in Rehoboam's actions in this chapter. Though he solicited the opinion of his older advisors, it's clear he did not identify with them as much as he did the younger; again, notice his use of third-person versus first-person pronouns (v. 9). Had Rehoboam re-

14. Kendra Cherry, "What Is Groupthink?" June 24, 2016. Accessed Sept 5, 2016. <https://www.verywell.com/what-is-groupthink-2795213>

mained more objective and encouraged vigorous, respectful debate on the issue, perhaps he would have made a wiser decision.

In families, churches, and businesses, there can be intense pressure to conform to "keep the peace" and not "rock the boat" or be a "troublemaker." But at times, this only means we are expected to submit to stronger alpha personalities and allow them to have their way. Many a congregation has suffered because church leaders were either too assertive or not assertive enough. The same could be said for any type of group. Perhaps all of us would benefit if we remembered Paul's umbrella command when it came to interpersonal relationships, whether in marriage, parenting, or business—"Submit to one another out of reverence for Christ" (Eph 5:21 NIV).

Effective leaders do not perceive dissent as a threat. Rather, they (at the least) consider it an opportunity to affirm the dissenter's value to the group and (at the most) welcome it as a chance to discern flaws in their plan. Submission does not mean always giving in to the other side, but being respectful of others' opinions and valuing them as equal servants of Christ. Successful businesses in today's world encourage dialogue and differences of opinion; the church, however, is often slow to catch on to this, wrongly believing that dissent is the enemy of the community's shalom. But healthy disagreement today can spare us many headaches tomorrow.

The Northern tribes' response to Rehoboam was predictable. "To your tents, O Israel!" amounted to a repudiation of the Davidic dynasty[15] (cf. 2 Sam 20:1). "To your tents" had once functioned as an expression of release from military service (cf. 1 Sam 4:10; 2 Sam 20:22). But the saying had evolved as a proverb expressing dissatisfaction with the present administration, and we are left to wonder if ridding themselves of the house of David was what the Northern tribes had desired all along.[16]

In an ill-advised attempt to settle the dispute by force, Rehoboam sent Adoram, who as a young man had been an official in David's cabinet (2 Sam

---

15. "The ominous cry, which had been heard before, in Sheba's abortive revolt, answers Rehoboam with instantaneous and full-throated defiance. Rancorous tribal hatred is audible in it. Long pent up jealousy and dislike of the dynasty of David has got breath at last," (Maclaren, *Expositions*, 4:222).

16. Fritz, *1 & 2 Kings*, 143.

20:24) and later served as Solomon's overseer of forced labor (4:6). In retrospect, Rehoboam couldn't have chosen a worse person for this mission. Adoram was stoned, and the king fled for his life. Like "the shot heard round the world" at Concord, Massachusetts in 1775, or the firing on Fort Sumter in 1861, Adoram's assassination signaled the beginning of hostilities. And though this would be mostly a cold war,[17] things wouldn't thaw out for several decades.

In a last-ditch effort to keep the two factions united, Rehoboam mustered 180,000[18] troops from Judah and Benjamin to quell the rebellion. But on the eve of battle, the prophet Shemaiah[19] brought Rehoboam a message from the Lord: the division was a divine decree. Rehoboam had no business resisting any longer. Go home and deal with it. Thus, the king "is bluntly reminded who is really in charge of the future of Davidic rule."[20]

mentioned earlier how this political fumble by Rehoboam was only one thread in this tapestry; though his actions receive most of the attention from preachers and teachers, there is a more troubling dynamic at play in this chapter. Blame Rehoboam, yes. Chide the Israelites for petulantly taking their marbles and going home when they didn't get their way. But do not miss the fact that this all was the Lord's doing. Yes, this *division* was of Yahweh. The king didn't listen to the people, and the people refused to capitulate to a tyrant, "for it was a turn of affairs brought about by the LORD" (v. 15). It doesn't take a biblical scholar to realize that such a bold admission by the narrator is intended to make us sit up and reassess our assumptions about the narrative.

---

17. "Full-scale war does not appear to have broken out between Judah and the Northern tribes over their secession. Rather, border clashes between the two seem to have continued over a number of years (cf. 14:30), probably before and after the raid of Shishak," (Cogan, *I Kings*, 355).

18. Some scholars question this number. It must be conceded that the Hebrew '*elep* can mean "unit" or "clan," and not just "thousand." To compound matters, the LXX says Rehoboam mustered 120,000 troops, not 180,000. However, there had been 500,000 troops in Judah at the end of David's reign versus 800,000 in Israel (2 Sam 24:9), so 180,000 is not unbelievable.

19. Precious little is known about Shemaiah; he does not reappear in Kings, and his role in this passage seems minimal. But the author of Chronicles portrays him as a sort of court prophet (2 Chr 12:5–8) on the level of Nathan and Ahijah, and one who, along with Iddo, penned Rehoboam's biography (2 Chr 12:15).

20. Olley, *Message of Kings*, 134. "Remarkably Rehoboam who would not listen to good political counsel accepts the prophetic word," (Brueggemann, *1 & 2 Kings*, 160).

How, then, are we to reckon the schism of Israel? Who is to blame? It seems a paradox when we realize, "Rehoboam is fatally responsible even for what God is seen to have already decreed."[21] The conundrum is not unlike Moses and Pharaoh. Who hardened the heart of the king of Egypt? "You can look at what happens from different angles and see both the reality of human freedom and decision making and the reality of divine sovereignty and the fulfilling of the divine will."[22] As has often been illustrated, divine sovereignty and human responsibility are but two pedals on a bicycle. God was at work to divide Israel as he swore to do through Ahijah the prophet, and so he pushed Rehoboam's buttons as he had Pharaoh's.

Only to the wicked does this seem unfair; to the righteous, this is comforting (cf. Ps 18:25–26). For one thing, I want a God who is large, in charge, and never caught off guard. For another, I want to know he can work with both willing and unwilling instruments to accomplish his agenda. Maclaren reminds us, "The greatest crime in the world's history was at the same time the accomplishment of God's most merciful purpose. Calvary is the highest example of the truth, which embraces all lesser instances of the wrath of man, which He makes to praise Him and effect His deep designs."[23]

But there are two deeper realities I want us to notice. *First, Rehoboam was not forced to react as he did.* He had the choice to respond righteously, and the division of Israel would have materialized *in spite* of him, rather than *because* of him. God's will does not fatalistically resign anyone to sin. We cannot thwart God's purposes, but neither do we have to be a part of making a bad situation worse. If God sees fit to use human sin for his purposes, let it always be someone else's sin he uses!

Second, the same divine will that capitalized on Rehoboam's folly also intervened to prevent further folly. Dead set on forcing reconciliation in Israel, Rehoboam and his 180,000 troops were sent home by the prophet Shemaiah. To his credit, Rehoboam listened—a little too late in the narrative, but he listened. So it is that while divine sovereignty sometimes gives us enough rope with which to hang ourselves, it also sometimes intervenes in an attempt to save us graciously from ourselves. "That is clearly a footprint of grace."[24]

---

21. Wallace, *1 Kings*, 80.

22. Goldingay, *1 and 2 Kings for Everyone*, 59.

23. Maclaren, *Expositions*, 4:221.

24. Davis, *1 Kings*, 132.

For the church in any age, it is imperative that we trust in God's sovereignty and act accordingly. Regardless of the threats breathed against us, we must remember this: "Big men (especially royal, arrogant ones) are simply little servants of Yahweh's word. Contrary to our fears, human stupidity is not running loose but is on the leash of God's sovereignty."[25] God has sworn that his every promise to us will be fulfilled. That includes the promise that the wicked will never inherit his kingdom; that he shall supply our every need in Christ; that heaven and earth will pass away before his Word does; and that if we are faithful to the point of death, a crown of life awaits us. How magnificent and freeing it is to resign ourselves to his sovereignty by walking righteously and responsibly before him!

1 KINGS 12:25-33

Jeroboam's first order of business as king (930–909) was to fortify his capital at Shechem, and he later did the same at Penuel, a location five miles west of the Jordan River (Gen 32:31; Judg 8:8–9) that provided a protective buffer against threats to the east[26] and served as an alternate royal residence akin to Camp David.[27]

While Jeroboam's fortification endeavors were arguably spiritually neutral, it was his second order of business that left the narrator hotter than a hornet. In what was, at least in Jeroboam's mind, a politically expedient move necessary to solidify his rule,[28] the king had alternative worship centers established at Dan and Bethel, each one complete with the image of a golden calf.

Dan and Bethel represented polar ends of the Northern Kingdom. Bethel lay on Ephraim's border with Benjamin, some eleven miles north of Jerusalem,

---

25. Ibid., 129.

26. "Jeroboam's fortification was designed doubtless to secure Gilead, which had remained loyal to David in Absalom's revolt," (Gray, *I & II Kings*, 290).

27. Josephus, *Antiquities* 8.225. Some have suggested that Penuel was built up as a fallback position when Shishak later attacked from the west (Robinson, *First Book*, 155–56), but if so, it offered little help, since the Egyptian potentate also conquered that site according to his list (Cogan, *I Kings*, 358). Alternatively, Allan suggests that Jeroboam was forced to relocate because Levites in Shechem conspired against him (Nigel Allan, "Jeroboam and Shechem," *VT* 24 [1974]: 353–57).

28. "Jeroboam's early actions are a mirror to expose motives and priorities, to point to what happens when pragmatism and self-protection are put before trust and following God's ways," (Olley, *Message of Kings*, 139).

and it was a traditional worship site dating to the time of Abraham and Jacob[29] (Gen 12:8; 28:11–19; 35:1; cf. Judg 4:5; 20:26–27). Dan lay on Israel's northern boundary, and it too had a religious history[30] (Judg 18:27–31), but one considerably more dubious than Bethel. Thus, Bethel continued to be a prominent locale in the Northern Kingdom (Hos 10:5; Amos 7:13); for one thing, Bethel benefited from a better location—Israelites making the trip to Jerusalem would find Bethel a more convenient destination.

Scholars are not in agreement as to what exactly these calves represented. In many ancient Near Eastern religions, bulls and calves were symbols of fertility and power, but were seldom, if ever, used to depict a god as much as represent a god's attributes. In the case of the Arameans and Assyrians (Israel's northern neighbors), calves or bulls were considered the "the pedestal or footstool on which the deity stood"[31]—not unlike the cherubim atop the Ark of the Covenant functioning as God's footstool (1 Chr 28:2). Based on this understanding, some scholars believe Jeroboam never intended the calves to be an act of unfaithfulness to the covenant, and that the negative light in which Jeroboam is cast in this section is really just the fault of a grouchy narrator with a bone to pick.[32]

There are, however, several facts that blow holes in such an interpretation. *First, there is no question that we are to see in this calf story a reflection of the original golden calf story of Exodus 32.*

- Like Aaron (Exod 32:2–4), Jeroboam oversaw the construction of the calves (v. 28).

- Like Aaron (Exod 32:4), Jeroboam announced, "Behold your

---

29. "Jeroboam may easily have fancied, and have tried to persuade others, that Jehovah would reveal Himself to the descendants of Jacob in this sacred place just as well as He had done to their forefather," (Keil, *Commentary*, 199).

30. Archaeologists have discovered the remains of Jeroboam's high place at Dan. "The sanctuary complex was about 195 by 145 feet and featured a large altar in an open-air courtyard," (Walton, *Bible Background*, 369).

31. Monson, "1 Kings," 57; cf. Walton, *Bible Background*, 368.

32. "Thus what may have been an innocent and well meaning liturgical alternative to Jerusalem is promptly subjected to a heavy-handed theological caricature and critique. Thus immediately we are told, 'this thing became a sin' (12:30). Note well, we are not given any theological reason for the judgment that it is a sin, except that it caused the people to worship elsewhere, other than in Jerusalem," (Brueggemann, *1 & 2 Kings*, 161; cf. Jones, *1 and 2 Kings*, 1:258).

gods, O Israel, who brought you up out of the land of Egypt (v. 28).

- Like Aaron (Exod 32:5), Jeroboam established a new altar and a new feast (vv. 32–33).[33]

Second, the calves were too closely identifiable with the idolatry of Israel's neighbors. "Such a symbol had to create problems for those who were just progressing in the biblical understanding of God. All around Israel, and in the numerous Canaanite enclaves within its territory, were half-Yahwists to whom the calf or bull was the symbol of male fecundity. Officially or unofficially, Baalism was in the land; it was destined in the days of Ahab to gain the mastery. Thus the golden calf could have done nothing but confuse and mislead."[34] How we worship God is of critical importance, and doing so in ways that are "culturally relevant" often lead to unimaginable consequences. Slippery slopes are dangerous for a reason.

Finally, what Jeroboam thought *he was doing matters little.* "Sincerity—if that is what it is—is not enough."[35] The argument that Jeroboam was not establishing worship of another god in Israel (which isn't sound, based on 14:9) only neutralizes the first commandment. The second commandment still clearly prohibited the crafting of any image as a symbol or representation of the God of heaven (Exod 20:4–5; Deut 5:8). Whether he broke the first commandment or the second, the narrator is dismayed that Jeroboam violated any of them in the first place[36] (cf. Hos 8:5; 10:5–6). Whether he is abandoning the worship of the true God, or simply perverting Israel's worship, the end result is the same. "Here Jeroboam miscalculated and substituted human wisdom for divine direc-

---

33. And as if we needed any more evidence, "the significance of the names borne by Jeroboam's sons, Nadab and Abijah, echoing the names of Aaron's sons, Nadab and Abihu, should not be underestimated," (Cogan, *I Kings*, 363).

34. DeVries, *1 Kings*, 162. House adds, "Israel's monotheistic faith was not an easy sell at any time, so Jeroboam's actions made it harder for Yahwism to survive in any recognizably distinct form," (*1, 2 Kings*, 185).

35. Provan, *1 & 2 Kings*, 112.

36. "Inasmuch as Pentateuchal law prohibited the use of all images in the worship of YHWH, any breach of orthodox practice was branded idolatry, whatever the intention of the worshiper may have been," (Cogan, *I Kings*, 363).

tion. Although God may have allowed the kingdom to be divided politically, he intended no theological schism."[37]

But Jeroboam's apostasy was not limited to the calves. The narrator also records that he established alternate temples on high places at Dan and Bethel (cf. Deut 12), installed non-Levitical priests (cf. Deut 18:1–8; Judg 17:10–13; 2 Chr 11:13–15), and instituted a new feast to rival the Feast of Booths, typically celebrated in the seventh month in Jerusalem (cf. 8:2; Lev 23:33–43; Deut 16:13–17). Some explain this decision by speculating that the harvest in northern Israel must have come a month later than in environs farther south, immediately around Jerusalem,[38] so it might make more sense to delay the feast. Another scholar suggests Jeroboam simply abandoned Solomon's solar calendar and revived the old Canaanite one,[39] and so of course the festival would have changed.

But all of this is a cover for the fact that "each of these actions defied and broke God-given requirements in the law and implied that civil matters were considered more important than religious principle and practice."[40] Kings of neighboring nations appointed new priests, established new calendars, and built new worship sites, but such was not the prerogative of Israel's king; this was the sole domain of Yahweh. If Solomon's disobedience cost him, how much more will his own unfaithfulness cost Jeroboam?

Jeroboam was God's anointed for Israel and the bearer of divine blessing; Hens-Piazza notes that his "rise to kingship is one of the most trouble-free and uncontested recorded in the accounts of the northern monarch in the books of

---

37. Patterson, "1, 2 Kings," 743.

38. Wiseman, *1 and 2 Kings*, 156; cf. S. Talmon, "Divergences in Calendar-Reckoning in Ephraim and Judah," *VT* 8 (1958): 56–67. Gray, however, counters, "The distance between Jerusalem and Bethel is not so marked as to occasion the difference of one month in harvest, and in fact rain is actually earlier at Bethel, which is higher than Jerusalem, so that this would occasion a somewhat earlier harvest," (*I & II Kings*, 292–93).

39. Julian Morgenstern, "The Festival of Jerobeam I," *JBL* 83 (1964): 109–18.

40. Wiseman, *1 and 2 Kings*, 156. "Political agendas and cultural pressures have an enormous power to distort adherence to faith in God and obedience to a divinely ordered way of life," (Konkel, *1 & 2 Kings*, 255). Jeroboam used religion as a manipulative tool for power, and white Democrats who campaign in African-American pulpits, as well as Republicans who pay lip service to the Religious Right, carry on Jeroboam's dangerous legacy. "There is a lot to be said for separation of church and state, not to protect the state but to protect the church," (Goldingay, *1 and 2 Kings for Everyone*, 60).

Kings."[41] But the promises of God were not enough for him. "The heavens will stand without our rearing brickwork pillars to hold them up. But it takes much faith to trust God's bare word, and we are all apt to feel safer if we have something for sense to grasp."[42] Jeroboam could not be convinced that the people of Israel truly supported him; they would surely assassinate him and defect to Judah if they went to worship at the Temple one too many times. Though he was king of ten tribes, he secretly considered Rehoboam to be his "lord" (v. 27).

All that was required to secure his kingdom was Jeroboam's obedience, but he could not give it. The prophetic word had encouraged him to do "as David my servant did" (11:38); instead, the actions he takes in vv. 28–33 all arise from doubt in the veracity of God's word.[43]

1 KINGS 13

In the final five weeks of his presidency, George W. Bush visited Iraq to sign a new security agreement. During the trip, he and Iraqi Prime Minister Nouri Maliki were hosting a press conference when Iraqi journalist Muntadar al-Zaidi stood up, called President Bush a dog, and threw his shoe at him. The journalist later received three years in his prison, but most in America found the incident comical. Political enemies of President Bush had a field day with the story (*Newsweek* reporter Michael Hirsh called it "somehow appropriate"), and even Bush supporters exhibited little outrage or indignation, despite the fact that al-Zaidi's deed was the Middle Eastern equivalent of flipping a dignitary the bird—or worse.

Less than a year later, in September 2009, President Obama gave a speech to a joint session of Congress on his then-proposed health care reform legislation. During the speech, when President Obama claimed his plan would not provide free health coverage for illegal immigrants, Representative Joe Wilson of South Carolina interrupted from his seat with a loud, "You lie!" A lot of resulting criticism of Wilson was just political posturing by Democrats, but the Congressman's outburst was certainly a "Did he really just do that!?" moment. For what it's worth, Representative Wilson later apologized to the president. Without any political commentary, I mention these incidents because they help us appreciate

41. Hens-Piazza, *1–2 Kings*, 127.

42. Maclaren, *Expositions*, 4:225.

43. Wray Beal, *1 & 2 Kings*, 184. Jeroboam's "problem was not that orthodoxy was dull or boring, but that it was unnerving," (Davis, *1 Kings*, 138).

the scandal of a prophet confronting Jeroboam in the midst of the king performing a very kingly duty.

The narrator did not mean for a chapter break to occur in the middle of his
story.[44] During this illegitimate feast on the fifteenth day of the eighth month,
while Jeroboam was leading worship at Bethel's illegitimate altar, an anonymous
prophet rudely interrupted festivities with a proverbial thrown shoe and an outburst tantamount to, "You lie!" This stunt was an affront to every standard of
decency and decorum. Yet if this story teaches us anything, it's that God's Word
is greater than any power, any standard or sense of propriety, or any politician's
agenda. But that's not all. This story also reinforces the timeless truth that one
must be obedient to that Word or suffer the consequences, a message that perfectly summarizes 1–2 Kings.[45]

Indeed, the phrase "word of the LORD" is key to this story, appearing elev-
en times (vv. 1, 2, 5, 9, 17, 18, 20, 21, 26, 32), more than any other chapter of the
Bible.[46] The prophet from Judah cried out against the altar. He spoke of a time
three hundred years in the future when a king named Josiah, a descendant of
David, would desecrate this altar (a taboo akin to burning the American flag) by
burning human corpses upon it, an act that "would so utterly corrupt it that it
would be difficult to ever use it again."[47] To confirm that his message was indeed
heaven-sent, a sign would accompany it: "Behold, the altar shall be torn down,
and the ashes that are on it shall be poured out" (v. 3).

Jeroboam unwittingly contributes additional proof that this message is
from God. Despots don't like it when their spotlight is stolen. Jeroboam growled
at the prophet and screamed, "Seize him!" But the words were scarcely out of his
mouth when his hand "dried up, so that he could not draw it back to himself"

---

44. D. W. van Winkle, "1 Kings XII 25-XIII 34: Jeroboam's Cultic Innovations and the
Man of God from Judah," *VT* 46 (1996): 101–14.

45. G. Michael Hagan, "First and Second Kings," in *A Complete Literary Guide to the Bible*,
eds. Leland Ryken and Tremper Longman III (Grand Rapids: Zondervan, 1993), 191.

46. Olley, *Message of Kings*, 139, n. 24. Additionally, the Hebrew *derek* (*way, road*) occurs
twelve times, and *shwb* (*turn, return*) occurs sixteen times. Thus this story confronts us with
which "way" or "path" we will take, and a reminder that the direction we "turn" can have life-and-
death implications.

47. Walton, *Bible Background*, 370. "The cure is violent and bloody: the only sacrifice
pleasing to God on this altar will be the human one of the very priests that have ministered
there," (Auld, *I & II Kings*, 89).

(v. 4), perhaps a condition known today as cataplexy in which a shock to the nervous system causes muscle rigidity.[48] But however it manifested itself physiologically, Jeroboam's withered arm was a sign of God's anger (cf. Zech 11:17). "Thus Jeroboam experienced in the limbs of his own body the severity of the threatened judgment of God."[49] Also, as the prophet had predicted, the altar "was ripped apart, and the ashes poured from the altar" (v. 5 HCSB), making both the altar and Jeroboam's sacrifice ritually unclean (cf. Lev 6:10–11) in much the same way that allowing the American flag to touch the ground disqualifies it from future service.

Justifiably panicked, Jeroboam pleaded with the nameless prophet to pray on his behalf so that his arm might be healed, and the prophet did so. God's miraculous healing further confirmed that all this was from the Lord (note that this is the third sign—a significant biblical number—to Jeroboam in the passage). No doubt grateful, the king invited this prophet to dine with him, but the prophet steadfastly refused. Wiseman explains why: "If the man of God were to make an agreement or show fellowship ('eat bread', vv. 7, 18) with the king, that would have been tantamount to a withdrawal of judgment."[50]

It seems to us as arbitrary or inane that God would require the prophet to return home a different way than he came. The perceived inconvenience of doing so is compounded when we realize that a major highway ran from Jerusalem to Bethel, and to require the prophet to return home a different way meant he had to forgo the interstate for a washed-out dirt road. But in obedience to the divine word, the unnamed prophet did just that.

Meanwhile, an old prophet in Bethel[51] (also unnamed) heard of what had happened when his sons "returned from church." After inquiring as to what di-

---

48. Walton, *Bible Background*, 370.

49. Keil, *Commentary*, 204.

50. Wiseman, *1 and 2 Kings*, 158. "Apparently the prophet's own conduct was to symbolize Yahweh's total rejection of worship at Bethel," (Hubbard, *First and Second Kings*, 79). A parallel passage exists where Samuel is invited to dine with Saul in the aftermath of the latter's disobedience (1 Sam 15:24–31).

51. "His association with Bethel makes it likely that he was not only *in* Bethel but also *of* Bethel, loyal to Jeroboam's new regime," (Inrig, *I & II Kings*, 107; emphasis his). "As the man of God's rejection of the invitation of Jeroboam was also doubtless reported, the local prophet may have resented what he regarded as an insult to the king and patron of the shrine to which he was attached. That he had a sinister motive is suggested by the statement that he lied (v. 18)," (Gray, *I & II Kings*, 300). The Northern prophet's dedication to king and country outran his allegiance to

rection the first prophet had taken, the old prophet of Bethel caught up on his donkey to the Judean man of God who was resting under an oak tree. When the Judean prophet was invited to the home of the Bethel prophet, he objected again, relating the divine command.

But then a twist—the old prophet informs his Southern counterpart that a new word of Yahweh has gone out. "I am also a prophet, just like you. And an angel came to me with a message from GOD: 'Bring him home with you, and give him a good meal!'" (v. 18 Msg). So that we know the truth, however, the narrator informs us that the old prophet of Bethel was lying. "His motivation is not made clear, but if he is a sympathizer of Jeroboam, he may have wanted to negate the word of judgment against Bethel by showing up the man of God as false."[52]

With false assurance, the Judean prophet trusted this new "word of the LORD" and returned with the old prophet to Bethel. But during their meal, the old prophet was suddenly seized by the Spirit with a prophetic word—a bona fide word from Yahweh, a message of judgment, and for the Judean prophet! He who had faithfully discharged his responsibility at first was now judged for failing to complete it. He would die on his way home and be denied dignity as to his final resting place[53] (cf. Gen 47:29–30; 50:25).

Sure enough, as he returned to Judah, the formerly-faithful prophet was attacked by a lion—known to inhabit Palestine until at least the thirteenth century A.D., and particularly the region of Bethel (cf. Amos 3:4). But lest we judge this to be simply a random accident, the narrator informs us that the lion stood guard over the body, but did not devour it, nor did it attack a perfectly delectable donkey. "Like the famous Balaam incident (Num. 22:21-41), this strange sight painted a contrast: unlike the disobedient prophet, the beast bent its will to God's sovereign will."[54] Passers-by were understandably struck by the odd scene, and news quickly reached the old prophet in Bethel.

Yahweh, a reminder that patriotism is as often a vice as it is a virtue. Had he been true to God and the Law, he would have never had anything to do with Jeroboam's syncretic agenda, nor would his sons have attended the blasphemous altar dedication at Bethel.

52. Fretheim, *First and Second Kings*, 79.

53. "It was important to Hebrews at this time that after death their bodies should lie in the family grave. For this not to happen was looked upon as a sign of divine displeasure," (Robinson, *First Book*, 161).

54. Hubbard, *First and Second Kings*, 81. This is not the only tie between this narrative and Balaam's; note the similar phrase used by the prophet (v. 8) and by Balaam (Num 22:18; 24:13).

No doubt profoundly saddened over his culpability, the old prophet of Bethel retrieved his colleague's body and buried him in his own family tomb. In addition, he charged his sons to bury him with the Judean prophet, choosing to identify with him in death, "impossible to distinguish bone from bone,"[55] now realizing that the word of judgment spoken against Bethel (and all the Northern Kingdom) was a potent word that would surely come to pass.

The grave also became a symbol of the fraternity of all the prophets from both North and South. "The individuals mirror their kingdoms, and their tragedy portends the tragic destiny awaiting Israel and Judah. Israel has become unfaithful. Judah can speak the word that Israel needs to hear; but if Judah, too, following Israel's lead, compromises its worship (as history shows it will), then both are doomed to overcome their separation only in death. Judah will be buried in an alien land, and Israel will be saved only so far as it is joined to Judah."[56]

At the risk of reading too much into this story, its symbolism is ripe. Jeroboam is often thought to be represented by the donkey—a dumb animal standing helplessly by the prophet's corpse like Jeroboam standing by the shattered altar earlier in the chapter.[57] Jeroboam is also like the Judean prophet, listening to bad counsel out of personal uncertainty rather than to the unadulterated prophetic word (cf. 12:28).[58] Like the Judean prophet, Jeroboam will not be buried in the family cemetery (cf. 14:13), a terrible fate for any Israelite to contemplate. And ironically, this will not be the last time in Kings that we read of lions (or bears) acting as agents of God's judgment in Bethel's neighborhood (cf. 2 Kgs 2:24; 17:25–26).

But literary symbolism eventually gives away to moral revulsion. Like Olley, we are tempted to wonder aloud, "Is not death too strong a punishment for what

---

55. Cogan, *I Kings*, 372. "At the time of death, bodies were laid on the benches, and after decomposition was complete, the bones were gathered into a repository hollowed out beneath one of the benches. Over time, this repository came to hold all the bones of family members long dead, and when an individual's bones were placed therein, that individual was dissolved into the collective ancestral heap," (McCane, "Burial," *NIBD* 1:509).

56. Jerome T. Walsh, "The Contexts of 1 Kings XIII," *VT* 39 (1989): 368.

57. James K. Mead, "Kings and Prophets, Donkeys and Lions: Dramatic Shape and Deuteronomistic Rhetoric in 1 Kings XIII," *VT* 49 (1999): 202.

58. House, *1, 2 Kings*, 189.

appears to be a minor misdemeanour?"[59] What kind of God sends a lion to maul his messenger for violating *Simon Says*? Yet, that is precisely the point. "The man of God's complete subjection to the divine purpose can only be tested through laying on him conditions that may seem unreasonable and burdensome to him."[60]

Yahweh's Word possesses a life and potency and tenacity all its own. It cannot be manipulated or co-opted for other purposes. Rather, that Word flows from the mouth of Yahweh and—in spite of deception, disobedience, or death—does not return empty to him[61] (cf. Isa 55:10–11; Mark 4:26–29). All are subject to God's Word; no mortal is above it. The actions of the Judean prophet earlier in the story confirmed the word of God. But in an ironic twist, the false prophet of Bethel *also* confirmed the word of God. "The divine word will win out, whatever the wayward actions of men, even prophets, may be!"[62] And if prophets cannot escape Yahweh's potent word, neither will kings.

In addition, this narrative warns us against accepting any rationale, no matter how benign or logical, that contradicts the Word of God. The apostle Paul warns the church, "Let God's curse fall on anyone, including us or even an angel from heaven, who preaches a different kind of Good News than the one we preached to you" (Gal 1:8 NLT). The Judean prophet had pure motives and acted in good faith when he returned with the Bethel prophet, but none of that mattered. The Scriptures are adequate for us; seeking something more is a repudiation of God's authority over our lives. Robinson's thoughts are worth reflection:

---

59. Olley, *Message of Kings*, 142. Nelson is even more incredulous: "As a moral tale it is patently offensive. Trickery triumphs over the servant of God and the lying prophet is rewarded in the end. Is this a crude, insensitive God who violates our ideas of justice?" (*First and Second Kings*, 83).

60. DeVries, *1 Kings*, 171.

61. Fretheim, *First and Second Kings*, 81.

62. Burke O. Long, *1 Kings* (Grand Rapids: Eerdmans, 1984), 148. In the words of Crenshaw, "Here one sees the true prophet become false to his commission, and the 'false prophet' takes up the genuine word of God and lets it fall with shattering force upon the erring man of God," (James L. Crenshaw, *Prophetic Conflict: Its Effect upon Israelite Religion* [Berlin: de Gruyter, 1971], 48). "The focus of the story must not be placed on the obedience or disobedience of the man of God or prophet. The story is not centered on these men, but on the word of God they speak about Jeroboam. The key effect of the story is a *double* prophetic witness against Jeroboam, from the leadership of *both* kingdoms, and so forceful that even a false prophet has seen the light though the true prophet has failed," (Fretheim, *First and Second Kings*, 81; emphasis his).

> If he were a true prophet, then God would have communicated directly with him and not through an intermediary. His paying attention to the prophet therefore called in question the validity of all that he had said and done at Bethel. In this way he was disloyal to his own prophetic vocation and dishonoured God who had sent him. The only way in which the validity of the message he had delivered to Jeroboam could be safeguarded was for him to be treated by God as a disobedient traitor. So on his way home he died and in such a manner as men could only interpret as the direct intervention of God. The meeting with the lion was no accident.[63]

That God's Word will not return to him empty is a great hope for his people. Jesus attested that heaven and earth would be brought to nothing, but his Word never would (Matt 24:35). Not even our unfaithfulness can thwart the divine will (cf. John 11:49–52). But by our radical obedience, we certainly testify to the authenticity and potency of the Word. "The preacher-prophet must be so committed to the transcendent truth of what he proclaims that his very own life is affected by it."[64] In an age when people increasingly want to know who is telling the truth, radical obedience becomes the acid test (cf. Deut 12:2–6).

The failure of the Judean prophet's obedience highlights all the more the perfect life of our Lord.

> In all of history there was only one Prophet who kept God's rules in every minutia. He would not be distracted from God's stern pathway, not even by religion's greatest authorities. He too was doomed to die, but for the sins of others rather than for sins of his own. In his grave he sanctified the death of many others—of all those who call him not just "man of God" but "Son of God." The paradox of the Judahite man of God, compelling as it is, is but a faint illumination of that greater paradox, the absolute obedience and the saving death of Jesus Christ.[65]

---

63. Robinson, *First Book*, 162.

64. DeVries, *1 Kings*, 174.

65. Ibid.

One final point merits mention. The Judean prophet's fearlessness before the tyrant Jeroboam is commendable. His is a fortitude every Christian should aspire to. But while he in one moment was faithful while under threat, he let his guard down in another over something as "trivial" as which way to go home and whether to do so directly. "This pattern is instructive: sometimes we have courage to face major crises but lack sense for subtle dilemmas. We can muster defiance for the danger of the hour but cannot find discernment for the ploy of the moment."[66] Let us not prove faithful in large things, but lax in small ones. Let us be deliberate as to the path we take and the direction we turn—such could be a matter of life and death.

1 KINGS 14:1-20

Not long after the prophet had denounced the altar at Bethel, Jeroboam's son, Abijah,[67] became gravely ill. It was not uncommon in ancient times for a seer of some sort to be consulted on whether full health would be recovered; in fact, this won't be the only time in Kings this is done (1 Kgs 17:17–24; 2 Kgs 1:2–4; 5:1–19; 8:7–15; 20:1–11). Jeroboam had a lot of confidence in the prophet Ahijah since the latter had prophesied that Jeroboam would be king in the first place (11:29–39). But many years had passed since that day, and Ahijah was now a lot older and more feeble.

In a rather bizarre move, Jeroboam counseled his wife to go in disguise to Ahijah at Shiloh. But why? Was there now tension between king and prophet? Was he afraid his recent apostasy would color the prophetic word spoken? Did he really think the disguise would fool a man who talked with God? Did Jeroboam believe the prophet's powers of discernment wouldn't be great enough to penetrate a shawl or wig or the eyeglasses-and-fake-moustache routine?[68] His wife

---

66. Davis, *1 Kings*, 154.

67. Abijah's age is never given, and the Hebrew *yeled* or "child" (v. 12) can refer to infants, toddlers, older children, or even adults (3:25; 2 Kgs 4:18; cf. Gen 21:8; Exod 2:3; Ruth 1:5; 4:16), while *na'ar* or "boy" (vv. 3, 17) is limited to teen and adult men (Gen 22:12; Judg 8:20; 1 Sam 20:21; 2 Sam 18:5).

68. "It looks as if they [i.e., Jeroboam and his wife] have some rather primitive ideas about prophets—prophets may be able to look into the future but not be able to see what is going on in the present. They discover they are wrong," (Goldingay, *1 and 2 Kings for Everyone*, 67). "Although the motifs of disguise and blindness are mutually exclusive, they are used here to enforce the reliability of the divine message," (Fritz, *1 & 2 Kings*, 155).

came bearing gifts of bread, cakes, and honey—a common act by those seeking
the services of a seer (cf. 1 Sam 9:7–8; 2 Kgs 5:5; 8:8–9)—but neither God nor a
man of God can be bought off with a Mrs. Fields gift basket. In fact, I believe this
is the point of this narrative, that Jeroboam's future is determined by the will of
God and cannot be bought, manipulated, or influenced unduly in any way. Even
personal righteousness (i.e., that of Abijah) is guarantee of nothing; how much
more so will Jeroboam's inexcusable apostasy merit the strongest condemnation
heaven can utter? God will not be mocked (Gal 6:7).

Elsewhere in the Old Testament where the theme of royal disguise appears
(e.g., 1 Sam 28:8–19; 2 Chr 35:20–27), it is to underscore that "whatever the
king may think, it is God and not the king who determines the course of events."[69]
Long ago, Ahijah had told Jeroboam that his rule would be established by God.
But Jeroboam had failed to trust and obey, and as we know, there is no other
way to secure a kingdom or be happy in Jesus, but to trust and obey. Now, feeble
Ahijah had the difficult task of making known to the queen the fate of her family.

The prophetic word began with a biting indictment of Jeroboam's sins.
God had exalted him as leader, but instead of becoming a king in David's footsteps, Jeroboam had incited the wrath of heaven by his idolatry. Jeroboam might
have believed he wasn't guilty of promoting other gods besides Yahweh since he
arguably intended the golden calves only to be representative of the true God.
But in this case, there was a chasm deep and wide between intent and action,
perception and reality, and that chasm led to the abyss. Jeroboam was guilty of
crafting "other gods and metal images" which provoked[70] God's anger (v. 9; cf.
Deut 4:25; 9:18; 31:29; 32:16, 19, 21; Judg 2:12). Because he had effectively
cast Yahweh behind his back, Jeroboam's dynasty would be treated similarly.

The judgment was not just for Jeroboam, but for "every male" of his house.
This phrase, however, is just a nicer way of expressing what the Hebrew literally
says—"he who urinates against a wall" (cf. KJV; see also 16:11; 21:21; 2 Kgs 9:8;
14:26). There is an intentional link between urine and dung in v. 10, and lest we
think a holy God has developed a potty mouth in need of being washed out with

---

69. Provan, *1 & 2 Kings*, 119. Nelson adds, "Disguise is a symptom of understanding only
in a surface way our broken relationship with God," (*First and Second Kings*, 95).

70. Davis points out that the same Hebrew term translated "provoking" (v. 9) is used in
1 Samuel 1:6–7 of Peninnah's treatment of "poor, childless Hannah whenever Elkanah's family
went to Shiloh to worship. Peninnah made it a point to ridicule and belittle Hannah, to irritate,
aggravate, and exasperate her," (*1 Kings*, 161).

soap, we must allow this divine vulgarity to underscore the gravity of Jeroboam's wickedness. God's point is obvious: "Jeroboam's house smells; radical action is needed to deal with this sanitation problem."[71]

But the scatological references are not the most offensive aspect. The most repugnant part of this pericope is the death of Abijah. Why should the child suffer for the sins of the father (cf. 2 Sam 12:14; John 9:2)? For anyone who has stood in a hospital with parents as their son or daughter succumbed to a brain tumor; for anyone who has sat in the ER after a horrific car accident; for anyone who has delivered a eulogy before a miniature casket, this part of the story is too much to bear. Punish Jeroboam, yes. Punish him for his idolatry, his arrogance and presumption, for his lack of faith. But why must his son have to die? And to compound matters, why is Abijah's death *because* of his virtue (v. 13) and not *in spite* of it?

For whatever reason, it was God's will in the Old Testament "that the sins of the parents may be visited upon the children and the grandchildren, to the third and fourth generation 'of those who reject me'" (Exod 20:5; Deut 5:9). We are not told what virtue Abijah possessed that enabled him to escape the curse of his father and die prematurely, thus all our speculation is exactly that.[72] But as twisted as it may sound to our modern ears, Abijah's death was actually an act of grace, for he alone of Jeroboam's house would be given a proper burial. The rest would be consumed out in the open by dogs and birds (v. 11)—a shameful thing in that culture (cf. Deut 28:26; 1 Sam 31:8–13), as it would be in ours.

> In the ancient world desecration of the deceased put in jeopardy the well-being and repose of the person in the underworld. If a body was not buried, the spirit could not pass into the netherworld and would roam the earth causing problems to the living. The body gave the dead person identity in the netherworld. In Babylonian thinking burial gave the spirit a

---

71. Provan, *1 & 2 Kings*, 119. "Vulgarity and scatology are weapons in the rhetorical arsenal of prophecy, and, from the perspective of the writer of 1–2 Kings, we cannot find fault with the language without finding fault with God himself, since Ahijah claims to be speaking the words that Yahweh delivered to him (1 Kgs. 14:7, 11). Yahweh uses shocking language when he calls useless men 'those who piss against the wall' and speaks of an idolatrous royal house as a pile of [s—t]," (Leithart, *1 & 2 Kings*, 105).

72. The rabbis believed Abijah had been responsible for removing the guards preventing faithful Israelites from going to Jerusalem for the feasts (Wiseman, *1 and 2 Kings*, 161).

place to reside once the body transitioned to the netherworld
through decomposition. With no identity in the world of the
dead, the individual would find no rest, receive no care, and
have no hope. No punishment could be greater than to be consumed by roaming dogs and fowl.[73]

That, however, was not all—Jeroboam's punishment was not limited to
himself and his house, but the entire Northern Kingdom. Yahweh would "strike
Israel as a reed is shaken in the water, and root up Israel out of this good land
that he gave to their fathers and scatter them beyond the Euphrates" (v. 15).
Indeed, the history of the Northern Kingdom would be one of instability ("a
rattled reed," cf. 2 Kgs 18:21; Ezek 29:6; Matt 11:7; Luke 7:24) and ultimate
exile ("rooted up," cf. Deut 29:27–28; Jer 12:14) from which she'd never return.
Sometimes our disobedience negatively impacts not just ourselves and our families, but the entire community.

Jeroboam's wife returned to Tirzah (seven miles northeast of Shechem)
with a mother's broken heart. "The son will die and the mother herself will become the messenger of death. She is condemned to carry death into the house,
since the son will die the moment she returns."[74] The nation mourned and buried
Abijah, and the word of the Lord was fulfilled, for it stands forever.

---

73. Monson, "1 Kings," 62; cf. Cogan, *I Kings*, 380. In ancient thought, "when one wishes
to deprive the recent dead of the possibility of retaining their individual and/or social identity,
one must destroy their body/corpse," (Tzvi Abusch, "Ghost and God: Some Observations on a
Babylonian Understanding of Human Nature," in *Self, Soul and Body in Religious Experience*, eds.
A. I. Baumgarten, J. Assmann, and G. G. Stroumsa [Leiden: Brill, 1998], 374). Abusch goes on to
explain, "When a corpse was left unburied and/or was destroyed by animals, fire, or the like, the
dead person would lose his human identity and human community. He could no longer be inte-
grated into the structured community of the dead and thereby into the ongoing and continuous
community of the living and the dead. [...] Some texts suggest that those dead who were left
unburied and had their corpses destroyed are relegated to the formless and chaotic world sometimes associated with steppe and winds, may even become a part of the demonic world that is
neither human nor god, male nor female, and/or may even lose all semblance of existence and
be transformed into formlessness and even nothingness. Put differently, even the actual ghost
thus loses its human identity and existence," (Ibid., 375). He further observes the stark contrast
between Greek and Semitic views of cremation—while the Greeks viewed cremation as freeing
the ghost to enter the afterlife, Semites viewed it as destroying the ghost, "for the ghost attached
itself in some peculiar way to the body," (Ibid., 376).

74. Fritz, *1 & 2 Kings*, 155.

After more than two decades of rule, Jeroboam himself died and was buried. "That he 'slept with his ancestors' only means that the announced devastation is on hold for now. But only for now."[75] A ruler with so much promise, one handpicked by God as Saul had been, reigned in folly because he cared too much about popular opinion and not enough about heaven's. Indeed, "secular historians would regard much about the career of Jeroboam as a success. The biblical writer sees him only as a failure."[76]

1 KINGS 14:21-31

Starting here, you will wish Kings had a split screen at times. One minute, the narrator's focus is on the Northern Kingdom; the other, it is on the South. In fact, chapters 15–16, "Nine monarchs are passed over—if not in silence then at least more than succinctly—at an average of seven and a half verses per head!"[77]

After retiring Jeroboam to his grave, the narrator's view shifts south to Rehoboam, whose reign (930–913) ended before that of his rival in the North. Jeroboam's sin in establishing an alternative worship site is underscored when the narrator yet again reminds us that Jerusalem was "the city that the LORD had chosen out of all the tribes of Israel, to put his name there (v. 21).

During Rehoboam's reign, Judah was not faithful to the Lord, but rather provoked him as Jeroboam did with his idolatry. The influence of Israel's pagan neighbors had begun under Solomon and is invoked by the narrator with mention of Rehoboam's mother (Naamah the Ammonite[78]). Like the nations around them, and the Canaanites before them,[79] Israel established high places, pillars,[80]

---

75. Brueggemann, *1 & 2 Kings*, 180.

76. Inrig, *I & II Kings*, 117. "The only thing that matters is whether you worshiped Yahweh alone. Were you contented with the real God? We think [1 Kings 14:]19 is only a throwaway bibliographical note. Actually, it's a disturbing world view," (Davis, *1 Kings*, 165).

77. Auld, *I & II Kings*, 105.

78. "Our chronicler seems to insist on queen mother Naamah's origins, for he repeats his note at the end of the chapter (vv.21,31). This quietly links Rehoboam's failures to his father's indulgence in foreign liaisons (11:1–8)," (Ibid., 100).

79. "It is easy for us to think that the deuteronomists were obsessed with an unreasoning and unreasonable hatred of Canaan. In fact, they and the prophets engaged in a life-or-death struggle for the soul of Israel," (Robinson, *First Book*, 172).

80. Several such stone pillars have been uncovered by archaeologists at Gezer, Hazor, and Arad. Some of them had basins at their feet where offerings were poured out by their followers

Asherim, and cult prostitution as a part of their worship (vv. 23–24). Yahweh had demanded that these be banished from the Land (Exod 34:13; Deut 12:3; 23:17–18), but they were not.

In Kings, there are several references to Asherah (1 Kgs 14:15, 23; 15:13; 16:33; 18:19; 2 Kgs 13:6; 17:10, 16; 18:4; 21:3, 7; 23:4, 6–7, 15), at times indicating the pagan fertility goddess or, at others, the object of worship at high places and shrines (i.e., Asherah pole, Asherim). As a goddess, Asherah may have been considered by apostate Israel to be the consort of Yahweh; in Canaanite mythology, she was the consort of the chief god, El. The Asherah pole was likely some sort of fake tree that represented a sacred grove where Asherah was thought to reside.[81]

Naamah wielded an impressive measure of influence on her son, and many of her successors would do the same. The first to hold this lofty position was Bathsheba, whom Solomon held in great esteem and allowed to sit at his right hand (2:19). Not a lot is known from Scripture about the position of queen mother (Hebrew *gebira*) among the Israelites, but "this title implied a certain dignity and special powers."[82] The *gebira* "apparently even wore a crown emblematic of her position (Jer 13:18)."[83] It seems the *gebira* held power by virtue of being the mother of the heir-apparent; their influence only grew after the deaths of their husbands and the ascendancies of their sons. That this position was an important one in Judah is seen in the fact that every mother of the king is named except for Joram and Ahaz (possibly because their mothers had died before their sons became king[84]). For whatever reason, there seems to have been no such position in the Northern Kingdom.[85] I guess the stereotype is true—southern boys love their mommas more!

(Walton, *Bible Background*, 372). "Given that we are dealing with a fertility cult, these 'pillars' may well have been phallic symbols," (Provan, *1 & 2 Kings*, 122).

81. Curtis, "Canaanite Gods and Religion," *DOTHB* 140–41; cf. Day, "Asherah," *ABD* 1:483–87; Wyatt, "Asherah," *DDD* 99–105.

82. de Vaux, *Ancient Israel*, 1:117.

83. Patterson, "1, 2 Kings," 755.

84. Wiseman, *1 and 2 Kings*, 50.

85. "Apart from Zeruah the mother of Jeroboam (1 K. 11:26), the mothers of the kings of Israel are not named. In 2 K. 10:13 the term *gebirā* is applied to Jezebel, but the word is spoken by a prince of Judah. Perhaps the dynastic instability of the northern kingdom did not allow this institution to develop there to the extent that it did in Judah," (Opperwall-Gallch, "Queen Mother," *ISBE* 4:8).

As punishment for Rehoboam's faithlessness, God sent the scourge of Pharaoh Shishak (known historically as Sheshonq I) against Jerusalem in 925.[86] Rehoboam was not an unfortunate victim of international political forces working against him. Rather, according to the narrators of Kings and Chronicles, Shishak was the divine means of punishing Rehoboam (2 Chr 12:5). Clearly, the diplomatic relationship between Israel and Egypt had soured since Solomon had struck an alliance with Pharaoh and married his daughter. Biblical historian John Bright postulates that relations chilled late in Solomon's reign when the twenty-first dynasty was overthrown by Shishak of Libya.[87] Shishak was more ambitious than his immediate predecessors,[88] and so he sought to expand Egypt's influence in Asia (conquest seems not to have been a goal), which necessitated access to Palestine's lucrative trade routes. The alliance between Hiram and Solomon had especially "dealt a most severe blow to Egypt's economic independence."[89]

In what Leithart calls "a preview of exile,"[90] Shishak looted the Temple, the palace, and terrorized the surrounding countryside (including the Northern Kingdom). The Karnak Inscription claims that Egypt captured 150 places during this campaign in Palestine, though Jerusalem is oddly never mentioned. Most of the destroyed locales were located in the Northern Kingdom and the Negev.

---

86. "The formal *casus belli* was probably a border-incident – incursions across Egypt's East-Delta boundaries by Semitic tribesmen whom it pleased Shoshenq to consider as Judean subjects committing hostile acts. The signal for war was apparently one such skirmish at the Bitter Lakes, directly followed by an all-out Egyptian attack. So much may be deduced from the fragments of a victory-steal from Karnak," (K. A. Kitchen, *The Third Immediate Period in Egypt [1100–650 B.C.]*, 2nd ed. [Warminster, England: Aris, 1986], 294). Shishak may have been a scourge for Rehoboam in other ways; since he harbored Jeroboam in Egypt for so long, it's possible he was partly responsible for instigating the schism between Israel and Judah (Chaim Herzog and Mordechai Gichon, *Battles of the Bible* [Toronto: Stoddart, 1997], 126–27). For more on Shishak, see Kitchen, *Third Immediate Period*, 287–302.

87. John Bright, *A History of Israel*, 4th ed. (Louisville: Westminster John Knox, 2000), 233.

88. "It is obvious that the construction of fortresses and chariot cities, such as Gezer, Beth-Horon and Baalath, which were carried out by Solomon in the later years of his reign, were the results of the aggressive policy pursued by Shishak against the Kingdom of Israel, in marked contrast to the line followed by the kings of the preceding Twenty-First Dynasty," (Benjamin Mazar, "The Campaign of Pharaoh Shishak to Palestine," in *Volume du Congres: Strasbourg, 1956* [Leiden: Brill, 1957], 57).

89. Herzog, *Battles*, 127.

90. Leithart, *1 & 2 Kings*, 108.

Though he had once been Jeroboam's benefactor, Shishak now ravaged Israel, arguably because "Jeroboam refused to admit the suzerainty of the Pharaoh, contrary to what he had consented during his revolt and the days he had spent in Egypt."[91] In the Negev, Shishak destroyed several fortified cities first constructed by Solomon, explaining "why Rehoboam was compelled to erect a new line of fortifications which encircled the Shephelah and the mountains of Judah."[92]

The narrator uses the occasion to offer up an anecdote concerning the erosion of Solomon's glory in Israel. Whereas he had had shields of gold for his guards, these were carried off by Shishak as spoil, and Rehoboam could only afford replacements of bronze[93] (that's what you get for having cut-rate shield insurance!). Worse, so paranoid was he of losing them that he kept them under lock and key when not used for ceremonial purposes. We obviously have come a long way (and in a painfully short amount of time) since Solomon's day when silver was as common as rocks (10:27). As we witness Shishak ride off victoriously into the sunset with great booty and bling, House notes that a disturbing trend has established itself. "Paying invaders to leave will become standard practice in Judah. Idolatry has political consequences."[94]

Notice of Rehoboam's reign ends with the standard formula in which the narrator directs the reader to other sources, then notes the king's burial and successor. He also reminds us that there was war (or more precisely, a general spirit of hostility[95]) between Rehoboam and Jeroboam throughout their reigns.

Conspicuously missing from the account of Rehoboam's reign is a prophecy (as was seen earlier in the chapter) predicting doom for David's house because of his grandson's disobedience. As we will continue to witness, God's commit-

---

91. Mazar, "Campaign of Pharaoh Shishak," 63.

92. Ibid., 66.

93. "The splendor is fading. But the pomp and ceremony must continue. And if we cannot have shields of department store quality, we shall have ones of discount store variety. The show must go on," (Davis, 1 Kings, 170).

94. House, 1, 2 Kings, 195. Raiding the Temple to pay invaders also becomes a painful theme in Kings (15:18; 2 Kgs 14:14; 16:8; 18:15–16; 24:13), climaxing in the destruction of the Temple itself (2 Kgs 25:13–17).

95. "Probably the word referred to a 'cold war' of anger and suspicion between north and south. Perhaps an occasional border skirmish erupted as the two armies maneuvered for tactical advantage or control of territory," (Hubbard, First and Second Kings, 86).

ment to the house of David was strong, and he graciously gave the giant-killer's descendants a longer leash than their counterparts in the North.

That said, God did send discipline Rehoboam's way. Whereas Solomon had been able to stockpile riches and enjoy peace for most of his reign, his son was looted by enemies and knew only warfare. Unlike David and Solomon, Rehoboam failed to keep the country united. The Lord had promised to preserve David's throne, but he had also sworn to mete out fatherly discipline to the unruly (2 Sam 7:14).

1 KINGS 15:1-8

Rehoboam's son, Abijam[96], reigned 913–910. The narrator identifies his mother as "Maacah the daughter[97] of Abishalom" (v. 2), also known as *Micaiah* (2 Chr 13:2). Josephus says she was the daughter of Tamar,[98] who was the daughter of Absalom (2 Sam 14:27), making Maacah David's great-granddaughter.

Like Rehoboam, his father, Abijam was wicked, since "his heart was not wholly true to the LORD his God." As will become standard for Judah's kings, his righteousness is compared with that of David.[99] But unexpectedly, the narrator tells us that God is faithful to the Davidic dynasty for David's sake and in spite of Abijam's evil. "God keeps his promises even when David's descendants do not."[100] It is for that reason that God maintains a lamp for David in Jerusalem. In the Old Testament, *lamp* is symbolic of one's posterity (cf. Prov 21:4). Though a man may be dead and gone, his life and work were not "extinguished" if he had descendants in the land of the living (cf. 2 Kgs 8:19; 2 Chr 21:7). Our own phrase *eternal flame* bears much the same meaning, one of continued remembrance.

---

96. It is interesting that though he is known as *Abijam* ("My father is Yam," the Canaanite god of the sea), the Chronicler (2 Chr 13:1–22) knows him as *Abijah* ("My father is Yahweh").

97. It's highly likely that *daughter* here means *granddaughter* (the term can mean any female descendant), and that *Abishalom* is a variant of *Absalom*. For more on the issue of Maacah/Micaiah's identity, see Cogan, *I Kings*, 392–93; Sweeney, *I & II Kings*, 191.

98. Josephus, *Antiquities* 8.249.

99. "David serves as a paradigm for southern kings (1 Kgs 11:33, 38; 14:8; 15:11; 22:43; 2 Kgs 10:30; 12:2; 14:3; 15:3, 34; 16:2; 18:3; 22:2). His paradigmatic value is not dependent on a perfect life (cf. Uriah), but one oriented to YHWH's ways, especially regarding worship," (Wray Beal, *1 & 2 Kings*, 211).

100. House, *1, 2 Kings*, 196.

Ironically, no specific sin on Abijam's part is mentioned, so we cannot evaluate him any further, but the narrator does in fact go out of his way to mention David's sin with Bathsheba and the consequent murder of Uriah. To anyone familiar with that story, it is abundantly clear that "David's Torah righteousness is deeply compromised in that event, as the prophet Nathan has made clear (2 Sam 12:10-11)."[101] This, then, is the beauty of what Brueggemann calls the "Davidic Nevertheless."[102] It is not because of David's moral superiority that God has mercy and compassion on Jerusalem time and again, but because of David's stubborn faith that responded[103] to God's stubborn grace. "Why don't the kingdom and people of God vanish into the mists of history? Because God will not permit it. He has decided that his kingdom *will* come. Grace is not only greater but more stubborn than our sins."[104]

And therein we see the gospel in living color in the Old Testament, a place where one would never expect to find it. Just as Abraham was justified by his faith, so David's throne is secured by his. In so doing, the morality of Abraham and David become moot points, while the grace of God takes center stage (cf. Deut 7:7–8). For us, as for Israel's and Judah's kings, "sin is inevitable, but repentance and return remain a possibility before the Lord."[105]

We, too, can lay claim by grace to a similar "nevertheless," the one Paul celebrates in Romans 8:37–39—"No, in all these things we are more than conquerors through him who loved us. For I am sure that neither death nor life, nor angels nor rulers, nor things present nor things to come, nor powers, nor height nor depth, nor anything else in all creation, will be able to separate us from the love of God in Christ Jesus our Lord."

Twice in his closing comments on Abijam, the narrator speaks of war with the Northern tribes. In the first mention, he speaks of it as a "war between Rehoboam and Jeroboam" (v. 6). In the second, he notes that

---

101. Brueggemann, *1 & 2 Kings*, 188.

102. Ibid.

103. "The faithfulness of a king's heart does not depend upon a life of perfection but upon a life governed by repentance and return. David, who sinned, paid for his evil choice and set his heart on the Lord once again," (Hens-Piazza, *1–2 Kings*, 151).

104. Davis, *1 Kings*, 172; emphasis his.

105. Hens-Piazza, *1–2 Kings*, 152.

"there was war between Abijam and Jeroboam" (v. 7). Some scholars consider one of the statements to be an inadvertent, redundant addition by a later editor.

Yet the narrator's double mention might be intended to stress that this is not just Abijam's war, but one he inherited from his father. In fact, the chapter mentions "war" four times (vv. 6, 7, 16, 32), highlighting how it was an ongoing struggle (again, think of the Cold War or the War on Terror). The Chronicler notes that Abijam defeated Jeroboam around 912 and established a buffer between Israel and Judah by seizing "Bethel, Jeshanah and Ephron, with their surrounding villages" (2 Chr 13:19 NIV). Nonetheless, Israel and Judah remained mired in conflict, with neither side giving much way.

1 KINGS 15:9–24

Asa's reign (910–869) likely included a three-year co-regency with his son, Jehoshaphat, arguably due to Asa's illness in his old age.[106] While he reigned forty-one years on Judah's throne (only Manasseh would reign longer, 2 Kgs 21:1), the throne of Israel saw six different monarchs. At the beginning, Asa's grandmother, Maacah, remained in the position of queen mother.[107] But he soon deposed her "because she had made an abominable image for Asherah" (v. 13), an image believed to have been pornographic in nature (e.g., phallic shaped).

Though the narrator's comments on Asa are not totally positive—he didn't remove the high places—it's true that he was Judah's best king since at least Solomon and possibly David. Unlike his father, "the heart of Asa was wholly true to the LORD all his days" (v. 14; cf. v. 3). In fact, the narrator of Kings gives greater honor only to Hezekiah and Josiah. Asa expelled the cult prostitutes, tore down the idols of his predecessors, ousted Maacah from her position of influence, and burned the queen mother's Asherah image in the Kidron[108] (cf. Deut 9:21). Asa also restored some of the Temple's treasures.

---

106. Edwin R. Thiele, *The Mysterious Numbers of the Hebrew Kings*, rev. ed. (Grand Rapids: Kregel, 1983), 83–87.

107. Despite being called Asa's *mother* (v. 10), the Hebrew term can also denote one's grandmother (cf. NIV).

108. The Kidron was a brook that ran east of Jerusalem, separating the Temple mount from the Mount of Olives, and eventually flowed into the Dead Sea. Since it served as the city dump of sorts, this would not be the last time the Kidron became the center of righteous idol purging (2 Kgs 23:4–15; 2 Chr 29:16; 30:14).

However, no good deed goes unpunished. Despite Asa's faithfulness, he did not enjoy the peace Solomon had—"there was war between Asa and Baasha king of Israel all their days" (v. 16).[109] Baasha, the Northern king (more on him soon), antagonized Judah by fortifying Ramah. Located 5½ miles north of Jerusalem, Ramah was a Benjaminite[110] city on the border of Ephraim (Josh 18:25; Judg 4:5) that lay at the intersection of two important military/economic routes, one running north-south (giving access to the hill country of Ephraim) and the other east-west (giving access to the Mediterranean coast). By fortifying that city, Baasha essentially pigeon-holed Asa in Jerusalem without a means of escape (v. 17).

In retaliation, Asa solicited the help of the Aramean king, Ben-hadad I (c. 900–860). The Chronicler explicitly condemns Asa's appealing for help to a Gentile instead of Yahweh (2 Chr 16:7–10), but the narrator of Kings is more subtle with his criticism. Asa took the Temple treasures previously donated (v. 15) and offered them to Ben-hadad as a "present" (v. 19) or "gift" (HCSB, NIV). Davis finds himself marveling at why translators launder Asa's money for him—"It is a bribe"[111]—and the Hebrew word's usage elsewhere in the Old Testament (some twenty-two times) confirms this (e.g., Deut 27:25; Ps 26:10; Ezek 22:12). In addition to the subtle scorn of Asa's "gift," the narrator also invites us to ponder the righteousness of a son of David asking a pagan king to break his covenant with a fellow Israelite (cf. Ezek 17:11–21). "In light of this biblical mentality I doubt that Kings regards Asa's pitch to Ben-hadad as simply a bit of neutral politics."[112] It would not be the last time faith in God was scuttled in favor of a "more pragmatic approach."

To get Baasha off Asa's back, Ben-hadad attacked the territory of Naphtali and, moving north to south, conquered four locations: Ijon, Dan, Abel-beth-

---

109. "The Chronicler records that before the outbreak of hostilities between Baasha and Asa, Asa faced and defeated an invasion led by Zerah the Ethiopian (2Ch 14:9–15). Zerah was probably a commander in the forces of the Egyptian pharaoh Osorkon I (914–874 BC)," (Patterson, "1, 2 Kings," 759).

110. "The city [of Jerusalem] lies on the southern edge of Benjamin's tribal territory. A plateau at the center of this territory interconnects with roads from all directions. Jerusalem's well-being depended upon the fate of this plateau because the city lacked convenient access roads to the coastal plain and Jordan Valley. Immediately after the United Monarchy dissolved, great battles between Israel and Judah erupted in this region," (Monson, "Temple of Solomon," 2, n. 3).

111. Davis, 1 Kings, 175.

112. Ibid.

maacah, and Chinneroth (on the western shore of the Sea of Galilee).[113] Obviously, Baasha was forced to abandon his building program at Ramah and redirect resources to the north to ward off the threat. And this wasn't an act of charity on Ben-hadad's part; Aram gained lucrative access to the Mediterranean coast and Egypt via the Jezreel Valley and established hegemony over both Israel and Judah. In fact, with this move, the Arameans solidified a foothold in the Northern Kingdom and would remain an antagonist for the next two centuries.[114]

Meanwhile, Baasha retired to Tirzah, and Asa seized the building materials at Ramah and used them to fortify Geba and Mizpah. Geba was located six miles northeast of Jerusalem on the road to Jericho, and Mizpah was south of Bethel and northwest of Jerusalem, a site that provided "a good base on the north-south highway from which to control the Descent of Beth-horon."[115] The locations of Geba and Mizpah tell us that Asa was intent on creating a decent buffer between Judah and Israel so that Jerusalem could not be blockaded quite so easily in the future.[116]

Asa's biography ends with a note that "he was diseased in his feet" towards the end of his life (v. 23). Jewish rabbis in the Talmud identified the ailment as gout, but Wiseman argues that such a malady was uncommon in ancient Palestine and Egypt. "It is more likely, in view of Asa's age, the severity of the disease and death within two years, to have been a peripheral obstructive vascular

---

113. Archaeologists have uncovered evidence of the destruction of some of these cities dating to this period (cf. Cogan, *I Kings*, 403, n. 2; Amnon Ben-Tor and Doron Ben-Ami, "Hazor and the Archaeology of the Tenth Century B.C.E.," *IEJ* 48 [1998]: 1–37).

114. It can be dizzying trying to keep up with the shifting international alliances in Kings, but it's not that different than alliances today. For example, ponder the shifting alliances between the U.S., Great Britain, France, Germany, Russia, Japan, Iraq, Iran, etc. during the twentieth century.

115. Gray, *I & II Kings*, 322. "Asa literally moved his own northern border past Ramah, about 3.5 km (2 mi) deeper into Benjaminite territory, by fortifying Geba and Mizpah, two villages set on the hill abutting and controlling the main north-south approach to Jerusalem," (Zevit, "1 Kings," 708).

116. At the sites of Geba and Mizpah, "There are expansive remains and evidence of massive fortification and administrative architecture exposed in modern excavations. In some places the walls are four to six meters (thirteen to nineteen feet) thick. These features bear witness to the strategic position of the town and Asa's determination to define the border once and for all. Two of the gates were preserved to a height of several meters and sections of the city wall towered fifteen meters (nearly forty feet) above ground level," (Monson, "1 Kings," 68; cf. Zorn, "Nasbeh, Tell En-," *NEAEHL* 3:1100).

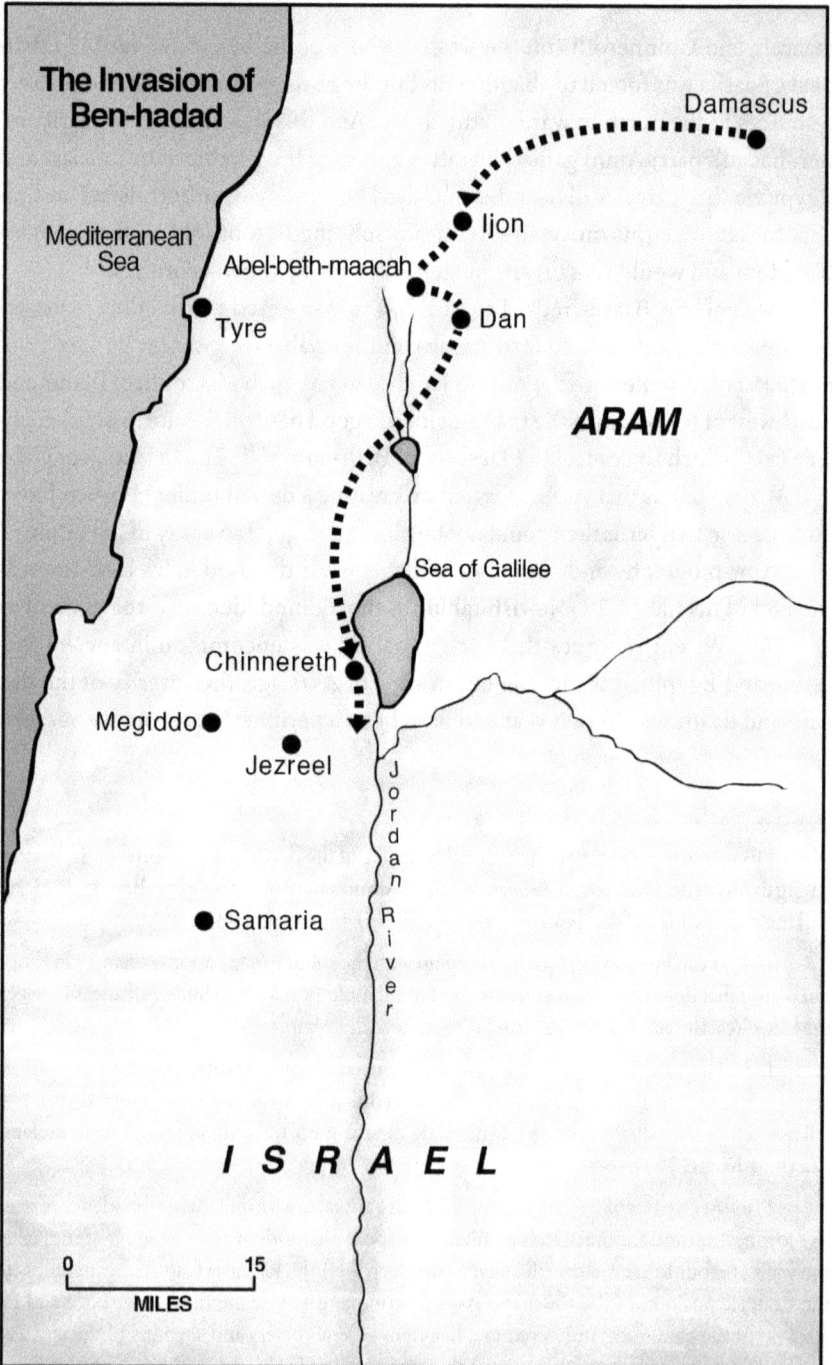

The Invasion of Ben-hadad

disease with ensuing gangrene."[117] Other suggestions include dropsy[118] or a sort of venereal disease,[119] understanding "feet" as a euphemism for genitalia. The nature of the ailment aside, the Chronicler shamed Asa for seeking help from his doctors instead of the Lord (2 Chr 16:12). For whatever reason, and breaking with what was customary in ancient records (including the Chronicler), the narrator of Kings never interprets royal illness as a sign of divine displeasure[120] (cf. 2 Kgs 15:5; 20:1–11).

What are we to make of Asa? In regards to his righteousness, he started strong—the Chronicler seems to indicate that his failures did not come until much later in his reign. As was the case with Solomon and Jeroboam, Asa failed to trust the Lord in *all* things, opting to walk by sight and not by faith (2 Cor 5:7). When faced with a threat, appealing to the enemy of your enemy for help (particularly with sacred riches) may make all the sense in the world, but biblical faith is fundamentally at odds with the sense of this world (cf. 1 Cor 1:25). God kept alight the lamp of David, however, despite the spiritual frailty of his descendants. Only a God of grace remains faithful even when we are faithless (2 Tim 2:13).

Asa's biography closes with Judah delivered from the threat of her Northern brethren. But things have changed.

> One cannot help but notice that whereas Solomon very much had the upper hand in his treaty with Hiram of Tyre (1 Kgs. 5; 9:10–14), Asa is quite clearly the suppliant in regard to Ben-Hadad of Aram. He does not even receive any help with the stones and timber for the building work that results from the treaty (v. 22; cf. 5:18)—he has to resort to the imposition of forced labor upon his Judean citizens. Nor can it escape our attention that, whereas Solomon's political arrangements contributed to the maintenance of the empire, Asa's strategy results in the loss of parts of Israel to a foreign king (v. 20).

---

117. Wiseman, *1 and 2 Kings*, 168–69; cf. Andrew de Vries and Abraham Weinberger, "King Asa's Presumed Gout," *New York State Journal of Medicine* (Feb 1975): 452–55.

118. Robinson, *First Book*, 177.

119. Patterson, "1, 2 Kings," 761; Jeremy Schipper, "Deuteronomy 24:5 and King Asa's Foot Disease in 1 Kings 15:23b," *JBL* 128 (2009): 643–48.

120. Though in Asa's case, scholars aren't so restrained—"His ailment is only one symptom of his loss of trust in the Lord," (Auld, *I & II Kings*, 107).

Faithfulness like Solomon's no longer brings Solomon's glory in its wake. These are different times—times of humbling for David's descendants (11:39).[121]

One of the troubling themes of the post-Revolution period of American history is the Founders' ambivalence to the issue of slavery. Thomas Jefferson's lofty "all men are created equal" rings a little hollow when you recall that he owned approximately six hundred slaves in his lifetime. George Washington seemed to dislike slavery in principle: he freed all of his slaves in his last will and testament, though conspicuously not in his lifetime. Indeed, the Founders were split on the issue of slavery, and often along geographical lines— John Jay and Benjamin Franklin owned slaves, but became abolitionists later in life. It was a concession, however, to the *northern* states (the North didn't want the South skewing the census by counting all their slaves as people while, at the same time, treating them as property) that the Constitution valued a slave at only three-fifths of a person[122]—an insulting clause that was only rectified by the Fourteenth Amendment.

In reality, the Founders were content to kick the can of slavery down the road for someone else to deal with. The reason is that many of the Founders believed slavery would die out on its own within twenty years of the Constitution's ratification anyway.[123] Yet the graves of more than 600,000 Civil War dead (accounting for nearly half of all American deaths in all wars combined) proved such to be worse-than-wishful thinking. The Founders' refusal to address directly the issue of slavery only exacerbated the problem.

With Asa, there begins a troubling trend in Judah that will linger until—indeed, will hasten—her downfall, destruction, and exile. With the exception of two kings—Hezekiah and Josiah—the righteous rulers of the Southern Kingdom always failed to root out the idolatrous high places. Though some were personally opposed to idolatry and set their hearts to seek the Lord, it was not their policy to exterminate pagan worship from the suburbs surrounding Jerusalem. Content they must have been to kick the can down the road, to sweep the is-

---

121. Provan, *1 & 2 Kings*, 125–26.

122. Lawrence Goldstone, *Dark Bargain: Slavery, Profits, and the Struggle for the Constitution* (New York: Walker, 2005), 123–29.

123. Ron Chernow, *Alexander Hamilton* (New York: Penguin, 2004), 238–39.

sue under the rug, hoping it would take care of itself at some later date. "Let it be someone else's problem." And though Hezekiah and Josiah are celebrated by the narrator for doing what other kings had been unwilling to do, their efforts proved too late to make a lasting difference in Judah's fate.

How is a kingdom lost in four hundred years? In part, by refusing to tackle thorny issues head-on in favor of hoping they go away on their own. But the thing is, they almost never go away on their own. Instead, they fester, rot, and lead to the decay of the community. The author of Hebrews warned his own community, "Watch out, brothers, so that there won't be in any of you an evil, unbelieving heart that departs from the living God. But encourage each other daily, while it is still called today, so that none of you is hardened by sin's deception" (Heb 3:12–13 HCSB).

The inspired writer knew that sin grows in a heart until that heart becomes hard and bears the fruit of doubt in God and a departure from him. How much better if we deal ruthlessly with those things that lead to sin and hard-heartedness! Sin, like cancer, doesn't go away on its own. It must be rudely and ruthlessly rooted out if we are ever to be healthy again. This is as true for families, churches, and business as it is for individuals—a truth Judah learned the hard way. "Father, give us leaders who never stop short of rooting out the high places, no matter how sacred they may be."

1 KINGS 15:25-32

The narrator's attention backs up about forty years in time and shifts north to Israel and will not leave until the final chapter of 1 Kings. We are introduced to the reign of Nadab, Jeroboam's heir (14:20). Nadab was a case of "like father, like son"—a common theme among the Northern kings. Because of his wickedness, he only served something over twelve months in 909–908.[124]

In 908, Israel laid siege to the Philistine town Gibbethon, located a dozen miles from the Mediterranean coast. Gibbethon was a strategic border town on the western edge of the hills of Judah, and its capture would allow Israel to "drive a wedge between Judah and Philistia and thus to undermine the economic position of Judah as well."[125]

---

124. Robinson, *First Book*, 178.

125. S. Yeivin, "Did the Kingdoms of Israel Have a Maritime Policy?" *JQR* 50 (1959–60): 218. During this period, Judah, Philistia, and Phoenecia may have had some sort of trade

During the siege, Nadab was assassinated by Baasha of Issachar (likely a military commander), and the rest of Jeroboam's family was summarily exterminated, fulfilling Ahijah's prophecy[126] (14:10–11), "and this fulfilment of the prophecy provided a salutary example of the deuteronomic teaching that God quickly punishes all who are disobedient to his will."[127]

A note stating that Nadab received a royal burial is conspicuously absent[128] (cf. 14:31), and he is in fact the first of six northern kings to be assassinated (16:9–10, 18; 2 Kgs 15:10, 14, 25, 30). Also, with Nadab's assassination, a lengthy period of instability commences in Israel. Six different men would reign over the Northern Kingdom in less than thirty years as opposed to just one in Judah during the same period. What is more, all of Judah's kings were descended from David, while dynasties in Israel were often short-lived.[129] We cannot help but wonder if the extreme internal instability that came to characterize the Northern Kingdom was a result of God's judgment on her wickedness.

---

agreement with one another. Israel's seizure of Gibbethon would have disrupted such trade. Less likely, Robinson believes the town had been seized by the ever-expansionistic Philistines on the occasion of Jeroboam's death (*First Book*, 179). Sweeney hypothesizes that the attack was "an attempt to extend Israel's power into the coastal plain, perhaps by recovering territory that once belonged to Dan (see Josh 19:44; 21:23)," (*I & II Kings*, 196).

126. "Baasha's father is named Ahijah, as was the prophet who predicted the doom of the house of Jeroboam (cf. 14:9–16). Though they are not the same individual, the identical names provide a touch of irony to the whole episode," (Patterson, "1, 2 Kings," 762).

127. Robinson, *First Book*, 179. "The revolt may have been an outworking of inter-tribal or regional power struggles, a feature of clashes in the period of judges—and of many conflicts in history up to today. Jeroboam's family was from Ephraim in the central hill country, the dominant tribe, while Baasha is from *Issachar*, one of the tribes from the region of Galilee which included the strategic Jezreel valley," (Olley, *Message of Kings*, 157; emphasis his). However, "Theologically, the political realities or personal conflicts behind the coup matter not at all," (Wray Beal, *1 & 2 Kings*, 214).

128. "Since Nadab was removed by murder, he was probably buried where he was killed, that is, far from the family grave," (Fritz, *1 & 2 Kings*, 170).

129. "Over the centuries, a conspicuous number of adventurers (e.g., Omri, Jehu, Pekah) emerged from the ranks of the Israelite army; with the support of their forces, these usurpers succeeded in wresting the throne from the incumbents," (Cogan, *I Kings*, 407).

1 KINGS 15:33–16:7

Nadab's assassin, Baasha, set up his capital at Tirzah (a site Gray calls "well-watered and strategically significant"[130]), seven miles northeast of Shechem on the downhill road to Beth-shean in the Jordan Valley. He reigned for twenty-four years (908–886) and is the first of several Northern kings to seize power via assassination. Any hopes of spiritual reform are immediately dashed. Like his predecessors, he was wicked in Yahweh's eyes and copied Jeroboam's apostasy. But this is not the only way in which the narrator invokes Jeroboam's memory.

A prophet, Jehu son of Hanani, brought a message of judgment from Yahweh to Baasha. Like Jeroboam, Baasha had been hand-picked by God and "exalted [...] out of the dust" to the throne (cf. 1 Sam 2:8; Ps 113:7, cf. Ps. 40:2). The word translated "ruler" (Hebrew *nagid*) is indicative of one divinely appointed to rule or lead, and was used of David (1 Sam 25:30), Jeroboam (1 Kgs 14:7), and Hezekiah (2 Kgs 20:5). It is not very different from the concept of *messiah*.

But despite being Yahweh's anointed, Baasha responded by perpetuating spiritual rebellion, and the people only continued in "provoking [God] to anger with their sins" (v. 2). Thus, a prophet of God again appeared, bearing a message of judgment and punishment. God's wrath would be poured out on the house of Baasha as it had on Jeroboam.[131] "Appropriately, he faced the same humiliating judgment as the two worst kings in the northern monarchy, Jeroboam and Ahab (vv. 3-4; 1 Kings 14:10-11; 21:24; 2 Kings 10). No long line of heirs would succeed him, and no fine state burial would honor his passing. Instead, his family would be totally annihilated and their corpses shamefully scavenged by hungry dogs and buzzards."[132] In short, Baasha's destiny was the worst imaginable by someone in the ancient world. But the divine warning seems to have had no effect on him.

The rest of the divine account of Baasha's reign is what we would expect. He died and was buried in Tirzah; his son reigned in his place. What is unexpect-

---

130. Gray, *I & II Kings*, 326. "The city's location enables easy communication and troop movement during the years of warfare with Asa and Ben-hadad," (Wray Beal, *1 & 2 Kings*, 220–21). In Song of Solomon 6:4, Tirzah is remembered for its natural beauty—*Tirzah* means "pleasure" or "beauty" in Hebrew. It was a place "of great natural beauty with extensive gardens and groves encouraged by its abundant water supply (one of the best in Israel)," (G. Lloyd Carr, *The Song of Solomon* [Downers Grove, IL: InterVarsity Press, 1984], 146).

131. Walsh notes several parallels between Ahijah's condemnation of Jeroboam in 1 Kings 14 and Jehu's condemnation of Baasha (*I Kings*, 214).

132. Hubbard, *First and Second Kings*, 90.

ed, however, is that we are told that, along with Baasha's spiritual rebellion, he was also punished because he had destroyed the house of Jeroboam (v. 7)—an odd detail considering God had raised him up to do just that. One commentator suggests that the *also because* of v. 7 can be rendered *despite that*, meaning Baasha was condemned because of his wickedness, even though he had ended the house of Jeroboam.[133] However, another scholar reasonably posits, "It is one thing to displace a rival; it is another thing to use God's commission as an excuse for carrying out selfish ambition. Baasha's perpetuation of Jeroboam's sins betrays his improper motivations. Although he had raised up Baasha in spite of his murderous intention, God in no way condoned Baasha's deeds."[134] This would not be the last time a holy God would punish a former instrument of his discipline (cf. Isa 10:5–19; Jer 27:1–7).

1 KINGS 16:8–14

Though Baasha managed to reign for a quarter-century, his son, Elah (886–885), fared no better than had Nadab, reigning for a few months during two different years. I imagine that, like Nadab's, there were any number of reasons for Elah's assassination, though the fact that God had judged and condemned the house of Baasha was enough reason for the narrator. But "at least Nadab was assassinated during a military campaign rather than during a drinking spree!"[135] The context of his demise may signal something to us about Elah's weakness or indulgence.

It seems half of Israel's chariot force was stationed at Megiddo and the other at Tirzah (and later, Samaria).[136] There, a chariot commander assassinated Elah. While the king was enjoying a red Solo cup party in the home of one of his servants (whom Wiseman identifies as a sort of prime minister[137]),

---

133. James A. Montgomery, *A Critical and Exegetical Commentary on the Books of Kings* (New York: Scribner's, 1951), 282.

134. Patterson, "1, 2 Kings," 763. Olley (*Message of Kings*, 159, n. 31) also points out that, though it was God's will to bring to an end the house of Jeroboam, regicide was still a sin (cf. 1 Sam 24:6; 26:9; 31:4; 2 Sam 1:1–16; 4:1–12). It is thus possible for an act to be according to God's plan (e.g., Judas' betrayal of Jesus) and still be a sin.

135. House, *1, 2 Kings*, 201.

136. Yigael Yadin, *The Art of Warfare in Biblical Lands: In the Light of Archaeological Discovery* (London: Weidenfeld, 1963), 301.

137. Wiseman, *1 and 2 Kings*, 171.

Zimri dispatched Elah. The terse biography of Elah's reign is underscored by Barnes—"Surely he did more in his two-year reign than attend private parties, but historical treatments are naturally quite selective in their emphases. This last point certainly gives pause to leaders of any age!"[138]

Though Zimri likely eliminated Elah's family so as to minimize the chances of any kinfolk[139] seeking blood vengeance, his thoroughness unwittingly fulfilled God's word spoken through his prophet, Jehu. The dedication of the family of Baasha to idols brought them only destruction and death.

> Both Jeroboam and Baasha tried to create dynasties in Israel and in each case their sons were killed by usurpers and then the whole family annihilated. Such wholesale murders were not exceptional. They were the common practice of the time, and regarded as a necessary precaution to prevent further opposition in the state centring [sic] on some member of the former royal family. However, the deuteronomists were moralists and made these sad events the basis for moralizing. They concluded that the dynasties had been set aside because of the disloyalty of their founders to the religious traditions of Yahweh, and that this had been foretold by a prophet.[140]

1 KINGS 16:15-20

In what has to be one of history's shortest regencies, the assassin Zimri reigned a whopping seven days[141] in 885. After learning of Elah's assassination, Omri abandoned the siege against the Philistines at Gibbethon and hurried some forty miles north to Tirzah,[142] the capital. Omri quickly took control of the

---

138. Barnes, *1-2 Kings*, 141. "The account pays its final disrespect to this pathetic king by omitting all information about Elah's death, burial, or successor to the throne," (Hens-Piazza, *1-2 Kings*, 156).

139. The word translated "relatives" (v. 11) is the Hebrew *go'el*, "a term elsewhere used for a close relative whose duty it was to assist needy kinfolk (Lev. 25; Num. 35; Ruth 4:4-5, 10)," (Hubbard, *First and Second Kings*, 91).

140. Robinson, *First Book*, 181.

141. Jewish legend says that Barenaked Ladies' "One Week" was played at Zimri's funeral.

142. Tirzah lay thirty-six miles north of Jerusalem and seven miles north of Shechem. Archaeologists have unearthed evidence of a well-fortified city dating to the early days of the

city, at which point Zimri set fire to the palace, choosing death by conflagration over execution by Omri. If only in my mind, I imagine Zimri's demise resembled that of Denethor at Minas Tirith in *The Lord of the Rings: The Return of the King*.

Lost in the quagmire of political intrigue and spiritual bankruptcy is the fact that Israel had been laying siege to the Philistine town of Gibbethon for a quarter-century now (whether off-and-on or sustained) with no progress. Repeatedly frustrated by their efforts to take the city, Israel eventually walked away from it with nothing to show. We're left with the impression that the town remained in the Philistines' possession. "Twenty-four years of supplies, death, blood—all wasted."[143] Slowly but surely, the Promised Land so graciously given to Israel is eroding from her hands because of spiritual unfaithfulness and political chaos.

Though Zimri was a rather minor figure in Israel's memory, it seems his name became synonymous with political treachery (not unlike America's Benedict Arnold or Aaron Burr). Later in Kings, he is invoked by Jezebel in an insult to Jehu's rebellion (2 Kgs 9:31). But he is not so minor as to escape condemnation by the divine narrator. Though he reigned only seven days on Israel's throne, he was a "'week' king."[144] Of course, Zimri was condemned, but not for seven days of evil; the narrator's comment is a diagnosis of his entire life.

1 KINGS 16:21-28

When Zimri's week-long reign went up in flames, the Northern Kingdom descended into civil war. On one side was "Tibni the son of Ginath," and on the other was Omri. The fact that Omri's ancestry isn't mentioned by the narrator may indicate that he was a commoner, perhaps not even an Israelite.[145]

> No mention is made of his family so his origins must have been obscure and humble. He was a self-made man who chose soldiering as a career. This probably meant that his family pos-

---

Northern Kingdom (Chambon, "Far'ah, Tell el- [North]," *NEAEHL* 2:433–40).

143. Leithart, *1 & 2 Kings*, 118.

144. Davis, *1 Kings*, 189.

145. Montgomery suggests that Omri came from South Arabia—"Omri and Zimri were evidently mercenaries of non-Israelite stock," (*Book of Kings*, 290). Patterson believes Omri's close association with the Phoenicians indicates he was a Canaanite ("1, 2 Kings," 765; cf. Gray, *I & II Kings*, 330).

sessed no land. He rose to command the army by his own ability. Clearly he was the kind of leader to whom the Israelites
had looked for help in the old days when the tribal league was
threatened by enemies. To call him a judge would be an anach-
ronism, but he did possess many of the personal characteristics of a judge, and the gifts which made him a leader whom
men would follow in difficult times.[146]

After a four-year struggle (cf. vv. 15, 23), somehow Omri seized the throne.
We are not told what became of Tibni—whether he died naturally or in battle,
was assassinated,[147] had a "skiing accident," woke up with a horse head in his bed
sheets, or decided to take early retirement.[148] Regardless, Omri became king of
Israel and reigned a grand total of a dozen years (885–874). He was Israel's sixth
king in less than fifty years (by comparison, recall that Saul, David, and Solomon
had reigned for forty years each).

I find it intriguing that Omri receives such scant mention in Kings,[149]
quickly relinquishing the spotlight to his infamous son, Ahab. But secular history remembers Omri as a powerful ruler, one who established a dynasty that
lasted forty-eight years (in contrast, Israel had seen three different dynasties in
the five decades before Omri). "One might say that Omri came to the fore not
a moment too soon, for fifty years of instability had left Israel helpless to defend
herself from hostile neighbors."[150]

As had Solomon, Israel's new king benefited from a lack of regional su-
perpowers. Assyria was just starting to threaten her neighbors to the west, and
Aram would soon give Israel headaches during Ahab's reign , but not yet. Closer
to home, "Omri's policy for Israel's recovery was patterned in its major features
on that of David and Solomon; it called for internal peace, friendly relationship

---

146. Robinson, *First Book*, 184.

147. The LXX mentions that Tibni's brother, Joram, died with him, suggesting a violent
death; cf. Josephus, *Antiquities* 8.311.

148. Indeed, one scholar argues that Tibni "was divested of whatever royal authority he
previously held" without dying (J. Max Miller, "So Tibni Died [1 Kings xvi 22]," *VT* 18 [1968]:
392–94).

149. Davis calls Omri's biography in Kings "as scintillating as an obituary," (*1 Kings*, 191).

150. Bright, *History*, 240.

with Judah, close ties with the Phoenicians, and a strong hand east of the Jordan, particularly against the Arameans."[151]

The Mesha Inscription or Moabite Stone (a stele discovered by a missionary in Transjordan in 1868) tells of how Omri conquered Moab and made them into a vassal state, and he was the first Northern king to make peace with the Southern Kingdom. Omri also arranged for his son to marry the princess of Tyre and thus forge an alliance with an important trading partner, increasing Israel's economic opportunities. "The alliance was mutually advantageous. Tyre was at the height of her colonial expansion (Carthage was founded later in the century); being partly dependent on imports of food stuffs, she offered Israel both an outlet for agricultural products and numerous commercial opportunities. Tyre, for her part, desired both a counterbalance to the power of Damascus and the reactivation of trade with Israel and, via Israel, with the lands of the south."[152]

We are never told why Omri decided to relocate the capital from Tirzah twelve miles west to Samaria, but the new site had much to commend it. It was certainly a more advantageous location, both politically and militarily—the city sat on a hill three hundred feet higher in elevation than the surrounding plain and was "eminently defensible."[153] It also offered better economic opportunities since it was connected to major trade routes to the north, west, and south. In exchange for the site, Omri paid Shemer a premium of 150 pounds of silver (worth about $15-20 million today) for roughly 160 acres of real estate. Excavations have uncovered the palace at Samaria and confirmed that Omri was indeed the initial builder.[154] The city walls were five feet thick and well made. All in all, Samaria cemented Omri's greatness as a ruler. Like David, he gave Israel a new capital and a new dynasty, as well as renewed hope for the future.[155]

In every way imaginable, Omri is the first strong king of Israel since (and is arguably superior to) Jeroboam. He strengthened the military, stabilized the economy, and made great strides in international relations. So great was Omri's power that the Assyrians—thirty-five years after his death—referred to Israel as

---

151. Ibid., 241.

152. Ibid., 241–42.

153. Wray Beal, *1 & 2 Kings*, 224.

154. Avigad, "Samaria (City)," *NEAEHL* 4:1302–3.

155. Leithart notes several parallels between David and Omri. "Unlike David, however, he does not walk in the ways of Yahweh but worships idols (1 Kgs. 16:26)," *(1 & 2 Kings*, 119).

"the house of Omri" (though the irony is that the reference was to Jehu, who had assassinated Omri's grandson and ended the Omride dynasty). A full century after his dynasty had been extinguished, Assyrian documents still referred to Israel as "the land of Omri."

None of that matters, however, in divine history. All the narrator is interested in is Omri's faithfulness to God and the Law, of which there was none. In fact, he is notorious for doing "more evil than all who were before him" (v. 25)—the statement in Micah 6:16 makes us wonder if Omri and Ahab officially codified Israel's apostasy. Like Jeroboam and Baasha, Omri received from God a chance for a fresh start in Israel, but when it came to idolatry, it was just business as usual. "And if you want to know more about him, you can search the public archives on your own time," the narrator concludes in disgust.

1 KINGS 16:29-34

If Omri was bad, Ahab was worse; if the narrator was disgusted with Omri, he got that nasty, pre-vomit taste in his mouth while writing about Ahab. In itself, it is an ominous omen that Ahab is the seventh king of the Northern Kingdom, and he would indeed bring completion or wholeness to Israel's sins in unparalleled ways. It should come as no surprise that the seventh king of Judah, Ahaziah, "is explicitly compared to Ahab for his wickedness" (2 Kgs 8:27), and the seventh after Ahaziah is Manasseh, "who is the most Ahab-like of the southern kings" (2 Kgs 21:3, 13). "In each case, the seventh king in the sequence is the object of prophetic condemnation, and the seventh king's sins bring an interruption or end of the dynasty of which he is a part. The kings in this sabbatical seventh slot bring the sins of Israel and Judah to completion, and the Lord of the Sabbath brings rest through judgment."[156]

Omri's son reigned for twenty-two years (874–853), but maintaining the apostasy of Jeroboam was child's play for him (v. 31). Ahab married Jezebel, the princess of Tyre and Sidon and daughter of their ruler, Ethbaal (c. 887–856).[157] As princess, she also may have served as the high priestess of Baal. As with Solomon, Ahab's choice of spouse became a corrupting influence in Israel. Patterson

---

156. Ibid., 120.

157. Ethbaal was the ruler of Sidon who overthrew the Tyrian dynasty of Hiram and united the two Phoenician cities. He assassinated Hiram's descendant and reigned for thirty-two years, dying at age sixty-eight (Josephus, *Against Apion* 1.123).

correctly surmises that, "No more notorious husband-and-wife team than Ahab and Jezebel is known in all the sacred Scriptures."[158] In so many ways, their wickedness was unprecedented.[159]

Upon her nuptials, Jezebel introduced her patron god to both her husband and her adopted country. Whereas there once had been only an altar and calf in Bethel and Dan, there is now a temple of Baal and an Asherah pole in Samaria, both of which survived for many years (cf. 2 Kgs 10:23; 13:6); while Jeroboam had sinned in reducing Yahweh to an image, a violation of the second commandment, Ahab and Jezebel were attempting to replace Yahweh with Baal as the patron god of Samaria in every way imaginable. Indeed, "the sins of the northern kingdom have multiplied."[160]

And lest we are tempted to think that these changes were merely cosmetic, Monson reminds us that "Israel's acceptance of Canaanite religion was far more insidious than cultic activity alone. It represented the adoption of an entire worldview replete with human-like gods of vice and a self-serving despot who turned upside down the cosmology of the Bible and the ethics of biblical law."[161] As we will discover in the record of Ahab's reign (especially in the narrative of Naboth's vineyard), the worldview of the son of Omri was at complete odds with what was reflected in the Law of Moses and traditions of Israel.

Like his father, historians remember Ahab as a gifted ruler and formidable military opponent. In 853, a significant international alliance opposed the Assyrian ruler Shalmaneser III at the battle of Qarqar (more on that in chapter seven), and Ahab is noted for his significant contributions to the fray. "The '2,000 chariots and 10,000 troops of Ahab the Israelite' comprise the second largest contingent of the coalition against the Assyrian attack. Ahab's military and civic structures are well represented at excavated sites such as Megiddo, Hazor, Tel Dan, Samaria, Dothan, and Jezreel. They include storage facilities, palaces with

---

158. Patterson, "1, 2 Kings," 767.

159. "By comparison, Jeroboam's was a pastel evil, Ahab's a darker, deeper hue. Jeroboam's state cult is like drinking polluted water; Ahab's imported paganism is like sucking raw sewage. Neither is good, but one is worse than the other," (Davis, 1 Kings, 197).

160. Provan, 1 & 2 Kings, 129.

161. Monson, "1 Kings," 72; cf. William G. Dever, "'Will the Real Israel Please Stand Up?' Part II: Archaeology and the Religions of Ancient Israel," BASOR 298 (1995): 37–58.

characteristic Phoenician masonry, large solid city walls, and pillared buildings associated with chariotry."[162]

Closer to home, Ahab established peace with the Philistines (cf. 15:27; 16:15) and maintained control of Moab across the Jordan. "Thus, Ahab achieved a truce on all borders, and in some areas even secured allies, in order to meet the Aramean threat in the [North]."[163] But to the narrator, worldly greatness paled in comparison to spiritual fidelity to the first two commandments.[164] It seems a leader can establish a strong national defense, a vibrant economy, and enjoy massive popularity among the masses, yet still be a complete failure in God's eyes.

A final anecdote is deployed by the narrator to illustrate the lengths of Ahab's unprecedented evil. "During the time of Ahab, Hiel from Bethel rebuilt the city of Jericho. It cost Hiel the life of Abiram, his oldest son, to begin work on the city, and it cost the life of Segub, his youngest son, to build the city gates. This happened just as the LORD, speaking through Joshua son of Nun, said it would happen" (v. 34 NCV).

Many years before, Joshua had cursed Jericho as a victorious Israel stood amidst its ruins and rubble. "Anyone who tries to rebuild this city of Jericho will be cursed by the LORD. The one who lays the foundation of this city will lose his oldest son, and the one who sets up the gates will lose his youngest son" (Josh 6:26 NCV). In the intervening period, it seems Jericho was resettled (cf. Josh 18:21; Judg 3:13; 2 Sam 10:5; 1 Chr 19:5), but it never became an established, fortified city (which Joshua had sworn should never occur) until Ahab's day, and the archaeological record supports this.[165] As the divine Landowner,

---

162. Monson, "1 Kings," 72.

163. Thiel, "Ahab (Person)," ABD 1:101.

164. It is not unusual for modern biblical scholarship to take issue with the inspired narrator's negative appraisal of Ahab: "The portrait of Ahab and his dynasty (the 'House of Ahab') has been negatively distorted in the OT tradition primarily because of his religious policies which were seen as a danger to the traditional worship of God in circles loyal to Yahweh. His skillful foreign policies, which provided Israel with strength, security, and prosperity, which safeguarded peace and the balance of power, and which, finally, contributed to the (temporary) containment of Assyrian expansionism, may be inferred from the few sources that yield reliable historical data. However, his contributions in this regard were ignored in the decidedly theological perspective of the OT witnesses," (Ibid., 1:103).

165. Kenyon, "Jericho," NEAEHL 2:680.

God allowed the city to be inhabited, but the walls he kept for himself. When Hiel laid the foundation (the first step in city building) and erected the gates (the last step), he lost his oldest and youngest sons[166]—just as Joshua had said.

This detail is important for a few reasons. *First, it further underscored Ahab's hostility to the word of God.* Several scholars believe Ahab was directly or indirectly behind the building project at Jericho.[167] It is speculated that Ahab's wars against Moab (cf. 2 Kgs 1:1; 3:5), just across the Jordan from Jericho, made fortifying the site a national security issue[168] (recall that Jeroboam's Penuel, also five miles from the Jordan, had been sacked by Shishak fifty years prior). But the Old Testament consistently mocks the defenses of man against the will of God (cf. Nah 3:12). Van't Veer reflected on this passage by saying, "It is inevitable that the steadily growing bond with Baal should be coupled with a sinful emancipation from the Word of God, and thus also from Yahweh, Israel's God. The rift between Israel and Yahweh is clearly illustrated when Ahab gives the order to rebuild Jericho."[169]

Second, Hiel's foolish building venture portrays Ahab as actively reversing the conquest of Canaan under Joshua, "an undoing of God's gift of the land."[170] Gazing on the smoking ruins of a city delivered into his hands by the Lord, Joshua swore that it should never be rebuilt as a citadel lest the enemies of God's people regain concentrated urban power in the Promised Land.[171] The enemy could not be allowed a foothold, and that is why the systematic extermination of the Canaanites

---

166. At one time, the dominant interpretation was that this alluded "to the practice of 'foundation sacrifice' wherein a child was killed and entombed into the foundation of a new building as an act of piety to assure the well-being of the new structure" (Brueggemann, *1 & 2 Kings*, 204). In more recent times, however, this interpretation has been abandoned for the more realistic explanation that Hiel's sons died as punishment for Hiel violating Joshua's curse.

167. Davis, *1 Kings*, 198; Gray, *I & II Kings*, 335; Walsh, *1 Kings*, 219. See especially M. B. Van't Veer, *My God is Yahweh: Elijah and Ahab in an Age of Apostasy*, trans. Theodore Plantinga (St. Catharines, Ontario: Paideia, 1980) 9–26.

168. Jewish tradition remembers Hiel as Ahab's commander of the army (Louis Ginzberg, *Legends of the Jews*, 2nd ed., trans. Henrietta Szold and Paul Radin [Philadelphia: Jewish Publication Society, 2003], 992).

169. Van't Veer, *My God*, 10.

170. Fretheim, *First and Second Kings*, 92. "The firstfruits of the Israelite conquest, Jericho would be, as it were, the *last* city to be rebuilt in the land, and at a fearsome cost," (Barnes, *1–2 Kings*, 147; emphasis his).

171. Brueggemann, *1 & 2 Kings*, 204.

and their idols was so important. But now, rather than exterminate idolatry, Ahab sanctioned its unprecedented expansion. Instead of leaving pagan centers of power in ruins, he rebuilt them. Under this new king, "Israel no longer conquers the Canaanites but instead embraces their religion and courts their fate."[172]

Finally, the Jericho story perpetuated the narrator's insistence that *God's word stands forever and will surely come to pass* (Isa 55:11), that Yahweh means what he says. A six-centuries-old curse on Jericho remained violently potent since it had originated from the mouth of the Lord. And if Hiel had spurned the divine warning and paid dearly for it, how much more so would Ahab, Jezebel, and all Israel suffer unless repentance and restoration were sought?

We are left, then, with a very bleak picture of Israel's spiritual fortunes at the end of 1 Kings 16. But just when we might think God has fallen silent or failed to act, he proves that he is up to the task, that he has created a person to rise to the occasion. God meets the worst of evil with the best of his power. Seasons of great wickedness see the rise of God's greatest servants.

Enter Elijah.[173]

---

172. Provan, *1 & 2 Kings*, 131.

173. "With [1 Kings 17] we arrive at an abrupt and decisive interruption of the royal narrative, a pause to consider the *prophetic counterforce* in Israel's life," (Brueggemann, *1 & 2 Kings*, 207; emphasis his). "It is a remarkable feature of the Book of Kings that suddenly here at the end of the sixteenth chapter the speed with which we have been moving through history of both kingdoms slows down and the next seventeen chapters are taken up with very detailed account of events which occur mainly in North Israel during more than one generation. God obviously regarded the threat posed by Baal religion was so serious that it required a decisive and quite distinct answer," (Wallace, *1 Kings*, 103).

TALKING POINTS

T ony Bennett claims that if he ruled the world, every day would be the first day of spring. Me? I'd outlaw diabetes and make bratwurst choles-terol-free. None of us like being governed by superior forces. We love the idea of being our own boss, of retiring and not having anyone tell us what to do. We bandy about, "It's a free country," as if it's our constitutional right to do whatever we want without consequences. But the reality is we want everyone *else* kept in check. And though the most democratically-minded politicians seem driven to obtain and preserve power by hook or crook, this passage reminds us that not even kings are outside the bounds of God's sovereignty—nothing in all creation is, for Christ alone is "the ruler of kings on earth" (Rev 1:5). "Across these accounts, [...] the repetitive refrain 'did what was displeasing in the sight of the LORD' discloses more than divine dissatisfaction. 'The sight of the LORD' suggests God's constant vigilance and watchfulness over these events."[174] Re-hoboam tried to salvage a divided kingdom, and Jeroboam attempted to silence the prophetic voice, but it is the Lord alone "who works all things according to the counsel of his will" (Eph 1:11). All the kingdoms of man will eventually crumble, but their fall is harder and faster when it is forgotten that God is God and we are not. Reflecting on this section of Kings, Inrig reminds us, "It is the word of God, not the power of the king or even the person of the prophet, that shapes events in the nation."[175]

A s Kings goes on to demonstrate, Jeroboam's apostasy—the improper worship of the Lord—became the root of both Israel's wickedness and decline.[176] Twenty-three times, the narrator will invoke "the sin of Je-roboam."[177] Fretheim notes "that all of Jeroboam's sins are connected to worship in some way. There are no signs that he violated the principles of justice for the

---

174. Hens-Piazza, *1–2 Kings*, 161.

175. Inrig, *I & II Kings*, 111.

176. John Holder, "The Presuppositions, Accusations, and Threats of 1 Kings 14:1–18," *JBL* 107 (1988): 27–38.

177. 1 Kings 13:34; 14:16; 15:30, 34; 16:2, 7, 19, 26, 31; 22:52; 2 Kings 3:3; 10:29, 31; 13:2, 6, 11; 14:24; 15:9, 18, 24, 28; 17:21–23; 23:15.

oppressed upon which his rebellion was grounded (with God's approval)."[178] Given the harsh judgment leveled against Jeroboam, this should make us pause and reflect on our own worship habits. Scripture is clear that God is especially sensitive to unauthorized changes to how we worship him. We are not free to make just any changes we want to the prescribed worship practices God has given us—even small modifications or "tweaks" made with good intentions can be dangerous.[179] "God simply will not accept worship that distorts who he is, worship that is the product of human creativity or political expediency."[180] If we believe God to be Creator, Redeemer, Lord, and Judge, it is perhaps best to do exactly what he has commanded. If improper worship eventually led to judgment in Israel, why would we think it will be different for us?

D oubt in God's provision is the root of our rebellion, and this has been true since Adam and Eve sinned in Eden. We do not obey because we do not trust. Spend some time reflecting on those sins that so often trip you up. Are they not all tied, some way or another, to a weak faith in God's ability to provide for us? Anxiety and worry occur when we don't believe that God really cares for us more than the flowers or the birds. Seeking payback on those who have wronged us betrays our lack of confidence in God's promise to right every wrong. Jeroboam was promised a kingdom, and had he trusted the Lord, his throne would have been no less secure than David's. Once king, however, Jeroboam did not trust God to unite his kingdom, but sought human, idolatrous alternatives instead. Confessing that God's Word stands forever means trusting God to do what he has promised and getting out of his way.

---

178. Fretheim, *First and Second Kings*, 77.

179. "Jeroboam professed to retain the worship of Jehovah, and to introduce only a small alteration in setting up a symbol of Him. He would vehemently have asserted that he was no idolater, and would have shuddered at the very notion of bowing down to the gods of the nations, but in less than fifty years a temple to the Sidonian Baal rose in Samaria, and his worship, with its foul sensuality, was corrupting all Israel. [...] Let no one say: 'Thus far and no farther will I go.' There is no stopping at will on that course, any more than a man sliding down a steeply sloping sheet of smooth ice can pull himself up before he plunges over the edge into the abyss below," (Maclaren, *Expositions*, 4:231–32).

180. Inrig, *I & II Kings*, 106.

T here is much in this section (and in the whole of Kings, for that matter) that warns against weak, ineffective leadership. *First, wise leaders
must be selfless.* While selfless leadership can foster unity, self-serving
leadership eventually leads to division. The counsel of Rehoboam's more mature advisors was to serve the people so that they would be loyal (12:7), and
Jesus illustrates this principle perfectly (Mark 10:43–45; cf. Ezek 34; Matt 9:36;
John 10:11, 14–16; Acts 20:38; 1 Pet 5:2–4). *Second, wise leaders must lead
with trust, not fear.* When he uttered his unfortunate bravado, the Israelites realized they could not trust Rehoboam to have their best at heart. Jeroboam, too,
attempted to consolidate his power because he did not trust his people not to
abandon him (nor did he trust God to keep his kingdom secure). "Wise leaders
realize that they must earn the support of followers, not demand or coerce it."[181]
Finally, wise leaders must seek the wisest counsel. Notice that, in Rehoboam's
moment of truth, he sought the counsel of his advisors, young and old, but never once inquired of the Lord. "The issues before [Rehoboam and his advisors]
were critical and decisive for their future. Yet no priest was invited, no prayer was
offered, no reference at all was made to God and his will, even by the elders."[182]
Wise leaders know that, though they may seek the advice of others, they must
seek the Lord's will above all else (Jas 1:5).

---

181. Inrig, *I & II Kings*, 98.

182. Wallace, *1 Kings*, 80.

6

TRUE GRIT

n 1968, a serial novel ran in *The Saturday Evening Post* that would later be hailed by several critics as being among the best American novels. Charles Portis' *True Grit* tells the story of Mattie Ross' determination to find her father's murderer and bring him to justice. After shooting Frank Ross in cold blood, Tom Chaney had slipped into the Indian territory of Oklahoma and was beyond the reach of the authorities in Fort Smith, Arkansas. To capture the outlaw, Mattie Ross solicited the help of U.S. Marshall Rooster Cogburn, a man whom she had been assured had "grit." "He's a pitiless man," she's told. "Double-tough, and fear don't enter into his thinking."[1]

In 1969, the novel was adapted to the big screen with John Wayne playing the role of Cogburn. In my opinion, the character is quintessential Wayne—grizzled, caustic, determined—and his performance in the film landed him his sole Oscar in a career comprising over 140 leading roles. It's a shame the Duke didn't live long enough to star in a feature film on the life of Elijah. As I read Portis' novel and whenever I reflect on the stories of Israel's prophet, I'm struck by the similarities between Cogburn and Elijah. Grizzled, caustic, determined—Wayne would have been perfect for the lead role of the prophet from Tishbe.

In every way, Elijah was the man for Israel's hour. So far, "we have lacked a prophet to address the house of Omri, but now a prophet bursts onto the scene with a vengeance."[2] When faithfulness to Yahweh was at an all-time low, a prophet with true grit emerged from virtually nowhere. Grizzled, caustic, deter-

---

1. Charles Portis, *True Grit* (New York: Overlook, 1968), 25.

2. Provan, *1 & 2 Kings*, 132.

mined—these are the classic traits that have become synonymous with Elijah. He was a man's man and prophet's prophet. Considering the large shadow he casts across the rest of Scripture, it might surprise you to learn that Elijah's life does not consume much of Kings. Aside from these three chapters, he appears briefly at the end of 1 Kings 21, and then in the opening two episodes of 2 Kings.

However, those committed to God's will and Word don't have to be around for very long to make an impact. Jesus compared his followers to salt, and salt—no matter how late it arrives at the party—always makes a difference.

1 KINGS 17:1-7

In his debut on the stage of Scripture, Elijah could not have been more uncouth had he tried. In an offensive move somewhere between insulting Ahab's momma and flipping the bird at Jezebel, Elijah showed up to declare a ban on rain until he said so.[3] And then, just as suddenly and mysteriously as he had entered the scene, Elijah disappeared.

I've been fascinated with v. 1 for a long time. There is no lead-up to Elijah's story. We're given no insight into his background. We're told he's a Tishbite from Tishbe in Gilead, but modern scholars haven't the foggiest clue where that is.[4] The narrator might as well have claimed the prophet hailed from Timbuktu.

When Elijah entered Ahab's throne room to deliver his message, the announcement of his very name had to have stuck in the king's craw. I can imagine Ahab's executive secretary buzzing in to say, "Mr. Ahab, sir, there's a Mr. Elijah here to see you," and Ahab flushing red with anger. Elijah's name means, "Yahweh is my God," which told Ahab all he needed to know about the prophet's opinion of the royal Baal cult.

---

3. In Deuteronomy, dew and rain are evidence of God's covenant blessings (11:11, 14; 28:12; 33:28), and their absence is evidence of God's curse for covenant unfaithfulness. "Thus Elijah's pronouncement enacts a covenant curse upon Israel because they have broken the covenant," (Wray Beal, *1 & 2 Kings*, 232). The Greek historian Meander noted a significant drought that occurred during the reign of Jezebel's father, Ethbaal (Josephus, *Antiquities* 8.324).

4. Patterson's explanation comes closest to an actual theory. He suggests Elijah was from Tishbe in Naphtali (cf. Tobit 1:2), but that Elijah had become a settler in Gilead (east of the Jordan), that Elijah's family had relocated there during Baasha's wars with the Arameans ("1, 2 Kings," 771). Wiseman contends that Tishbe is said to be in Gilead to distinguish it from the one in Naphtali (*1 and 2 Kings*, 176).

Ahab would have also considered Elijah's prediction of drought to be threatening to the throne. In ancient times, "royal responsibility for rain is not unlike contemporary presidential responsibility for the economy. The measure of an effective king is rain that produces [crops]. In this simple assertion the capacity to administer rain and therefore life is taken from the king. The king is made a political irrelevance, void of any critical function for society."[5]

Elijah's message would have also been threatening to Israel's new national religion. In the worldview of Ahab and Jezebel, Baal sent dew in the summer and rain in the winter to nourish the earth since he was the god of fertility. Worshipers of Baal gave him the title "rider of the clouds," one that uniquely belongs to Yahweh (Ps 104:3; Isa 19:1; Nah 1:3). Servants of Baal sought his favor in exchange for plenteous crops, fertile wombs for women and livestock, and anything else they desired to prosper and multiply. Baalism was like a Miracle Grow/fertility drugs one-stop-shop.

I know what you're thinking: "Doesn't the land of Israel often go long periods without rain?" Yes, yes it does. "So how could anyone believe in a rain god during regular seasons of drought?" Those are excellent questions, and I should preface my answer with a reminder that people don't like to let cold, hard reality get in the way of terrible theology.

Baalites (like Ahab and Jezebel) would say that Baal was put to death each spring by Mot, the god of death, only to be resurrected again and bring rain to the land.[6] Israel depended on the rainy season each year (October-March) to get it through the dry season (April-September)—seventy percent of annual precipitation in modern Israel falls between November and February alone. Growth in the dry season was supplemented by each morning's dew.[7] Thus, if the dew and rain didn't come when it was supposed to, Israel would suffer, and three years of no rain would create a terrible famine. In Elijah's story, then, the true God of heaven took Baal and Mot to task, proving Yahweh alone held power

---

5. Brueggemann, *1 & 2 Kings*, 209.

6. Day, "Baal (Deity)," *ABD* 1:546; Herrmann, "Baal," *DDD* 134. "As proof positive that power belongs to YHWH and not Baal, the drought will last much longer than a one-yearly cycle (18:1), the agricultural period associated with Baal's ability to bring the rains once again," (Wray Beal, *1 & 2 Kings*, 232).

7. "The dew (often falling as heavy as drizzle in some regions of Palestine) was also a sign of God's favor to his covenantal people (Dt 33:28; Pr 19:12). However, it could be withdrawn from a thankless and apostate people (Hag 1:10)," (Patterson, "1, 2 Kings," 770).

over rain and drought, life and death. Just as the ten plagues in Egypt were really about the God of Israel versus the gods of Egypt (not Moses versus Pharaoh), the story of Elijah is really about God versus Baal (not Elijah versus Ahab).[8] Of Elijah's warning of drought, Dillard sums it up nicely: "There could be no clearer way to throw down the gauntlet to the worship of Baal."[9]

During my final two years of high school, I participated in speech and debate competitions, and the debate resolution my senior year was on U.S. agricultural policy. That experience, plus living in rural areas and going to church with farmers and ranchers for much of my life, has made me realize how remarkably stable America's food supply is, yet how susceptible American farmers remain to drought, even in the twenty-first century. No rain means no crops and no feed for the animals, which affects most everything else.

Several years ago, a lack of rain in Middle Tennessee where I lived at the time forced area farmers to truck hay in from Wisconsin. Needless to say, this drove their costs through the roof. For a lot of reasons, Americans remain somewhat insulated from the adverse effects of drought. In fact, when suburbanites see *drought* in the headlines, their immediate thought is often, "Great, now I won't be able to water my lawn as much as I want." But for farmers and ranchers, the devastation of drought is much more immediate and severe.

Considering that virtually 100% of ancient Israel's economy was directly dependent on agriculture, the threat of drought was especially grave. If Elijah had screamed, "I have a bomb," as he went through airport security at LaGuardia a week after 9/11, he could not have incited a greater combination of animosity and fear than he did here in Ahab's throne room. In the worst way imaginable, Elijah's declaration made him persona non grata. Later, we're told Ahab had been searching for Elijah while the latter had been AWOL, probably thinking that getting rid of the prophet would end the drought since Elijah was "the cause."

---

8. "The Canaanites' equating of fertility with the presence of a live and vibrant Baal, who as the storm god sent the life-preserving rains onto the land, and their equating of drought and famine with the periodic death of Baal, set the stage for the stories in 1 Kings 17–19," (Alan J. Hauser, "Yahweh Versus Death—The Real Struggle in 1 Kings 17–19," in *From Carmel to Horeb: Elijah in Crisis*, ed., Alan J. Hauser [Sheffield: Almond Press, 1990], 11). To this, House adds, "Elijah must find a way to expose Baal as a nonentity and at the same time reestablish Yahweh as sovereign in the people's minds," (*1, 2 Kings*, 211).

9. Raymond B. Dillard, *Faith in the Face of Apostasy: The Gospel According to Elijah & Elisha* (Phillipsburg, NJ: P&R, 1999), 18. Likewise, Wallace calls it "a declaration of war on the whole set-up in Israel," (*1 Kings*, 107).

The prophet's prediction now delivered, Yahweh commanded Elijah to depart for a stream called Cherith in Transjordan.[10] There, Elijah was sustained by God with water from the brook and food brought to him by ravens.[11] As long as I've known this story, I've imagined Elijah subsisting on meager rations, not unlike the Israelites living off of manna in the wilderness. The mental picture left me quite sympathetic of Elijah. "Poor guy," I thought. "There couldn't have been much joy in his meals—it was for the birds!"

However, Elijah lived in a time when only the wealthy could afford to have meat as a part of their regular diet. The narrator, then, by telling us that the ravens brought bread and meat to Elijah, intends for us to see this exiled prophet feasting like a king while the rest of Israel suffered during the drought and resulting famine. And while many might have been lucky to have one substantive meal each day, Elijah was feasting morning and night.[12] And one scholar reminds us that brooks and streams (i.e., wadis) in that part of the world were seasonal, meaning they ran dry when the rain ceased and even pools would not have survived a drought.[13] But Cherith yielded water for Elijah for a long time. Unlike Baal, God knows how to take care of those faithful to him!

But things weren't this way forever. Eventually, the brook dried up, and Elijah was called away by God yet again. Elijah could have sat by Cherith and pouted about the loss of water and food. Why had God stopped providing? Had he, like Baal, been defeated by Mot, god of death? Or, worse, was God's withdrawal of provision a sign of his displeasure with Elijah?

When God removes a blessing, we too often chalk it up to divine impotence or dissatisfaction. But God is anything but powerless, and though he might be

---

10. In the Middle Ages, Cherith was identified with the Wadi Qelt, located north of Jericho on the west side of the Jordan, but LaSor claims this can't be correct; "this location is flatly contradicted by the biblical description in 17:3." Instead, he offers up Wadi Yabis, which empties into the Jordan about five miles south of Pella, as an alternative site in the highlands of northern Gilead, but concedes that it "is hardly more than careful speculation" ("Cherith, the Brook," *ISBE* 1:641; cf. Younker, "Cherith, Brook of," *ABD* 1:899).

11. To make the story more believable, some scholars once argued that *ravens* here actually referred to a band of black Arabs east of the Jordan who brought Elijah food (Gray, *I & II Kings*, 339). But this seems more outlandish than the bird theory. For one thing, though Ahab searched far and wide for Elijah (18:10), he could have never interrogated the ravens! (My thanks to Dr. Dale Manor of Harding University for offering this insight in a private conversation).

12. Provan, *1 & 2 Kings*, 133.

13. Cogan, *I Kings*, 426.

displeased with us at times, a dried-up stream can just as easily mean that the Lord has greater work for us to do. On the other hand, comfort and ease often insulate us from assuming the risk of obedience to the divine call.

1 KINGS 17:8–24

With Cherith now a dry stream bed, Yahweh commanded Elijah to go to Zarephath, a Phoenician town located eight miles south of Sidon and eighty miles north of Samaria. The irony of this location is that it, like Cherith, was beyond the domain of Ahab, but was also in Jezebel's backyard and thus on Baal's home turf. In other words, "Here is a region, some might have thought, over which Israel's God could have no authority."[14]

If I had been Elijah, it would have been more than a little disconcerting to hear God say, "Go to this place because I've arranged for a widow to take care of you there."[15] When you think of a widow, you might be tempted to conjure up the image of this little old lady who appears very unassuming, but is, in fact, worth millions. But widows in ancient times were on the opposite end of the social spectrum (cf. Exod 22:22; Deut 10:18; 14:29; 24:17–21; 26:12–13). Their economic hopes hovered somewhere between "high school drop-out" and "homeless."[16] Some widows were forced into prostitution as a means of providing for themselves. So when Elijah was told about the circumstances of his new benefactor, it couldn't have been faith-inspiring—"As with the ravens, the prophet is finally dependent, not only upon God but also upon such a lowly one,

---

14. Provan, *1 & 2 Kings*, 133.

15. "The story presupposes that there was some external sign that differentiated widows, who were typically poor, from other women, perhaps some item of dress (Gen. 38.14)," (Zevit, "1 Kings," 712).

16. Hiebert draws parallels between the widow (Hebrew *'almānâ*) and the immigrant (Hebrew *gēr*) in the Old Testament. Both "existed on the fringes of society. In a society where kinship ties gave one identity, meaning, and protection, both the *'almānâ* and the *gēr* had no such ties. Unlike, the *gēr*, however, the *'almānâ* lived in this liminal zone as a woman. Not only was she bereft of kin, but she was also without a male who ordinarily provided a woman with access to the public sphere. [. . .] The wicked take advantage of the *'almānâ* because they fear no reprisals from outraged family members. Yahweh takes special care of the *'almānâ*, supplying the role of the missing male kin who would have been concerned for her well-being and economic support," (Paula S. Hiebert, "'Whence Shall Help Come to Me?': The Biblical Widow," in *Gender and Difference in Ancient Israel*, ed. Peggy L. Day [Minneapolis: Fortress, 1989], 130, 137; cf. Leeuwen, "אַלְמָנָה," *NIDOTTE* 1:413–15; Holwerda and Opperwall-Galluch, "Widow," *ISBE* 4:1060–61).

for his basic needs."[17] His journey to Zarephath was probably less "Blue Skies and Rainbows" and more "Farther Along" and "Ready to Suffer."

When Elijah came upon this widow, the narrator says she was "gathering sticks," and I think we are to imagine her hunched over at the city gate, scrounging for random branches for a fire. A lot of traffic would have passed through the gate each day, and people would have dropped things. Whether intentionally or coincidentally, the narrator's depiction of this widow reminds us of another widow, Ruth, who stumbled upon God's providence while also foraging for a meager meal.

The widow's plight is illustrated by Elijah requesting a morsel[18] of bread, only for the widow to respond that she has none, that she is indeed preparing for herself and her son a last supper of sorts. She is at the end of her rope—"Caught between the demands of ancient hospitality and the harsh reality of famine, she reacts with an oath and fatalistic resignation."[19] But Elijah speaks to her fear by reasserting his request for bread. Though she has but only a handful of flour and a little oil, her meager gift—when coupled with faith—will bring a bountiful return. Elijah brought a word from Yahweh, an assurance that her flour and oil would not run out, and Yahweh's word came to pass.

The irony is that "Grain and oil were two of the major exports of the city of Zarephath. The fact that they were in short supply is an indication of how severe the drought was. They are also two of the most basic commodities for survival. As staple products they represent the major arena where fertility can be observed."[20] Even in enemy territory, the Lord proved himself quite capable of caring for those whom Baal had forgotten.

So far, Yahweh has soundly proven his superiority to Baal in Israel and Phoenicia. He can provide for his prophet and for the poor when they have nothing. Baal is no match for the Lord's providence. But there remains one last lingering question: What of death? "Is there a 'border' that [the

---

17. Fretheim, *First and Second Kings*, 99.

18. Lest we think Elijah is requesting a feast, the word translated "morsel" (v. 11) in Hebrew means "a bit, crumbs," etc. (*HALOT* 983; cf. Gen 18:5; Lev 2:6; 1 Sam 2:36; 28:22; Ezek 13:19).

19. Nelson, *First and Second Kings*, 110.

20. Walton, *Bible Background*, 377.

Lord] ultimately *cannot* cross, a kingdom in which he has no power? When faced by 'Mot,' must the LORD, like Baal, bow the knee?"[21]

Sometime later, the Zarephath widow's son became sick and died. Any woman who lost her husband in ancient times was placed in a difficult circumstance, but those without children faced a particularly grim future (cf. Ruth 1:3–5; 1 Tim 5:4). So we should empathize with her as she believes her world to be crashing down around her. There is pain and bitterness and incredulity in her voice when she said to Elijah, "Why did you ever show up here in the first place—a holy man barging in, exposing my sins, and killing my son?" (v. 18 Msg).[22]

As all of us are prone to do, the widow exhibited amnesia in her hour of grief. While she blamed her son's death on Elijah's presence, the fact remained that both she and her son would at this point be dead had it not been for Elijah.

> Her immature faith struggles with the tragedy, and she assumes the death is God's punishment for some unknown sin in her life. She believed Elijah's saintly presence in her home had somehow drawn God's attention to her. If he had not come, God would have continued to overlook her sin, and her son would not have died. It is sad to see the same distorted belief expressed today in the midst of suffering. "What did I do to deserve this?" is a question pastors and counselors hear too often from confused people facing tragedy.[23]

Elijah carried the widow's deceased son to the upstairs room the prophet had been occupying during his time in Zarephath. He laid the child out on the bed and then "stretched himself upon the child three times." In a very tender moment of painful honesty, the prophet pleaded with God to restore life to the boy, and "the LORD listened."

---

21.   Provan, *1 & 2 Kings*, 134; emphasis his. "In the absence of Baal who lies impotent in the Netherworld, Yahweh steps in to assist the widow and the orphan, and this is even done in the heartland of Baal, Phoenicia," (F. C. Fensham, "A Few Observations on the Polarisation between Yahweh and Baal in I Kings 17–19," *ZAW* 92 [1980]: 234). Wray Beal notes the emphasis on life throughout this narrative (*1 & 2 Kings*, 235–36).

22.   "Hospitality to the man of God should have brought blessing on the widow's house and the clearest form that blessing could take was immunity from the natural disasters of life. The opposite proved to be the case," (Robinson, *First Book*, 202).

23.   Russell Dilday, *1, 2 Kings* (Waco: Word, 1987), 205.

Nelson reminds us that "Elijah's deed is more a matter of prayer (vv. 21b–22) than of magic."[24] Any suggestion that Elijah's stretching out over the boy (v. 21) was merely the performance of CPR—that the child had simply stopped breathing and was not actually dead medically[25]—misses the point. What had been dead was now alive by Elijah's petition and Yahweh's power. Baal had been powerless to end the drought; he had also been powerless to return a son to his mother. But "by restoring the boy's life, Yahweh is again showing his power in the realm considered to be Baal's central arena,"[26] (cf. 1 Sam 2:6). How joyful the widow must have been to receive her son back to life! The miracle confirmed for her that Elijah was who he said he was, and that Yahweh indeed would do all he had promised.

U nlike Baal, God knows how to take care of those faithful to him, and this narrative exemplifies how God responds to our needs. It may be that we are appointed in the will of God to suffer, to starve, or even to die. But he who swore to provide for our every need in Christ does just that. "Where can I go from your presence?" David asked. Where can we go that casts us beyond Yahweh's ability to deliver? Certainly not the grave (Ps 139:7–12). In fact, there seems to be a corollary between our circumstances and God's involvement in our life: the direr our situation becomes, the more he makes himself known.[27]

Paul believed as much—"Indeed, we felt that we had received the sentence of death. But that was to make us rely not on ourselves but on God who raises the dead. He delivered us from such a deadly peril, and he will deliver us. On him we have set our hope that he will deliver us again" (2 Cor 1:9–10). Kingdoms are never lost for lack of resources or opportunities, but for lack of faith. In the New Testament, Jesus drew attention to this widow's faith (Luke 4:25–26), something that didn't sit well with his hometown church-goers, and this merits our reflection. Relying on ourselves, and not the Savior, to supply our every need robs us of seeing God at his best. Perhaps we fear dire circumstances so much

---

24. Nelson, *First and Second Kings*, 111.

25. It's clear the boy's breath had left him (v. 17), and in Hebrew thought, when breath leaves a person, death has arrived (cf. Job 34:14–15).

26. Walton, *Bible Background*, 377.

27. "Thus, as the challenges by death grow in intensity, God himself becomes more actively involved in the life-sustaining process, no longer commanding others, but himself taking the initiative against death and overcoming death's challenges," (Hauser, "Yahweh Versus Death," 22).

because we know God will show up in them, and we believe, as the widow did, that some sin will then be exposed. We forget that God already knows our sin, and not all dire circumstances are due to sin in the first place.

Rather than always seeking to punish someone somewhere, God instead always acts to glorify himself (John 9:3), and acting to confirm the veracity and potency of his Word is one such way of gaining that glory. In the widow's final words, she confessed her trust in Elijah's prophetic ministry (v. 24). Perhaps, as we face dire circumstances of our own, we should not focus on what we did to deserve such misfortune, but rather seek opportunities to magnify Christ in our suffering and so confirm his Word to the lost.

1 KINGS 18:1-19

After nearly three years[28] of drought, it was time for Elijah to confront Ahab and Jezebel once again. At God's direction, Elijah emerged from hiding.[29] The irony, however, is that all this time, "Elijah has been living only a few miles from Jezebel's home town, [yet] he has not been discovered. Ahab, like Baal, is impotent. He can do nothing."[30]

---

28. "In the New Testament (Jas. 5:17), it is said that the drought lasted three and a half years, but this number is symbolic. Three and a half was a half of seven, the sacred number of the sabbath. In some Jewish literature three and a half was used to symbolize disaster," (Robinson, *First Book*, 199). "The significance of this number becomes apparent when we consider the agricultural practices in ancient Israel. The threat of crop failure led the farmers of this land to plant, harvest, and store their grain in a strategic way. The grain harvest from the current year was placed into storage for the following year as a buffer against famine. Thus the Israelite family would eat the grain they had harvested from their fields the previous season. If a drought ruined the crop from the current growing season, they had the insurance of a one-year grain reserve. Since the famine described in our text had lasted into the third year, those reserves had expired," (John A. Beck, "Geography as Irony: The Narrative-Geographical Shaping of Elijah's Duel with the Prophets of Baal [1 Kings 18]," *SJOT* 17 [2003]: 295).

29. Davis argues that Elijah's hiding in 1 Kings 17 should not be seen as such. "The disappearance of Elijah spells the absence of the word of God from the life of Israel. Israel's judgment is the drought of the land and the silence of the Lord. Scripture always treats the withdrawal of God's word and the silence of his voice as an agonizing judgment (see 1 Sam. 28:6, 15; Ps. 74:9; Amos 8:11–12)," (*1 Kings*, 207; cf. DeVries, *1 Kings*, 218).

30. Provan, *1 & 2 Kings*, 136.

We are introduced to a righteous servant of God named Obadiah. Though he served as the administrator[31] of Ahab's palace, "Obadiah feared the LORD greatly" (v. 3). At considerable risk to himself, he secreted away a hundred prophets— their opposition to Ahab and Jezebel being as much political as it was religious— in various caves in Israel and kept them alive with small rations of bread and water. There are over two thousand known caves in the region of Mount Carmel (cf. Amos 9:3), so the plausibility of Obadiah pulling this off is unquestioned.[32]

Ahab sent Obadiah out on a mission to find water and grass for his horses and mules. In his memoirs of the battle of Qarqar, Shalmaneser III recalled how Ahab had contributed two thousand chariots to the coalition that resisted the Assyrian monarch. Considering there would be at least two horses per chariot (and likely three), Ahab had a lot of hungry, thirsty equines in his charge, and three years of drought could not have been easy on them.

While searching, Obadiah stumbled upon the prophet and fell on his face in disbelief. Elijah bid him to bring Ahab to him, but Obadiah believed that to be a death wish. Ahab had left no stone unturned in his pursuit of Elijah—"There is no nation or kingdom where my lord has not sent to seek you. And when they would say, 'He is not here,' he would take an oath of the kingdom or nation, that they had not found you" (v. 10).[33] So talented had Elijah been at hide-and-seek[34] that Obadiah fully expected the prophet to disappear once again as soon as he

---

31. Obadiah's role in Ahab's administration seems to have been economic in nature, similar to Joseph's role in Pharaoh's service (Gen 41:40, 47–57; 47:13–26). "The function of the 'one who is over the house' in Egypt consisted in management of all the Pharaoh's assets and streams of income. He administered his houses, his fields, his storehouses, his herds, etc.," (Izabela Eph'al-Jaruzelska, "Officialdom and Society in the Book of Kings: The Social Relevance of the State," in *The Books of Kings: Sources, Composition, Historiography and Reception*, eds., André Lemaire and Baruch Halpern [Leiden: Brill, 2010], 483).

32. "Even Obadiah is more effective than Baal, because he provides water to prophets of Yahweh. Prophets may be hiding in caves and in Gentile territory, but even there Yahweh provides food," (Leithart, *1 & 2 Kings*, 133).

33. In the ancient Near East, it was common for nations to have extradition treaties with one another in the cases of insurrectionists or runaway slaves. "In Ahab's eyes, Elijah was a fugitive from justice, inasmuch as his words and deeds had threatened the regime; thus, Ahab could call upon allied kingdoms to extradite Elijah if he were found in their territory," (Cogan, *I Kings*, 438).

34. "Elijah had so frequently successfully eluded Ahab's officers that he gained a reputation as the possessor of supernatural powers," (Robinson, *First Book*, 206).

had fetched the king, and then there would be no more Obadiah. But Elijah gave his word that such would not happen,[35] and Obadiah did as he was told.

Obadiah's faithfulness to Yahweh and the servants of Yahweh must not be discounted. He is one of countless individuals who play very minor supporting roles in the biblical epic, yet whose faithfulness played no small part in the advancement of God's purposes in the world.[36] His fear is understandable—he claims three times Ahab will kill him (vv. 9, 12, 14)[37]—yet it is starkly juxtaposed with Elijah's cool, confident, calm demeanor. The gritty prophet had just spent three years being provided for by the hand of Yahweh, so he fears no power of hell, nor scheme of man.

When Ahab laid eyes on the prophet, he greeted him by calling Elijah the "troubler[38] of Israel." In the deluded mind of Israel's king, Elijah was solely to blame for the dire situation Israel in which found herself—politicians are skilled in shifting blame and passing the buck. In Hebrew, the verb form of *troubler* meant "to entangle, put into disorder, bring disaster, throw into confusion, ruin."[39] Just as Achan had once brought trouble (and almost ruin) on Israel (Josh 6:18; 7:25; cf. Saul, 1 Sam 14:29) and had to be eliminated for the good of the

---

35. "His instruction to Obadiah to proclaim 'Elijah is here' translates literally from the Hebrew (*hinneh 'eliyahu*), 'Behold, Yahweh is my God.' Hence, the prophet is requiring of this servant much more than the disclosure that Elijah has been found. The prophet requires of Obadiah what he will eventually require of the people of Israel—to proclaim a faith in Yahweh and thus denounce a pledge of fidelity to this royal power and its Baalistic backing," (Hens-Piazza, *1–2 Kings*, 175–76).

36. Brueggemann encourages, "We may well reread the Bible with attention to 'minor' figures who live at the edge of the narrative in dangerous, faithful ways," (*1 & 2 Kings*, 221).

37. "This is ironically parallel to the conundrum the Phoenician widow faced in 17:18. When a prophet of God shows up, the situation often escalates to life-or-death levels," (Barnes, *1–2 Kings*, 155).

38. "The 'troubler' is one who disturbs the well-being of the community by acting for self against healthy social relationships. The prophets were often perceived as troublers because they dissented from conventional reality and raised awkward questions. Thus Hosea is dismissed as a 'fool' who is 'mad' (Hos 9:7); Jeremiah is reckoned to be a traitor for undermining the war effort (Jer 38:4). And surely Elijah is a profound social disturbance. The work of prophets is to raise questions and expose what is taken for granted when it is in fact destructive," (Brueggemann, *1 & 2 Kings*, 222).

39. *HALOT* 824. Gray intriguingly notes that "the verb is found in Arabic denoting the pollution of water by mud," (*I & II Kings*, 349).

community, so Ahab believed Elijah's life must be snuffed out if the drought was to abate. But Ahab's sin had blinded him to the fact that he, not Elijah, was the Achan in this particular story, and Elijah says as much: "I have not troubled Israel, but you have, and your father's house, because you have abandoned the commandments of the LORD and followed the Baals" (v. 18).

Christians sin, and thus we must always be willing to heed rebuke humbly when it is justified. But for every occasion when repentance is necessary, there are many more when the faithful are falsely accused of being the problem. It is the world's favorite tactic—to slander the elect as troublers of the community. Indeed, Satan is the great accuser who loves to malign the people of God "day and night" (Rev 12:10). When this happens, we must not concede or capitulate, but remain firm in our resolve, confident that no one can succeed in bringing a false charge against the elect if it is God who justifies (Rom 8:33).[40]

In our culture, anyone who upsets the peace of the community for any reason is often perceived as the troubler. But what if it is the status quo that is troubling?[41] What if the "troubler" is seeking to restore the shalom God so desperately desires for each of us? In reflecting on this very principle, Brueggemann invokes the Civil Rights protesters of the 1960s. Just as America is popularly assumed to be a place of "liberty and justice for all," kings in ancient times were responsible for social justice and the general welfare of their subjects. Likewise, protesters of the Civil Rights era "were thought to be disturbers of the peace, when in fact it was accepted, distorted social relationships that caused trouble of a deep, unnoticed kind."[42]

In families and churches, as well as businesses and communities, truth-tellers can be mistaken for troublemakers. A word of reproof, rebuke, or exhortation can be readily interpreted as evidence of prejudice, bitterness, or arrogance. But individuals committed to "truthing in love" (Eph 4:15) are crucial to the shalom of any family, church, or community. A church no longer continuing in the apostles' doctrine; a contentious marriage headed toward irreparable dissolution; a

---

40. "We entrust ourselves to the God who judges justly, the God who will vindicate those who trust in him and are able to resist the paralyzing scapegoating of those who are enemies of the gospel," (Leithart, *1 & 2 Kings*, 133, n. 1).

41. "Is it the instrument of divine judgment who causes the pain, or those who have provoked that judgment? It is easy to blame God for our suffering when we have caused it ourselves," (DeVries, *1 Kings*, 219).

42. Brueggemann, *1 & 2 Kings*, 222.

society hell-bent on betraying its heritage, silencing dissenters, and suppressing the truth—who will rise to trouble a troubling status quo?

For his part, Elijah had had enough of Ahab's slander. To expose the king's god as a fraud, the prophet challenged Ahab and the false prophets of Baal and Asherah, those held in such high esteem by the queen of Israel, to meet him for the greatest contest of all time. The conflict at Carmel would prove to be one of the most dramatic scenes in Scripture.

1 KINGS 18:20-46

Located in northwestern Israel about thirty miles south of the Bay of Acre on the Mediterranean coast, Mount Carmel and the Carmel Ridge divide Israel's coastal plain in half, and at times served as the border between Israel and Phoenicia. Like many other mountains in antiquity, it was considered sacred; it was the site of an ancient altar to Israel's God and also, at this point, a shrine to Baal.[43] It was here that a lone prophet of Yahweh and a multitude of prophets of Baal faced off against one another.

Elijah's initial question to his audience was, "How long will you go limping between two different opinions?"[44] (v. 21). The verb translated "limping" is used only two other times in Scripture. The first (2 Sam 4:4) is in reference to Jonathan's son, Mephibosheth, who was crippled. The other is later in v. 26, "describing the way the Baal priests 'danced,' apparently a pun ridiculing their behavior."[45] Literally, Elijah was asking, "How long will you hobble on two crutches?" The body politic in Israel was sick and lame, torn in two directions—Baal versus Yahweh—and attempting to rely on both of them. The people's silent response

---

43. "While both the LORD and Baal had made a claim on this mountain, the ruined altar of the Israelite God made it clear who was king of this hill. It belonged to Baal. And the duel with Elijah was to occur on their home field. But [...] on the very spot where they were most confident of success, the prophets of Baal failed," (Beck, "Geography as Irony," 299). "It is possible that the contest took place at the foot of the mountain rather than on its summit. Sacred mountains usually featured the places of worship at their base rather than at the summit, which would have been considered holy ground inaccessible to the populace. Elijah eventually ascends to the summit to offer his prayer for rain (v. 42)," (Walton, *Bible Background*, 378).

44. "The Hebrew idiom here is akin to our English expression 'sitting on the fence,'" (Barnes, *1–2 Kings*, 156).

45. House, *1, 2 Kings*, 219, n. 22.

to Elijah's question amounted to a concession that the prophet was right, so Elijah sought to settle everything once and for all.

The prophet's proposal called for two altars, two bulls, two sacrifices, but no fire. With everything prepared, each group would call on Baal or Yahweh respectively, requesting that their altars be kindled with divine fire. Surely with an entourage of 450 sycophantic prophets, Baal could be persuaded to perform. The storm god of Canaan had to have a few lightning bolts laying around that could be spared for his dedicated servants—he was, after all, thought by the ancients to be the god in control of fire and lightning.[46]

But no fire would be coming from Baal. Elijah had accused Israel of limping between two opinions; now, and for several hours, the prophetic frauds "limped[47] around the altar that they had made" (v. 26). Elijah derided[48] their pathetic attempts to start the fire, and paraphrase translations really bring out the salty spite the Tishbite laid upon them: "'Pray louder!' he said. 'Baal must be a god. Maybe he's day-dreaming or using the toilet or traveling somewhere. Or maybe he's asleep, and you have to wake him up'" (v. 27 CEV).

George E. Saint-Laurent observes, "Elijah has good reason to refer to Baal being 'pre-occupied' in terms of the Baal-cycle, which speaks of a very busy god indeed, concerned about a wide variety of matters, from the building of his castle, to the defeat of his rivals, to the satisfaction of his prodigious sexual appetite. There is also a basis for the mocking suggestion that perhaps Baal is 'on a journey.'" He goes on to cite various stories of Baal not being at home when expected and of the god being fatigued and needing sleep.[49]

---

46. Leah Bronner, *The Stories of Elijah and Elisha: As Polemics Against Baal Worship* (Leiden: Brill, 1968), 54–65.

47. H. H. Rowley, "Elijah on Mount Carmel," *BJRL* 43 (1960): 204–5.

48. Of Elijah's attitude, Maclaren offers this warning: "Sarcasm is not the highest weapon, and the 'spirit of Elijah' is not the spirit of Jesus; but the exposure of the absurdity of idolatry is legitimate, and even ridicule may have its place in pricking wind-distended bladders. A man throttling a serpent may be excused using anything that comes handy for the purpose. But, at the same time, the right attitude for us as Christians in the presence of that awful fact of idolatry, is neither contempt nor scientific curiosity, but pity deep as Christ's, and earnest resolve to help our darkened brethren," (*Expositions*, 4:256–57).

49. George E. Saint-Laurent, "Light from Ras Shamra on Elijah's Ordeal upon Mount Carmel," in *Scripture in Context: Essays on the Comparative Method*, eds. Carl D. Evans, William W. Hallo, John B. White (Pittsburgh: Pickwick, 1980), 133–34. He concludes, "The discovered literature of Ras Shamra has become our principal source for understanding a strangely fascinating

Indeed, the activity rendered as "busy" in some translations (e.g., NCV, NIV, NKJV) appears in the Old Testament only here and literally meant "to go away" or "to go to the side," but was, in fact, Hebrew slang for a bowel movement.[50] And the taunt that he was asleep was likely a jab that Baal had been done in for the year by Mot (sleep often being a metaphor for death). As noon came and went, the prophets began slashing their wrists (an act well-attested in ancient religious rites) in a mournful effort to trigger Baal's sympathy or resurrection from the dead (cf. Lev 19:28; 21:5; Deut 14:1; Jer 16:6; 41:5). But "there was no voice. No one answered; no one paid attention" (v. 29).[51]

This, in fact, is a damning indictment on idolatry. False gods, whether ancient or modern, fail miserably to deliver or redeem us when such is most needed. There is no voice. There is no answer. No one pays us any attention.[52] Nearly three thousand years ago on Carmel's hillside, it was a false god's failure to start the fire. Today, this reality takes other forms. The idol of politics and government will always leave us feeling forsaken and ignored. The idol of materialism will always leave us feeling forsaken and ignored. Relationships. Health. Pleasure. Work. Anything or anyone that becomes our ultimate passion and pursuit will leave us empty, unless that One is he who has loved us since before the foundation of the world. When our despair is deep and need is great, we'll cry out for aid, but there will be no voice, no answer. No one will pay attention.

---

religion which previously could speak to us only through the compositions of its archenemies, the sacred writers of Israel. Now we can understand the full thrust of anti-Baalistic polemics as well as the broad meaning of Baalism itself as a deification of the forces of nature through mythology," (Ibid., 134–35).

50. *HALOT* 1319; cf. Gary A. Rendsburg, "The Mock of Baal in 1 Kings 18:27," *CBQ* 50 (1988): 414–17.

51. Brueggemann notes, "The Hebrew has the flat negative particle *'ain* five times! None, not any ever! Baal is absent, silent, indifferent, unresponsive, uncaring, unwilling to answer. His devotees are abandoned and on their own. They cried aloud, they cut themselves, they raved… nothing!" (*1 & 2 Kings*, 224).

52. "The problem with Baal (as with idols more generally; see Ps. 115:3–8; Isa. 44:10, 17; Jer. 10:5) is not that he is distant and removed (he does that well!), but that he does not listen or speak or feel or act or care," (Fretheim, *First and Second Kings*, 105).

E ventually, Elijah had experienced enough amusement, and so he called the people to come closer, lest they think he had fooled them with sleight of hand. They repaired the traditional altar of Yahweh on Carmel, one that had fallen into disrepair in recent times under Ahab and Jezebel's watch. The prophet took twelve stones—representing the tribes and thus Israel's "identity as the LORD's people" (cf. vv. 30–31; Exod 24:4; Josh 4:1–9)[53]—to remake the altar and dug a trench large enough to hold 3½ gallons of water. With the sacrifice arranged, Elijah then requested that twelve jars of water be poured over all of it. Everything was soaked; the excess water filled the trench around the altar.

With that, the prophet turned his eyes to heaven and prayed. He invoked the names of the patriarchs, a reminder (not so much to God as to those present at Caramel) that Israel had a history with this God. He called upon Yahweh to act so as to make himself known to Israel, to validate the prophet's deeds, and to turn his people back to the Lord. Desiring that God would make himself known and thereby reclaim the lost is among the noblest prayers we can offer.

In response to the gritty prophet's prayer, the fire of Yahweh (commonly presumed to have been a lightning bolt, which would have amounted to beating Baal at his own game) descended in dramatic fashion and consumed everything. "The burnt offering and the wood and the stones and the dust, and licked up the water that was in the trench" (v. 38). In Israel's collective memory, fire was often indicative of the presence of the holy (Exod 3:2; 24:17), as well as divine approval of the sacrifice (Lev 9:24; 1 Chr 21:26; 2 Chr 7:3). So all-consuming was this fire from heaven that not even the altar survived. As Yahweh had claimed Sinai as his mountain via descending fire (Exod 19:18), he now did so with Carmel. "What seems at first to be a battle between two competing gods turns out instead to be a contest between God and an empty delusion."[54]

After the roar from heaven, the people fell to the ground, confessing Yahweh as the only God (cf. Deut 4:35, 39; 7:9; Pss 95:7; 100:3; 105:7). Elijah ordered the execution[55] of the false prophets; such bloodshed may offend our twenty-first-century sensibilities, but it served two purposes. First, Jezebel's slaughter of Yahweh's prophets (vv. 4, 13) had to be avenged. Second, Elijah was

---

53. Provan, *1 & 2 Kings*, 138, 142.

54. Nelson, *First and Second Kings*, 121.

55. The verb used here occurs some fifty-one times in the Old Testament for slaughtering a sacrifice on the altar. In the same way, this execution was a ritual slaughter under the watch of Yahweh.

leading Israel in a recommitment to the covenant, one that demanded the execution of all false prophets (Deut 13:1–5). Into the Kishon ran the blood of the slain prophets; the medieval Jewish philosopher Gersonides claimed that this was "so that their blood would not pollute the land; and on this account, it was spilled into the wadi that would carry it far off."[56]

E lijah's command to Ahab to eat and drink before the rain comes (v. 41) seems odd, but the instruction was part of a covenant renewal ceremony, not unlike the meal on Sinai (Exod 24:9–11). Ahab's cooperation presents us with an intriguing reality. From v. 19, it seems Jezebel was the catalyst for Baal-worship in Israel; she clearly wore the pants in her family. Ahab will prove himself quite capable of meriting condemnation for himself, but his willingness to turn back to Yahweh here should not go without notice. His heart was not completely evil.[57]

With such an impressive display of divine sovereignty, the Lord was now ready to restore rain to Israel. Elijah went up near the summit of Carmel and assumed a prone position with his head between his knees. In this posture, he prayed fervently (Jas 5:18) that Yahweh would end the drought and send rain to Israel (cf. Deut 28:12). He then instructed his servant to climb the summit seven times and report back as to what he saw. The first six times? Nothing. On the seventh? A cloud, but no larger than a man's fist.

And just like that, where there had just been a cloudless sky, the heavens quickly darkened "with clouds and wind, and there was a great rain" (v. 45). This wasn't a light afternoon shower—I like to imagine that what descended on Israel was what we would call in the South a "gully washer." And with this sudden tor-

---

56. Quoted in Cogan, I Kings, 444. "Like Jesus' warnings about hell, the story is meant to leave us horrified and to make us face the possible consequences of making the wrong choice about whether to follow the real God, who has made himself known to us," (Goldingay, 1 and 2 Kings for Everyone, 88).

57. "Ahab's eating and drinking on Mount Carmel, in the aftermath of Yahweh's decisive display of power against the forces of Baalism, confers divine approval upon Ahab's kingship. Just as the sacred meal on Mount Sinai was a reassuring sign of the deity's acceptance and affirmation, so Ahab's sacred meal establishes his role as Yahweh's representative. Ahab's eating and drinking on the mountain seals the covenant and legitimizes his kingship," (Kathryn L. Roberts, "God, Prophet, and King: Eating and Drinking on the Mountain in First Kings 18:41," CBQ 62 [2000]: 644; cf. Walsh, 1 Kings, 286).

rent, Yahweh's victory over Baal is made complete.[58] "God sustains and protects his prophets, while Baal lets his die. Yahweh feeds the orphans and widows and raises the dead, while Baal lets the needy suffer and requires Anat to raise him from death. Yahweh can send fire or rain from heaven, but Baal cannot respond to his most valiant worshipers. A god like Baal is no God at all. A God like Yahweh must be God of all. Rain is not just rain here, but evidence of the Lord's absolute sovereignty over nature and human affairs."[59]

Elijah instructed his servant to inform Ahab to beat a path home, lest the rain catch him.[60] And only then are we treated to one of Scripture's most impressive scenes—the sight of Elijah outrunning Ahab's chariot down the slippery, muddy slopes of Carmel and on to Jezreel, about seventeen miles away. Leithart reminds us, "A runner before a king is a herald and a king's servant [cf. 1:5], and Elijah returns to Jezreel to announce that the blessing of Yahweh has returned to the land and to proclaim the return of the king to one of his chief cities."[61] Admittedly, it is an odd scene—Elijah running before Ahab's chariot as if he is the kings' servant. But it is fitting and appropriate if we are right in the conclusion that (for now) Ahab has committed himself to Yahweh as God.[62]

---

58. "From the moment Elijah steps into the presence of Ahab (18,16), through the time when the Baal prophets are on center stage, we do not find a drop of water. The only liquid we hear about is their own blood being shed in an act of imitative magic as they seek to release rain from the sky. And in an ironic twist, when the rain comes they are not there to see it. Rain only arrives after they are removed from Mount Carmel and executed in the Jezreel Valley (18,40). By contrast, water is regularly mentioned in association with the representatives of Israel's God. Obadiah has water to give the prophets he has hidden (18,4.13) and Elijah appears to have plenty of water to pour on the intended sacrifice (18,33-35)," (Beck, "Geography as Irony," 300).

59. House, *1, 2 Kings*, 221.

60. "In antiquity the [Kishon] river swelled during the winter months and flooded the entire region between Megiddo and Nazareth, making passage nearly impossible. This is the reason the prophet urged Ahab to return to Jezreel without delay (18:44)," (Monson, "1 Kings," 80).

61. Leithart, *1 & 2 Kings*, 136; cf. Robert L. Cohn, "The Literary Logic of 1 Kings 17–19," *JBL* 101 (1982): 341. In a similar way, kings believed their patron deities ran before their chariots in battle (Monson, "1 Kings," 81; cf. Walton, *Bible Background*, 379). If this image is at play, then Elijah's running before Ahab's chariot represented that God's blessing now rested on the king.

62. "We think it much more likely that, having won Ahab's sympathy in his triumph on Carmel, he [Elijah] now sought to exploit the situation in face of Jezebel's opposition in Jezreel, well knowing the support that Ahab needed against that dominant lady. Furthermore Elijah, through whose agency the rain was coming, wanted to exploit popular opinion in the queen's presence when the rain actually did come," (Gray, *I & II Kings*, 361).

1 KINGS 19

Among the most puzzling paradoxes of the spiritual life is that our greatest lows often follow on the heels of our greatest highs.[63] In the immediate aftermath of such a great victory for the Lord's cause in Israel, Elijah fell off the cliff into a spiritual abyss and almost never recovered. The prophet had no desire to continue his ministry, but rather resigned himself to death. His Boss, however, refused his resignation. Only God's faithfulness kept Elijah from perishing in the abyss, proving that the Lord's most meaningful work is done when we are at our worst—not our best (cf. 2 Cor 12:9).

Upon his return to his winter palace at Jezreel, Ahab informed his wife of what had happened at the contest on Carmel, and particularly of the massacre of Jezebel's prophets. Ahab had come dangerously close to giving all religious authority in Israel to Elijah and endorsing the national revival, so Jezebel had to act fast. In retaliation, she coldly and calculatingly sent a messenger to Elijah, swearing to dump his corpse in the waters of the Kishon (just like the other prophets) within twenty-four hours.

Elijah's response surprises us. From a man who had just faced down hundreds of prophets, summoned fire from heaven, and spurred a national revival, we would expect more courage and fortitude—and not a little swagger. But our gritty prophet is no more, transformed by fear into a coward.[64] Like Obadiah, he knows the queen is capable of fulfilling her vow. At Jezebel's threat, Elijah fled for his life over a hundred miles south to Beersheba.

Since mention of her marriage to Ahab at the end of 1 Kings 16, this is really the first we have heard from Jezebel. Though she plays a minor role in Kings, it is no surprise that she is one of Scripture's leading bad girls, "as worthy an opponent as God's servants ever face in Scripture."[65] Jezebel seems to have a much more dominant personality than her husband; with her threat to Elijah, she accomplished her ultimate goal: getting the trouble-making prophet to leave the

---

63. "The ensuing narrative has been a biblical example in many analyses of emotional collapse and depression," (Olley, *Message of Kings*, 178). This passage is of particular importance for ministers; every discussion I've ever heard on ministerial burnout has considered this narrative.

64. Contra Allen, who argues that Elijah was broken but not afraid of Jezebel (Ronald Barclay Allen, "Elijah the Broken Prophet," *JETS* 22 [1979], 195–201).

65. House, *1, 2 Kings*, 222.

country.[66] The turnaround is striking: "In three short verses the writer has totally changed the flow of the story. Victory seems to be transformed into defeat, the brave prophet into a cowering refugee, and the victory over death and Baal into an opportunity for death to reassert itself through Jezebel's oath to take Elijah's life."[67]

Leaving his servant at Beersheba (twenty-five miles southwest of Hebron), Elijah went another "day's journey" into the desert and collapsed under a broom or juniper (NASU) tree.[68] That Elijah went beyond Beersheba—the southern terminus of the Promised Land and as far from Jezebel as he could get without leaving Israel or Judah—alone into the wilderness may indicate that "he has given up his ministry altogether."[69] There under the tree, he begged God to take his life; it was only a matter of time before he died anyway. Bizarrely, "having wrested from Jezebel the chance to have him assassinated, he now bares his neck to God and asks him to be the executioner!"[70] But Elijah recognizes none of this absurdity. Rather, "he lies down in the shade of a bush with [...] the prayer that many have quietly repeated since: not to wake up again in the morning."[71]

I make no excuses for Elijah, and certainly not for myself. But I know what it is to feel so empty and forsaken that you want to go to sleep and never awake. Though, unlike the prophet, I have never had anyone actively seeking to take my life, I wanted mine to end nonetheless. I first felt it in college when my dad passed away suddenly and unexpectedly. I felt it again when my son did the same. In between those two tragedies, I frequently found myself beset by depression and lacking a will to continue living because the challenges and trials before me—

---

66. Merecz presents a convincing case that Jezebel was bluffing in an attempt to get Elijah to leave Israel (Robert J. Merecz, "Jezebel's Oath [1 Kgs 19,2]," *Bib* 90 [2009]: 257–59). "The threat is a convention because if Jezebel had actually intended to arrest Elijah she would have sent her bailiffs and not her messenger, giving him a day's head start," (DeVries, *1 Kings*, 235).

67. Hauser, "Yahweh Versus Death," 63. "The message of death sent by Jezebel effectively immobilizes as a prophet of Yahweh the very one who had earlier been inspired by the word from Yahweh to show Yahweh's power over both Baal and death. That a message threatening death has so much power to affect Elijah is one means the writer has used to express again the power of death as a foe of Yahweh," (Ibid., 61).

68. This bush or shrub can grow up to twelve feet and is found in abundance in the deserts of Sinai and Palestine (Harrison, "Broom Tree," *ISBE* 1:550).

69. House, *1, 2 Kings*, 222; cf. DeVries, *1 Kings*, 235.

70. Auld, *I & II Kings*, 123.

71. Ibid.

financial, physical, ecclesiastical, relational—seemed insurmountable. Looking back, I made three crucial mistakes that Elijah also made, as we are about to see.

While the prophet slept, a divine messenger appeared in answer to his prayer.[72] Miraculously, there appeared beside Elijah a cake and some water. He was commanded to eat, and then he fell asleep again.[73] Again, an angel appeared and woke him, ordering him to eat once more. Through this provision, God was preparing Elijah for a forty-day journey to Horeb or Sinai, a mountain that had not been a part of Israel's history since the time of Moses.[74]

I n choosing to flee instead of fight, and in giving into fear versus faith, Elijah made three crucial mistakes. *First, he forgot to think theologically* and, for the first time in the narrative of his life, merely reacted to circumstances.[75] Thinking theologically would have helped him realize that God was no less powerful after Carmel than he had been before. The same Yahweh who had protected and provided for him then would do so now. In fact, the *cake* provided to Elijah in v. 6 is a verbal link to 17:13 and God's provision for the prophet via the widow of Zarephath. Moreover, the Israelites had made cakes out of the manna they received in the wilderness (Num 11:8), and this was not the first time that miraculous provision had been made by God in the region of Beersheba (Gen 21:8–21).[76]

Down by six runs in the bottom of the ninth inning, a baseball team can more easily rally to victory if they think, "We've won games like this plenty of times; why should this one be any different?" In the same way, Christians can

---

72. Brueggemann reminds us, "Sleep (when the guard is down) is a time when the inscrutable powers of God work their will with us," (*1 & 2 Kings*, 234).

73. "You cannot isolate the spiritual from the physical for we are body, mind and spirit. The greatest and the best Christians when they are physically weak are more prone to an attack of spiritual depression than at any other time and there are great illustrations of this in the Scriptures," (D. Martin Lloyd-Jones, *Spiritual Depression* [Grand Rapids: Eerdmans, 1965], 19).

74. There are, in fact, several points of contact between this story in 1 Kings 19 and the life of Moses (cf. Mal 4:4–5). See Cogan, *I Kings*, 456–57; Patterson, "1, 2 Kings," 782. "In scriptural tradition Elijah has come to occupy a position as a successor to Moses in prophetic authority. The narrative of Elijah creates an association with Moses as a prophet with a distinguished mission in the life of Israel," (Konkel, *1 & 2 Kings*, 308).

75. Provan, *1 & 2 Kings*, 144.

76. Wray Beal notes parallels between this narrative and that of Hagar and Ishmael in Genesis 21:14–21 (*1 & 2 Kings*, 252).

weather the terrible circumstances of the present by recalling God's past faithfulness and provision. If Elijah had viewed his circumstances through the lens of God's previous acts, he might not have so easily succumbed to fear.

Second, Elijah exposed an inordinate pride that had taken root in his heart as a result of his ministry successes (vv. 4, 10, 14). This was the product of not thinking theologically. In the frustration he spewed forth to the Lord, it's clear the prophet considered himself God's #1 all-time all-star; none of the gains made would have been possible without him; Elijah was indispensable to what Yahweh was doing in Israel.[77] And if Elijah was about to be offed, the Lord might as well throw in the towel.

Placed in such stark terms, such a mindset seems too absurd to be possible. Surely no one could actually think that. But they can; I've thought that before. I think nearly every one of God's servants has thought this at some point—that we are indispensable to God's work. But such thinking inevitably leads to depression, burnout, and collapse, and for the simple reason that we were never meant to carry the weight of the world successfully. We aren't wired that way.[78] Pride gives way to stress, and stress gives way to falling off the cliff as Elijah did. Inrig warns, "When people get big and the Lord gets small, we are headed for trouble!"[79]

Finally, Elijah stopped believing he was in a special relationship with God, and thus was "no better than my fathers" (v. 4).[80] "Elijah's memory is selective indeed. The resistance of one woman has in Elijah's mind turned massive victory into overwhelming defeat. [...] Somewhere between exaggerated self-loathing and exaggerated self-importance—both partly the product of selective memory—there is a quiet place where Elijah must rest content with who he is and what he has done. The key is to remember his past with the LORD."[81]

My dad often liked to say that we serve a Commander-in-Chief who has never known defeat. Despite what we might think, *setback* is not a part of God's vocabulary. Paul did not claim that we are conquerors, but "more than conquer-

---

77. "Elijah had come to bask in the glow of the spectacular. He may have fully expected that because of what had been accomplished at Mount Carmel, Jezebel would capitulate and pagan worship would come to an end in Israel—all through his influence!" (Patterson, "1, 2 Kings, 782).

78. "The despair of Elijah demonstrates the frailty of human strength and the power of God that is liberated within human weakness," (Konkel, *1 & 2 Kings*, 302).

79. Inrig, *I & II Kings*, 159.

80. Cogan, *I Kings*, 451.

81. Provan, *1 & 2 Kings*, 145.

ors," and we are such, not because of any inherent goodness or skill on our parts, but "through him who loved us" (Rom 8:37). Yes, it is God's favored election of his people that makes us victors. Because we are in a special relationship with him, you and I are winners automatically. Elijah lost sight of this and panicked.

I n a cave[82] at Sinai, Elijah found shelter. It was then that he heard the Lord speak: "What are you doing here, Elijah?" We must remember that Yahweh, like any good attorney, never asks a question to which he doesn't know the answer. Rather, he often asks such questions to beckon us out of self-deception and into self-disclosure (e.g., Gen 3:9; 4:9). Elijah's reply was textbook narcissism, too often a byproduct of depression. The prophet professed his zeal for God and declared himself the lone righteous soul in Israel. But "in his response to the divine mediator, he does not count even on the angel who has ministered to him."[83]

At this, God beckoned him to the opening of the cave, and as he had done with Moses, he now did with Elijah. The Lord's presence passed by Elijah at Sinai. The presence was followed by a great wind, an earthquake, and fire, but Yahweh was actually not present in any of these physical phenomena. The fire, however, was followed by a whisper, and it was in this gentle whisper[84] that Yahweh again asked, "What are you doing here, Elijah?"

Elijah's reply was the same as before, with only a very subtle shift in emphasis.[85] To this, the Lord responded with a three-pronged commission: anoint a

------

82. "In fact, the author denominates the refuge as 'the cave' (hammĕʿārāh), probably indicating the place on the mountain where Moses stood (Exod 33:21) when Yahweh passed by (ʿōbēr, v 22) as he now passes by (ʿōbēr, 19:11) before Elijah," (Cohn, "Literary Logic," 342).

83. Brueggemann, 1 & 2 Kings, 235.

84. A lot of scholarly attention has been focused on the meaning of the great wind, the earthquake, and the fire, and how God spoke through none of them, but only through the whisper. Hubbard (First and Second Kings, 101) suggests that, "like heralds who precede a king, the three natural phenomena announced the imminent arrival of Yahweh." Instead of a whisper, Brueggemann believes there was "no voice, no sound, but an eerie silence laden with a sense of holiness," (1 & 2 Kings, 236). There is also the issue of what this theophany says about God; many scholars suggest it is a reminder that God does not always work through spectacular fireworks, but quietly and behind the scenes.

85. "The first time this statement of defense is presented to the audience, the emphasis falls on Elijah's feelings (informative) but the precise reiteration exhibits Elijah's inflexibility and

new king over Aram, a new king over Israel, and a new prophet at Abel-meholah. In these three individuals, God would continue to accomplish his will for Israel and the world. He then concluded with a stark reminder to his despondent prophet: you aren't the only one living righteously. You are not alone. "I'm preserving for myself seven thousand[86] souls" (v. 18 Msg). Obadiah had secreted away a hundred such faithful men. And another named Micaiah would become a burr under Ahab's saddle in due time.[87]

The Lord's command in v. 15, "Go, return on your way," was essentially a directive for Elijah to resume his prophetic ministry, the ministry the prophet had tried to abandon when he fled Beersheba for the wilderness. What is more, the divine instruction to anoint a Gentile named Hazael as king over Aram constituted a demonstration that Yahweh was sovereign, not just over Israel or Judah, but over all the nations of the world. Even today, there is not a ruler of men that does not answer to our cosmic King (Rev 1:5).

As would be revealed later, God would use first Jehu, then Hazael, to judge the house of Ahab and end the international prestige Israel had enjoyed under the Omride dynasty. "Victory will come, in other words, as a result of political process—not through obviously spectacular demonstrations of divine power. It will arrive, not as a result of Elijah's efforts, but through the efforts of others."[88]

On the other hand, via Elisha's ministry, the Lord would continue to show his deep concern for those intent on serving him faithfully. Even today, the Lord uses

---

egocentrism (elucidating)," (Russell Gregory, "Irony and the Unmasking of Elijah," in *From Carmel to Horeb: Elijah in Crisis*, ed., Alan J. Hauser [Sheffield: Almond Press, 1990], 134).

86. Robinson claims that *seven thousand* here "is not to be taken literally. It is symbolic, made up of the combination of seven, the number which expresses completion [...] and thousand, the number which expresses magnitude. The point being made was that many struggles lay ahead but that God would ensure the survival of his faithful people," (*First Book*, 222).

87. "There are many Elijah's who today find their varied ministries on behalf of the church and world utterly beyond their own power. Burnt out, exhausted, tired of the unresponsive crowd, at the point of opting out. Perhaps time is needed: refreshment, nourishment, redirected or renewed ministry balance. But renewed ministry also comes in the recognition that it is not accomplished alone. There is a great company who have not bowed their knee to Baal, who are refreshment on the road. And in the company's midst is the one who carries his cross – and calls the company to the same task. The company walks with YHWH in their midst as Emmanuel, the Suffering Savior. Only in this is ministry empowered and accomplished with joy," (Wray Beal, *1 & 2 Kings*, 257–58).

88. Provan, *1 & 2 Kings*, 146–47.

his messengers and servants to bring a warning word of judgment and punishment to the wicked, yet a reassuring word of love and providence to the righteous.[89]

In yet another Mosaic connection, just as the lawgiver did not live to see Canaan, Elijah did not live to see the divine word fulfilled[90]—but it *was* fulfilled. Upon his rapture to heaven, Elijah's ministry passed to Elisha, and the latter played a part in the accession of Hazael and Jehu over Aram and Israel, respectively. God's servants must remember that God's plan is to be fulfilled in his own time, that we must play our role as instructed. We must remember that, though we might live and die without seeing all that God will do, we can take our final breath confident that the Word of the Lord will surely come to pass (Matt 24:35).

In the meantime, we can rest assured that we serve a Lord who knows what it is like to be frustrated and weakened. Jesus was attended by angels in the desert (Matt 4:1–11; cf. Luke 22:43), as was Elijah. And like the prophet, he left servants behind to continue the work. But he did not leave them as orphans. The Lord has never abandoned his people, and he never will (cf. Ps 91:11–13).

When we panic, feel defeated, and believe all is lost, let us do as Elijah did. Let us have a talk with the Lord. Let us recommit ourselves to his work and trust in his sovereignty. And let us leave the dark cave of self-pity behind for the fields ripe for harvest. "Therefore, my beloved brothers, be steadfast, immovable, always abounding in the work of the Lord, knowing that in the Lord your labor is not in vain" (1 Cor 15:58).

n response to Yahweh's reassurances, Elijah made the journey to Abel-meholah (located about twenty miles south of the Sea of Galilee) to anoint Elisha; this is the only time in Scripture that a prophet anoints his own successor. He found his protégé plowing with oxen[91] (cf. 1 Sam 11:5–6; Amos 7:14–15). His choice of Elisha as his prophetic successor was expressed by cast-

---

89. "Yahweh's appearance along with wind, earthquake, and fire also pictures what Yahweh will do with Israel. He is going to shake Israel down, but after he will speak quietly to his people, like a husband wooing back his wayward bride (Hos. 2:14–20)," (Leithart, *1 & 2 Kings*, 142, n. 3).

90. "Elijah must be content with being part of the plan and not *the plan itself*," (Provan, *1 & 2 Kings*, 147; emphasis his).

91. The twelve yoke of oxen may indicate that Elisha came from wealth and was thus giving up a lot to become Elijah's protégé, though it's possible "that certain tasks in farming were carried out collectively," (Fritz, *1 & 2 Kings*, 200).

ing his cloak on Elisha, a costly garment (cf. Josh 7:21, 24) that clearly identified its bearer as holding the prophetic office (cf. Num 20:25–28; 2 Kgs 1:8; 2:13–15; Zech 13:4). In so doing, he passed on to Elisha not only his mission, but also the divine ability to accomplish it.[92]

Before Elisha accepted the invitation to be Elijah's protégé and successor, he asked first to bid his family farewell, to which Elijah responded with something similar to "I have no problem with that," or, "Just remember you must follow me afterward."[93] Elisha's selection was proof that God had not yet given up on Israel, and Elisha's final celebration with his family was evidence that he was making a clean break with his former life. He had slaughtered, not sold, his oxen; once he put his hand to this new plow, he wouldn't look back (Luke 9:61–62).[94]

92. Konkel, 1 & 2 Kings, 304.

93. Hubbard, First and Second Kings, 103. "This is a strong challenge, possibly a rebuke to Elisha's request to say good-bye to his parents. At least, Elijah's response represents a sharp rhetorical reminder of how momentous Elisha's career change will be. Jesus likewise reminds us forcefully to 'count the cost' carefully if we are thinking of becoming his disciples (see Luke 14:25–35)," (Barnes, 1–2 Kings, 167).

94. Fretheim, First and Second Kings, 111. "Following God involves strenuous demands. Though a disciple of Christ, like a disciple of Elijah, must continue to live in this world, he can no longer be of it. There is only one direction for a disciple to go: forward—and that without misgivings and regrets. If he cannot make this commitment, it is better that he should stay home with his oxen," (DeVries, 1 Kings, 240; emphasis his).

TALKING POINTS

I t is easy to miss both the intimacy and the potency of God's word in Elijah's life. "In this stage of his ministry he is so near to God and so continually sensitive to what he says, that every significant movement he makes is prefaced by a command from God telling him to do exactly what he does," (cf. 17:3, 9; 18:1).[95] But there is also a potency when Elijah speaks *for* Yahweh. Elijah's mouth sparked drought, secured a widow's provision, raised the dead to life, and summoned fire from heaven—and it was because he spoke God's word. When we speak the same Word—in churches, in classes, in homes, in society, in life—do we actually expect anything to happen?[96] How quickly we forget that the Word is a dangerous weapon (Eph 6:17; Heb 4:12) and ought to be handled responsibly, but also expectantly. Like Elijah, let us develop an intimacy with God's Word, but also an expectation of its potency.

T o non-Christians, the theme of Yahweh versus Baal in these chapters and Elijah's insistence that Israel choose (18:21) can seem strange. We live in a country where the ability to choose one's own religion is a cherished liberty, and for good reason. But in a fallen world, religious freedom also brings with it the rise of tolerance, and a perverted definition of tolerance at that. "Tolerance has come to imply that it does not matter what one believes and has been used even to exclude religious faith from the 'public world.'"[97] It is imperative, then, that Christians confess—in word and deed—that one's religious convictions matter a great deal, and that those convictions ought to inform

---

95. Wallace, *1 Kings*, 108.

96. Ibid., 115.

97. Olley, *Message of Kings*, 176. Earlier, he noted, "In many places today Christian worship is practised alongside traditional rituals or contact with shamans or other spirit mediums, especially in times of sickness or trouble. In the secularised West the combination may be more subtle: the God and Father of our Lord Jesus Christ is seen as important in church and family life, but somehow in the worlds of business, politics, international conflict or religious diversity different rules apply: one must follow 'the way of business' or 'market forces'; 'love of enemies' is 'unrealistic'; God 'does not belong' in business or politics; faith 'belongs to your private life'. Elijah challenges every generation: if Yahweh is the only God, he is God of every sphere of life in every place in every age," (Ibid., 173).

and pervade every arena of life, for our God pervades every sphere of life. In a culture where God has been banished to the hidden corners of life, we must become walking testimonies to the fact that all of life begins, is sustained by, and ultimately returns to God (Rom 11:36).

f there's one solid piece of ministry advice in this section, it comes from 1 Kings 19. Elijah, in the depths of despair, wanted nothing more than to abandon his ministry completely and die. Servants of the Lord today can despair also. Sometimes the challenges seem too great. Other times, we believe ourselves too damaged or maligned ever to be of further use to God. But the same truth Elijah learned is the one we must accept. *No one's ministry is over until the Lord says so.* Whatever challenges stand in our way, and no matter how negatively others speak of us, the Lord alone is the one who decommissions us from service. Such resolve will be easier to sustain if we are constantly focused on what God has done for us in the past. Like Cherith and Zarephath, there have been times when the Lord provided focus when it seemed all hope was lost. Like Zarephath and Carmel, the Lord has done wondrous things through us and for us when it seemed the impossible was just that. "He has delivered us from such a deadly peril, and he will deliver us again. On him we have set our hope that he will continue to deliver us" (2 Cor 1:10 NIV).

've had more than a few senior saints wag their fingers in my face and warn that the Lord's church is just one generation away from extinction. The implication seems to be that if I and my contemporaries mess this up, all that the Lord's church has accomplished since Pentecost will be for not. I'm convinced such people mean well, but if you've ever muttered something similar to a younger Christian, I hope you'll get on your knees and repent right now. Such egotistical hogwash is little better than Elijah moaning in the cave that he's the only righteous soul left, and what will be after him? Do not be deceived; God has always kept "seven thousand" in reserve who are faithful to him (cf. Isa 10:20–23; 11:11–16; Amos 9:8). Jesus swore that the defenses of hell would never prevail against the church, that we would never be in retreat (Matt 16:18). The church may grow unfaithful. She might dabble in apostasy. Her witness may go silent and her love grow cold—but the church shall never go extinct. Remember that the next time you grow fearful of what is to come. The future of Christ's bride is always bright, not because of your faithfulness or mine or that of our children, but because of her Husband. Even when we are faithless, he is faithful (2 Tim 2:13). As long as there's a Christ, there will be a church of Christ.

7

PERDITION'S FLAMES

I
n 1851, Herman Melville released the classic novel *Moby-Dick*. Anyone with
even a passing familiarity with American literature recognizes the book's
opening words, "Call me Ishmael." One of the principal characters in Melville's tome is Ahab, captain of the whaling vessel *Pequod* and the book's primary
antagonist.

Even if it meant the destruction of his ship and crew, Ahab was intent on
catching the white whale named Moby Dick. "Aye, aye!" cries Ahab in the novel,
"and I'll chase him round Good Hope, and round the Horn, and round the Nor-
way Maelstrom, and round perdition's flames before I give him up."[1] Ahab, then,
represents the depraved fanatic who will stop at nothing—whether it be the loss
of his own life or the destruction of the community—to achieve his selfish desires, and often in the face of sound advice.

Melville's Ahab isn't that different from his biblical counterpart: an uncompromising, borderline-fanatical pagan intent on seeing his own will become a
reality in the world. Ahab and his wife, Jezebel, are now synonymous with wickedness, and for good reason. The narrator's scorn is unequivocal; we've already
been told that Ahab was worse than any king before him (16:30), and that epi-
taph is judicious in light of the stories we are about to read. In fact, the narrator's
comments about him at the end of 1 Kings 16 provide a grid for understanding
these next three episodes. Remember the three things we learned about Ahab
from the anecdote of Hiel and Jericho?

- Ahab was hostile to the word of Yahweh.

---

1. Herman Melville, *Moby-Dick* (New York: Knopf, 1988), 182.

- Ahab sought to reverse the Conquest of Canaan.

- In spite of Ahab's best efforts, the word of Yahweh stands forever.

What we'll discover is that these three realities help us understand the stories of 1 Kings 20–22. In his treaty with Ben-hadad, Ahab proved himself hostile
to the word of Yahweh. In his seizure of Naboth's vineyard, he sought to reverse
the Conquest of Canaan. And in his demise at Ramoth-gilead, Ahab learned that
despite the best efforts of the wicked, the word of Yahweh stands forever.

However, what exacerbates the disdain of the divine narrator above all else is
a recognition that Ahab, though unrighteous, was not an inept king. His immatu-
rity in the Naboth narrative notwithstanding, secular history remembers him as a
capable, even formidable, ruler. And though he was no friend of the Lord of heav-
en, I'm not convinced Ahab was ever an all-in Baal worshiper—his two sons and
his daughter bear names reflective of Yahweh. But one must be "all in" with God
or not in at all. There is no in-between. Yahweh demands *exclusive* allegiance—
something Ahab could never surrender, and that is why he is remembered as a
pagan. One is left to wonder how Israel's history might read today had Ahab not
spent so much of his life petulantly chasing his self-will round perdition's flames.

1 KINGS 20

Early in Ahab's reign, the nation of Aram felt pressure to their north in the
form of the ascendant Assyrian empire. Aram's trade routes had been severed by
wars with Asshurnasirpal II (c. 884–860) and Shalmaneser III (c. 859–825), and
when Omri had conquered Moab, Aram lost access to the King's Highway trade
route in Transjordan. Also, Israel and Tyre had forged an alliance when Ahab and
Jezebel tied the knot, jeopardizing Aram's alliance with the Phoenicians.[2] But if
Ben-hadad, Aram's king, could subdue Israel, he would regain access to trade via
Mediterranean ports and Phoenician trading vessels in Tyre. Moreover, making
a vassal out of Ahab would give Ben-hadad additional military resources if/when
Assyria attacked from the north. The king of Aram also knew Israel was coming
off a three-year famine; Samaria surely could not endure a lengthy siege. What
did Aram have to lose?

---

2. A stele of Ben-hadad II discovered at Aleppo was dedicated to Baal of Tyre, suggesting
a treaty relationship between the Arameans and Phoenicians (Frank Moore Cross, "The Stele
Dedicated to Melcarth by Ben-Hadad of Damascus," *BASOR* 205 [1972]: 36–42).

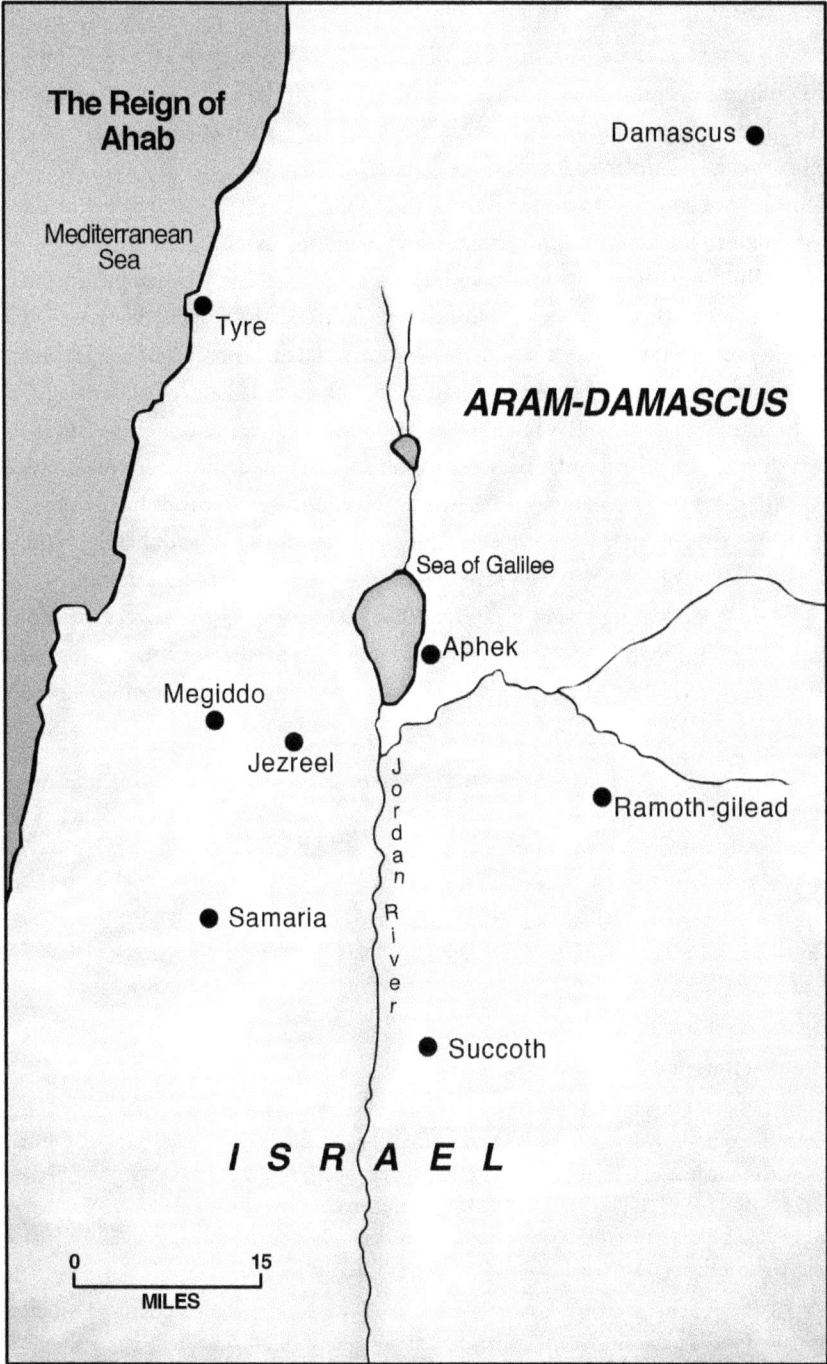

The Reign of Ahab

Mediterranean
Sea

Damascus ●

● Tyre

ARAM-DAMASCUS

Sea of Galilee

● Aphek

Megiddo
●

● Jezreel

Jordan
River

● Ramoth-gilead

● Samaria

● Succoth

I S R A E L

0   15

MILES

The text says Ben-hadad[3] came against Samaria with thirty-two "kings," which in all likelihood were tribal chieftains[4] or modern-day mayors (cf. Num 31:8; Judg 8:5; Jer 25:24). They were kings in the sense that they ruled individual city-states, similar to Canaan's realpolitik in Joshua's day. That said, it was a significant accomplishment for Ben-hadad to forge so sizable a coalition and is a testament to the powerful influence Aram's king possessed.[5]

While most translations speak of this as a siege, the ESV is appropriately vague in saying that Ben-hadad "closed in on Samaria and fought against it." Provan suggests "put pressure on" is a more appropriate translation of the Hebrew.[6] As the story unfolds, it becomes apparent that Samaria is hardly "under siege" as we think of it—the threat is real, but this isn't the Alamo. For one thing, messengers shuttled back and forth between Ahab and Ben-hadad over some distance. Consider also that Ahab was able to muster seven thousand troops from throughout Israel, that they were able to assemble in or near Samaria, and that they didn't engage the enemy until they were at least some distance from the capital.[7]

Ben-hadad smugly sent a demand to Ahab using language very common for its day: "Your silver and your gold are mine; your best wives and children also are mine" (v. 3).[8] For Ahab to surrender his wives alone would seem to some to

---

3. Several kings of Aram carried the name *Ben-hadad* (it was likely a dynastic throne-name denoting divine adoption), so it is difficult to know for sure which historical king we are dealing with. But Cogan's suggestion that it is Ben-hadad II (aka Adad-idri or Hadadezer) is quite plausible (*I Kings*, 474; cf. Cross, "Stele," 36–42; Kitchen, "Ben-Hadad," *NBD* 129).

4. Jones speculates that these were princes and chiefs of North Arabian tribes (*1 and 2 Kings*, 2:339). The Hebrew *melek* occurs about 2,500 times in the Old Testament and though it often means "king," it essentially means a "ruler of varying status," (*HALOT* 591).

5. Monson, "1 Kings," 84.

6. Provan, *1 & 2 Kings*, 154.

7. It was once suggested by Yigael Yadin and others that "booths" (v. 12) is actually a place name, Succoth (the Hebrew word can mean either), located about thirty miles away on the eastern side of the Jordan ("Some Aspects of the Strategy of Ahab and David [I Kings 20; II Sam. 11]," *Bib* 36 [1955]: 332–51). But for a king to be directing his army from so far away seems unlikely, plus the fact that the Hebrew contains the definite article *the*, making it unlikely that it is referring to a place (cf. we wouldn't say, "I'm going to *the* Atlanta").

8. In accounts of their defeat of their enemies, Assyrian kings Esarhaddon and Ashurbanipal used very similar language: "I carried off as booty: his wife, his children, the personnel of his palace, gold, silver, (other) valuables, precious stones, garments made of multicolored trimmings and linen, elephant-hides, ivory, ebony and boxwood, whatever precious objects there

be an abdication of the throne (cf. 2:22; 2 Sam 16:21), but to Ben-hadad's demands, Israel's king gladly and quickly acquiesced.

But then Ben-hadad altered the terms, "making them more extensive (everything you value), intrusive (search your palace), and immediate (this time tomorrow)."[9] This Ahab rejected; rather than just being greedy, Ben-hadad's negotiation tactics might have been designed intentionally to pick a fight as opposed to settling peacefully. When Ahab put the matter to the elders of the people, they also thought Ben-hadad's demands unreasonable.

Ben-hadad's response is what you'd expect from the neighborhood bully who's grown up and inherited an army. "May the gods punish me and do so severely if Samaria's dust amounts to a handful for each of the people who follow me" (v. 10 HCSB).[10] To this, Ahab replied with an ancient, four-word proverb that meant, "Don't count your chickens before they hatch." (One will notice that prewar rhetoric hasn't evolved much in three thousand years.) At that, Ben-hadad ordered his soldiers to their battle stations.

And this is where things get really fascinating. An unnamed prophet appeared with a message from Yahweh,[11] and it was intended primarily for Ahab (the second-person pronouns in v. 13 are singular). "You see that massive army that stands against you? I'm going to defeat it today on your behalf so that you know I'm real and that I'm your God."[12] Note specifically the phrase, "I will give it into your hands" (v. 13), an oft-repeated line in the holy war passages of Joshua (2:24; 6:2; 8:1, 18; 10:8, 19). The Lord instructed Ahab first to send out to battle 232 "servants of the governors of the districts," which is a complicated phrase

---

were in his palace, (and) in great quantities," (*ANET* 291).

9. Provan, *1 & 2 Kings*, 151–52.

10. Jones explains the meaning: "Samaria is threatened with total devastation, for Benhadad's army is so numerous that it will be able to carry away the dust of Samaria in handfuls," (*1 and 2 Kings*, 2:341).

11. "Oracular revelation of battle tactics occurs in holy war contexts (1 Sam. 14:36–37; 23:1–4, 10–12), and the phraseology of the passage echoes such contexts. YHWH will deliver the enemy 'into your hand' (see Deut. 2:24, 30; 3:2; 7:24; 20:13; 21:10; Josh. 6:2; 8:1, 18; 10:8; Judg. 4:7, 14; 7:7–9; 1 Sam. 23:4–5; 2 Sam. 5:19); the battle's outcome is 'so you will know that I am YHWH' (see Exod 6:7; 7:5; 10:2; 14:4; 16:12)," (Wray Beal, *1 & 2 Kings*, 265).

12. In Ezekiel, written roughly the same time as Kings, this phrase occurs over sixty times and carries the same importance. God has always acted primarily that we might know he is real and holy.

indicating the translators weren't sure how to render the Hebrew. Other versions aren't much help—cf. "junior officers under the provincial commanders" (NIV) or "young commandos of the regional chiefs" (Msg).

Whatever these young men were, it's unlikely they were trained warriors. It would have been very out of character for Yahweh to demonstrate his power by sending Army Rangers or Navy SEALs in the first wave (cf. Exod 14:14; Judg 7). In a general sense, the Hebrew *na'ar* means "servant" (e.g., Gen 18:7; 22:5; Num 22:22; 2 Sam 13:28) or "child" (Gen 37:2; Judg 13:5; 1 Sam 4:21) and can refer to trained military personnel[13] (e.g., 2 Sam 2:14; 4:12; 17:18; 20:11). But Provan points out that the term "elsewhere in Kings never requires such a military sense"[14] (cf. 3:7; 11:17, 28; 14:3, 17; 18:43; 19:3). In fact, the same term is used of David in 1 Samuel 17:33. There, as here, God was using his "foolishness" to shame the world's military "wisdom" and prove the battle always belongs to him.

What we are left with is an impressive scene. While Ben-hadad enjoyed a kegger in his tent with his allies and officers (he drunkenly issues incoherent orders in v. 18), 232 young Israelite servants—wielding all the military shock and awe of a Cub Scout troop—threw the Aramean camp into a tizzy. The seven thousand that made up Israel's army (v. 15) were sent out to mop up the carnage,[15] and Ben-hadad was forced to beat a path back to Damascus on horseback with his tail between his legs.

At the end of the battle, the nameless prophet reappeared with a warning for Ahab: Don't get too comfortable; Ben-hadad would return in the spring (cf. 2 Sam 11:1) with a vengeance. Meanwhile, Ben-hadad's advisors blamed the defeat on the fact that Israel's god held a military advantage in the hill country; on the plains, however, Aram's gods would prove superior (cf. Judg 1:19). But such ignorance only blinded Aram to the truth, and just as Elijah's victory at Carmel demonstrated Yahweh's superiority over Baal, the next battle would demonstrate his sovereignty over Aram's pantheon.[16]

---

13. de Vaux, *Ancient Israel*, 1:220–21; B. Cutler and J. MacDonald, "Identification of the NA'AR in the Ugaritic Texts," *UF* 8 (1976): 27–35. It must be noted, however, that the term's militaristic nuance is primarily derived from Egyptian and Ugaritic sources, not the Old Testament (cf. Hamilton, "נַעַר," *NIDOTTE* 3:124–27).

14. Provan, *1 & 2 Kings*, 155.

15. Provan argues that "who shall begin the battle?" (v. 14) is better rendered "who will finish the battle?" The verb translated "begin" (cf. "start" NIV) literally means "tie up" (Ibid.).

16. "In the polytheistic setting of the ancient Near East, gods were generally considered

The king's advisors also counseled Ben-hadad to relieve his thirty-two allies of command over their own troops and replace them with Aram's own commanders, streamlining the chain-of-command and giving everyone a common
objective. Perhaps in their panic—so the reasoning went—the allied chiefs had
abandoned their allegiance to Ben-hadad, failed to act in concert with one another, and adopted an "every man for himself" mentality.

Both Ben-hadad and Ahab, however, had missed the day's real lesson: Military size matters not at all if Yahweh is for/against you. Neither is he bound by
space or time (Pss 90:2; 139:7–12). He is equally potent against all enemies, foreign or domestic, and can destroy all challengers with the breath of his mouth,
on their turf or his.

S ure enough, come spring, Ben-hadad invaded Israel again and met her at
Aphek. There are about five Apheks mentioned in the Old Testament.
The most likely candidate here is the city in Asher, east of Galilee, and
located on the road to Damascus (cf. Josh 19:30; Judg 1:31), meaning this "second battle is considerably further north than the first."[17] The Arameans had mustered another large army; Israel's force, meanwhile, is described by the narrator
as "two little flocks of goats" (v. 27).[18]

But those for whom Yahweh fights are never outnumbered or led like lambs
to the slaughter. The anonymous prophet again informed Ahab that God would
fight for his people, this time to teach the Arameans a lesson. "They not only
make up a massed horde facing Israel, but a foolish, misguided horde; they stag-
ger at Aphek as much from false premises (v. 28) as they did at Samaria from

as having defined territorial jurisdiction, just as political leaders would have. This jurisdiction
could be divided up along national lines (each nation having its patron deities) or by topograph-
ical areas or boundaries (rivers, mountains, lakes, plains), as here construed. The fact that Israel was a mountainous country and that the capital cities, Samaria and Jerusalem, were both in
mountain regions, would fuel the speculation that Yahweh's jurisdiction was in the mountains,"
(Walton, *Bible Background*, 381).

17. Provan, *1 & 2 Kings*, 156.

18. One scholar argues that the passage should be translated, "The Israelites encamp-
ed opposite them (covering) an area of the size of two clearings of goats, while Aram filled the
land," though this admittedly leaves the meaning of the verse essentially unchanged (Amitai Ba-
ruchi-Una, "Two Clearings of Goats [1 Kings 20:27]: An Interpretation Supported by an Akkadian Parallel," *JBL* 133 [2014]: 247–49).

drink."[19] Aram falsely presumed that Yahweh was limited to the hills, and the God of Israel is always interested in setting the record straight when it comes to his consistent character and transcendent glory.

After a week of military standstill (a duration perhaps intended to remind us of Jericho), the two sides went at it. Israel defeated 100,000 and sent the rest fleeing for the safety of Aphek's fortified walls. But in another event deliberately reminiscent of Jericho, the city wall collapsed, claiming another 27,000[20] casualties—though some commentators think Israelite guerrillas sabotaged the wall.[21]

Meanwhile, a panicked Ben-hadad holed up in an "undisclosed location" in the heart of the city.[22] His aides reminded him that the kings of Israel were known to be trustworthy (literally, "kings of loyalty"), and that if Ben-hadad played the part of a prisoner-slave eager to do Ahab's bidding, he might escape with his life. Thus, Ben-hadad and his entourage paraded before the Israelites in sackcloth and with nooses around their necks[23] (the ancient equivalent of putting on an orange jumpsuit and handcuffing yourself), playing the part of captured slaves and expressing their willingness to submit and serve. Sure enough, Ahab fell for the ruse, inviting the Aramean into his royal chariot to parlay as a brother (v. 32; cf. 9:13). What is most unfathomable for me is that Ahab did not even treat his rival as a subordinate or defeated foe, but as an equal. In their nego-

---

19. Burke O. Long, "Historical Narrative and the Fictionalizing Imagination," *VT* 35 (1985): 415.

20. Since the Hebrew *'elep* can mean "unit" instead of "thousand," it's possible that Israel struck down one hundred infantry units in battle and another twenty-seven units in the city (cf. George E. Mendenhall, "The Census Lists of Numbers 1 and 26," *JBL* 77 [1958]: 52–66; de Vaux, *Ancient Israel*, 1:216). Additionally, the verb translated "struck down" (v. 29) "ranges [in meaning] from hitting to killing" (Van Dam, "נָכָה," *NIDOTTE* 3:103), so these numbers could indicate total casualties, and not just the death toll.

21. Gray, *I & II Kings*, 381. "The massive walls of ancient Israelite cities required large foundations that could be undermined by sapper work as depicted in many Assyrian reliefs. Sections of the large walls at Megiddo, Mizpah, Lachish, and even the Millo of Jerusalem could easily kill two dozen 'units' of defenders," (Monson, "1 Kings," 87–88).

22. This "was most likely a fortified space within the citadel of the city. A Hittite historiographic document describes an associate of the king going into the 'inner chamber' and sitting before him on the right. The context implies a throne room or some portion of the king's secure quarters," (Ibid., 88; *COS* 1.72).

23. "Both Assyrian and Egyptian reliefs depict captives from Syria with a tether bound around the neck," (Walton, *Bible Background*, 382).

tiation,[24] Ben-hadad promised to restore the cities Aram had seized from Israel, as well as give Israelite merchants access to the markets in Damascus. It seems Ahab was on a "Make Israel Great Again" kick.

From a political standpoint, Ahab's new treaty with Ben-hadad was incredibly shrewd and would no doubt pay dividends for years to come. He gained a formidable ally against Shalmaneser and the Assyrians (the pivotal Battle of Qarqar likely took place shortly after this episode). Ahab also gained access to Damascus markets for his merchants, which would, in turn, provide more tax revenue for the crown. "Spiritually, however, the deal confirmed Ahab's bankruptcy and led Yahweh to foreclose on his reign."[25]

At this point, one would think the story would be over. However, "Biblical narrative sometimes sneaks up on the reader to deliver an unexpected blow."[26] And this is indeed where the story's point crashes home like a Chuck Norris roundhouse kick to the face. At Yahweh's instigation, a prophet[27] (the same from vv. 13, 22, 28?) told a fellow prophet to strike him, but the fellow prophet refused. For his disobedience, it was prophesied that the disobedient prophet would be mauled by a lion (cf. 13:24), and that's exactly what happened. The first prophet then found someone else to strike him, and it left a wound near his eyes which allowed him to don a bandage as if he were a wounded soldier.

As he approached Ahab, the disguised prophet "confessed" to allowing a POW to escape, and the penalty would be either the "soldier's" life or a fine of

---

24. "Ahab and Ben-Hadad were apparently rearranging the terms of a previously existing treaty, perhaps enacted as a result of the action detailed in 15:18–20," (Patterson, "1, 2 Kings," 790). Similar treaties between the kings of Arpad and Assyria have been discovered (*ANET* 532–33; 659–61).

25. Hubbard, *First and Second Kings*, 108. "Ahab's failure on points of deuteronomic law means that, despite his victory, he is judged on the familiar refrain of covenant obedience," (Wray Beal, *1 & 2 Kings*, 263).

26. Nelson, *First and Second Kings*, 137.

27. The mention of the "sons of the prophets" is a reference to the prophetic guild that existed in Israel and would become more prominent in Elisha's day (2 Kgs 2:3–7, 15; 4:1, 38; 5:22; 6:1; 9:1). It may be that these were the same prophets sheltered by Obadiah (18:4). Josephus identifies the anonymous prophet here as Micaiah (*Antiquities* 8.389), though there is no way we can know this for sure. Josephus theorized that since Ahab and Micaiah obviously had no love lost for one another in 1 Kings 22, the two had to have had a history.

a talent of silver (cf. Exod 22:7–13).[28] Since he could never pay such an exorbitant sum (cf. Matt 18:23–24), his penalty would be death (cf. Acts 16:27). Ahab responded with something akin to, "Yep, those are the options for your punishment. You choose."[29] At that point, the "soldier" removed his disguise, and Ahab instantly recognized him as one of the prophets.[30] Ahab was then chastised for showing clemency to Ben-hadad, whom Yahweh had "devoted to destruction" (v. 42). Just as Ahab was so willing for the soldier to lose his life for allowing his prisoner to escape, so God would exact Ahab's life as a penalty for letting Ben-hadad off the hook.

Modern readers of this story will likely wonder why it was such a big deal for Ahab to show clemency toward Ben-hadad instead of executing him. Indeed, to our twenty-first-century sensitivities, the former is far more preferable.[31] But whenever Israel went out to battle at the Lord's command, they were expected to operate under the rules of holy war. One of the primary rules of holy war was that everything placed under God's ban (Hebrew *hērem*) must die (Deut 7:2; 20:16–18; cf. Lev 27:29; Josh 6:17–21; 1 Sam 15:7–9, 18–23; Isa 34:5). The phrase "devoted to destruction" (v. 42) translates the Hebrew *hērem*, meaning Ben-hadad had been devoted to destruction by the Lord! However, that begs the question: how was Ahab expected to know his struggle with Ben-hadad was holy war? Consider that:

---

28. "This was the price of two or more slaves in Mesopotamia and Egypt. Such a large sum of money, though exorbitant, is in keeping with the penalties recorded in other ancient Near Eastern cultures," (Monson, "1 Kings," 89; cf. Wiseman, *1 and 2 Kings*, 192).

29. "It is interesting that while the king has a reputation for mercy (v. 31) and shows mercy to Ben-Hadad, his judgment in this wounded man's case is anything but merciful," (Walton, *Bible Background*, 382).

30. It's thought that the prophets bore some identifying mark on their person. The prophet Zechariah had a wound or mark of some kind on his back identifying him as a man of God (13:6). In Isaiah 44:5, the mark seems to have been on the hand. If, however, the anonymous prophet of 1 Kings 20 had this identifying mark on his head (cf. Ezek 9:4), it would explain why Ahab recognized him when the bandage was removed.

31. "Ahab was acting according to the enlightened morality common to kings of all ages, but this did not save him from the deadly effects of misplaced priorities and the failure to pay proper attention," (Nelson, *First and Second Kings*, 137). "As we know, however, the Bible rarely preaches reasonableness and accommodation in our walk of faith, and that certainly is the case here," (Barnes, *1–2 Kings*, 173).

- Ben-hadad intended to reduce Samaria to rubble; for ancient Israel, the threat of utter destruction must be met with utter destruction.

- The battle of Aphek amounted to a reenactment of Jericho—seven days and the walls collapse.

- Yahweh had given Ahab the battle strategy, as he often did with Moses, Joshua, Gideon, etc.

- Yahweh gave the Arameans into the Israelites' hands because the battle belongs to the Lord (cf. Josh 6:2, 16; 8:1, 18; Judg 7:2; 18:10; 1 Sam 23:4; 24:4).[32]

The ultimate reason Ahab should have known better is that the anonymous prophet had made clear Yahweh would give Israel victory so that Ahab would know that Yahweh was the Lord—not Baal. This concept saturates the account of the Exodus (cf. 6:7; 7:5, 17; 10:2; 14:4, 18; 16:12; Deut 29:6), but in Joshua–Kings, occurs only here. In other words, God was acting to glorify himself and make himself known to Ahab. Ahab, however, used his God-given victory as an opportunity to gratify himself and achieve his own purposes. As he had proven with his order to resurrect Jericho, Ahab had nothing but scorn for Yahweh's word, which amounts to scorn for Yahweh's Name—something God jealously protects. Every king of Israel was expected to be well versed in the traditions of the covenant people of Yahweh (Deut 17:18–20), and the concept of holy war was a major tenet of that tradition. Thus, "far from being tricked by God, Ahab is implicitly faulted for not steeping himself in the law as a good king would."[33]

Ben-hadad was Yahweh's prisoner, not Ahab's, and Yahweh alone had the power of life or death over the Aramean king, not unlike the story of Saul and Agag (1 Sam 15). And just as the soldier in the parable had allowed someone else's prisoner to escape, and thus must pay the price, so Ahab had allowed someone else's prisoner to escape, and thus must pay the price. It may be absurd to us to think that God expected Ahab to execute Ben-hadad, and it appeared no less cockamamie to the fellow prophet when the first prophet commanded him to

---

32. Leithart, *1 & 2 Kings*, 150. Wray Beal lists additional ties between this text and the holy war passages of the Old Testament, concluding, "The presence of several of these elements makes 1 Kgs 20 an unmistakable holy war. Ahab fails to reckon the spoils belong to YHWH, and he is judged on the deuteronomic law of *hērem*," (*1 & 2 Kings*, 268).

33. Fretheim, *First and Second Kings*, 115–16.

strike him in the name of the Lord. But what kind of king keeps covenant with defeated pagan enemies but not with his Lord? God expects to be obeyed, regardless of how (ir)rational his commands may seem. In the parable, the prophet deftly drew Ahab into his story just as Nathan had done with David (2 Sam 12:1–15), and thereby the Lord led the king into self-judgment.

Arguably the saddest part of this story is that Ahab ignored the opportunity given him to repent. For one thing, the prophet approached Ahab unsolicited—God was offering the king grace! And just as the soldier in the parable could have paid the talent of silver and repented, contrition on the king's part would have secured mercy from Yahweh. Instead, however, he responded with sullen anger and stubborn resentment. He forgot "that every word from God is an act of grace, an invitation to conversation because it is an invitation to conversion."[34] This unknown prophet had sought out Ahab at God's command; he had come to the king unsolicited. As is often the case, God's judgment is mercy in disguise—something Ahab might have recognized had he not been petulantly pursuing his self-will "round perdition's flames."

1 KINGS 21

Naboth and his vineyard is a pivotal moment in the flow of Kings. Whereas the narrator previously had been satisfied to mention and dismiss rulers within a terse few verses (e.g., 1 Kgs 15–16), he has slowed the pace of storytelling considerably and taken his time while the spotlight lingers on the Omride dynasty. As Ahab's power grows, especially in light of both his victory over Aram and Elijah's inexplicable silence in the preceding story, the reader is left to wonder if this king of Israel will ever be punished for his unprecedented evil.[35] Judgment sounded forth at the end of the previous chapter, but where is the hammer? Indeed, Ahab's wickedness crescendos with this appalling story of might making right, of power seizing what it wants by hook or crook.[36]

---

34. Leithart, *1 & 2 Kings*, 150.

35. "Ahab's actions in the two chapters summarize his apostasy: he loves Gentiles and their gods while hating faithful Israelites and their God. He fails to carry out holy war against Ben Hadad, but prosecutes it instead against Naboth and his house (2 Kgs. 9:26). He does not know how to fight enemies, and, to say the same thing, he does not know how to protect friends," (Ibid., 154).

36. Even House observes that, so far, "Of all Ahab's failings the text has never accused him of oppression or brutality against his people," (*1, 2 Kings*, 231).

But just when we start to think Yahweh has grown impotent or indifferent regarding Israel's sin, or that Elijah has succumbed to the futility of his calling, the reenergized prophet crashes onto the scene with a damning message direct from heaven. Might doesn't make right. As long as Yahweh—not Baal—is Lord of heaven, unprecedented evil will always meet an abhorrent end.

Game on.

The story takes place in Jezreel, where a man named Naboth owned a vineyard. Jezreel was located in the territory of Issachar (Josh 19:18) and overlooked the Jezreel Valley. Excavations have revealed it was a decent-sized town in Naboth's day, since it served as Ahab's winter retreat (18:46), being at a lower elevation than Samaria, some twenty-three miles to the southwest.

The double mention of Jezreel in v. 1 reinforces that this place was Naboth's ancestral hometown, which is a crucial detail in the narrative,[37] as is the fact that he seems to be a part of the local aristocracy (v. 12). Naboth's refusal to sell his land is rooted in more than a "Daddy won't sell the farm" sentimentality. The word translated "forbid" (v. 3) indicates that the sale would have been a profane thing in God's eyes, a desecration of a divine gift (cf. Num 36:7–12; Josh 22:29; 1 Sam 12:23; 26:11; 2 Sam 23:17).[38]

Land was a big deal in ancient Israel—and if you pay attention to contemporary politics in the Levant, it still is. It had been promised to Abraham and his descendants in perpetuity (Gen 17:8), but only as tenants; Yahweh was still the Landowner (Lev 25:23). The tribes of Israel had received their various inheritances from the Lord once Joshua's campaigns were completed (Josh 13:1–7); they were stewards of what God had given them. "It was therefore not open to individuals to sell land in perpetuity, and complicated laws existed that were designed to keep land in the family and to prevent its accumulation in the hands of a few," (cf. Lev 25:8–34; Deut 25:5–10).[39]

In his book, *God's People in God's Land*, Christopher Wright makes this very intriguing observation: "Although admittedly an argument from silence, it

---

37. Cogan, *I Kings*, 476.

38. Ibid., 478.

39. Provan, *1 & 2 Kings*, 157. Robinson also points out that "it is quite possible that the tombs of his ancestors were situated on the ancestral family land. To sell such land would have been a shameful act of impiety and betrayal," (*First Book*, 236).

is nevertheless an impressive fact that the whole Old Testament provides not a single case of an Israelite voluntarily selling land outside his family group [...] This silence of the text is matched by the absence as yet of any inscriptional evidence from Palestine of Israelite sale and purchase of land, though there is abundant evidence of such transactions from Canaanite and surrounding societies."[40] The very fact, then, that Ahab made an offer for Naboth's vineyard demonstrates what little regard the king had for God's Law (cf. Isa 5:8; Mic 2:1–2).

What's worse, Ahab had plans to turn this beautiful vineyard—something that took time and diligence to cultivate properly—into an unremarkable vegetable garden. It would be like plowing up beautiful rose bushes to make way for kale. Ever eaten kale? That abominable Lettuce of Lucifer tastes like insecticide. Leithart points out that the only other place in the Old Testament that uses the term *vegetable garden* is Deuteronomy 11:10, in reference to Egypt. "Symbolically, Ahab's intention is to turn the vineyard of Israel into an Egyptian vegetable patch, and this is consistent with his entire policy of 're-Canaanitization' of Israel. Ahab wants to 'drive out' Naboth and 'take possession' (1 Kgs. 21:19, 26), as Israel once did to the Canaanites (Gen. 15:7; Num. 13:30; Josh. 18:3; Judg. 2:6). Like the crowds that follow Moses from Egypt, Ahab wants to return to slavery and idolatry."[41]

Leithart's point becomes more potent when we consider how Israel was often portrayed as a vineyard (Ps 80:8–11; Isa 5; Matt 21:33–43). "Israel was a land of vineyards. Even today, traveling through the central hill country of Israel during the right season, one can see abundant evidence of fruitful vines." As a vineyard, ancient Israel belonged to her creator and owner. God loved his vineyard and proved it by preparing the Promised Land and planting Israel there— Israel was his elect nation, and he providentially cared for her as a husbandman nurtures his vines and grapes.[42] With his plan to purchase Naboth's vineyard (i.e., Israel, God's possession) and turn it into a vegetable garden (ungodly Ca-

---

40. Christopher J. H. Wright, *God's People in God's Land: Family, Land, and Property in the Old Testament* (Grand Rapids: Eerdmans, 1990), 56.

41. Leithart, *1 & 2 Kings*, 154–55. "This story perhaps more than any other makes clear what the deuteronomists believed to be at stake in the fight to prevent Israel from becoming one more Canaanite community," (Robinson, *First Book*, 237).

42. "Vine, Vineyard," in *Dictionary of Biblical Imagery*, eds. Leland Ryken, James C. Wilhoit, and Tremper Longman III (Downers Grove, IL: InterVarsity Press, 1998), 914–15.

naan/Egypt), Ahab was no better than a despot stealing a poor man's beloved lamb and serving it for dinner (2 Sam 12:1–4).[43]

His offer to Naboth rebuffed, Ahab did what all great and powerful kings do when they don't get what they want—he went to his bedroom and pouted (cf. 20:43), all along sobbing, "No one loves me!"[44] When his wife asked why Ahab was acting like a child, he told Jezebel all that had happened. Her response is chilling, in effect saying, "Don't you worry about it, sweetie. I'll take care of it." In fact, her rhetorical question in v. 7 contains an emphasis on *you* and *I* in the Hebrew text—"Is this how *you* act as king over Israel? Get up and eat! Cheer up. *I'll* get you the vineyard of Naboth the Jezreelite" (NIV; emphasis mine).

Behind Jezebel's scornful question of her husband lay a wholly different view (a Canaanite one) of power and property than the one Yahweh inscribed within the Torah (cf. Deut 17:14–20; 1 Sam 8:11–18). In regards to property, and as mentioned previously, the Law made clear that Yahweh owned the land, and Israel was his tenant. Israel's pagan neighbors, however, believed that all property was owned by the crown, with the citizens living on it as tenants— essentially, "all land was on grant from the king."[45]

In terms of power, *God* was Israel's king. The mortal on Israel's throne was merely Yahweh's agent to administer justice and lend a hand to the downtrodden. We have no greater example of this paradigm than when Solomon adjudicated the case of the two prostitutes (3:16–28). In short, the king of Israel didn't sit atop the totem pole, and he certainly was not above the law, but was *primus inter pares*— first among equals. On the other hand, as a Phoenician princess and daughter of a pagan priest, "Jezebel would not have been accustomed to such niceties."[46]

Indeed, it's clear in the text that Jezebel was the one with the real power; Ahab was her puppet.[47] The queen got to work mailing letters[48] to the aristocra-

43. Drinkard notes several parallels between 1 Kings 21 and 2 Samuel 11 ("Omri Dynasty," *DOTHB* 759).

44. Jewish legend also claims that Ahab went on a Twitter rant on this occasion.

45. Walton, *Bible Background*, 383. "Jezebel [...] may not have known (or cared) much about the Torah, but she certainly knew about the 'divine right of kings' (at least in Phoenicia)," (Barnes, *1–2 Kings*, 177).

46. Walton, *Bible Background*, 383; cf. DeVries, *1 Kings*, 257.

47. "Though the letter of instructions had borne the seal of the king, the elders reported back to the queen; obviously, they knew who had penned the letters," (Cogan, *1 Kings*, 481).

48. Though she uses Ahab's seal in v. 8, a seal has been discovered bearing Jezebel's name,

cy (cf. Deut 16:18) of Jezreel with instructions to bring trumped-up charges of blasphemy and treason against Naboth, a crime which carried the death penalty (Exod 22:28). Everything was to be done according to the letter of the Law.[49] Amazing that the one time Jezebel or Ahab show any concern for Israel's Law, they do so for their own selfish gain! "Ahab and Jezebel, however, miss the most important factor in the situation: there is a God from whom no secrets are hid, a God before whom all the thoughts and intentions of the heart are open and revealed."[50]

A kangaroo court was called into session,[51] Naboth was found guilty of blasphemy, and a righteous man was stoned to death in cold blood (cf. Lev 24:16). According to 2 Kings 9:26, Naboth's sons were executed with their father, meaning no heirs existed to inherit the property, so it defaulted to the crown. With that, Jezebel informed an elated Ahab that the vineyard was now his to enjoy, and he quickly confiscated the ownerless land.

The question has been asked how exactly Naboth could be accused of blasphemy against God and king,[52] and especially how this would entitle the throne

---

dating to the ninth or eighth century. "There is, of course, no basis for identifying the owner of our seal with this famous lady, although they may have been contemporaries, and the seal seems worthy of a queen. Moreover, Jezebel is a rare Phoenician name, nowhere previously documented other than in the Old Testament," (N. Agivad, "The Seal of Jezebel," *IEJ* 14 [1964]: 275).

49. "The charge against Naboth was twofold: he had blasphemed both God and the king. The penalty for such action was death by stoning (Dt 13:10–11; 17:5) outside the city (Lev 24:14; Dt 22:24). Proper procedure called for at least two witnesses (Dt 17:6; 19:15). They were to lay their hands on the accused (Lev 24:14) and cast the first stones (cf. Jn 8:7). Since death by stoning was the responsibility of the whole community, the rest of the people were to take up the stoning," (Patterson, "1, 2 Kings," 795).

50. Leithart, *1 & 2 Kings*, 156.

51. Just as the Law demanded (cf. Num 35:30; Deut 17:6; 19:15), two "witnesses" (cf. Matt 26:60) came forward to convict Naboth. The translations variously call them "worthless men" (ESV), "wicked men" (HCSB), "stool pigeons" (Msg), "troublemakers" (NCV), and "scoundrels" (NIV), while the Hebrew literally reads "sons of Belial" or "sons of no-good" (cf. Judg 19:22; 1 Sam 10:27).

52. "The curse is thought to be a mighty and damaging word whose power unfolds independently of its immediate context. The curse against God violates the sanctity of Yahweh and infringes upon the sphere of God alone to which no human being must have access. The curse against the king diminishes his actions and status and subsequently is harmful to the people, whose well-being is closely connected to that of the king. The accusation against Naboth therefore blames him alone for all the misfortunes that have occurred to the people and have necessitated the assembly in the first place. God had to answer the infringement of his proper

to confiscate his property upon his death. The traditional explanation is that, in ancient times, property of a criminal defaulted to the state[53] (cf. 2 Sam 16:4; Ezra 10:8; Ezek 45:8; 46:18). But no provision for such a thing exists in the Law of Moses, and it doesn't explain how Naboth could plausibly (if unjustly) be open to the charge of blasphemy.

Thus one scholar proposes that the allegation laid at Naboth's feet was that he had defaulted on an oath to sell his vineyard to Ahab and had sworn to do so by the name of Yahweh, and that failure to do so was blasphemy against God and the king. As a result, he was to be executed, and according to standard legal codes of the ancient Near East, his property would forfeit to the person to whom Naboth had previously sworn to sell it.[54] This explanation makes the most sense in the context, but Naboth had undoubtedly never sworn to do any such thing; his allegiance to the name of Yahweh was the very reason he refused to sell!

Whenever I read this story, I can't help but confuse Ahab with a spoiled little rich kid who jealously covets another little boy's bike. He throws a tantrum until his mother asks what's wrong, and then she proceeds to have the other little boy beaten up and his bike confiscated so that her brat of a child can have what he wants.[55] This travesty of justice triggered another showdown between king and prophet. Note that God told Elijah exactly where he could find the king—despite the immoral power play, the narrator still calls it the "vineyard of Naboth" (v. 18). "Royal manipulation does not alter the true identity of the land!"[56]

Elijah bore a message that Ahab's blood would be lapped up by the same dogs that had lapped Naboth's; in fact, all of Ahab's family was destined for the dogs (2 Kgs 9:25–26, 36–37; 10:10–11, 17).[57] Arguably, no greater disgrace in

---

sphere with an act of punishment, while the king could no longer guarantee the prosperity of his people," (Fritz, *1 & 2 Kings*, 213).

53. Nahum M. Sarna, "Naboth's Vineyard Revisited (1 Kings 21)," in *Tehillah le-Moshe: Biblical and Judaic Studies in Honor of Moshe Greenberg*, eds. Mordechai Cogan, Barry L. Eichler, and Jeffrey H. Tigay (Winona Lake, IN: Eisenbrauns, 1997), 122–25.

54. Francis I. Andersen, "The Socio-Juridical Background of the Naboth Incident," *JBL* 85 (1966): 46–57.

55. "Ahab's 'going down' to Naboth's vineyard may be compared to Abraham's 'walking through the land' (Gen 13:17; cf. Josh 24:3), both symbolic acts of acquisition through actual traversal of the property newly acquired," (Cogan, *I Kings*, 481).

56. Brueggemann, *1 & 2 Kings*, 260.

57. Elijah's curse did not mean that Ahab would die in Jezreel as some infer, for the fulfill-

HOW TO LOSE A KINGDOM IN 400 YEARS

death existed in the mind of an ancient Israelite (cf. Deut 28:25–26; Ps 68:23; Jer 16:4). In ancient times, dogs did not enjoy the "man's best friend" status they do today. Rather, they were considered "unclean scavengers worthy of scorn."[58] According to Jewish tradition, whenever *Old Yeller* was shown in theaters during Ahab's reign, the audience cheered at the end. A contemporary Assyrian curse declared, "Let dogs tear his unburied body to pieces."[59] In Homer's *Iliad*, as Achilles stands over the dying Hector, he boasts, "You the dogs and birds will rip apart shamefully […] the dogs and birds will devour you wholly."[60]

After killing Osama bin Laden, it's rumored that members of SEAL Team 6 riddled his corpse with magazine after magazine of bullets. If this is true, they were no doubt giving outlet to a decade of frustrated American vengeance (and this may partially explain why images of bin Laden's body were never released). In World War II, the Japanese would desecrate the bodies of American soldiers by cutting off the penis and stuffing it into the dying GIs mouth. Either of these shocking, horrific images gets us close to the ancient concept of one's remains being given over to the dogs.

Ahab's response was a hostile one—"My enemy! So, you've run me down!" (v. 20 Msg). Perhaps Elijah had been absent for so long that Ahab had thought the prophet had met his demise. But any reports of his death had been greatly exaggerated! The prophet's arrival impressed on Ahab that he couldn't escape the judgment of Israel's God. The king could pitch a fit and have his rival executed in order to seize a coveted vineyard, but he remained subject to the divine Landlord. Because the king had provoked the wrath of Yahweh in such an unprecedented way, the house of Omri would become like that of Jeroboam and Baasha. "I […] will cut off from Ahab him that pisseth against the wall, and him that is shut up and left in Israel" (v. 21 KJV; cf. 14:10–11; 16:3–4). From the world's perspective, Naboth was a nobody. But in the Lord's eyes, he was a righteous member of the covenant community and a bearer of the *imago Dei*, so his illegal execution trig-

---

ment of this prophecy took place in Samaria (22:38), and the Hebrew construction can simply mean "in the place of" or "instead of" (cf. Eccl 3:16; Isa 33:21; Ezek 6:13; Hos 1:10). Thus, Provan suggests translating Elijah's words as, "Instead of dogs licking up Naboth's blood, dogs will lick up your blood—yes, yours!" (*1 & 2 Kings*, 160).

58. Monson, "1 Kings," 92.

59. Walton, *Bible Background*, 383.

60. Homer, *Iliad* 22.335, 354.

gered the collapse of a dynasty. Yahweh was intent on consuming Ahab with his holy anger like an out-of-control wildfire.

And lest we deem Yahweh to be too vengeful for doling out a $50,000 punishment for a 50¢ crime, the narrator reminds us that Ahab and Jezebel had been unprecedented in their evil. Not since the previous inhabitants of the Promised Land had there been such evil in Canaan (vv. 25–26). Just as God had done with the Amorites, he would now, in his righteousness, vomit out of the land a wicked king and queen for trying to procure property illicitly. Given their political and administrative skill, "We might have expected 'the House of Omri' to be more durable than the preceding dynasties, but the practice of a public ethic of exploitation is the death knell for any regime in Israel."[61]

But then the twist comes. Just when we feel led to believe that Ahab has no conscience, no soul, no remorse—he repents! I like to imagine that Elijah sang all eighteen verses of "Just As I Am" until Ahab walked down the aisle. He engaged in all the typical ancient practices associated with grief and remorse (Num 14:6; Josh 7:6; Judg 11:35; 2 Sam 1:2; 3:31). God saw his heart and had mercy; he informed Ahab through the prophet that he would delay Ahab's judgment, just as he would later do for Nineveh (Jon 3:10) and Hezekiah (2 Kgs 20:5–6, 11).

The careful reader will note that this is the first time in Kings that God has sworn judgment in someone's lifetime; in previous episodes, God's wrath was poured out on the offender's son (Jeroboam/Nadab, Baasha/Elah). "Presumably we are to take it that Ahab's sins were so very bad that *he could* have expected judgment on his house in his lifetime. Now, however, he has humbled himself, and thus he is to be treated as a normal, rather than a spectacular, sinner."[62] Due to God's grace, Ahab would live another few years, and his sons about fourteen after that. Even an unprecedented degenerate—when he repents—can receive mercy, for God desires that no one perish in his wrath (Ezek 18:32; 2 Pet 3:9).

1 KINGS 22:1-40

In 853, a major battle was fought between Shalmaneser III of Assyria and a coalition force of twelve nations at a place called Qarqar, located on the Orontes River some 150 miles north of Damascus. The coalition that opposed the Assyrian king was headed by Ahab of Israel, Ben-hadad of Aram, and Iarhuleni of

61. Brueggemann, *1 & 2 Kings*, 260–61.

62. Provan, *1 & 2 Kings*, 159; emphasis his.

Hamath. Coalition forces totaled 3,940 chariots, 1,900 cavalry units, and more than 60,000 infantry. Meanwhile, Shalmaneser had at his disposal little more than half the chariot force as his opponents and roughly the same cavalry units[63] (the size of his infantry is unknown). Not surprisingly, Shalmaneser in his memoirs claimed he had won this battle, but a "study of subsequent history suggests that the western coalition succeeded in their major objective. It was not until ten or twelve years later, after the confederacy had eroded, that Shalmaneser finally shows any indication of control in the region."[64]

The treaty struck in 1 Kings 20 had survived for about three years, likely because Israel and Aram needed one another since their hands were full with Assyria. But soon after the battle of Qarqar, the city of Ramoth-gilead had still not been returned to Ahab and Israel per the terms of the treaty struck in 20:34. This Levitical city of refuge in the territory of Gad (Deut 4:43; Josh 20:8; 21:38) was thirty-six miles north of modern-day Amman, Jordan, and in ancient times was located on the Transjordanian King's Highway used by traders. When occupied by Israel, Ramoth-gilead protected the Northern Kingdom from enemies to the east; it had been a major administrative center in Solomon's day (4:13). But according to Josephus, it had been seized from Israel by Ben-hadad I during the reign of Omri.[65] Ironically, this episode would not be the last in which Ramoth-gilead would feature in the downfall of Ahab's house (cf. 2 Kgs 9:1–15; 2 Chr 22:2–6).

While on a diplomatic trip to Samaria,[66] Jehoshaphat king of Judah pledged his willingness to go to war with Ahab in an effort to recapture Ramoth-gilead. Ahab likely thought his chances of taking Ramoth-gilead were good, based on his strong showing at Qarqar. But Jehoshaphat wisely insisted on inquiring of Yahweh before going into battle. At his request, Ahab summoned four hundred prophets (likely a remnant of those represented at Carmel, cf. 18:19, 40) to tip

---

63. "Reliefs of Shalmaneser's reign show that a cavalry unit included two horses and two riders, one soldier serving as driver, holding the reins of both horses in one hand and a shield protecting both riders in the other, while the second soldier served as the archer. This system of cavalry fighting did not permit the Assyrians to exploit to the full the speed of their horses, and thus the cavalry was deprived of his chief advantages—striking power and the ability to surprise," (M. Elat, "The Campaigns of Shalmaneser III against Aram and Israel," *IEJ* 25 [1975]: 29).

64. Walton, *Bible Background*, 384.

65. Josephus, *Antiquities* 8.398–99.

66. An alliance between Israel and Judah had been established with the marriage of Ahab's daughter, Athaliah, to Jehoshaphat's son, Joram (2 Kgs 8:18).

him off as to the battle's outcome.[67] Their take? Yahweh had already given Ramoth-gilead into Ahab's hands.

The king's request of these prophets was actually a common one among monarchs of the ancient Near East. In an inscription from around the ninth century, the king of Hamath described the assurances Baal had given him about his upcoming battle: "Don't be afraid! Since I have made you king I will stand beside you!"[68] In his own various military incursions against the Philistines, David had often sought God's instruction before battle (1 Sam 23:2–4; 2 Sam 5:19–25). However, as far as the Old Testament goes, "this is the earliest reference to the consultation of prophets prior to battle, a function that had previously been in the purview of priests," (cf. Num 27:21; Judg 20:27–28; 1 Sam 30:7–8).[69]

But the prophets' positive report[70] seemed a little bit too convenient for Jehoshaphat's conscience. Unanimous decisions might be God's work, but not always in the way we want or expect. "Isn't there a prophet of the LORD here? Let's ask him what we should do" (v. 7 NCV).[71] This is significant: "Against Ahab's sheer pragmatism, Jehoshaphat asks about *the will of Yahweh*."[72] Ahab objected to such a notion. "As a matter of fact, there is still one such man. But I hate him. He

---

67. Abraham Malamat, "A Forerunner of Biblical Prophecy: The Mari Documents," in *Ancient Israelite Religion: Essays in Honor of Frank Moore Cross*, eds. Patrick D. Miller, Jr., Paul D. Hanson, and S. Dean McBride (Philadelphia: Fortress, 1987), 42. "Ahab apparently knows the Lord is not with him in this battle, as stated in his response to Micaiah son of Imlah (vv. 8, 15–16). But Ahab has determined his course of action irrespective of the outcome of the consultations. It seems the function of the royal prophets was to sanction the decisions of the king rather than provide actual guidance," (Konkel, *1 & 2 Kings*, 351).

68. Monson, "1 Kings," 92–93; cf. *COS* 2.35.

69. Cogan, *I Kings*, 490.

70. "The writer, in describing the scene so vividly, is putting across an important message: how delusive a whipped up enthusiasm for anything can become, if it is artfully managed! Bring in the expert in advertising and public relations. Invent the slogans and the songs. Repeat, repeat and repeat. The real quality and worth of what is being offered matters less and less. Moreover, if the issues at stake are serious, religious, or political, people can become immersed in error, a prey to the charlatan, and oriented around self-destruction, and as with Micaiah, dissent and protest will too often find themselves dealt with by brute force," (Wallace, *1 Kings*, 164).

71. "Jehoshaphat is probably spiritually attuned enough to know that the word of God does not come with the message, 'Everything is perfectly okay. You're okay just the way you are,'" (Leithart, *1 & 2 Kings*, 160).

72. Brueggemann, *1 & 2 Kings*, 268; emphasis his.

never preaches anything good to me, only doom, doom, doom—Micaiah son of Imlah" (v. 8 Msg). To which Jehoshaphat seems to have responded with a meek, "Aww, don't talk like that."

While Micaiah was being summoned, a prophet named Zedekiah seized the spotlight by theatrically demonstrating (cf. Jer 19:1, 10–12; 28:10–11; Ezek 4) the beatdown Ahab was sure to give the Arameans.[73] In this case, iron horns represented brute power and overwhelming military might (cf. Deut 33:17; Dan 8; Mic 4:13; Zech 1:18–19). The Assyrian king Esarhaddon bragged that he had led his troops like a wild ox, and Ashurbanipal depicted his enemies as being gored by the horns of his goddess, Ninlil.[74] All signs seemed to be pointing to a smashing victory for Ahab and Jehoshaphat. Except Yahweh had not yet spoken.

Or had he?

For the final time in Ahab's life, there is a dramatic showdown between his petulant self-will and the word of Yahweh. The messenger sent to fetch Micaiah didn't hesitate to remind the prophet what was expected of him (v. 13). Everyone else had spoken a favorable word, and Micaiah had better fall in line if he knew what was good for him. But Micaiah's response is a bold example of the resiliency required of every man and woman of God: "As surely as the LORD lives, I can tell him only what the LORD tells me" (v. 14 NIV). Like Balaam (Num 23:12, 26; 24:12–13), Micaiah was bound up in the will of heaven.

When prompted by Ahab to say whether Ramoth-gilead should be attacked, Micaiah surprises us by affirming what the other four hundred prophets had said. Yes! Yahweh had given the city into Ahab's hands already. It was as good as his. It's arresting to us that "Micaiah's first words to Ahab are exactly those of the other prophets [cf. vv. 12, 15]. If he can tell the king only what the LORD tells him, why is he confirming the message of prophets who are (we suspect) false? Something is not quite right."[75]

---

73. "His prophecy is probably drawn from Deut. 33:13–17, where Moses blesses the tribes of Ephraim and Manasseh, the two dominant tribes in the north [...] Yahweh makes promises to the tribes of Joseph through Moses, and since Ahab rules the kingdom of Joseph, Zedekiah reasons, he can be confident of victory," (Leithart, *1 & 2 Kings*, 159). It seems taking verses out of context has been a thing for over three thousand years.

74. *ANET* 292, 300.

75. Provan, *1 & 2 Kings*, 163.

But then the story takes yet *another* turn. We would expect someone like Ahab (a king whose heart was anything but sensitive to the ways of the Lord) to grin from ear to ear, call for his armor, and ride off into dubious battle. But he doesn't. He instead cried, "Baloney!" on what Micaiah had spoken: "How many times do I have to tell you to speak only the truth to me in the name of the LORD?" (v. 16 ncv).[76]

The prophet responded with the truth—Israel would be scattered like sheep without a shepherd, a common metaphor indicating the death of a king. Without a king to lead, a nation would be destroyed by division and ruin (Num 27:16–17; Jer 23:1–2; Ezek 34:1–6; Zech 13:7; Matt 9:36; 26:31).[77] Implicit in Micaiah's words may be a judgment on Ahab that he had not been the shepherd to his people he should have been (cf. 2 Sam 5:2; 7:7).

And then Micaiah dramatically pulled back the cosmic curtain to give Ahab (and us) a glimpse at what had really happened behind the scenes. Micaiah knew the throne room scene he described had actually taken place because he had literally stood in the presence of this council, as did all of God's prophets when they were commissioned to speak the divine word (Pss 103:20–21; 148:2; Jer 23:18–22; Amos 3:7). What follows has few parallels in Scripture. The prophet claimed to have stood in the midst of the divine council in heaven, before Yahweh on his throne. The Lord asked his council how Ahab might be enticed to attack Ramoth-gilead; in the midst of the debate, "a spirit came forward and stood before the LORD," offering to deceive the king through his prophets. This proposal met with Yahweh's approval (vv. 21–22).

There is obviously a lot to untangle in this scene. First, for the uninitiated, the divine council scene is confusing to some. Second, why does an omniscient God like Yahweh need anyone's advice (cf. Acts 17:25)? Finally, am I the only one disturbed by the thought of God—who cannot lie (Tit 1:2; Heb 6:18; Jas 1:17)—deceiving someone? Though I cannot agree with his characterization or conclusion, Nelson gives expression to this awkward image of our Lord: "There

---

76. "Micaiah's reputation for presenting contrary prophecies seems to have raised the suspicion that this time he was lying," (Cogan, *I Kings*, 491).

77. Wiseman, *1 and 2 Kings*, 199. A contemporary Babylonian proverb claimed, "A people without a king (is like) a sheep without a shepherd," (W. G. Lambert, *Babylonian Wisdom Literature* [Oxford: Clarendon, 1960], 232).

is a certain hardness to this God who brushes aside ethical niceties to effect the divine purpose, who even lies for the good of the people."[78]

It's important to realize that the divine or heavenly council theme was a common one in the religious traditions of ancient Egypt, Canaan, and Mesopotamia. It's also one the Bible alludes to from time to time.[79] While in pagan religions the divine council was made up of greater and lesser gods, the Old Testament portrays Yahweh on his throne surrounded by angels and spirits—"the sons of God" (e.g., Job 1:6; 2:1; 38:7). The concept is not that dissimilar from the idea of a medieval court where a king and/or queen are surrounded by advisors, assistants, friends, fawning fans, and others seeking royal favors.

But there is a distinct difference between these scenes and the true divine council in heaven—God does not actually need anyone's advice or counsel as if he is on the horns of a dilemma and requires brighter minds to help him untangle nasty knots. The appearance of Yahweh asking for "advice" is meant metaphorically, a trope borrowed from a war council where a king and his advisors plot how best to attack and defeat the enemy. But instead of plotting how to deliver Aram into the hands of Israel, the Lord desires a means to bring about Ahab's death. "God has planned to act against Ahab who is seen as being led to his intended doom through the strategies suggested by trusted advisors (the prophets) that will coincide with his natural inclinations."[80]

Finally, as to the disturbing idea that God is deceiving Ahab, note that it is a deceiving spirit that goes out to manipulate the king through his prophets—God himself is not deceiving anyone. This dynamic is exactly what Paul discussed in his second letter to the Thessalonians. For those who do not love or practice the truth, "God sends them a strong delusion so that they will believe what is false, so that all will be condemned" (2 Thess 2:11–12 HCSB; cf. Ps 81:12). If we love God and seek him, we need not worry that he will deceive us (Ps 18:25–26).

> That YHWH can act in deception should not leave his people wary, as if they stand before an arbitrary God. There is, instead, the knowledge that YHWH acts towards his people as they themselves act and deserve. As one's heart remains responsive

78. Nelson, *First and Second Kings*, 153.

79. e.g., Job 1:6; 2:1; Psalms 82:1; 89:6–7; 103:19–20; 148:1–2; Zechariah 6:5–8; cf. 1 Timothy 5:21; Hebrews 1:6; 12:22; Revelation 5:11–12; 7:11–12; 14:10.

80. Walton, *Bible Background*, 439.

to YHWH, as was David's, one is led in "paths of righteousness
for his name's sake". Instead of fear there is praise, certainty of
YHWH's commitment to his people and his sure promise. But
to those who stand as YHWH's enemies he is a powerful opponent who – yet after many attempts towards redemption –
will use even deception to execute judgment.[81]

To put it more plainly, though God cannot lie, he is not above "pushing
our buttons"[82] in order to accomplish his will. Though it is possible to act against
God's ideal or circumstantial will, no one can thwart his ultimate will. Part of
what makes God gloriously omnipotent is that he is able and willing to use human selfishness and sin to accomplish his good pleasure. Just as he hardened
Pharaoh's heart—and allowed Pharaoh to harden his own heart—in order to
glorify himself and accomplish his will (cf. Exod 7:3–5, 13–14, 22; 8:15, 19;
9:12; 14:1–14), so God used Ahab's petulant self-will to trigger the king's own
"disaster" (v. 23).[83] Truly, "The king's heart is a stream of water in the hand of the
LORD; he turns it wherever he will" (Prov 21:1).

And if we remain doubtful as to the Lord's integrity in this matter, we
should realize, "Deception exposed is no longer deception but something more
complicated. It hands over to the person whom one intends to deceive the capacity of choosing whether to be deceived or not. Therefore, despite the strong
rhetoric in Micaiah's vision, the *effect* of the vision, once it has become a matter
of public knowledge, is just the opposite."[84] To put it more succinctly, "What
better deception than telling the simple truth if people are predisposed not to

---

81. Wray Beal, *1 & 2 Kings*, 289–90.

82. "The idea, familiar in Greek tragedy, that 'he whom God wishes to destroy he first
makes mad', hence the instrument of his own destruction, was even more familiar to the ancient
Hebrew," (Gray, *I & II Kings*, 403). Olley notes the famous parallel in Greek mythology of Croe-
sus, king of Lydia, who asked the Delphi oracle if he should attack Persia. "The message was that
if he attacked he would destroy a great kingdom. Too late he discovered that the 'great kingdom'
he destroyed was his own," (*Message of Kings*, 201).

83. "Both the false prophets and the king are culpable in their resolve to carry out their
own purposes, irrespective of God's guidance. This is not a situation of being unknowingly mis-
led. Their deception lies in the belief they can deny the word of Yahweh and succeed," (Konkel,
1 & 2 Kings, 352).

84. Jeffries M. Hamilton, "Caught in the Nets of Prophecy? The Death of King Ahab and
the Character of God," *CBQ* 56 (1994): 658, n. 18; emphasis his.

receive it?"[85] Though he brought a false message, Micaiah also brought a true message, and the irony is that both came directly from Yahweh. In other words, Yahweh is above reproach since he tells Ahab, "I allowed these prophets to lie to you in order to trigger your destruction. Now that you know what will happen, choose for yourself whether you love me and the truth versus your petulant self-will and self-delusion."[86]

In response to Micaiah's pronouncement, Zedekiah put down his iron horns and slapped the man of God across the cheek, which was as humiliating an act then as it is now (cf. Job 16:10; Ps 3:7; Lam 3:30; John 18:22). Under the Code of Hammurabi (§§ 202–5), such an act was punishable by fine or flogging. To add insult to injury—literally, in this case—Zedekiah made it known that *Micaiah* was the one lying in Yahweh's name. The prophet simply responded with something along the lines of, "Oh yeah? Then how come I can see into the future to the time when you cower in a closet like a little girl?" (v. 25; cf. 20:30).

Ahab had Micaiah sentenced[87] to incarceration and fed meager rations until he returned "in peace," to which Micaiah retorted, "If you return in *peace* and not in *pieces*, I'm no prophet."

> Throughout the ancient world it was believed that prophets not only proclaimed the message of deity but in the process unleashed the divine action. It is no wonder, then, that a prophet negatively disposed toward a king must somehow be controlled lest he bring about all sorts of havoc. In Assyrian king Esarhaddon's instructions to his vassals he requires that they report any improper or negative statements that may be made by anyone, but he specifically names prophets, ecstat-

85. Barnes, *1–2 Kings*, 187.

86. "The divine will is carried out within the freely chosen actions of all the individuals involved. Ahab is not deceived; he fully knows that his prophets are lying and is told why they are lying. There is every reason for Ahab to have chosen differently, but he has passed the point of no return. He operates under delusion, a self-imposed blindness. The divine message plunges him headlong into judgment. This judgment does not violate Ahab's volition; it comes because of it," (Konkel, *1 & 2 Kings*, 362).

87. Prisoners in ancient times were typically not imprisoned for lengthy periods, but rather until their case could be adjudicated. Here, "Micaiah is being imprisoned to await the outcome of his prophecy and the battle—that will constitute his hearing and trial," (Walton, *Bible Background*, 439).

ics and dream interpreters. One can perhaps understand why a king would be inclined to imprison a prophet whose very words might incite insurrection or impose doom.[88]

For his part, Micaiah had no issue staking his prophetic integrity on the veracity of his words—the very method Moses had established long ago (Deut 18:21–22; cf. Jer 28:6–9).

When the Israel/Judah coalition met Ben-hadad's army at Ramoth-gilead, Ahab encouraged Jehoshaphat to enter the fray in his royal robes, while Ahab himself went incognito, surely guaranteeing that Judah's king—not Israel's—would be the easier target. Josephus claims Jehoshaphat put on Ahab's own royal garments.[89] And just as Ahab arguably hoped, the Aramaeans gave chase to Jehoshaphat, but only because they mistook him somehow for Ahab. They had been given direct orders to seek out Ahab in battle and eliminate him—imagine the irony of Ben-hadad, the king whose life Ahab had spared (20:34), now ungratefully gunning for Ahab's head. When the Aramaeans discovered their mistake, they let Jehoshaphat go.[90]

"But a certain man drew his bow at random and struck the king of Israel between the scale armor and the breastplate" (v. 34). In this singular statement are no less than three supposed "coincidences" the narrator invites us to contemplate. *First, it was "a certain man" who drew his bow.* I imagine this to have been any ole Joe among Ben-hadad's archers. It wasn't an elite warrior, a member of Aram's A-Team, nor was this a highly trained special-ops assassin. It wasn't Chuck Norris, Jason Bourne, James Bond, or anyone else from Langley or MI-6. It was a certain man, known only to the Most High God, who drew in his bow the fatal arrow that delivered ultimate disaster to Ahab.

Second, the narrator tells us this archer "drew his bow at random." He did not aim specifically at Ahab.[91] He wasn't aiming at anyone, apparently. He was

---

88. Ibid.

89. Josephus, *Antiquities* 8.412.

90. The Chronicler interprets Jehoshaphat's cry as a prayer to God, who answered by drawing the Arameans away from Judah's king (2 Chr 18:31). Later, Jehoshaphat was rebuked by the Lord for participating in the battle (2 Chr 19:2).

91. Behind the ESV's "at random," the Hebrew means "in his simplicity," i.e., without par-

merely one of hundreds of archers who loosed their quivers into the sky, hoping the arrows struck a foe and not a friend. "The soldier had no notion whom he had killed. But Yahweh knew, because Yahweh was singularly devoted to this assassination."[92] As per the sovereignty of heaven, this random arrow from this anonymous archer found its mark in Ahab's body. "Elijah predicted what would happen (1 Kgs 21:19), the king ignored Micaiah's warning, and Ahab paid the price for both his complicity in the killing of Naboth and his rejection of the Lord's merciful word. He could not hide from the results of his own decision."[93] In other words, what appeared to have been dumb luck was a carefully orchestrated act of the divine will.

Finally, the arrow found its place "between the scale armor and the breast-plate." I mean, really! What are the odds? At various sites in the ancient Near East, body armor has been excavated showing interconnected scales and plates, worn as a sort of sleeveless vest with a scale-armor kilt beneath it. Not many gaps would have existed in this armor, and those that did would have been small indeed.[94] Yet this arrow "just happened" to strike Ahab in one of the very few places where he was most vulnerable. Again, what would have appeared to anyone else as dumb luck was a carefully orchestrated act of the divine will.[95]

Knowing he had been mortally wounded, Ahab commanded his driver to wheel around and carry him behind the lines, from whence he watched the remainder of the battle. As the day turned to night, Ahab bled out in his chariot, and Israel's army dispersed to a thousand hills like sheep without a shepherd (v. 36)—just as Yahweh had said. Ahab was buried in Samaria; his chariot was washed in the pool of Samaria,[96] allowing dogs and local whores to frolic in his

---

ticular aim; cf. NRSV "unknowingly" (Wiseman, *1 and 2 Kings*, 201; cf. 2 Sam 15:11). "Such a combination of elaborate precautions, phenomenal luck in escaping determined enemies, and cruel mischance is meant to teach the inevitability of the judgement and the will of God," (Robinson, *First Book*, 248).

92. Brueggemann, *1 & 2 Kings*, 275.

93. House, *1, 2 Kings*, 240.

94. Yadin, *Art of Warfare*, 15. A relief from the tomb of Thutmose IV of Egypt (1411–1397) shows a charioteer pierced by an arrow in the same gap in his armor (Ibid., 192–93, 196).

95. "Against our divinely ordained fate, we humans and our schemes are powerless, even if they seem as well devised as those of Ahab," (Fritz, *1 & 2 Kings*, 220).

96. Among the excavations of the royal palace in Samaria, there has been discovered in the northwest corner a pool measuring sixteen by thirty-three feet (Avigad, "Samaria [City],"

blood—just as Yahweh had said. "In life, Ahab had associated with whores—that is, with idolaters—and so also in death."[97] With that, the narrator dispenses with Ahab, and if you read between the lines, you can almost discern a caustic, "Good riddance!"[98]

T his final episode of Ahab's life is a cautionary tale regarding the consequences of unbelief and scorn for the Word of God. Like Melville's Ahab, this king of Israel became so antagonistic to the truth and wallowed so deeply in self-delusion that he became incapable of believing God's word, even when it was spoken for Ahab's good—perhaps especially when it was spoken for his good. Note Ahab's defiance in this final narrative versus his humility when confronted in Naboth's vineyard (21:27–29).

I know people—and you do, too—who have been so antagonistic to God's revealed will that they cannot believe his Word when spoken for their good. They have no love for the truth, and so God hands them over to be deceived and deluded again and again (cf. Rom 1:24–28). Even in their delusion, however, God sends messengers into their life to shake them back to reality, and though a part of them knows the warning to be valid, they fail to act so as to prevent disaster. This is how churches die, nations crumble, families split, and marriages fail: through selfishness and self-delusion, they slowly lose their ability to believe God's Word and trust his will.

The tragedy of Ahab is made more depressing by the realization that he was a capable king in so many other ways. Despite a three-year drought and defeat by the Arameans (both triggered by Ahab's apostasy), Israel was mostly secure during his reign. Here at the end, the narrator reminds us of Ahab's many building projects (v. 39). As excavators have uncovered the sites of Hazor, Megiddo, Jezreel, Tirzah, and Samaria, all of them exhibit impressive fortification and engineering skill dating to Ahab's reign. "The intricate images of architecture, lions

---

NEAEHL 4:1303).

97. Hubbard, *First and Second Kings*, 120.

98. Notice that "Ahab rested with his fathers" (v. 40) may seem confusing since the phrase normally refers to a king dying peacefully. In fact, it causes DeVries to conclude that "the real Ahab died peacefully in Samaria, probably in ripe old age," rather than in battle (*1 Kings*, 269). However, all the narrator might mean is that, upon Ahab's death, dynastic succession passed from father to son without issue (Sweeney, *I & II Kings*, 262).

and bulls, cherubs, lotus flowers, mythical scenes, and women were common in the Levant, Cyprus, and particularly in Phoenicia. These finds are a concrete manifestation of the syncretistic and excessive practices of Ahab described in 1 Kings. A house with ivory paneled walls would have represented opulence and indulgence taken to unprecedented levels. Further evidence of great wealth among the kingdom's aristocracy was uncovered at Shechem. There a large house with wealthy contents is a good parallel to Ahab's ivory house."[99]

But all the wealth and opulence and administrative acuity and military success in the world are worthless if one does not trust the Word of the Lord and obey it. There is, after all, no other way to be happy in Jesus.

1 KINGS 22:41–50

We've already been introduced to Jehoshaphat in the previous narrative, but here the narrator turns his full attention to Asa's successor, and we realize it has been a while since we heard anything from Judah (15:9–24). "But then, compared to Israel, little has been happening! Revolution and war, apostasy and prophetic intervention—all this has passed the southern kingdom by."[100]

Jehoshaphat (872–848) served as a co-regent with his father for the first three years of his reign (recall Asa's foot disease, 2 Chr 16:12), while his final five years saw his son, Joram, as a co-regent. No known reference to Jehoshaphat exists in ancient secular literature. Like his father, he was a righteous king, but failed to exterminate the scourge of idolatry in Judah completely (v. 43). One thing in his favor is that he wiped out the practice of prostitution at the cult shrines and high places (cf. 15:12; Deut 23:17–18).

In addition to tolerating idolatry to some degree, it seems the narrator is equally disgusted with Jehoshaphat's cozy relationship with Ahab and Jezebel— his son married their daughter (2 Kgs 8:18). It's possible that all the narrator means (v. 44) is that Jehoshaphat negotiated a truce[101] in the sixty-year-long civil war between the two kingdoms. Nonetheless, righteous Jehoshaphat's close ties to the Omrides is disconcerting. "Perhaps he thought it a suave move in face of the resurging Assyrian menace under Ashurnasirpal II and Shalmaneser III. But

---

99. Monson, "1 Kings," 95.

100. Provan, *1 & 2 Kings*, 167.

101. "The verb form [of 'made peace,' v. 44] suggests the initiative was his and he was likely the weaker partner of the alliance," (Olley, *Message of Kings*, 207, n. 65).

it was a spiritual, moral, national disaster. Jehoshaphat seemed to be long on piety and short on sense."[102]

The Chronicler remembers Jehoshaphat as a strong, righteous leader who established several forts and garrisons in Judah (2 Chr 17:2), increased military conscriptions (17:12–19), launched a religious campaign to educate the people in the Law (17:7–9; 19:4), and was responsible for several social reforms (19:3–11). But the Chronicler also tells us of how Jehoshaphat was chastised for his cozy relationship with the house of Omri (2 Chr 19:1–2).

The narrator of Kings also tells us that Jehoshaphat held influence over Edom, just as Solomon had. But he didn't have Solomon's luck (9:26–28) when it came to maritime trade.[103] When Jehoshaphat's ships were destroyed while in port at Ezion-geber (on the Gulf of Aqaba), Ahab's son proposed a joint venture,[104] something to which Jehoshaphat did not agree. Through the prophet Eliezer, Chronicles explains that the ships' destruction was because Jehoshaphat had built them in collaboration with Ahaziah (2 Chr 20:35–37). Duly warned, Judah's righteous king knew better than to attempt such folly a second time.

---

102. Dale Ralph Davis, *2 Kings* (Ross-shire, Scotland: Christian Focus, 2005), 140.

103. "It can be assumed here that Jehoshaphat made an attempt to renovate the ships used by Solomon, but because they proved unseaworthy they could not be taken out of the port of Ezion-geber," (Jones, *1 and 2 Kings*, 2:374).

104. "Ahaziah with his Phoenician connections could have provided experienced sailors," (Robinson, *First Book*, 251).

TALKING POINTS

The statement in 1 Kings 20:23 on the lips of the Arameans—"Their gods are gods of the hills, and so they were stronger than we. But let us fight against them in the plain, and surely we shall be stronger than they"— seems theologically primitive. But it offers a word of warning for God's people in any age. We, too, can be tempted to think that God is potent in some areas of life, but ineffective or uninterested in others. "Religion, we say, will help sometimes; but there are troubles in which some far more definite assistance is required; our God is a God of the hills, but beware, O Christian, of the plain."[105] Though such a confession might never make it to our lips, we might subscribe to a more subtle form of this pagan theology, as Benjamin Franklin did. He once wrote the preacher George Whitefield, "I rather suspect, from certain circumstances, that though the general government of the universe is well administered, our particular little affairs are perhaps below notice, and left to take the chance of human prudence or imprudence, as either may happen to be uppermost."[106] The reality, however, is there is not a molecule, atom, or speck of dust in the universe that is beyond God's concern or control. If he notices when birds fall from the sky and has numbered the hairs on our heads (Matt 10:29–31), we can be sure God reigns in merciful majesty over both the hills and the plains.

Perhaps the most comforting truth of 1 Kings 22 is that God can use delusion, ineptitude, falsehood, and evil to accomplish his grander purposes for his people. Christians are conditioned to think that all calamity and confusion are from a source other than God. Though this may be true in one sense, it is not so in another. To ignore the semantic merry-go-around and cut to the chase, God uses both good and evil events, failure and success, righteousness and wickedness, truth and deception to bring about his will (cf. Rev 16:14). God used deluded false prophets to bring judgment on Ahab's house, liberate Israel from a tyrant's rule, and affirm the divine word spoken by Elijah and Micaiah. Regardless of the blunders of church officials, the political deception of civic lead-

---

105. J. Gresham Machen, *What Is Faith?* (Grand Rapids: Eerdmans, 2011), 68.

106. Arnold A. Dallimore, *George Whitefield*, vol. 2 (Westchester, IL: Cornerstone, 1980), 452.

ers, or the blatant evil of rogue regimes, "we know that for those who love God all things work together for good, for those who are called according to his purpose" (Rom 8:28; cf. Eph 1:11). To guard against being deceived ourselves, we must make sure we love God and love the truth (2 Thess 2:10–12). This begins with fostering a heart desperate for the truth in any situation and at all costs.[107]

R ather than trust and obey the Lord, like Ahab, people often adopt disguises in a dubious attempt to circumvent the divine utterance; to hedge their bets; to have their cake and eat it too. As objective observers, we recognize Ahab's disguise was an exercise in futility: if Micaiah had lied about everything, Ahab had nothing to worry about. On the other hand, if Micaiah had been right about Ahab's doom, no disguise could effectively conceal the king. Years earlier, a prophet had tricked Ahab and decreed his miserable destiny (20:35–43); here, Ahab believed himself capable of fooling a prophet (or worse, that prophet's God!) and so escaping said destiny. But like Saul and Jeroboam's wife, Ahab's disguise was exposed by an all-seeing eye. Our attempts at camouflage are more subtle than that. We exchange horrible concepts like "adultery" and "homosexuality" for more PR-friendly labels like "affair" and "alternate lifestyle." "Sin" has been reconceptualized as a "mistake." Fundamentally bad, Scripture-denigrating decisions are said to be "Spirit-led" and an opportunity to "step out in faith." We're no better than real estate agents advertising crack houses as "homes with character." It is no wonder, then, that a prerequisite for any right relationship with God is shedding our "disguises," owning up to and being open about our sins, and allowing the sunlight of truth to sanitize our corrupted hearts. Where there is equivocation over sin and fraternity with falsehood, deception, and disguises, there can be no fellowship with He who has 20/20 vision.

---

107. "Ahab is a forerunner of all leaders who say 'tell me the truth' but expect affirmation and reject criticism, leaders who surround themselves with likeminded people. If that is dangerous on the human level of leadership and management, how much more when it shuts out any 'word of God' that is uncomfortable, questioning present attitudes and actions. Wise are leaders who are open to well-founded criticism, and Christian leaders who are open to having their understanding of Scripture corrected," (Olley, *Message of Kings*, 203).

8

TRANSITIONS

Transition can intimidate us. Transitioning into a new job can be exciting, but with it comes an avalanche of anxiety and uncertainty. Will this work out? Should I have left my old job? Will I make friends here? Am I even qualified for this position?

Transitioning into a new season of life can be exciting, but with it comes a dose of melancholy and more than a little regret. Will we miss the old days more? Will we become so miserable in our new circumstance that we just mark time until a new season arrives?

Transitions in leadership and power can be especially tense. A new boss in the office. A new eldership in the church. A new president or political party in power in Washington. It's not unusual for more than a few people to claim the sky is falling whenever a powerful CEO (e.g., Steve Jobs, Lee Iacocca) steps down or a new president (e.g., Presidents Obama and Trump) is sworn in. Roughly half the people will think the future is bright when change comes; the other half will claim that brightness is a giant meteor hastening our global demise.

The transition from 1 to 2 Kings sees the death of Ahab and the rise of his two sons, Ahaziah and Jehoram. The wicked king is dead, but his dynasty remains. New leaders always bring with them the hope of renewal and reform—of change we can believe in. Should we get our hopes up? Will we be disappointed?

The transition also sees the rapture of Elijah and the rise of his successor, Elisha. What will become of God's work in Israel?[1] Elijah has meant more to Israel than her entire military—can Elisha even begin to fill those formidable shoes?

---

1. "Elijah has demonstrated Yahweh's sovereignty over Baal (1 Kgs 17–19). The unnamed prophets showed that the Lord rules hill and valley (1 Kgs 20). Elijah and Micaiah claimed that

The chapters that deal with transition present us with many changes. But there is one thing that doesn't change throughout: God's word and God's work.[2] They cannot be overcome. He still speaks and acts among his people to accomplish his will. That's not bad advice for us—his people—either, when we find ourselves drowning in transition. Keep calm and keep speaking God's Word and doing his work. The more things change, the more some things ought to stay the same.

1 KINGS 22:51–2 KINGS 1:18

First Kings ends at an arbitrary point. Though Ahaziah's story continues in 2 Kings 1, the final three verses of 1 Kings 22 give the conventional notice of his reign (853–852).[3] In a nutshell, he was just as wicked as Mom and Dad.

After a brief note about Moab's rebellion (a detail that will be picked up in 2 Kings 3), we learn that Ahaziah was injured when he fell out of a window in his palace.[4] And I love Leithart's insight here—"Strikingly, 2 Kings begins, as does 1 Kings, with a sick king, confined to bed. Both David and Ahaziah receive prophets on their deathbeds, but the results are quite different."[5]

As was common in ancient times, Ahaziah ordered messengers to go and inquire of a deity as to whether he would recover. But the rub is that Ahaziah wished to inquire of Baal-zebub in Ekron[6] (a Philistine town near the coast, sixty

---

the Lord punishes sin and directs battles (1 Kgs 21–22). But the prophets' messages fall on deaf ears, and truth must be taught all over again in each new situation," (House, *1, 2 Kings*, 244).

2. "The critical truth is this: *when God's leader is removed, everything of God remains.* Transition times are times to refocus on the unchanging God," (Inrig, *I & II Kings*, 203; emphasis his).

3. "The two years of Ahaziah were of less than a twelve-month duration, according to our calender [*sic*]; he came to the throne in Jehoshaphat's seventeenth year (22:52) and died in his eighteenth year (2 Kgs 3:1)," (Mordechai Cogan and Hayim Tadmor, *II Kings* [Garden City, NY: Doubleday, 1988], 21).

4. "The excavations in Samaria have demonstrated that the royal palace at this time did have a second story. The style of architecture featured open areas, and the lattice described here would have been a wooden grid offering both shade and air circulation," (Walton, *Bible Background*, 385).

5. Leithart, *1 & 2 Kings*, 165.

6. "Later in 2 Kgs this motif of the search for healing from a foreign deity becomes common (cf. 2 Kgs 5, 8). The point of these stories is to demonstrate that only in Israel is the true God to be found," (T. R. Hobbs, *2 Kings* [Waco: Word, 1985], 9). A jar from the seventh century was uncovered at Ekron in 1997, bearing the name *Baal* (Seymour Gitin and Mordechai Cogan, "A

miles southwest of Samaria), rather than seeking a word from Yahweh (cf. Amos 5:5–6; Lev 19:31). The Philistines seem to have had a reputation in the Old Testament for divining and/or healing diseases (cf. 1 Sam 6:2; Isa 2:6). By seeking help outside Israel, the king may have also been trying to keep the severity of his injury from leaking to the press, "lest it tempt his rivals to overthrow him."[7] But one imagines the Holy One of Israel looking upon Ahaziah in disgust, asking, "What am I? Chopped liver?" Suffice it to say that God's incredulity[8] over being passed over in favor of a false god (cf. Deut 4:35; 12:30) is a major point of tension in this passage.

The name *Baal-zebub* means "lord of the flies" and is thought by more than a few scholars to be "a satirical corruption of Baalzebul," which means "Baal the prince."[9] Incidentally, it is also a moniker for Satan in the New Testament (Matt 10:25; 12:24, 27; Mark 3:22; Luke 11:15, 18–19). If the name is not a satirical corruption, it may refer to the god's "ability to drive away flies who carry disease and infection,"[10] but there remains no reference to a god named Baal-zebub outside of Scripture.

Except for a brief appearance at the end of Naboth's story, we have not heard a peep out of Elijah since he anointed Elisha as his successor in 1 Kings 19:19–21. An angel inspired Elijah to intercept Ahaziah's messengers and deliver Yahweh's assessment of the situation. Ahaziah would not recover; his days were numbered. The phrase "you shall surely die," repeated three times in the narrative (vv. 4, 6, 16), may look rather ordinary in English, but "it is in fact a quite se-

---

New Type of Dedicatory Inscription from Ekron," *IEJ* 49 [1999]: 193–202).

7. Hubbard, *First and Second Kings*, 136.

8. In Hebrew, there is an emphatic double negative in Elijah's rhetorical question, "Is it because there is *no* God in Israel…?" (v. 3; emphasis mine). "Yahweh alone is God and therefore the only one to be approached for counsel or help; to acknowledge Yahweh as the only God precludes the possibility of appealing to any other god," (Fritz, *1 & 2 Kings*, 230).

9. Fretheim, *First and Second Kings*, 132; cf. Wray Beal, *1 & 2 Kings*, 294–95; Brueggemann, *1 & 2 Kings*, 284; Gray, *I & II Kings*, 413. "Such a use of corrupted names conveying more of the writer's or speaker's opinion of the character than its proper meaning is common in the OT," (Hobbs, *2 Kings*, 8).

10. Walton, *Bible Background*, 385; Herrmann, "Baal Zebub," *DDD* 154. "Abundant parallels of 'fly-gods' are available in classical and patristic literature. […] Because of their power over flies, these deities could send or retract plagues and diseases, and the increased activities of flies in high summer probably indicated that they were essentially sun-gods," (Jones, *1 and 2 Kings*, 2:377). See also Arvid Tangberg, "A Note on Ba'al Zĕbūb in 2 Kgs 1,2.3.6.16," *SJOT* 6 (1992): 293–96.

vere, absolute, and formal pronouncement of a death penalty from which there is no escape or reprieve."[11] Elsewhere in the Old Testament, the phrase is used by God for violating his will (Gen 2:17; 3:3; Exod 21:12–17)—"These parallels attest to the severity and firmness of the prophetic utterance to the king."[12]

The messengers returned to the king with Elijah's memo, and as soon as they described his appearance, Ahaziah knew exactly who he was dealing with—"There is something roughhewn and perhaps forbidding in his distinctive look."[13] It seems prophets (or at least Elijah) wore iconic apparel (cf. Zech 13:4; Matt 3:4). The king responded to Elijah's message as we would expect any biblical tyrant to do: he sent a detachment of troops to silence the Troublemaker once and for all. The text tells us that Elijah "was sitting on top of a hill," perhaps a reference to Carmel. The unit's commander demanded[14] he come down in the name of the king, but Elijah declined. "If I am a man of God,[15] let fire come down from heaven and consume you and your fifty" (v. 10). No sooner were the words out of his mouth than they came to pass. Elijah had summoned fire once before on Carmel; doing so again confirmed him as God's man, "a true possessor and proclaimer of God's word."[16]

Ahaziah, who doesn't strike me as the sharpest tool in the shed, sent another detachment to do his bidding. His momma had once succeeded in intimidating Elijah; but here, our gritty prophet is aloof to imperial power (Sirach 48:12). Again, the commander demanded Elijah come down in the name of the king.[17]

---

11. Brueggemann, *1 & 2 Kings*, 284.

12. Ibid.

13. Alter, *Ancient Israel*, 732.

14. "It must be noted that the demand made of Elijah was wrong. A king had no right to ask such allegiance and his actions should always be subordinate to God's word (cf. 1 Sam. 10:25). God was protecting his word and his servant," (Wiseman, *1 and 2 Kings*, 206).

15. "[Elijah]—and the narrative—regard the title 'man of God' as one of immense authority, well beyond royal control," (Brueggemann, *1 & 2 Kings*, 286).

16. House, *1, 2 Kings*, 244.

17. "Everything is the same, except the royal imperative. In v. 9 it was 'come down.' Now in v. 11, it is 'come down *quickly*.' The adverb intensifies royal urgency, no doubt because of the intensification of royal anxiety. But to no avail. Royal imperative will not impinge upon prophetic authority," (Brueggemann, *1 & 2 Kings*, 286; emphasis his).

Again, Elijah gave him a thumbs down. Again, fire fell from heaven.[18] Again, fifty-one Israelite army wives became widows.

Ahaziah sent a third detachment, but this commander was wiser and more submissive to Elijah's status as a man of God. Falling to his knees, he begged Elijah's mercy and favor—the verb translated "entreated" (v. 13) literally means "be gracious to."[19] "The captain personifies the insight that acceptance is the only appropriate response to the man of God as the representative of God's will. The example of the other two captains, in contrast, serves to demonstrate the infinite superiority of divine power over that of humans."[20]

With the angel's blessing, Elijah accompanied the commander back to Samaria. But his message remained the same: Ahaziah would die. And he did, for the word of the Lord stands forever, and when it goes forth, it does not return to him empty (Isa 55:11). "The king, emblem of power and wealth, is dead, unable to resist the harsh pronouncements of the God of countertruth."[21] Following Ahaziah's death, his brother, Jehoram, became king.

A haziah's presumption that he could order a man of God around like he was yet another palace lackey is one of the more comical moments in Kings. Provan writes, "Not for the first time in Kings, a negative oracle addressed to a king elicits an attempt to capture the prophet who delivered it (cf. 1 Kgs. 13:1–7; 17:1–4; 18:9–10; 22:1–28). The prophetic word, however,

---

18. "The fire is less a divine means to protect the prophet than a public demonstration of the power of Israel's God in a situation where that power (to heal) has been called into question and a public verification of Elijah as mediator of this power [...] It is almost as if in approaching Elijah (on a hill) they approach the reality of God himself (see Exod. 19:18)," (Fretheim, *First and Second Kings*, 133).

19. Fretheim, "חָנַן," *NIDOTTE* 2:203. Josephus records that this third officer was "wise," "of a mild disposition," and "spake civilly to [Elijah]," (*Antiquities* 9.25). "Elijah, like his God, is to be entreated, and not commanded," (Auld, *I & II Kings*, 152).

20. Fritz, *1 & 2 Kings*, 231.

21. Brueggemann, *1 & 2 Kings*, 292. "Notably, the narrative has no interest in the fall of the king with which the narrative began (1:2). The king will not die from his injury. He will die, rather, because Yahweh plays for keeps, and will tolerate no alternative loyalty. The narrative is abrupt. In v. 7, the king responds to the prophetic declaration of death. But here there is a tone of finality to the prophetic word. The king does not speak, offers no rebuttal. He promptly dies in the next verse!" (Ibid., 287).

cannot be brought under human control. A man of God, precisely because he is a man *of God*, cannot be coerced by a mere king."[22]

Not only does our God exercise absolute sovereignty over all creation, but he also directs events for the benefit of his servants when it is his sovereign good pleasure to do so. Not a hair on the prophet's head can be harmed without God's permission. Meanwhile, the Ahaziahs of the world exercise as much control over the divine word as they do their own health.

And that, in fact, leads us to the main point of the story. Like little kids who are distracted by shiny objects, we can become easily enamored with heaven's pyrotechnics and miss their reason. More than for Elijah's protection, the fire from heaven represented God's judgment against Ahaziah for seeking a divine word outside of Israel and her God. When God's people solicit a word of counsel or direction outside of Scripture and its Author, we risk the same judgment. Leithart explains, "One would not want an amateur performing a quadruple bypass, but the post-Enlightenment reliance on experts is often a form of practical idolatry, a version of consulting Baal-zebub instead of Yahweh. Elijah could well challenge churches that rely on Freud for counseling, on Marx or Weber for their sociology and politics, on Madison Avenue for their evangelistic planning with the question, 'Is there no God in Israel, that you go to inquire of Baal-zebub of Ekron?'"[23]

Concerning the question posed three times in this story—"Is there no God in Israel?" (vv. 3, 6, 16)—Fretheim makes an excellent observation: "The purpose of the question is not simply to make a claim for the Lord, but to get these individuals themselves explicity [*sic*] or implicitly to downgrade the godness of Baal."[24] In other words, it's not enough to say God is our best source of refuge and strength, but that he is our *only* source of refuge and strength. The world might be satisfied with a #1 ranking on Yelp; God, however, ruthlessly seeks to put all competitors out of business forever.

The Alpha and Omega brooks no rivals.

2 KINGS 2:1-12

"If you knew you had only twenty-four hours to live, what would you do?" I once asked this of a Bible class, and I received the expected pious responses:

---

22. Provan, *1 & 2 Kings*, 169; emphasis his.

23. Leithart, *1 & 2 Kings*, 168.

24. Fretheim, *First and Second Kings*, 134.

- "I'd call all my kids and tell them I love them."
- "I'd pray and read my Bible."
- "I'd spend the day repenting of all I'd done wrong."

As a diabetic, I'd probably eat as many root beer floats as I could stomach. Why not?

I find myself fascinated with how Elijah spent his last day on earth. Knowing that his ministry was at an end, he and Elisha made a journey from Gilgal[25] to Bethel to Jericho to the other side of the Jordan.[26] At each place, Elijah begged Elisha to leave him be (vv. 2, 4, 6; cf. Matt 26:38–45), but Elisha would not be deterred from following his mentor to the end (Brueggemann notes that *leave* in these three verses has the force of *abandon*[27]). At Bethel and Jericho, the prophetic community came out to greet them. When they asked Elisha, "Do you know today's the day?"[28] he responded with something like, "Yes; don't remind me" (vv. 3, 5).

When they arrived at the Jordan, Elijah rolled up his cloak, or outer garment, and parted the river with it. In every way, we are observing here a reversal of Joshua's Conquest. As the Jordan was parted so that Israel could enter the Promised Land, so it is now parted so that Elijah and Elisha could technically leave the Promised Land.[29]

─────────────

25. That this is the same Gilgal as the one where Israel camped after crossing the Jordan (Josh 4:19) is not certain. Unlike that Gilgal, the one described in 2 Kings 2:2 is at a higher elevation than of Bethel (cf. "went down to"). Thus, this Gilgal has been tentatively identified with a site seven miles north of Bethel (Iain Provan, "2 Kings," in *Zondervan Illustrated Bible Backgrounds Commentary*, vol. 3, ed. John H. Walton [Grand Rapids: Zondervan, 2009], 119; cf. Boyce M. Bennett, Jr., "The Search for Israelite Gilgal," *PEQ* 104 [1972]: 111–22).

26. The journey from Bethel to Jericho is about twelve miles and would have taken about half a day. The Jordan River was another five miles beyond Jericho.

27. Brueggemann, *1 & 2 Kings*, 294.

28. In the Hebrew text, the prophets' use of *take away* is the same Hebrew verb as is used in Genesis 5:24 for Enoch's rapture to heaven.

29. "Gilgal, Bethel, and Jericho are associated with Israel's original arrival in the land. Israel camps at Gilgal when it first enters the land, and there the Israelite men are circumcised and Israel celebrates the first Passover in the land (5:1–12). Bethel is associated with the city of Ai and was destroyed along with Ai during the conquest (8:9, 12, 17), and Jericho, of course, is the site of the great battle where the walls tumble down. Each of these cities, in short, is associated with Joshua's conquest. Under the idolatrous Omride dynasty, Israel moves, as it were, backward in time, as the Omride kings promote the worship of Canaanite gods, particularly Baal. With his

Before being taken up to heaven, Elijah granted Elisha one request. Elisha responded, "Please let there be a double portion of your spirit on me" (v. 9). It may seem as if Elisha was asking for double Elijah's mojo or moxie, but he was actually requesting the inheritance due the firstborn, which was twice as much as every other share (cf. Deut 21:15–17). Elisha, however, did not have property in mind so much as prophetic prowess and leadership. "This reception of the double share identified Elisha as the first-born among the prophets, that is, as the one entitled to become the new leader of the prophetic guilds in the place of the departed leader."[30]

In response, Elijah assured his protégé that the request would be honored if Elisha's gaze did not shift during what he was about to witness. "What Elijah implies is that Elisha's status as successor depends on his ability to see and comprehend the spiritual world. If he possesses the ability of a visionary to penetrate into the heavenly world, his request will be granted; if he cannot demonstrate that he has that ability, his request will not be granted."[31]

For only the second time in history, a mortal was raptured to heaven without seeing death. Elijah was taken up (literally in the Hebrew) "in the storm[32] of the heavens." While beholding the spectacle, all Elisha could say was, "My father, my father! The chariots of Israel and its horsemen!" (v. 12). What did he mean by those words? Obviously, it's possible Elisha was merely commenting on what he saw (v. 11).[33] But the fact that Jehoash will later utter the same words

---

departing itinerary Elijah demonstrates this reversal, preenacting the exile of Israel and Judah on the far side of the Jordan. Like the exile later in Israel's history, however, this reversal of the conquest sets the stage for a new conquest," (Leithart, *1 & 2 Kings*, 172).

30. R. P. Carroll, "The Elijah-Elisha Sagas: Some Remarks on Prophetic Succession in Ancient Israel," *VT* 19 (1969): 405. "With Elijah's ascension to heaven, prophetic responsibility to hold Israel accountable for covenant fidelity is transferred to Elisha," (Konkel, *1 & 2 Kings*, 379).

31. Jones, *1 and 2 Kings*, 2:385.

32. "Earlier God had spoken to Elijah after a storm of sorts was over (1 Kgs 19:11–13). Also, this scene may be one last time where Yahweh proves stronger than Baal, for once again the Lord conquers death (cf. 1 Kgs 17:7–24), and once again he rules the storms instead of the supposed storm god Baal. Thus, rich irony, not unlike that so evident in the Mount Carmel episode, prevails to the end of the Elijah accounts," (House, *1, 2 Kings*, 259).

33. Lundbom absurdly contends that, rather than a miraculous rapture to heaven, Elisha was crying out that the king of Israel's chariot had swooped in, kidnapped Elijah, and was now carrying him off to his death (Jack R. Lundbom, "Elijah's Chariot Ride," *JJS* 24 [1973]: 48).

at Elisha's deathbed, an occasion lacking literal chariots and horses of fire, may indicate that another meaning is in order.

In both ancient biblical and secular literature, chariots and fire represented the presence of deity (Exod 3:2; 19:18; Ps 68:17; Isa 66:15–16; Ezek 1:15–21; 10:15–18), and often in a military context (Hab 3:8). Every day of Israel's advance to the Promised Land was considered a military march, one led by the pillar of cloud and fire (Exod 13:21–22; 14:19–20; Num 10:33–34; 14:13–14). The whirlwind, too, is often associated with God's appearing (Job 38:1; 40:6; Pss 18:9–15; 29:3–9). Robinson adds:

> Chariots had played a considerable part in the fortunes of the Israelite tribes in the early days of their settlements in Canaan. The Canaanites had then possessed chariots and this had given them weapon superiority over the Israelites. So the Israelites had been confined to the hill-country where chariots could not be used effectively. They could not settle at all on the plains where their foot-soldiers were no match for the enemy chariots. At that time the Israelites had neither the expertise for using chariots nor the economic resources to be able to maintain them. Thus chariots came to be for Israel the symbol of overwhelming military force, and when under David and Solomon, the kingdom grew strong and powerful, that power was displayed by the building of chariot cities which housed large forces of chariots. These were regarded as one of the greater bulwarks for the defence of the nation. The association of chariots with the prophets Elijah and Elisha may be pointing to them as fulfilling the same function, i.e. defending the nation against its enemies.[34]

Secular history remembers Ahab for his military might, particularly his many chariots at the battle of Qarqar. But in 1 Kings 20, the Arameans were under the impression that they would enjoy a distinct advantage over Israel's military if they fought on the plains where Aramean chariots would rule the day; Israel's God, so they thought, was effective only in the hills. They didn't realize

---

34. J. Robinson, *The Second Book of Kings* (Cambridge: Cambridge Univ. Press, 1976), 25–26; cf. James G. Williams, "The Prophetic 'Father': A Brief Explanation of the Term 'Sons of the Prophets,'" *JBL* 85 (1966): 344–48.

that Israel had chariots and horses of a different kind[35] (Deut 20:1). Thus, Elisha's parting words to his mentor affirmed that "Elijah's prophetic powers and spiritual depth [were Israel's] true strength,"[36] and only because they came from the Lord (cf. Deut 17:16; Isa 31:1; Rom 8:37–39; Eph 6:10–17).

As he watched his mentor being raptured to heaven, Elisha "took hold of his own clothes and tore them in two pieces" (v. 12), which was a common public expression of grief in ancient times (cf. Gen 37:34; 2 Sam 1:11; 13:31; Job 1:20). That Elijah departed this life in such a fashion surely points to his uniqueness as a man of God. Nothing like him would be seen in Israel for a long time.

The sudden, unexpected death of my father during my college years was quite traumatic. Dad was more than a dad; he was a mentor, confidant, and friend. I was looking forward to a lifetime of partnership with him in our service to God. As it turned out, Dad was also a linchpin in my life, one who held a lot of things together. With his passing, those things came undone.

Several months after his death, one of my professors asked me to visit his office. He could tell I was still struggling to keep my head above water in the ocean of grief. He knew the wrong person had been at the center of my life. So, as we talked in his office, he pulled a pen from his drawer and several paper clips, looping the paper clips on the pen. He explained, "Too often, one person in our life keeps many things from falling to the ground." The pen represented my father, and the paper clips all the things I had "hung" on him through the years. One paper clip represented his leadership role as a father; another, that of friend. He was my preacher. He was my financial supporter. In sum, I had structured my life so that nearly every arena depended on him. And when my professor yanked the pen away, and the paper clips clattered to his desk, I realized my mistake.

I lost it. I wept bitterly—more so than I had in weeks.

---

35. Patrick D. Miller, Jr., *The Divine Warrior in Early Israel* (Cambridge, MA: Harvard Univ. Press, 1973), 134–35.

36. House, *1, 2 Kings*, 258. "Elijah does not simply ride Yahweh's chariot, but *is* Yahweh's chariot, the prophet who bears God's presence and serves as the true protector of the land. Elisha confesses that the true power, the true defense of Israel does not lie with the kings or with his horses and chariots but with his master Elijah," (Leithart, *1 & 2 Kings*, 176; emphasis his). See also M. A. Beek, "The Meaning of the Expression 'The Chariots and the Horsemen of Israel' (II Kings ii 12)," in *The Witness of Tradition: Papers Read at the Joint British-Dutch Old Testament Conference held at Woudschoten, 1970* (Leiden: Brill, 1972), 1–10.

Inrig encourages us to "value people who have gone before you, but let your trust and focus be on the Lord alone."[37] Times of transition can intimidate us, and the loss of someone significant not only brings grief and heartache, but also a strong sense of disorientation. Elijah's rapture left a huge void in Israel. Elisha's utterance, "My father…," represented a lot of paper clips. But no matter how significant someone may be in our lives, their passing ought to help us realize how important it is to rely ultimately on the Lord. In times of transition, there is one thing that never changes: God's Word and God's work.

The final words of the Old Testament contain an enigmatic promise of Elijah's return. "Behold, I will send you Elijah the prophet before the great and awesome day of the LORD comes. And he will turn the hearts of fathers to their children and the hearts of children to their fathers, lest I come and strike the land with a decree of utter destruction" (Mal 4:5–6).[38] There arose, then, a belief among the Jews that Elijah would return to earth as a precursor to the coming of the Messiah. Even today, Jews offer this prayer at meals, "May God in his mercy send us the prophet Elijah," and a seat is reserved for Elijah at the Passover table.[39]

Elijah did come as a forerunner of Christ, but he did so in the form of John the Baptist (Matt 11:13–14; Luke 1:17; cf. John 1:21). After John's death, the apostles acknowledged that many believed Jesus to be John or Elijah resurrected (Matt 16:14). And while hanging on the cross, onlookers misinterpreted Jesus' cry of abandonment in the Hebrew tongue to be a summons for Elijah to come and rescue him (Matt 27:46–47), presumably with the chariots and horsemen of Israel. Elijah's importance to Israel's story is never more clearly demonstrated

---

37. Inrig, *I & II Kings*, 211.

38. "The figure of Elijah appears to stand behind the representation of the two prophets in Rev. 11:1–6, who stop the rain and kill with fire those who try to harm them," (Provan, *1 & 2 Kings*, 170). "A mixture of images is woven into the description of these two witnesses. The references to the witnesses calling down fire, shutting up the heavens so it cannot rain, and striking the earth with plagues (Rev. 11:5–6) recall the work of Moses and Elijah. […] Earlier John symbolized the whole church by seven lampstands (Rev. 1:20), but the two witnesses are depicted as lamps corresponding to the work of Moses and Elijah. The churches of Asia are given the function of Moses and Elijah to prepare the way for the coming of the Lord, when the kingdoms of this world become exclusively his own," (Konkel, *1 & 2 Kings*, 311–12).

39. Ibid., 310.

than when he, along with Moses,[40] appeared transfigured on either side of Christ on the mountain (Matt 17:1–3), Moses and Elijah representing the Prophets and the Law, respectively.

Elijah, then, not only came to embody all the prophets of Israel, but also what they represented beyond all else: God's attempt to reconcile with his people. The passage in Malachi spoke of Elijah turning hearts back to God, lest people perish in the way of his wrath (cf. Sirach 48:10), and this thinking may have been why people thought Jesus was summoning the prophet—as a rescue from the divine wrath they thought Christ so justly deserved. Yet, as we have seen, Elijah was flawed—no less or more than you and me. So we should be grateful that one much greater than Elijah—God in Christ—came to reconcile us to the Father and spare us from divine wrath (2 Cor 5:18–21).

2 KINGS 2:13–25

Elijah now gone, Elisha picked up his departed master's cloak—as well as the proverbial prophetic mantle—and used it to part the Jordan again. "Elisha thereby demonstrates both to himself and to the witnessing prophets that Elijah's mantle has indeed passed to him."[41] The author of Kings does not linger on what happened to Elijah; he quickly shifts his narrative focus to Elisha and his ministry. Elijah may have departed, but Yahweh remained, and he would equip his servant to discharge his prophetic ministry. Israel had not suffered a setback when Moses died and Joshua assumed leadership; nor would she suffer a setback with Elisha at the prophetic fore.

Though mentioned in the latter chapters of 1 Kings, this is our first extended look at the prophetic guild or "sons of the prophets." Originating with Samuel (1 Sam 10:10; 19:20), the prophetic guild was a community of prophets and prophets-in-training in Israel—think of it as part training school, part trade fraternity. Though they seem to have had some connection with Elijah, their connection with Elisha will be even stronger (e.g., 4:1; 6:1; 9:1). They were not the same as the prophets who served the king (1 Kgs 22:5–12); the prophetic guild was quite "anti-establishment."

---

40. Indeed, Elijah's mysterious departure from this life "invested him with the quality of eternal life, surpassing even Moses, the father of all prophets, who died and was buried (albeit by God himself: Deut 34:5–6)," (Cogan, *II Kings*, 33–34; cf. Wray Beal, *1 & 2 Kings*, 306).

41. Fretheim, *First and Second Kings*, 138.

When members of the guild saw Elisha return without his mentor, they acknowledged that something fundamental had changed in Elisha—"The spirit of Elijah rests on Elisha" (v. 15)—but they were not aware that Elijah was gone for good. Instead, they begged Elisha to sanction a search party. It seems Elijah was prone to be caught up by the Spirit and taken to out-of-the-way places (cf. 1 Kgs 18:12). Elisha finally gave in and allowed such, but the search was fruitless.[42]

The remaining anecdotes of the chapter affirm Elisha's prophetic potency was no less than Elijah's. The city of Jericho was suffering from bad water—one of the reasons Jericho was an attractive site in the first place was its access to abundant spring water[43]—and we can't help but wonder if this had something to do with Joshua's curse (Josh 6:26).

In 1967, Ian M. Blake suggested that the Ain es-Sultan spring that provides water to the Jericho site was contaminated and radioactive from Joshua's Conquest until the time of Elisha.[44] Given that the Jericho site receives an average of less than two inches of rain per year, this perennial spring provided much-needed irrigation for surrounding fields.[45] This explains why the men of the city told the prophet, "the water is foul and the country suffers from miscarriages" (v. 19 NJB), and may clarify how Hiel's children died (1 Kgs 16:34)—the word translated "unfruitful" (v. 19 ESV) can also refer to abortion or miscarriage.[46]

Whatever was wrong with the water of Jericho, God was powerful enough to cleanse it, and he mercifully and unilaterally reversed the curse of Jericho through Elisha. At the initiative of Yahweh, the prophet threw salt in the local

---

42. Provan wonders aloud, "Perhaps it is the retrieval of a body for burial (cf. 1 Sam. 31:11–13), rather than recovery of a living person, that they have in mind," (*1 & 2 Kings*, 174). This, however, seems unlikely since the prophets speculated that the Spirit of the Lord had moved Elijah. "The episode may constitute the narrator's acknowledgement that the ascent is indeed strange and inexplicable. The other prophets have no categories for it. In order to reassure those who hear the narrative, this three-day search is one additional assurance. The entire exchange serves, in the end, to enhance the authority of Elisha," (Brueggemann, *1 & 2 Kings*, 299).

43. W. J. Drumbell, "Jericho," in *Major Cities in the Biblical World*, ed. R. K. Harrison (Nashville: Nelson, 1985), 133.

44. Ian M. Blake, "Jericho (Ain es-Sultan): Joshua's Curse and Elisha's Miracle—One Possible Explanation," *PEQ* 99 (1967): 86–97.

45. Provan, "2 Kings," 121.

46. *HALOT* 1492; cf. Hamilton, "שָׁכֹל," *NIDOTTE* 4:105–6.

spring to purify it, and then the water was miraculously desalinated.[47] In ancient times, it seems salt was used to symbolize a break from the past (cf. Lev 2:13; Num 18:19; Judg 9:45; Ezek 16:4; 43:24),[48] and here it serves that very function. No longer did Jericho stand under Yahweh's curse—the spring was healed and fertility restored (cf. Gen 20:17).

In the next scene, Elisha was passing through Bethel when forty-two[49] boys of the town began taunting him and his baldness, regarded as a disgrace in the Old Testament (cf. Lev 19:27; 21:5; Isa 3:17, 24). Recall that Elijah had been one hairy dude (1:8), so "Elisha's baldness would be a stark contrast and perhaps suggest to some that he could never have the same powers as his master. This taunt would therefore be a disavowal of his prophetic office and calling and would be strikingly refuted by the immediate fulfillment of his curse."[50] In response, Elisha cursed them (not in the sense of foul language, but of praying for God to mete out consequences) and two bears—common in ancient Israel—appeared and mauled[51] them (cf. Hos 13:8). Note that Elisha did not specially call out two bears; rather, he called upon God to do something about the situation, and God did.

Elisha's actions here are often perceived to have been cruel and vindictive.[52] That said, there are a few mitigating facts that must be acknowledged. First, in

---

47. Daniel Sperber, "Weak Waters," *ZAW* 82 (1970): 114–16.

48. Gray, *I & II Kings*, 427–28.

49. It's possible that the number *forty-two* here symbolically represents something else, rather than being a literal number (cf. 10:14; Rev 11:2; 13:5).

50. Walton, *Bible Background*, 387. "He is no longer a servant of Elijah, but has taken Elijah's place. He is due, and must demand, appropriate respect. To tolerate less is to invite insult. Shouting an insult to the Lord's prophet approaches hurling an insult at the Lord. Such behavior warrants immediate chastisement," (Hens-Piazza, *1–2 Kings*, 237).

51. Irwin notes that the Hebrew verb used "has the sense of 'split open' and [...] likely indicates that the boys were severely injured if not killed," (Brian P. Irwin, "The Curious Incident of the Boys and the Bears: 2 Kings 2 and the Prophetic Authority of Elisha," *TynBul* 67 [2016]: 24).

52. "This is in every respect a puerile tale, and serves as a gauge of the moral level of the dervish communities from which the strictly hagiographical material in the Elisha cycle emanated. [...] There is no serious point in this incident, and it does not reflect much to the credit of the prophet. [...] The supposition that Elisha invoked the name of Yahweh to curse the boys, with such terrible consequences, is derogatory to the great public figure, and borders on blasphemy," (Gray, *I & II Kings*, 428–29). "The early rabbis were so outraged by this story that they felt constrained to assert it never really happened. Their formulation, 'neither bears nor forest,' became

the Old Testament, the Hebrew phrase translated "young lads" (v. 23 NASU; other translations' "small boys" is inappropriate) can refer to a male aged twelve to
thirty years old (cf. 1 Sam 16:11–12; 2 Sam 14:21; 18:5)—in other words, "old
enough to show respect for God's prophet."[53] There was simply no excuse for
their behavior.

What is more, Bethel in Kings is in some ways the epicenter of apostasy (cf.
1 Kgs 12:29), and as we saw with the unnamed prophet in 1 Kings 13 or with
Elijah in 2 Kings 1, disrespecting God's prophets brings with it the risk of immediate retribution[54] (cf. Deut 7:10; 18:19). Along this line, the Old Testament
consistently presents wild animal attacks as punishment for covenant violators
(Deut 32:24; Amos 5:18–19). In Genesis 1:28, God had granted to man dominion over all the animals; attacks, then, were seen by ancient Israel as a suspension
of that primeval blessing.[55] Add to this the connection in this passage between
Bethel and Jericho; while Jericho experienced the removal of its curse because of
the people's positive response to Elisha, Bethel has its curse perpetuated because
these boys did not receive the prophet warmly.[56]

Finally, Elisha's "baldness" may not be literal, but an allusion to the fact that
he was (in the mind of the boys) decidedly *not* as good as his predecessor. Elijah
was associated with hair so much that the phrase "a hairy man" told Ahaziah exactly whom he was dealing with (1:8). Thus, the boys taunt Elisha: "You're not the
prophet we need, the miracle-worker we're used to."[57] But their snap judgment is
wrong. Dead wrong. Elisha is everything Elijah was and more. Thus, "the incident

---

idiomatic in Hebrew for a cock-and-bull story," (Alter, *Ancient Israel*, 739). Contra Konkel: "The
mauling of the youthful mob is not vindictive anger on behalf of Elisha but divine judgment for
culpable denial of the divine purpose. The bears are no less divinely appointed than the whale
that swallowed Jonah," (Konkel, *1 & 2 Kings*, 382).

53. House, *1, 2 Kings*, 260, n. 23.

54. Provan, *1 & 2 Kings*, 175.

55. Irwin, "Curious Incident," 27–28.

56. "The juxtaposition of Jericho and Bethel shows that the state of curse need not be
permanent. By their positive response to the prophetic word, the people of Jericho are able to
shed the mantle of divine curse. By contrast, the way in which the people of Bethel continue to
reject and ridicule the prophet means that the curse remains with them and becomes even more
severe," (Ibid., 32).

57. David E. Fass, "Elisha's Locks and the She-Bears," *JRJ* 34/3 (1987): 25–26.

puts Israel on notice. This Elisha is dangerous and is not to be trifled with, not by small boys, not by kings, not by anybody, for he has the spirit of Elijah."[58]

2 KINGS 3

One of my favorite directors when it comes to cinematic unexpected endings is M. Night Shyamalan. His films, particularly *The Sixth Sense*, *Signs*, and *The Village*, set the audience up to believe one thing, only to be hit hard with a twist at the end. When the viewer goes back to watch the film a second, third, and fourth time, clues to the surprise ending are more conspicuous, and the viewer becomes more adept at spotting said clues the first time around in subsequent films.

Something similar could be said for films with no clear resolution at the end (e.g., *The Birds*, *Dr. Strangelove*, *The Ides of March*). Though they deny the viewer the satisfaction of tying up loose ends, these very loose ends offer an opportunity for deeper reflection—*Dr. Strangelove*, for example, was a satirical lampoon/criticism of the Cold War philosophy known as MAD or mutually-assured destruction. On the other hand, nice and tidy endings are far less likely to trigger reflection.

The narrative of 2 Kings 3 is an abrupt departure from what the reader might expect. With Elisha having taken up Elijah's prophetic mantle, we would anticipate the narrator to continue focusing on Elisha's ministry, and the prophet does make an appearance in the story, but his role is a brief (albeit important) one. Resumption of Elisha's story will be delayed until the next chapter.

To complicate matters, the story of 2 Kings 3 ends rather suddenly without any clear resolution. I've seen several films, and so have you, that had a most surprising ending or concluded without any clear resolution to the plot. We were left with the same feeling as someone trying to solve a Rubik's cube whose sides were never color-matched to begin with! It's helpful to know at the outset that this passage contains echoes of 1 Kings 22, and we must pay attention to the similarities between the two chapters "if we are to understand what is happening in this rather puzzling narrative."[59] Yes, the narrative ends abruptly without any clear resolution; I believe it does so for a reason, for the point of this passage is a critical one.

---

58. Brueggemann, *1 & 2 Kings*, 299.

59. Provan, *1 & 2 Kings*, 181.

Upon Ahaziah's death (1:17), his brother assumed the throne of Israel. Jehoram (852–841) is remembered by the narrator as a wicked king, but not quite
to the degree of his infamous parents.[60] "Nevertheless," the narrator says, "he *clung*
to the sin of Jeroboam" (v. 3; emphasis mine). Elsewhere, the Old Testament uses
this verb to describe a positive clinging—of a man to his wife (Gen 2:24), of Ruth
to Naomi (Ruth 1:14), and of Israel to Yahweh (Deut 10:20). Here, Jehoram is
depicted as one who just couldn't let go of Jeroboam's idolatrous legacy.

We are then introduced to Mesha, king of Moab. Though Omri and Ahab
had subjugated Moab for two generations, in the aftermath of Ahab's death, Israel was preoccupied with Aram and Assyria to the north, and Mesha seized
the opportunity to rebel. In fact, notice of Moab's rebellion in 2 Kings 1:1 was
meant to underscore the fading glory of the Omride dynasty. While Omri and
Ahab had proven themselves to be strong military rulers, their successors did
not. Ahaziah and Jehoram were what we would call "girly men."

Mesha is identified as a sheep breeder who paid an annual tribute of
"100,000 lambs and the wool of 100,000 rams" to Israel (v. 4; cf. Amos 1:1). This
amounted to a significant windfall for the Omrides, and when it ceased because
of Mesha's rebellion, the economic consequences in Israel would have been enormous. In the Moabite Stone, Mesha records how he drove Israel out of the towns
of northern Moab (e.g., Madeba, Ataroth, Nebo, and Jahaz) and built up several
of them into fortified cities. Not content to accept the economic loss of Moab's
rebellion, Jehoram decided to attack with a coalition of the willing. As his father
had done previously (1 Kgs 22:1–5), he solicited Jehoshaphat's assistance, as
well as Edom's (a vassal-state of Judah, cf. 1 Kgs 22:48; 2 Kgs 8:20). Jehoshaphat
eagerly placed Judah's troops at Jehoram's disposal.[61] Surely Yahweh would give
Israel victory over Moab as he had in the days of Ehud (Judg 3:15–30).

---

60. Though Jehoram is commended for putting away "the pillar of Baal," it had been reestablished in the temple of Baal in Samaria at some point in his reign (10:26–27), perhaps by
his mother. "Jehoram is presented, then, as tolerating the Baal cult while not himself necessarily
participating in it," (Ibid.).

61. "The immediate response of Jehoshaphat indicates a complete willingness to go to war;
his response suggests that he was firmly under the thumb of the North, so that Jehoram's question
in v. 7 is in effect a requirement of his subordinate ally," (Brueggemann, *1 & 2 Kings*, 307). Contra Hubbard, who perceives Jehoshaphat being motivated by his own interests. "A revived Moab
threatened the security of Judah's eastern frontier. Jehoshaphat may even have wanted to settle the
score with Moab for an earlier invasion (2 Chron. 20:1–29)," (*First and Second Kings*, 145).

Since the region of Moab directly across from Israel had recently been for-tified by Mesha with several strongholds, Jehoram and his allies took the long, out-of-the-way route in order to attack Moab from the rear (which was less forti-fied and had the element of surprise). The plan was to go around the Dead Sea's south end and approach Moab via the wilderness of Edom, which required "a circuitous march of seven days" (v. 9) of at least 130 miles and depleted the ar-my's resources, especially the water supply. This development did not bode well for Jehoram; note that the apostate king and his troops are almost destroyed, not by a formidable military, but by a simple lack of water. Rebellion against God complicates *everything*!

Stuck in the dry desert with nothing to drink, Jehoram began to lament that Yahweh had brought them out only to be defeated (note that the Lord had never sent them into battle in the first place, nor had he been consulted). Meanwhile, unwilling to throw up his hands and blame God, Jehoshaphat asked to consult a prophet. We are thus treated to an important contrast between the spiritually weak versus spiritually mature. One is quick to blame God when selfish plans go awry; the other calmly seeks a word from the Lord at the first sign of trouble (cf. Prov 28:1).

It is here that Elisha makes his cameo in the story, and though it is brief, it's not an insignificant one. He is identified as the one "who poured water on the hands of Elijah" (v. 11), a phrase that somehow pegs Elisha as Elijah's servant and legitimate heir to his ministry. Konkel says the act of "'pouring water over the hands' was apparently a gesture of respect shown by a servant to his master or a host to his guest."[62]

When the kings had their audience with Elisha, it's clear the man of God had no love lost for Israel's monarch. Indignantly, he asks, "What do you and I have in common? Go consult the puppet-prophets of your father and mother"[63] (v. 13 Msg). Jehoram's response is equally indignant and rather presumptuous. "No; it is the LORD who has called these three kings to give them into the hand of Moab." Again, when was Yahweh consulted about this expedition?

In the Old Testament, there is a connection between music and prophecy (1 Sam 10:5–11) or the Spirit of the Lord coming upon someone (1 Sam 16:16, 23), and in ancient times, prophets were known to "receive ecstatic utterances

---

62. Konkel, *1 & 2 Kings*, 394.

63. "The utter disrespect for the house of Omri is rarely more clearly expressed," (Hobbs, *2 Kings*, 36).

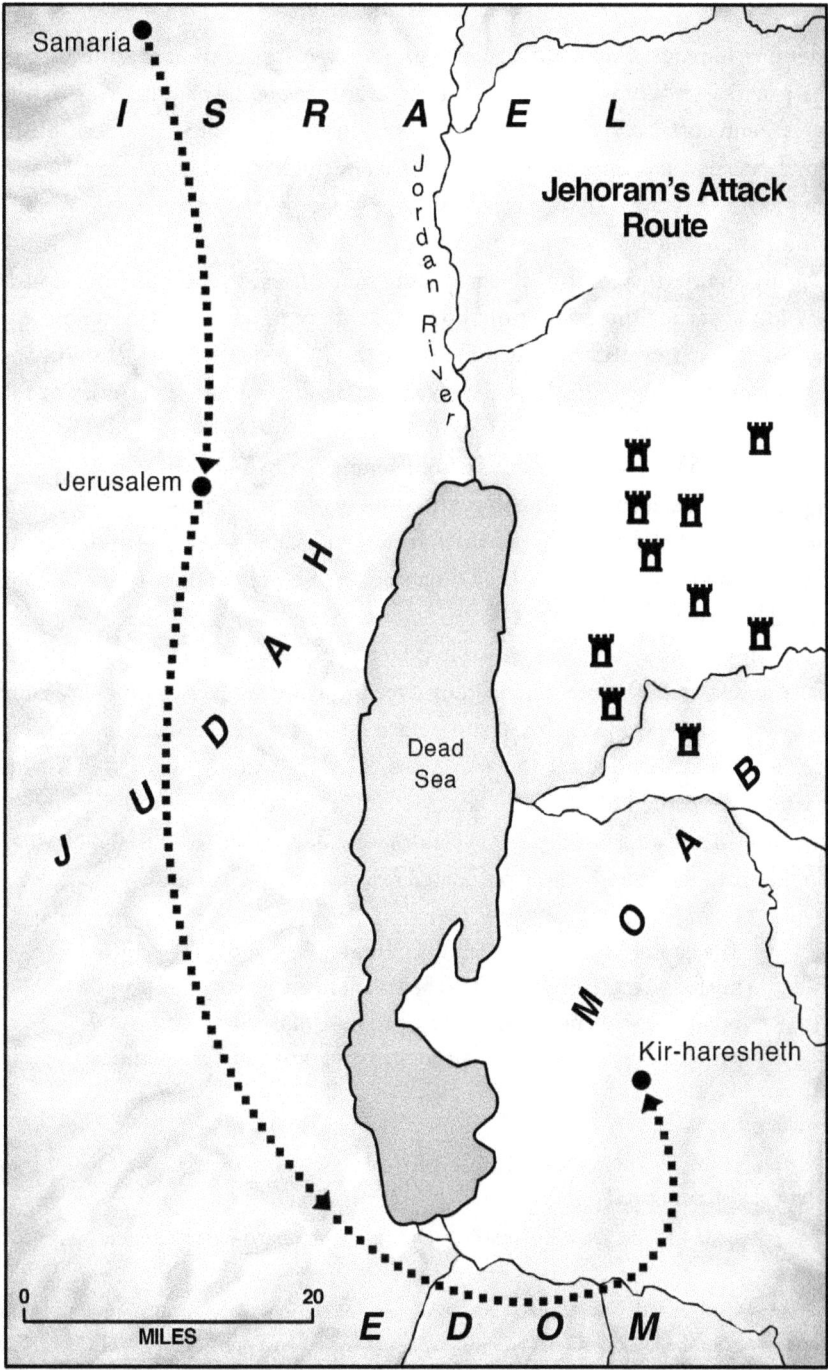

Samaria

_I   S   R   A   E   L_

Jordan River

Jehoram's Attack Route

Jerusalem

_J   U   D   A   H_

Dead Sea

_M   O   A   B_

Kir-haresheth

0   20

MILES

_E   D   O   M_

after hearing music and would then speak out of a sort of trance."[64] But though this practice was common, it does not necessarily mean Elisha was trying to trigger a Pentecostal revival when he sent for a musician (v. 15). Rather, "Elisha simply wanted soothing music played so that he might be quieted before God—after having been visited by three great kings—and thus to be brought to a mood conducive for God to reveal to him."[65]

By divine inspiration, Elisha prophesied that God would miraculously provide water for the expedition, but it would come without rain or storm—and this wasn't even the most difficult thing God would do for Jehoram and Jehoshaphat! Yahweh would also deliver the Moabites into their hand. The following morning, the Lord made good on his promise. Not only did this water mean salvation for Israel in terms of quenching their thirst, but the water's red appearance deceived the Moabites into thinking that the kings of Israel, Judah, and Edom had had a falling out, their armies had slaughtered one another, and the camp had been deserted. They then rushed in, thinking their enemies' spoil would be easy pickings.

But the Moabites were ambushed by a ready coalition force and the rout was on. Just as Elisha predicted, "they overthrew the cities, and on every good piece of land every man threw a stone until it was covered. They stopped every spring of water and felled all the good trees, till only its stones were left in Kir-ha-reseth[66] [the capital of Moab, cf. Isa 15:1; 16:7; Jer 48:31, 36], and the slingers surrounded and attacked it" (v. 25). Such severe devastation to the land of Moab would prevent it from being repopulated too easily.

> The ecological destruction was intended to cripple the econo-
> my for years. The springs and fields could eventually be cleared
> of stones, but needing to do so would make it a long, slow
> process to reestablish a productive agriculture. Sometimes

---

64. House, 1, 2 Kings, 263. cf. Robert R. Wilson, Prophecy and Society in Ancient Israel (Philadelphia: Fortress, 1980), 33–35, 103–6, 129–30.

65. Leon J. Wood, The Holy Spirit in the Old Testament (Grand Rapids: Zondervan, 1976), 118.

66. Kir-hareseth was "located about seventeen miles south of the Arnon Gorge and eleven miles east of the Dead Sea" and was "strategically situated on a promontory overlooking the Dead Sea," (Provan, "2 Kings," 127–28). The steep slopes made Kir-hareseth especially difficult to conquer.

springs would find other, less usable outlets and fields would be so damaged as to have greatly reduced fertility. The cutting down of trees would have even more devastating effects on the ecological balance. Not only would shade and wood supply be lost, but topsoil erosion would increase and the loss of forestation's contribution to the environment would accelerate the development of wasteland conditions. Some fruit trees (such as the date palm) take twenty years of growth before they become productive. Agricultural devastation and deforestation were typical tactics of invading armies seeking to punish those they conquered and as an attempt to hasten their surrender. The Assyrian records and reliefs especially detail punitive measures that include felling trees, devastating meadowlands and destroying canal systems used for irrigation.[67]

Then the narrative takes a very strange, most unexpected turn that has left generations of interpreters scratching their heads in discombobulation. *Everything* seemed to be going Israel's way. Her slingers had surrounded the capital "and pelted Moabites patrolling the walls with a deadly barrage of stones. Often crack marksmen (Judg. 20:16), the slingers shot either handpicked pebbles (1 Sam. 17:40) or ones rounded to resemble large olives (2 Chron. 26:14)."[68] All that remained was a final, all-out assault, and the Moabite rebellion would have been extinguished. Indeed, Mesha sensed that his cause was lost and tried unsuccessfully to break through the lines with seven hundred swordsmen where Edom's king was fighting—a place Mesha presumably considered to be the weakest part of the line.

---

67. Walton, *Bible Background*, 388. Several commentators point out that the felling of good (i.e., fruit) trees went beyond the bounds of holy war protocol in Deuteronomy 20:19–20. In other words, they argue, when Elisha had said "you shall" (v. 19), it had been a prediction of what would be done, not a divine sanction (an important distinction). On the other hand, the Deuteronomy prohibition had to do with building siege works, not general devastation of the land (Hobbs, *2 Kings*, 37).

68. Hubbard, *First and Second Kings*, 147–48. Archaeologists have uncovered several large slinger stones (de Vaux, *Ancient Israel*, 1:244). According to Assyrian sources, slingers often operated "in pairs behind the archers" and "were particularly effective in attacks on a city, for they could direct high-angled fire up steep slopes," (Yadin, *Art of Warfare*, 297).

But expectations of an Israelite victory suddenly evaporated. This will not be a beatdown of Jericho proportions. Like a cocky prize fighter poised to deliver a death blow to his opponent, Israel instead suffers a roundhouse knockout punch to the face from a Moab that was on the ropes. "[Mesha] took his oldest son who was to reign in his place and offered him for a burnt offering on the wall. And there came great wrath against Israel. And they withdrew from him and returned to their own land" (v. 27). And with that, the story concludes without so much as a moral lesson, a "now you know the rest of the story," or Porky Pig saying, "Th-Th-Th-Th-Th-... That's all, folks." We are thus left with a slew of questions:

- Why would Mesha sacrifice his son?

- Whose wrath came against Israel—Mesha's? That of his god, Chemosh[69]? Yahweh's? The Moabites?

- Why did this force Israel to withdraw? If they were forced to withdraw with a tie—or worse, in defeat—did this render Elisha's prophecy unfulfilled—or worse, inaccurate?

I won't pretend to know all the answers to these questions; I admit this passage is among the worst Gordian knots I've ever encountered in Scripture. But if we unpack these questions one at a time, I believe the passage begins to make a lot of sense, though some of our questions will remain unanswered.

In the Moabite Stone referenced above, Mesha claims that disaster (i.e., Israel's conquest under Omri/Ahab) came upon Moab because "Chemosh was angry with his land." By offering his son on the wall (cf. Lev 18:21; 1 Kgs 11:7; Jer 32:35), therefore, Mesha was attempting to appease his god's wrath (cf. Mic 6:6–7). In this understanding, then, Chemosh's fury turned against Israel and forced them to withdraw without conquering the city.[70]

But this interpretation presents its own set of thorny problems, primarily the issue of a false god defeating the army of Yahweh, a notion the author of

---

69. Chemosh was the primary god of the Moabites (cf. Num 21:29; Jer 48:46); the Moabite Stone mentions him twelve times. Just as Yahweh had chosen Israel, Moab believed Chemosh had chosen them as his special people. Solomon had built an altar to Chemosh (1 Kgs 11:7), but in Jeremiah 48:7, the prophet announced Yahweh's ultimate destiny for Chemosh.

70. Gray, *I and II Kings*, 438; Jones, *1 and 2 Kings*, 2:400; J. B. Burns, "Why Did the Besieging Army Withdraw? (2 Reg 3:27)," *ZAW* 102 (1990): 187–94.

Kings would have categorically rejected.[71] False gods have no efficacy or potency
for the reason that they are false. It's just as difficult to believe that the narrator
of Kings would endorse "a link between child sacrifice and divine action—as if
this practice, which other passages describe as abhorrent to the Lord (cf. 2 Kgs.
16:3; 17:17; 21:6), was in this one instance acceptable."[72] And finally, though
the Bible elsewhere refers to the Lord's wrath against sinners (Num 18:5; Deut
29:27; Josh 9:20), there is the fact that elsewhere in Kings (2 Kgs 5:11; 13:19),
the Hebrew *qesep*, translated "wrath," is always a human anger, not divine.

This leads us to the solution of identifying the wrath as belonging to Moab,
meaning the child sacrifice "inspired Moab's army to fight more fiercely or that it
caused Israel such indignation and sickness of heart that they lifted the siege."[73]
Along these lines, Hubbard believes that the narrator's statement indeed referred
to Chemosh's fury, but that it was meant sarcastically; that Israel only *thought*
Chemosh had turned the tide of the battle in Moab's favor in response to Mesha's sacrifice. "If so, this would have been the scene: the king's sacrifice inspired
the Moabites to fight more fiercely; it also spooked Israel into believing that the
new ferocity was a sign of Chemosh's intervention. Thus the [narrator's] remark
portrayed Israel's poor spiritual condition. Even the word of Yahweh's prophet
Elisha failed to reassure her (vv. 16-19). Israel turned and went home. Her unbelief turned what seemed to be certain victory (vv. 24-25) into defeat."[74]

Hubbard's understanding makes the most sense if only because it satisfies
more questions than it raises. It's unconscionable that a false god had any true
power over Israel; on the other hand, knowing what we know about Jehoram's
(and Israel's) spiritual condition, one easily imagines the king making some
faulty assumptions instead of trusting the word of Yahweh's prophet and pressing the fight. And if God was behind this turn of events, inspiring the Moabites

---

71. "It must be inferred that only the wrath of Yahweh, who grants deliverance, can cause
army foes to retreat. In Deuteronomistic theology the cause must be a failure of Israelite faith,"
(Konkel, *1 & 2 Kings*, 397).

72. Provan, *1 & 2 Kings*, 186.

73. House, *1, 2 Kings*, 264.

74. Hubbard, *First and Second Kings*, 148; cf. Davis, *2 Kings*, 49. "This is not to ignore the
fact, of course, that at another level it is certainly the Lord whose hand must be seen in this reversal for Israel, for it is always he who gives other nations their victories in Kings (cf., e.g., 2 Kgs. 5:1;
23:26–27; 24:1–4, 10–17). The Moabites' anger would have counted for nothing, had God not
ordained that it should count for something," (Provan, *1 & 2 Kings*, 186).

and depleting the fortitude of Israel as punishment for their idolatrous world-view, such was clearly his prerogative to do so.

A s noted earlier, this story bears several similarities to the one in 1 Kings 22 in which Ahab and Jehoshaphat attacked Aram.

- In both narratives, Ahab and Jehoram are simply known as the "king of Israel," rather than their given names.

- In both narratives, there is an alliance between Israel and Judah, and Judah's response to the invitation to war is nearly identical in both episodes (cf. v. 4; 1 Kgs 22:4).

- In both instances, Jehoshaphat wonders aloud if there is no prophet to speak for Yahweh (v. 11; cf. 1 Kgs 22:7); though, admittedly, Jehoshaphat does not insist on a word from the Lord *before* commencing operations against Moab as he had Aram.

- In both narratives, men of God lure kings into battle by speaking a prophetic word.

The greatest similarity, however, might be a principle that leaves us a bit nervous. It's that God's message cannot be exploited or controlled at our whim. Yahweh reveals his will on his terms, not ours. He is not a genie to be manipulated by formulaic ritual, but rather is sovereign over all things.

In 1 Kings 22, Micaiah was sent to deceive Ahab into going into battle and told him so! Though Ahab knew he was being lured into a trap, he went anyway! In the most bizarre and unexpected of ways, the Lord's will came to pass. Here, Elisha had prophesied that Moab would be given into Israel's hand. Later, when the battle turns, "We are given no hint that Elisha had overstepped his authority or that the Lord had changed his mind."[75] Hence our nervous head-scratching. Has the word of the Lord failed?

Note the precise prediction Elisha gave: "[The Lord] will also give the Moabites into your hand" (v. 18). It's clear Jehoram heard what he wanted to hear. His enemy would be given into his hand, but this does not equate to automatic victory. Indeed, this passage is an important one in our understanding

---

75. Auld, *I & II Kings*, 159.

of the relationship between divine sovereignty and human responsibility. That God ordains a future does not make it automatically come to pass. Instead, Israel's king interpreted Elisha's prophecy subjectively.

> There is in his [Elisha's] prophecy, nevertheless, a certain economy with the truth. All that he said about the Moabite campaign was true, but the whole truth was not spoken. Some crucial information (about its end) was withheld—information whose absence led the recipients of revelation (and the reader) to have quite mistaken expectations about what would happen. The LORD did hand Moab over to the kings (3:18)— but only up to a certain point. After that point, he handed the kings over to Moab. In the light of 1 Kings 22, we can scarcely doubt that this was his intention from the start. Total victory was never on the agenda, in spite of the way Elisha's words might have been construed. Once again a wicked Israelite king has been lured to disaster, this time not by a lying spirit speaking through false prophets, but by the Spirit of God revealing partial truth to a true prophet.[76]

Imagine that God appeared to you and promised your team would win the big game. Victory was guaranteed. As a player on the team, would you still suit up? Of course. Would you still try to play your best? You should. Assurance of victory isn't license for laziness. If anything, confidence of the outcome should spur you to give extra effort. And this is never more imperative than when the game seems not to be going your way. When a crucial penalty flag is thrown, a dispiriting turnover occurs, a wild pitch triggers bedlam—*those* are the moments when we must double down on our belief that victory is assured, rather than question whether we have been bamboozled.

Jehoram and his allies were assured of victory over Moab, but just as it was in their grasp, they allowed it to be snatched away. This was not because the Lord's word failed, but rather Israel's faith in that word. When the king of Judah had found himself perplexed, Jehoshaphat sought a word from the Lord in Elisha. But when faced with his own confounding shift in the wind (the sudden fury of Moab), Jehoram slinked back to Samaria in defeat. Note also that Jehoram never sought God's direction until he found himself in trouble (v. 13),

---

76. Provan, *1 & 2 Kings*, 183–84.

a reminder of how easy it is to use God's sovereignty as an excuse to falter and fail versus trust and obey. And maybe we deserve defeat when we ride into battle without God's initiative in the first place.

When it seems God's Word has failed, that his promise will come up short, we must double down, press on, and make it so. And not with some sense that God needs our help in sustaining his integrity, but with a realization that the Lord might be testing us. When met with even the most stubborn resistance, God's people continue to act as if God's Word is true until hell's gates give way. This, I believe, is the point of 2 Kings 3: the hope of God's people is always in his Word.[77]

And in this way, the story points to the gospel. When things look their bleakest, Jesus' church should recall his words in order to understand what is before them. Perhaps the apostles wouldn't have been so despondent on Saturday if they had recalled or understood their Lord's many promises to raise himself on Sunday (John 2:18–22; 20:9). Faith that God's Word will not fail moves us to act confidently and decisively in order to see that Word fulfilled. The seeming death of his sovereignty is never but a testimony to our near-sightedness and a reminder that his ways are infinitely beyond ours.

> Second Kings 3 does not leave us with an arbitrary God, but it certainly does not reveal a tame God. This story leaves us precisely where the whole of Scripture leaves us: utterly dependent upon the God who is sovereign love and sovereign good. This odd and mystifying story urges us to take this one stance in life: trust him, remembering that the greatest surprise ending is the double surprise of the gospel—the shocking horror of the Son of the King crucified outside the walls by his own "fathers" and the wild joy of a risen Lord.[78]

---

77. Davis, 2 Kings, 41.

78. Leithart, 1 & 2 Kings, 183.

TALKING POINTS

t is the American Way to pull ourselves up by our own bootstraps. Independence, self-sufficiency, and power are arguably the three pillars of the American Dream. But all three of these prove to be at significant odds with the God of Israel. King Ahaziah's reluctance to inquire of the Lord cost him his life. His determination to order Elijah around like a whipping boy only exposed the pathetic limits of his royal power. His successor, Jehoram, learned the hard way that any number of things can go wrong with a military expedition into the desert. And while God can provide streams of water to a dry, thirsty land—to say nothing of delivering formidable enemies into the hands of his people—the one thing he will *not* do is force a blessing on those who refuse to trust completely in him. If we actually believe that every blessing in life comes from God, then we must also rely on him exclusively to sustain those same blessings and ultimately employ them for his glory, "for from him and through him and to him are all things" (Rom 11:36).

t is instructive to note," Patterson says, "that even though Elijah knows this day will be his last on earth, his concern is that the Lord's work will continue after his passing; so he wants to assure himself of the progress of his 'seminary students.'"[79] In what was likely his final letter, Paul exhorted Timothy, "What you have heard from me in the presence of many witnesses, commit to faithful men who will be able to teach others also" (2 Tim 2:2 HCSB). I am in no way endorsing a line-of-succession concept as is found in Catholicism or Mormonism. On the other hand, none of us should be so enamored with ourselves and our role in the church that we believe ourselves invaluable or irreplaceable. Nothing could be further from the truth; we are all disposable. Though we will one day go the way of all the earth, the work of the Lord will always continue until Christ returns. To that end, like Elijah and Paul, we should be diligent in helping to raise up the next generation of strong, faithful leaders. Those who follow us need to witness our reliance on the Lord, our uncompromising commitment to his Word, and our passion for discharging Christ's commission in our communities.

79. Patterson, "1, 2 Kings," 813.

T here is arguably no chapter in Kings more worthy of prolonged consideration than 2 Kings 3. A narrative with no clear resolution, perhaps such is a reminder to us that "the point" of a story can easily be found in how the story plays out and not just in how it ends. Jehoram made the mistake of not starting his campaign with the end in mind. Fundamentally, all war in Israel had to be holy war, or war to the glory of God. Jehoram, however, entered into battle with selfish motives. As a result, he values the divine word in the moment, but doesn't want to submit to it long term. "Jehoramites view the word of God as something for emergency only, but not for normal days. God is simply the airbag in the disasters of life—which you hope you never have to use."[80] We must not follow his example; rather, Paul counsels us to do all things in God's Name (i.e., by his authority) and to his glory (Col 3:17; 1 Cor 10:31)—wise advice that can expose selfish motives and poor practices. If Jehoram had been committed to doing things in God's Name for God's glory, 2 Kings 3 would have concluded quite differently.

---

80. Davis, 2 Kings, 45.

9

BLUE-COLLAR PROPHET

In Portis' novel, Rooster Cogburn is unquestionably portrayed as a man of true grit. But the book's title is as much an apt description of Mattie Ross as it is Cogburn. A fourteen-year-old girl braved the harsh conditions of December in Oklahoma to see to it personally that her father's murderer paid for his crime. Though the story's narration is set many years after its events, one can tell Mattie Ross still possessed all the grit of Cogburn—and arguably more.

Elijah is unquestionably among the grittiest of the prophets. But as we will discover in this section of Kings, Elisha had as much claim to this label as did his predecessor. In fact, we are left to wonder if whether Elisha had a greater singular impact on righteousness in Israel. Whereas the uncouth Tishbite often led an isolated existence, Elisha presided over a flourishing prophetic community. Elijah performed his fair share of miracles, but Elisha worked more. While the camel-clothed prophet was always persona non grata with kings, Elisha's relationship with the throne was less strained—at least, most of the time. Elisha's prophetic ministry was certainly not inferior to that of his mentor, and Elijah never had the impact on international events that Elisha had.

To a handful of scholars, some of the stories in the Elisha cycle seem to be absentminded reruns from the Elijah Chronicles (e.g., 1 Kgs 17:17–24; 2 Kgs 4:18–37). But our narrator is no dunce; he expects us to see in Elisha a mirror reflection of Elijah's ministry.[1] Just as the Lord's Spirit and power had rested mightily on Elijah, they too rested on his successor. God had not left himself without a witness or a mouthpiece when his chariots of fire raptured Elijah

---

1. Hagan, "First and Second Kings," 188.

home. Throughout these narratives, at stake is whether there is still a "prophet in Israel" (3:11; 5:3, 8; 6:12). Elisha's ministry answers with a resounding, "Yes!"

2 KINGS 4:1-7

These accounts do not further the history of national Israel per se, but rather illustrate the power and authority of Elisha, his compassion for individuals, and his significance to the preservation of a faithful remnant. Elisha does the work of God, the true King of Israel (Deut 10:18). In theory, the duty of the king in ancient cultures was to provide for justice, protection, and the well-being of the people (cf. Ps 72:1–7). But in the fading days of the Omride dynasty, the responsibilities of the king of Israel were instead discharged in particular times and places through this formidable man of God.[2]

The first narrative of 2 Kings 4 concerns an unnamed woman whose deceased husband had been a member of the prophetic community. Jewish tradition identified her as the widow of Obadiah, the steward of Ahab who had protected the prophetic community in Elijah's day (1 Kgs 18:3–4). According to the theory, her debt was a result of the money Obadiah had borrowed to provision those same prophets.[3] Regardless of whether this is true, "These followers of the covenant would have paid a high price for their commitment in the hostile environment of the official Baal cult. The time and sacrifice required to support this movement against the prevailing economic forces left little reserve when the family provider died. Even in normal times families could become so indebted that some members were given as servants to their creditors."[4]

In the ancient Near East, it was standard practice to enslave debtors in default (Lev 26:39; Neh 5:5; Isa 50:1; Amos 2:6; 8:6; Mic 2:9; cf. Code of Hammurabi §§ 117, 119, 213). Under the Law of Moses, however, this enslavement could not be indefinite (Exod 21:2–3, 7; 22:25–27; Deut 24:10–13), though it's dubious that this woman's creditor would have cared much for the Law (cf. Amos 2:6; 8:6; Mic 2:9). In fact, it's possible the woman's sons had been pledged as collateral for the debt.[5]

---

2. Konkel, 1 & 2 Kings, 412.

3. Josephus, Antiquities 9.47; Ginzberg, Legends, 1026.

4. Konkel, 1 & 2 Kings, 412.

5. Hobbs, 2 Kings, 50.

We are left, then, with the image of a widow who was likely suffering for her (and her husband's) faithfulness to Yahweh. Would Yahweh deliver her? The widow appealed to Elisha,[6] the leader of the prophets, for help, since a creditor was threatening to enslave her children to pay her outstanding debts. This woman's grief over losing her husband was bad enough (remember that this was a male-dominated society where widows had very few options available to them), but slavery "would be a dismal end for a family that had already endured so much."[7]

At Elisha's command, the widow collected as many vessels as possible in order to store oil. Her obedience led to a miraculous providence[8] in which a small amount of reserve oil in her pantry filled up countless vessels, which were then sold to pay the widow's debts, and with money to spare! In her abject poverty, Elisha sought to prepare her to receive an unthinkable, abundant blessing.[9]

The story bears a striking resemblance to that of Elijah and the widow of Zarephath (1 Kgs 17:8–16). Because of their relationship with men of God, both widows benefited from a miracle concerning oil in their kitchens. The similarity is again a reminder that Elisha's ministry was in no way inferior to Elijah's.

This narrative (and those that follow) also affirmed the God of Israel remained committed to relieving the plight of the poor.[10] In fact, there are faint echoes of Ruth and Boaz in this scene. Just as God provisioned the needs of widows Ruth and Naomi through the kinsman-redeemer Boaz, God did the

---

6. "In the Bible, appeals for help are almost always addressed to the Lord or the king. This one, however, is addressed to the man of God, Elisha," (Yael Shemesh, "Elisha and the Miraculous Jug of Oil [2 Kgs 4:1–7]," *JHS* 8 [2008]: 7).

7. Konkel, *1 & 2 Kings*, 413.

8. "It is emphasized that the miracle was performed in Elisha's absence. It was by the power of God and not by any sleight of hand," (Gray, *I & II Kings*, 441).

9. "The prophet is neither imperious nor paternalistic. He does not produce gold from somewhere else, even if he could, but respects the widow's integrity and dignity. She may start with the smallest possible contribution, but she is an active participant in the solution and is not overshadowed by Elisha. She owns the problem and the way forward. Elisha's brief words covering both immediate need and future livelihood (v. 7) thoughtfully bring together two aspects often separated in popular thinking. Catering for present and future, however, is the practice of many agencies involved in welfare and development work. Elisha follows a God who does not simply solve problems but cares for people," (Olley, *Message of Kings*, 230).

10. "God's meeting of the needs of both the widow and Elisha is in keeping with his concern for the downtrodden of society, such as widows, orphans, and the poor (Dt 10:18–19; Ps 82:3–4; Isa 1:23; Jas 1:27)," (Patterson, "1, 2 Kings," 822).

same for this unnamed widow through Elisha. The prophet indeed functions as a kinsman-redeemer here as he aids relatives/friends facing economic ruin (cf. Lev 25:35–55).[11]

Finally, this is an illustration of the beautiful relationship between providence and obedience. God was compassionate and mighty enough to deliver this poor widow from her dire circumstances. In his mercy, Yahweh delivered to her a word from the Lord through Elisha that offered a way out of her trouble. This story and those that follow are collectively a hymn of praise to God's faithfulness.

But obedience was also necessary for the deliverance to be consummated. In fact, this will become a theme throughout Elisha's ministry—the providence of Yahweh effected by obedience to the prophetic word (cf. vv. 3, 7, 29, 38, 41, 43). So while God deserves all the credit for the mercy he shows to his people in dire circumstances, we must also concede the fact that faith, like the one exhibited by the widow, can make all the difference.[12]

2 KINGS 4:8-37

Another anecdote highlighting the potency of Elisha's ministry concerns a "wealthy woman" living in Shunem, a town in the tribal territory of Issachar (Josh 19:18) on the eastern end of the Jezreel Valley, some four miles north of Jezreel. Elisha traveled a circuit (cf. 1 Sam 7:15–17) on a major trade route between Carmel and the Jordan. This woman wanted to provide a special place for Elisha to lodge when he passed her way.

While most residential rooftops in ancient Israel would have been flat with a light, lattice-like, walled structure, the Hebrew phrase in v. 10 suggests a structure with stouter walls—distinguishing between what we might think of as a screened-in porch versus an actual room in the house. Whereas Elijah had found hospitality in the home of a husbandless woman and her son (1 Kgs 17:17–24), Elisha finds the same in the home of a childless woman and her husband.[13]

So touched was Elisha by this woman's generosity that he determined to return her kindness. He asked if she happened to be in need of any political favors

---

11. Provan, "2 Kings," 129.

12. "The movement of the narrative is from *prophetic command* (4:3-4) to the *obedience of the woman* (4:5-6) that transforms her situation," (Brueggemann, *1 & 2 Kings*, 320; emphasis his).

13. For parallels between this narrative and 1 Kings 17, see Cogan, *I Kings*, 432.

(v. 13),[14] but her response effectively meant, "I'm doing fine since I have family and friends nearby"—though this would not always be the case (8:1–6). But then Gehazi mentions that the woman was childless, and her husband was old, insinuating that they suffered from the same predicament as Abraham and Sarah (Gen 18:1–15). Though the woman was wealthy, riches could not provide what a child could. "The birth of a son was not only essential for the survival of the family in ancient Israelite society but also meant the greatest fulfillment in the life of a woman."[15] So Elisha magnanimously promised she would cradle such a son within a year. Similar to Sarah's response (Gen 18:12), she protested the impossible—"Don't deceive me and get my hopes up like that" (v. 16 NLT). But the narrator's pithy report (v. 17) confirms the potency of Elisha's prophetic voice.

The narrative then fast-forwards several years to a time when the child would have been old enough to work in the fields during harvest. Suddenly he was afflicted with some sort of head injury, its cause unknown.[16] Concussion? Cerebral hemorrhage or malaria? Heat stroke (cf. Ps 121:6)? Meningitis?[17] We aren't told. The child was carried to his mother where he died in her arms, and we are left in shock over the sudden passing of this promised son, the hope he embodied, and the joy he had undoubtedly brought to his parents.

In a powerful, symbolic act, the woman laid her son's body on the bed in Elisha's room. "By closing the door, she conceals the death as though to keep it frozen in dramatic time, to prevent the death process from going any further. Her evasive reply to her flustered husband [...] forestalls his setting in motion the next stage of death, mourning and burial."[18] Her husband's question puz-

---

14. "His suggestions of intervening with the king or military commander show that Elisha has come into a position of political influence, perhaps enhanced by his involvement in the Moabite campaign," (Konkel, *1 & 2 Kings*, 414).

15. Fritz, *1 & 2 Kings*, 251. "It is impossible to overestimate the cruciality of a son in that ancient, patriarchal world. A son guaranteed economic surety in time to come, and lack of a son was a social stigma to a woman. It may well be that the woman in our narrative thinks otherwise, but Gehazi voices conventional perceptions," (Brueggemann, *1 & 2 Kings*, 322).

16. "Like Isaac, another son born after an annunciation, this child is threatened with death out in the open," (Alter, *Ancient Israel*, 747).

17. Donald J. Wiseman, "Medicine in the Old Testament World," in *Medicine and the Bible*, ed. Bernard Palmer (Exeter, Great Britain: Paternoster, 1986), 28.

18. Nelson, *First and Second Kings*, 173–74; cf. Gray, *I & II Kings*, 445. "As long as the secret could be kept, the issue was between her and Elisha. Once the death was public knowledge, the mourning rites would begin and in the general view either Elisha would be accounted a false

zles us—he's perplexed that his wife would visit a prophet when it wasn't a New Moon or Sabbath (i.e., a day of rest), which seems to have been the custom[19] (cf. Amos 8:5). Does he lack compassion or faith or both?

The woman set out at a frenzied pace (v. 24) in search of Elisha at Carmel, about twenty-five miles from Shunem. The man of God knows she's coming, but does not know the reason because "the LORD has hidden it from me" (v. 27). "This is a most interesting statement in view of what has just occurred in 2 Kgs. 3, where Elisha's knowledge of the future was similarly incomplete. God is not a vending machine that pours out oracles when primed with prophetic pennies."[20]

Equally interesting is both the assertiveness and humility of this woman. She refuses to share her plight with Elisha's servant; only the man of God can help. And she is not shy about her pain: "Did I ask you for a son, my lord? And didn't I say, 'Don't deceive me and get my hopes up'?" (v. 28 NLT; cf. 1 Kgs 17:18). "She is quite clear that a promise of blessing, when unqualified by any warning of trouble, should work out in an uncomplicated way."[21] But she says all this in a posture of humility and deference. Grasping the feet (v. 27) was a display of self-abasement and entreaty, and though it occurs only here in the Old Testament, we see it demonstrated in the New (Matt 28:9).

When he grasped the situation, Elisha sent Gehazi posthaste to Shunem, armed with Elisha's staff, and with explicit orders not to stop for any reason. When he arrived, Gehazi was to lay Elisha's staff on the child's face. Perhaps the staff, a symbol of Elisha's God-given prophetic power (cf. Exod 4:1–3; 17:8–13), was a means of intervention, an interruption of the decaying process, and an expression of faith that God had not yet spoken the final word.

But this is not enough for the woman; she won't allow Elisha to remain behind. She insists he come, recognizing he possesses the power she needs. It is embodied in the man of God; she does not believe in prophetic power by proxy

---

prophet or the woman a greater sinner. Even if Elisha were a true prophet, it would have been taken as a mark of the limitation of his prophetic inspiration that he could have consorted with such a woman. What was at stake was Elisha's credibility as a prophet," (Robinson, *Second Book*, 44).

19. Keil, *Commentary*, 311, n. 1; Cogan, *II Kings*, 57.

20. Provan, *1 & 2 Kings*, 189.

21. Ibid., 189–90. "She had not asked for a son; it was Elisha that had promised one to her. Was now her great gift from God to be snatched from her and so leave her in a worse state than before? It would have been better never to have had a son than to have such joy taken away so quickly!" (Patterson, "1, 2 Kings," 825).

(cf. Luke 7:6–10).[22] And in an ironic twist, she uses Elisha's own words against him (v. 30; cf. 2:2). Also, Elisha's orders to Gehazi proved fruitless anyway; nothing happened when he did as Elisha commanded.

In a scene directly reminiscent of Elijah at Zarephath, the man of God entered the room of death alone upon his arrival. He prayed, he stretched himself out on the child, the child was raised to life,[23] and a son was returned to his mother. The final verse of the narrative is as terse in its report as was v. 17, suggesting that the woman was not at all surprised that this man of God in Israel could reclaim life from Sheol.

I t took me a while to summon the willingness to engage this text, to reflect on and write about it. Halfway through the life of this book project, my two-year-old son unexpectedly passed away of no known cause. Thus, the scene of a mother clutching the lifeless body of her only-begotten, supremely-beloved son hit too close to home. Writing about the widow of Zarephath and the loss of her son was also difficult, but this one more so. And it just occurred to me why.

The Shunammite woman's faith and character humiliates, informs, and challenges my own. "She refuses to accept her child's death or at least refuses to do so until the prophet himself says nothing can be done. Her faith stands out in a history filled with descriptions of persons who reject belief and obedience."[24] She is, without question, among the most striking characters in the Old Testament.

There is an undercurrent of stubborn humility in this text—a woman of grace who refuses to be pushed aside, marginalized, or put in her place. She, not her husband, takes the initiative to build the room for Elisha. She lingers outside the room, with Gehazi acting as intermediary, when Elisha inquires if he can bless her in some way. And with her son's corpse in her arms, she stubbornly believes God can do something about it. She will not rest until she has spoken directly to the man of God. So it's not a Sabbath or New Moon—what of it!? She

22. "She understood that it is the person of the prophet who carries authority that cannot be extended beyond the prophet's own person. There is no transfer of power to a totem, for this power is a person-to-person phenomenon," (Brueggemann, *1 & 2 Kings*, 324).

23. "The boy 'sneezed' to indicate that 'the breath of life' had returned to his nostrils. The number seven may have indicated the completeness of the restoration," (Robinson, *Second Book*, 46).

24. House, *1, 2 Kings*, 267–68.

must inquire of the Lord, and she will reject the etiquette imposed on her by her husband and by Elisha until God has spoken.

To be sure, there are other remarkable qualities in this woman. For one, she was a gracious practitioner of hospitality toward the people of God. God blesses all who offer bread or a cup of cold water to those who "have gone out for the sake of the name" (3 John 7); hospitality has always been an identifying mark of the saints (Heb 13:2).

But it is the persistence of this woman's audacious faith that makes the greatest impression upon me. First skeptical that she would ever have a son, she is quickly convinced that a God who could give life once could give it again. Though Gehazi was at first successful in being a buffer between her and Elisha (v. 15), in the second scene, he fails (vv. 26–27), for her audacious faith overrides every propriety. Neither does she indulge alternatives. She does not consult the god of Ekron as did Ahaziah. She has no expectation that Elisha's "magic staff" can work a miracle, for the power she needs is not magical but divine. This woman insists her help can come only from the Lord, the maker of heaven and earth.

If those last words sounded familiar, it's because they come from Psalm 121, the second of the Songs of Ascent. Traditionally, it has been understood that these were hymns sung by Israelites as they made the pilgrimage to Jerusalem for the feasts (e.g., Passover, Pentecost, Booths). As a pilgrim would see Jerusalem on the horizon, he would also notice the pagan high places in the hilltops surrounding the City of David. "I lift up my eyes to the mountains—where does my help come from? My help comes from the LORD, the Maker of heaven and earth" (Ps 121:1–2 NIV). The psalm goes on to celebrate the protection God alone can bring. He does not sleep on the job; he will not allow evil to overwhelm us. On his watch, "the sun shall not strike you"—an ironic statement, given the fate of the Shunammite's son. The psalm then ends with this promise: "The LORD will watch over your coming and going both now and forevermore" (Ps 121:8 NIV).

It requires an audacious, persistent faith to believe this promise when it seems evil has blanketed your life and the Keeper of Israel (Ps 121:4) has fallen asleep or become distracted. But if faith is evidence of things not seen, it is also a refusal to accept evil as the final score until God's last word has sounded. And in this story, we have a remarkable example of a woman who refused to accept the evil finality of death without allowing God to have the last word.

Nearly three thousand years later, God's people still cling to the audacious promise that death is not the end. We refuse to yield our loved ones to its grip until God has spoken the final word—one coming from the voice of the archangel (1 Thess 4:16).

2 KINGS 4:38-44

On another occasion, during a famine,[25] Elisha was at Gilgal and directed his servant to prepare a stew for the members of the prophetic guild—it may be that Elisha was teaching a Bible class of some sort (cf. Ezek 8:1; 14:1; 20:1). One of the prophets brought some wild gourds (the LXX identifies them as wild cucumbers[26]) he had gathered, and they were mixed into the stew, though no one knew "what they were" (v. 39). But when some of them tasted the stew, they were horrified, exclaiming to Elisha, "There is death in the pot!"[27] Elisha calmly cured what was wrong by summoning flour and throwing it in, not unlike his remedy of salt for the toxic water at Jericho (2:19–22).

The narrator also tells us of a man from Baal-shalishah[28] who brought Elisha "first fruits" of barley loaves and ears of grain, offerings usually reserved for Israel's priests (Num 18:13; Deut 18:4–5).[29] Since they were still in the midst of famine, Elisha ordered that the food be distributed among the members of the prophetic community. Gehazi balked at the idea of being able to satisfy a hundred appetites with so little, but Elisha commanded him to distribute the food anyway. In a miracle that functions as a shadow of Jesus feeding the five and four thousand, all the prophets "ate and had some left," proving "God is in the business of taking what seems inadequate and multiplying it, with excess."[30]

---

25. This famine, likely a covenant curse (cf. Deut 11:16–17; 28:3–6), lasts through 8:6.

26. Also known as the "Apple of Sodom" (cf. Deut 32:32), this gourd was "a strong purgative and known to be fatal. The addition of flour to the potage absorbs the bitterness and makes it edible," (Konkel, *1 & 2 Kings*, 416).

27. Just as we hyperbolically disparage disgusting food in various ways, Hobbs claims this phrase "is not to be taken literally, but is a natural reaction to something which tasted bitter," (*2 Kings*, 53).

28. Scholars are unsure about the location of Baal-shalishah. Some locate it in the territory of Ephraim (Provan, "2 Kings," 131–32).

29. "In this case, however, the man brought it to Elisha, bypassing in protest the apostate northern religious leaders at the sanctuary nearby at Bethel," (Hubbard, *First and Second Kings*, 152).

30. Olley, *Message of Kings*, 232.

t's unclear if Elisha worked a miracle in the episode involving the wild gourds. The prophets' protest could be interpreted as meaning the stew was simply terrible in taste, not that it was fatal. But what is clear is that this serves as an example of Elisha's divine wisdom—he knows what to add, even though no one knows what was put in the stew.

In the final episode, Elisha demonstrates an unwavering trust in God's providence. Though in the middle of famine when food was scarce, the prophet was confident his God could and would care for his servants, and in a miraculous way if necessary. This rounds out Elisha's personality—he is not just a messenger of judgment, but also an agent of God's magnanimous provision.

In both stories, we also see echoes of Elijah's ministry. Just as God used Elijah and flour to deliver the righteous (the widow of Zarephath), so he used Elisha to do the same. And just as God did for the widow through Elijah, he worked through Elisha to make sure there were ample provisions for the righteous when there was seemingly little to go around—abundance where there had previously been poverty. Also in both stories, we see God protecting the prophets from harm and providing for their needs, just as he had done for Elijah at Cherith and Zarephath, and just as he had done for other men of God through Obadiah (1 Kgs 18:1–15). In every way, this blue-collar prophet from Abel-meholah was as formidable as was his predecessor, the man of God from Tishbe.

2 KINGS 5

The story of Naaman is arguably the most famous of Elisha's life recorded in Scripture. It's certainly a central tenet of children's Sunday school curriculum, and its echoes of baptism qualify it as a favorite of preachers. But there is so much more to this story that it is not done enough justice if relegated to kids' classes and random allusions in half-hour homilies. The narrative perpetuates a few themes from Elisha's ministry: that God's sovereignty reaches beyond Israel (1 Kgs 17:8–24), and that he is not one of many gods, but the one true and only God (1 Kgs 18:20–40).[31]

The story takes place during Jehoram's reign in Israel, possibly only a few years before Jehu's revolt (Hobbs tentatively dates it to 850–843[32]). We are introduced to Naaman, commander of Aram's army. He had been responsible for

---

31. Provan, *1 & 2 Kings*, 191; Wray Beal, *1 & 2 Kings*, 333.

32. Hobbs, "Naaman (Person)," *ABD* 4:968.

Aram's recent victories over Israel—perhaps at Ramoth-gilead (1 Kgs 22)?—because of Yahweh's blessing. In an impossible-to-confirm report, Josephus identifies Naaman as the one who had killed Ahab.[33] Specifics aside, it's easy to envision Naaman as the toast of Damascus and the king's prized warrior. There was only one hitch in his giddy-up. He had leprosy.[34]

The leprosy of the Old Testament is not what you likely may have been led to believe. I was always taught that it was identical to what is now known as Hansen's disease—a highly contagious malady in which limbs rot off and other deformities occur. But notice that Naaman is not disfigured, nor is medical quarantine required; he was welcomed into the presence of the kings of Aram and Israel without reservation, indicating "his distress is more aesthetic than contagion."[35] In addition, Hansen's disease isn't known to have existed in the ancient Near East before the time of Alexander the Great, when his army brought it back from India.

The Hebrew word translated "leprosy" here was "a generic term for a variety of cutaneous diseases, most of which were benign, with one being malignant in character" and often served "as a comprehensive designation for a wide variety of skin afflictions in the same general sense that 'cancer' is employed to describe both sarcomas and carcinomas."[36] While Hansen's disease is the malignant form of leprosy, benign forms included acne, psoriasis, and vitiligo.[37]

That said, though the disease may not have been as awful in its physical consequences, it still would have (in the eyes of the reader, ancient and modern) lent to its victim the stigma of ritual uncleanness and divine judgment (cf. Lev 13–14;

---

33. Josephus, *Antiquities* 8.414.

34. "The fame and valor of Naaman is expanded three times to emphasize his distinction: He is a great man before his lord; he is of high renown because of the victories he has won; he is a hero of valor (v. 1). He also has one other distinction; he is a leper. This one single word at the end of a string of accolades compromises all the others," (Konkel, *1 & 2 Kings*, 427).

35. Ibid., 428. For more on leprosy in the Old Testament and in antiquity, see Wright and Jones, "Leprosy," *ABD* 4:277–82; Gordon J. Wenham, *The Book of Leviticus* (Grand Rapids: Eerdmans, 1979), 189–214; E. V. Hulse, "The Nature of Biblical 'Leprosy' and the Use of Alternative Medical Terms in Modern Translations of the Bible," *PEQ* 107 (1975): 87–105.

36. Harrison, "צָרַע," *NIDOTTE* 3:846.

37. Ibid. "The great cultural aversion to skin diseases may be that in appearance and sometimes odor they resemble the rotting skin of the corpse and are therefore associated with death. This natural revulsion adds considerably to the victim's outcast status when combined with the quarantine that is ritually rather than medically motivated," (Walton, *Bible Background*, 390).

Num 12:10–15; 2 Sam 3:28–29; 2 Kgs 15:5). It seems quarantine for lepers in biblical terms was done for religious or aesthetic, not medical, reasons. Recall the stigma that AIDS possessed until the last decade, and you have an idea of the ignominy leprosy had in Naaman's day. In addition, we cannot discount the fact that Naaman considers his leprosy to be more than a nuisance; indeed, he is willing to travel to enemy territory with only the hope for a cure.[38] Thus "on three counts Naaman is an 'outsider': a foreigner, an enemy general and a 'leper.'"[39]

On one of Aram's many raids into Israel,[40] a young girl had been captured and became a servant in Naaman's household. When she learned of her master's disease, she seemed to lament sincerely that he did not know the man of God in Israel capable of healing leprosy. It is nothing short of remarkable that this young girl, stolen away so far from her home, had this much compassion for her owner.[41]

At Naaman's behest, the king of Aram (probably Ben-hadad II) sent him to Israel laden with gifts[42] and a letter of introduction to the king of Israel (Jehoram), though the king interpreted it as a setup: "Am I a god with the power to bring death or life[43] that I get orders to heal this man from his disease? What's going on here? That king's trying to pick a fight, that's what!" (v. 7 Msg).

---

38. Hens-Piazza, 1–2 Kings, 259.

39. Olley, Message of Kings, 234.

40. This was a period pock-marked by hostilities between Aram and Israel. In the next chapter of 2 Kings, we will read of military raids by Aram into the heart of the Israelite countryside (6:8) and of a siege of Samaria (6:24–7:20).

41. "Perhaps the book's first readers would have noted that the girl in the text is an exile too. Despite her captivity, she is not bitter or unhelpful. Rather, she shares what she knows about the Lord and the prophet out of concern for Naaman and her mistress and desire to see God's glory magnified. In this way she acts like Daniel, Mordecai, Ezra, Nehemiah, and other exiles who care for the spiritual and physical well-being of their conquerors," (House, 1, 2 Kings, 272).

42. Early on, a talent was roughly equal to the load one man could carry; by Naaman's time, a talent had been standardized to about seventy pounds, or three thousand shekels (cf. Exod 38:25–26). To put it in perspective, the amount of silver Naaman brought with him was five times what Omri paid for Samaria (1 Kgs 16:24). The six thousand shekels of gold was about equal to "the combined annual wages of six hundred common laborers," (Provan, "2 Kings," 134). Walton estimates the total amount of Naaman's treasure at about $750 million (Bible Background, 390–91).

43. "It is an impossible demand for someone who is not God, for someone who cannot kill and bring back to life (v. 7; cf. Deut. 32:39; 1 Sam. 2:6; Hos. 6:1–2). This is a significant statement in the context of the story as a whole," (Provan, 1 & 2 Kings, 191).

I've always wondered why Ben-hadad sent Naaman to the king of Israel and not directly to Elisha—had Naaman been unclear in v. 4 when he had relayed the servant girl's news to the king of Aram? Unlikely. Rather, Ben-hadad likely worked from the assumption that all prophets were in the employ of the king. "He does not know that true prophets do not work for money, nor are they paid by the king, nor does the king have authority over them. Thus, sending Naaman to Israel's king does Naaman no good."[44]

At this point, Elisha interceded. He beckoned the king to send Naaman to visit him "that he may know that there is a prophet in Israel" (v. 8)—an ironic statement since the king of Israel was obviously ignorant of such a fact.[45] But when Naaman arrived at Elisha's house, it was Elisha's page—not the prophet himself—who bore the message. If Naaman would wash in the Jordan seven times, he would be completely healed of his leprosy.

When we consider how much of a VIP Naaman was, we can perhaps understand his rage. First, he thought himself important enough to merit special attention, that any prophet should be at his beck and call.[46] He expected Elisha himself to show up and wave his hand ritualistically over Naaman's leprosy as if conducting an exorcism. Instead, he got the equivalent (in his mind) of "take two aspirin and call me in the morning."[47] "He expected Elisha, the practitioner, to make the difference, while Elisha is careful to remove himself from such a role."[48]

---

44. House, 1, 2 Kings, 272.

45. "No doubt, behind J[eh]oram's oversight lay the long-standing antagonism of the royal palace toward true prophets such as Elisha. Since Ahab, the northern monarchy preferred simply to ignore them," (Hubbard, First and Second Kings, 154).

46. "Like so many other characters in Kings, Naaman seems to think that prophets are very much in control of their prophetic gift, able to say and do as they choose, and having a responsibility to please their superiors (e.g., 1 Kgs. 22:13). [...] To Naaman, the LORD is only a local deity at the beck and call of the prophet. It is the prophet who is the healer, not the god. Why has he refused to do his job?" (Provan, 1 & 2 Kings, 192).

47. Brueggemann, 1 & 2 Kings, 333.

48. Walton, Bible Background, 391. "[Elisha's] appearance could have led Naaman to conclude that the miracle was by his power alone. In Elisha's absence the miraculous power was credited to its true source. Healed and restored, Naaman acknowledges YHWH's sovereignty over all gods: no god exists but in Israel," (Wray Beal, 1 & 2 Kings, 335).

Second, the thought of dipping in the Jordan—when his native Abana and Pharpar[49] were so much better—was simply too much to bear. "He bore a diplomatic letter and a huge gift and had traveled many miles just to get there. He expected to be honored."[50] Even today, some expect God to work through flash and fireworks instead of boring, "ordinary" ways.

Had his servants not intervened to reason with their master, Naaman might not have ever been cleansed. But they did. Here, they serve the same narrative function as the young Israelite slave girl: nameless, they are used by God to speak a word of grace and direction to a very proud man.[51] Naaman needed to get out of his own way, and God used the people in his life to gently, subtly help him do just that.[52]

With that, Naaman made his way to the Jordan. At this point, it occurs to me that I've always imagined Naaman going to the Jordan as if it were the community swimming pool—i.e., it was right around the corner from Elisha's house; at worst, it was just a few blocks away. But in fact, the Jordan was about thirty miles from Samaria, a destination that would have required at least a day's journey.[53] Perhaps this distance was meant to impress upon Naaman that his healing would be effected by the power of the God of Israel and not by the sleight-of-hand magic of a prophet.

---

49. "The Abana and Pharpar were two rivers of the Anti-Lebanon Range, the first descending from Mount Amanah into plain of Damascus, the second descending eastward from the heights of Hermon," (Konkel, *1 & 2 Kings*, 429). In his visits to Damascus in 1891 and 1901, George Adam Smith attested to the beauty of the area surrounding the Syrian city (*The Historical Geography of the Holy Land*, 25th ed. [New York: Harper, 1966], 429–30).

50. Hubbard, *First and Second Kings*, 154.

51. "In Hebrew 'to me' is the first phrase in Naaman's complaint in 5:11," (Leithart, *1 & 2 Kings*, 194).

52. "Beyond our expectations, through persons we might least suppose, the Lord continues to manifest power and healing on the road to winning our confession of faith as well. Since the least among us, the servants, are often God's greatest agents, it behooves us to pay attention to those individuals in our own lives," (Hens-Piazza, *1–2 Kings*, 265).

53. "There is no easy, direct route from Samaria to the Jordan. He probably would have gone back the way he came: north to Dothan, through the Dothan Valley to the Valley of Jezreel, from Jezreel through the Gilboa pass to Beth Shan and then on to the Jordan," (Walton, *Bible Background*, 391).

Once there, Naaman dipped seven[54] times, as commanded. It's important to note here that he was not healed on the second, fourth, or sixth time; only when he had done all "according to the word of the man of God" (v. 14) was he healed. Even today, God's cleansing, deliverance, or salvation is not total until we have done what he has commanded us to do.

Rather than continuing on home to Damascus, Naaman backtracked to Samaria in order to thank the prophet properly. He declared Yahweh of Israel to be the one and only God and offered Elisha the gifts he had brought with him. But the man of God refused, for he understood that it was God who had done the healing, and neither the divine word, nor divine power, can be bought off (cf. Acts 8:18–24). Hobbs reminds us, "Elisha's refusal to accept Naaman's gift is particularly remarkable, since the story is set in a time of famine (4:38; 7:1–20)."[55]

But here's where things get interesting. Naaman's request for two mule loads of dirt (v. 17) is a detail that was for some reason omitted from the Sunday school curriculum of my childhood. I've had the opportunity to ask a few hundred adults—all veterans of Sunday school themselves—if they remember this part of the story from their childhoods, but they too were surprised by it. What possible use did Naaman have for two mule loads of Samaritan soil?

In October 2016, I was saddened to hear of the sudden passing of Dennis Byrd. A former professional football player for the New York Jets, Byrd was killed one Saturday morning when a car swerved into his lane and hit him head-on. He was pronounced dead at the scene. Byrd's life was a remarkable one. Playing college football at Tulsa, Byrd had been considered a long-shot to succeed in the NFL, but the Jets took a chance on him, and he proved them right, posting seven sacks his rookie season. However, in November 1992, Byrd collided with a teammate during a game against the Buffalo Bills and was paralyzed. Doctors said he would never walk again. Eighteen months later, however, Byrd did just

---

54. In biblical symbolism, *seven* represented wholeness, completeness, or perfection (cf. Jenson, "שֶׁבַע," *NIDOTTE* 4:34–37). "Seven days is the period of quarantine prescribed for those with various skin diseases in Lev. 13–14 (cf. 13:4, 5, etc.), and such legislation may be influencing the choice of words in this verse. At the same time, there is another numerical link here, this time with the story of the Shunammite woman in 2 Kgs. 4:8–37, whose son, in the course of his 'healing,' sneezed seven times," (Provan, *1 & 2 Kings*, 195). Provan goes on to point out other links between the stories of the Shunammite woman and Naaman. For the significance of *seven* in the ancient world, see John J. Davis, *Biblical Numerology* (Grand Rapids: Baker, 1968), 115–19.

55. Hobbs, *2 Kings*, 66.

that. The rest of his life was spent out of the public eye, but he would on occasion be called on to inspire groups of people with his improbable story.

One detail from the 1994 film about his life, *Rise & Walk*, stood out to me, a boy of only nine when I first saw it. Byrd would take some dirt out of a coffee can before each game he played and sprinkle it on the turf as he ran out of the tunnel. The dirt was from Oklahoma where he had grown up, and the practice was Byrd's way of reminding himself that whatever became of him in life, he was still just a humble farm boy from the Sooner State.

> I had always told myself that if I ever made it, if I ever got to the point where I was leaving Oklahoma behind, leaving my roots, I'd take some of those roots with me, something I could always have, something I could actually hold onto and touch, something to constantly remind me of where I came from. I had brought a can with me. Nothing fancy, just an old Folger's coffee can. I bent down and filled it with dirt, the same dirt I'd sweated and bled into back when I wasn't sure what I'd become, when all I had was a vague dream. Now that dream had come true. I was going to play professional football. I was going to live in New York City, farther from Mustang[, Oklahoma] than mere miles could measure. And I was bringing some of that soil with me.[56]

From his statements, Naaman appears to be a converted monotheist (vv. 15, 17). "Clearly, then, Naaman confesses what Israel fails to confess: the sovereign, saving God is the only God and therefore deserves worship."[57] Moreover, Israel's God had just healed him of arguably the most dreaded disease in the ancient Near East. Add to that the prevalent Old Testament idea of all the Promised Land being "holy ground," while other nations are "unclean" (cf. Hos 9:3; Amos 7:17), and it seems Naaman wanted some soil to take home to serve as a reminder that "Yahweh, he is God!" (Isa 44:6; 45:5–6, 18) and of what that God had done for him[58]—what Fretheim calls "a tangible and material tie to the com-

---

56. Dennis Byrd, *Rise and Walk: The Trial and Triumph of Dennis Byrd* (New York: HarperCollins, 1993), 76.

57. House, *1, 2 Kings*, 314.

58. "This report may indicate that although Naaman's public duties as the king's 'right-hand man' might cause him to bow down to the state god, he wanted to build a personal altar to

munity of faith Elisha represents."[59] A man who not too long before had had a very negative view of Israel's rivers was now quite fond of her dirt! Like Naaman, you and I could benefit from icons that remind us of God's presence and past faithfulness to us.

But the surprises aren't done. In yet another detail omitted from the Bible classes of my youth, Naaman explains that despite his authentic conversion, he'll need to continue going with the king of Aram to worship in the "house of Rimmon" (i.e., the temple of Hadad, Aram's chief god).[60] Bizarrely, Elisha tells him to "Go in peace." Considering that idolatry is "a First Commandment concern so important for the narrator,"[61] one wonders how the man of God could have so casually told the Aramean, "Don't worry about it. Do what you have to do," (cf. Exod 4:18; Judg 18:6; 1 Sam 1:17). The fact that this bothered Naaman so much says to me (and likely said to Elisha) that Naaman was fully converted. By every other metric, "his heart is newly, and really, wed to Yahweh."[62]

The final plot twist occurs when Naaman heads for home. Just as the Aramean entourage had disappeared over the horizon, Elisha's servant, Gehazi, ran to catch up with them. He couldn't believe the prophet had refused Naaman's generous offer of payment, so he hatched a story about Elisha being visited at the last moment by unexpected guests, two members of the prophetic guild from the nearby hill country. Could the former leper spare a talent of silver and two new outfits? "Take two talents," insisted Naaman, and he sent Gehazi back to Elisha laden down with the treasure.[63]

I find myself marveling at Gehazi's restraint. Recall that Naaman had originally come loaded with lots of gold, ten talents of silver, and ten changes of

Yahweh," (Patterson, "1, 2 Kings," 831).

59. Fretheim, *First and Second Kings*, 153.

60. Jonas C. Greenfield, "The Aramean God Rammān/Rimmōn," *IEJ* 26 (1976): 195–98.

61. Fretheim, *First and Second Kings*, 153.

62. Burke O. Long, *2 Kings* (Grand Rapids: Eerdmans, 1991), 73.

63. "A talent of silver is three hundred years of wages (for someone making thirty to thirty-five thousand a year, that would be like getting about ten million dollars), and Naaman doubles it. Gehazi is trying to set himself up for life," (Walton, *Bible Background*, 391).

clothes. The servant never mentioned the gold and asked for only ten percent of Naaman's silver, and for a "good cause." What could be wrong with that?

Everything, according to Elisha. Gehazi managed to get his ill-gained loot to his home and hide it. But when he returned to the prophet's side, Elisha had that all-knowing look on his face.[64] The exchange (v. 25) reminds me of one too many I had with my mom as a guilty teenager—"What did you do?" "Nothing!" "Where did you go?" "Nowhere!"

Elisha condemned his servant's greed, especially when so many were in need. Moreover, Gehazi had exploited God's power and God's prophet for his own enrichment and glorification. In short, he had stolen the glory from God and marred the integrity of the man of God. And with that, Gehazi was struck with leprosy and dismissed from serving Elisha. In an ironic twist only the Bible could pull off, "He commits fraud against a stranger and is made a stranger as a result. He sins against a Gentile and is put in the place of a Gentile."[65]

A   s of late, the issue of Syrian refugees and their entry into the U.S. has become a lightning rod for controversy. The nation of Syria has been ripped apart by civil war since 2011, and a million of its citizens have fled the country for refuge in Europe and the U.S., according to the United Nations High Commissioner for Refugees.[66] Meanwhile, America's willingness to accept these huddled masses from the Middle East has been quite reserved, mostly out of national security concerns.

I don't want to downplay the risks posed by accepting Syrian refugees into the U.S., and the story of Naaman offers up no direct moral imperative on this issue. Nonetheless, when my mind connected "Naaman the Syrian" with Syrian refugees, it made me think twice about perhaps the most neglected message of this story. The narrator introduces us to a Syrian, an enemy of God's people,

---

64. "Presumably Gehazi has calculated that Elisha will not be aware of what has happened. He knows, after all, that the LORD sometimes conceals things from him (4:27). Unfortunately for him, however, Elisha has on this occasion 'seen' only too clearly," (Provan, *1 & 2 Kings*, 193).

65. Leithart, *1 & 2 Kings*, 196.

66. This figure does not reflect the 4.8 million that have found refuge elsewhere in the Middle East (e.g., Turkey, Lebanon, Jordan, Iraq, and Egypt) and the 6.6 million who remain in Syria, but have been displaced from their homes because of the civil war.

and one in dire straits. As Naaman journeyed through the Northern Kingdom in search of Elisha, he likely passed the smoldering remains of his prior raids. Moreover, Naaman is a leper, and arguably nothing else came close in ancient times to rendering people "unclean" and giving their peers the impression that they were under God's judgment. Naaman was an outsider in every way imaginable.

Yet, it is the outsider in this story that is healed and praised, while an insider, Gehazi, is humiliated and punished. "The insider has experienced God's judgment; the outsider has received salvation. The outsider has become an insider and the insider an outsider. The boundary lines of the community of faith are less clear than the insiders often suggest."[67] This confronts us, the elect of God, with a disturbing truth. Though you and I are privileged to be of the elect as Christians, we can also falsely appropriate this to our nationality and thus forfeit our ability to see every person as one created in God's image. Put another way, we are part of God's chosen people because we are in Christ, not in America.

In this passage, Gehazi is no better than Jonah; he is incensed that mercy would be shown to a Gentile (v. 20; cf. Jon 4). His excuse that the money is necessary for supporting the prophetic guild is ludicrous if we remember that Elisha is quite capable of providing by God's power (4:38–44). No, Gehazi was just a selfish, greedy, racist Israelite, presuming that God's mercy was available "to him and his group in a way it does not apply to those wicked Arameans."[68]

This was Jesus' point when he invoked Naaman in his hometown synagogue, noting that he was the only leper healed, though "there were many lepers in Israel in the time of the prophet Elisha" (Luke 4:27). The next few verses demonstrate that such a claim did not go over well—the audience became livid and tried to throw Christ off a cliff.

I feel the need to repeat one more time that nothing in 2 Kings 5 requires us to admit as many refugees into the U.S. as desire to come here, and especially while throwing caution and responsibility to the wind. I know that foreign refugees from predominantly Muslim countries pose a threat, no matter how remote. But I also know that American Christians haven't always been that welcoming of immigrants, no matter their religion or country of origin. It is sinfully human to be suspicious of people not like us, and I have more than once witnessed the ugly fruit of racism and xenophobia appear on the lips of the elect. Since the complaint of the Grecian widows in Acts 6:1 and the tension between

---

67. Fretheim, *First and Second Kings,* 155.

68. Konkel, *1 & 2 Kings,* 435.

Jews and Gentiles, the church has seen more than its fair share of bigotry—real or imagined. Olley makes this excellent observation:

> The story that started with the positive results of a lowly, captive girl's witness ends not with the account of her master's healing but with the judgment on a person who was not open to God's free compassion to an outsider, even an enemy (*this Aramean*, v. 20). In a similar way, Jesus' "eating with tax-collectors and sinners" was a contributing human factor towards his crucifixion. The story of Acts points to struggles and tensions as Gentiles became Christians, while Revelation is a message of warning and hope to Christians in danger of succumbing to cultural pressures, with much on wealth. How much human rivalry and conflict is associated with derogatory labelling ("this Aramean") that places the other in a different and lower category of human and excuses showing love to another who is also made in the image of God?[69]

Naaman's story, in sum, reminds us that outsiders—in dire circumstances and willing to submit humbly to the Lord[70]—are closer to the kingdom of heaven than insiders who have been part of the community of the elect their entire lives (cf. Matt 21:31). Refugees have as much right to the gospel as you and I. "How are they to believe in him of whom they have never heard? And how are they to hear without someone preaching?" (Rom 10:14). And since it is easier to evangelize them in our own country as opposed to entering war-torn Syria as missionaries, we ought to take advantage of the opportunity for however many come to the U.S.

At the same time, members of the elect community can find themselves on the outside looking in if they allow their compassion and humanity to be overridden by hatred, suspicion, and envy. And do not be deceived; just as Elisha had supernatural knowledge of what Gehazi had done, so God has perfect knowl-

69. Olley, *Message of Kings*, 237; emphasis his.

70. It is important to note that "Naaman follows up his conversion with actions that embody his transformed heart and spirit. He greets Gehazi graciously. His focus is upon the well-being of the other—that of both Gehazi and Elisha. Immediately, he responds to need with an unquestioning and unconditional generosity—all signs of a heart now fixed upon the Lord," (Hens-Piazza, *1–2 Kings*, 264).

edge of what is in our hearts. Before we seek to make the U.S. secure, we would do well to secure our own hearts and bring them into subjection to the Lord Jesus Christ (2 Cor 10:5), for from the heart spring the issues of life (Prov 4:23).

2 KINGS 6:1–7

Elisha's ministry was growing, as evidenced by the statement that the prophetic guild had outgrown its meeting house[71] (v. 1). They thus sought and procured permission from the man of God to build a larger place near the Jordan. While some of them were felling trees near the river, the axe head flew off the handle wielded by one of the prophets.

He was instantly filled with dismay, for the axe had been borrowed. The prophet wielding this axe had likely had to leave collateral or a pledge of some kind until he returned the tool; the Law certainly demanded that he make restitution (Exod 22:14–15). His predicament, in other words, is not unlike someone living paycheck to paycheck who has wrecked a rental car and declined the collision insurance while having no other protection. Iron was expensive in ancient times; according to 1 Samuel 13:19–22, iron was very rare in Israel two hundred years earlier, and it likely hadn't changed much since. In addition to this, given the famine in Israel, the prophet was likely poor. Someone was going to be paying out the nose.

Elisha calmly asked where the head had fallen into the Jordan, and the man of God threw a stick into the river, causing the axe head to float and the prophet to retrieve it. The narrator invites us to appreciate how much the laws of gravity were bent when he refers to the axe head as "the iron" (v. 6). But the greater point is that Elisha was able to redeem the man from certain economic ruin, as he had the widow (4:1–7).[72]

---

71. Wray Beal notes that the Hebrew text implies a formal gathering place "in which inferiors sit before a superior to listen, worship or be taught" (*1 & 2 Kings*, 341; cf. Gen 43:33; Ezek 8:1; 14:1). In other words, this was a meeting, not dwelling, place. In latter times, other prophetic and monastic communities would gather and thrive near the Jordan, such as the Qumran community, which provided us with the Dead Sea Scrolls.

72. "Elisha's instruction to 'take it up' (6:7) echoes his instruction to the Shunammite woman to 'take up' her son (4:36), suggesting that by saving the ax head Elisha gives the man new life," (Leithart, *1 & 2 Kings*, 200).

R egarding miracles, Fretheim notes that they "are concentrated at two points in the Old Testament—the exodus complex of events and Elijah/ Elisha stories—both crucial turning points in the history of the people of God."[73] Indeed, the bulk of God's amazing acts of power seem to come in the days of Moses, as well as Elijah and his successor. In both contexts, the miracles reflect God's power to establish a new beginning for his people and sustain them through any hardship.

Most significant here is the care God gives to the needs of individuals. Whether physical harm (death, leprosy) or financial hardship (oil, axe heads), Elisha is God's agent to make known God's concern for the "least of these" of Israelite society. God's concern is poured out on both men and women, rich and poor, friends, and enemies, Israelites and Gentiles, the cautious and the negligent.[74]

And this concern continues in the New Testament. On one occasion when taxes needed to be paid, Jesus ordered Peter to cast a hook into the sea. The fish he reeled in contained the necessary shekel to send the IRS. Paul promised the Philippians, "My God will meet all your needs according to the riches of his glory in Christ Jesus" (Phil 4:19 NIV). God does his best work when his people are in dire straits. We need only pray in faith, and then stand back to watch God perform his glorious work.[75]

2 KINGS 6:8–23

On another occasion, during one of many periods when Aram and Israel were at each other's throats,[76] Aram's king became suspicious that he had a mole in his midst. It seems on several occasions Elisha was feeding the king of Israel military intelligence[77] concerning Aram (the relationship between monarch

---

73. Fretheim, *First and Second Kings*, 156.

74. Olley, *Message of Kings*, 240.

75. "God's power invades the world of the ordinary to effect strange reversals. The lowly are raised to places of honor (Luke 1:51–53). The unrighteous are justified (Luke 18:9–14). The lost are found (Luke 15:3–10). The dead are raised. These are as much incredible reversals as is iron that floats," (Nelson, *First and Second Kings*, 185).

76. "Periodic military action between Israel and Aram has occurred since 1 Kgs 15, and Aram's border conflicts (v. 23) and frequent warring (v. 8) may reflect the tenuous relationship between the two countries during Jehoram's reign," (Wray Beal, *1 & 2 Kings*, 342).

77. Wiseman believes such intelligence was gained through informants (cf. 5:3) instead of divine power (*1 and 2 Kings*, 222). But, though prophets often gave military advice in the an-

and prophet apparently had thawed since 3:13–14). Aram's king was intent on flushing out the mole, but one of his aides informed him that it was the prophet's doing, that Elisha was repeating even those things unknowable to anyone (v. 12; cf. Eccl 10:20). So Aram's king sent his men to Dothan,[78] located some twelve miles north of Samaria, to eliminate Israel's man of God.

At this point, we have to stop and marvel at the stupidity of this king of Aram. If Elisha indeed knew his most intimate decisions, then the man of God in Israel would also know that troops were on their way to Dothan. "Does he really think that Elisha will not 'see' what is happening? Does he really think that he can constrain God's prophet by force?"[79] Such is a reminder that reason and logic are seldom a part of the decision making of the godless.

Early the next morning, when Elisha's servant (Gehazi?) saw the Arameans bivouacked around the city, he panicked and ran inside to tell his master. Elisha's response to the news, however, was one equally of profound faith and insight. With a prayer, the prophet asked Yahweh to open his servant's eyes, to allow them both to see the same thing[80]—a divine army had surrounded the prophet's home (cf. 2:11); Elisha was not in danger.[81] Elijah had been divinely protected

---

cient Near East, "the information given by Elisha is far more specific than the examples known from other literature," (Walton, *Bible Background*, 392). In an embellished version of the story, Josephus claims the Arameans planned to ambush Israel's king while he was hunting, so Elisha warned him not to go (*Antiquities* 9.51).

78. "The story seems to assume that Syria already controlled much of northern Israel, for Dothan lies to the south of the valley of Jezreel, in the northern foothills of the Ephraimite hill-country," (Auld, *I & II Kings*, 174). At the site of Dothan, "Archaeological investigation has confirmed the existence of a major settlement dating from the Iron Age II period, complete with an impressive many-roomed building that may have been an administrative center. This building was, however, destroyed at some point in the ninth century B.C., in the course of the ongoing Israel/Damascus conflict described in 2 Kings," (Provan, "2 Kings," 136).

79. Provan, *1 & 2 Kings*, 198.

80. "The statement must have bewildered the servant, because he can see and he can count. There is a large host outside and two inside. The prophet's arithmetic is clearly out of touch with reality. The prophet and his servant are hopelessly outmanned," (Brueggemann, *1 & 2 Kings*, 346).

81. Provan notes that "mountain" (v. 17) or "hill" (NIV) is singular, meaning the Arameans had surrounded the city in the hills, but the divine army had surrounded Elisha on the mound or hill of the city, which towers some two hundred feet above its surroundings (*1 & 2 Kings*, 199; cf. Joseph P. Free, "The Excavation of Dothan," *BA* 19 [1956]: 43–48).

from royal threat (1 Kgs 17:1–24; 18:1–15; 19:1–18; 2 Kgs 1:1–15), and so would Elisha.[82]

When the Arameans attacked, and with the eyes of his servant *opened*, Elisha asked God to *close* those of his enemies, at which point he led the blinded troops into a trap in Samaria. The image of the old man leading these elite military men into the city like the fabled pied piper is rather comical. Since they were obviously capable of following Elisha (vv. 19–20), it may be that this blindness was actually a deceived or disoriented condition of some sort (cf. Gen 19:11).[83] Once inside the capital city, Elisha prayed for their "sight" to be restored.

Note that these men were prisoners of Elisha, which explains why he refused the demand of Israel's king to execute them on the spot (cf. Deut 20:10–11).[84] Rather, the prophet fed them and sent them home to Aram (cf. Prov 25:21–22). And lest we wonder if Elisha's amnesty is no better than Ahab's, we should remember that "no holy war ban has been declared in this case (contrast I Kings 20:31–42), so the rules of civilized warfare apply."[85] Finally, it's not insignificant that the Arameans no longer raided Israel after this (v. 23).

As was the case with Naaman, Elisha's actions here were meant to prompt evangelism. His hope was that these soldiers would return to Aram declaring the Lord's greatness. God has done the same with us; he invites us to the Table each week to remind us of what he has done for us in Christ; once blind, we now see. "For he has rescued us from the dominion of darkness and brought us into the kingdom of the Son he loves, in whom we have redemption, the forgiveness of sins" (Col 1:13–14 NIV).

---

82. "Elisha, more than any other of the early prophets, repeatedly resorts to miraculous powers. His master Elijah was obliged to flee for his life when Ahab sought to kill him, but Elisha when mortally threatened can immediately count on chariots of fire and mysterious cavalry," (Alter, *Ancient Israel*, 757).

83. Stol argues that this was a condition known as day-blindness or hemeralopia (Marten Stol, "Blindness and Night-Blindness in Akkadian," *JNES* 45 [1986]: 295–99), something akin to having difficulty seeing in bright light after having your eyes dilated.

84. "Elisha, as he does for so much of his ministry, stands on the side of life. The reason he provides for not killing the captives suggests some rule of war by which prisoners, particularly those captured without battle, are spared and enslaved," (Wray Beal, *1 & 2 Kings*, 344).

85. Nelson, *First and Second Kings*, 187.

A t Yalta in 1945, Winston Churchill asked Joseph Stalin to respect the religious freedoms of Eastern Europeans, to which Stalin, who was an atheist, smirked and asked, "How many [military] divisions does the Pope have?" The illegitimacy of Catholicism aside, such a ridiculous remark reveals that Stalin was more obtuse than even Ben-hadad. The king of Aram rightly perceived Elisha to be a threat, but foolishly believed the prophet could be eliminated. Stalin, on the other hand, believed the supernatural to have no power in this world at all. The delusion here is as comical as it is deep-seated.

Konkel notes, "The focus of the whole story is on vision, particularly the ability to see beyond usual perception. [...] It is a story about the difference between sight and vision, about being controlled by the temporal or by the transcendent. Political powers are subordinated to the sovereignty of God."[86] Though we might not ever have the ability to see physically the army of the Lord, we can have no doubt that our God comes to our aid when we are in trouble.

Nothing under heaven can withstand us when we wield the most formidable weapon in our arsenal: prayer. In his discussion of the Christian armor (Eph 6:10–20), the apostle Paul presents prayer in the Spirit as the catalyst that makes effective the armor of God. When we see other powers at work in the world (e.g., political machinations, economic turmoil, moral hostility against the church), we must believe and pray and worship and act as if faith is the victory that overcomes the world (1 John 5:4).

As countless other biblical stories demonstrate, prayer opens our spiritual eyes to what God is doing in the world and rouses us to be a part of it. So Fretheim concludes, "There are moments in the life of a people when the insights and prayers of key individuals are decisive in human affairs, even miracu-

---

86. Konkel, *1 & 2 Kings*, 456. "This narrative makes the same point as the Book of Kings as a whole. Kings of nations, be they of Judah or Israel, Assyria or even Babylon, were never really in control of the history of God's people. Only God was. In this case God gave victory to the people. In the larger story the people were to experience total, humiliating defeat at the hands of the Babylonians, but again under the power and control of God. The awesome power of government, be it totalitarian or democratic, is something of a joke when compared to the horses and chariots of Yahweh, operative through the word of God's true spokesperson. To a world terrified by the possibility of destruction, the church continues to affirm God's power and to assert, with eyes opened by Easter's new life, 'Fear not, for those who are with us are more than those who are with them' (v. 16)," (Nelson, *First and Second Kings*, 187–88).

lously so. Such a salutary effect may not always come to be, but one prays as if it would make all the difference in the world."[87]

2 KINGS 6:24–7:20

In Steven Soderbergh's 2011 movie *Contagion*, actor Matt Damon plays a father in Minneapolis named Mitch Emhoff whose wife and stepson fall victim to the MEV-1 virus and die. In the film, the virus becomes an epidemic overnight, claiming 2.5 million lives in the U.S. and 28 million abroad in just a matter of weeks. One of the scenes shows Emhoff and his surviving daughter, Jory, going to the supermarket in search of food, only to find that the store has been looted and virtually picked clean. Only because the film deals with the breakdown of social order during an event like an international health crisis was the scene believable. I remember watching the film for the first time, thinking, "That's almost impossible to imagine happening in this day and time."

Scenes of massive food shortages are familiar to Americans, but only via news reports from countries far away. As a kid, I remember images of famine coming from Somalia and, later, reenacted in the movie *Black Hawk Down*. Most recently, Venezuela has been rocked by massive food shortages and skyrocketing inflation; food is on the shelves of their grocery stores, but almost no one can afford to buy it. My point here is that the scene we are about to be treated to in Kings may seem foreign to us, but only because we are a blessed people living in a blessed land—a claim Old Testament Israel could also make, but only as long as she remained faithful to the Lord and his Law.

Sometime after the Aramean troops returned in humiliation (v. 23), Ben-hadad II brought his army to besiege Samaria yet again.[88] Whereas he had been rebuffed by Ahab in 1 Kings 20, he now was able to inflict such suffering on the capital city that food became scarce. The narrator tells us that such "delicacies" as donkey heads and dove poop[89] were being sold for exorbitant pric-

---

87. Fretheim, *First and Second Kings*, 158. He goes on to suggest that prayer empowers God to act, a nuance I would not agree with, but the implications of which are intriguing: "Elisha's use of prayer as a vehicle for divine action, even twice addressing God with a 'please' (vv. 17–18), is seen to be important. His prayer is efficacious—a means in and through which God gets things done in the world. Thereby *God* has access to power and resources that would not otherwise be available," (Ibid.; emphasis his).

88. For a description of typical siege conditions in ancient times, see Josephus, *Wars* 5.10.3.

89. Some claim *dove dung* is a euphemism for edible seed pods (Cogan, *II Kings*, 79; Kon-

es—the five silver shekels for dove dung (v. 25) would represent more than a month's wages for the average laborer.[90] I cannot fathom a hunger so desperate that I'd give half a month's salary for half a liter of bird poop. Not much better is the report of Babylonians desperately gnawing on leather straps during a siege in the year 650.[91] Israel's plight was as plausible as it is horrible.

Samaria's dire straits is further illustrated by the testimony of a woman to the king: she and a friend agreed to boil the first woman's baby and eat him (cf. Deut 28:53–57; Lam 2:20; 4:10; Ezek 5:10), but when it came time to cannibalize the second woman's son, she had hidden him. Some believe such an extreme act to be fictional, but examples of the same exist in our own day. From the severe Soviet famine of 1932–33 come horrific stories of cannibalism, including the cannibalization of children by their parents.[92] The same, and worse, also occurred during the Nazi's siege of Leningrad in 1941–43.[93]

When he heard the mother's complaint, King Jehoram tore his clothes in grief in a humiliating display of impotence and vowed to punish Elisha.[94] As we have already seen, it was the king's obligation in ancient Israel to attend to the needs of the poor (Ps 72:1–4). But the king had been powerless to save in his battle against Moab; powerless to save when Naaman appeared; powerless to prevent Aramean raids; now, he was powerless to save his people from famine. He does not lead his people in national repentance or prayers for deliverance,

kel, *1 & 2 Kings*, 450). But this isn't necessary—a similar fate for a besieged city is exemplified in 18:27, as well as other historical sources (cf. Hobbs, *2 Kings*, 79; Wray Beal, *1 & 2 Kings*, 351).

90. Wiseman, *1 and 2 Kings*, 223. A dead donkey's head cost eighty silver shekels (v. 25), more than half the cost of a live horse in Solomon's day (1 Kgs 10:29). By comparison, a slave could be bought for thirty shekels (Exod 21:32).

91. Cogan, *II Kings*, 79; cf. *ANET* 300. Other similar stories from antiquity exist. Pliny the Elder mentions a siege by Hannibal in which a mouse began selling for two hundred denarii (*Natural History* 8.82).

92. Robert Conquest, *Harvest of Sorrow: Soviet Collectivization and the Terror–Famine* (New York: Oxford Univ. Press, 1986), 257–58.

93. Harrison E. Salisbury, *The 900 Days: The Siege of Leningrad* (Cambridge, MA: DeCapo, 1985), 474–81.

94. "After all, Elisha let the Arameans go (6:23), enabling them to regroup and mount this debilitating siege. And Elisha has (to date) done nothing to alleviate the siege," (Wray Beal, *1 & 2 Kings*, 351). "The king's diversionary response is to apprehend Elisha and seek to execute him. He holds the prophet responsible for the trouble, completely unwilling and unable to recognize his own deep complicity in the suffering just reported," (Bruegemann, *1 & 2 Kings*, 357).

nor does he send for Elisha in search of a "thus saith the Lord." He waits for God to act, but he also blames God's servant for Israel's problems—just as Ahab had done (1 Kgs 18:17). Jehoram isn't a "buck stops here" sort of leader. He doesn't doubt God's omnipotence, but he doesn't trust in his omnibenevolence, either. "Evident is the desperation and anger of someone who has relied on his own position and abilities and not on following Yahweh but who now finds the situation outside his control and so seeks to deflect blame. Tragically he is an example of those who are quick to say God is responsible (vv. 27, 33) but have no sense of their own accountability."[95]

We're familiar with the cliché ethics question, "Would you steal in order to feed your family?" But the mere idea of a mother opting to cannibalize her infant for the sake of survival tests the limits of belief. Indeed, cannibalism in the Old Testament is a sign of the breakdown of social order, that things have been turned upside down, and devouring one's children "is both cultural and religious suicide, for it is through the children that the covenant with Yahweh is kept alive."[96] Note that the woman is more outraged by her friend's fecklessness than she is filled with guilt or shame over her hideous act. "The normal compassion of motherhood is subordinated to the desperation to survive."[97] All this is intended to trigger in our minds a recall of Deuteronomy 28:53–57. The covenant curses Moses invoked on Israel predicted this exact situation, should Israel ever be unfaithful. And just as the word of the Lord stands forever, this is how we have arrived here; "Samaria was finally paying for her sins."[98]

Meanwhile, Elisha and the elders of the community were in the house of the prophet (having a home Bible study? a prayer meeting?). With prophetic

---

95. Olley, *Message of Kings*, 245.

96. Stuart Lasine, "Jehoram and the Cannibal Mothers (2 Kings 6.24-33): Solomon's Judgment in an Inverted World," *JSOT* 50 (1991): 35.

97. Konkel, *1 & 2 Kings*, 450. Later, he adds, "War creates a perversion of values so that good and evil in particular circumstances become entirely blurred," (Ibid., 462).

98. Hubbard, *First and Second Kings*, 161. "This gruesome description of the curse of the covenant is not a vengeful punishment of an insulted God. This description is the inescapable reality of war and the dreadful consequences of the anarchy that war perpetuates. Failure to honor the divine order of the covenant leaves the people at the mercy of the nations. They suffer in the ways of all other nations. [. . .] The curses of Deuteronomy, exemplified in these stories of Elisha, describe a society outside of the order that God has designed. This is not what God has chosen for his people; the house of Omri chose the ways of the nations for themselves," (Konkel, *1 & 2 Kings*, 456–57).

foresight, Elisha could see the king's messenger headed towards his home bearing a message of death, and that the king was not far behind. Elisha gave his guests instructions to shut the door and prevent the messenger from entering, hoping "perhaps [to] forestall the messenger's murderous attempt until Elisha could deliver an encouraging word to the king."[99] At this point, it's a tad confusing what happens, but Josephus reconstructs a plausible scene:

> "But," said [Elisha], "when he that is commanded to do this comes, take care that you do not let him come in, but press the door against him, and hold him fast there, for the king himself will follow him, and come to me, having altered his mind." Accordingly, they did as they were bidden, when he that was sent by the king to kill Elisha came: but J[eh]oram repented of his wrath against the prophet; and for fear he that was commanded to kill him should have done it before he came he made haste to hinder the slaughter, and to save the prophet; and when he came to him he accused him that he did not pray to God for their deliverance from the miseries they now lay under, but saw them so sadly destroyed by them.[100]

The man of God calmly informed the king that, in less than twenty-four hours, the siege would lift and the famine abate; food prices (though still inflated[101]) would begin to return to normal, there would be no need for cannibalism, and Israel would be saved. The king's lieutenant[102] was skeptical, however. To his lack of faith, Elisha responded that the lieutenant would see the deliverance, but not be among the delivered, "for to mock the prophetic word is to mock the LORD."[103]

---

99. Patterson, "1, 2 Kings," 839. "The elders (v. 32) function as witnesses to the prophetic word, but also as a humorous signal of the impotence of royal power, thwarted by some old men holding a door shut against it!" (Nelson, *First and Second Kings*, 189).

100. Josephus, *Antiquities* 9.60–70.

101. Walton, *Bible Background*, 394.

102. B. A. Mastin, "Was the ŠĀLÎŠ the Third Man in the Chariot?" in *Studies in the Historical Books of the Old Testament*, ed. J. A. Emerton (Leiden: Brill, 1979), 125–54.

103. Provan, *1 & 2 Kings*, 201.

Elisha sets a powerful example here; once again, he "remains unperturbed at the ranting of the king."[104] As he had in 2 Kings 3, the prophet sets a standard for all men of God. In times of great tension, stress, or calamity, keep calm and minister the Word.

t's then that the scene shifts to four lepers living at the gate of Samaria—i.e., the fringe of the community (cf. Lev 13:11, 46; Num 12:14–15). The way in which they express their options would be hilarious if it weren't so sad— "One, we can stay in the city and die. Two, if we stay here, we die. Three, if we defect to Aram, we might live or die." As the day was ending, they decided to roll the dice and cast their lot with the army of Ben-hadad II.

Imagine these four men, then, and their bewilderment as they entered the camp to find it abandoned. In a stunning miracle, the Lord had created the audible illusion (cf. 2 Sam 5:24) that the armies of the Hittites and Egyptians were closing in on Aram, at which the Arameans had fled their camp in terror just as the lepers arrived. The Hittite and Egyptian empires, it should be noted, had long outlived their glory days at this point and wouldn't have struck terror in a Boy Scout troop—"but that is just the point. This panic is induced by God, not logic."[105] The camp, then, was found "as it was" (v. 7).

Throughout the night, the four lepers partied like it was 1999. Food and drink were plentiful; they looted tent after tent for gold, silver, and clothes. But we are left to wonder if these lepers with their loot are no better than Gehazi, Elisha's greedy servant. Will they think only of themselves when others are in need?

Sure enough, their consciences overtook them: "We are not doing right. This day is a day of good news. If we are silent and wait until the morning light, punishment will overtake us. Now therefore come; let us go and tell the king's household" (v. 9). They passed word to the king through the gatekeepers of what they had found in the Aramean camp.

Jehoram's initial reaction was one of skepticism. "It's a trap," he thought. "The Arameans have abandoned their camp in order to draw us out into the open" (cf. Josh 8:3–23; Judg 9). "Despite hearing Elisha's prophecy, the king does not consider the events YHWH's work; nor does he consult with the

---

104. Konkel, *1 & 2 Kings*, 458.

105. Nelson, *First and Second Kings*, 190.

prophet."[106] Surely, the king thought, the deserted camp and its treasures was another Trojan horse. Yet, when he sent out scouts all the way to the Jordan to verify, they found that the Arameans had indeed beat a path back to Damascus, scattering their belongings along the way (vv. 14–15).

The people of Israel, then, plundered the camp and food prices stabilized, just as Elisha had predicted. But in the mad rush for food, the king's lieutenant—the one who had doubted the prophetic word—was trampled to death. The refrain of Kings resounds once again: the word of the Lord stands forever.

At the center of this narrative is the question, "How should God's people respond to hardship and suffering, especially on a community or national level?" Fretheim identifies different strategies or responses to hardship employed by various players in this drama:

1.   The women: "Cope with the disaster in whatever way one can; extreme situations may call for extreme measures."

2.   The king: "Blame God, lose hope, and kill the prophet."

3.   The lieutenant: "Doubt that God can ameliorate the situation."

4.   The lepers: "Act imaginatively and with some abandon regarding one's own life, and spread the 'good news' that miraculously becomes available, even if one is not fully cognizant of the theological issues involved."[107]

He then contrasts these with the response of the prophet, Elisha, who trusts "that God has Israel's best interests at heart and will bring salvation."[108] If there is ever a question whether one man can make a difference, this blue-collar prophet answers assertively. Through him, God offered a promise of miraculous deliverance to his people, one that could be claimed or realized by all those who believed. Elisha was salt and light to his world—a preservative of God's values and a beacon of hope in very dark times.

---

106. Wray Beal, *1 & 2 Kings*, 353.

107. Fretheim, *First and Second Kings*, 160–62.

108. Ibid., 162.

In the same way, God offers hope to the hurting of any age through the hands and feet of his people. Christians ought never to respond to disaster with a "eat or be eaten" philosophy, nor should they lose heart and turn on God. Rather, may we always be bastions of faith, hope, and love—even if the heavens fall and the mountains collapse into the sea, for we are confident that he who notices the death of a sparrow has his eye trained on his creation and ultimately works for us, not against us. Wherever there is heartache, disaster, suffering, pain, and the question, "Where is God?" may the answer be found in the presence of the church. If we are not present to preserve God's values and offer a beacon of hope, our fallen world will resort to the most abhorrent behavior imaginable, as this story illustrates all too starkly.

And like the lepers, as we exult in the riches of Christ Jesus that we have unexpectedly stumbled upon, let us not neglect to carry back to the city good news of the deliverance God has wrought. Funny how, in 2 Kings 7, it is lepers— the deplorables of society—who bear witness to the gospel; God, too, chose the foolish and weak and deplorables of the world to bear witness to his gospel (1 Cor 1:18–31) to a society cannibalizing itself. This story of the siege of Samaria, then, is a call for the church to be about her Father's business. "We are not doing right. This day is a day of good news. If we are silent and wait [...] punishment will overtake us" (v. 9).

2 KINGS 8:1-6

Before the famine that we were introduced to in the previous narrative (as well as in 4:38), and probably not long after raising her son back to life, Elisha had warned the Shunammite woman of the impending disaster. He predicted that it would last seven years, a number that communicates intensity as much as it does duration.[109] Accordingly, she sought refuge among the Philistines,[110] similar to how Naomi's family had sought refuge among the Moabites during the

---

109. Hubbard, *First and Second Kings*, 164.

110. Aharoni notes of the Philistine coast, "as far down as the Gaza region [rainfall] still suffices for growing good crops of grain on the plains," (Yohanan Aharoni, *The Land of the Bible: A Historical Geography*, trans. A. F. Rainey [London: Burns, 1967], 23). Recall that Isaac had also sought refuge among the Philistines during a famine (Gen 26:1). Considering that this woman's husband was likely deceased (cf. 4:14), and that the Philistine coast was less dependent on rainfall and near Egypt (the world's breadbasket during hardship, cf. Gen 12:10; 41:53–57; 42:1–5; 47:4), it makes sense that this woman relocated.

period of Judges (Ruth 1:1–2). Upon her return to Israel, however, the Shunammite woman discovered that her land either had been forfeited to the crown or
had passed to the crown to be held in trust. She thus appealed to have it returned
to her and her son, the rightful heir to the property.

The king (never identified, probably Jehoram) was hearing Gehazi[111] tell of
all the great things Elisha had done; while Gehazi was heralding the prophet's
greatest hits, the woman "just happened" to walk up with her appeal to have her
land returned. We should not be surprised at this; Hobbs reminds us that "expro-
priation of land by the powerful is a constant target of the prophets' attack," (e.g.,
Isa 5:8).[112] But here, the king of Israel acted as the fair and just ruler he was intended to be.[113] He appointed an official to return not only the land, but also to credit
its seven-year yield to her.[114] If this king was Jehoram, we have before us a stark
contrast to the example of his father and his land-grabbing tendencies (1 Kgs 21).

Throughout the book of Joshua, there is tension as to whether the commander of Israel will fill the shoes Moses left behind. Indeed, often in Joshua,
Moses is known as the "servant of the LORD." Only at the end of the book is
Joshua given that same moniker (Josh 24:29). Likewise, since Elijah's rapture,
the reader has been wondering if his prophetic successor would fill his shoes. Is
Elisha a legitimate man of God? Thus, this incident concerning the Shunammite
woman "offered final, climactic authentication that Elisha was a genuine prophet
of Yahweh. It showed that Elisha carried great influence even when absent. More
important, it presented the persuasive witness of a former skeptic and opponent,
the king of Israel. Thus, in effect, this episode validated the claims made about
Elisha in earlier passages. Those who associated with Elisha enjoyed God's blessing, even in the prophet's absence."[115]

---

111. "This scene is either a 'throwback' to Gehazi's preleprosy days or his leprosy was, like
Naaman's, a type that did not require him to remove himself from society," (House, *1, 2 Kings*,
282, n. 72). Patterson believes this "story hints at the possibility that Gehazi has repented of his
sins and has been restored to a place of usefulness for God," ("1, 2 Kings," 843).

112. Hobbs, *2 Kings*, 101.

113. In the Law, God made clear his intention for the king to care for widows and orphans (cf. Deut 10:18; 24:19–20; 2 Sam 8:15; Ps 72:1–4, 12–14; Isa 1:17; Jer 7:6–7).

114. "Generally a person would not expect to receive back income from the land for the
period of absence. That would be considered the reimbursement to those who had kept the land
up and worked it," (Walton, *Bible Background*, 395).

115. Hubbard, *First and Second Kings*, 165. "Though Elisha's advice to leave the land

ith the narrator of Kings having shown so much emphasis on monarchs, it's nice to see some attention given to the regular Joes of this
world. Konkel notes that, unlike Elijah, nearly all the stories of Elisha "do not provide a political history but are examples of the sovereign work of
God through his prophet during times of apostasy and conflict."[116] Our Lord is
as intimately concerned about your needs and mine as he is those of the world's
VIPs. "You can be sure that God will take care of everything you need," boasted
the apostle Paul (Phil 4:19 Msg)—a promise to which we can lay claim because
of a resurrection (just like the Shunammite woman). No person or problem is
too small for the God of Israel, and these stories about the deeds of the blue-collar prophet confirm that.

But lest we think Yahweh to be merely a cosmic concierge, we must note
that God's power worked in Elisha for a particular purpose. In the waning days
of the dark Omride dynasty, and in a nation of Israel that seemed completely
inept at spiritual revival, Yahweh was determined not to leave himself without
witness. Elisha's miracles exhibited that there was a man of God in Israel—an
ambassador whose very presence proved that the Lord had not quit on his people, though they had certainly quit on him (cf. 2 Tim 2:13).

By extension, Elisha's ministry not only attested to the divine presence, but
also divine sovereignty. God was greater than Baal or any other rival. Sure, he can
direct the course of international events in ways no other can, but he is equally
able to touch tenderly the life of a solitary person whenever he chooses.

This last fact is one I believe the church cannot—must not!—lose sight
of. If not vigilant and disciplined, we can become wrapped up in the culture
wars—championing pro-life judges, a biblical definition of marriage, or other
such causes—until we falsely conclude that God only acts in the world against
"big" things and in "big" ways; that God's work and way are always on a grand
scale and aimed at dominions and strongholds and all the pagan "isms" known
to us. And while it is true that no force can stand against him, the same Lord who
worked his will through widows, servant girls, and impoverished prophets—the
same Lord who spoke to Elijah in a still, small voice—is the same Lord who

---

caused the woman's problem, his reputation now brings about a resolution to her crisis upon
her return. Hence, even in Elisha's absence, the goodness of his deeds continues to bring life,"
(Hens-Piazza, *1–2 Kings*, 279).

116. Konkel, *1 & 2 Kings*, 447.

today does as much or more to advance his kingdom through servants in the heartland as he does heads of state in the capital.

It is of no small significance that four times in 8:1–6, resurrection from death to life is mentioned. Ours is a gospel of just such a resurrection. At the center of the Christian faith is the conviction that God does the impossible, that he injects abundance and life into places where there was once only poverty and death. And he does so more often through the meek and lowly than the high and mighty. His kingdom, after all, was launched in a backwater province—not the capital—of a mighty empire.

Though Elijah fought the good fight against evil in Israel, Elisha's ministry was no less effective. And so in this war against the evil spiritual powers, let us be content when God uses us for minor surgical strikes instead of shock and awe campaigns. Let us show as much compassion for the single mother wanting to abort yet another pregnancy as we do concern for the nomination of pro-life judges; as much care for the homosexual adrift in these morally-confused times as we do criticism for the enemies of godly sexuality. Let us remember that God is sometimes content to effect change one soul at a time.

TALKING POINTS

I n the stories of Elisha, Gehazi's attitude and actions mirror those of Christians today to a degree that should make us all uncomfortable. We first meet him in the story of the Shunammite woman. Like Gehazi, we have been tasked by our master to accomplish a particular mission, but we too often fail, and perhaps because we rely on our own power and not the Lord's. In the Gospels, "some of Jesus' followers invest great faith in his ability to heal—and even to raise from the dead—when present [...]. Nevertheless, the highest commendation is reserved for those who believe that only his words are necessary," (cf. Mark 5:21–24, 35–43; Luke 7:1–17; John 11:17–37).[117] Later, in 2 Kings 4, Gehazi considered a gift of food as too little to feed so many; in the Gospels, the apostles balked over an identical situation (John 6:9). In the Naaman narrative, Gehazi is elitist and greedy, miffed that God would show favor to an enemy of Israel. He sought to parlay God's glory for his personal gain, and it backfired. Again, in the Gospels, the apostles proved themselves to be elitists at times (Luke 9:51–56), as well as greedy (John 12:1–6). At times, we must consider less-than-righteous individuals in Scripture and view them as a mirror. Like Gehazi and the apostles, do we sometimes doubt that God's command to act brings with it God's power to achieve? Like Gehazi and the apostles, do we sometimes doubt God's ability to provide for our every need (cf. 2 Cor 9:10)? Like Gehazi and the apostles, are we sometimes guilty of elitism and greed, miffed at the thought of God showing favor to our enemies?[118]

---

117. Provan, *1 & 2 Kings*, 190.

118. "The conversion of Naaman the Aramean is one of the examples Jesus uses to show what faith must mean for the Christian and their understanding of the Bible. His rebuke of the religious leaders of his day shows their propensity towards cultural blindness; they fail to recognize their own faithlessness and condemn whatever does not conform to their own interpretations. [...] The crowd at Nazareth has a faith much like that of Gehazi. Though they think themselves to be the true followers of the Scriptures, they are not prepared to hear the Scriptures. They can no more accept Jesus as the servant of Isaiah than Gehazi can accept Naaman the Aramean as one who belongs with the sons of the prophets as he himself does," (Konkel, *1 & 2 Kings*, 435–36).

The story of Naaman has several lessons to teach us about salvation. *First, God loves and seeks to save all people.* God's favor is not limited to those who believe they have an exclusive claim to his affection. It was no small scandal that God would show such concern for an Aramean officer who had experienced such victory over Israel. But *scandalous* is the perfect adjective for God's grace. *Second, God's grace was mediated to Naaman through his servant.* In the same way, each of us is to be an agent or instrument of God's salvation to others (Rom 10:14–15; 1 Cor 3:6). For the lost, this is also a reminder that God seeks to reach us through the most unlikely of people. It is also proof that salvation is not something we achieve by our own effort, but a gift granted to us by another. *Third, God's mercy is only effectual in a humble heart.* Note the build-up of Naaman's résumé by the narrator in 5:1; the final phrase, however, reminds us that Naaman is proud, yet broken. Like Naaman, many are not open to the gospel until trial or tragedy descends. In 5:14, it's made clear that Naaman becomes like a young boy. In the New Testament, we are reminded that a new birth is necessary for salvation (John 3:1–18), that we must become like little children if we are to enter the Kingdom (Matt 18:1–5). *Fourth, God's salvation does not immediately bring perfect knowledge on how to live the Christian life.* Though Naaman confesses his faith in Israel's God, he also seeks pardon for continuing to join his master in worshiping in a pagan temple. Elisha knows that Naaman cannot yet grasp the ins and outs of monotheism; the prophet knows that while conversion is immediate, maturity is not. *Finally, God's salvation is total only when we do as he has commanded.* There was no special magic inherent in dipping seven times; its efficacy was only in the fact that this was the number God ordained. So it is today that we cannot be saved apart from obedience to the Lord's plan of salvation (Acts 22:16; Rom 6:17–18).

One disturbing question lingers concerning the story of the siege of Samaria and the two cannibalistic mothers. Why did God or Elisha allow circumstances to become so dire before acting to deliver Israel? The question, when worded more broadly, is a timeless one—how could a loving, powerful God allow such evil atrocities to take place? First, God should not be blamed for the deeds of the wicked. Each of us was created as a free moral agent, at liberty to obey or rebel in any situation. But second, this narrative portrays Jehoram as a faithless and ineffectual king. At any time, he could have called upon God to deliver his people; perhaps the question should not be, "Why did

God wait so long to act?" but, "Why did Jehoram wait so long to seek help?" Sometimes dire circumstances fall upon us for the purpose of bringing us back to God; the longer we refuse his loving call, the longer we perpetuate the disaster around us. Well did Paul remind us that "the 'right time' is now, and the 'day of salvation' is now" (2 Cor 6:2 NCV).

10

THE GRAPES OF WRATH

There's always been one scene in Mel Gibson's *Braveheart* that has stood out to me. In the aftermath of the Battle of Stirling, one in which Scotland unexpectedly routed the English, William Wallace stands on a hilltop surveying the bloody battlefield as his men chant his name. Whereas before the battle, Wallace's face was streaked with woad dye and his kilt neatly pressed, he is now a mess of blood and sweat and dirt. "War is hell," William Sherman once said, and those words (plus Wallace's bloody, sweaty face) are what I think of when I read this section of Kings.

There's a lot of turmoil and upheaval in this part of Kings; the bloody revolt led by Jehu in Israel (2 Kgs 9–10) is conspicuously juxtaposed with Jehoiada's relatively peaceful installation of Joash as king in Judah (2 Kgs 11). Kings are shot in the back, queens are hacked to pieces in the palace courtyard by their subjects, and foreign warlords gnash at the land with iron teeth. Indeed, "These chapters carry us deep into the paradox created by human and divine violence as it intersects with God's will for peace."[1]

It is indeed a paradox—and a disturbing one—that a God of love, mercy, and peace would instigate the violence we are about to witness. If war is hell, and God is in heaven, what should one have to do with the other? It helps if we recall that God's grace and wrath, his mercy and his judgment, are really two sides of the same coin. It is impossible to treasure, even evaluate, the depths of grace without being all too familiar with wrath. What good is being saved if we aren't aware of what we've been saved from? And though God began to visit the

---

1. Nelson, *First and Second Kings*, 197.

covenant curses on Israel in these chapters, we must remember such were meant
to be restorative, not punitive on Yahweh's part.

Put another way, kingdoms start to disappear when we fail to recognize
and respond to grace. Israel in these chapters illustrates that. In spite of God's
magnanimous blessings, Israel refused to obey. Though he raised up saviors to
deliver them from hostility and oppression, Israel refused to obey. Though he
purged idolatry from her midst and gave her a clean slate, Israel refused to obey.
And though the Lord time and again gave evidence that he means what he says,
that his word will surely come to pass, Israel refused to obey.

Yet, in these chapters, we'll discover that God always goes out of his way to
find any rationale to forgive and bless his people. If one excuse does not allow
him to preserve his holiness while blessing his people, he'll simply find another
reason. God always has more grace than we have sin (Rom 5:20). But when the
cup of God's wrath reaches its limit and begins to splash over the sides, he must
act in his fury to punish sin. It is God's grace *and* his holiness that force him to
tread in a winepress the grapes of his wrath in order to serve the cup of judgment.

And Israel is becoming ripe for judgment.

2 KINGS 8:7-15

For the first time in Kings, a man of God visits a foreign capital, and though
Elisha is in enemy territory, he comes and goes as he pleases, a testament to "the
high respect in which God's prophet was held."[2] In 842, Ben-hadad II, the puny
king of Aram and Ahab's former ally/nemesis, heard Elisha was in town and
wanted to inquire of the Lord via the prophet whether he would recover from his
illness. Earlier (6:8–23), Ben-hadad had learned the hard way that Elisha had a
close relationship with God, and he now wanted to take advantage of this.[3] One
cannot help being struck by the irony "that a foreign king knows well enough to
consult the Lord," while Ahab's son, Ahaziah, had thought so little of Yahweh
that he had instead inquired of Baal-zebub (1:2).[4]

---

2. Patterson, "1, 2 Kings," 844.

3. Josephus claims that Ben-hadad fell ill when he learned that Yahweh had thwarted his
efforts against Israel in 2 Kings 6 (*Antiquities* 9.87).

4. Provan, *1 & 2 Kings*, 205.

Though the alert reader should have been anticipating his arrival since 1 Kings 19:15, Hazael's[5] entrance onto the scene is surprisingly subtle. Consistent with his demeanor in the text, he was of quite humble origins; he calls himself a dog (v. 13; cf. 1 Sam 24:14; 2 Sam 9:8). "Apparently he has no proper claim to power and no pedigree that would give entitlement."[6] Thus, and not surprisingly, on a statue of the Assyrian king Shalmaneser, there is a condescending reference to Hazael as the "son of a nobody,"[7] which was apparently an epithet often used of usurpers by ancient propagandists.

Bringing with him an extravagant honorarium (v. 9), Hazael located Elisha and delivered the inquiry. But in a very unexpected turn of events, Elisha answers with an apparent lie (v. 10), and the audience is left to wonder if a deceiving spirit has again gone out from the presence of the Lord as it did in 1 Kings 22.[8] Elisha's on-the-record reply was, "You shall certainly recover." But no sooner were the words out of his mouth than he conceded that the king would die.

With that, Hazael stared at Elisha with a dumbfounded expression until he dropped his eyes in embarrassment.[9] Elisha then began to weep because he had been given a vision of all Hazael would do to Israel during his forty-year reign. He would leave a trail of destruction and holocaust in his wake; the gory assault on women and children would be especially horrific[10] (cf. Hos 10:14; 13:16;

---

5. At a site in northern Syria was found an inscription reading, "Our lord Hazael," and dates to about forty years after the events of this chapter (Unger, "Hazael," *NUBD* 541).

6. Brueggemann, *1 & 2 Kings*, 372.

7. *COS* 2.113G.

8. "Great ingenuity has been applied by interpreters (going back as far as the transmitters of MT) to exonerate Elisha from the suspicion of advocating a lie. The reader with moral scruples may wish to consider this as Elisha's first impression, superseded by the vision (cf. 'shown') he next reports. But the pair of grammatically emphasized verbal phrases clearly contrast the lie ('certainly recover') and the truth ('certainly die'). The reader is reminded of the pattern followed by Micaiah in I Kings 22:15, 17. The lie is for Ben-hadad, the truth for Hazael," (Nelson, *First and Second Kings*, 193; cf. Cogan, *II Kings*, 90; Konkel, *1 & 2 Kings*, 454, n. 18). House offers up a simpler explanation, one that preserves Elisha's integrity: "The truth is that Ben-Hadad *could* recover yet will not because Hazael will kill him and take his place," (*1, 2 Kings*, 283; emphasis his).

9. "Hazael's discomfort probably betrayed his fear that Elisha knew his secret plan to seize the Syrian throne soon," (Hubbard, *First and Second Kings*, 166).

10. An Assyrian poem heralding the victories of Tiglath-pileser I celebrates this atrocity (Mordechai Cogan, "'Ripping open Pregnant Women' in Light of an Assyrian Analogue," *JAOS* 103 [1983]: 755–57).

Amos 1:3, 13). Hazael claimed to be too much of a nobody ever to be guilty of such atrocities. But "Hazael's denial will prove to have a hollow ring, for subsequent Scripture records that he often oppressed God's people (8:28; 9:14–15; 10:32–33; 12:17–18; 13:3, 22)."[11] Only after Hazael's death would Israel find relief from the Aramean onslaught (13:24–25).

When Hazael returned to his ill master's side, he gave him Elisha's "good news" about the king's recovery. But the next day, and perhaps under the guise of dabbing his boss' forehead with a damp towel, Hazael suffocated the king[12] with something similar to the pillow-over-the-face routine. And since there was no CSI unit around to conduct a special investigation, nor a coroner to perform an autopsy, everyone believed Ben-hadad died of natural causes. The king is dead; long live the king.

O ne wonders what application could be derived from such a story. Indeed, the image of Hazael hovering over his master with the damp cloth of death seems more at home in an episode of *The Sopranos* or a film directed by Martin Scorsese than it does Holy Scripture. But as Cogan writes, "This prophetic message asserts that YHWH controls the destiny of all nations, and in particular of Israel and its neighbor Aram."[13]

If the Lord exerted such sovereignty over powers of yesteryear, there is no reason to believe he doesn't do so even today. Whether it's personal trial or political unrest, turmoil often leaves us wondering if God is really in control. Like an-

---

11. Patterson, "1, 2 Kings," 844. "From this point on Hazael emerges as the most serious Syrian threat to date to both Israel and Judah. Hazael's reign inaugurated a period of political chaos in which Syria moved outward and eastward to threaten the borders of both Israel and Judah," (Hobbs, *2 Kings*, 106). "Hazael's destructive attacks on sites such as Rehov in Galilee and Gath and Zeitah in Philistia are seen in excavated destruction layers that are dated securely by radiocarbon dating. After fighting off Shalmaneser III of Assyria, Hazael successfully cut off Israel and Judah on three sides and reopened his own trade links to the Mediterranean Sea. In 805 B.C. his kingdom was destroyed by another Assyrian king, Adad-Nirari III," (Provan, "2 Kings," 84). For more on Hazael and Israel, see Bright, *History*, 254–55.

12. Josephus, *Antiquities* 9.92.

13. Cogan, *II Kings*, 92. "Here the word of God impels a wicked deed for the strange purpose of bringing doom to Israel. Yahweh is not powerless, as some exiles were tempted to conclude, but rather one whose own purposes have made it necessary to declare war on the people of promise," (Nelson, *First and Second Kings*, 195).

cient Israel, we are often tempted to interpret adverse circumstances as proof of God's impotence, which only pushes us deeper into our unfaithfulness. Doubt in God's sovereignty exacerbates our calamity. The less we believe he knows what he's doing, the more likely we are to grab the reins of life and run into the ditch.

The problem, however, is never with God's willingness to care for us, nor his ability to control events. The problem is most always with our desire to obey. The ominous storm clouds on Israel's horizon were of Israel's own making; how might have her history been different if she had trusted in God and yielded to his voice? How might our lives be different if we follow the advice of that old hymn and learn that "there is no other way to be happy in Jesus but to trust and obey"?

2 KINGS 8:16-24

Since the end of 1 Kings, the focus of the narrator has been almost exclusively on the Northern Kingdom. But we are here introduced to the son of Jehoshaphat, thirty-two-year-old J(eh)oram, bearing the same name as his brother-in-law and Northern counterpart,[14] and whose reign (853–841) began with a five-year co-regency with his father.[15] Thiele reasonably suggests that Jehoshaphat, knowing the risks of joining Ahab in military action at Ramoth-gilead (1 Kgs 22:32–37), made Joram a co-regent before the battle.[16]

Though Joram's father and grandfather had been righteous, he shares more than a name with his brother-in-law—he was also wicked like Ahab's family. "The family of Ahab has now deeply infected both kingdoms (see 11:18; 21:3) [...] Looking back, one can understand why the narrator gave so much space to Ahab."[17] According to 2 Chronicles 21:2–4, and possibly at the prompting of his wife, Athaliah, Joram murdered all his rivals to the throne (including his six

---

14. In this book, I have retained *Jehoram* for the Northern king and *Joram* for the Southern king to avoid confusion.

15. The biblical data seems contradictory at first glance; 2 Kings 1:17 says Jehoram of Israel became king in the second year of Joram of Judah, while 8:16 says Joram of Judah became king in Jehoram of Israel's fifth year. The narrator likely means that Jehoram of Israel became king during the second year of Joram's co-regency with Jehoshaphat (852), and Joram of Judah became *sole* king in Jehoram of Israel's fifth year (847–846) (Thiel, "Joram [Person]," *ABD* 3:949–50).

16. Thiele, *Mysterious Numbers*, 100.

17. Fretheim, *First and Second Kings*, 166.

brothers).[18] But again, we are reminded that Judah and her kings benefit from greater grace than does Israel, and all because of God's promise to David "to give a lamp to him and to his sons forever" (v. 19; cf. 1 Kgs 11:34–39; 15:3–5). "Yahweh's 'Davidic plan' is still in force and the wickedness of some two-bit Ahab-clone in Judah isn't going to overthrow it."[19]

The nation of Edom had been subject to Judah since the wars of David (2 Sam 8:2). But during Joram's reign—arguably right after his father's death—Edom rebelled[20] (recall that Moab had rebelled against Israel a few years prior following the death of Ahab). In response, Joram led Judah's forces to meet the Edomites at Zair.[21] But things didn't go well, and when Judah's king found himself surrounded, he had no choice but to break through enemy lines and scamper home to Jerusalem with his tail between his legs. Though God had sworn to give a lamp to David's sons, he had also promised to discipline them with the "rod of men" (2 Sam 7:14; cf. Ps 89:32).

The Edomites' victory at Zair inspired the town of Libnah, a Levitical city in Judah (Josh 21:13) located on the Philistine border, to rebel also.[22] The narrator uses their successful revolt to underscore just how bad things are going for Joram. He's not unlike the football coach who, already on the hot seat, loses to the heavy-underdog, cupcake team scheduled for Homecoming. He just can't win because God is disciplining him as a son of David—"the empire is slowly being trimmed back."[23] And with that, the narrator scornfully dispenses with Joram via his conventional style.

---

18. "The purge would have silenced any opposition to the pro-Israelite policies of the king and his wife. It also presages the activities of this queen in [2 Kings] 11," (Hobbs, 2 Kings, 103).

19. Davis, 2 Kings, 139.

20. Josephus claims the Edomites assassinated the Judean-appointed ruler (cf. 3:9) and installed their own (Antiquities 9.97). "Judah had always tried to dominate Edom in order to control the route to the port of Ezion-geber," (Robinson, Second Book, 75).

21. The location of Zair is unknown, though Provan identifies it with Zoar, which was southeast of the Dead Sea ("2 Kings," 145); others (less plausibly) interpret it as Seir, a location northeast of Hebron (Liwak, "Zair [Place]," ABD 6:1038).

22. "This is the only notice of a city breaking with the central rule in Jerusalem. [. . .] Apparently the military weakness of Judah gives an important border fort opportunity to advance its own interests," (Konkel, 1 & 2 Kings, 474). Note that it had returned to the fold by the time of Hezekiah's reign (19:8).

23. Fretheim, First and Second Kings, 166. "Like Israel's loss of its Moabite vassal (2 Kgs

The Chronicler includes additional information (2 Chr 21). Joram received a letter from a not-yet-raptured[24] Elijah rebuking the Southern king for his alliance with the house of Ahab. The Philistines and Arabians—the same people who had once paid tribute to Joram's father, Jehoshaphat (2 Chr 17:11)—attacked Joram (cf. Joel 3:4–8, 19; Amos 1:6–8). The battle cost him the lives of his sons, save his youngest, Ahaziah (2 Chr 22:1).[25] Joram lost his own life as well because of an incurable intestinal disease,[26] and he was not buried in the royal tombs. Disdainfully, the Chronicler adds, "he departed with no one's regret" (2 Chr 21:20).

2 KINGS 8:25-29

The death of Joram of Judah brought his youngest son, Ahaziah,[27] to the throne in the critical year of 841. The twenty-two-year-old lasted only a matter of months, for he was wicked like the other Omrides. He was particularly influenced by his mother, Athaliah. In addition to her role as queen mother, she and her relatives also served as Ahaziah's top advisors (2 Chr 22:3–4).

Ominous storm clouds appear on the horizon when we note that Ahaziah came to the throne in Jehoram of Israel's twelfth year (v. 25; cf. 3:1). In the pre-

---

3:1–27), this humiliation at the hands of the Edomites demonstrates how weak Judah has become since the glory days of David and Solomon," (House, 1, 2 Kings, 285).

24. Gleason L. Archer, Encyclopedia of Bible Difficulties (Grand Rapids: Zondervan, 1982), 226–27; Martin J. Selman, 2 Chronicles (Downers Grove, IL: InterVarsity Press, 1994), 435–36.

25. Josephus, Antiquities 9.102.

26. "While the cause may have been a malignant tumor of the descending colon or the rectum, the breakdown of intestinal function suggested by the text could well indicate the presence of bacillary dysentery. Caused by one species or other of the bacillus Shigella, it is marked by the usual symptoms of dysentery but can also exhibit a necrotic inflammation of the mucous membrane of the colon. A separation of dead intestinal tissue and sloughing off of the rectum probably marked the last agonizing moments of this unfortunate king," (Harrison, "Disease," ISBE 1:957–58).

27. Ahaziah of Judah bore the same name as his mother's brother and Ahab's son (1 Kings 22:51–2 Kings 1:17). He was also known as Jehoahaz (2 Chr 21:17). "The fact that at this period we have kings with the same names—Jehoram and Ahaziah in Judah and Ahaziah and Jehoram (Joram) in Israel—speaks of the friendly relations between the two nations. Both royal houses were extending the courtesy of naming heirs to the throne after each other," (Thiele, Mysterious Numbers, 101).

vious year, 842, Hazael took charge of Aram. In 841, Shalmaneser III of Assyria defeated the Arameans, and Jehu led his coup against the Omrides of Israel.[28]

Needless to say, there was a lot of upheaval and uncertainty in the ancient Near East in the year of Ahaziah's ascension. We are left to wonder: "Is the house of David, mixed up with Ahab's house through marriage, to be caught up in the coming judgment after all? Or will the promise to David hold?"[29]

To set the stage, the narrator recounts a time when Ahaziah of Judah and Jehoram of Israel attacked the Arameans at Ramoth-gilead.[30] Though once pre-occupied with Moab (2 Kgs 3), Jehoram now realized Aram posed a greater con-tinuous threat. "Once the Arameans were beaten and the Gileadite border safely established on the Yarmuk River, the field became clear for an attack upon Moab, the reduction of which was a sound assumption in those circumstances. Besides, the previously mentioned economic importance of the Ramoth region certainly was an additional motive for making it a primary objective."[31]

There was also arguably the issue of wanting to avenge his father's defeat (1 Kgs 22). Like his father, Jehoram was wounded in battle; unlike his father, however, his injuries were not fatal. While recuperating at Jezreel[32] (recall that Ahab's winter palace was there), his nephew, Ahaziah, came to visit him. Neither would return home alive.

---

28. When Shalmaneser victoriously camped at Mount Carmel in 841, he names Jehu, not Jehoram, as the offerer of tribute on behalf of Israel (Alberto R. Green, "Sua and Jehu: The Boundaries of Shalmaneser's Conquest," *PEQ* 111 [1979]: 35–39).

29. Provan, *1 & 2 Kings*, 207.

30. It's unclear if Ramoth-gilead was in Israel's or Aram's control when Jehoram and Aha-ziah went to battle (cf. 9:14–15). Archaeologists have confirmed that Ramoth-gilead constantly changed hands between Israel and Aram during the dynasties of Omri and Jehu (Provan, "2 Kings," 146–47).

31. Herzog, *Battles*, 173.

32. It's possible Jezreel served as Israel's primary military base (Provan, "2 Kings," 147; Olley, *Message of Kings*, 254, n. 10). "En route from Ramoth Gilead to Israel, it is the first major city which would provide refuge from Joram. It also serves a dramatic purpose. It puts the king at the very place where Ahab expropriated Naboth's vineyard, and it sets in motion the series of events which culminate in the destruction of that apostate dynasty," (Hobbs, *2 Kings*, 105).

2 KINGS 9

Some years earlier (but what seems as if several lifetimes ago for the reader of Kings), God had visited Elijah in the depths of the prophet's despondency and given him a peek at the divine agenda for Israel. Elisha would succeed Elijah, Hazael would replace Ben-hadad, and an unknown son of Nimshi, one named Jehu, would assume the throne of Israel. The Omrides would not afflict Israel forever; the days of the house of Ahab were numbered.[33] Elijah had personally tapped Elisha as his protégé, but for whatever reason, he had anointed neither Hazael nor Jehu as ordered. Upon his rapture to heaven, he had left some important things undone.

To anoint[34] Jehu as the next king of Israel, Elisha sent an unnamed prophet to Ramoth-gilead. He was to waste no time in discharging his orders—"tie up your garments" equates to "drive straight through and don't stop for any reason." Once the anointing had been performed, the prophet was to flee home, for he would then be technically guilty of an act of treason (cf. 1 Sam 16:1–13).

Somehow, the prophet recognized Jehu (whether by prophetic power or past experience) and asked for a private word. In his anointing, he expanded on what Elisha had told him to say. Jehu was to be Yahweh's instrument of vengeance[35] against the Omrides, and particularly Jezebel, for the bloodshed they had committed. The first (Jeroboam) and second (Baasha) dynasties of the Northern Kingdom had ended in bloody coups; a third (Omri/Ahab) would be added to it. All males—the Hebrew of v. 8 literally reads "everyone who urinates against the wall" (cf. 1 Kgs 14:10; 21:21 KJV)—were to be executed, and Jezebel

---

33. García-Treto draws attention to the fact that *house* is a key word in 2 Kings 9–10, occurring eighteen times, both in reference to the "house of Ahab" (six times) and the "house of Baal" (five times), (Francisco O. García-Treto, "The Fall of the House: A Carnivalesque Reading of 2 Kings 9 and 10," *JSOT* 46 [1990]: 47–65). Thus the narrator is emphatically presenting Jehu as the one bringing an end to these two houses that have been a scourge to Israel for so long.

34. "Jehu is the only king of the Northern Kingdom (Israel) to have been anointed, perhaps to indicate that he should follow in the Davidic tradition, as Saul had been anointed by Samuel (1 Sam. 9:16; 10:1); David by Samuel, to mark the Spirit of God endowing him for the task (1 Sam. 16:12–13); and Solomon by the high priest Zadok and Nathan the prophet (1 Kgs 1:45). Such anointing was symbolic and probably confined to Hebrew practice," (Wiseman, *1 and 2 Kings*, 232).

35. "Only here in Kings is emphasis placed on Yahweh as an avenging God, using as he does a human agent as the avenger of blood (cf. Gen. 4:24; Rev. 6:10). This concept was strong in the Davidic tradition (2 Sam. 4:8; 22:48; cf. Pss 9:12; 79:10)," (Ibid., 233).

was to be scorned most of all (v. 10; cf. Deut 28:25–26; 1 Kgs 21:23; Jer 8:2; 16:4, 6; 22:19; 25:33).

"Such an odd visitation could easily have disrupted the camp and troubled the soldiers"[36] (cf. 1 Sam 16:4), so Jehu must have received some quizzical looks from his comrades when he exited the room. "What was all that about?" they asked, to which Jehu tried to diffuse the awkwardness with something akin to "You know how crazy[37] some of the prophets can be." But his fellow officers didn't buy it (perhaps the oily head sparked their suspicions) and pressed him further. When Jehu told them that he had been anointed king, the men laid their garments out in honor[38] on an impromptu throne of bare steps (what we would call "the red carpet treatment") and celebrated with blasts from a shophar. They were now complicit in this plot against the throne of Israel.[39]

From here, Jehu will go on to exterminate the house of Ahab and secure his rule over Israel. Seven violent acts are narrated in 2 Kings 9–10:

1.   the assassination of Jehoram

2.   the assassination of Ahaziah

---

36. House, *1, 2 Kings*, 287. "In the ancient Near East priests often play significant political roles, but no prophets from the ancient Near East are known to have played the same role as these Israelite kingmakers. Nonetheless, throughout the ancient world it was believed that prophets not only proclaimed the message of deity but in the process unleashed the divine action. In Assyrian king Esarhaddon's instructions to his vassals, he requires that they report any improper or negative statements that may be made by anyone, and he specifically names prophets, ecstatics and dream interpreters. It is no wonder, then, that a prophet negatively disposed toward a king must somehow be controlled lest he bring about all sorts of havoc. One can perhaps understand why a king would be inclined to imprison such a prophet, whose very words might incite insurrection or impose doom," (Walton, *Bible Background*, 396).

37. The word translated "mad fellow" (ESV) or "crazy person" (HCSB) in v. 11 has varied meanings in the Old Testament, ranging from insanity resulting from trauma (Deut 28:34) to what we would consider to be mental retardation (1 Sam 21:13). It seems the prophets were especially prone to being called crazy (Jer 29:26; Hos 9:7). So the word is simply used in 2 Kings 9:11 "as a demeaning and derogatory reference to one who was already known to be somewhat crazy. Jehu's comment reveals that the man was well known by the group of officers," (Hobbs, *2 Kings*, 115).

38. "The act of spreading out the garment was one of recognition, loyalty and promise of support (cf. the people to Christ in Matt. 21:8; Luke 19:36)," (Wiseman, *1 and 2 Kings*, 234).

39. "As the Israelite army brought Omri to power (cf. 1 Kgs 16:15–16), the army will also bring about the downfall of his dynasty," (Barnes, *1–2 Kings*, 254).

3.   the assassination of Jezebel

4.   the execution of Ahab's seventy sons

5.   the execution of Ahaziah's forty-two relatives

6.   the purge of all remaining loyalists to Ahab

7.   the execution of the devotees of Baal[40]

Ahab and Jezebel hadn't exactly been dearly-beloved monarchs in Israel; instead, "resentment over the rule of Ahab and his son J[eh]oram was likely widespread. [...] The intermittent wars with Damascus, together with the sometime alliance with Damascus against Assyria, costly public projects, and an extravagant royal lifestyle (1 Kgs 22:39), were all contributing factors to the political and social malaise, of which the lingering presence of Queen Jezebel and her entourage was a constant reminder."[41] Or, to put it more succinctly, "The anointing lit the fuse of the explosives already prepared."[42]

As previously mentioned (8:29), Jehoram had been wounded in battle at Ramoth-gilead and retreated to the royal winter residence at Jezreel to recuperate. Once Jehu had been anointed as the next king, he wasted no time in putting the town of Ramoth-gilead on lockdown (v. 15) and making a mad dash for Jezreel, about forty-four miles away.

The lookout in Jezreel saw Jehu coming and relayed the news to the king, who in turn commissioned a messenger to ride out and learn what news Jehu brought. The specific question, "Is it peace?" is an interesting one. On the sur-

---

40. "The focus moves from acts against individuals to whole groups, and the reader is given the impression of that snowballing violence that is so characteristic of revolution," (Nelson, *First and Second Kings*, 200).

41. Cogan, *II Kings*, 120. "Violent dynastic changes in Israel can frequently be traced to dissatisfaction with foreign military policies, which led army officers to take matters into their own hands (cf. e.g. 1 Kgs 16:8–10, 15–18; 2 Kgs 15:25). Though not explicitly stated, the immediate cause of Jehu's insurrection was the inconclusive outcome of the renewed war with Aram-Damascus by Joram, during which the king himself was wounded (2 Kgs 9:14–15a). On top of this, the combined Israelite-Judaean armies had been forced to retreat from Moab just a few years earlier (2 Kgs 3:27), allowing Mesha to strengthen his position in Trans-Jordan," (Ibid., 119–20). Of course, all of this is secondary; Jehu's coup was primarily the work of Yahweh's will.

42. Olley, *Message of Kings*, 258.

face, the messenger was only asking, "Did we win or lose?" But this will become a refrain throughout this chapter; the Hebrew *shalom* occurs nine times in 2 Kings 9 (cf. vv. 11, 17–19, 22, 31). For now, Jehu shot back, "What do you anti-shalom people have to do with shalom?"[43]

Jehu gave the messenger the opportunity to fall in line with Jehu's men; perhaps the messenger could read the writing on the wall, for he did so quickly, as did a second messenger Jehoram sent out. Eventually, the watchman in Jezreel recognized that it must be Jehu at the head of the battalion since he was driving so erratically.[44]

Finally, Jehoram and Ahaziah decided to go and see for themselves what Jehu had to say. Each in his own chariot—possibly indicating they did not expect any danger—they rendezvoused with Jehu on Naboth's old property (v. 21), at which point ominous music should be playing in your head if it isn't already[45] (cf. 1 Kgs 21:20–24). "Is it peace, Jehu?" Jehoram asked, or, "Is everything all right?" Jehu responded by calling Jehoram's mom a slut and then shot him in the back.[46] OK, that's not exactly what happened, but it's close. Jehu invoked "the whorings and the sorceries" of Jezebel, adultery being a common biblical metaphor for idolatry (cf. Exod 34:16; Lev 17:7; 20:5; Num 15:39; Deut 31:16). Sorcery (cf. Deut 17:2–7; 18:10–12; Jer 27:9), on the other hand, is something not yet explicitly mentioned concerning Jezebel, though it is certainly believable.

The larger issue, however, was expressed in Jehu's curt reply, "How can there be peace…?" (v. 22 NIV). Shalom in Israel had not existed as long as Ahab's family had occupied the throne, so Jehu's retort could as well have been worded, "Peace? You wouldn't know what peace was if it slapped you in the face" (cf. 2 Sam 16:10; 19:22). Only when the sinful, idolatrous, repugnant legacy of Ahab had been purged from the Northern Kingdom could God's people experience well-being and harmony again. And it began with Jehoram being shot through the heart with Jehu's arrow. Jehu ordered the king's body be dumped on Naboth's

43. Nelson, *First and Second Kings*, 201.

44. "His reputation as a reckless driver must have stayed with him all his years in the army, and was by now widespread," (Hobbs, *2 Kings*, 116).

45. "When we learn that Naboth's piece of land is the meeting place of Jehu and the kings, we know in our bones what the outcome will be," (Auld, *I & II Kings*, 185).

46. "In v. 23, J[eh]oram's recognition of 'treason' borders on the ironic, for the term used by the king bespeaks treachery, when the Omri dynasty itself has been endlessly treacherous and duplicitous toward Yahweh," (Brueggemann, *1 & 2 Kings*, 386).

property and invoked the word of the Lord, that God had sworn to "repay [Ahab] on this plot of ground" (v. 26). The Hebrew verb *shalem*, translated "repay," literally means "to make peace" since it is from the same root as *shalom*.[47] "Hence the words underscored the nature of Jehu's mission, namely, through violence to restore the 'peace' between Yahweh and Israel."[48]

When Ahaziah[49] saw that his uncle had been assassinated, he too tried to flee in the direction of Beth-haggan (a town several miles south of Jezreel en route to Samaria), but he was shot at Ibleam (ten miles south of Jezreel), so he turned northwest and died at Megiddo (the Chronicler adds that Ahaziah made it all the way to Samaria, but was found and brought to Jehu at Megiddo where he was executed[50]).

W   ith Jehoram and Ahaziah sleeping with the fishes, Jehu made his way into Jezreel and was greeted by Jezebel, who had dressed to the nines for the occasion. One wonders if she was attempting to seduce[51] Jehu or if she was choosing to face her demise with every bit of defiance she could muster.[52] Regardless, she looked the part of the whore that she was (cf.

---

47. Nel, "שָׁלַם," *NIDOTTE* 4:130–35.

48. Hubbard, *First and Second Kings*, 173.

49. "Nowhere is Ahaziah or the Southern dynasty mentioned, neither in the governing oracle of Elijah (1 Kgs 19:15-16) nor in the specific mandate to Jehu (2 Kgs 9:6-10). Ahaziah is apparently implicated in the 'sins of the North' and therefore is killed alongside J[eh]oram for his collusion and the broader collusion of the Southern dynasty in the vagaries of the Omri dynasty in the North. No extravagant prophetic rhetoric is used of him in order to justify his death, simply, 'Shoot him also,'" (Brueggemann, *1 & 2 Kings*, 387).

50. In the Tel Dan inscription, it is Hazael of Aram who claims to have killed Ahaziah. For the discrepancy concerning Ahaziah's death, see Iain Provan, V. Philips Long, and Tremper Longman III, *A Biblical History of Israel* (Louisville: Westminster John Knox, 2003), 372–73, n. 46.

51. Barré believes Jezebel was attempting to seduce Jehu, but by commanding that she be thrown from the window, "Jehu is portrayed as completely impervious to Jezebel's charms. Indeed, Jezebel's seductive designs backfired. Instead of swaying him to join forces, she ignited the seething hatred that he had earlier expressed in his encounter with her son," (Lloyd M. Barré, *The Rhetoric of Political Persuasion: The Narrative Artistry and Political Intentions of 2 Kings 9–11* [Washington: Catholic Biblical Assoc. of America, 1988], 79; cf. Simon B. Parker, "Jezebel's Reception of Jehu," *Maarav* 1 [1978]: 67–78).

52. "This is no attempt to seduce the rebel. Rather, she does these things to look like,

Ezek 23:36–49). "So framed, she was the portrait of a haughty, stylish queen, defiant and unrepentant to the end."[53]

Her greeting was consistent with the theme of the story—"Is it peace?"—but by invoking the name of Zimri (1 Kgs 16:8–20), she spitefully insinuated that Jehu was just another Israelite upstart that wouldn't last long, a "seven-day wonder."[54] Even to the bitter end, the establishment is committed to scorning the maverick upstarts.

Jehu responded to Jezebel's scorn by calling on her eunuchs[55] to toss her out of the window, which they did. And in a scene that would make Quentin Tarantino quite proud, "Her blood spattered the wall and the horses, and Jehu trampled her under his horse's hooves" (v. 33 Msg). Jehu coolly responded with "What's for dinner," and in an ice-cold scene, sat down to dine in the palace as if the day had been business as usual. It's possible that the meal was a political fundraiser of sort—an attempt to win the support of the nobles of Jezreel[56]—but "he was apparently carrying on as if nothing amiss had taken place."[57]

Inexplicably, Jehu had a change of heart about Jezebel's demise and ordered her to be buried since she was royalty. But when the undertakers went to retrieve the body, they found only her skull, hands, and feet. Through Elijah, God had scornfully predicted that Jezebel's remains would be left to the dogs (1 Kgs 21:23) "so that her spirit would wonder restlessly forever. Thus she has received

---

and die like, a queen," (House, *1, 2 Kings*, 290). "Cosmetic treatments also could demonstrate a certain level of authority when they were combined with fine clothing or robes of office. Thus the beleaguered queen Jezebel put on a brave front in the face of the advancing army of the rebel general Jehu by painting her eyes and adorning her head (2 Kgs 9:30)," (Matthews, "Cosmetics," *NIBD* 1:754–55).

53. Hubbard, *First and Second Kings*, 173.

54. Provan, *1 & 2 Kings*, 211.

55. "It was common practice in the ancient world for the king to have a harem (cf. 1 Kings 11:3) and for the harem to be provided with guards. These guards were typically eunuchs (castrated human males), so that the king could be sure that the males who were in close proximity to his women were not capable of sexual relationships with them," (Provan, "2 Kings," 151).

56. Kathryn L. Roberts, "God, Prophet, and King: Eating and Drinking on the Mountain in First Kings 18:41," *CBQ* 62 (2000): 632–44.

57. Barnes, *1–2 Kings*, 261.

the most severe punishment that was imaginable in ancient Israel,"[58] and that's exactly what happened. The word of the Lord stands forever.

2 KINGS 10:1-28

In the narrative of Ahab, we had been introduced to only one wife, Jezebel. So it is with no little surprise that this chapter begins with mention of seventy sons that belonged to the former king (v. 1; cf. Judg 9:5). Were these all sons of Ahab? Unlikely. It's possible Ahab had fathered all these through his harem. But it is more probable that these included his grandsons and other male relatives with a claim to the throne. Regardless, the point here is that "these are the people from whom a successor to Jehoram would normally be chosen, and Jehu confronts this threat head on."[59]

To the rulers and aides who had guardianship over these princes, Jehu sent a letter—an echo of Jezebel's letters concerning Naboth—challenging them to select one and place him on the throne as Jehoram's successor (not unlike Goliath's challenge to Saul). The ruling class of Samaria knew they would be no match for Jehu[60]—note the intensity of the phrase "exceedingly afraid" (v. 4) or "absolutely terrified" (Msg)—so they replied, "We're your biggest supporters. Your word is our command" (v. 5).

That's when Jehu gave the command that they execute (or did he?[61]) the seventy sons of Ahab and bring them to Jezreel. The scene is reminiscent of

---

58. Fritz, *1 & 2 Kings*, 287. "Jezebel's end is as pathetic as any zealous prophet of Yahweh could wish: the pampered child of a Tyrian king becoming nothing more than food for scavenging Israelite dogs," (Barnes, *1-2 Kings*, 261). "There may be a political angle to this fulfillment of the curse: nothing recognizable of Jezebel's body is left, nothing for any potential loyalists to venerate (as the Bolsheviks reduced the murdered family of the Czar to ashes for just this reason)," (Alter, *Ancient Israel*, 777).

59. Provan, *1 & 2 Kings*, 214. Konkel believes *seventy* here is not arithmetic, but rather a metaphor to express totality (*1 & 2 Kings*, 479; cf. F. C. Fensham, "The Numeral Seventy in the Old Testament and the Family of Jerubbaal, Ahab, Panammuwa and Athirat," *PEQ* 109 [1977]: 113-15). "The large numbers would certainly cover all those likely to seek reprisals or have any legitimate claim to the throne," (Wiseman, *1 and 2 Kings*, 238).

60. "A contest is being proposed, in which the outcome will determine who is truly in the right with God. The leading officials deduce from what has happened so far (two kings have not resisted him, v. 4) what the authors will later tell the reader—that Jehu is in the right, and God is with him. They do not, therefore, allow the contest to proceed," (Provan, *1 & 2 Kings*, 217-18).

61. Jehu's order to "take the heads of your master's sons and come to me" may have been

when two of David's men brought him the head of David's rival/Saul's son, Ish-bosheth (2 Sam 4:8), not to mention the severed-head-in-a-basket sequence in *Braveheart*. Baskets of severed heads arrived in Jezreel the next day in accordance with Jehu's request, and they were arranged into two grisly piles at the city gates, imitating an Assyrian practice of silencing detractors.[62] Jehu then gave a speech, in effect saying, "You didn't do this; I did. But this is to fulfill Yahweh's word against Ahab." Translation: "I have a lot of people on my side, including God."

En route to Samaria from Jezreel, Jehu intercepted a delegation of Ahazi-ah's relatives from the South. One wonders if the delegation's story—relatives in town for a family get-together (v. 13)—was true; Provan calls it "unconvincing." I think the fact that this took place at Beth-eked[63] (v. 12) is meant to spark ques-tions: "Why are they north of Samaria, on the Jezreel road, if (as we suppose) they have come from Judah?" Provan asks.[64] For whatever reason, Jehu gave the order that all forty-two be executed.

One might cry "Foul!" at the thought of these "innocents" from Judah be-ing unceremoniously exterminated, but this was a time for judgment on Ahab's house and all his allies.[65] On the other hand, Jehu crossed paths with Jehonadab

---

intentionally ambiguous, since the Hebrew term translated "heads" (as in English) can refer both to a leader and to one's skull (Leithart, *1 & 2 Kings*, 222). Wray Beal argues, "The request's am-biguity is intentional: Jehu does wish the sons dead, but he also desires deniability (which he asserts in the next scene)," (*1 & 2 Kings*, 378).

62. Cogan, *II Kings*, 113; Patterson, "1, 2 Kings," 857–58. "Besides scaring the people, this display also informs the Jezreelites that Samaria is now under the usurper's power. The *coup* has indeed succeeded, and any counterattack is useless," (House, *1, 2 Kings*, 292; emphasis his).

63. The exact location of Beth-eked is disputed; Walton's suggestion that it is located around the plain of Dothan makes sense (*Bible Background*, 398).

64. Provan, *1 & 2 Kings*, 215; cf. Hobbs, *2 Kings*, 128. Konkel adds, "It is hardly possible that the associates of Ahaziah are unaware of the events in Jezreel, and this is not the road they would use if they are simply going there to greet him. It may be that this is a resistance movement intercepted by Jehu," (*1 & 2 Kings*, 480).

65. "The group intercepted by Jehu consisted of Judean soldiers on their way north, by an inconspicuous route, to avenge the death of their king and his cousins," (Hobbs, *2 Kings*, 128). Contra House, "Jehu mercilessly slaughters these men without any real justification for doing so, unless he reasons that since Israel's and Judah's royal houses are related these individuals might have some claim to the throne. Even this possibility stretches the limits of credibility, and it is probably these murders that cause Hosea to condemn what occurs in Jezreel (Hos 1:4–5). The prophecies of Elijah and Elisha say nothing about killing *David's* descendants," (*1, 2 Kings*, 293; emphasis his).

the Rechabite[66] and spared him, inviting him to join his coup —"he gave him his hand" (v. 15) was a means of pledging allegiance to someone (cf. 1 Chr 29:24; Ezra 10:1–5, 19; Lam 5:6). Together, they exterminated the remaining loyalists to Ahab's dynasty in Samaria.[67] Jehonadab is spared Jehu's wrath because he is on the Lord's side; the family and friends of Ahab are not, and so they are extinguished (vv. 11, 17).

H aving purged the successors and supporters of the previous regime, Jehu turned his murderous attention to Ahab's prophets and priests. He fooled them into thinking that he would be a bigger Baal fan than Ahab had ever been and mandated that everyone assemble for a grand worship service[68] (vv. 18–19), one that reminds us of Elijah's own assembly of Baalites (1 Kgs 18:20–40). Into the temple of Baal, the faithful crammed themselves like sardines (v. 21). The priests entered dressed in their trappings, and Jehu gave orders to search through the assembly to ensure no Yahwistic interlopers were present (v. 23).

But while the sacrifice was being offered, Jehu had the temple surrounded by eighty of his royal escort.[69] At his signal, they rushed in and murdered everyone.

---

66. The Rechabites in Jeremiah are known for their asceticism and covenant faithfulness (Jer 35:1–19), which spared them from the Babylonian onslaught. Rechab was a Kenite (1 Chr 2:55) and possibly a descendant of Moses' father-in-law (Keil, *Commentary*, 349). See also Frank S. Frick, "The Rechabites Reconsidered," *JBL* 90 (1971): 279–87.

67. Josephus claims that Jehu and Jehonadab were old friends (*Antiquities* 9.132).

68. "Part of the rhetoric that accompanied the promises of new kings in the ancient world was that they would be more devoted to the national or local gods than their predecessors. This often included commitments to repair, restore, enlarge or embellish the sanctuary. This strategy would gain the support of the priesthood and the pious populace, and, hopefully, bring divine approval of the new reign as well. It was politically correct for the king to take his place as royal patron and foremost of the supporters of the local deity. It is possible that Jehu is calling for an enthronement celebration in which he will take the throne as the vassal of Baal, whose enthronement as king of the gods would likewise be recognized. To be absent from such an event could easily be considered treason," (Walton, *Bible Background*, 398).

69. These eighty men "appear as the royal escort of a king (1 Sam 22:17), who in addition to their normal guard duties (2 Kgs 11:4, 6), also paraded in state ceremonies (1 Kgs 14:27–28). Pretenders to the throne considered it essential to appear in public accompanied by a squadron of outrunners, cf. 2 Sam 15:1; 1 Kgs 1:5," (Cogan, *II Kings*, 115–16).

They left the bodies unburied,[70] desecrated the image of Baal, demolished the temple Ahab had built (1 Kgs 16:32), and turned it into a public porta-potty.[71] "One could hardly imagine a more thorough expurgation of Baalism. For now, Baalism has no place in Israelite culture. What Elijah began Jehu has finished."[72]

Highlighted by the narrator is the gullibility of the Baalites, the slyness of Jehu, and the impotence of Baal. Though Jehu had had Jezebel assassinated, the Baalites thought he was their ally! And though Jehu had promised that he had a "sacrifice to offer to Baal" (v. 19), the word translated "sacrifice" can mean "slaughter" (23:20; 1 Kgs 13:2), and thus Jehu may have been engaging in double entendres. But the bigger point is Baal's impotence. The name *Baal* is mentioned sixteen times in vv. 18–28, but he couldn't so much as lift a finger to protect his most devout followers. "Thus Jehu wiped out Baal from Israel" (v. 28).

One more thing—for all the archaeological excavations done in Samaria, the temple of Baal has never been found. True, it could be that it simply hasn't been found *yet*. But it's also possible that this stands as testimony to the thoroughness of Jehu's purge.

T hough the divine narrator seems to approve of the cleansing Jehu brought to Israel, one wonders what we are really intended to think about Jehu. For one thing, his coup is a bloody one. "Seldom has history witnessed a more thorough blood purging of a previous royal family and favored religious order than this."[73] As mentioned before, seven violent acts are

---

70. This is what is meant in v. 26 by "the guard and the officers cast them out" (Cogan, *II Kings*, 116; cf. Morton Cogan, "A Technical Term for Exposure," *JNES* 27 [1968]: 133–35).

71. "The narrator uses three strong verbs to characterize the destructive action undertaken: they *burned...*they *demolished...*they *destroyed*. The action reflects the use of pent-up hatred against the symbols of the despised regime that had been oppressive and exploitative," (Brueggemann, *1 & 2 Kings*, 399; emphasis his). There is a point of connection between the reference to the house of Ahab as those who "pisseth against the wall" (9:8 KJV; 1 Kgs 21:21) and the comment here that Jehu turned the house of Baal into a public toilet (Sweeney, *I & II Kings*, 339).

72. House, *1, 2 Kings*, 294–95. "It was the practice to rebuild temples on the sites where they had traditionally been because it was believed that the god had revealed the location and it was holy ground. By making it into a latrine area (or perhaps a garbage dump), Jehu was insuring that it would never be the site of a temple again. This greatly reduced any possible resurgence of the official Baal cult in Samaria," (Walton, *Bible Background*, 399).

73. Leon Wood, *A Survey of Israel's History* (Grand Rapids: Zondervan, 1970), 321.

narrated in 2 Kings 9–10; "the path to Jehu's reign is soaked in the blood of his victims."[74] Elsewhere, Jehu is condemned "for the blood of Jezreel" (Hos 1:4). In contrast, David (the gold standard in Kings) opted to bide his time when he was anointed instead of eliminating Saul the quick and easy way—which he had the opportunity to do on at least two occasions (1 Sam 24; 26; cf. 2 Sam 1).

There is also the issue of Jehu's seeming duplicity. When he addressed the citizens of Jezreel with two piles of severed heads flanking the city gates, he made it appear as if the beheadings had been the unequivocal will of God (10:9–10), though no such divine decree can be found.[75] Add to that Jehu's seeming distrust of everyone and repeated demands for others to prove their loyalty (9:15, 32; 10:6), and Jehu has all the makings of an insecure tyrant.

So while Jehu may have been the Lord's broom to sweep away the house of Ahab from the earth, it seems he zealously overreached. Perhaps, like the narrator, we ought to celebrate the Lord's word coming to pass while also protesting the hijacking of the sacred in order to sanction the violent. Nothing is more deplorable than a despot shedding innocent blood in God's name.

> Clearly the object which he had in view was not merely fulfilment of prophecy, but securing the throne; and there was more passion, as well as selfish policy, in his massacres, than befitted a minister of the divine justice, who should let no anger disturb the solemnity of his terrible task. Such dangers ever attend the path of the great men who feel themselves to be sent by God. In our humbler lives they dog our steps, and religious fervour needs ever to keep careful watch on itself, lest it should degenerate unconsciously into self-will, and should allow the muddy stream of earth-born passion to darken its crystal waters.[76]

---

74. Fritz, *1 & 2 Kings*, 285.

75. "Jehu is not totally honest at this point, for he leaves the impression that the men were killed not by his command but by divine decree. His goal is to make the people believe that opposing Jehu is the same as opposing God," (House, *1, 2 Kings*, 293).

76. Maclaren, *Expositions*, 5:10.

2 KINGS 10:29-36

Despite being Yahweh's anointed and having cleared the land of Baal-worship (v. 28), Jehu did nothing about the golden calves at Dan and Bethel,[77] meaning he was no better spiritually than his predecessors. Rather, he continued in the apostasy and idolatry instituted by Jeroboam. Such "shows the impurity of his 'zeal,' which flamed only against what it was for his advantage to destroy, and left the more popular and older idolatry undisturbed. Obedience has to be 'all in all, or not at all.' [...] We often think it enough to remove the grosser evils, and leave the less, but white ants will eat up a carcass faster than a lion."[78]

Yahweh rewarded Jehu by promising that his great-great-grandson would sit on Israel's throne (his dynasty, lasting about a century, would be the longest of the Northern Kingdom), but such a promise was not enough to secure Jehu's loyalty to the Lord. As a result, God chastised Israel through the sword of Hazael of Aram[79] (c. 842–802). The entire Transjordan region was no match for Hazael's savagery, and "the loss cost Israel her protective buffer zone with [Aram] and control of the lucrative trade routes in Transjordan."[80]

Historically, we know that the Assyrian ruler Shalmaneser had bested Hazael in two attacks on Aram, the first about 841 and the second about 838. But later, the Assyrian king was preoccupied with enemies foreign (to his east, 839–828) and domestic (a revolt at home, 827–822) and thus was not available to harass Aram—no Assyrian did until Adadnirari III in 806. At the end of 2 Kings 12, we find Hazael rampaging through the Promised Land with no one to stop him (12:17–18; cf. 2 Chr 24:23–24). No wonder Elisha had sobbed at the thought of what Hazael would do (8:11–12). Add to that the fact that Jehu

---

77. "Literarily, the mention of Jeroboam's calves reintroduces Jeroboam's 'sins' after preoccupation with Baal-worship since 1 Kings 22:52. It implies that another apostasy still plagued Israel—and with Jehu's help," (Hubbard, *First and Second Kings*, 179).

78. Maclaren, *Expositions*, 5:13.

79. "Humiliation of Israel at the hands of foreign powers was especially pronounced during Jehu's reign," (Wood, *Survey*, 322). "Hazael's military successes are equated unequivocally with God's act of cutting off from Israel the entire Transjordan, described in classic Deuteronomistic terms (Deut. 3:12–13). Historians point out that Syria's victories depended on a relaxation of Assyrian pressure, but for this narrator, God's intent to punish was the causative factor," (Nelson, *First and Second Kings*, 205).

80. Hubbard, *First and Second Kings*, 179.

was allied with Assyria—a famed Black Obelisk depicts Jehu offering tribute to Shalmaneser in 841[81]—and we can understand Hazael's fury.[82]

In this way, Jehu's reign proves very disappointing. That most of the narrator's attention focuses on his usurpation of the house of Ahab and the purge of Baal (while mentioning virtually nothing about his actual tenure on the throne) demonstrates that Jehu made no other meaningful reforms in Israel, that his reign was as much a wasted opportunity as Jeroboam's had been. One can almost hear a labored sigh from the narrator as he refers us to the royal archives if we want to know anything else about Jehu's twenty-eight years (841–814) on the throne (vv. 34–36).

But we cannot move on in the story of Kings without realizing *why* Jehu was such a disappointing sovereign. "His reform was soon seen to be political and selfish rather than born of any deep concern for God (v. 31)."[83] In this way, Jehu is no different from other immoral rods of Yahweh's anger.[84] The annals of history are full of those who co-opted the Lord for their own purposes, and though God used them to his glory, he also disposed of them in their shame. Attempt to use God for your own ends, only to discard him when he no longer suits your purposes, and you will find yourself used by God for his ends, only to discard you when you no longer suit his purposes. "No one makes a fool of God" (Gal 6:7 Msg).

There is one more detail about Jehu's reign we must observe, and it is arguably the most important takeaway from his life. His coup of Omri's house and

---

81. Michael C. Astour, "841 B.C.: The First Assyrian Invasion of Israel," *JAOS* 91 (1991): 383–89.

82. "What may have made Hazael the angriest is the possibility that Jehu may not have been *forced* to ally himself with Shalmaneser III. Elat [M. Elat, "The Campaigns of Shalmaneser III against Aram and Israel," *IEJ* 25 (1975): 30] argues that the black obelisk 'shows the bearing of tribute only from those kings or countries which submitted without resistance, and perhaps at their own initiative.' If so, Jehu may have been taking what he considered were preventative measures, or he may have been supporting the enemy of his enemy. Whatever his motives, the result was that when Assyria left the region Jehu was left to face an angry Hazael, and by Jehu's death in 814 B.C. he 'had lost the whole of Transjordan south to the Moabite frontier on the Arnon (2 Kings 10:32 f.; cf. Amos 1:3),'" (House, *1, 2 Kings*, 296; emphasis his).

83. Patterson, "1, 2 Kings," 859.

84. "God will do to the house of Jehu exactly as he did through Jehu in the elimination of the Omrides—and for the same reasons. They are traitors to their own cause in not maintaining zeal for Yahweh," (Konkel, *1 & 2 Kings*, 488).

purge of Baal proved "once again the power of the prophetic word. Not one of Elijah's predictions about Ahab and Jezebel fail to come true."[85] But of course, for the Word of the Lord stands forever and will surely come to pass.

2 KINGS 11-12

With Jehu having usurped the throne of the Northern Kingdom, the narrative spotlight shifts south again to Judah. Upon the death of her son, Ahaziah, Queen Athaliah[86] began to consolidate her power by assassinating "all the royal family" (v. 1), much like Medea in Greek mythology. Barnes aptly calls Athaliah a "'Judean Jehu'—someone in the dynasty-killing business."[87] We can also imagine that she has quite a bit of her mother, Jezebel, in her genes. Equally concerning is that, when the narrator last focused on Judah, there was an "ominous lack of any restatement of the Davidic promise in 8:25–27. Have the two houses become so identified in intermarriage (8:18, 27) that a distinction is no longer to be maintained between them?"[88]

Not at all. Note here the conspicuous absence of the typical introduction/ conclusion given for Judah's rulers (e.g., "in the x year of y, king of Israel, a the son of b, king of Judah, began to reign"), indicating the narrator in no way considered Athaliah to be a legitimate ruler, but rather an interruption or usurper of the Davidic line.[89] Events would shortly prove that David's lamp had not been extinguished.

One of the royal lineage, a year-old infant named Joash, was saved from Athaliah's purge by his aunt, Jehosheba. Adding to the irony of the story is Jehosheba's relationship to Athaliah—"The narrative carefully notes that the

---

85. House, 1, 2 Kings, 296.

86. Recall that Athaliah was the daughter of Ahab and Jezebel (cf. Cogan, II Kings, 98; Keil, Commentary, 355), wife of Joram of Judah, and daughter-in-law of Jehoshaphat. "That Athaliah is an Omride (8:18, 26) anticipates that the fate prophesied against the Omrides similarly awaits her," (Wray Beal, 1 & 2 Kings, 388).

87. Barnes, 1 & 2 Kings, 272. Sweeney notes that since her son, Ahaziah, had been eliminated, her privileged position as queen mother was now in jeopardy (I & II Kings, 344).

88. Provan, 1 & 2 Kings, 219.

89. Auld, I & II Kings, 194. "Although the reign of Athaliah is seen in this way, and although the southern monarchy is now restored, there is an emerging sense in these narratives of the postponement of the inevitable," (Hobbs, 2 Kings, 145).

queen's own daughter was her undoing."[90] Since she was not a full Israelite, Athaliah was prohibited from entering the Temple. So Jehosheba hid him in a bedroom—either the high priest's residence (2 Chr 22:11) or (less probable) a storage room that housed bedding[91]—in the Temple precinct until he was seven. Here, Joash lay under the watchful, protective eye of God. Only then did Jehoiada, the high priest and Jehosheba's husband (2 Chr 22:11), believe the time was right to stage a coup and return a son of David to Judah's throne.

Jehoiada's plan involved the Carites (v. 4), foreign mercenaries hired to serve as a royal bodyguard, similar to the U.S. Secret Service.[92] And though there is no mention of them in Kings, "The Chronicler (2 Ch 23:1–2) lists the names of the officers whom Jehoiada took into his confidence concerning the existence of the rightful king and with whom he entered into covenant to unseat Athaliah. The Chronicler also adds that these men gathered the Levites and family heads and brought them to Jerusalem."[93]

At Jehoiada's instigation, these men swore to carry out the plot to protect Joash and make him king. The scheme was well planned. Since it would go down on the Sabbath, when there was a ceremonial changing of the guard, no one in the palace would think anything about troop movements, etc. Since some find Jehoiada's plan as described by the narrator (vv. 5–7) to be a little convoluted, the following reconstruction might help.

> One company of Carites was to guard the palace. It was a company which normally came on duty on the Sabbath. A second company was to stand guard at the Gate of Sur, the location of which was unknown. A third company was to stand guard at the palace or city entrance and offer support to the palace guard if needed. In addition to this, two platoons were to stand

---

90. Cogan, *II Kings*, 126. Bruggemann believes Jehosheba to be Athaliah's step-daughter (*1 & 2 Kings*, 408; cf. Josephus, *Antiquities* 9.141). Elsewhere in the Old Testament, similar ironies exist: Pharaoh's daughter delivered Moses from Pharaoh (Exod 2:1–10), and both Jonathan and Michal protected David from their father's murderous plots (1 Sam 19).

91. Keil, *Commentary*, 356.

92. Cogan says the Carites were like the Swiss Guard for rulers of Judah (*II Kings*, 126). In the LXX of 2 Samuel 20:23, they are called "Kerethites" and associated with the Pelethites, as they are in 1 Kings 1:38, 44.

93. Patterson, "1, 2 Kings," 863.

guard at the temple to protect the king. These platoons were from among those who normally did not come on duty on the Sabbath.[94]

Jehoiada wasn't willing to take any chances: "Whoever approaches the ranks is to be put to death" (v. 8). Mention of the weapons of David (v. 10; cf. 2 Sam 8:7) reminds us that the shepherd-king's lamp had not gone out in Jerusalem; God had been faithful. Athaliah's reign of terror had been as illegitimate as it was unpleasant. A son of David was now poised to take back the crown! Surrounded by the temple guards, the high priest anointed and crowned Joash as king before the people, who "clapped their hands and said, 'Long live the king!'" (v. 12). In every way possible, Athaliah was "caught off guard" by this "changing of the guard" and its implications.

> When she looked in upon the ceremony in the temple, what she saw stunned her, for there was the boy of seven, the new boy king, standing in the place of honor with all the markings of royal office and royal authority. She could tell at a glance what had happened without her knowing. The little boy who had been hidden now was available in public as an agent of power. Perhaps he had been so well hidden that she had forgotten him; certainly she had not seen him since the early days of his life. In a flash, she knows everything. Above all, she knows her own ambitions are finished and her life is now in jeopardy. She knows what winners do with losers in ruthless royal combat, for she knew about the North and the ideological passion embraced there by Jehu.[95]

When she discovered the commotion and saw what was really going on, she shrieked "Treason! Treason!" (cf. 9:23)—talk about the pot calling the kettle black!—and ripped her clothes in grief (v. 14). But she was immediately seized by the guards, drug back to the palace "through the horse's entrance" (cf. 23:11; Neh 3:28; Jer 31:40), and cut down like a cur dog—much like her mother's demise (9:27–37). Note, however, that on this day, Athaliah is the only

94. Hobbs, 2 Kings, 140; cf. Cogan, II Kings, 127; Patterson, "1, 2 Kings," 863.

95. Brueggemann, 1 & 2 Kings, 410–11.

person executed. Compared to Jehu's bloodbath, the coup staged by Jehoiada was remarkably restrained and relatively bloodless.[96]

Jehoiada used the occasion to rededicate the kingdom of Judah to the covenant made at Sinai, as well as to remind the people and Joash of their covenant obligations to one another. As Jehu had done, the people then demolished (cf. Deut 12:2–3[97]) the temple of Baal located two miles south of Jerusalem[98] (one built by Athaliah and her husband[99]) and struck down its priest, Mattan. With the coup of Jehu and rise of Joash, Baalism had been uprooted throughout Israel and Judah. The people[100] established Joash on his throne and rejoiced that rule over Judah had been restored to the house of David (vv. 19–20).

T hus Joash (835–796) began to reign in Jerusalem. He was a righteous king because of the positive influence of the high priest, Jehoiada. Sadly, however, and like the righteous kings before him, Joash allowed the high places and the practice of idolatry in the countryside to remain.

Since there had not been a righteous king in Jerusalem since the death of Jehoshaphat, and Athaliah's sons had frequently raided it for idolatrous purpos-

---

96. "For Jehoiada, and we may assume Jehosheba, actions flow from trust in God's promises and the continuation of the covenant relationship including the Davidic dynasty. There is no personal power-play using religion for one's own purposes. They are unable to predict the results, but action must be taken, done thoughtfully. There is violence, but it is minimized; there is leadership, but it is sensitive to the wider population and embraces their support. Their faith, attitudes and actions provide a mirror for reflecting on what leads to 'calm' for communities, cities and nations," (Olley, *Message of Kings*, 272; cf. Nelson, *First and Second Kings*, 214).

97. Brueggemann calls attention to "the sequence of strong, negative verbs in the command of Moses [in Deuteronomy 12:2–3], the very verbs enacted by Jehoiada," (*1 & 2 Kings*, 416).

98. Yigael Yadin, "The 'House of Ba'al' of Ahab and Jezebel in Samaria, and that of Athaliah in Judah," in *Archaeology in the Levant: Essays for Kathleen Kenyon*, eds. Roger Moorey and Peter Parr (Warminster, England: Aris, 1978), 127–35.

99. Josephus, *Antiquities* 9.154.

100. "The people of the land" (vv. 13–14, 18)—a phrase that occurs more than seventy-three times in the Old Testament—will arise often in 2 Kings to ensure the continuity of the Davidic dynasty (14:21; 21:23–24; 23:30). These were likely civic leaders and aristocratic landowners (Jer 1:18; 34:19; 37:2; cf. Ezek 22:29) and "commonly thought to be covenantal, conservative Yahwists of a political bent who resisted the enhancement of the royal office at the expense of the 'elders,'" (Brueggemann, *1 & 2 Kings*, 536; cf. Jones, *1 and 2 Kings*, 2:483–84).

es (2 Chr 24:7), Joash decided to renovate[101] the 125-year-old Temple,[102] using funds from taxes and donations.[103] The date of the commencement of these repairs is unknown, but by the king's twenty-third year (814), nothing had been done. Joash commanded that no more donations be accepted, to which the priests agreed, but they still seemed unwilling to commence the renovation project (vv. 7–8). "We are not yet told why there is such inactivity. The priests were apparently 'sitting on' the money collected for the project and were not mobilizing the workmen."[104]

So Jehoiada put what amounted to a giant cash box[105] at the altar located at the Temple's entrance (cf. 2 Chr 24:8). Here the priests deposited all the money they collected; when the chest was full, the high priest and royal secretary counted the funds themselves and then gave it directly to the Temple repairmen, something Barnes likens to having double signatures on church checks.[106] Such

---

101. "After this long hiatus in the story of the temple, the narrator makes it a major theme in the closing half of 2 Kings," (Leithart, *1 & 2 Kings*, 229; cf. 2 Kgs 14:14; 15:35; 16:8–18; 19:1, 14–19; 20:5, 8; 21:4–8; 22:3–7; 23:1–12; 24:13; 25:9, 13–17). "To neglect a temple in the ancient world was to neglect its deity and to risk his or her disapproval and the possible undermining of a king's legitimate authority to rule. [...] Conversely, a deity's approval of the ruling king was often communicated in the ancient Near East through the construction of a temple or, if a major shift in political power was taking place, through the renewal or renovation of an existing temple. This construction or renovation of a temple, it was believed, would bring peace and prosperity to all the inhabitants of the kingdom. It is against this background that Joash's actions are to be understood, as the Davidic dynasty sought to reestablish itself in the aftermath of Athaliah's coup," (Provan, "2 Kings," 159; cf. Brueggemann, *1 & 2 Kings*, 420).

102. The craziest thing about this fact is that Jehoiada was born around the time the Temple was built (2 Chr 24:15). It should be noted also that this chapter contains the greatest concentration of the phrase "the house of Yahweh" in the Old Testament—twenty-two times in this chapter and eighteen in the parallel of 2 Chronicles 23–24 (Olley, *Message of Kings*, 269, n. 60).

103. Traditionally, Temple income came from an annual census tax (Exod 30:11–14), payment for vows made (Lev 27:1–25), and free-will offerings (Lev 22:18–23; Deut 16:10).

104. Brueggemann, *1 & 2 Kings*, 420.

105. To speak of *money* during this time period is a bit anachronistic, since coins are not known in the biblical world until Ezra 2:69 (Hamburger, "Money, Coins," *IDB* 3:423–35). Rather, the Hebrew *kesep*, translated "silver," can refer "to all manner of precious artifacts or valuables for monetary exchange," (Konkel, "כָּסֶף," *NIDOTTE* 2:683).

106. Barnes, *1–2 Kings*, 280.

a practice—one of collecting donations as worshipers entered a temple to worship—was quite common in the ancient Near East during this time.[107]

It is insinuated by the narrator that the priests (with the exception of Jehoiada) collecting the Temple funds had not been honest this entire time, explaining why renovations hadn't taken place until Joash was thirty years old—and Wiseman wonders if the fracture between Jehoiada and Joash didn't occur at this time.[108] Note that the Temple repairmen, however, were honest dealers and thus not expected to account for funds paid to them (v. 15).

Meanwhile, Hazael of Aram launched a military campaign to the south against the Philistine city of Gath. Since it lay less than twenty-five miles from Jerusalem, it's understandable that Hazael's arrival sent a shiver down Joash's spine. Besides this being a military threat, Hazael likely was seeking to expand his access to trade routes. There is no extra-biblical mention of this campaign, but it may have been triggered by Jehu's death in 814 in Israel.

Sure enough, after his victory at Gath, Hazael put Jerusalem in his sights, but Joash paid him off by raiding the Temple and royal treasuries, though not before the Arameans clobbered a superior force of Judah's troops in battle (2 Chr 24:24). "Ironically, what Joash collected in 2 Kgs 12:4–16 he now spends."[109] The bribe worked; we're told "Hazael went away from Jerusalem" (v. 18). But "in this way, [Joash] unwittingly acted like his great-great-grandfather Asa did when confronted by an earlier Aramean king, Ben-hadad I."[110]

For his salvation, Joash paid a startlingly high cost, and not just financially. We have to wonder why he would bribe the neighborhood bully like this instead of appealing to heaven for help. This is not the first, and will not be the last, time a righteous king demonstrates such an appalling lack of faith. Was Joash still righteous at this point? The narrator had told us that the king "was right in the eyes of the LORD all his days because Jehoiada the priest instructed him" (v. 2),

107. A. Leo Oppenheim, "A Fiscal Practice of the Ancient Near East," *JNES* 6 (1947): 116–20; Victor Hurowitz, "Another Fiscal Practice in the Ancient Near East: 2 Kings 12:5–17 and a Letter to Esarhaddon (Las 227)," *JNES* 45 (1986): 289–94.

108. Wiseman, *1 and 2 Kings*, 251.

109. House, *1, 2 Kings*, 303.

110. Barnes, *1–2 Kings*, 281.

possibly insinuating that after Jehoiada's death, Joash came under the influence of ungodly advisors (2 Chr 24:15–18).[111]

Yet, we cannot be too hard on Joash; when disaster strikes in our world, we too often jettison our faith and values, wrongly believing that it is up to us to get ourselves out of trouble. We fall victim to the "If I don't, it won't" mindset. When the choice is between fear and faith, we too often choose fear.

Joash paid for his fear, and not just financially or spiritually, but also with his life. At the age of forty-seven, he was assassinated by two servants,[112] Jozacar and Jehozabad (both foreigners, 2 Chr 24:26). Though the narrator of Kings is silent on the issue, the Chronicler tells us that he was cut down because he had had Jehoiada's son, Zechariah, stoned to death (2 Chr 24:20–22).[113] "Joash becomes so unpopular at the end of his life that he is denied burial in the tomb of his ancestors."[114]

2 KINGS 13:1–9

The latter half of Joash's reign in Judah saw two kings on Israel's throne. Jehoahaz, Jehu's son, assumed the throne upon his father's death (the same year Joash began Temple renovations) and reigned seventeen years (814–798). Like all the other Northern kings, he was wicked, since he perpetuated the apostasy of Jeroboam. Thus, "under normal circumstances we might expect the appearance of a prophet to announce the end of Jehu's house (cf. 1 Kgs. 14:6ff.; 16:1ff.; 21:21ff.). These are not normal circumstances, however. The divine promise to Jehu (2 Kgs. 10:30) is functioning like the earlier promise to David (2 Sam. 7:1–17), and the Israelite royal house is, for the moment, being treated like the Judean."[115]

But as chastisement, Yahweh continually gave Israel into the hands of Aram's kings, Hazael and Ben-hadad III (c. 802–780). Through the prophet Amos,

---

111. Provan, *Biblical History*, 374, n. 56.

112. It seems palace intrigue did not die with Athaliah. "The fact that it was 'his servants' who killed the king suggests that within the palace, acute tension continued between factions competing for control of the levers of power," (Brueggemann, *1 & 2 Kings*, 422–23).

113. "The tragedy is deepened when we consider that Joash and Zechariah had known each other from childhood," (Leithart, *1 & 2 Kings*, 231, n. 7).

114. House, *1, 2 Kings*, 304.

115. Provan, *1 & 2 Kings*, 227.

Yahweh accused these two Aramean kings of having "sinned again and again, and I will not let them go unpunished! They beat down my people in Gilead as grain is threshed with iron sledges. So I will send down fire on King Hazael's palace, and the fortresses of King Ben-hadad will be destroyed" (Amos 1:3–4 NLT). As previously mentioned, Assyria's attention was occupied elsewhere during this time, so Aram remained unchecked.

But here's where we are in for a surprise. As in the days of the judges (e.g., Judg 2:11–23), Israel's king appealed[116] to the Lord's mercy and God heard him—"the LORD provided a deliverer for Israel, and they escaped from the power of Aram" (v. 5 NIV). In spite of the warning of Proverbs 28:9, it seems "that sometimes Yahweh's pity over the distress of his people trumps the wickedness of the one seeking him for relief."[117]

Who was this deliverer or "savior" (ESV)? Is it a reference to Elisha?[118] If so, it's a rather cryptic one when Elisha has been no stranger to the story of Kings, and it's been several decades since we last heard from Israel's man of God. However, identifying this deliverer with Elisha would be consistent with the promise of Deuteronomy 18:15–19, and it is also true that "his last prophecy would set Israel's deliverance in motion."[119]

Less likely is that this savior was a foreign ruler who distracted Israel's enemies. Around 806, the Assyrian king Adadnirari III led a campaign against Aram that ended with a siege of Damascus and the exacting of tribute.[120] Jehoash[121]

---

116. The verb translated "sought the favor of" (v. 4) occurs elsewhere in Kings only in 1 Kings 13:6, where Jeroboam asked the Lord for healing. One is left with the impression that Jehoahaz wasn't penitently seeking help as much as experiencing a "jailhouse conversion" in order to get out of a bad situation.

117. Davis, 2 Kings, 189. "God is moved to compassionate action as people experience oppression, even when their situation is an outworking of his anger! This juxtaposition of compassion and judgment is expressed with great pathos in the dramatic confrontation and promise of Hosea 11, addressed to rebellious Israel, and comes together most powerfully on the cross where love and justice meet," (Olley, Message of Kings, 279).

118. Gray, I & II Kings, 538–39; House, 1, 2 Kings, 305–6; Hobbs, 2 Kings, 167–68; Konkel, 1 & 2 Kings, 525.

119. Hubbard, First and Second Kings, 187.

120. Benjamin Mazar, "The Aramean Empire and its Relations with Israel," BA 25 (1962): 115; A. R. Millar, "Adad-Nirari III, Aram, and Arpad," PEQ 105 (1973): 161–64; Menahem Haran, "The Rise and Decline of the Empire of Jeroboam ben Joash," VT 17 (1967): 267–68.

121. Aelred Cody, "A New Inscription from Tell al-Rimah and King Jehoash of Israel,"

(Jehoahaz's son) and Jeroboam II[122] (Jehoahaz's grandson) are also mentioned as possible nominees for the "savior" label. In the end, there's no real way of knowing, and in one sense it doesn't matter. Regardless of who it was, God was behind this deliverer (cf. Judg 3:9, 15; Ps 107:19–20), graciously remaining faithful to a faithless people.[123]

Unfortunately, "God's gracious intervention makes no difference to Israel's religious outlook."[124] Idolatry—particularly the Asherah pole first established by Ahab (1 Kgs 16:33)—continued to flourish in Samaria. As a result, though the nation was delivered from Aramean assault ("Israel lived in safety again as they had in former days," v. 5 NLT), they continued to limp along in a severely weakened state. Israel possessed only ten chariots and ten thousand soldiers; "no field battle could have been won with such a small contingent."[125]

But in our frustration with ancient Israel, let us not pass up this opportunity to reflect upon and give thanks for God's faithfulness to his people. Both Israel and Judah had long before forfeited their right to deliverance. Yet, we serve a God who is always willing to deliver when we cry for mercy. "For the LORD your God is a merciful God. He will not leave you or destroy you or forget the covenant with your fathers that he swore to them" (Deut 4:31). In the darkest spiritual blackness imaginable, the light of grace continues to shine, guiding us home to Yahweh's heart.

CBQ 32 (1970): 336–37.

122. Robinson, Second Book, 121–22.

123. The anonymity of the savior in this passage may be meant to shift "readers' attention from a human deliverer sent by Yahweh to Yahweh himself as the 'deliverer,'" (John W. Olley, "2 Kings 13: A Cluster of Hope in God," JSOT 36 [2011]: 204).

124. Provan, 1 & 2 Kings, 228. "As in the times of Amos, it seems that the more the Lord does to change Israel's habits the more the people choose a destructive path (cf. Amos 4:6–12)," (House, 1, 2 Kings, 306).

125. Fritz, 1 & 2 Kings, 309. By means of comparison, "A normal ratio of chariotry to infantry on such campaigns was from 1:30 to 1:50. Ahab fielded a force of 10,000 infantry and 2,000 chariotry at Qarqar," (Hobbs, Jehoahaz [Person]," ABD 3:659).

2 KINGS 13:10-25

Jehoahaz's son, Jehoash,[126] reigned sixteen years[127] (798–782). Second verse, same as the first—he continued Jeroboam's apostasy of idolatry. Israel's circumstances began to improve under Jehoash and continued under his son, Jeroboam II. But though Jehoash was a capable leader, particularly in war (he recovered the cities Aram had previously taken from Israel, v. 25), his success was due only to God's grace. Thus his only real significance to the narrator was his connection with Amaziah, king of Judah, which we will learn about in the next chapter in Kings.

t was during the reign of Jehoash, however, that a person of great worth to Israel passed away after fifty years of ministry, and that individual was Elisha. When he heard that the aged prophet was on his deathbed, Jehoash visited him. Intriguingly, he uttered the same cry upon his arrival that Elisha had when Elijah was raptured to heaven: "My father, my father! The chariots of Israel and its horsemen!" (v. 14; cf. 2:12). In recent memory, Israel had been devastated by the Arameans (cf. vv. 3–7; 10:32–33), and Jehoash recognized Elisha as the savior Yahweh had provided Israel (v. 5),[128] but the prophet leaves behind no

---

126. Though known as *Jehoash* here, his name was the same as Joash, his Southern counterpart. Jehoash's name is preserved in a stele discovered in northern Iraq on which Adadnirari III lists him as a tributary (Stephanie Page, "A Stela of Adad-nirari III and Nergal-ereš from Tell al Rimah," *Iraq* 30 (1968): 139–53). As with Jehoram of Israel and Joram of Judah, I will use *Jehoash* to refer to the king of Israel and *Joash* to refer to the king of Judah. "The difference in the form of the name is due to peculiarities in regional pronunciations of [Hebrew] during the biblical period. Both forms are found in Kings because the author tended to write names as he found them in his sources," (Ziony Zevit, "2 Kings," in *The Jewish Study Bible*, eds. Adele Berlin and Marc Zvi Brettler [Oxford: Oxford Univ. Press, 2004], 747).

127. Based on the note in v. 1, we would expect Jehoash to have ascended Israel's throne in the thirty-ninth year of Joash of Judah, not the thirty-seventh (indeed, some LXX manuscripts read "thirty-ninth"). Wiseman (*1 and 2 Kings*, 256) suggests the difference of two years can be accounted for by recognizing a two-year co-regency for Jehoahaz and Jehoash (cf. Gray, *I & II Kings*, 540, n. a). Thiele, however, argues that here the narrator began using a different way of reckoning the reigns of the Northern kings—non-accession year versus accession year (*Mysterious Numbers*, 111).

128. "It is divine intervention through the prophets, after all, that has from the beginning ensured Israelite survival in the face of superior Aramean forces (cf. 1 Kgs. 20:1–34; 2 Kgs.

successor as Elijah had done. What hope did Israel have after Elisha's passing?[129] The king is desperate.

The dying prophet instructed the king of Israel to take a bow and loose an arrow out of the window to the east.[130] Elisha then prophesied that Israel would finally win victory over the dreaded Arameans and instructed the king to seize a fistful of arrows and strike the ground. For whatever reason, the king only struck the ground three times, at which point Elisha got angry, insisting the king should have struck the ground twice as much as he did (though, in the king's defense, he had never been told how many times to do so). Now, instead of vanquishing Aram once and for all, the king would win only three times.

That Israel's fate would be determined by shooting and smashing arrows seems rather bizarre to modern readers, but Elisha's instructions reflected an ancient divination practice known as belomancy. Provan explains its many forms: "A number of different instructions might be attached to a set of arrows, which were then fired. The instruction on the arrow that flew the furthest, or was found first, would be obeyed. Alternatively, the instructions on the first arrow drawn from a quiver would be taken, or the arrows could be thrown to the ground and the practitioners would travel in the direction they pointed as they settled."[131]

Though infrequently mentioned, it does seem that this was practiced in Palestine during Elisha's day. And while the Lord had outlawed various forms of divination in Israel (Deut 18:10–11), it seems Elisha saw in the loosing and

---

6:8–7:20)," (Provan, 1 & 2 Kings, 228). "The prophet is the man whose prayer is better than chariots and horsemen. Trust in the words of the prophet means that horses and chariots can be abandoned," (Beek, "Meaning of the Expression," 8). With Elisha's passing, "Israel must rely on lukewarm kings whose prayers (v. 4) are undercut by their obdurate sin (vv. 2, 6, 11)," (Nelson, First and Second Kings, 218).

129. Leithart notes that *hand* "is used repeatedly in the chapter: several times it describes the power of Aram (13:3, 5, 25), but 13:16 uses the word four times to refer to the hand of Jehoash. It is through *his* hand that Israel will be saved, but only so long as his hand is guided by the hand of the prophet," (1 & 2 Kings, 233; emphasis his).

130. The Aphek later mentioned in v. 17 was likely the same from 1 Kings 20:26–30, which was in the same direction that Jehoash shot the arrow.

131. Provan, "2 Kings," 162. He adds, "Ezekiel 21:21 provides us with a description of this kind of divination, picturing the king of Babylon standing at a crossroads and trying to determine how to proceed by shaking or tossing arrows, consulting his idols, and inspecting the liver of an animal," (Ibid.). See also Samuel Iwry, "New Evidence for Belomancy in Ancient Palestine and Phoenicia," *JAOS* 81 (1961): 27–34.

smashing of arrows an indication of what God had in store for his people[132] (cf. Exod 17:8–13; Josh 8:18; 1 Kgs 11:29–32; Jer 18). Perhaps in his order to launch the arrow and strike the ground, the prophet was reiterating the certainty of God's word, that it would surely come to pass, and was testing Jehoash's enthusiasm and commitment to that word. It's certainly clear that Elisha linked "his prophetic power to the ensuing action" when he placed his hand on the king's as the arrow is loosed.[133]

This would explain why the king is chastised by the dying prophet. How did the king know how many times he ought to strike the ground? He didn't know precisely, but "he must have known that the striking was symbolic and showed that he had not the will or the character to be God's instrument for the task that was being laid upon him."[134] Elisha was trying to pass on to him the power to defeat the enemies of God's people; thus when a prophet tells you to strike the ground with arrows, you do so enthusiastically, knowing the act might have profound implications for yourself and all God's Israel. But like his predecessor, Ahab, Jehoash lacked the gusto necessary to prosecute holy war to the fullest.

In what has to be one of the strangest stories in the Old Testament, the narrator tells us that a marauding band of Moabites showed up during a burial. Panicked and fleeing to safety, the pallbearers tossed the dead body into Elisha's tomb; upon contact with the prophet's corpse, the deceased "revived and stood on his feet" (v. 21; cf. Sirach 48:13–14).

> Like Elijah before him, Elisha has been a powerful force for life with a capacity to transform circumstances of death. Thus he is the one who turned deathly water whole (2:19-22), who gave life to the besieged widow (4:1-7), who rescued the pot of food from death (4:38-41), who fed the hungry (4:42-44), who healed the foreign leper (5:14), who recovered a lost ax head (6:1-7 [sic], who turned war to feast (6:7-23), who provisionally ended famine (7:1), and who turned out the deathly dynasty of Omri (9:1-37). Quintessentially, he is the one who raised the

---

132. Of such symbolic acts, Robinson writes, "Sometimes [...] the event itself is arbitrarily created in order to be a miniature of that larger activity of God which it initiates," (H. Wheeler Robinson, *Inspiration and Revelation in the Old Testament* [Oxford: Clarendon, 1946], 35–36).

133. Wray Beal, *1 & 2 Kings*, 410.

134. Robinson, *Second Book*, 125.

son of the Shunammite woman from death to life (4:32-37), a wonder subsequently reckoned as a "great thing" in Israel (8:4-5). The present text functions as something of a reprise on this entire memory of ministry. The power of life has been operative in Israel through this enigmatic figure and is at work yet.[135]

It's possible that this brief aside is meant to offer hope to Israel. It will not be long before the nation, like the anonymous man in this anecdote, is thrown into its grave (the verb translated "thrown" in v. 21 is the same as "cast" in v. 23 and 17:20). But the Lord will not allow death to have the final word; coming into contact with God's Man always offers life, and in abundance (John 10:10; Eph 2:5)![136]

D espite the scourge of Hazael, Yahweh could not bring himself to cast Israel from his presence—at least, not yet. Israel had been unfaithful to the covenant of Sinai, so according to ancient Near Eastern theology, God had every right to turn his back on Israel: "You didn't keep your end of the bargain; I won't keep mine."

But instead of voiding the contract, it seems God chose to search for a loophole—a reason, any reason—that would allow him to forgive and forget. And he found such a loophole when he remembered "his covenant with Abraham, Isaac, and Jacob"[137] (v. 23; cf. Deut 9:27). It is not insignificant that this is the only mention of the patriarchs in all of Joshua–Kings, with the exception of Elijah's prayer on Carmel (1 Kgs 18:36). "In these many ways YHWH shows himself gracious and merciful, even towards an apostate people. That YHWH so acts arises out of his character," (Exod 34:6–7; Num 14:18; Neh 9:17; Pss 86:15; 103:8; 145:8; Joel 2:13; Jon 4:2; Nah 1:3).[138]

---

135. Brueggemann, *1 & 2 Kings*, 432–33. "The Elisha cycle began with a (scandalous) episode in which he summoned bears to kill forty-two boys. Now, at the end of the cycle, his bones perform the opposite act of reviving the dead," (Alter, *Ancient Israel*, 794).

136. "Clinging to the prophet is the way of life, but what happens to that life when the prophet dies and stays dead? Israel will not be saved by any ordinary prophet or by any extraordinary one. Israel needs a prophet who would give life on the other side of the grave by triumphing, once for all, over the grave," (Leithart, *1 & 2 Kings*, 236).

137. Provan, *1 & 2 Kings*, 229.

138. Wray Beal, *1 & 2 Kings*, 412–13.

So it is that, due to God's gracious will, the Northern Kingdom turns a corner.[139] During his sixteen years on the throne, Jehoash indeed witnessed the Aramean threat wane. Hazael had been a formidable foe, just as Elisha had predicted. But Hazael's son, Ben-hadad III, was not as competent as his warrior-father. For one thing, unlike during Hazael's reign, Assyria again began to harass Aram once Adadnirari III (c. 811–783) became king. Thus, Jehoash was able to reclaim lost territory—likely cities west of the Jordan (cf. 10:32–33), including Lo-debar and Karnaim (Amos 6:13)—and defeated Ben-hadad three times in battle—again, just as Elisha had predicted.[140]

But two Assyrian inscriptions infer that, in 796, Jehoash paid tribute to Adadnirari.[141] If this is so, it is quite clear how Jehoash planned to gain victory over Aram: by buying off the enemy of his enemy, rather than waging holy war under the banner of Yahweh. Why dally in the ambiguities of biblical faith when one can make alliances with the ungodly to achieve the desired outcome?

Why? Because faith is the victory that overcomes the world. Because faith is the only proper response to a God who looks for any excuse or loophole available to forgive and bless his people in Christ. Because when faith meets grace, death is brought to life.

But radical faith is not something Jehoash can offer. So "there are hints now of a darker future, a future in which Israel will have to do without their great protector Elisha; a future of defeat and exile in a foreign land. It is the end of an era in which two mighty prophets have walked the land. What will happen now?"[142]

---

139. "Such a revival of the sick body of Israel and the dynasty of Jehu is neither accidental nor automatic. It happens solely at the will of God. [...] The writer invites the reader to look back to the distant past in interpreting the recent past and the present. God has acted, but only out of his own desire, quite uninfluenced by the actions of others, kings or commoners. Thus it is that Joash restored so much territory to Israel and defeated Hazael and Ben Hadad (v 25). Such actions are firmly grounded on the prior activity of God (v 23). The pattern of complete dependence upon Yahweh is clear," (Hobbs, *2 Kings*, 172–73).

140. "Three times, however, is not enough. Elisha reckoned 'five or six' to be adequate (13:19). Thus even in success, the regime fails to enact the full prophetic promise. The narrative is restrained and tells us nothing more of the matter. The wording of the last sentence, however, suggests that three-times success carries in it long-term failure. Kings should pay more attention to prophets!" (Brueggemann, *1 & 2 Kings*, 434).

141. Page, "A Stela of Adad-nirari III," 139–53; Stephanie Page, "Joash and Samaria in a New Stela Excavated at Tell al Rimah, Iraq," *VT* 19 (1969): 483–84.

142. Provan, *1 & 2 Kings*, 227.

TALKING POINTS

n his Apocalypse, the apostle John saw the ascended, glorified Christ "tread the winepress of the fury of the wrath of God the Almighty" (Rev 19:15). This same Christ, John claimed, would strike the nations with a sharp sword and rule them with an iron rod. Fierce, indeed, is the wrath God will pour out upon evil and wickedness on the final day (Rom 1:18; 2 Thess 1:8). Jehu's wrath poured out on the house of Ahab, the people's wrath poured out on Athaliah and the temple of Baal, and Hazael's wrath poured out on a weakened Israel are all forerunners of this divine wrath. However, in our response to wickedness, Christians are called to leave room for God's wrath (Rom 12:19). Our model is not Jehu, but Christ, who wept at the thought of Israel's punishment for rejecting him (Luke 19:41–44). Likewise, the thought that there were enemies of Jesus and his cross brought tears to Paul's eyes (Phil 3:18). Because the capacity for overreaction and lack of restraint is so high (as Jehu's bloody purge proves), Christians are prohibited from taking matters into their own hands. As difficult as it is, we are to pray for our enemies and wish the best for them. "Judgment is real, but the message is not a denial of compassion. It is one's fellow human beings who are to suffer."[143]

n Joash, it is clear we are dealing with a special child, one who holds an important place in God's grand scheme. If nothing else, the infant prince represented a candle in the wind, the flickering wick of David's lamp. But as "weak as he may allow it to become, the Lord will not allow the flame to die. The lamp of David could not be extinguished,"[144] (cf. Ps 89:36). Elsewhere in Scripture, we see God's plan hang by a slender thread (e.g., Exod 2:1–10; Matt 2:1–23). In his Apocalypse, John saw a dragon seeking to devour a baby boy being born, yet that child was carried by angels to safety into the desert (Rev 12:1–6). To be clear, such moments illustrate the importance of God's agents standing in the gap[145]

---

143. Olley, *Message of Kings*, 252.

144. Inrig, *I & II Kings*, 274.

145. "[The story of Joash] teaches us how God watches over His purposes and their instruments when they seem nearest to failure, for one poor infant was all that was left of the seed of David; and how, therefore, we are never to despair, even in the darkest hour, of the fulfilment of His promises. It teaches us how much one brave, good man and woman can do to change the

(e.g., Moses' parents, Jehoiada and Jehosheba, the Magi, the angels). But they are a greater testament to the fact that the future is always sustained by God's power and love. This, then, is the greatest safeguard in the church's possession—our ace in the hole. God has a plan, and God is powerful enough to see that plan come to pass. He also loves us infinitely. God's power and love are a great hope to the church in dark times. If nothing else, they give us the strength to obey the Lord Jesus Christ and risk our lives to do his will in the world, regardless of the cost.[146]

Too often, our lives are riddled with trouble and conflict, and sometimes due to our sin. An important theme in this section is peace, and particularly the fact that true peace comes only when in a right relationship with God (cf. Jer 7:9–11; 8:11; 33:6). At the end of Athaliah's reign of terror, there is a note that "the city was quiet" (v. 20). The statement reminds us of the common refrain of Judges, "the land had rest," after the defeat of Israel's enemy (3:11, 30; 5:31; 8:28)—but note that a similar statement is not made after Jehu's coup. "The term [i.e., rest] in such usage does not mean simply a stillness at the end of the day. Rather it means the restoration of the elemental, reliable, reassuring governance of Yahweh after things had fallen into chaos and confusion. Thus the term makes a profound theological claim for 'the God of order' with a reestablished governance and control. The world is again seen to be coherent. The center will hold. The processes of chaos and disorder have been overcome. All is well and all shall be well."[147] That same rest or peace, realized in Judah after the elimination of Athaliah, can be ours when we, too, turn back to the Lord and seek to honor him in every area of life.

---

whole face of things, and how often there needs but one man to direct and voice the thoughts and acts of the silent multitude, and to light a fire that consumes evil," (Maclaren, *Expositions*, 5:19).

146. "The wonder of our story, as with the other narratives, is that risks are run by those willing to run such risks for the sake of newness they cannot yet see. The hiding of the baby is an act of profound hope that refuses to give in to the fearful brutality of the status quo," (Brueggemann, *1 & 2 Kings*, 414).

147. Ibid., 413.

This section of Kings contains a rich repository of characters who offer up a smorgasbord of moral lessons. The rise of Hazael in Damascus is a warning that God will, from time to time, raise up rods of his anger to discipline his people—but that discipline will not last forever. In good times and bad, God's people can put their faith and hope in the fact that God is in complete control of every international event and works them for our good and his glory. In the gratuitous violence of Jehu, himself a rod of God's anger against the house of Ahab, we have a warning against vindictive retribution and the bloody excess it produces. As Christians, it is better to forgive than to avenge. In the deaths of Jezebel and Athaliah, we are reminded that a person reaps what they sow. Mother and daughter had been responsible for the murders of so many, and they eventually felt the assassin's sword themselves. God is not mocked. Jehoiada, on the other hand, demonstrates a responsible orientation to power. "Jehoiada is a heroic priest, and heroic precisely because he does not grasp for power but helps to reestablish legitimate royal power."[148] From the life of Joash, we learn the importance of making our faith our own. The boy king was faithful as long as his mentor, Jehoiada, lived. But once the priest died, Joash's faithfulness declined, and so did Judah. Finally, as we gaze on Elisha on his deathbed, we are reminded of the power of one man's faith to lead and deliver a nation. Even in death, the person of Elisha brought life to Israel—but for how much longer?

---

148. Leithart, *1 & 2 Kings*, 228.

11

THE ELEVENTH HOUR

A nyone who has spent time as a caregiver for the terminally ill has perhaps witnessed an eleventh-hour rally—a sudden surge of energy, rise in adrenaline, or increased lucidity that makes it appear as if the patient will recover. Such a rally is often nothing more than a cruel source of false hope; rather than recovery, it often means death is imminent. In their book, *Final Gifts*, authors Patricia Kelley and Maggie Callahan note that an eleventh-hour rally is evidence of a "near-death awareness" in the patient.[1]

Second Kings 14–17 represents just such an eleventh-hour rally for Israel. With the death of Elisha, we get the uneasy feeling that the Northern Kingdom cannot last very long. If he was indeed the savior God had provided to deliver his people from oppression, how much longer can Israel survive now that Elisha is no longer in the land of the living?

But then we read of Jeroboam's four decades of peace and success, the likes of which the North has not seen since her split with the house of David. However, don't get your hopes up: rather than a sign of vibrancy, such a rally will prove to be one last demonstration of grace on God's part before the end comes. Indeed, "God's compassion and saving acts are cited more often in these chapters (13:5, 23; 14:25–27) than God's anger (13:3; compare the predominance of anger in 1 Kings 14:21–16:34."[2]

The Northern Kingdom also benefited from a half-century lull in Assyrian hegemony over the region. But the great bully of the North awoke from its slum-

---

1. Maggie Callanan and Patricia Kelley, *Final Gifts: Understanding the Special Awareness, Needs, and Communications of the Dying* (New York: Simon & Schuster, 1992).

2. Fretheim, *First and Second Kings*, 187.

ber when Tiglath-pileser III came to power in 745. He first took care of business in the east and then turned his attention to Aram and Israel in 743. It would be another twenty years until Israel collapsed before the Assyrian war machine, but for those two decades, the Northern Kingdom was essentially on life support.

Woven into the narrative are stories of war, strife, revolution, and incompetence at the highest levels of government—not at all unlike what we read about in our newspapers today. But "what is unfamiliar is the insistence that God was playing some intentional role (14:25; 15:12) in all these events, which are seen through the evaluative lens of sin and divine response. God willed only good for this people Israel. God was bound to them by ties of covenant and compassion (13:4–5, 23; 14:26–27). Yet obdurate sin (13:2, 6, 11; 14:24; 15:9, 18, 24, 28) demanded punishment (13:7; 15:37)."[3]

Such a reality gives me hope on two levels. On the one hand, it's comforting to know that God extends his grace to us right up to the very end. The thief on the cross was not the first, and will certainly not be the last, to experience this reality. God never gives up on anyone until a last breath has been taken.

On the other hand, it is comforting also to know that, for good or bad, God remains involved in the activity and direction of history. In times of war, strife, revolution, and incompetence, it helps to know that there is a Lord reigning sovereign over the chaos, imposing his will in the world.

2 KINGS 14:1–22

The ninth king of Judah was Amaziah, whose twenty-nine-year reign (796–767) included a quarter-century co-regency with his son, Azariah, beginning about 792.[4] Amaziah was a good king, but not quite as good as David (v. 3). Rather, like his father, Amaziah tolerated the idolatrous high places and pagan cults of Judah, and we must concede that "the qualified praise of Amaziah portends some future disaster."[5]

What he didn't tolerate were his father's murderers (12:20). It was common practice in the ancient Near East to execute all assassins, as well as their families.[6] Yet, Amaziah is commended for remaining faithful to the Law of

3. Nelson, *First and Second Kings*, 222.

4. Thiele, *Mysterious Numbers*, 113–15.

5. Hobbs, *2 Kings*, 178.

6. Greenberg, "Avenger of Blood," *IDB* 1:321. The Assyrian king Esarhaddon made his

Moses by punishing only the assassins themselves (vv. 5–6; cf. Deut 24:16; Jer 31:29–30; Ezek 18:2–4). Thus the narrator is emphatic that the king chose to follow the standards of God's Law rather than stooping to those of the world. In any age, those who follow the Word of the Lord will distinguish themselves from their peers. "Ironically though, the very ones he spared may be those who are later responsible for his death."[7]

Among Amaziah's exploits is that he wiped out ten thousand Edomites in the Salt Valley "and took Sela[8] by storm" (v. 7; cf. 2 Sam 8:13), neither of which was a small feat.[9] On the heels of his Edomite victory, Amaziah decided to challenge Jehoash, king of Israel. Judah had just successfully expanded its territory to include Edom; remember that Judah had *lost* its control of Edom during the reign of Joram (8:20–22). In other words, it may seem as if Amaziah, high on his recent acquisition of Edom, became even more land-hungry and coveted Israel to the north. But the Chronicler again sheds additional light on the situation.

Before commencing the Edomite campaign, Amaziah had mustered 300,000 troops and hired another 100,000 mercenaries from Israel (2 Chr 25:5–6) for the low, low price of 100 silver talents.[10] But an unnamed prophet warned the king that God would not be with these Northern troops; Amaziah was to take *only* soldiers from Judah into battle. Amaziah obeyed and sent the Northern mercenaries home. The Northern troops, however, were outraged; though they had been paid their fee, they were missing out on much more in the form of the

---

vassals swear that, in the event of a coup, they would execute the perpetrators, along with their descendants (*ANET* 534–41; cf. Moshe Weinfeld, *Deuteronomy and the Deuteronomic School* [Oxford: Clarendon, 1972], 89).

7. Hens-Piazza, *1–2 Kings*, 327.

8. The Valley of Salt was located either in the Negev or in the region south of the Dead Sea (Hobbs, *2 Kings*, 179). Sela has often been identified with Petra, a location that "lay amid the seemingly impregnable rocks and cliffs of the Wadi Musa," (Patterson, "1, 2 Kings," 876).

9. "The control of Edom was not only important to the prestige of Judah, but was also essential to her commercial prosperity, since a hostile Edom could cut off Judah from her southern port Elath. The logical conclusion of Amaziah's victory over Edom was to retake and reopen Elath, which was in fact done by Azariah (2 K. 14:22)," (Caldecott and Payne, "Amaziah," *ISBE* 1:109). Hens-Piazza (*1–2 Kings*, 328) believes "this brief note about Amaziah's victory over Edom may actually serve less to inform about this battle and more as an explanation of Amaziah's curious challenge to the king of Israel that follows," and she might be right.

10. That figure represents a bit over three tons of silver, but this would have hardly been an exorbitant amount per soldier.

spoils of war they would have collected once Edom was defeated. In their rage, the Northern mercenaries raided and looted "cities of Judah, from Samaria to Beth-horon, and struck down 3,000 people" (2 Chr 25:13). If they were to miss out on looting in Edom, they would seize spoil from Judah instead.

Intriguingly, the Chronicler reveals Amaziah included Edomite gods in his worship after the victory at Sela (2 Chr 25:14–16, 20). In an age where military victories were believed to have been symbolic of one nation's god defeating the god(s) of other countries, we can only marvel at Amaziah's stupidity in worshiping a pantheon whose divine derrières had just been handed to them.[11] But again, an unnamed prophet arrived with a message of judgment. Amaziah cut him off in the middle of the sermon, but not before the man of God offered this final warning: "God has made up his mind to throw you out because of what you've done, and because you wouldn't listen to me" (2 Chr 25:16 Msg).

So imagine the "recipe" for disaster we have before us. We have a semi-righteous king who is:

- smarting over divine rebuke

- fresh off a resounding victory against Edom

- celebrating the annexation of more territory

- seeking to avenge the marauding behavior of his former friends-for-hire

Allow these "ingredients" to marinate in the heart of a king, and it's not difficult to imagine the snafu that plays out. Recall, also, that Jehoahaz (the previous king of Israel) had had only ten thousand troops at his disposal (13:7), the same number Amaziah had defeated in the Valley of Salt (v. 7)—how much resistance could Jehoash of Israel now muster if Amaziah attacked?[12] Well, for one, Amaziah seems to have forgotten the 100,000 Northern mercenaries he had

---

11. Actually, worshiping the deities of defeated enemies was common in ancient times (Walton, *Bible Background*, 447), which only goes to show you just how absurd idolatry is.

12. Wood reminds us that, in actuality, Israel might have been rather formidable as a result of her alliance with Assyria, and that Amaziah did not realize this (*Survey*, 350–51). "Clearly the sorry military status of Jehoash in [13:7] has now been quickly overcome, so that Israel has adequate military power of horses, chariots, and soldiers," (Brueggemann, *1 & 2 Kings*, 430).

just ticked off. Indeed, to Amaziah's call to war[13] (cf. 1 Sam 17:4), Jehoash responded with all the jitters Chuck Norris might have while roundhouse-kicking a chihuahua. The proverb he retorts with (vv. 9–10)—something that was common in ancient Near Eastern discourse—was meant to say, "You are way out of your league attacking me. You are feeling invincible because of your victory over Edom. But I'm not Edom."

We should hardly be surprised that Amaziah ignored Jehoash's sound advice, and the two kings met in battle at Beth-shemesh, located within the territory of Judah some fifteen miles west of Jerusalem. The clash ended before it essentially began—according to Josephus, the men of Judah didn't even fight before they fled before Jehoash's army, and they left their king to fend for himself.[14] Judah was routed, and Israel's troops gave chase to Jerusalem, where they opened up a gap about the size of two football fields in the city's north wall.[15] Meanwhile, Jehoash looted the Temple and royal treasuries,[16] and Amaziah was captured and deported to Samaria in chains along with other POWs.[17] From this point until early on in Azariah's reign (son of Amaziah), the Northern Kingdom ruled over Judah.[18]

Following Jehoash's death (vv. 15–16), it seems Amaziah was released from prison and returned to his throne in Jerusalem (observe the odd notation in v. 17). The text never says so explicitly, but we know he had already returned to the

---

13. "The challenge is remarkable, because during the Omride dynasty it was consistently made clear that the Northern state was the stronger party with whom the South was docilely cooperative," (Ibid., 440).

14. Josephus, *Antiquities* 9.199–200.

15. "Jerusalem's northern wall, its most crucial, was thus extensively breached and the city immediately rendered defenseless (steep ravines helped protect Jerusalem on the western and eastern sides, as well as to some degree on the narrow southern side)," (Barnes, *1–2 Kings*, 293). Amaziah's son, Azariah, would later rebuild the Corner Gate and add a watchtower (2 Chr 26:9), perhaps mindful that this was the weakest point of Jerusalem's defenses.

16. Jehoash likely didn't pilfer much; recall that Hazael had looted the treasuries just ten years prior (12:18).

17. "The Assyrian records show that often the family of the defeated king was carried off and kept under guard at the Assyrian court as hostages for the good behavior of the king who was allowed to remain on his throne. They might also be held for ransom at a later date. In the present case, the identity of the Judaean hostages is not stated; but one may surmise that they belonged to the nobility," (Cogan, *II Kings*, 157).

18. Provan, *Biblical History*, 269.

city of David when he futilely fled his assassins to Lachish, a fortified town thirty miles to the southwest that served as Judah's "second capital" and a buffer between Jerusalem and the Philistines.[19] After his death, Amaziah was given a royal burial in Jerusalem, but it seems the people of Judah weren't exactly sad to see him go.

Rather, they too eagerly "took Azariah, who was sixteen years old, and made him king instead of his father Amaziah" (v. 21). For one thing, Amaziah's apostasy and hubris had cost Judah her security and her treasure. That Amaziah's corpse was borne to Jerusalem on horseback (v. 20), and not in a coffin or litter, was a final insult—imagine President Kennedy's body being taken from Dallas to Washington in a dump truck—or dragged behind one—and you get the point.

If something about Amaziah's and Jehoash's reigns seems incongruent to you, you're not the only one. On the one hand, we are told that Amaziah is righteous (v. 3) and Jehoash is wicked (13:11). But it is Jehoash who is victorious in battle, while Amaziah is humiliated. Amaziah, then, may represent one who is partly righteous, yet spiritually calloused and driven by his own self-interest. Put another way, Amaziah's ambition outran his faith. And though Jehoash was evil, Yahweh was not above disciplining the dynasty of David at the hands of their wicked Northern cousins.

2 KINGS 14:23-29

Jeroboam the son of Jehoash[20]—designated by many biblical historians as Jeroboam II to differentiate him from the North's first king—was by far the North's longest-reigning monarch (793–753), though he was only a co-regent with his father until 782.[21] The narrator's assessment of his spirituality (v. 24) reminds us that sometimes the wicked succeed and prosper—Josephus claims Jeroboam II "was also the cause of ten thousand misfortunes to the people of Israel."[22]

---

19. Tufnell declares Lachish to have been one of the most important cities in Judah c. 900–700 (Olga Tufnell, "Lachish," in *Archaeology and Old Testament Study*, ed. D. Winton Thomas [Oxford: Clarendon, 1967], 304).

20. Archaeologists have discovered a seal from this period, one that reads, "Belonging to Shema, servant of Jeroboam," (Cogan, *II Kings*, 160).

21. Wray Beal, *1 & 2 Kings*, 409.

22. Josephus, *Antiquities* 9.205.

Indeed, it was during his reign that we first meet the prophet Jonah, he of big fish fame. This same Jonah predicted that the territory of Israel would expand under the reign of Jeroboam II. Hamath was located over one hundred miles north of Damascus on the Orontes River and was the traditional northern terminus of Canaan proper (cf. Num 13:21; 34:8; Josh 13:5; Ezek 47:15). The Sea of the Arabah is a reference to the Dead Sea (cf. Deut 3:17; 4:49; Josh 3:16; 12:3). Later on in the passage, we learn that Damascus also returned to Israel's possession under Jeroboam (v. 28). In other words, and presumably by virtue of military victories (e.g., Amos 6:13–14), Jeroboam[23] managed to restore the boundaries existent in Solomon's day (cf. 1 Kgs 8:65), most notably the territory seized by Hazael (10:32–33).[24]

Though Jeroboam II enjoyed peace and prosperity, the narrator dismisses him rather quickly. We know only a little of what happened on the international scene during this time, but it's clear that neither Aram nor Assyria posed much of a threat to Israel and Judah. Here's why:

- A few years before Jeroboam II became king, the Assyrian king Adadnirari III (c. 811–783) had conquered Damascus, neutralizing the Aramean threat to Israel.

- Later in Jeroboam's reign, the Assyrian Shalmaneser IV (c. 783–773) perpetually had his hands full with a defensive war against Urartu to the north (modern-day Armenia).

- Shalmaneser's brother and successor, Ashurdan III (c. 773–755), was a weak king. According to Assyrian records, his reign was beset with plague, domestic unrest, and a general air of lethargy when it came to military expeditions.

Secular peace, however, does not equate to spiritual vitality—"Israel used the time of her respite to weave the rope with which she was soon to be hanged."[25] The ministries of both Hosea and Amos date to the reign of Jeroboam II, and both of these prophets were critical of the rise of apostasy and the death

---

23. Haran believes Jeroboam's territorial expansion occurred late in his reign (Menahem Haran, "The Rise and Decline of the Empire of Jeroboam ben Joash," *VT* 17 [1967]: 266–97).

24. An Aramaic inscription found at Dan is said to be evidence of Israel's expansion during the reigns of Jehoash and Jeroboam II (Konkel, *1 & 2 Kings*, 533–34).

25. Robinson, *Second Book*, 133.

of justice they witnessed in Jeroboam's day.[26] They argued that though Israel felt safe and secure in her prosperity, she was actually hanging on by a thread but for the grace of God. The discovery in A.D. 1910 of the Samaria Ostraca (ceramic or pottery inscriptions dating to Jeroboam's reign) has confirmed a spike in tax revenue during Jeroboam's reign (indicating a strong economy[27]), but also a rise in Israel's wickedness. "The personal names they recorded thereon show an advance in apostasy in that for every eleven personal names compounded with Yah seven now include Baal."[28] The narrator explicitly mentions that there was still suffering in Israel during this time, and no one bothered to help these victims of Jeroboam's "peace" (v. 26). Israel's spiritual apostasy had taken its toll; the seed of Abraham was in dire straights and was beyond human help. Indeed, the end for Israel lay just three decades beyond Jeroboam's death.[29]

Nonetheless, we are told that Yahweh had not yet decided to "blot out the name of Israel from under heaven"[30] (v. 27; cf. Deut 9:14; 29:20), which is why he gave Jeroboam success. The image comes from the Egyptian practice of washing an already-written-upon papyrus clean so that it could be used again.[31] God was rewarding Israel *in spite* of her sin in hopes of reclaiming her and bringing her to repentance, a policy he still pursues with us (cf. Rom 2:4; 2 Tim 2:13).

---

26. "What sins do the people commit during these years? Hosea says they are spiritual adulterers (Hos 1:2; 4:1), thieves (4:2), and ungrateful children (11:1–7). In short, there is 'no acknowledgment of God in the land' (Hos 4:1). God desires mercy (Hos 6:6) and monotheism (Hos 13:4) but receives only meaningless sacrifice and idolatry. Likewise, Amos finds oppression of the poor (Amos 2:6), injustice (2:7), and immorality (2:8). The people love wealth more than kindness (4:1–3), ease more than righteous character (6:1–7)," (House, *1, 2 Kings*, 326–27).

27. "Vast areas of productive agricultural land, from the prairies of Bashan (Amos 4:1) to the plantations of Carmel (1:1), produce abundant harvests of grain, wine, and oil (Hos. 7:14). The Transjordan caravan routes are under Israelite control as well as the Jezreel Valley and the Sharon Plain," (Konkel, *1 & 2 Kings*, 531).

28. Wiseman, *1 and 2 Kings*, 264.

29. Leithart details a structure that points to Jeroboam II's reign being the "beginning of the end" in the mind of the narrator, just as the reign of Jeroboam I had been the beginning of Israel's new identity (*1 & 2 Kings*, 238).

30. "This statement must be understood in the context of what the Lord *has* said about judgment upon Israel in the book of Kings[.] Israel will go into exile for its sins (1 Kgs. 14:15–16), but this will not be the end of Israel (1 Kgs. 8:33–51). God's covenant promises are still in force (2 Kgs. 13:23)," (Provan, *1 & 2 Kings*, 240; emphasis his).

31. Menahem Haran, "Book-Scrolls in Israel in Pre-Exilic Times," *JJS* 33 (1982): 168–70.

2 KINGS 15:1-7

From the chronological data, Azariah (aka Uzziah[32]) joined his father as a co-regent at just sixteen years of age when his father was deported to Samaria by Jehoash, helping us understand Azariah's lengthy reign of over a half-century (792–740). In fact, Azariah may have been a vassal of Jeroboam II in the early years of his reign, a yoke that was not thrown off until the death of Azariah's father, Amaziah.[33] The co-regency seems to have lasted for about twenty-five years, making Azariah about forty-one when he assumed sole rule of Judah. That he did not avenge his father's assassination—as Amaziah had avenged *his* father's (14:5)—may implicate Azariah in the plot.[34]

Like his father, Azariah is memorialized as a good king, yet one who did not remove the scourge of idolatry from life in Judah; Amos 2:4–5 indicates that many of the sins of the North plagued the South also. The narrator's comments on Azariah are brief. We are told that Yahweh struck Azariah with leprosy, which forced the king to live in separate quarters[35] (cf. 7:3; Lev 13:11, 46; Num 12:14–15). This made it necessary for Jotham, Azariah's son, to become a co-regent for the final decade of his father's reign. It may seem odd that Naaman's leprosy did not require him to retire from public life, yet Azariah's did. While it might be that Azariah's condition was more severe, Hobbs notes that "it probably has more to do with the social role of the king in society. A monarch whose skin (i.e., outer limits) was thus affected would have been a very inadequate symbol of the Davidic ideology."[36]

For whatever reason, the Chronicler provides much more information about Azariah's reign, which informs us of just how strong a ruler he was:

- To the north, the prosperous reign of Jeroboam II in Israel secured Azariah's northern border.

---

32. "This alternation has been taken as evidence for Azariah's having assumed a throne name when he began his single rule in Judah after the death of Amaziah; or it was the name associated with the king during his leprosy," (Cogan, *II Kings*, 165).

33. Nadav Na'aman, "Azariah of Judah and Jeroboam II of Israel," *VT* 43 (1993): 227–34.

34. Cogan, *II Kings*, 159.

35. Josephus claims these quarters were outside Jerusalem (*Antiquities* 9.227). Auld considers this arrangement to have constituted a kind of living death (*I & II Kings*, 206).

36. Hobbs, *2 Kings*, 194.

- To the south, Azariah kept a firm hand over Edom and expanded Judah's holdings at Elath[37] (14:22; 2 Chr 26:2).

- To the east, we know the Ammonites paid tribute to Azariah (2 Chr 26:8).

- To the west, Azariah subjugated the Philistines, retaking Gath (2 Chr 26:6–7; cf. 2 Kgs 12:17).

Azariah also fortified Jerusalem in the aftermath of Jehoash's assault (14:13; cf. 2 Chr 26:9, 15) and implemented reforms in agriculture and the military[38] (2 Chr 26:10–14).

Despite these highlights, however, the Chronicler also includes the reason for his leprosy. On one occasion, Azariah attempted to offer incense on the Temple altar, something only the priests were allowed to do (Num 16:40). He did so out of an arrogant intoxication over his many military successes. For his transgression, Yahweh struck him with leprosy (2 Chr 26:16–20). Josephus claims Azariah's arrogant act also triggered the famed earthquake spoken of in Amos 1:1 and Zechariah 14:5.[39] Supposedly, the earthquake ripped an opening in the Temple, "and the bright rays of the sun shone through it, and fell upon the king's face, insomuch that the leprosy seized upon him immediately."

Though Azariah was buried in the city of David, his body was not laid to rest in the royal tombs (2 Chr 26:22–23), likely due to the leprosy. In A.D. 1931, an ossuary was discovered on the Mount of Olives with an inscription in Aramaic, dating to the first century A.D. It read, "Hitherto were brought the bones of Uzziah, king of Judah. Do not open."[40] The year of his death was also when Isaiah received his dramatic call to ministry (Isa 6:1–8), meaning "the presumed period of national uncertainty was immediately met by the calling of one of the most famous prophets of Old Testament times."[41]

---

37. Elath was an Edomite port located at the end of the King's Highway used by traders. Lost to Edom by Joram of Judah (8:20–22), Azariah was only able to reclaim the port after his father had defeated the Edomites (14:7).

38. Archaeological discoveries confirm Azariah's improvements to agriculture and defense (H. G. M. Williamson, *1 and 2 Chronicles* [Grand Rapids: Eerdmans, 1982], 336–37).

39. Josephus, *Antiquities* 9.225.

40. E. L. Sukenik, "Funerary Tablet of Uzziah, King of Judah," *PEQ* 63 (1931): 217–21.

41. Barnes, *1–2 Kings*, 301.

2 KINGS 15:8–12

After reigns of twenty-eight, seventeen, sixteen, and forty-one years by his predecessors, Zechariah assumed the throne of Israel (753) for less than a baseball season, a signal of "how completely YHWH removes his blessing as the dynasty ends."[42] In addition to this internal instability, international pressure returned. "After the death of Jeroboam II, Assyrian hegemony started to spread quickly across the entire Near East. The ruling class of Israel was split over their attitude to the Assyrian Empire, and the resulting factions represented political choices: submission or resistance."[43]

Zechariah was as wicked as his predecessors.[44] Consistent with the prophecy that Jehu's dynasty would see only four generations (10:30; cf. Amos 7:9), he was assassinated by Shallum[45] at Ibleam[46] (cf. NIV's "in front of the people"). Josephus adds spice to this royal intrigue by claiming Shallum was a friend of Zechariah.[47]

The Lord may have promised not to blot out Israel, but one gets the impression that the "accumulated wrath" of Yahweh is about to burst forth from heaven upon the house of Jehu.[48] Once Jehu's lineage is wiped out, things get worse as "Israel's political scene becomes increasingly chaotic."[49] And while some may wonder why Zechariah was permitted *just* six months compared to his father's

---

42. Wray Beal, *1 & 2 Kings*, 428. Israel's "own chaos is a sign that God is in the process of destroying her," (Davis, *2 Kings*, 222).

43. Fritz, *1 & 2 Kings*, 330.

44. "Social and moral decay, vividly chronicled in Amos, has its effect in the political upheavals that come with the death of Jeroboam," (Konkel, *1 & 2 Kings*, 549).

45. "If 'son of Jabesh' points to Shallum's place of origin, it would indicate that he was a Transjordanian Gileadite. A later Gileadite plot would take the life of King Pekahiah (v. 25)," (Patterson, "1, 2 Kings," 882). Sweeney considers Shallum's murderous motivation to have been a desire to bring an end to Jehu's dynasty and its alliance with Assyria in favor of one with Aram (*I & II Kings*, 371).

46. East of the Jezreel Valley, Ibleam was located in the territory of Issachar, but inhabited by Manasseh. "There is a certain poetic justice here in that the last of the house of Jehu was killed at Ibleam, near which Jehu had so brutally massacred princes of the royal house of Judah when he usurped the throne of Israel," (Gray, *I & II Kings*, 562).

47. Josephus, *Antiquities* 9.228.

48. Provan, *1 & 2 Kings*, 241.

49. House, *1, 2 Kings*, 329.

four decades, those in awe of God's amazing grace marvel at Zechariah being given *so* much time to repent.

2 KINGS 15:13-22

"Thirty days hath September, Shallum, June, and November..." Wait, that's not right. Nevertheless, Shallum's reign lasted a single moon cycle before Menahem[50] came from Tirzah (the former capital, 1 Kgs 16:8–10) and assassinated the assassin, putting an end to the coup d'état. "So short is [Shallum's] reign that the author even fails to assess his merits or lack of redeeming characteristics."[51]

I n his own revolt against the upstart Shallum, Menahem (752–742) came against the town of Tiphsah, a commercial center located far to the north on the Euphrates[52] (1 Kgs 4:24). Menahem sacked Tiphsah and its neighboring countryside because its citizens refused to capitulate to the new king. The atrocity of ripping open the stomachs of pregnant women is recorded as a way of demonstrating Menahem's cruelty—indeed, the act "is unparalleled for brutality by any Israelite."[53] This war crime was a practice of Israel's neighbors: Aram (8:12), Ammon (Amos 1:13), and Assyria (Hos 13:16). While "it may be that Menahem emulated Assyrian practice in order to demonstrate his power

---

50. Josephus identifies Menahem as a general in Zechariah's army (*Antiquities* 9.229). If so, "he may have been avenging Zachariah's death, as well as furthering his own interest in assuming the throne," (Wood, *Survey*, 328).

51. House, *1, 2 Kings*, 330. Despite the claims of some scholars, Wiseman notes, "There is no reference to Shallum as 'a son of a nobody' in the Assyrian annals," (*1 and 2 Kings*, 269).

52. Wiseman disagrees with this identification, preferring the LXX's *Tappuah*, a town on the Ephraim border according to Joshua 16:8, located fourteen miles from Tirzah (Ibid., 269–70; cf. Jones, *1 and 2 Kings*, 2:523). However, to the argument that it is unlikely Menahem would be fighting so far north on the Euphrates, Hobbs responds that such an idea "is not as far-fetched. This was, after all, the northeastern limit of the expansion under Jeroboam (14:28), and such an expedition by Menahem on behalf of Zechariah, Jeroboam's son, would have been to either regain or strengthen those outer limits. The evidence one way or the other is not completely convincing, but Tiphsah cannot be lightly dismissed," (*2 Kings*, 197; cf. Provan, *Biblical History*, 376, n. 71; Haran, "Rise and Decline," 284–90).

53. Wiseman, *1 and 2 Kings*, 269; cf. Josephus, *Antiquities* 9.231.

and to stifle opposition,"[54] all it really did was illustrate how Israel had become as wicked and vile as the enemies who surrounded her.

The narrator remembers Menahem as just as evil as his predecessors. He did nothing to remove the idolatry begun by Jeroboam I. Presumably as punishment for his wickedness, the Assyrian king Pul (known historically as Tiglath-pileser III,[55] cf. 1 Chr 5:26) came against Israel around 743.[56] Menahem was able to buy him off with a tribute of a thousand talents (thirty-seven tons) of silver,[57] but it was money he had collected by taxing the wealthy in Israel[58] (it seems Menahem was an "Occupy Wall Street" kind of guy). Assyrian annals and a stele inscription both record Menahem's tribute payment.[59] This sum not only got the Assyrian king off his back, but it also enticed Tiglath-pileser to support Menahem's claim to the throne (v. 19),[60] which would have been somewhat tenuous since he had seized it by so unsavory of means.

"The coming of Tiglath-pileser III to the throne (745–727) inaugurated a new stage in the history of Assyria and the ancient Near East as a whole."[61] The first half of the eighth century had seen Assyria plagued by weak kings and internal strife. But with the ascendancy of Tiglath-pileser from the ashes of revolt, Assyria became power hungry, campaigning against her enemies in all four di-

---

54. Jones, *1 and 2 Kings*, 2:524.

55. *Pul* was the name taken by Tiglath-pileser III after he conquered Babylon in 729.

56. The year 743 is given by Thiele (*Mysterious Numbers*, 118–23), but this date is disputed. Other scholars posit 740 and 737 as the year in which Tiglath-pileser came against Israel and received tribute from Menahem (Louis D. Levine, "Menahem and Tiglath-pileser: A New Synchronism," *BASOR* 206 [1972]: 40–42).

57. "Such a sum compares well with other sums extracted from vassals by [Tiglath-pileser III], as is evident from his records," (Hobbs, *2 Kings*, 199; cf. *COS* 2.114E).

58. The individual toll of fifty shekels of silver was at the time the cost of a slave in Assyria (D. J. Wiseman, "The Nimrud Tablets, 1953," *Iraq* 15 [1953]: 135, n. 1). Unger suggests this led to widespread anti-Assyrian sentiment in Israel (Merrill F. Unger, *Israel and the Aramaeans of Damascus* [Grand Rapids: Baker, 1980], 99).

59. *COS* 2.117A–2.117B.

60. *ANET* 283–84.

61. Cogan, *II Kings*, 176.

rections.[62] In two different campaigns (743–738 and 734–732), he and his army entered the region of Syro-Palestine.[63]

Menahem's solicitation to Tiglath-pileser for help, then, was as dangerous as it was foolish. From now on, it would be Assyria—not Aram—that would harass Israel until she was destroyed and deported. Winston Churchill once quipped, "An appeaser is one who feeds a crocodile, hoping it will eat him last." Churchill is famous for being an outspoken critic of England's earlier policy of appeasing Hitler; he knew such actions could end only in sorrow, and the same could be said for Menahem's appeasement of the aggressive Assyrians.

For his part, the prophet Hosea condemned Menahem's alliance with Assyria. "Israel is eaten up; the people are mixed among the other nations and have become useless to me. Israel is like a wild donkey all by itself. They have run to Assyria; They have hired other nations to protect them. Although Israel is mixed among the nations, I will gather them together. They will become weaker and weaker as they suffer under the great king of Assyria" (Hos 8:8–10 NCV). So if you listen carefully to Menahem's appeal for help, you can hear the final, desperate gasps for air from a dying Northern Kingdom.

2 KINGS 15:23-26

Upon Menahem's death,[64] Pekahiah, his son, assumed the throne for two years (742–740). Like those before him, says the narrator, he was wickedly

---

62. "The Assyrian campaigns of the next four decades [beginning with Tiglath-pileser] not only assumed a new intensity but also covered greater distances in more numerous directions than ever before," (William W. Hallo and William Kelly Simpson, *The Ancient Near East: A History*, 2nd ed. [Fort Worth: Harcourt, 1998], 129).

63. "While the biblical narrative has him preoccupied with Israel and Judah, in fact he had no continuing interest in such small states. His policy aims were to have access to the Mediterranean Sea and to establish trading lines with Egypt. It so happened that it was necessary to pass through (and control) territory in the states of Israel and Judah in order to achieve larger policy aims. He is the first in the line of Assyrian kings who will dominate these smaller states in brutal ways for the next century," (Brueggemann, *1 & 2 Kings*, 454).

64. "Only in the instance of Menahem is reference made that he was buried with his ancestors (v. 22). This is a likely consequence of his son Pekahiah's initiative as he takes his father's place on the throne. In the other four summaries, there is no mention of where the rulers are laid to rest. The silence surrounding their burial location, along with the unsettling ways each of them came to their end, conveys the impression of the unrest that now afflicts the whole nation," (Hens-Piazza, *1–2 Kings*, 338).

consistent with Jeroboam I's apostasy. His reign was cut short when Pekahiah's military commander, Pekah, and a detachment of troops assassinated him in Samaria[65]—note that this was the third bloody coup in thirteen years. The identities of Argob and Arieh, who also died, are not without doubt, though it's likely they were Pekahiah's sons.[66] An alternative suggestion is to interpret "with Argob and Arieh" as "near the eagle and the lion," a reference to guardian figures or protective deities in the palace.[67] If this latter interpretation is correct, Pekahiah died under the gaze of the false gods in whom he had put his trust.

2 KINGS 15:27-31

On the surface, the chronology of Pekah's reign (752–732) is confusing. If he began his twenty-year rule in 740, when Pekahiah was assassinated, this would take us to 720, two years beyond the fall of Samaria and leaving no room for Hoshea's time on the throne. It seems Pekah's "reign" (which probably refers to the period of his military power and not just his time on the throne in Samaria) overlapped with that of Menahem and Pekahiah. Thiele proposes that Pekah reigned in Gilead[68] as a rival (cf. v. 25) beginning in 752, around the same time Menahem seized the throne in Samaria[69] (cf. 1 Kgs 16:21–22), a situation that may be reflected in Isaiah 9:19–21. It could be that Rezin, king of Aram, was behind Pekah's rival rule.[70] If this is so, Pekah was likely the rival that worried Menahem, prompting him to ally with Tiglath-pileser as insurance.[71] Whatever

---

65. Josephus, *Antiquities* 9.233–34.

66. Provan, *1 & 2 Kings*, 242. Jones believes these are place names (*1 and 2 Kings*, 2:527). Viviano claims the names are a scribal error ("Argob and Arieh [Persons]," *ABD* 1:376).

67. M. J. Geller, "A New Translation for Kings XV 25," *VT* 26 (1976): 374–77.

68. "This agriculturally rich and strategically vital territory, recovered by Jeroboam II after decades of Aramaean domination (14:25), became the base for a new Israelite elite which fought to seize power in Samaria," (Cogan, *II Kings*, 178).

69. Thiele, *Mysterious Numbers*, 124, 129; cf. H. J. Cook, "Pekah," *VT* 14 (1964): 121–35. Less likely is the fact that Pekah simply considered Menahem and Pekahiah to be illegitimate heirs of Jeroboam II and Zechariah and factored the reigns of Menahem and Pekahiah as his own (Nadav Na'aman, "Historical and Chronological Notes on the Kingdoms of Israel and Judah in the Eighth Century B.C.," *VT* 36 [1986]: 74–82).

70. B. Oded, "The Historical Background of the Syro-Ephraimite War Reconsidered," *CBQ* 34 (1972): 162.

71. Seale and Harrison, "Pekah," *ISBE* 3:735.

the case, sometime around 740, Pekah assassinated Pekahiah and assumed total possession of Israel's crown.

Pekah supported the apostasy of Jeroboam I.[72] We can also assume that he was anti-Assyrian in his policies[73] since it was in his day (733) that Tiglath-pileser III seized several Israelite towns, including "Ijon, Abel-beth-maacah, Janoah, Kedesh, Hazor, Gilead, and Galilee" (v. 29; cf. 1 Kgs 15:20), as well as the territory of Naphtali.[74] In the year prior, 734, the Assyrian king captured the Philistine city of Gaza in order to neutralize any hope of assistance from Egypt. In 732, the year after his march through Galilee, Tiglath-pileser III besieged Damascus for forty-five days, inflicting heavy casualties, executing Rezin, king of Damascus, and ultimately taking the city.[75]

Having annexed these towns in northern Israel, Tiglath-pileser claims to have taken 13,520 captives[76] and deported them far, far away to Assyria. Deportation was the punishment of choice for Assyria; "by this means Assyrian kings could not only increase their labor force for building projects or the development of uncultivated land in order to increase the food supply, but also reduce the possibility of further opposition among the subjugated peoples."[77] In

---

72. "This is the last of some 15 times where we have found this Deuteronomistic refrain used against a northern king," (Barnes, *1–2 Kings*, 307).

73. "Pekahiah's appointment of Pekah to be a chief officer may have been an attempt to placate a rival party. The usurpation and troubled times that followed may suggest that there was an anti-Assyrian party that remained submerged during the rule of the fiery Menahem," (Patterson "1, 2 Kings," 885). "Pekah was a fiery anti-Assyrian; his predecessors' policy of truckling to Assyria was to him and his Gileadite patriots a betrayal of Israel's national interests, a threat to its independence, and thus a policy to be reversed at all costs. This he attempted to do by creating an anti-Assyrian confederacy, of which he and Rezin king of Damascus were the principal leaders," (Seale and Harrison, "Pekah," *ISBE* 3:735).

74. Bob Becking, *The Fall of Samaria: An Historical and Archaeological Study* (Leiden: Brill, 1992), 15–19.

75. K. Lawson Younger, Jr., "The Deportations of the Israelites," *JBL* 117 (1998): 201–14.

76. *COS* 2.117C.

77. Provan, "2 Kings," 172. He adds, "Tiglath-pileser III made deportation of this kind a major feature of his imperial policy, and it was imitated often by subsequent rulers. It is estimated that between a quarter and a half million people were deported during the reigns of Assyrian kings. With only occasional exceptions, they were deported to environments similar to those from which they originated—some to cities, others to underpopulated rural areas, and still others to regions of the empire depopulated by an earlier deportation after a rebellion. One

addition to the captured peoples and their cities, Hazor and Megiddo were razed to the ground.[78]

This invasion by the Assyrians was a result of Ahaz's appeal to Tiglath-pileser for a diversion when Pekah and Rezin besieged Jerusalem (16:5–9), an event we'll examine in short order. Presumably out of discontent for allowing a foreign power to run roughshod over the Northern Kingdom, Hoshea rose up and assassinated Pekah. In his memoirs, Tiglath-pileser III notes that the people of Israel "overthrew their king Pekah and I placed Hoshea as king over them."[79]

T o say that things are rapidly declining in Israel would be an understatement. Whereas Jehu's coup had been divinely ordained, those of Shallum, Menahem, and Pekah were not. Theologically and politically, the Northern Kingdom was in chaos at this point. "Murderous and volcanic, they incinerate their rulers. Their kings fall one by one, and no one pays any attention to me" (Hos 7:7 Msg; cf. 13:10–11). At times in 2 Kings 15, it seems Israel had more assassins than she did kings.[80]

To this political instability, add war crimes and heavy taxes, and one realizes the end cannot be far off. "In effect, the end of God's promise to Jehu (v. 12) lifted Israel's stay of execution. Besides her apostasy, the series of coups showed her flagrant disregard for God's will in choosing kings (cf. Hos. 8:4). On both accounts she was ripe for judgment."[81]

Sin has a compounding effect, which can hasten the divine wrath; Paul illustrates as much in Romans 1:18–32. As one of my college professors put it, "The lost become more lost." And neither you nor I are immune from the same fate. When we become as far gone as Israel was at the close of 2 Kings 15, only extraordinary faithfulness and wisdom on our part (plus extraordinary grace on God's) can get us out of such a mess. Seldom do those three things converge, and

major consequence was that Assyrian cities in particular became cosmopolitan and multilingual," (Ibid., cf. H. W. F. Saggs, *The Might That Was Assyria* [London: Sidgwick, 1984], 124–30).

78. Amid the ruins of the destruction of Hazor, there was found a wine jar with the words "belonging to Pekah," (Y. Yadin, "Hazor," in *Archaeology and Old Testament Study*, ed. D. Winton Thomas [Oxford: Clarendon, 1967], 257).

79. *ANET* 284; *COS* 2.117C.

80. Davis, *2 Kings*, 223.

81. Hubbard, *First and Second Kings*, 201.

Kings will soon prove it can be too little, too late. Better, I suppose, never to find ourselves in so hopeless a predicament in the first place.

2 KINGS 15:32–38

Jotham's[82] sixteen-year reign (750–732) began when he was a quarter-century old. Chronologically, he was a co-regent with Azariah (Uzziah) for about eight to ten years, due to his father's leprosy. Like his father, he was a good king. But also like too many before him, he failed to root out idolatry and unauthorized worship in Judah, though the Chronicler remembers him as a mighty man who "ordered his ways before the LORD his God" (2 Chr 27:6). In any event, the narrator of Kings denies him a comparison with David. Judah prospered during his reign, but this led to a spiritual apathy that ripened into apostasy during the reign of Jotham's son, Ahaz.

Jotham's building programs are only briefly noted by our narrator (v. 35), but we are given more information by the Chronicler (2 Chr 27:1–9). In addition to a gate in Yahweh's house (Jer 20:2; Ezek 9:2), one that separated the palace from the Temple[83] (cf. 2 Chr 27:2), Jotham repaired some of Jerusalem's walls (presumably the portions damaged by Jehoash). He also established new towns in Judah and erected additional defenses,[84] and was successful in subduing the Ammonites and extracting tribute from them for three years (2 Chr 27:5). This no doubt pleased the Tobiads, a powerful Judean family in Transjordan that would flex its political muscles during the reign of Ahaz.[85]

Jotham's years as sole ruler seem to have come to an end in 735, but his son's reign did not "begin" until 732, suggesting that these years saw a co-regen-

---

82. A signet ring was discovered at Ezion-geber bearing the name *Jotham*, and though there is no other identification (e.g., "the king"), this actually makes it more likely this is the same Jotham who ruled Judah (Kuntz, "Jotham [Person]," *ABD* 3:1021).

83. "It is intriguing that Jotham should give attention to the boundary marker between temple and palace when it is precisely the transgression of that boundary for which 2 Chronicles 26:16–21 blames his father," (Provan, "2 Kings," 173).

84. One such location might be Ziklag, which shows signs of being fortified during this period (Eliezer Oren, "Ziklag—A Biblical City On The Edge Of The Negev," *BA* 45 [1982]: 155–66). "It is clear from that evidence that his construction projects added considerably to the defenses of the country. Such a move was undoubtedly necessary in the very disturbed times which characterized his reign," (Hobbs, *2 Kings*, 204).

85. B. Mazar, "The Tobiads," *IEJ* 7 (1957): 229–38.

cy in Judah (cf. "the twentieth year of Jotham," v. 30). While Jotham's international diplomacy was anti-Assyrian, pro-Assyrian factions in Jerusalem apparently succeeded in putting Ahaz in power, pushing Jotham into retirement until his death in 732.[86]

It was during the waning days of Jotham's reign, the narrator says, that Judah began to be harassed by the kings of Israel and Aram (v. 37). Though the narrator of Kings is sparse with details about this conflict, especially its cause, this has not stopped scholars from positing their conjectures. For a long time, the scholarly consensus[87] has been that Israel and Aram were attempting to force Judah into an anti-Assyrian coalition. When Judah would not join, Rezin and Pekah sought to do so by force, with plans to place "the son of Tabeel" on the throne in Jerusalem (Isa 7:6). But Oded dissents from the prevailing opinion: "We do not know of a single clear-cut, indisputable example of a war fought against a state in Syria or Palestine because it refused to join an anti-Assyrian alliance; whereas there is no lack of opposite examples."[88] Oded goes on to suggest convincingly that the Syro-Ephraimite War had more to do with regaining sovereignty over Transjordan.[89] Regardless of the political reasons for the war, however, the Lord intended it to be a test for Jotham's son, Ahaz.

2 KINGS 16

Not since the illicit reign of Queen Athaliah had Jerusalem seen a ruler as wicked as Ahaz, Jotham's son. Like his father, Ahaz reigned just sixteen years (732–715). Rather than following David's righteous path, as his predecessors had done, Ahaz was as wicked as were the kings in the North (a statement made only of Ahaz and Joram, son of Jehoshaphat). Notably, Ahaz is the first Judean king since Solomon to worship at the high places[90] (Jer 7:31; 19:5; 32:35). And

---

86. Schultz, "Jotham (Person)," *ISBE* 2:1140.

87. W. F. Albright, "The Son of Tabeel (Isaiah 7:6)," *BASOR* 140 (1955): 34–35.

88. Oded, "Historical Background," 154.

89. Ibid., 157; cf. Roger Tomes, "The Reason for the Syro-Ephraimite War," *JSOT* 59 (1993): 55–71.

90. The phrase "under every green tree" (v. 4) is a euphemism for the sexual rites that often took place upon the high places (Susan Ackerman, *Under Every Green Tree: Popular Religion in Sixth-Century Judah* [Atlanta: Scholars, 1992], 152–63). "Normally the terminology of verse 4 describes what the people still did under a generally 'righteous' king (12:3; 14:4; 15:4, 35), but

as if his idolatry wasn't enough, he is particularly remembered for engaging in the deplorable practice of child sacrifice (v. 3; 2 Chr 28:3; cf. Lev 18:21; Deut 18:9–10; Ezek 16:20–21; 20:26–31). This rite, one done in worship to the god Molech, was often conducted in the Valley of Hinnom[91] in a structure known as Topheth[92] (Isa 30:33; Jer 7:31).

Unlike past notes of unfaithfulness, absent here is any mention of David.

> It has been some time, in fact, since we have heard this prom-
> ise cited in relation to Judah. This is disconcerting. The last
> time it was absent from the account of a wicked king's reign
> (Ahaziah's) we saw the Davidic house brought to the brink of
> extinction. What are we to expect now, when a Judean once
> more follows the detestable ways of the nations and when we
> are reminded, not of the LORD's promise to David, but of his
> "driving out" of the nations before the Israelites because of
> their sins? Is the Davidic promise no longer in force? Is Judah
> is [sic] to be "driven out" of the land for its sins?[93]

There are only two anecdotes from Ahaz's reign that the narrator cared to preserve in his account, and both highlight the king's covenant unfaithfulness. The first is his foolish alliance with Assyria, and the second is his unauthorized Temple renovations.

As punishment for Ahaz's evil, the kings of Aram (Rezin) and Israel (Pekah) attacked Jerusalem (cf. Isa 7:1), but could not conquer the city. Their plan was to depose Ahaz and install "the son of Tabeel" as a puppet ruler (Isa 7:6) in their anti-Assyrian alliance.[94] This conflict is known to modern historians as

---

here the verbs are singular—Ahaz himself engages in this worship," (Davis, *2 Kings*, 228).

91. "The valley's reputation for extreme wickedness gave rise to the employment of its name as a term for the eschatological place of punishment of the wicked (1 En. 27:1ff.; 54:1ff.; 56:3–4; 90:26), a designation confirmed by Christ himself (Mt 5:22, 29–30; 10:28; 18:9; 23:15, 33; 25:41)," (Patterson, "1, 2 Kings," 891).

92. John Day, *Molech: A God of Human Sacrifice in the Old Testament* (Cambridge: Cambridge Univ. Press, 1989), 15–28.

93. Provan, *1 & 2 Kings*, 245.

94. Mazar argues that this "son of Tabeel" was a member of the powerful Tobiad family that resided in Transjordan ("The Tobiads," 236–37). In addition to Israel and Aram, Edom, Philistia, and Tyre were also part of the alliance (2 Chr 28:17–18).

the Syro-Ephraimite War.[95] Though their main objective was not accomplished, Rezin and Pekah succeeded in inflicting tremendous damage on Judah. Rezin reclaimed the town of Elath for Edom (v. 6; cf. 14:22), and Pekah slaughtered 120,000 of Judah's troops, including Ahaz's son, Maaseiah; the king's commander of the palace, Azrikam; and the king's second-in-command, Elkanah. They also took captive an additional 200,000 women and children (2 Chr 28:6–8; cf. Isa 9:19–21). The Edomites and Philistines also joined in the fun, making raids and annexing territory from Judah[96] (2 Chr 28:17–18).

Seeking relief from the hostility of his northern neighbors, Ahaz made the very foolish decision to appeal farther north for help from Assyria (cf. Isa 7:10–16; Exod 23:22). He began his appeal with *servant* to portray himself in a subservient, dependent light, while *son* was meant to conjure fatherly feelings in Tiglath-pileser[97] (v. 7). Such an intervention would have profound political and religious consequences for many years. "Despite ample evidence of such action in the past (Exod. 15:2–12; Deut. 2:31–37; 3:1-3; 7:1–2; Judg. 6:1–16; 1 Kgs 20, 22), Ahaz disregards this aspect of the covenant relationship and forges an alliance. Thus he rejects the God of the covenant, and alienates himself and his people from that God."[98]

Ahaz's appeal for Assyrian help was granted, and I'm sure his monetary gift[99] (v. 8) helped Tiglath-pileser make up his mind. The Assyrian war machine ramped up against Aram and Israel—Damascus was captured, Rezin was killed (v. 9), Israel was invaded, and Pekah was assassinated (15:29–30).

---

95. Cazelles, "Syro-Ephraimite War," *ABD* 6:282–85; Norman K. Gottwald, *All the Kingdoms of the Earth: Israelite Prophecy and International Relations in the Ancient Near East* (New York: Harper, 1964), 148–62.

96. "Already in 2 Kings it has been seen that the loss of land is a theme of judgment (see on 1:1; 3:4–5; 10:32–33; 12:17–18; 13:3–4)," (Hobbs, *2 Kings*, 211).

97. Cogan, *II Kings*, 187.

98. Wray Beal, *1 & 2 Kings*, 442. Ahaz "acts not as a covenant believer but as a shrewd politician," (Davis, *2 Kings*, 229). Davis then offers up a satirical rewrite of the classic hymn "My Jesus, I Love Thee" that Ahaz might have sung: "My Tig, I bribe thee, you know I'm your man; for thee Yahweh's promises I view as mere sand. You mighty oppressor, my savior art thou, if ever I needed you, dear Tiglath, 'tis now," (Ibid., 230).

99. "No doubt, this action [bribing Tiglath-pileser] is to be interpreted as both a part of Ahaz's crime and a part of his punishment," (E. Theodore Mullen, Jr., "Crime and Punishment: The Sins of the King and the Despoliation of the Treasuries," *CBQ* 54 [1992]: 242).

Later, Ahaz was summoned to Damascus[100] for some face time with the
Assyrian emperor (according to Tiglath-pileser's memoirs, this was a meeting
with all his new vassals). While on this business trip, Ahaz began to admire a
particular altar in Damascus (possibly one in the temple of Rimmon, 5:18) and
provided Uriah the priest with blueprints to build one exactly like it in Jerusalem. The word translated "pattern" is conspicuous in Old Testament passages
related to the Tabernacle and Temple (Exod 25:9, 40; 1 Chr 28:11–12; 18–19),
suggesting Ahaz erroneously believed himself qualified to tinker with the divine
blueprint.[101] Upon his return to the capital, the king was so delighted with the
replica that he replaced the traditional bronze altar[102] in the Temple with this
idolatrous incarnation (cf. 2 Chr 28:22–23).

Not content with rearranging the furniture and stripping the Temple to pay
tribute (vv. 17–18), Ahaz unilaterally altered Temple practices (v. 15). "Never
before has a Judean king taken it upon himself to redesign the Solomonic temple
in such a way. The days of Solomon's glory seem farther and farther behind us."[103]
For all intents and purposes, Ahaz scorned the Davidic heritage of his fathers
and wanted nothing more than to be thoroughly Assyrian.[104] He is the Southern
Kingdom's version of Jeroboam I (1 Kgs 12:26–33).[105]

Scholars are divided as to whether Ahaz should be censured for removing
and replacing Solomon's altar. They note that neither Hezekiah nor Josiah removed it in their reforms. Rather, it is Ahaz's faith in foreign kingdoms and not

---

100. Nelson believes the narrator was less interested in Ahaz's foreign policy and more
so in his religious activities, using the former to set up a discussion of the latter (*First and Second
Kings*, 225).

101. "The altar is specified in Exod. 27 and, although the word *tabnit* [Hebrew for 'pattern'] is not used, YHWH clearly sets a standard governing the altar's construction," (Wray Beal,
1 & 2 Kings, 442). In other words, messing with the Temple altar was above Ahab's pay grade.

102. It is thought that Ahaz repurposed this bronze altar for use in the idolatrous practice
of divination (cf. 2 Sam 2:1; 1 Kgs 22:6–17; 2 Kgs 19:1–7; 22:11–20) (J. W. McKay, *Religion in
Judah under the Assyrians, 732–609 BC* [Naperville, IL: Allenson, 1973], 8).

103. Provan, *1 & 2 Kings*, 246. Robinson is more sympathetic: "Maybe Ahaz discovered
at Damascus that new liturgical fashions had come into vogue there and he was simply concerned that his own temple should not appear to be old-fashioned," (*Second Book*, 150).

104. Wray Beal, *1 & 2 Kings*, 443.

105. Davis notes that there are several parallels in this text between Ahaz and Jeroboam
(*2 Kings*, 232–33).

his fathers' God for which he is to be condemned, so they argue. "While Ahaz continues Yahwistic worship at the temple, such worship is conducted in subservience to a foreign king and god. This is the evil of Ahaz's altar."[106]

n August 1953, U.S. and British intelligence deposed the quasi-democratically elected Iranian Prime Minister Mohammed Mossadegh through a coup d'état code-named *Operation Ajax*, preferring instead a dictatorship headed by Mohammad Reza Pahlavi. In so doing, the U.S. unwittingly began a half-century of hostile relations with one of the Middle East's most powerful nations,[107] and the consequences have simply compounded upon themselves: the 444-day Iran hostage situation in 1979–81; the Iran-Iraq War of the 1980s, during which the U.S. gave aid to the Iraqis, led by a charismatic leader named Saddam Hussein[108] (aid which led to two Persian Gulf wars and the rise of ISIS); today's concern over Iran's nuclear program—let me know when you get the picture.[109]

Ahaz was not the first king of Judah, nor would he be the last, to seek foreign aid from an enemy of God's people; even his righteous son, Hezekiah, would be condemned for a too-cozy alliance with Babylon (20:17–18). Indeed, the prophets are full of examples where God wrung his hands in frustration as his people sought alliances to bail themselves out of trouble instead of trusting in their Sovereign Lord to guard, guide, and protect.

---

106. Wray Beal, *1 & 2 Kings*, 439. But later, she admits, "Tellingly, however, that new altar is never spoken of as 'before YHWH'. To move the altar is grave business and this gravity is reflected in an unusual word order that places the noun ('bronze altar') before the verb ('he moved'; v.14)," (Ibid., 440). She also invokes the narrative of Joshua 22, noting that it "reveals assumptions that no other altar of burnt offering is to be made lest it be used for false worship that supplants the tabernacle altar," (Ibid., 442).

107. David Talbot, *The Devil's Chessboard: Allen Dulles, the CIA, and the Rise of America's Secret Government* (New York: Harper, 2015), 227–43.

108. Alan Friedman, *Spider's Web: The Secret History of How the White House Illegally Armed Iraq* (New York: Bantam, 1993).

109. In March 2000, then-Secretary of State Madeleine Albright issued a semi-apology for America's involvement in the 1953 coup, saying, "The coup was clearly a setback for Iran's political development. And it is easy to see now why many Iranians continue to resent this intervention by America in their internal affairs," (Malcolm Byrne, "Introduction," in *Mohammad Mosaddeq and the 1953 Coup in Iran*, eds. Mark J. Gasiorowski and Malcolm Byrne [Syracuse, NY: Syracuse Univ. Press, 2004], xiii).

> When Israel and Judah saw how sick they were, Israel turned
> to Assyria—to the great king there—but he could neither help
> nor cure them.
>
> Hos 5:13 NLT

> The people of Israel have become like silly, witless doves, first
> calling to Egypt, then flying to Assyria for help.
>
> Hos 7:11 NLT

> What have you gained by your alliances with Egypt and your
> covenants with Assyria? What good to you are the streams of
> the Nile or the waters of the Euphrates River?
>
> Jer 2:18 NLT

Israel's and Judah's propensity to bribe "allies" to bail them out of trouble provides a cautionary tale to God's people today to be cautious about the alliances we enter into for our own protection. Such partnerships are often justified using human reasoning versus holy discernment. How many historical examples must be marshaled to teach us that trust in human government is misplaced? Though there should never be a separation between God and government or biblical principles and civic administration, there should forever remain a separation between church and state, for history has proven that whenever the church and the state have been bedfellows, it has always proven terrific for the state and apostasy for the church.

In recent memory, the American church's seemingly unconditional allegiance to the Republican party has made for some awkward alliances, including the backing of a Mormon presidential candidate in 2012 and a self-confessed and unapologetic adulterer in 2016, the latter being on record as bragging that he had never found it necessary to ask God for forgiveness. Such individuals, Scripture says, stand unequivocally under God's condemnation and curse, and the godly shouldn't be caught anywhere near their platform.

The mistakes of U.S. foreign policy in Iran (and elsewhere!) over the last half-century continues to bear ugly, rotten fruit. An argument can be made that, out of economic greed (one primarily related to oil), the U.S. betrayed its democratic values in sponsoring the 1953 Iranian coup.

In the spiritual realm, misplaced trust and unholy alliances will produce ugly, rancid fruit for the godly. Paul once warned, "Don't become partners with those who reject God. How can you make a partnership out of right and wrong? That's not partnership; that's war. Is light best friends with dark? Does Christ go strolling with the Devil? Do trust and mistrust hold hands?" (2 Cor 6:14–15 Msg). Our trust should be in the God of Israel alone, the Creator of the universe, the Father of our Lord and Savior Jesus Christ, and with him alone do we partner for the purposes of his universal glorification and our eternal good. Invested in anyone or anything else, we risk the inevitable betrayal of our most cherished values.

B oth in his engagement in child sacrifice, as well as his appeal for Assyrian military aid, we get a glimpse at arguably the greatest flaw in Ahaz's character. Simply put, rather than holding to the traditional values of his people, the king was *too* open to foreign influence in every arena of his life.

When he notes that Ahaz sent a "present" to the king of Assyria (v. 8), the narrator's scorn is scarcely disguised. The word elsewhere in the Old Testament means "bribe," something that was expressly forbidden in ancient Israel (Exod 23:8; Deut 10:17; 16:19; 27:25; cf. 1 Sam 8:3; Isa 5:23; Ezek 22:12). In Proverbs, this word is considered "a corrupt act, a perversion of justice" (Prov 17:23; cf. Ps 15:5).[110] At the same time, Isaiah mocked Tiglath-pileser as a hired razor (Isa 7:20) and criticized Ahaz for his lack of faith. For what it's worth, Tiglath-pileser reported this gift to the IRS as tribute, rather than payment for services rendered,[111] an acknowledgment that he saw this as Judah surrendering her sovereignty to him.

Once upon a time, it was argued that Ahaz's subservience to Assyria obligated him to build the aforementioned altar in Jerusalem (e.g., "I didn't want to do it; I was just following orders"). But recent research has exposed the fact that Assyria did not force its religion on her vassal states.[112] What is more, 2 Chronicles 28:23 indicates Ahaz built this altar in order to honor the gods of Aram, not Assyria.[113] Even if the new altar was not borne out of a desire to impress

---

110. Hayim Tadmor and Mordechai Cogan, "Ahaz and Tiglath-Pileser in the Book of Kings: Historiographic Considerations," *Bib* 60 (1979): 491–508. They cite examples of Sargon II and Sennacherib similarly accusing the Babylonians of bribery in order to foment insurrection.

111. Oded, "Historical Background," 165.

112. Morton Cogan, *Imperialism and Religion: Assyria, Judah and Israel in the Eighth and Seventh Centuries B.C.E.* (Missoula, MT: Scholars, 1974); McKay, *Religion in Judah.*

113. Cogan, *Imperialism*, 72–77; McKay, *Religion in Judah*, 6–10; Menahem Haran, *Tem-*

superiors, Ahaz clearly cared too much about contemporary developments in religion and too little about acting in Judah's long-term interests, to say nothing of serving Yahweh faithfully.

Thus, I find House's eulogy of Ahaz to be spot-on: "He leaves a legacy of appeasement and syncretism unmatched to this time. Assyria can count on him for money, loyalty, and zealous acceptance of their gods. Judah's king seems genuinely pleased to serve a powerful master who can deliver him from regional foes. No doubt he feels safe, but the historian duly notes the ways in which he has exceeded Jeroboam's wickedness."[114]

Ahaz's legacy in Scripture is also similar to Ahab's. He made covenants with the wrong people, and this, in part, led to his unprecedented wickedness. If Ahaz had put his faith solely in the Lord, he would have discovered the Divine Warrior willing and able to deliver him from all enemies, foreign and domestic. But as it is, he allied himself with one bully to save himself from another, jumping from the frying pan into the fire (Isa 7:1–8:10). "He is an accommodator and compromiser; we might term him a religious pragmatist. Such pragmatism will never evoke hard, courageous acts or policies that rely upon a single, overriding commitment."[115] Doubt and rebellion versus trust and obedience always cost us more in the final analysis.

2 KINGS 17

The final king of Israel, Hoshea, occupied the throne for nine years (732–723). Bizarrely, we are told that he was evil, "yet not as the kings of Israel who were before him" (v. 2). It is a strange and bitter irony that arguably the most righteous king of the Northern Kingdom (which, granted, isn't saying much) was also the last. The Jewish rabbis claimed Hoshea allowed citizens of Israel to worship in Jerusalem[116] (cf. Jehoram's reforms, 3:2), something Jeroboam's calves had been designed to prevent. But this appears to have been too little, too late.

---

ples and Temple-Service in Ancient Israel (Oxford: Clarendon, 1978), 135–36, n. 6.

    114. House, *1, 2 Kings*, 338.

    115. Brueggemann, *1 & 2 Kings*, 467. He adds, "Ahaz has traded sovereigns and has done so in a moment of anxiety that, from a Yahwist perspective, is insane and suicidal," (Ibid., 468).

    116. Alexander Rofé, *The Prophetical Stories* (Jerusalem, Magnes Press, 1988), 98, n. 50.

The new Assyrian monarch, Shalmaneser (c. 727–722), threatened Israel[117] again and reaffirmed Hoshea as his vassal[118] in 727. This was a nice arrangement until Israel's king appealed to Pharaoh So—likely to be identified with Osorkon IV[119] (c. 730–715)—for relief in 725. Hosea the prophet criticized this move (5:13; 7:8–16; 8:9), "since it is opposed to the ideology of Holy War which demanded trust in Yahweh as the norm and trust in numbers or allies as a sign of unfaithfulness."[120] Because So/Osorkon was weak militarily, Egypt was of no help to Israel.

The funny thing is that kings usually don't take too kindly to disloyalty, and even less kindly to not getting the money they think they're owed. So Shalmaneser punitively hauled Hoshea off to prison, decimated the region around Samaria,[121] and besieged the capital for two years.[122] Shalmaneser actually died soon after the city's fall, so his brother and successor, Sargon II (c. 722–705), finished the job.[123] Ten of Israel's tribes were exiled to the upper Tigris/Euphra-

---

117. By this point, most of the Northern Kingdom had been absorbed by Assyria so that "Israel" really amounted to the hill country of Ephraim and the city of Samaria.

118. "Presumably Hoshea functioned as a puppet ruler for the Assyrians, in a manner similar to Gedaliah in the south after the deportation of Judah," (Hobbs, *2 Kings*, 203).

119. Kitchen, *Third Intermediate Period*, 372–75. Alternatively, Green prefers to identify So with Piankhy (Alberto R. W. Green, "The Identity of King So of Egypt—An Alternative Interpretation," *JNES* 52 [1993]: 99–108), and Christensen claims he is Tefnakht I (Duane L. Christensen, "The Identity of 'King So' in Egypt [2 Kings XVII 4]," *VT* 39 [1989]: 140–53; cf. John Day, "The Problem of 'So, King of Egypt' in 2 Kings XVII 4," *VT* 42 [1992]: 289–301). Others believe "So" to be a city versus a person (Hans Goedicke, "The End of 'So, King of Egypt,'" *BASOR* 171 [1963]: 64–66).

120. Hobbs, *2 Kings*, 229.

121. "The strategy of the Assyrian invasion was to paralyze the country, then to circumscribe the capital city after its military and economic support had been taken away. The same strategy is seen in the later invasions of Judah's Shephelah by both Sennacherib and Nebuchadrezzar," (Ibid., 230).

122. "The 'three years' indicated (17:5; 18:10) means all of one year and some part of both the preceding and following. This means that the siege lasted a minimum of fourteen months," (Wood, *Survey*, 333, n. 93).

123. Both Kings and the Babylonian Chronicle (*COS* 1.137) name Shalmaneser as the conquering king, but Sargon claims no less than eight times in his annals to have conquered Samaria (*COS* 2.118E; K. Lawson Younger, "The Fall of Samaria in Light of Recent Research," *CBQ* 61 [1999]: 461–82). It's possible that Sargon merely laid claim to some of Shalmaneser's

tes valley, never to return. In Assyrian annals, Sargon claims he deported 27,290 captives,[124] a number not including women and children. As we will later learn, other refugees escaped to Judah, seeking sanctuary in Jerusalem.

In yet another bitter irony, the meaning of Hoshea's name is "salvation." It is actually an alternative moniker for the name *Joshua* (cf. Num 13:8, 16). Whereas one Joshua oversaw Israel's entrance and conquest of the Promised Land, another watches helplessly as the same Israel exits the land in shame and is scattered to the four winds.[125] Samaria had been besieged twice before (6:24; 1 Kgs 20:1), but unlike the previous occasions, no salvation from Yahweh would be forthcoming.

t is here that the narrator pauses his story and offers extended commentary on Israel's collapse,[126] something that is common throughout Joshua–Kings (cf. Josh 1; 23; Judg 2:10–23; 1 Sam 12:6–25; 2 Sam 7; 1 Kgs 8:22–53). He begins by echoing the Lord's deliverance of Israel out of Egypt, the event that had triggered the covenant between Yahweh and his people. But instead of being faithful to the covenant, Israel had done the very thing the Lord had warned about in Leviticus–Judges: they had adapted the religious practices of their predecessors and neighbors. Emphasis[127] here is placed on:

- *Worship at the high places.* The mention of two extremes, "from watchtower to fortified city" (v. 9), emphasizes that cities and towns, large and small, eventually housed shrines to idolatry.

- *Ignoring the warnings of the prophets.* Since the death of Elisha, few prophet have been known in the Northern Kingdom, though Amos and Hosea certainly ministered during its latter days (and Jonah, too, is a possibility). The narrator notes that despite these prophets, the people were "stubborn" (v. 14), a term

---

accomplishments for political purposes (Provan, "2 Kings," 176).

124. *ANET* 284; *COS* 2.118E.

125. Auld, *I & II Kings*, 211.

126. "A network of evaluative nerves from all over the Book of Kings gathers into a central ganglion at this point," (Nelson, *First and Second Kings*, 228).

127. "This event [i.e., Israel's exile] has been anticipated in earlier narratives, and here the use of repeated words and phrases pounds the point home," (Fretheim, *First and Second Kings*, 192).

that actually refers to the back of the skull, which is turned towards a person in rejection and disrespect (cf. 2 Sam 22:41; Jer
18:17). The same concept, often presented as *stiff-necked*, occurs
prominently in Exodus (32:9; 33:3, 5; 34:9) and Deuteronomy
(9:6, 13; 10:16; 31:27).

- **Disobedience of the Law of Moses.** In addition to the worship of
idols, there is also mention here of astral worship (v. 16; cf. Deut
4:19; 17:3), divination, and sorcery[128] (v. 17; cf. Deut 18:10).
Archaeology has confirmed the practice of worshiping the heavens in Israel during this period in Israel.[129]

Prominent at the end of the section is mention of Jeroboam, the Northern Kingdom's first king. He is faulted with driving "Israel from following the
LORD" (v. 21) by introducing the idolatrous golden calves at Dan and Bethel.
And as long as there was a Northern Kingdom, the scourge of idolatry was embraced whole-heartedly. Two hundred years prior, Yahweh had sworn to punish
Israel if she did not turn from idols and repent; they never did this, "So Israel was
exiled from their own land to Assyria until this day" (v. 23). Thus, the destruction of Samaria shouldn't surprise us; it is "dramatic only in the sense that it is
Israel's final scene. God's grace alone has delayed the fall this long."[130]

The rest of 2 Kings 17 serves as an epilogue to the Northern Kingdom.
With those tribes exiled far away, the land was repopulated with peoples[131] from:

- **Babylon** was the famed city on the Euphrates in what is now

---

128. "Whereas to the modern ear such terms often conjure up the 'spooky' and the ab-
normal, the OT advises avoidance of them because of their inherent tendency toward apostasy.
[...] The OT criticism against such activity is that its center of focus is the manipulation of forces
beyond the human by the human. The OT's alternative is trust in the God of creation," (Hobbs,
2 Kings, 235).

129. Provan, "2 Kings," 180.

130. House, *1, 2 Kings*, 340.

131. "The five nationalities noted in 17:24 correspond with Mesopotamian locations
conquered by Sargon II in the latter part of the eighth century," (Konkel, *1 & 2 Kings*, 578).

southern Iraq. Deportees from Babylon likely were taken when Sargon defeated the Babylonian ruler Merodach-baladan in 710. In 689, Sennacherib destroyed the city and deported some of its residents.[132]

- *Cuthah* was located twenty miles northeast of Babylon and later became one of the most important cities of the Babylonian Empire. The city was the center of worship of Nergal (v. 30), chief deity of the Mesopotamian underworld (similar to the god Hades in Greek mythology). It is thought that Cuthah joined Babylon, led by Merodach-baladan in their revolt against Assyria (20:12–19).[133]

- *Avva* was probably an Elamite city, though others place it between Aleppo and Antioch.[134]

- *Hamath,* located on the Orontes River, was sacked by the Assyrians in 720.[135]

- *Sepharvaim* was a place of uncertain location.[136]

It's unlikely that these peoples came to the region of Samaria all at once, but rather over the course of time. Because these new residents did not know Yahweh, nor fear him, the narrator says, the Lord gave them over to wild animals[137] (cf. Lev 26:21–22; Deut 32:24; 1 Kgs 13:24; 20:36)—"a sign that He still owned

---

132. Marc Van De Mieroop, *A History of the Ancient Near East, ca. 3000–323 BC*, 2nd ed. (Malden, MA: Blackwell, 2007), 255. Scripture also alludes to deportations from Babylon to Samaria by Esarhaddon and Ashurbanipal (Ezra 4:2, 9–10).

133. Meier, "Cuth (Place)," *ABD* 1:1221.

134. Lewis, "Ivvah," *ISBE* 2:943.

135. Vos, "Hamath," *ISBE* 2:65; *ANET* 284.

136. After listing and dismissing four possibilities, Bush concludes, "In the present state of our knowledge the identity and location of Sepharvaim remain unknown," ("Sepharvaim," *ISBE* 4:399).

137. In latter times, Jews would sneeringly refer to Samaritans as "proselytes of the lions," (Wiseman, *1 and 2 Kings*, 286).

Canaan."[138] The political solution was to send a priest from among the exiles to teach the land's new residents how to worship the god of the land properly.[139]

The rest of the text goes on to explain how these mongrel Israelites produced a perverted form of Yahwism that would come to be despised by true Israel in the days of Ezra, Nehemiah, and even Christ. It is here that the Jews' ethnocentric hatred of Samaritans (e.g., John 4:9; 8:48) has its roots. The irony of the political solution was that such a priest was most likely not a Levite (1 Kgs 12:25-33) and thus not even remotely qualified to teach or lead the people. On the other hand, if the priest was a Levite, such is also ironic in that "a priest exiled for his apostasy [is] now returning to teach the customs of his God to those who replaced him."[140]

To compound matters, the people merely assimilated their own religious heritage with what the priest taught them—worship to Yahweh was merged with that of the gods Succoth-benoth, Nergal,[141] Ashima, Nibhaz, Tartak, Adrammelech, and Anammelech[142] (the latter two being notorious for receiving child sacrifice). The narrator's sarcasm is no more biting than when he says these new people "feared the LORD" (vv. 32–33). "Any attempt to 'fear the Lord' while serving other gods on the side is not really fearing the Lord at all."[143] Indeed, his directness returns with, "They do not fear the LORD" (v. 34), though Yahweh had called them to do so (vv. 35–39). Their "fear" of the Lord, though perhaps sincere, only perpetuated apostasy to future generations (v. 41). Not until a king named Josiah would the Northern Kingdom be purged of its idolatry (23:15–20).[144]

---

138. Hubbard, *First and Second Kings*, 207.

139. This was not the only time Sargon adopted such a policy (Shalom M. Paul, "Sargon's Administrative Diction in II Kings 17 27," *JBL* 88 [1969]: 73–74).

140. Hobbs, *2 Kings*, 238.

141. "Nergal was the god of war, death and pestilence at his principal shrine at Cutha, his symbol being a lion," (Wiseman, *1 and 2 Kings*, 287).

142. Provan, "2 Kings," 182.

143. Nelson, *First and Second Kings*, 232.

144. "What is clear by the end of the chapter, then, is that the exile of Israel has not led to any improvement in the religion of the people who dwell in the land. They pursue their path of 'worshiping' the Lord while serving their idols. Nothing has changed," (Provan, *1 & 2 Kings*, 250–51).

TALKING POINTS

O n one occasion, Jesus asked rhetorically if a king would go to war against a superior foe without first counting the cost (Luke 14:31– 32). It's worth a moment's pause to consider if Jesus had Amaziah in mind. Amaziah had shown restraint and discipline in punishing his father's assassins, but that same self-control did not translate to international affairs, where he became a humble "thistle" bragging before a mighty "cedar." God-loving people can do stupid things if they don't use the wisdom God gave them. One could argue that as the lights went out in Europe on the eve of World War I, it was because various nations did not count the cost of a world war. When Christians become as arrogant and aggressive as Amaziah, the same fate awaits us. A person who is always "standing for the truth" can just as well be a jerk who happens to be biblically literate. Christians who consider themselves most indispensable to a church's life are actually the most injurious. Instead, Paul encourages us, "Don't think you are better than you really are. Be honest in your evaluation of yourselves, measuring yourselves by the faith God has given us" (Rom 12:3 NLT).

S uccess can blind us to sin. It's possible to confuse good times as confirmation that we're doing something right. Though Jeroboam II was Israel's longest-ruling and most prosperous king, the nation's survival hung by a slender thread. It was during Jeroboam's reign that Amos prophesied: "Israel will be hauled off to exile, far from home" (Amos 7:17 Msg), so much so that his message was interpreted as a threat against Jeroboam himself (cf. 7:11–12). Throughout Amos, we see Israel bragging about her military prowess (6:13) and economic prosperity (6:1), but the reality is that she was rotten from within. "Therefore," Barnes writes, "let us not lose sight of such sobering realities: In any era, a long and seemingly successful career, whether in politics, academia, or even ministry, may not necessarily indicate the unequivocal seal of God's approval on an individual or that individual's accomplishments. Maybe it is, after all, quite appropriate that we find here little discussion about the accomplishments of King Jeroboam II of Israel, but a fair amount about the love and faithfulness of his (and our) God."[145]

---

145. Barnes, *1–2 Kings*, 298.

M ake no mistake about it: I'm proud to be an American. But while I consider myself blessed to live in the best country in the world, it is nonetheless troubling and embarrassing to admit that some rather horrific abuses have been committed in our name by those claiming to protect us from our enemies. The cruelty of Menahem is not isolated; war crimes have been perpetrated by every country on every continent in every time, even by Americans. Citizens of the U.S. were shocked by revelations in 2004 of abuse at Abu Ghraib in Iraq—the offenders were dishonorably discharged and sentenced to military prison. In the Kandahar massacre of March 2012, sixteen civilians were murdered and six others wounded by Army Staff Sergeant Robert Bales in Afghanistan. Nine of his victims were children. In 2013, he received life in prison without parole. In 2006, a teen girl in Al-Mahmudiyah, Iraq was raped and murdered, as well as her family, by five U.S. soldiers (they later received multiple life sentences). The church serves as the conscience of the state (Matt 5:13–16), and thus she must faithfully speak truth to power, especially when it comes to violations of human rights.[146] If Christians fail to advocate that all people bear the image of God, no one else on earth will be left to herald such a truth.

---

146. "Whether in the form of a confrontation, denouncement, or brazen evaluation and judgment, the responsibility of religious officials before the powers of state is clear. Whether in the presence of priest, rabbi, minister, deacon, or the believing faithful, those who serve the state and the political process must always know that 'there is a prophet among them,'" (Hens-Piazza, 1–2 Kings, 285).

12

A WOLF IN THE FOLD

My little boy died on December 8, 2015. About 1:15 am, my wife ran into the room, telling me Daniel wasn't breathing. I bolted awake and rushed to perform CPR on him while ordering her to call 911. When the medics arrived, we both watched in shock as they attempted to revive our little boy. After twenty minutes, they rushed him to a nearby hospital, and we followed in our own vehicle. All the way, we prayed and held out hope that something could be done to resuscitate him. Once at the hospital, I watched for another twenty minutes as the doctors and nurses tried everything. But I then asked the lead doctor, "Is there any hope?" He grimly shook his head. "How long will they continue to work on him?" I asked. "As long as you want."

It was then that I did the most difficult thing I've ever done in my life. I asked them to stop working on my son. It had been an hour since we had found him lifeless. I then did the second most difficult thing I've ever done—I walked the twenty feet to the ER waiting room and told my wife that Daniel was gone.

In the midst of life's many dangers, toils, and snares—the fog of spiritual warfare—it often appears as if God has abandoned us, that his will has been thwarted, or that he isn't the smartest strategist on the battlefield. But the fog of war only makes it *seem* like that. The reality is that God's knowledge and presence are perfect and total. He is aware of every detail, every circumstance, every scenario. On the battlefield, it is absolutely critical that soldiers obey the orders of the commander. Discipline and obedience are no light thing in the military. But the ability of a soldier to obey and follow directives is absolutely dependent on how much trust he has in his superior. Where there is no trust, discipline will break down and obedience will erode.

In the previous chapter of 2 Kings, we witnessed the destruction and exile of Israel. Decades of prophetic warnings had fallen on deaf ears; now, decades of prophetic doom had come to pass. Samaria was gone, and with it, ten of Israel's tribes. How much longer would Jerusalem and Judah hold out? Could they turn things around spiritually? Or was the fate of the North inevitable for the Southern Kingdom? How much longer would David's lamp remain kindled?

The apostle John tells us that faith, or trust, is the victory that overcomes the world (1 John 5:4), and indeed, the theme of faith echoes throughout the narrative of Hezekiah. The verb rendered "trust" (Hebrew *bātah*) occurs eight times in 2 Kings 18 alone (vv. 5, 19–22, 24, 30), and it dominates chapters 19–20 as well. In question is whether Hezekiah will trust in the God of his fathers, not only when his world is collapsing around him, but also when things are going well. Does he—and all in Jerusalem—have a faith that overcomes the world? Will they continue to trust and obey in spite of the fog of war? Or will Israel's fate become Judah's?

2 KINGS 18:1-12

The chronology surrounding Hezekiah's coronation is quite complicated, leading Patterson to dub it "the knottiest of all chronological problems in the Scriptures."[1] In the simplest terms possible, the problem is this:

- From vv. 9–10, it seems Hezekiah began his reign in 729 or 728.

- But v. 13 places Sennacherib's invasion—an event we can accurately date to 701—in Hezekiah's fourteenth year, meaning his coronation would have been in 715.

- Yet, 16:1–2 seems to indicate that Ahaz, Hezekiah's father, died in 720, meaning Hezekiah would have become king at that time.

We are thus left with three different dates for the beginning of Hezekiah's reign. Patterson suggests that Hezekiah became co-regent with his father, Ahaz, in 729. Then, in 720, Ahaz put the government solely in Hezekiah's hands, and then Ahaz died in 715, making 701 Hezekiah's fourteenth year as sole king of Judah. Despite his own attempt to resolve Hezekiah's chronological conundrum,

---

1. Patterson, "1, 2 Kings," 903.

however, Patterson still concludes: "The harmonization of these data remains a thorny problem."[2]

Regardless of when exactly his reign began, Hezekiah[3] (715–686) went on to cast a dynamic, often-unappreciated shadow across the pages of Kings. In many ways, there has not been a king as righteous[4] and faithful since David. Indeed, the narrator piles on a heap of praise with, "There was none like him among all the kings of Judah after him, nor among those who were before him" (v. 5).

Hezekiah's résumé of righteousness included destruction of the idolatrous high places[5] in Judah, including pillars and Asherah poles. But it's also said that he busted up the bronze serpent constructed by Moses (Num 21:5–9).[6] At some point, the people had turned that snake into an idol named Nehushtan and worshiped it. Copper and bronze snakes used in worship have been found throughout the ancient Near East; they often accompanied worship of the goddess Asherah.[7] Though not mentioned in Kings, Hezekiah's other religious reforms

---

2. Ibid. Other scholars account for the discrepancy by blaming it on everything from scribal errors to miscalculations (House, *1, 2 Kings*, 358). For all of his admirable work in confirming the historicity of the chronology of Kings, Thiele's explanation concerning the chronology of Hezekiah must be rejected. He claims the narrator mistakenly attributes twelve years of reign to both Jotham and Pekah, which throws the numbers off, leading him to conclude, "the synchronisms between [Hezekiah] and Hoshea [must] be recognized as late and artificial," (*Mysterious Numbers*, 174). For an excellent rebuttal to Thiele on this matter, see Leslie McFall, "Did Thiele Overlook Hezekiah's Coregency?" *BibSac* 146 (1989): 393–404.

3. A seal bearing Hezekiah's name was discovered near Hebron (Ruth Hestrin and Michal Dayagi, "A Seal Impression of a Servant of King Hezekiah," *IEJ* 24 [1974]: 27–29).

4. "The comment is entirely favorable, and therefore a rare accolade. It contrasts very sharply with the many negative comments on the kings of the northern nation in the previous chapter," (Hobbs, *2 Kings*, 251). From an unexpected place comes confirmation of Hezekiah's widespread reforms. Dating to his reign, archaeologists have confirmed the standardization of the shekel, which attests to efforts to eliminate unfair business practices (cf. Mic 6:11) (William G. Dever, *What Did the Biblical Writers Know and When Did They Know It? What Archaeology Can Tell Us about the Reality of Ancient Israel* [Grand Rapids: Eerdmans, 2001], 226–27).

5. "The destruction of local shrines (even Yahwistic ones) has received remarkable confirmation in the findings at Tel Arad. The Iron Age Temple found at the site was during this time devoid of sacrifice," (Hobbs, *2 Kings*, 251–52). At Beersheba, Aharoni discovered a stone altar, the stones of which had been repurposed to repair a wall during the time of Hezekiah, confirming his reforms (Yohanan Aharoni, "The Horned Altar of Beer-sheba," *BA* 37 [1974]: 2–6).

6. Jacob Milgrom, *Numbers* (Philadelphia: Jewish Publication Society, 1990), 459–60.

7. Karen Randolph Joines, "The Bronze Serpent in the Israelite Cult," *JBL* 87 (1968):

included repairing the Temple and celebrating Passover (2 Chr 29–31), some of
which was prompted by the prophet Isaiah.[8]

Hezekiah also proved himself mighty in war by throwing off the Assyrian
yoke in 705 (Judah had likely been paying tribute for a half-century) and humiliating the Philistines.[9] Whereas Ahaz had forfeited territory to the Philistines
(2 Chr 28:18–19), Hezekiah regained it. Defeat of the Philistines carried a distinct economic advantage. Since Tiglath-pileser III (745–727), the Philistines'
seaports had been controlled by Assyria. It was perhaps after Sargon II died in
battle that Hezekiah attacked the Philistines and gained access to international
trade with Egypt.[10] And as he had with David, "The LORD was with [Hezekiah];
wherever he went out, he prospered" (v. 7; cf. Josh 1:7–8; 1 Sam 16:18; 18:5, 12,
14–15; 2 Sam 5:10; 1 Kgs 2:3). It's been a while since we read such a statement
about a king in Jerusalem, but as we are about to discover, Hezekiah wasn't just
another king in David's lineage.

With Hezekiah's righteousness firmly established, the narrator turns his
gaze once more to the north to the fate of Israel. He reminds us that it was early
on in Hezekiah's reign that the Assyrians had besieged Samaria, taking the city
three years later and deporting its citizens. This happened "because they did not
listen to the voice of the LORD their God but violated His covenant—all He
had commanded Moses the servant of the LORD. They did not listen, and they
did not obey" (v. 12 HCSB). There is here a direct contrast being drawn between
Hezekiah and Hoshea; one listened and obeyed the word of the Lord (vv. 3–6),
and the other did not.[11]

245–56.

   8. Concerning Hezekiah's reforms, Alter speculates, "The motive may have been political
as well as religious, for an extensive cult in Jerusalem would clearly consolidate the power of
the Judean king. [...] In Rabshakeh's provocative speech, he appears to play to this resentment
by describing the removal of the high places as an offense against YHWH," (*Ancient Israel*, 812;
M. Weinfeld, "Cult Centralization in Israel in the Light of a Neo-Babylonian Analogy," *JNES* 23
[1964]: 202–12.).

   9. In his annals, Sennacherib lists the Philistine kings of Ashdod, Gaza, and Ekron as Assyrian allies whom Hezekiah had imprisoned (*COS* 2.119B).

   10. Nadav Na'aman, "Sennacherib's 'Letter to God' on His Campaign to Judah," *BASOR*
214 (1974): 25–39.

   11. Brueggeman, *1 & 2 Kings*, 492.

But the narrator leaves us wondering—would Jerusalem prove capable of rebuffing the Assyrian war machine? Would Hezekiah, despite his righteousness, suffer the same fate as Hoshea?[12] Is the king's obedience too little, too late? Had the time come for the lamp of David to be extinguished?

2 KINGS 18:13-37

Beginning in this section is a story about Sennacherib and Hezekiah that runs through end of 2 Kings 19. With the exception of Solomon building the Temple (a seven-year endeavor), no one event receives as much attention in Kings as does this singular conflict. Its importance—both spiritually and historically—cannot be understated.

In 1830, a British colonel named Robert Taylor unearthed in Nineveh what has become known as Taylor's Prism or the Annals of Sennacherib. Originally composed in the early-seventh century, the prism details the military exploits of Sennacherib of Assyria, particularly those against Jerusalem and Hezekiah. In the account, Sennacherib boasts of shutting Hezekiah up in Jerusalem "like a bird in a cage." But conspicuously absent is any mention of victorious conquest—and for good reason, which the biblical record goes on to explain.[13] Once you learn the "rest of the story," you'll realize why this pompous Assyrian omitted certain details from his memoirs.

More significant than the story's historical value, however, is the spiritual lesson it taught Judah. The battle belongs to the Lord! God's people had no reason to fear foreign threats as long as they were faithful to the Lord. Hezekiah trusted not in chariots or horseman, but in the name of Yahweh. Sadly, a century later, Jerusa-

---

12. "The Assyrian victory over the north was itself possible only because it was the will of God that Assyria should execute judgment on a sinful people. Yet we cannot forget that it was under the best of the northern kings that judgment fell (2 Kgs. 17:2). Is it possible that Hezekiah's reforms have come too late to make any difference? Are we now to read of the end of Judah?" (Provan, *1 & 2 Kings*, 253–54).

13. "Nowhere in his own account of his campaign does Sennacherib claim to have taken Jerusalem, nor even to have received tribute from Hezekiah in the immediate aftermath of the siege. He tells us only that after his return to Nineveh (whose occasion he does not describe), Hezekiah sent tribute. His silence on the way in which the siege ended when compared to what he says in this same account about other kings in the region requires some explanation, and our biblical sources give us some hints in the direction of this when they tell of a mysterious reversal suffered by the Assyrians while Jerusalem lay at their mercy (v. 35)," (Provan, "2 Kings," 193–94).

lem would face another empire, Babylon, and would crumble before them because a new administration thought the answer was found in a big army, not a big God.

Indeed, the theme of trust dominates this story. As previously mentioned, *trust* in Hebrew occurs nine times (18:5, 19–22, 24, 30; 19:10) and *deliverance* occurs eleven times (18:29–30, 32–35; 19:11–12). Though unrecorded in Kings, Chronicles preserves Hezekiah's speech to the people of Jerusalem on the eve of Sennacherib's siege: "Be strong and courageous. Do not be afraid or dismayed before the king of Assyria and all the horde that is with him, for there are more with us than with him. With him is an arm of flesh, but with us is the LORD our God, to help us and to fight our battles" (2 Chr 32:7–8).

From historical inscriptions, we know the Assyrians often lampooned their enemies for trusting in their gods or in their own strength. True to form, Hezekiah's trust in Yahweh will be scrutinized, mocked, and blamed for the predicament in which Jerusalem finds itself. In every way imaginable, faith in God and faith in empire are at odds with one another,[14] for the central question of the narrative is, "In whom will you trust?" (v. 20), or "On whom do you rely for deliverance?"

S ennacherib ascended the throne of his father, Sargon II, in 705. Sargon had been killed in battle—"his body captured by the enemy, not recovered and not buried,"[15] which was considered such a scandalous disgrace that Sennacherib disowned his dear, deceased daddy—and Assyria's vassal

---

14. Leithart, *1 & 2 Kings*, 256. "It is the insistence of this narrator (and of Isaiah in a parallel tradition) that, in the unequal struggle between the empire and the government of Judah, Yahweh is the 'great equalizer.' That is, Yahweh must be taken into account in policy formation because the public, international process is not merely one of raw power. The capacity to take Yahweh into account as an active player goes under the rubric of 'faith' or 'trust.' [...] It is easy for us to imagine that in the ancient world, such a dimension of faith was more credible than it would be in the modern world. But we must not misunderstand and assume that even in that ancient world, with its military, political, and economic realities, 'faith' was such an obvious decision. It was then, as now, an act or a cluster of acts that ran against what seemed to be the pertinent factors of Realpolitik. That is, faith was no more an easy choice then than it might be now. Thus the text does not call for something easily embraced, but celebrates this king who took the hard choice," (Brueggemann, *1 & 2 Kings*, 495).

15. Cogan, *II Kings*, 221; cf. Hayim Tadmor, "The Campaigns of Sargon II of Assur: A Chronological-Historical Study (Conclusion)," *JCS* 12 (1958): 97–98.

states revolted one after the other as they began to smell blood in the water. Merodach-baladan of Babylon was the first to do so, and Judah wasn't far behind.

> He [Hezekiah] became the moving force in a new coalition composed of Philistia, Judah, Edom, and Moab. The Philistines were evidently reluctant to join, so following the very same policy Israel and Syria had tried on Judah thirty years earlier, Hezekiah attacked them, deposed their king, and installed a man who would take his orders. Behind this policy one discerns the hand of Egypt, promising help and support. Isaiah was bitterly opposed to the entire proceeding: Egypt was worse than useless and Assyria could be left to God. The secret politicking and conniving were a bold-faced affront to God that could only bring disaster.[16]

Meanwhile, Sennacherib proved to be anything but a weakling. The new king of Assyria subdued Babylon and subsequently launched his military campaign against Hezekiah (his third of eight total campaigns) by first targeting the fortified cities of Phoenicia, Philistia, and Judah; the cities listed in Micah 1:8–16 may have been his targets[17] (cf. Isa 1:4–9). He defeated Tyre and caused the leaders of Byblos, Arvad, Ashdod, Moab, Edom, and Ammon to make nice and offer tribute. By the time Sennacherib turned his lonely eyes to Jerusalem, he had tallied over 200,000 prisoners of war, 46 fortified cities, and countless small villages.[18]

At his base at Lachish,[19] about thirty miles southwest of Jerusalem, Sennacherib received a message from the king of Judah. Hezekiah had panicked and

---

16. John N. Oswalt, *The Book of Isaiah, Chapters 1–39* (Grand Rapids: Eerdmans, 1986), 10.

17. In one Assyrian document, Sennacherib mentions successful attacks against Azekah and Gath (Na'aman, "Sennacherib's 'Letter to God,'" 25–39).

18. *COS* 2.119B.

19. Archaeologists have uncovered much evidence at Lachish of the city's destruction at the hands of Sennacherib. "The main Assyrian attack was carried out in the southwest corner of the city—the only part of the city not protected by a deep valley—where a siege ramp of boulders was erected to allow the approach of the Assyrian forces. The city was eventually captured and burned to the ground," (Provan, "2 Kings," 185–86). There is also a stone panel from the Assyrian palace in Nineveh that depicts the city's siege (David Ussishkin, "The 'Lachish Reliefs'

now offered to "buy off" Sennacherib. By now, this is a negotiating tactic we've seen too often in Kings, and from a "real-world" perspective, the offer makes sense—Hezekiah's Phoenician and Philistine allies had all fled, and Egypt was unreliable (as Isaiah had warned). Sennacherib responded with an absurd ransom: three hundred talents of silver and thirty talents of gold, equal to $5 billion in today's money. To pay it, Hezekiah raided his personal bank account, not to mention the Temple. In humiliation, he was even forced to scrape gold from the Temple's doors and doorposts (cf. 12:17–18; 16:7; 1 Kgs 15:18).

But such an immense ransom was not enough for Sennacherib; for the first time in Kings, the unwritten rules are broken. Hezekiah had been a ringleader of rebellion against Assyria, and now he had to pay; he had to be made an example of. Sennacherib seems to have wanted nothing less than for the populace to depose Hezekiah and allow Sennacherib to place his own puppet on the throne.[20] The king's three-man delegation, backed by Assyrian soldiers, went to Jerusalem to meet with Hezekiah's own three-man team of negotiators.

The parlay met at what the narrator calls "the conduit of the upper pool, which is on the highway to the Washer's Field" (v. 17). Such a detail is meant to do more than grant us our geographical bearings or to invoke Hezekiah's tunnel or the vulnerability of Jerusalem's water supply. Though we are uncertain of its exact whereabouts,[21] the upper pool was outside of the city. But that isn't the locale's real significance. In a scene absent from Kings, but present in Isaiah, the prophet had called upon Hezekiah's father, Ahaz, to trust in God and rebuff the enemy when threatened. It had been at "the conduit of the upper pool on the highway to the Washer's Field" that Yahweh had promised Ahaz, "It shall not stand, and

---

and the City of Lachish," *IEJ* 30 [1980]: 174–95). Today, that panel can be seen in the British Museum in London.

20. "Tyre's king has already been replaced, and Assyria's historical pattern was to place Assyrians on the thrones of rebellious states," (House, *1, 2 Kings*, 362). "The previous attempt to unseat illegally the house of David in the days of Hezekiah's father, Ahaz, had been overruled by God (Isa 7:1–16). Sennacherib's efforts to unseat the godly Hezekiah would fare no better. When it was time for a sinful Jerusalem to fall, it would happen at divine direction (2 Ch 36:14–17), and even then the house of David would be sovereignly sustained until the coming of the Messiah (Isa 7:1–9:7; Mt 1; Lk 1:26–37, 67–69; 2:4–11)," (Patterson, "1, 2 Kings, 917).

21. Ussishkin places the Assyrian war camp northwest of Jerusalem (and the upper pool was close by), the same place where Titus and the Romans would camp eight hundred years later before the destruction of Jerusalem in A.D. 70 (David Ussishkin, "The 'Camp of the Assyrians' in Jerusalem," *IEJ* 29 [1979]: 137–42).

it shall not come to pass" concerning the Syro-Ephraimite threat (Isa 7:3, 7–9). The Lord even offered Ahaz a sign to prove the integrity of his promise; when Ahaz refused, the Lord famously promised an immaculate conception anyway as validation of his power (Isa 7:14). If this narrative link is intentional by the narrator, we are meant to wonder whether Hezekiah will respond as his father did, or will he exchange his fear for faith? Again, the entire narrative of Sennacherib's threat to Jerusalem poses this question to the reader—in whom is your trust?

The Rabshakeh's[22] speech is worth special attention since it was "a masterpiece of deception and psychological warfare."[23] The Assyrians employed mind games as a part of their overall battle strategy,[24] and the Rabshakeh particularly sought to demonstrate Sennacherib's superiority to the God of Israel. Here, "the juxtaposition of the word of 'the great king' and the word of Yahweh now becomes a deliberate feature of the narrative."[25] The Rabshakeh's speech can be summarized by these main points:

---

22. It's worth noting that *Tartan, Rabsaris*, and *Rabshakeh* are titles, not given names (cf. NIV). Respectively, they translate to "supreme commander" (second only to the king; often the crown prince), "chief officer" (possibly head of the king's bodyguard), and "field commander" or "provincial governor" (Walton, *Bible Background*, 405; Wray Beal, *1 & 2 Kings*, 467). Since the Rabshakeh traditionally never took part in military campaigns, the fact that he speaks for the delegation here may indicate that he alone knew Hebrew. "He may well himself have been of Aramean or Israelite origin, for although his first speech in 18:19–35 reveals many parallels with the Neo-Assyrian annals, he clearly not only knew the local language but also displayed good knowledge of Judean customs," (Provan, "2 Kings," 188–89).

23. Wiseman, *1 and 2 Kings*, 295. Wiseman also mentions "a relief from Khorsabad showing an Assyrian officer standing on a siege-machine and holding a scroll as he addresses defenders on the wall," (Ibid., n. 8). In his examination of the Rabshakeh's speech, Hyman concludes, "Commentators who focus on the qualities of the speech describe it as abusive, rude and disrespectful, threatening and ridiculing, insolent, scornful, and blasphemous, a taunt, clever propaganda and a powerful harangue. The speech is all of these and more. All these terms are fitting descriptions of the speech which the Rabshakeh delivers to achieve his immediate goal—to intimidate Hezekiah and his people. The Rabshakeh succeeds convincingly because his speech is a masterful example of rhetorical intimidation in the political-military arena. However, the Rabshakeh's persuasive techniques fall short. While they succeed immediately in causing distress and intimidation, they do not reach their long term goal—the surrender of King Hezekiah even before a battle begins," (Ronald T. Hyman, "The Rabshakeh's Speech [II Kg. 18-25]: A Study of Rhetorical Intimidation," *JBQ* 23 [1995]: 214).

24. H. W. F. Saggs, "Assyrian Warfare in the Sargonid Period," *Iraq* 25 (1963): 148–54.

25. Hobbs, *2 Kings*, 257.

HOW TO LOSE A KINGDOM IN 400 YEARS

If you're depending on your ally, Egypt, to bail you out, you're a trusting fool (v. 21). "This metaphor portrays Hezekiah as leaning on a reed cane which is thin and splintered on top. Not only will the reed cane collapse and become useless because it is weak, but it will even pierce the palm of Hezekiah's hand when he leans upon it. Accordingly, the reed cane is worse than useless; it is actually damaging. By relying on Egypt—aptly depicted as a reed—Hezekiah places himself in jeopardy."[26] Recall that Hoshea of Israel had solicited Egypt for military aid before the collapse of Samaria (17:4). When Sennacherib had previously destroyed Ashdod on his way to Jerusalem, Ashdod's ruler escaped to Egypt. In fact, Israel, Judah, and her neighbors in the ancient Near East had repeatedly looked to Egypt for help time and again, and never had it panned out like they hoped. Little wonder, then, that Yahweh lampooned his people through Isaiah: "Ah, stubborn children [...] who set out to go down to Egypt, without asking for my direction, to take refuge in the protection of Pharaoh and to seek shelter in the shadow of Egypt! Therefore shall the protection of Pharaoh turn to your shame, and the shelter in the shadow of Egypt to your humiliation [...] Egypt's help is worthless and empty" (Isa 30:1–3, 7; cf. 31:1–3).

If you're depending on your god to bail you out, you're a trusting fool (v. 22). The Rabshakeh was conveying "the message that he is aware of what is happening to Judah. He seeks to convince the three aides that he is no mere ignorant foreigner but an astute observer who knows the true meaning of events taking place in Judah."[27] Yet, he erroneously believed that Hezekiah had torn down the pagan altars as an insult to Judah's God; what hope, then, did Judah have of being saved by this God when Hezekiah had angered him? Such a notion is further evidence that Sennacherib's plan was to convince the populace to depose Hezekiah on their own, saving Sennacherib the expense of a prolonged siege. If the people believed their king to be responsible for the most recent misfortune, Hezekiah ought to beware the Ides of March.

If you're depending on your army to bail you out, you're a trusting fool (vv. 23–24). The Rabshakeh was right; Judah's army was mostly infantry with few cavalry, and Sennacherib in his annals claims that many of Hezekiah's elite troops had deserted the army.[28] Even if Assyria supplied two thousand horses,

---

26. Hyman, "Rabshakeh's Speech," 216; cf. Ehud Ben Zvi, "Who Wrote the Speech of Rabshakeh and When?" *JBL* 109 (1990): 79–92.

27. Hyman, "Rabshakeh's Speech," 217.

28. *COS* 2.119B.

Judah couldn't provide the riders, and certainly not enough to make a difference in pitched battle. "That is the point of the offer. It indicates that Judah is bereft of manpower resources as well as every other kind of resource and therefore had better knuckle under to the empire. Indeed, Judah is so weak that its entire military force could not cope with one Assyrian military company. The odds are unthinkable for Judah, made more so by the fact that Egypt is no reliable military support. Judah is in principle defeated even before any conflict begins."[29]

At the end, the Rabshakeh topped off his lethal dessert sundae with this ripe cherry: "Do you think I've come up here to destroy this country without the express approval of GOD? The fact is that GOD expressly ordered me, 'Attack and destroy this country!'" (v. 25 Msg).[30] It was typical of Assyrian wartime propaganda to tell their enemies their gods were angry with them and that they should surrender.[31] But we cannot help but wonder if the Rabshakeh knew of Isaiah's prophecy that Assyria was the rod of Yahweh's anger (Isa 10:5–6; cf. 2 Kgs 19:25–26). One thing he certainly did *not* know was that Israel's chariots and horsemen were not of this world (2:12; 13:14). He also had not taken into account the strength of Hezekiah's great faith, the influence of Isaiah the prophet, or Yahweh's covenant faithfulness to his people. The Rabshakeh made one particularly egregious error when he used the title "great king" to refer to Sennacherib; when it appears elsewhere in the Old Testament, it almost always applies *only* to Yahweh (Pss 47:2; 48:2; 95:3; Mal 1:14) and no one else.

Hezekiah's delegation begged the Rabshakeh to parlay with them in Aramaic (the lingua franca of that time), not in Hebrew, lest the soldiers overhear the conversation and be frightened—to which the Rabshakeh began talking even louder. He promised those listening that if they would reject Hezekiah and accept Sennacherib's terms of surrender, they would be treated well (as op-

---

29. Brueggemann, *1 & 2 Kings*, 496.

30. "'I am not here because I personally seek a bigger kingdom or that I am vindictive because you are rebelling against me. Rather I am here to destroy this place because the Lord told me personally to come here. I surely would not come up here to destroy this place without the Lord on my side.' The justification based on the Lord's word is intended to effect a significant transformation. While Hezekiah was once the king who found favor with the Lord (18:3-7), now Sennacherib is the king chosen by the Lord. This rhetorical technique of aligning Sennacherib with the Lord and quoting Him serves simultaneously to convey blasphemy, bravado, audacity and support," (Hyman, "Rabshakeh's Speech," 220).

31. Cogan, *Imperialism*, 9–21.

posed to his threat in v. 27) and go into exile in a place not unlike their home
(vv. 31–32; cf. Deut 8:7–9). "The Assyrian king will be Israel's shepherd-king, a
composite of Moses, Joshua, and Solomon who will lead Judah to green pastures
beside the still waters, into a promised land flowing with wine, oil, and honey,"[32]
(vv. 31–32; cf. 1 Kgs 4:25). This was a classic Assyrian propaganda strategy—
pretending to have the good of regular Joes at heart, "but history has left no trace
of concrete evidence of any such benevolence."[33] Little wonder that Joseph Stalin
is supposed to have once remarked, "Sincere diplomacy is no more possible than
dry water or wooden iron."

The Rabshakeh concluded his disinformation campaign with a direct insult
to Israel's God: "The gods of our past victims could not save them; what makes
you think your god is any better?" (cf. Deut 4:33–34). Ironically, many of the victims listed (v. 34) had been conquered, not by Sennacherib, but by his predecessors. But the bigger point is that Sennacherib had just arrogantly insinuated that
Israel's God was just another worthless wimp, a girlie-god, a wannabe divinity.
"Yahweh is unable to save. By having the Rab-shakeh repeat this assertion, our
writer sets a trap to be sprung later. The whole incident now turns on this point."[34]

Remarkably, the soldiers and citizens said nothing. Hezekiah had ordered
them to remain silent, and this is exactly what they did—a testament to Hezekiah's skilled leadership and the people's respect for him. But this does not mean
that fear and despair did not settle over Jerusalem like a dense fog. The king's delegation returned to the city, where they tore their clothes over the blaspheming
of Yahweh's Name as they gave a report to Hezekiah.

---

32. Leithart, *1 & 2 Kings*, 256. "Implicitly, it claimed that Sennacherib himself would give
them the things Yahweh had promised. In effect, Sennacherib challenged Yahweh's right to have
Judah's exclusive loyalty. Thus, as Baal confronted Yahweh on Mt. Carmel (1 Kings 18), so Sennacherib now faced Yahweh on Mt. Zion," (Hubbard, *First and Second Kings*, 212).

33. House, *1, 2 Kings*, 363.

34. Hobbs, *2 Kings*, 259.

2 KINGS 19:1-19

When Hezekiah heard what the Rabshakeh had said, he grieved heavily and went to the Temple. "Hezekiah's attitude in the face of the Assyrian threat and taunting is to be contrasted with that of other kings, who in similar circumstances took a different course of action (see Ahaz, Zedekiah, and Jehoiakim)."[35]

Hezekiah also sent a delegation of VIPs to inquire of the Lord[36] through Isaiah. The bizarre proverb they mention (v. 3; cf. Hos 13:13) invokes the critical moment in the birthing process when the lives of both mother and infant are at the greatest risk; it "indicates that the moment of truth has arrived for Jerusalem but it does not have the strength to succeed."[37]

The word of the Lord came, assuring there was no reason to fear. He had plans[38] for Sennacherib (v. 7), which he would work out in due time. "Yahweh reassured the king concerning the Assyrians. They had blasphemed Him by in effect demoting Him, the Lord of all, to the level of other gods. Soon Yahweh would personally show Sennacherib His sovereignty over history. By executing a blasphemer outside Israel, Yahweh would prove Himself to be a cosmic, not a local, God."[39]

---

35. Ibid., 274. "The contrast between wicked Jehoram and pious Hezekiah, in their reaction to enemies at their gates, is particularly interesting. Jehoram tears his clothes and, unwilling to wait for God, looks to kill God's prophet (2 Kgs. 6:30–31). Hezekiah tears his clothes and humbly requests prophetic prayer," (Provan, *1 & 2 Kings*, 261).

36. "Again, the king's behavior is extraordinary in light of past kings. Before, the prophets sought the kings, only to be rebuked. Now, the king actually *wants* a prophetic word. He is not simply acting out of desperation," (House, *1, 2 Kings*, 366; emphasis his).

37. Fretheim, *First and Second Kings*, 202. "For a woman to carry a child to the moment of birth and then be unable to deliver it implied the most public humiliation possible for her, and since the Hebrews believed that suffering was a punishment for sin, it marked her off as a particularly wicked person. This was the nature of the humiliation to which Hezekiah and his people had been brought. The issue is whether Hezekiah or the Assyrians are going to be declared by events to be the true instrument of God at this time," (Robinson, *Second Book*, 178).

38. Note that, as is true of every one of the men of God in the Old Testament, Isaiah offered specific promises in order to confirm whether he was a true or false prophet (House, *1, 2 Kings*, 366). The three promises made were 1) Sennacherib would "hear a rumor," 2) "return to his own land," and 3) "fall by the sword in his own land" (v. 7). Each of these three promises would come true, though not in quick succession.

39. Hubbard, *First and Second Kings*, 213–14.

Meanwhile, the Rabshakeh rendezvoused with the Assyrians at Libnah, eight miles northeast of Lachish on the road to Jerusalem. This indicates that Sennacherib was pressing towards Jerusalem, drawing the noose tighter around the capital city. But Sennacherib soon heard a rumor that Tirhakah the Ethiopian was gunning for him. At this point, some scholars deride the factuality of this story because in 701, Tirhakah was not yet king and possibly still a child of nine or ten years of age. Kitchen, however, argues that Tirhakah was indeed an adult (there is no consensus on his birthday) at this time, albeit not yet king[40] (his royal ascendency did not occur until 690). If this is the case, it would be anachronistic (but not unheard of) to call him "king."

The reader has already been led to believe that Egypt will offer no assistance to Hezekiah, and none will be forthcoming from Tirhakah. Sennacherib claims in his annals that he made short work of the threat from the Egyptians at the battle of Eltekeh. "If Jerusalem were to see salvation, it would come without Egypt's help."[41]

Sennacherib then sent another message to Hezekiah (vv. 10–13) restating the futility of resistance. But while he had previously claimed God was too *powerless* to deliver Jerusalem, the Assyrian now alleged God was too *duplicitous* to do so (v. 10). Hezekiah had once been labeled the deceiver (18:29); now it is Yahweh. "Here is a much more direct attack on the LORD than the one in chapter 18, and one that displays monumental arrogance."[42] The places named in v. 13 are repeated from 18:34, but v. 12 lists four more notches in the Assyrian's gun barrel:[43]

- *Gozan*, east of Haran and northwest of Nineveh, sat on the Habor River[44] and had become the home of deportees from Samaria after the fall of the Northern Kingdom (17:6).

- *Haran*, the famous city of Abraham (Gen 11:31–32), was lo-

---

40. Kitchen, *Third Intermediate Period*, 383–87.

41. Hubbard, *First and Second Kings*, 214.

42. Provan, *1 & 2 Kings*, 258. "The letter meant to drown Judah's hopes with a second flood of historical reality. The Egyptian foray against Assyria was no cause for increased Judean confidence. The letter intensified the confrontation between Sennacherib and Yahweh. The two now faced each other one-on-one. This was the central issue at stake: Was Yahweh just another divine nonentity? Or was He a very different kind of God?" (Hubbard, *First and Second Kings*, 214).

43. Fretheim, *First and Second Kings*, 203.

44. LaSor, "Gozan," *ISBE* 2:547.

cated fifty miles east of Carchemish on the upper Euphrates River. It had been annexed by Assyria in the ninth century and destroyed by Ashurdan III as punishment for rebellion in 763.[45]

- **Rezeph** was the capital of an Assyrian province and situated in upper Mesopotamia on a trade route between Haran and Palmyra. Shalmaneser III had conquered it in 839.[46]

- **Telassar** was a site "on the banks of the middle Euphrates at its great western bend," approximately fifty-six miles east of Aleppo.[47]

When you receive news that triggers despair and rattles you to your core, how do you respond? When you feel threatened or targeted, what is your natural reaction? All of us often respond with a certain mixture of fear and rashness, and both can incite us to do some rather foolish things. We mistake irrational swagger for rational courage and confuse fear for caution.

When Sennacherib's message reached Hezekiah, he didn't rashly rush into battle, but neither did he rush around with the fortitude of Chicken Little. Personally, I would have much preferred it if he had responded with something like, "You can have my city when you pry it from my cold dead fingers." Instead, he "went up to the house of the LORD and spread it [the scroll bearing Sennacherib's threats] before the LORD" (v. 14), as if he wanted Yahweh to behold the Assyrian's audacity and hubris for himself. He then prayed. Hezekiah's prayer had four main points worth spotlighting:

First, Hezekiah praised the sovereignty of God. He was not foolish enough to think that Yahweh's dominion was limited to Israel. His presence may have hovered above the Ark of the Covenant, but this was merely where he sat enthroned (cf. 1 Kgs 8:27–30; 1 Chr 28:2; Pss 99:5; 132:7). His authority in fact was over "all the kingdoms of the earth," and his mighty hand reaches even now beyond the most distant solar systems to the ends of the universe. Our Father in heaven is no less mighty in Nepal, Nigeria, or Nebraska—to say nothing of galaxies far, far away.[48] When they faced their own threats in Jerusalem, the

---

45. Kobayashi, "Haran (Place)," *ABD* 3:59.

46. Thompson, "Rezeph (Place)," *ABD* 5:708.

47. Olivier, "Tel-Assar," *ISBE* 4:747.

48. "Yahweh is beyond comparison 'in all the kingdoms of the earth.' He is not like those gods defeated by Sennacherib. [...] Establishing Yahweh's superiority is confirmed by this ref-

first-century church copied Hezekiah. No sooner had the religious leaders commanded Peter and John to stop preaching Jesus than the church called a prayer
meeting that they addressed to the "Sovereign Lord" (Acts 4:24). When threats
arise against the people of God, it is important for the church to confess that
our Lord is in complete control; that he has not been caught off guard; that the
words, "I didn't see that coming," are not a part of the divine vocabulary; that
he will always work his perfect will for our good and his glory; that the entire
universe is upheld "by the word of his power" (Heb 1:3).

Second, Hezekiah confessed that God was his last resort. This might be the
most confusing aspect of his prayer, but Hezekiah invited God to take notice of
Israel's situation (cf. Pss 17:6; 71:2; 86:1; 116:2). Had God somehow "missed"
what had happened? Had he been temporarily distracted? Like Baal at Carmel,
had Yahweh taken a potty break or been "out to lunch" when Sennacherib came
against Jerusalem and made such blasphemous allegations? No. Instead, the
king's plea for God to incline his ear and open his eyes was a declaration of Hezekiah's faith. Seeking help from a God already inclined to help his people is never
redundant; rather, it is a declaration that we consider God our last resort. If you
were falsely accused of a crime and sentenced to prison or death, you would
jump up and down, flail your arms, and implore the judge to see and hear what
was happening—the judge would be your last resort. If you were diagnosed with
an untreatable terminal illness, but heard about a drug in clinical trials that held
at least some measure of hope for healing, you'd jump up and down, flail your
arms, and implore the doctors to see and hear your condition—that trial drug
would be your last resort. In the same way, we implore God to see our situation
and hear our prayer, not for his sake (as if he somehow had become distracted),
but for our own, since we always need reminding that God is our last resort.

Third, Hezekiah acknowledged the worthlessness of false gods. By recognizing the misplaced trust of Sennacherib's past victims, the king denounced
idols as worthless defenses against life's dangers, toils, and snares (Pss 115:3–8;
135:15–18; Isa 2:20; 40:19–20; 41:7; 44:9–20; Jer 10:3–10). Namath, Arpad,
Sephardim, Hena, and Ivvah lay in ruins because their trust had been in man-
made images of wood and stone. "Our hope is not in idols but in you, O Lord,"
Hezekiah confesses. He was not kissing up to God as much as reminding himself
and Israel where their hope rested, that if God did not come through for Israel,

---

erence to creation. Beyond the creator no greater power exists, and Hezekiah's faith rests in this
confidence," (Hobbs, *2 Kings*, 278).

they wouldn't be going anywhere else for help. When storms rage against us, our declaration of dependence must be explicit and constant. How easily our corrupted hearts believe that our salvation is because of something we've done! Noah had to enter the ark, David had to hurl the stone, and Israel had to cross the Red Sea, but salvation is always the Lord's! And we cannot allow ourselves to chase after other alternatives should God not give us the answer we desired.

Finally, Hezekiah asked God to save Israel for God's sake. He made his request very clear—"save us, please, from his hand." But his reasoning is what is noteworthy—"that all the kingdoms of the earth may know that you, O LORD, are God alone." Hezekiah did not play the "We have a covenant with you, so keep your promise" card, nor did he couch his request in terms of God needing to prove that he really loved his people. And though he could have done so legitimately, Hezekiah never used his own David-esque righteousness as a bargaining chip. No, Hezekiah's deepest concern was seeing God's Name glorified to the ends of the earth, that all the kingdoms of earth confessed Yahweh as God alone (cf. 1 Sam 17:45–47; 1 Kgs 18:36–37; Ps 79:1–10). "It is a memorable prayer, in which self-interest is for the moment left behind, and concern for the LORD's reputation, so besmirched by Sennacherib's slander, takes over."[49] When we find ourselves in dire straits and cry to God for help, it will be to our benefit to see our predicament as an opportunity for God to be greatly glorified (cf. Phil 1:20). In fact, asking for God to glorify himself in our present circumstances is a prayer that will be answered affirmatively 100% of the time. Anything far beyond that will ultimately lead to our tremendous disappointment. "God is the one Being in all the universe for whom seeking His own praise is the ultimately loving act. For Him, self-exaltation is the highest virtue. When He does all things 'for the praise of His glory,' He preserves for us and offers to us the only thing in all the world that can satisfy our longings. God is for us! And the foundation of this love is that God has been, is now, and always will be for Himself."[50]

49. Provan, *1 & 2 Kings*, 258. "Hezekiah certainly wants relief from Assyria, yet his main concern is God's reputation in the world. In other words, the king prays out of a relational sense of respect for God," (House, *1, 2 Kings*, 405).

50. John Piper, *Desiring God* (Sisters, OR: Multnomah, 2003), 49.

2 KINGS 19:20-37

In response to Hezekiah's prayer, the prophet Isaiah brought a message from Yahweh assuring the king his prayer had been heard in God's very throne room. Furthermore, Isaiah was there to inform Hezekiah of what the Lord of all the earth had already decreed concerning the Assyrian war machine and her blasphemous leader. In Yahweh's official response, three issues are addressed.

First, God made clear that it wasn't just the holy city of Zion that had been mocked, but rather the Holy One of Israel (an iconic phrase in the book of Isaiah). Rather than be intimidated by Sennacherib, Jerusalem scorned him by "[wagging] her head" (v. 21; cf. Job 16:4; Pss 22:7; 109:25; Jer 18:16). "Jerusalem is personified as a virgin daughter who tosses her head in disdain at the proud, once-powerful Assyrians, who believe they have made themselves great. Indeed they have been great, but their reputation will not be 'enhanced' by the rape of this virgin. Why? Because in insulting the virgin they have insulted the virgin's protector, who happens to rule the universe."[51]

Sennacherib was foolish to think that if he had been mighty enough to subdue foreign powers like Phoenicia and Egypt—if he had ascended Lebanon's mountains (v. 23) and dried up the Nile in Egypt[52] (v. 24)—then a backwater Podunk town like Jerusalem would be no match for him. But to mess with Zion was to mess with her God. Sennacherib had poked the wrong bear! It's as if God was saying, "Do you have any idea who you're messing with, Sennacherib? I'm Alpha and Omega. I'm the Commander of angelic armies. I'm the Holy One of Israel. I'm not some two-bit god from some third-world country."

Second, God reminded Sennacherib that he was not just the Defender of Israel, but also the Sovereign Lord of all the earth and the Screenwriter of all of history. Sennacherib foolishly believed he was responsible for the collapse of Judah's fortified cities, but it had really been the Lord's doing (cf. Isa 41:2; 45:1; Amos 9:7). The Assyrian king had no hope of even seizing candy from a baby without God's permission. By going up against the God of Judah, Sennacherib thought he was the lead actor in a one-man historical epic—a Kirk Douglas in his very own *Spartacus*. But the Assyrian king was about to discover quite rudely that he was just a supporting actor in a grander drama, a Yul Brynner in someone

---

51. House, *1, 2 Kings*, 369–70.

52. Though his plans for conquest probably included Egypt, Sennacherib would never add the land of the Nile to his trophy case. In fact, Assyria would not conquer Egypt until 671 under Sennacherib's son, Esarhaddon.

else's *The Ten Commandments.* "Did it never occur to you that I'm behind all this? Long, long ago I drew up the plans, and now I've gone into action" (v. 25 Msg; cf. Isa 14:24–27; 40:21; 46:10).

Finally, God informed Sennacherib of his specific plan for the self-designated Assyrian demigod. He knew when Sennacherib stood and sat, when he entered and exited, when he was naughty or nice. He also knew every blasphemous word the king had spoken in defiance of the Holy One of Israel. So the Lord was about to put a hook in his nose and a bit in his mouth like a stubborn barnyard ass[53] and send him right back where he came from (Ps 32:9; Prov 26:3; Ezek 19:4; Amos 4:1–3).

I don't pretend to be a Hebrew scholar (though I did stay at a Holiday Inn Express once). However, I believe God's words in v. 28 were meant to be purposefully offensive and condescending to Sennacherib's ears. Though the actual terms used might not have been profane, the image conjured by those words was certainly uncouth; you don't tell the most powerful man in the world you're about to put a hook in his nose and a bit in his mouth. Out of concern that I might unjustifiably transgress boundaries of propriety and decency, I will mostly leave to your own periphrastic imagination the full force of what God said here. But suffice it to say that the divine King wanted Sennacherib to know he was about to become Yahweh's whipping boy.

Elsewhere, Isaiah prophesied:

> After the Lord has used the king of Assyria to accomplish his purposes on Mount Zion and in Jerusalem, he will turn against the king of Assyria and punish him—for he is proud and arrogant. He boasts, "By my own powerful arm I have done this. With my own shrewd wisdom I planned it. I have broken down the defenses of nations and carried off their treasures. I have knocked down their kings like a bull. I have robbed their nests of riches and gathered up kingdoms as a farmer gathers eggs. No one can even flap a wing against me or utter a peep of protest." But can the ax boast greater power than the person who uses it? Is the saw greater than the person who saws? Can

---

53. "This image has parallels in Assyrian literature and iconography. Esarhaddon is depicted on a stele from Zinjirli in Syria as leading Baal of Tyre and Tirhakah of Egypt by a rope tied to a ring through their lips. Ashurbanipal claims to have pierced the cheeks of Uate' (king of Ishmael) with a sharp edged tool and put a ring in his jaw," (Walton, *Bible Background,* 406).

a rod strike unless a hand moves it? Can a wooden cane walk by itself? Therefore, the Lord, the LORD of Heaven's Armies, will send a plague among Assyria's proud troops, and a flaming fire will consume its glory. The LORD, the Light of Israel, will be a fire; the Holy One will be a flame. He will devour the thorns and briers with fire, burning up the enemy in a single night. The LORD will consume Assyria's glory like a fire consumes a forest in a fruitful land; it will waste away like sick people in a plague. Of all that glorious forest, only a few trees will survive— so few that a child could count them!

Isaiah 10:12–19 NLT

Returning to 2 Kings 19, two more important statements are made about Jerusalem's salvation. Judah's food supply—devastated by Sennacherib's tear through the countryside—would be sparse for two years, but would recover by the third year (vv. 29–31). Normally, people ate the previous year's harvest while the present year's was stored in the barn, always ensuring a year's supply as a buffer against drought or famine. But in the first two years after Sennacherib's defeat, they will have to eat that year's harvest. "This sign may not seem extraordinary at first, yet is remarkable considering Hezekiah is uncertain of three months of survival, let alone three years of recovery followed by an unspecified number of secure years. The sign means Judah has been healed from what appeared to be a terminal illness."[54] The recovery would be slow, but God would not forsake his people.

Furthermore, Sennacherib would not enter Jerusalem nor bring a siege weapon against it (vv. 32–33). Rather, the Divine Warrior would defend Jerusalem "for my own sake and for the sake of my servant David" (v. 34).[55] Yahweh here demonstrates his remarkable faithfulness to the Davidic dynasty (cf. 20:6; 1 Kgs 11:36); all former threats to David's lamp had been neutralized, and this new threat from Sennacherib would end the same. But also note that, consistent with Hezekiah's prayer, Yahweh would spare Jerusalem out of grace, and not

---

54. House, *1, 2 Kings*, 370. "For the present, Hezekiah and Judah had to live by faith; but when the deliverance was complete, and they were enjoying the fruits of their labours and of God's salvation, then they could look back on the weary years, and recognise more clearly than while these were slowly passing how God had been in all the trouble, and had been carrying on His purposes of mercy through it all," (Maclaren, *Expositions*, 5:58).

55. J. J. M. Roberts, "The Davidic Origin of the Zion Tradition," *JBL* 92 (1973): 329–44.

because Hezekiah's faithfulness somehow merited such a rescue—"the piety of even the most faithful offers no guarantee of deliverance."[56]

Just as the Lord had sworn, Sennacherib's humiliating defeat did not come by arrows or shields or siege mounds. In other words, his defeat didn't come with his boots on. Rather, a mysterious being from heaven (cf. Exod 12:12–13, 23; 2 Sam 24:15–16) brought a message of death to Sennacherib's camp in the dead of night. Nestled all snug in their field beds with visions of victory dancing in their heads, 185,000 Assyrian soldiers simply failed to wake up the next morning.[57] The One who had breathed life into their nostrils at birth now snatched it away by divine prerogative in order to defend his people and to glorify his own Name to the ends of the earth.[58] In 1815, Lord Byron eulogized the Assyrian despot's bravado in the poem, *The Destruction of Sennacherib*.

> The Assyrian came down like the wolf on the fold,
> And his cohorts were gleaming in purple and gold;
> And the sheen of their spears was like stars on the sea,
> When the blue wave rolls nightly on deep Galilee.
>
> Like the leaves of the forest when Summer is green,
> That host with their banners at sunset were seen:
> Like the leaves of the forest when Autumn hath blown,
> That host on the morrow lay withered and strown.
>
> For the Angel of Death spread his wings on the blast,
> And breathed in the face of the foe as he passed;
> And the eyes of the sleepers waxed deadly and chill,
> And their hearts but once heaved, and for ever grew still!
>
> And there lay the steed with his nostril all wide,
> But through it there rolled not the breath of his pride;

---

56. Provan, *1 & 2 Kings*, 260.

57. The Greek historian Herodotus recorded that mice chewed through the bowstrings and shield handles of the Assyrian army, forcing Sennacherib to withdraw (*Histories* 2.141). Josephus cites this report, discredits it, and instead says that the Lord sent upon the Assyrians "a pestilential distemper," (*Antiquities* 10.21).

58. The Chronicler records how indeed the Lord and Hezekiah received international praise for the defeat of the Assyrians (2 Chr 32:23).

And the foam of his gasping lay white on the turf,
And cold as the spray of the rock-beating surf.

And there lay the rider distorted and pale,
With the dew on his brow, and the rust on his mail:
And the tents were all silent, the banners alone,
The lances unlifted, the trumpet unblown.

And the widows of Ashur are loud in their wail,
And the idols are broke in the temple of Baal;
And the might of the Gentile, unsmote by the sword,
Hath melted like snow in the glance of the Lord.[59]

~~Sylvester~~ Sennacherib shut up Hezekiah in Jerusalem like a bird in a cage. But that bad ol' Assyrian putty tat couldn't finish off the yellow Tweety bird because it was not the will of heaven that he do so. In humiliation, Sennacherib returned to his capital alone with all the glory of Napoleon skulking away from Moscow. And "though he would conduct five more campaigns, no mention of another return to Judah is given."[60]

Twenty years later (January 681), the narrator informs us, while worshiping in the temple of his god, Nisroch,[61] Sennacherib's two sons assassinated him and fled in exile to Ararat (modern-day Armenia). Each year for the rest of their lives, Adrammelech and Sharezer had to endure a very awkward Father's Day—Hallmark doesn't make cards for sons who kill their daddies. But what is more, a mighty king of a mighty empire proved no match for the God of heaven. Like many of Israel's former kings, he had put his hope in his own gods and his own strength. But Sennacherib's divine benefactor, Nisroch, could not protect his servant from assassination in his own house. And with that, every one of God's words through Isaiah (v. 7) came to pass, for the word of the Lord stands forever.

Idols, particularly the false god of self-sufficiency, fill us with an inflated sense of self-worth and invulnerability. On the other hand, faith in God and in his Son awakens in us a longing to serve and work for something greater than

59. George Gordon Lord Byron, *Poems* (New York: Knopf, 1994), 19–20.

60. Patterson, "1, 2 Kings," 918.

61. Nisroch is not attested in Assyrian sources; perhaps Ashur (the chief Assyrian god) or Ninurta (Assyrian god of war) is meant.

ourselves: God's glory. And in the place of invulnerability, we are granted something more precious: immortality with he who has loved us since before the foundation of the world.

I n the aftermath of God's great deliverance of Jerusalem from the hands of Sennacherib, a hymn was written to commemorate the occasion. According to tradition, Psalm 46 is that hymn. The opening verses state confidently, "God is our refuge and strength, a very present help in trouble. Therefore we will not fear though the earth gives way, though the mountains be moved into the heart of the sea, though its waters roar and foam, though the mountains tremble at its swelling." Later, speaking of the city of God and the holy place of the Most High, the psalmist celebrates, "God is in the midst of her; she shall not be moved; God will help her when morning dawns." The end of the psalm calls on all to "Be still, and know that I am God. I will be exalted among the nations, I will be exalted in the earth!" Thus, the people of God can exult, "The LORD of hosts is with us; the God of Jacob is our fortress."

It is my practice to recite appropriate passages of Scripture to myself in times of trial or stress. From my childhood, my parents encouraged and aided me in memorizing large portions of the Word of God, wishing that I would hide them in my heart. And since Jesus responded to threats from Satan by reciting the sacred writings, I figure it is a good thing to do so the same.

My son died on December 8, 2015. About 1:15 am, my wife ran into the room, telling me Daniel wasn't breathing. I bolted awake and rushed to perform CPR on him while ordering her to call 911. When the medics arrived, we both watched in shock as they attempted to revive our little boy. The entire time, as we watched the medics work on him, and as we drove to the hospital, and as we prayed desperately to the God of Abraham, Isaac, and Jacob to preserve our son's life, I found myself reciting Psalm 46 over and over in my mind. I couldn't shake it. Providentially, I had been researching just days before the narrative of 2 Kings 18–19 and reflecting on Psalm 46 as a result.

The first verse of Psalm 46 was especially apropos: "God is our refuge and strength, a very present help in trouble." Our prayers that God would preserve our son's life that morning were not answered in the affirmative. And I have since spent not a little time wondering why the Lord saw fit to allow a perfectly healthy two-year-old boy to die without any apparent cause or reason, particularly one who brought so much joy and love to his family and friends. Even today, I remain helplessly broken and bereaved. Our son is dead, and my wife and I are left with as many questions as we have tears.

But one thing beyond question for us is that God will somehow glorify himself in this tragedy. In the days immediately after my son's unexpected passing, I often found myself lying prostrate in my bathroom floor or curled in the corner of my closet, sobbing uncontrollably. In the throes of a pain I previously did not know existed, I was at a loss as to what to say in prayer. Only by the help of the Holy Spirit did words come: "Be exalted, O Christ." The only respite for a heart stripped of every joy is the assurance that God will glorify himself in the worst of circumstances. "I will be exalted among the nations, I will be exalted in the earth!" Only with the assurance that God will glorify himself in all things can we find the strength to say, "God is our refuge and strength, a very present help in trouble. Therefore we will not fear…"

2 KINGS 20

Sometime before the siege of Jerusalem by Sennacherib,[62] Hezekiah became deathly ill, and the prophet Isaiah confirmed as much to him by saying something along the lines of, "I wouldn't buy any more green bananas if I were you."[63] We are never told the nature of the disease, but it seems to have involved some sort of inflammation or boil (v. 7; cf. Exod 9:9–11; Lev 13:18–20, 23; Deut 28:35), the same malady Job suffered (Job 2:7), possibly a condition known as pemphigus.[64]

More significant than *how* Hezekiah became ill is that he *is* ill. "One of the greatest blessings that God could bestow on any man was a long life, and such a life was regarded as a particular mark of God's blessing and approval. Equally one of the surest marks of God's disfavour, and therefore a sign of particular

---

62. Scholars are divided as to when this event took place. The text simply says "in those days" (v. 1), which could technically allude to any time during Hezekiah's reign—it can be used of both past and future events (e.g., Gen 6:4; Exod 2:11, 23; Deut 17:9; 19:17; 26:3; Jer 3:16, 18). Patterson ("1, 2 Kings," 922) places the date c. 713–712.

63. "Sick kings in 1–2 Kings normally die (1 Kgs. 14; 2 Kgs. 1), and their dynasties shortly follow them into the grave. […] Isaiah comes without bidding, and, more important, when Isaiah brings a message of death (20:1), Hezekiah does not turn his face to the wall and die. He prays, something that no other sick king does before (20:2–6)," (Leithart, *1 & 2 Kings*, 259–60).

64. Cogan, *II Kings*, 255. Levin believes Hezekiah suffered from a tuberculosis rash (Schneir Levin, "Hezekiah's Boil," *Judaism* 42 [1993]: 214–17); Barker, the bubonic plague (Margaret Barker, "Hezekiah's Boil," *JSOT* 95 [2011]: 31–42).

sinfulness, was a short life."[65] Why must Hezekiah, the most righteous king in Jerusalem since David, see his life end at just thirty-nine years of age?

Commentators are torn how to interpret the fact that Hezekiah "turned his face to the wall" (v. 2; cf. 1 Kgs 21:4) and "wept bitterly" (v. 3). Was he sulking as Ahab had done? Not at all. Rather, as Hubbard puts it, Hezekiah was "shutting out all distractions and focusing his attention on Yahweh alone."[66] And his weeping was surely a product of the king's frustration over being (from his perspective) punished in spite of his faithfulness. Any lingering reminder of Ahab is expelled by reflecting on the words of Hezekiah's prayer.

As Hezekiah did in previous episodes, he petitioned the Lord during this crisis, borrowing language from Deuteronomy (cf. 8:6; 10:12; 11:22; 19:9; 26:17; 28:9; 30:16). "Following the Israelite tradition of personal laments [cf. Pss 17:3–5; 26:1–5], he cites his own character, the Lord's mercy, and the past as the basis for why he might receive what he requests. All three happen to be true, so he does not speak arrogantly."[67] As became clear in the previous episode, Hezekiah knew how to pray effectively!

In response to Hezekiah's plea, the narrator tells us that God spoke to the prophet "before Isaiah had gone out of the middle court" (v. 4), a location between the palace and the Temple (cf. 1 Kgs 6:36; 7:8). In his mercy,[68] Yahweh informed Hezekiah that the king would be healed within three days, and that fifteen years would be added to his life.

> The prophetic response goes well beyond the sickness of the king. The oracle, congruent with that of 19:34, also assures well-being for the city with two decisive verbs, "deliver, defend." In light of this utterance, there can be no doubt that the illness of the king is understood as an ebbing of the power of the dynasty. The motivation for the reversal on Yahweh's part, moreover, is for David's sake and for "my own sake," a phrase echoing 19:34. The double phrase suggests a remarkable feature of Yahweh's commitment to Jerusalem. Yahweh has indeed

---

65. Robinson, *Second Book*, 192–93.

66. Hubbard, *First and Second Kings*, 218.

67. House, *1, 2 Kings*, 373.

68. "Our times are in God's hands (Ps. 31:15) and any lengthening of life is by his special blessing," (Wiseman, *1 and 2 Kings*, 305).

made promises to David and to David's dynasty that are now in play (see Ps 89:19-37). Yahweh will keep Yahweh's promises! Beyond that, however, Yahweh will save the city from Assyria for Yahweh's own sake, i.e., to defend the honor and reputation of Yahweh before the nations and the other gods. Yahweh's motivation is in part self-enhancement. The happy reality is that in this prophetic utterance, Yahweh's own sake and David's sake converge. The king will live and the city will be safe.[69]

To trigger the king's healing process, Isaiah summoned "a poultice of figs" (NIV) to place on the boil, likely to serve as an antibiotic to cure the infection. According to Pliny's Natural History, figs were believed to possess medicinal qualities in Roman times,[70] and a veterinary text recovered at Ugarit tells of using figs and other ingredients to heal horses.[71]

But Hezekiah, exhibiting a very different attitude than his father (Isa 7:10–14), requested a sign that God would indeed heal him, and when Isaiah posed two options to him, the king chose the more impossible of the two (cf. Josh 10:13–14; Judg 6:36–39). "If God can delay time, the time of his death can be delayed."[72] Instead of time speeding up, he wanted it to reverse by "ten steps." Ramm proposes that one of two things happened.

1.   The sun actually "backed up" (or, to be more scientific, the earth's rotation reversed).

2.   The backing up was a "supernatural superior mirage of the sun" that makes things appear to shift—an optical illusion, if you will, caused by the sun.

The first explanation arises from a natural reading of the text (which I prefer), but Ramm notes that 2 Chronicles 32:31 seems to restrict the sign to Judah and would not have been discerned globally. "It is not a problem as to whether God could do it, but whether this is the best interpretation of all the facts in-

---

69. Brueggemann, 1 & 2 Kings, 522.

70. Pliny, Natural History 22.7; 23.63; 23.122.

71. COS 1.106.

72. Fretheim, First and Second Kings, 205.

volved."[73] Though omitted here and in 2 Chronicles 32, Isaiah records Hezekiah's psalm of thanksgiving after being healed (38:9–20).

It is uncertain what is meant by the "steps" (v. 11) or "dial" of Ahaz (Isa 38:8). Sundials are known to have existed in Babylon and Egypt dating back to the fifteenth century, and since these steps are said to have belonged to Ahaz, it has been thought that such was a pagan symbol of some sort (perhaps a part of the upper chamber shrine mentioned in 23:12). But if it was pagan in nature, it's unlikely that such would have survived Hezekiah's reforms. More recent commentators have suggested that the steps of Ahaz were just that—steps, and not necessarily used to tell time, but that the sun naturally cast a shadow on them through a window.

About the same time Hezekiah was restored to health, Babylonian[74] ambassadors from Merodach-baladan arrived in Jerusalem. Merodach-baladan had proclaimed himself king of Babylon in 722 when Sargon II had ascended the throne of Assyria. The two kings fought like cats and dogs, with Sargon exiling Merodach in 710. Merodach-baladan returned from exile for several months in 704–703, but was again defeated and forced into exile permanently in Elam.[75] It's likely during this period of temporary return from exile in 704–703 that this second story takes place.

Hezekiah and Merodach-baladan were allies in their struggle against the Assyrian juggernaut; it was thus fitting for the one to send the other a "Get Well Soon" candy gram. To impress the ambassadors, Hezekiah "showed them all his treasure house," likely the repository of the spoils of war from Hezekiah's military successes, as well as tax revenues, trade profits, and other royal income—note that this story had to have taken place before Hezekiah was forced to empty the treasuries to pay Sennacherib (18:15–16). The spices mentioned were quite valuable and were also among those brought by the queen of Sheba (1 Kgs 10:2,

---

73. Bernard Ramm, *The Christian View of Science and Scripture* (Grand Rapids: Eerdmans, 1954), 162–63.

74. "For the first time in Kings we read of Babylonian activity, and while Hezekiah sees no threat, readers are aware of what followed a hundred years later," (Olley, *Message of Kings*, 334).

75. To learn more about Merodach-baladan, see J. A. Brinkman, "Merodach-Baladan II," in *Studies Presented to A. Leo Oppenheim, June 7, 1964* (Chicago: Univ. of Chicago Press, 1964), 6–53.

10); thus Wiseman believes these spices indicated Hezekiah enjoyed good trade with central Arabia.[76]

But Hezekiah didn't stop there. In fact, by the end of the tour, we're told, "There was nothing in his house or in all his realm that Hezekiah did not show them" (v. 13). Whether Hezekiah was wise to have thrown this Open House for the benefit of his Babylonian guests will be discussed in a moment. But Patterson reminds us that "Hezekiah's actions were common protocol to impress important foreign visitors, especially potential allies."[77] Just as not everyone gets to see the *entire* White House on the standard tour, Fritz reminds us, "The access of visitors to all parts of the palace seems not to have been the rule; the palace was usually reserved for the royal family and the royal household that had to fulfill its private and public duties."[78]

But if it was common practice to give a tour to impress VIPs, why was Hezekiah effectively censured[79] for doing so by the Lord? Though it is not explicitly stated, one wonders if Hezekiah's offense was one of pride (Prov 16:5, 18; 28:25–26; 29:23)—does the Chronicler hint at such (2 Chr 32:26, 31)? Notice what the narrator of Kings specifically says in v. 13—"And Hezekiah welcomed them, and he showed them all *his* treasure house, the silver, the gold, the spices, the precious oil, *his* armory, all that was found in *his* storehouses. There was nothing in *his* house or in all *his* realm that Hezekiah did not show them" (emphasis mine). The narrator's point was that this grand show-and-tell was all about Hezekiah, and Hobbs agrees: "The presence of so many personal suffixes on the buildings and contents of the various storehouses is significant in representing hubris on the part of Hezekiah. The model king is in fact one who will not set out to accumulate for himself such things (Deut 17:17). [...] Hezekiah now falls short of the Davidic ideal."[80]

---

76. Wiseman, *1 and 2 Kings*, 307.

77. Patterson, "1, 2 Kings," 925; cf. Christopher Begg, "Hezekiah's Display (2 Kgs 20,12–19)," *Biblische Notizen* 38/39 (1987): 14–18).

78. Fritz, *1 & 2 Kings*, 384.

79. "The mention of Jerusalem's fall to Babylon at a time when Assyria was the dominant power and immediate threat is clear evidence of the inspiration of Scripture and the trustworthiness of biblical prophecy," (Patterson, "1, 2 Kings," 926).

80. Hobbs, *2 Kings*, 294. "The exposure of all military and economic resources to those from 'a foreign land' (2 Kings 20:14–15) is an ominous portent of the future (Deut. 29:22–23). Inspection of the Promised Land by foreigners is a sign of judgment like that of Sodom and

What is more, two additional dynamics are at play. First, inspections of wealth in ancient times were sometimes conducted as part of a treaty in which two nations vowed to defend one another. Hezekiah was seeking help from the king of Babylon—not the King of kings—in his anticipated war against Assyria. No wonder, then, that Isaiah expressed so much displeasure over Hezekiah's conduct. Second, though Hezekiah would not have seen it as such, this tour for the Babylonians amounted in ancient thought as a transfer of ownership. "By letting these ambassadors see everything, Hezekiah has handed over the possession of everything in Judah to the enemy and has anticipated the exile. Though the disaster itself belongs to the future [...] the essential legal take-over has already ensured that exile will take place."[81]

Equally troubling is Hezekiah's response to Isaiah's prophecy. He does not seek intercession and a change of heart, as he had done when he was ill. Rather, with an indifference that reminds us of Eli (1 Sam 3:18), he seems resigned to the fate of his descendants.[82] But bearing in mind that this is not the end of what we know of Hezekiah—the visit of the Babylonians precedes Sennacherib's invasion—we ought to interpret Hezekiah's response as humble submission to the divine will and gratitude that Jerusalem would not be destroyed immediately.

The narrator's eulogy of Hezekiah (vv. 20–21) mentions "the pool and the tunnel" (NIV) the king built to provide water for Jerusalem. Such a project was likely undertaken as part of the defensive preparations for Sennacherib's siege (cf. 2 Chr 32:2–8). The tunnel's construction was an impressive engineering accomplishment for that time, since workmen began at opposite ends and managed to meet accurately in the middle. Discovered in 1880, the eighteen-hundred-foot-long tunnel redirected the flow of the Gihon Spring

---

Gomorrah," (Konkel, *1 & 2 Kings*, 611).

81. P. R. Ackroyd, "An Interpretation of the Babylonian Exile: A Study of 2 Kings 20, Isaiah 38-39," *SJT* 27 (1974): 341.

82. "There is no acknowledgment of his folly in trusting the riches of Jerusalem for deliverance, and there is none of his previous concern for the ongoing welfare of Jerusalem. By placing this narrative at the last in Hezekiah's account, his portrait ends in a less complimentary way than it began. Juxtaposed to positive accounts of the king, it prepares for the final chapters of Kings. Jerusalem's fall is certain, and even a righteous king contributes to its certainty. The only remaining questions are how and when Jerusalem will fall to Babylon," (Wray Beal, *1 & 2 Kings*, 483).

(outside the city walls) to the west side of Jerusalem and inside the city walls into the pool of Siloam, providing the city with another water source inside and denying one to invaders outside the walls. Today, visitors to this tunnel can see an inscription[83] from Hezekiah's time commemorating completion of the tunnel.

---

83. "[The day of] the breach. This is the record of how the tunnel was breached. While [the excavators were wielding] their pick-axes, each man towards his co-worker, and while there were yet three cubits for the brea[ch,] a voice [was hea]rd each man calling to his co-worker; because there was a cavity in the rock (extending) from the south to [the north]. So on the day of the breach, the excavators struck, each man to meet his co-worker, pick-axe against pick-[a]xe. Then the water flowed from the spring to the pool, a distance of one thousand and two hundred cubits. One hundred cubits was the height of the rock above the heads of the excavat[ors]," (*COS* 2.28).

TALKING POINTS

T hough Hezekiah represents a person of profound faith in God, not all of his actions demonstrated this. His rebellion against Assyria and attacks on the Philistines were evidence of his faith in God, but it seems Hezekiah went a little too far at times to hedge his bets. Hezekiah's tunnel (20:20) was but one of many preparations the king made for an inevitable siege with the Assyrians. He also built a new city wall, twenty-three-feet thick, around the Second Quarter of Jerusalem (2 Chr 32:5).[84] But all these preparations were made without much faith in God's ability to deliver. "At that time the people of Jerusalem depended on the weapons kept at the Palace of the Forest. You saw that the walls of Jerusalem had many cracks that needed repairing. You stored up water in the lower pool. You counted the houses of Jerusalem, and you tore down houses to repair the walls with their stones. You made a pool between the two walls to save water from the old pool, but you did not trust the God who made these things; you did not respect the One who planned them long ago" (Isa 22:8–11 NCV; cf. Pss 20:7; 33:16–22; 147:10–11; Isa 31:1). Even when Sennacherib came against the city, the king was all too eager to buy him off as had his predecessors. Hezekiah, then, represents a person who trusts the Lord, but not enough not to equivocate. Dad used to say we must often "put legs on our prayers," and I subscribe to the philosophy that we must pray as if it all depends on God, yet work as if it all depends on us. However, such work must be offered as a demonstration of trust, not an admission of doubt.

T ucked away in the clever rhetoric of the Rabshakeh was Sennacherib's seemingly generous offer to Jerusalem's citizens of a better home in another land. On the surface, such would have been difficult for many to pass up. Why continue to live in a war-torn land, one struggling to produce food for its people, one that might be sacked and turned into a wasteland at any moment? Why not, instead, accept this generous offer and live in peace and security for the rest of one's natural life? One, history never shows that the Assyrians

84. Benjamin Mazar and Gaalyah Cornfeld, *The Mountain of the Lord* (Garden City, NY: Doubleday, 1975), 176–77.

made good on such promises.[85] Moreover, a better life in another land is still life in another land—not God's Land, the Promised Land. How often do we settle for what's safe and secure, even if it means separation from God, and thus miss out on all the incredible things God has planned for us? Rejecting God's providence and protection robs us of God's promise. Doubt destroys.[86]

I n response to the Rabshakeh's irreverent, but persuasive, propaganda, the text reads, "The people were silent and answered him not a word, for the king's command was, 'Do not answer him'" (18:36; cf. Exod 14:14; Ps 46:10). How difficult it must have been for the populace of Jerusalem not to panic after hearing the Rabshakeh's speech. Their obedient silence, however, is a testament to the immense trust they had in their king. Such confidence would not have existed had Hezekiah not demonstrated his own resilient trust in the God of Israel. In times of threats and trial, strong leaders must demonstrate their own resilient faith in order to strengthen the timidity of their followers. Fathers and mothers who exude tremendous confidence in the Lord can help anchor entire families and clans. Church leaders who exude tremendous confidence in the Lord can help anchor entire congregations. Indeed, an abiding faith that God is who he claims to be, and will do what he has promised he will do, is the greatest gift we can bestow on those who follow us. The idolatry and sin of Israel's leaders cost them their confidence and faith; their lack of confidence and faith cost them their kingdom. May such not be said of us!

---

85. "God makes plain that he is the One to offer terms of life and death (vv. 32–34); Sennacherib cannot usurp that role," (Konkel, *1 & 2 Kings*, 607).

86. "All those who, like Sennacherib or the beast in Revelation 13, claim the trust and loyalty that belong to God alone, even if they control 'all the kingdoms of the world and the glory of them' (Matt. 4:8), must be answered as Jesus answered the tempter, 'You shall worship the Lord your God and him only shall you serve' (Deut. 6:13; Matt. 4:10). They may and must be so answered because in the end God will defeat them—Pharaoh, Sennacherib, Domitian. For Christians, the event which makes it possible to believe such incredible news is the resurrection of Jesus, the defeat of death itself. All the Old Testament victories of God, both historical and literary, serve as pointers to and signs of that cosmic Easter triumph," (Nelson, *First and Second Kings*, 242–43).

ennacherib and the Rabshakeh threw at Jerusalem every rhetorical and psychological device in their arsenal. Against anyone else, they would have been successful. But here they did not account for Hezekiah's faith, Isaiah's prophetic ministry, or the Lord's sworn commitment to deliver his people. When the world threatens us, we can be sure it has underestimated the same—our faith in God, our commitment to the Word, and the Lord's sworn commitment not to allow anything to prevail against his church. Likewise, God's response to Sennacherib at the end of 2 Kings 19 offers up three important truths the church must bear in mind when we are threatened by the powers of the earth. *First, the wicked are attacking God, not us.* We can't take it personally. If we do, we will be tempted to lash out in bitterness or shrink back in trepidation. But God informed Sennacherib that Judah and Jerusalem were mocking him in derision. And while the New Testament calls us to love our enemies and overcome evil with good, we are also expected to compassionately repudiate the wicked versus fearfully accommodating them. *Second, even when circumstances seem their worst, all is going according to his plan.* Sennacherib's blasphemy and hostility were only a part of God's grander purposes. And if the darkest day of human history can now be called Good Friday, then we can trust that even the wicked act only according to God's sovereign script, for he makes even the wrath of men to praise him (Ps 76:10). *Finally, God has sworn to punish evil powers, particularly those who stand against the church of Christ.* In flaming fire, Jesus will return one day to take vengeance on those who have persecuted his people and not obeyed his gospel (2 Thess 1:8). God will vindicate the righteous and punish the wicked, for his holiness and commitment to glorify himself demands it. In this—God's commitment to glorify himself—the Christian places his ultimate trust.

13

THE LAMP EXTINGUISHED

S even centuries before the death of Hezekiah, on the dusty plains of Moab and with a multitude of his countrymen before him, Moses delivered a farewell address of sorts before ascending nearby Nebo to die. His health was not poor, nor were his eyes dim. In fact, the final editor of Deuteronomy goes out of his way to say that Moses' body was not failing him and "his vigor [was] unabated" (Deut 34:7). But Moses had disobeyed the word of the Lord, and now he was to suffer the consequences. For all those created in the image of God, sin and disobedience unequivocally lead to death (Rom 6:23).

In fact, it was this very truth that Moses wanted Israel to take to heart. They had been a rebellious lot ever since Egypt had appeared in the rearview mirror. "Wait—" the lawgiver thinks. "That was another generation." The oldest of Israelites who stood before Moses on that day had been mere children during those faithless times. Few could scarcely remember the golden calf at Sinai or the ten spies' negative report at Kadesh. The parents of this new generation of Israelites lay buried in the desert sand because sin and disobedience always lead to death.

Towards the end of Deuteronomy, Moses pronounced a blessing on Israel if she were faithful to the Law. But he also called down curses. Though the blessing runs for fourteen verses, the curses make up more than fifty. Plague, drought, crop failure, war, despair, confusion, devastation, ridicule, humiliation, slavery, perpetual doom, and finally…exile.

> The LORD will bring a nation against you from far away, from the end of the earth, swooping down like the eagle, a nation whose language you do not understand, a hard-faced nation who shall not respect the old or show mercy to the young.

[…] They shall besiege you in all your towns, until your high and fortified walls, in which you trusted, come down throughout all your land. And they shall besiege you in all your towns throughout all your land, which the LORD your God has given you. […] And as the LORD took delight in doing you good and multiplying you, so the LORD will take delight in bringing ruin upon you and destroying you. And you shall be plucked off the land that you are entering to take possession of it. And the LORD will scatter you among all peoples, from one end of the earth to the other, and there you shall serve other gods of wood and stone, which neither you nor your fathers have known. And among these nations you shall find no respite, and there shall be no resting place for the sole of your foot, but the LORD will give you there a trembling heart and failing eyes and a languishing soul.

Deuteronomy 28:49–50, 52, 63–65

Centuries later, Moses' words came to pass. Israel had sinned. Israel had been unfaithful. Israel had been disobedient. So Israel must die. The prophet Zephaniah gave voice to the pain and fury of Yahweh: "Woe to her who is rebellious and defiled, the oppressing city! She listens to no voice; she accepts no correction. She does not trust in the LORD; she does not draw near to her God. Her officials within her are roaring lions; her judges are evening wolves that leave nothing till the morning. Her prophets are fickle, treacherous men; her priests profane what is holy; they do violence to the law" (3:1–4).

From a historical perspective, Judah in her final days became a pawn in the war games of Assyria, Egypt, and Babylon. Nineveh, the capital of the Assyrian Empire, was sacked by the Babylonians in 612. Egypt tried in vain to prop up her Assyrian ally, but the Assyrian-Egyptian alliance was broken by Nebuchadnezzar and the Babylonians at Carchemish in 605, and Judah (an Egyptian protectorate since 609) was formally subjugated by Babylon in 604. Though after this she flirted with independence at the instigation of Egypt, Jerusalem would never be sovereign again.

From a secular view, Judah was simply a victim of political circumstances. But the divine narrator of Kings makes clear in no uncertain terms that her collapse was for spiritual reasons, not political.[1] Again, Zephaniah gave voice to the

---

1. "Babylon's placement as the new imperial power in the Levant occurs by YHWH's

inner musings of the Lord: "Of Jerusalem I thought, 'Surely you will fear me and accept correction!' Then her place of refuge would not be destroyed, nor all my punishments come upon her. But they were still eager to act corruptly in all they did" (3:7 NIV).

At the onset of World War I, as one nation declared war on another, it was said that the lights went out all over Europe. In the final five chapters of Kings, we see the lights go out for Jacob's children and the lamp of Israel extinguished. Inrig prepares us for Judah's rapid decline: "As we come to the final chapters of 2 Kings, we are struck by how fast the end comes. Events rush downhill with increasing speed."[2] Six of Judah's final seven kings are wicked, though the goodness of the one—Josiah—rivals even David's righteousness (22:2). But even Josiah's faith is not enough to grant Judah a stay of execution and a reprieve from exile.

2 KINGS 21:1-18

As righteous as Hezekiah had been—that's how wicked his son Manasseh was.[3] His reign began at age twelve, likely meaning he shared the throne with his father as a co-regent for the first ten years, "making him the fifth consecutive Judean prince to begin reigning in this manner."[4] But if Hezekiah attempted to groom his son for the throne after his health scare, he failed spectacularly. All total, Manasseh reigned fifty-five years (696–642), the longest tenure of any monarch in Israel's history. But his longevity was not due to his righteousness as much as in spite of his lack of it. The narrator's disgust is as inconspicuous as muddy paw prints on a white Oriental rug. According to him, Manasseh:

- **Rebuilt the altars to Baal.** These had not been seen in Judah since the illicit reign of Athaliah (11:18). The horror was compounded by the presence of an Asherah pole, and in the Temple of all places (vv. 4–5; cf. Deut 16:21)!

- **Worshiped the stars and other heavenly bodies.** Despite pro-

---

hand, and through Babylon YHWH's judgment against Judah (20:16–18; 21:10–15; 22:16–17; 23:26–27) is effected," (Wray Beal, *1 & 2 Kings,* 515).

2. Inrig, *I & II Kings,* 360.

3. "Manasseh, uniformly and unambiguously, is the worst king of Judah in the valuation of the Deuteronomistic Historians," (Konkel, *1 & 2 Kings,* 624).

4. Wood, *Survey,* 364; cf. Thiele, *Mysterious Numbers,* 176.

hibitions both in the Law (Deut 4:19; 17:2–7) and by recent
prophets (Isa 47:13; Amos 5:26), Manasseh introduced the
practice of astral worship[5] (e.g., the Sun, the Moon, and possibly
Venus[6]). According to stamp seals unearthed by archaeologists
in Israel,[7] it prevailed long after his death into the twilight years
of Judah's existence (cf. Jer 7:18; 8:2; 19:13; Zeph 1:5).

- **Built pagan altars within the Temple complex.** This was unprecedented among the kings of Judah, and Fretheim helps us appreciate just how abominable this really was—"Such an infidelity
is like moving a mistress into the house to live with one's wife."[8]
Jerusalem and the Temple is where God had put his Name (v. 4),
and thus it was blasphemy in the worst way for any other deity to
be worshiped within its precincts.

- **Practiced child sacrifices** (cf. 1 Kgs 11:5; 2 Kgs 16:3; 17:17, 31;
Jer 7:31; 19:5; 32:35; Ezek 16:20–21). Though references to
this practice outside of Scripture are rare, they do exist. One Assyrian legal text describes a particular penalty in this way: "he
will burn his son to Sin (a lunar deity), and his daughter to Belet-
seri."[9] The Law explicitly prohibited this type of atrocity (Deut
18:9–14).

- **Engaged in sorcery, witchcraft, and necromancy.** These, too, were
a direct violation of the Law (cf. Lev 19:26; Deut 18:9–13). Sorcery and witchcraft were general forms of divination practiced
in ancient times (e.g., Isa 2:6; Jer 27:9; Mic 5:12); necromancy specifically concerned inquiring of the dead. In this way, not
only did Manasseh emulate Ahab and Jeroboam, but also Israel's
first king, Saul (1 Sam 28:3–25).

5. Jeffrey L. Cooley, "Astral Religion in Ugarit and Ancient Israel," *JNES* 70 (2011): 281–87.

6. McKay, *Religion in Judah*, 45–59.

7. Walton, *Bible Background*, 456.

8. Fretheim, *First and Second Kings*, 209. "Certainly the temerity of putting this object right in the temple of Yahweh itself, along with various illicit altars (vv. 4, 5), must have evoked a horrified reaction from the original readers," (Nelson, *First and Second Kings*, 249).

9. Walton, *Bible Background*, 456.

As you can tell, "It is hard to imagine a more damning critique."[10] And as is the case with Ahaz, while scholars of yesteryear tried to defend Manasseh by saying he was only placating the Assyrians (i.e., "I was only following orders"), that view is almost universally rejected today. "The abominable foreign practices of Manasseh are apparently totally voluntary. There is nothing to suggest this facilitates favor with his Assyrian masters."[11]

Note that Manasseh was not content to reinstitute old practices; he went further than his idolatrous predecessors. If previous wicked kings had been al Qaeda, Manasseh was ISIS. "Throughout 1–2 Kings, the narrator reports that the kings of Israel follow the ways of Jeroboam I, who 'made Israel sin' (1 Kgs. 14:16; 15:26, 30, 34; 16:2), a phrase used some twenty times in the book. Throughout the whole of 1–2 Kings, however, no king 'makes Judah sin' [...]— until Manasseh (2 Kgs. 21:11, 16)."[12] He was particularly hostile to the prophets of God—Jewish tradition (affirmed by Justin Martyr and Tertullian) maintained that Manasseh had Isaiah sawn in half[13] (cf. Heb 11:37).

The depths of Manasseh's depravity is underscored by the statement, "Manasseh led them [Israel] astray to do more evil than the nations had done whom the LORD destroyed before the people of Israel" (v. 9). So abhorrent and brazen and damnable were Manasseh's deeds that the narrator now considered Israel to be spiritually inferior to the nations God had driven out of Canaan. It's as if Manasseh had undone Joshua's Conquest and, "heedless of Moses," had repealed the entirety of Deuteronomy.[14] If the sins of the Canaanites had eventually reached God's limit (cf. Gen 15:14, 16), Israel could not long expect to escape the wrath of a holy God. "In him the cup of YHWH's patience is drained dry, making judgment inevitable."[15] Indeed, the narrator will go on to explicitly connect Manasseh's sins with the fall of Judah and Jerusalem (23:26; 24:3; cf. Jer 15:4).

---

10. House, *1, 2 Kings*, 378. "Every cult practice that is prohibited in the legal code of the book of Deuteronomy is here attributed to Manasseh," (Fritz, *1 & 2 Kings*, 390).

11. Konkel, *1 & 2 Kings*, 622.

12. Leithart, *1 & 2 Kings*, 264.

13. *Martyrdom and Ascension of Isaiah* 5:1; Josephus, *Antiquities* 10.37–39. "Here is a brutal reminder that when rulers do not recognize accountability to a God who requires justice towards all, the way is open to institutional violence of many forms, often directed to people of certain ethnicity, political or religious views, or social status," (Olley, *Message of Kings*, 342).

14. Wray Beal, *1 & 2 Kings*, 488.

15. Ibid., 494.

Manasseh was thus made into Judah's "Jeroboam," the figure
on whom was concentrated all the sins of the Davidic kings
and the people over whom they ruled. Fairly or not, his reign
is described as a fifty-five year orgy of apostasy. [...] Matters
for Judah have reached a critical point. Manasseh's apostasy
is so outrageous that it can lead only to national destruction
(cf. Zeph. 1:4–5). It has infuriated God to the breaking point
(vv. 6, 15), as had already happened with the Northern Kingdom (17:11, 17). [...] In the short term, Manasseh's sins will
provide tasks for Josiah's hopeful reform, but in the long term,
Kings insists that the die has already been cast. Even Josiah's
reform cannot stop the inexorable doom set in motion by
Manasseh, the worst king ever (22:17; 23:26).[16]

Manasseh is known to secular history by way of Assyrian records. Along
with several other kings, he is listed as a vassal of the Assyrian king Esarhaddon and was required to contribute timber and stone for building projects in
Nineveh. On another occasion, during the reign of Ashurbanipal, Manasseh provided soldiers for Assyria's campaign against Egypt.[17] In return, Manasseh was
likely able to hold on to his power and silence his opponents with the help of
Assyrian troops.[18]

Despite his hostility to God's messengers, Manasseh discovered that he
could not silence the divine word. Note that God could not remain silent while
evil remained so rampant. The prophetic voice once again spoke out against the
throne—God was bringing judgment against Judah because of Manasseh's unprecedented sin, and three powerful metaphors are used.

- *Tingling ears.* In the Old Testament, this represents how people
  receive bad news (cf. 1 Sam 3:11; Jer 19:3). Just as a loud noise
  leaves your ears ringing, the phrase is another way of expressing
  the terror or trembling that comes upon someone who hears what
  God has done[19] (cf. Exod 15:14; Deut 2:25; Isa 32:11; 64:2).

---

16. Nelson, *First and Second Kings,* 247, 251.

17. *ANET* 291, 294.

18. Konkel, *1 & 2 Kings,* 626.

19. Cogan, *II Kings,* 268–69. "The phrase means that the things to happen are so unbear-

- *Measuring line.* Though a measuring and plumb line were used in construction to determine if a wall was structurally sound (cf. Isa 28:17; 44:13; Amos 7:7–8; Zech 1:16), the Lord intended here to use them as instruments of destruction (cf. Isa 34:11; Lam 2:8). What is easily missed is that this is an allusion to the Northern Kingdom; God would use the same standards for Jerusalem that he had for Samaria to determine if the former should be torn down for being unsound (cf. 17:7–23).

- *Wiped dish.* If the measuring and plumb line highlighted the justice of God's punishment, this image portrayed the thoroughness of his wrath.[20] In an age with no refrigeration (and thus no leftovers), food remains were raked out of a dish and into the garbage. Thus, Yahweh vividly portrays Judah as a dish he is about to empty out into the trash and wipe clean. Nothing will remain when God's judgment is finished (cf. Jer 51:34); in fact, the term translated "wiping" is elsewhere rendered "blot out" (cf. Gen 6:7; 7:4; Exod 17:14; 32:32). Note that in this passage, the dish is also turned over, indicating the person dining has had enough. "Not only are a city and its people wiped out, but YHWH as well, has had his fill of Judah's sinning and can take no more."[21]

Like Ahab before him, Manasseh is convicted of being "an indiscriminate murderer. He drenched Jerusalem with the innocent blood of his victims" (v. 16 Msg; cf. 9:7, 26; Jer 7:5–7; Mic 3:9–11). As noted previously, some of these victims were no doubt the prophets of God. Whoever brought God's prediction of doom in vv. 10–15 likely paid the ultimate price. Conspicuous, too, is the fact that the prophetic activity so vibrant in generations before (Isaiah, Micah) and after (Zephaniah, Jeremiah) Manasseh is relatively silent during his reign. "None of the canonical prophets impinge on Manasseh's fifty-five years. The reign is characterized by a 'famine of the word of God.'"[22]

---

ably menacing that announcement of them will cause a jarring reaction, a pounding in the head, an unsettling reverberation among those who hear it," (Brueggemann, *1 & 2 Kings*, 533).

20. Olley, *Message of Kings*, 342. Hobbs says this phrase is "akin to the English 'wiping the slate clean,' but with the opposite effect!" (*2 Kings*, 307).

21. Cogan, *II Kings*, 269.

22. Hobbs, *2 Kings*, 307.

But there were other victims. In the mouths of the prophets who ministered late in Judah's life, *to shed innocent blood* was a phrase that "referred to oppression of the poor and the underprivileged,"[23] (e.g., Jer 7:6; 22:3, 17; Ezek 22:6, 25). In other words, there was a total collapse of spirituality, morality, and social justice during this dark period—what Hubbard calls "state-sponsored terror."[24] Nelson adds, "That totalitarian destruction of national religious institutions goes hand in hand with a disregard for judicial due process and the security of the average citizen should be no surprise to the modern reader. Manasseh's sins were not his alone. Sin is rarely an individual matter in the Old Testament."[25]

Manasseh's reign of terror left a deep bloodstain on Judah's garments that could not be cleansed or bleached. Later, it is "violence that is cited as one of the causes for Judah's exile (24:4). Naboth's blood cries out against Ahab for vengeance and calls up Jehu as the avenging angel. During the reign of Manasseh, blood cries from the ground of Jerusalem, and Nebuchadnezzar hears the cry."[26]

All too eagerly, the narrator dispenses with Manasseh with a brief eulogy.[27] Notably, he was not buried in the royal tombs, but in the garden of Uzza, and was succeeded by his son Amon. So far in Kings, deceased Judean monarchs have been buried "in the city of David." But beginning with Hezekiah (2 Chr 32:33), the death notice changes. Did the royal cemetery change locations due to lack of additional space? The reference to Uzza is ambiguous. Since Manasseh dabbled in astrology, is this reference to the Arabian goddess al-'Uzza, who was connected to Venus?[28] Or was it a private garden for Uzziah that now became a burial place for his descendants?[29] Wherever the tomb's location, it was almost

---

23. Cogan, *II Kings*, 269.

24. Hubbard, *First and Second Kings*, 223.

25. Nelson, *First and Second Kings*, 249.

26. Leithart, *1 & 2 Kings*, 264. "Jer 15:1–4 is evidence that the sins of Manasseh were burned into the memory of the prophetic tradition long after he had left the scene," (Hobbs, *2 Kings*, 307).

27. "Such a heinous king has a remarkably tame concluding regnal summary. Yet even here the magnitude of his sin intrudes, for he is the only southern king whose misdeeds are specifically noted in the closing summary," (Wray Beal, *1 & 2 Kings*, 491).

28. Konkel, *1 & 2 Kings*, 623; McKay, *Religion in Judah*, 24–25.

29. Walton, *Bible Background*, 407–8. "It is fitting that the name of the burial place of Manasseh, and of the son who walked in his ways, should carry connotations of spectacular judgment upon impiety," (Provan, *1 & 2 Kings*, 269).

certainly on royal property since the Chronicler claims Manasseh was buried in his palace (2 Chr 33:20).

Mysteriously absent from the Kings account of Manasseh is mention of his repentance late in life.[30] As punishment for his many sins, Chronicles claims that the Assyrians (likely Ashurbanipal) came and deported Manasseh to Babylon. "And when he was in distress, he entreated the favor of the LORD his God and humbled himself greatly before the God of his fathers. He prayed to him, and God was moved by his entreaty and heard his plea and brought him again to Jerusalem into his kingdom. Then Manasseh knew that the LORD was God" (2 Chr 33:12–13).[31] The Chronicler then goes on to describe the religious reforms Manasseh instituted in the Temple, including cleansing it of idols and restoring the altar he had replaced (vv. 4–5). But all of this seems to have been too little, too late. In other words, "the die had been cast."[32]

2 KINGS 21:19-26

Manasseh's son, Amon, inherited[33] the throne in his early twenties and lasted all of one Congressional term[34] (642–640). The note about his mother's

---

30. "From its exilic perspective, Kings underlines for its audience the awful consequences of idolatry, and it has been persuasively argued that part of the purpose of the work was to urge its exilic audience to look to the Lord with contrition and repentance. To include an account of the punishment and restoration of Manasseh would certainly have diminished the rhetorical force of the work. There is a note of hope in Kings, but it is decidedly muted in the aftermath of exile, where a summons to repentance is a more immediate concern. Chronicles, on the other hand, addresses a much later time and audience, and therefore draws a different (but complementary) lesson from the life of Manasseh, in emphasizing God's grace to a notorious sinner," (Brian Kelly, "Manasseh in the Books of Kings and Chronicles [2 Kings 21:1–18; 2 Chron 33:1–20]," in *Windows into Old Testament History: Evidence, Argument, and the Crisis of "Biblical Israel,"* eds. V. Philips Long, David W. Baker, and Gordon J. Wenham [Grand Rapids: Baker, 2002], 140).

31. Josephus, *Antiquities,* 10.40–45. Manasseh's prayer of repentance is allegedly preserved in the apocryphal book *Prayer of Manasseh.*

32. Hubbard, *First and Second Kings,* 223.

33. Manasseh seems to be the first king since Azariah not to name a co-regent. Gray speculates that this was due to Assyrian dominance: "So careful were the rulers of Assyria that there should be no leader round whom national resistance might rally that Manasseh is found twice as a hostage, probably, for the loyalty of his people, in Nineveh and Egypt. Thus we may understand why no co-regent was appointed," (*I & II Kings,* 647).

34. And probably less, given how Judah reckoned the length of a king's reign, not unlike

4444444
44444

name and origin speaks to Amon's upbringing. Though the location of Jotbah is uncertain, it's thought by some to have been outside of Israel in Arabia.[35] In other words, like Ahab and Manasseh, Amon had a strong feminine influence in his life from outside the covenant community. Add to that his father's wickedness, and we should not be surprised to read Amon "did what was evil in the sight of the LORD" (v. 20). As far as the narrator is concerned, this is another instance of "second verse, same as the first"—"There is little hope of redemption for Judah under this duplicate Manasseh."[36] The Chronicler adds, "he did not humble himself before the LORD," but rather "incurred guilt more and more" (2 Chr 33:23).

But unlike his father, Amon's story has a twist. Finally weary of the dark cloud hovering over the house of David, palace servants assassinated the king in 640. However, before they could go much further with their coup, "the people of the land" executed the assassins and established Amon's eight-year-old son, Josiah, in his place. "The people of the land" had once dispatched a previous sovereign (Athaliah) in favor of a boy king (Joash), and they did so again. As for Amon, he was buried beside his father in the garden of Uzza.

Why was Amon assassinated? The narrator does not tell us because, as far as he's concerned, wicked kings fully deserve whatever ignominious end they meet. But this doesn't keep scholars from speculating as to the immediate political reasons for Amon's death. For one thing, the fact that an eight-year-old replaces the deposed king "indicates that some faction puts him in place and probably actually runs the country for some time."[37] It's possible the assassins were either backers of Hezekiah's reforms or opposed to Assyria's political stranglehold on Judah (recall that Manasseh and Amon had been effectively vassals); we know that there was an uprising against the Assyrian king Ashurbanipal in the year Amon was murdered.[38] Meanwhile, in Egypt, Psammetik I (664–609) was

---

how Jesus was in the grave for "three days," when it was really one full day and parts of two others.

35. Gray, *I & II Kings*, 648; Jones, *1 and 2 Kings*, 2:601. Others place it in the area of Galilee (Frankel, "Jotbah [Place]," *ABD* 3:1020).

36. Wray Beal, *1 & 2 Kings*, 492.

37. House, *1, 2 Kings*, 380.

38. Malamat supposes that Amon's assassins hoped to join the revolt, only to be thwarted by the nobles of Judah (A. Malamat, "The Historical Background of the Assassination of Amon, King of Judah," *IEJ* 3 [1953]: 26–29; Lewis, "Amon [Person]," *ABD* 1:198).

growing more threatening, and Amon's political enemies might have intended to forge a stronger alliance with their neighbors on the Nile (cf. Jer 2:18, 36–37).[39]

In the end, it is impossible to know exactly why Amon was assassinated, just as it is sometimes impossible to know why current heads of state are struck down (e.g., the many theories as to who assassinated President Kennedy). What we can say for sure is that Amon was wicked, and in the mind of the divine narrator, he got what his wickedness deserved. What is also evident is that Jerusalem had become "a cauldron of competing ideological passions."[40]

2 KINGS 22:1–23:30

In January 1993, in the first round of the NFL playoffs, the Buffalo Bills found themselves being blown out by the visiting Houston Oilers 35-3. But backup quarterback Frank Reich engineered the most improbable comeback. In less than thirty minutes, Reich tied the game, and Buffalo won in overtime on a Steve Christie field goal. I didn't watch that game live, but I do remember other great comebacks in sports—I followed the Boston Red Sox's impossible recovery from being down 3-0 in the 2004 ALCS to the New York Yankees, only to pull off eight consecutive victories to win the World Series.

Josiah's reign reminds me of such an unlikely second-half comeback. Though the narrator spends only a chapter on the near-six decades prior to Josiah's reign, the horror of Manasseh and Amon must not be forgotten—"Against their dark, evil lives, Josiah's deep faith shone brightly as a truly extraordinary change."[41]

I confess that when I watch replays of great comebacks by the Dallas Cowboys, I always want to fast forward through the painful parts. Who would want to relive it? And the Red Sox's defeat of the Yankees in Game 4 of the 2004 ALCS is an emotional roller coaster (e.g., Dave Roberts stealing second in the eighth inning; David Ortiz's walk-off homer in extras). But few Boston fans remember that in Game 3, the Sox had been shelled by New York 19-8. Should I ever forget the agony of losing, the thrill of the comeback becomes less sweet.

---

39. The priestly establishment, whose "power and influence had been suppressed during Manasseh's long reign," may have also been culpable (Barnes, *1–2 Kings*, 355). Other reasons for Amon's assassination are posed by Miller and Hayes (J. Maxwell Miller and John H. Hayes, *A History of Ancient Israel and Judah*, 2nd ed. [Louisville: Westminster John Knox, 2006], 437).

40. Brueggemann, *1 & 2 Kings*, 536.

41. Hubbard, *First and Second Kings*, 224.

A fter his father's assassination, Josiah (640–609) was proclaimed king by the people of the land, though he was only eight years of age.[42] In addition, notice of his brief reign acts as a spoiler—"He dies at thirty-nine? *How? Why?*" This is arguably the response the narrator intends to elicit.

Unlike his father and grandfather, Josiah was a righteous man and followed in David's footsteps, not turning "aside to the right or to the left"[43] (v. 2). This very statement reminds us of Deuteronomy 17:20, "where the ideal king is one who does not 'turn' [same word in Hebrew as in 2 Kgs 22:2] from the law to the right or to the left. This is only the first of many references in 2 Kings 22–23 that link Josiah with the law of Moses in general and the figure of Moses in particular. For the authors of Kings, Josiah was the best of all kings, transcending even David and Hezekiah in his faithfulness to God."[44]

In 622, when the king was in his mid-twenties,[45] he commissioned his secretary and the high priest with restoring the Temple,[46] which had obviously not been a priority for many decades, and it had been almost two centuries since Joash's renovations. Hilkiah was to take money from the "general-purpose building fund" and use it for renovations. During the project, something very precious (and arguably believed up to that point to have been lost forever) was

---

42. Due to his young age, it's likely Josiah's policies were guided and implemented by guardian-advisors, perhaps the very "people of the land" who had made him king (Cogan, *II Kings*, 281).

43. "The right hand/left hand motif, which frequently expresses completeness or full participation on the part of the persons involved (cf. Eze 39:3; Da 12:7; Jnh 4:11; 2 Co 6:7), here stresses Josiah's singlehearted devotion to God's approved course of conduct for his life," (Patterson, "1, 2 Kings," 932).

44. Provan, *1 & 2 Kings*, 270; cf. Hens-Piazza, *1–2 Kings*, 383–84.

45. "His desire to serve the Lord surfaces even earlier according to the Chronicler, who states that Josiah begins to 'seek the God of his father David' in the eighth year of his rule (ca. 632 B.C.) and starts removing some 'high places, Asherah poles, carved idols and cast images' in about 628 B.C., his twelfth year as king (2 Chr 34:3). Therefore, it is not strange that in his eighteenth year the king senses an obligation to repair the temple, an impulse felt by Joash years earlier (cf. 2 Kgs 12:1–16)," (House, *1, 2 Kings*, 382).

46. "Restoration entailed both physical and ritual aspects. A neglected temple would need structural repairs and perhaps the restoration of pilfered furniture and accessories. It is possible that gold objects or gold plating on walls would need to be replaced. Then the temple would need to have its sanctity reestablished through appropriate rituals. Finally, it would need to be provided with funding and personnel so that it could operate," (Walton, *Bible Background*, 457).

found.[47] Hilkiah told Shaphan the secretary, "I have found the Book of the Law in the house of the LORD" (v. 8).[48]

When the contents of that book were read to Josiah, he tore his clothes in grief. In 19:1, Hezekiah had torn his clothes because of the threat against Jerusalem and God's Name being blasphemed by the Assyrians. Here, Josiah was no doubt grieved that God had been blasphemed by Judah's disobedience. When the royal reader got to the latter portions of Deuteronomy[49] and the covenant curses (28:15–68; 29:25–28), this probably didn't help either.[50]

His royal robes in tatters,[51] Josiah gave this directive: "Go, inquire of the LORD for me, and for the people, and for all Judah, concerning the words of this book that has been found. For great is the wrath of the LORD that is kindled against us, because our fathers have not obeyed the words of this book, to do according to all that is written concerning us" (v. 13). There are a lot of things I hope my children say at my funeral: "He was a wonderful dad." "He was a loving

---

47. In Jewish tradition, this scroll was considered unique because 1) Ahaz and Manasseh had destroyed all other scrolls, 2) this scroll had actually been written by Moses himself (Deut 31:24–26; cf. 2 Chr 34:14), or 3) the scroll had been found while open to Deuteronomy 28:36, which warned of exile (Zevit, "2 Kings," 771).

48. "It is not difficult to understand why the book may have been moved from its proper place beside the ark of the covenant (Deut. 31:26); Manasseh would not have wanted it there, nor would the priests have wanted to provoke him by leaving it there," (Konkel, *1 & 2 Kings*, 634).

49. Hubbard (*First and Second Kings*, 225) presents three solid reasons why we should equate Josiah's "Book of the Law" with Deuteronomy. First, the phrase "Book of the Law" occurs regularly in Deuteronomy (cf. 28:61; 29:21; 30:10; 31:26). Second, that Josiah was horrified when the book was read implies that the book threatened disaster to those who disobeyed its contents. Third, Josiah went on to restore worship to a central location in Israel—the Temple—which "fits the thrust of Deuteronomy better than any other book," (cf. Deut 12:11, 14; 16:2; 26:2).

50. In stark contrast, Josiah's son, Jehoiakim, would burn a message of judgment and warning from the Lord as if it were a week-old newspaper, and he certainly didn't tear his clothes in fear or grief (Jer 36:23–24). In fact, "tore" in 22:11 and "cut" in Jeremiah 36:23 are from the same Hebrew verb (*qara*). "Given the close connections between the literature of Deuteronomy and Jeremiah and given the same term in both cases, it is likely that the two texts are interrelated, offering the two classic responses of resistance and repentance to the authority of the scroll," (Brueggemann, *1 & 2 Kings*, 545; cf. Charles D. Isbell, "2 Kings 22:3–23:24 and Jeremiah 36: A Stylistic Comparison," *JSOT* 8 [1978]: 33–45).

51. "Josiah mourns when the written Torah is read, demonstrating what Huldah later describes as his 'tender' or 'fearful' heart (22:19; cf. Deut. 20:3; Isa. 7:4), the most responsive royal heart since the hearing heart of Solomon," (Leithart, *1 & 2 Kings*, 267).

husband." "He raised us to love Jesus, his church, and his Word." But for all the things I hope they say, I hope they do *not*—can*not*!—say: "Great is the wrath of the LORD that is kindled against us, because our father has not obeyed the words of this book."

To inquire of the Lord, several of Josiah's aides visited a prophetess named Huldah.[52] Beginning with the collapse of the Northern Kingdom, the population of Jerusalem seems to have tripled or quadrupled to the point that a "second quarter" (v. 14; cf. Zeph 1:10; Neh 3:9, 12) or district on the western hill of the city became necessary.[53] Refugees fleeing a destroyed Samaria and other Northern Israelite towns likely came to Jerusalem during Hezekiah's reign and found refuge in this second district, which overlooked the Hinnom Valley to the southwest and the Tyropoean Valley to the east.[54] In fact, Patterson implies that members of this neighborhood (including Huldah and her husband) were of "humble circumstances."[55]

The message they received was arguably not what they hoped to hear. Yahweh swore to bring on Jerusalem all the covenant curses Josiah had heard read from Deuteronomy (v. 16). The wrath of the Lord would be kindled and go unquenched against Jerusalem because of the centuries of idolatry and disobedience—"God's personalizing of the word (unlike the third person in 2 Kings 17:7–17) is striking: 'they have abandoned *me* ... provoked *me* to anger ... *my* wrath.'"[56] Wray Beal notes grammatical parallels between this oracle of judgment and those previously spoken against Manasseh (21:11–12), Ahab (1 Kgs 21:21), and Jeroboam (1 Kgs 14:10). Such a parallel, she believes, "is intentional and chilling: the word against Jerusalem is as certain of fulfilment as that given Jeroboam and Ahab. [...] YHWH's wrath will not be quenched. The final hurdle of sin has been broached and there is no hope of reprieve."[57]

---

52. Huldah is one of four prophetesses known in the Old Testament, the others being Miriam (Exod 15:20), Deborah (Judg 4:4), and Noadiah (Neh 6:14).

53. M. Broshi, "The Expansion of Jerusalem in the Reigns of Hezekiah and Manasseh," *IEJ* 24 (1974): 21–26; Avraham Faust, "The Settlement of Jerusalem's Western Hill and the City's Status in Iron Age II Revisited," *ZDPV* 121 (2005): 97–118; Shiloh, "Jerusalem: Topography," *NEAEHL* 2:705–6.

54. Provan, "2 Kings," 190.

55. Patterson, "1, 2 Kings," 935.

56. Fretheim, *First and Second Kings*, 214; emphasis his.

57. Wray Beal, *1 & 2 Kings*, 504.

But there was good news for Josiah personally—because of his repentance[58] and humility, Josiah would go to his "grave in peace" and not live to see
all the horrible things God had in store for his people (v. 19).[59] The word of the
Lord must come to pass—but he is merciful enough to delay the inevitable for
the sake of his righteous servants. "Of only two people in Kings is it said that
they 'humbled themselves': Ahab, the worst king of Israel, and Josiah, the best
king of Judah. In both cases promised judgment is deferred till after their death.
God's grace is open to all. Hezekiah had also received a word of delay beyond
his lifetime (20:16–19), although Josiah's concern for the whole city and people
shines through (vv. 13, 19)."[60]

D uring Josiah's reign, significant events took place on the world stage
that shifted the balance of power. In 627, the Assyrian king Ashurbanipal died, triggering an internal civil war and the final chapter in
Assyria's dominance. The next year, 626, saw the rise of Nabopolassar (father
of Nebuchadnezzar) in Babylon. With the help of his allies, the Medes, Nabopolassar cast off the Assyrian yoke and began harassing Assyria until the capitol,
Nineveh, fell in 612. During this same time, the Cimmerians and Scythians began harassing Assyria's northern border (cf. Jer 1:13).[61]

---

58. Literally, the Hebrew says Josiah's heart was *soft*. "This idiom is used in parallel to verbs
of fear and timidity; cf. Deut 20:3, Isa 7:4, Jer 51:46, 2 Chr 13:7. Here it describes Josiah, overcome by the warnings in the book of the Law read to him," (Cogan, *II Kings*, 284).

59. It is difficult to reconcile the promise that Josiah would die "in peace" when we see
him meet his demise, especially since elsewhere, dying in peace means dying of natural causes
(cf. Gen 15:15) and not by the sword (Jer 34:4–5). "But the holocaust facing Judah will be so
terrible that even normal burial following violent death (23:29–30) must be considered to be
'in peace' by comparison," (Nelson, *First and Second Kings*, 257; cf. P. S. F. van Keulen, "The Meaning of the Phrase *WN'SPT 'L-QBRTYK BSLWM* in 2 Kings XXII 20," *VT* 46 [1996]: 256–60).
Contra Cogan, who believes "these words of Huldah remain a striking example of unfulfilled
prophecy," (*II Kings*, 295).

60. Olley, *Message of Kings*, 350. Though Wray Beal offers this contrast: "The stakes are
much higher in Josiah's case. Ahab repented for only his own sin, and judgment concerned only
one dynasty. Josiah repents for the nation's sin, and judgment engulfs the whole nation," (*1 & 2
Kings*, 505).

61. H. F. W. Saggs, *The Greatness That Was Babylon* (New York: Mentor, 1962), 141–45;
cf. Bright, *History*, 313–16.

Meanwhile, Egypt began to flex her own muscles to the south, but showed little to no interest in Judah or Josiah, except in areas of commerce and trade—"albeit they expected to be able to move troops through Palestine when they wished to do so"[62] (a development that would prove momentous for Judah). "Thus, Josiah rules during years in which Assyria fades but also those in which Babylon is not yet ready to rule as far west as Judah and in a time when Egypt does not yet attempt to rule the smaller nations north of the border."[63] Free from international harassment, Josiah took point on several reforms in Judah.

T he reformation was launched with a covenant renewal ceremony in Jerusalem. Josiah had "the Book of the Covenant" (likely Deuteronomy) read to all the people and led them in rededicating themselves to the will of Yahweh, not unlike the covenant-renewal ceremonies led by Moses (Exod 24:3–8), Joshua (Josh 8:32–35), and Jehoiada (11:17). And then, as if directing cleanup of widespread nuclear waste,[64] the king gave instructions to Hilkiah and the priests that the Temple be scrubbed of all the trappings of idolatry—"the vessels made for Baal, for Asherah, and for all the host of heaven" (v. 4)—and had them burned in the Kidron Valley,[65] the area between Jerusalem and the Mount of Olives to the east. Their ashes, meanwhile, were carried to Bethel, one of the idolatrous shrines of the Northern Kingdom.

Idolatrous priests were deposed and humiliated, banned from serving in the Temple[66] (v. 9); idolatrous high places were destroyed; the Temple Asherah was ground to dust—just like the golden calf at Sinai (Exod 32:20; Deut 9:21)—and thrown into the graveyard. Chariots were burned and horses were retired that had once been a tribute to the sun god (thought to have been an

---

62. Provan, "2 Kings," 200–01.

63. House, *1, 2 Kings*, 382.

64. Notice the violent verbs used in this passage: "burned," "beat," "cast," "broke," "defiled," "broke down," "pulled down," "broke in pieces," "cut down" (23:6–19).

65. "Associated with idolatry since the time of Solomon (1 Kings 11:7), the Kidron Valley became during Josiah's reformation a convenient place to destroy cult objects, thus not only removing them from Jerusalem but also desecrating the valley itself as a religious site," (Provan, "2 Kings," 201).

66. "It is amazing to read that living quarters of the male shrine prostitutes had been constructed in the temple itself," (Inrig, *I & II Kings*, 348).

Assyrian practice, cf. Ezek 8:16); altars for celestial worship once prized by Ahaz and Manasseh were also destroyed. Prostitutes, mediums, necromancers, sorcerers—all these were immediately put out of business[67] (v. 24). Even the idolatrous shrines of Solomon on the Mount of Olives (1 Kgs 11:7) did not escape Josiah's notice (had they been spared in Hezekiah's purge?). The narrator also tells us that he "defiled Topheth[68]" (v. 10), the altar of Molech in the Hinnom Valley where parents had sacrificed their children to the flames to appease this faux god during the reigns of Ahaz and Manasseh (cf. 16:3; 21:6; Jer 7:31; 32:35).

At Bethel, Josiah tore down Jeroboam's idolatrous shrine to fulfill the word of the unknown prophet (1 Kgs 13:2). Unsatisfied that the place had been appropriately desecrated, he ordered that bones from nearby tombs be burned on the altar in order to defile it utterly. This campaign of cleansing did not end at Bethel, but was carried out throughout the territory of the Northern Kingdom,[69] and included the execution of the pagan priests on their own pagan altars (v. 20; cf. 17:29, 32; Deut 13:12–18). Walton explains that in the ancient Near East, "the worst criminals were not accorded a proper burial, and their bones were either burned or discarded. This was the worst possible thing for an individual, since one's spiritual existence was intertwined with their physical existence," meaning if the bones were destroyed—as Josiah does here—"the individual's existence was also extinguished."[70] Remarkably, however, Josiah left the remains of the unknown prophet and his Bethel colleague untouched (1 Kgs 13:31).[71]

Josiah's final reform was reinstating observance of the Passover. Apparently, not since the period of Judges had the Passover been observed as it was here. Hezekiah had observed the Passover also, but the narrator's point was that Josi-

---

67. "These actions remove not merely idolators [sic] but those who, because of their divination practices, compete with true prophets. The way is now clear for God's Word to flow directly to the people," (House, 1, 2 Kings, 390–91).

68. "Probably the word refers either to the stand over the fire upon which the child was placed or to the hearth as a whole," (Cogan, II Kings, 287).

69. "Both parts of the divided kingdom are reunited spiritually, if not politically. Both sections of the land return to fidelity to the Lord and to an emphasis on worship at a central sanctuary," (House, 1, 2 Kings, 389).

70. Walton, Bible Background, 410.

71. "The narrative pause identifies the two men buried together and the honour Josiah accords the pair. He thus affirms their ministries and acknowledges the inviolability of the prophetic word concerning the altar," (Wray Beal, 1 & 2 Kings, 509).

ah's observance was different than all Passovers before it because it was celebrat-ed, not among families in the villages (2 Chr 30:15–17; cf. Exod 12:1–10), but corporately in Jerusalem[72] (cf. Deut 16:5–6).

Thus the narrator concludes, "Before him there was no king like him, who turned to the LORD with all his heart and with all his soul and with all his might, according to all the Law of Moses, nor did any like him arise after him" (v. 25)—a startling commendation when we consider all the righteous kings who preced-ed Josiah. Even this most righteous king of kings, however, could not quench the burning anger of Yahweh. Auld gives voice to the question lingering in all our minds: "If the divine decision was in fact provoked by Manasseh (vv. 26–27), one might have expected Josiah's point by point unravelling of his—and all his predecessors'—tangled wrongs to tip the scales the other way."[73] But that's not what happened. The wrath kindled by Manasseh and those before him would not abate until Judah had become like her cousins to the north. And if there is an argument in the Old Testament against works-based salvation, this is it.[74] Not even Josiah's good works could deliver his people.

Yet, and I find this absolutely remarkable, Josiah conducted all these re-forms knowing the irrevocable and inevitable fate of Judah.[75] The surety of Jeru-salem's fall did not inspire apathy in Josiah, but action. The king sought to serve and please the Lord, not out of a tit-for-tat, "If we stop being naughty, he'll start being nice" mindset, but out of a desire to do what God had asked, and he there-by sets for us a stellar example to follow. Obedience that isn't a means to an end, but an end of itself, has always characterized the greatest of God's servants.

> Genuine faith transcends any desire for gain. The covenant re-lationship with the God of the Bible is no commercial arrange-

---

72. Nelson, *First and Second Kings*, 258.

73. Auld, *I & II Kings*, 227.

74. "The neat theological formula which insists that righteousness leads inevitably to suc-cess (I Kings 2:3) and repentance to forgiveness is fatally undercut," (Nelson, *First and Second Kings*, 260).

75. "Whether judgement can be forestalled is uncertain, but Josiah acts regardless be-cause reform is right. He could have rested in the assurance of his personal reprieve but he does not. His acts evidence singular commitment to YHWH (22:2; 23:25). […] He could easily have accepted his personal reprieve and left Israel to its deserved fate, but he does not. Some-thing moves him to the effort and expense of reform," (Wray Beal, *1 & 2 Kings*, 506, 511).

ment, no religious transaction entered into with the hope of personal benefit. It is a matter of fidelity and trust, irrespective of any desire for reward or fear of punishment. In this, Josiah is the Old Testament's best example of Deuteronomy's call, not just to fear God or obey God, but to love God with heart and soul and might (Deut. 6:5; cf. 23:25). For the original exilic readers of Kings, who had little or no hope of return to their homeland, the call was clear. Obey God's law and keep the faith, even if you can see no hope of reward.[76]

For all of his righteousness, Josiah's life came to a premature and (for Judah) devastating end. The narrator gives us only the bare facts: in 609, Josiah led a force to Megiddo,[77] an Egyptian fort, to intercept Pharaoh Neco II (c. 609–594), but Josiah was killed in battle. His corpse was carried back to Jerusalem, where he was buried, and his son, Jehoahaz, became king. The Chronicler specifically notes that Judah, led by Jeremiah, mourned their dead king like no other (2 Chr 35:24–25).[78] With Josiah's defeat at the hands of Neco, God's chosen people lost their independence and would not regain it until four and a half centuries later in the time of the Maccabees.

From secular history, we know a bit more. In 612, three years prior to Josiah's death, a coalition of Babylonians and Medes led by Nabopolassar (father of Nebuchadnezzar) had sacked Nineveh, forcing the Assyrian king Ashur-uballit II to retreat to Haran and putting the Assyrian Empire on life support. In 609, Neco allied with Assyria to counter the growing hegemony of Babylon, a development that troubled Josiah.

Throughout his reign, Judah had been free from the bullying influence of other nations. Bright suggests that Josiah, like Hezekiah, was pro-Babylon and feared an Egyptian-Assyrian alliance would once again jeopardize Judah's inde-

76. Nelson, *First and Second Kings*, 260.

77. Malamat notes that beginning around 616, Egypt used Megiddo as a logistics base in their support of Assyria ("The Twilight of Judah: In the Egyptian-Babylonian Maelstrom," in *Congress Volume: Edinburgh 1974* [Leiden: Brill, 1975], 125). The city controlled access to the Coastal Highway's entry into the Jezreel Valley, and "Josiah's decision to confront the Egyptian army there implies that he had captured Megiddo from either the Egyptians or the Assyrians prior to the battle," (Provan, "2 Kings," 203–4).

78. Josephus, *Antiquities* 10.78.

pendence.[79] House also speculates that Egypt posed a threat to Josiah's desire to reunite the two kingdoms of Israel under one rule.[80] But by supporting Babylon, Josiah ignored the clear warning Isaiah had posited (20:16–18).

It was while Neco was en route to Haran to rendezvous with Ashur-uballit that Josiah intervened, despite being warned by Yahweh not to do so (2 Chr 35:20–22)—a tradition preserved in the Apocrypha claims Jeremiah warned Josiah not to go to battle (1 Esdras 1:28). The battle of Megiddo cost Neco precious time, for he did not reach Haran in time to save Ashur-uballit from defeat at the hands of Babylon and Media.

T he metaphor of a great second-half comeback in sports doesn't fit perfectly with Judah's circumstances. In fact, it more closely resembles a vigorous third-quarter comeback, only for things to fall flat again in the fourth. It's the Boston Red Sox reeling off three straight victories in the 2004 ALCS, only to fall flat in Game 7. It's the Buffalo Bills drawing even with the Oilers, only to lose in overtime on a bonehead, what-were-you-thinking play.

With the exception of Hezekiah's reign, Judah had floundered for a long time. We get excited when we see the glimmer of hope that is Josiah, but the king dies ingloriously, and his kingdom is inherited by incompetent morons. In fact, the end comes so swiftly for Judah—in little more than two chapters and twenty years—that we are left with that sinking, what-just-happened feeling.[81] The lamp of Israel would soon extinguish.

2 KINGS 23:31–35

Jehoahaz's[82] reign (609) was scarcely long enough to merit mention, but "although he is neither the oldest nor the next in line, Jehoahaz is the choice

---

79. Bright, *History*, 324–25.

80. House, *1, 2 Kings*, 391. We later learn (23:36) that one of Josiah's wives was from Rumah in upper Galilee; "this northern location indicates Josiah took wives from the north to strengthen his associations there," (Konkel, *1 & 2 Kings*, 654).

81. Which was my reaction to Chris Davis' return of the Alabama field goal to score a touchdown for Auburn and win the 2013 Iron Bowl. Chris, if you're reading this, I pray you repent before it's too late.

82. *Jehoahaz* was likely his throne name (A. M. Honeyman, "The Evidence for Regnal Names among the Hebrews," *JBL* 67 [1948]: 13–25; de Vaux, *Ancient Israel*, 1:107–8); else-

of the people of Judah."[83] Like too many kings before him, he was evil in God's eyes.[84] His reign was cut short when he was deposed by Neco at Riblah[85] on the Orontes and deported to Egypt. In his place as king, Neco set up Jehoahaz's older brother, Eliakim, changing his name to *Jehoiakim* (the names are identical; Neco merely substituted *God* for *Yahweh*). It is thought that Jehoahaz continued the anti-Egyptian policies of his father, Josiah, but Jehoiakim was willing (at least initially) to toe the line.[86] Jehoahaz eventually died in Egypt (Jer 22:10–12).

In the ancient Near East, to give someone/thing a name demonstrated one's superiority (e.g., Gen 2:19–20; 17:5; Dan 1:6–7). In the more immediate context of Judah's last days (cf. 23:34; 24:17), "loss of name symbolizes loss of power. Judah no longer controls its own destiny. It is dictated to by others."[87] Provan then quips, "We are far away from the time when Solomon was thought worthy of Pharaoh's daughter."[88] Very far, indeed.

Adding insult to injury, Neco laid an indemnity demand on Jerusalem totaling one hundred talents of silver and a talent of gold.[89] This would have been worth over $3 million in today's coin, but was a rather modest sum compared

---

where in Scripture, he is listed as *Shallum* (cf. Jer 22:11; 1 Chr 3:15). Josiah's oldest son, Johanan, is never mentioned and is presumed to have died at this point, while Eliakim, two years older than Jehoahaz, was passed over, arguably because the people were reticent to do things "the Egyptian way."

83. Hens-Piazza, *1–2 Kings*, 390.

84. Gray (*I & II Kings*, 681) suggests his sin was going only too eagerly to Riblah to have Neco confirm his right to reign (i.e., trusting in Egypt's protection), but this is unlikely if Jehoahaz continued the anti-Egyptian policies of his father. Josephus claims Jehoahaz "was of a wicked disposition, and ready to do mischief, nor was he either religious towards God, or good-natured towards men," (*Antiquities* 10.83).

85. Located at the junction of two major military highways and "fortified by the Egyptians, [Riblah] served as their staging area for operations against the Assyrians. Later Nebuchadnezzar would make Riblah his headquarters for his western campaigns (25:6, 20)," (Patterson, "1, 2 Kings," 945).

86. Hobbs, *2 Kings*, 341. Malamat notes that the mother of Jehoahaz and Zedekiah was from Judah (2 Kgs 23:31; 24:18), while the mother of Jehoiakim was from Galilee, "most probably in territory under Egyptian control," ("Twilight," 126).

87. Provan, *1 & 2 Kings*, 281.

88. Ibid., 278.

89. The exact number of gold talents may be unknown; the Masoretic Text gives no number, while the LXX reads "one hundred."

to what had been demanded of Menahem (15:19) and Hezekiah (18:14). To pay the amount, Jehoiakim exacted[90] more taxes on the populace[91] (v. 35)—the same people who had promoted Jehoahaz to the throne over Jehoiakim. While not ideal, such doesn't seem too punitive or tyrannical (a king's gotta do what a king's gotta do) until we're told that Jehoiakim, while taxing the nation into economic oblivion, was building a brand new palace.[92] Little wonder, then, that Jeremiah predicted no one would be sorry when Jehoiakim died, and that he would be given a funeral fit for an ass (Jer 22:13–19).

2 KINGS 23:36–24:7

Like his brother and many kings before him, Jehoiakim (609–598) committed evil in God's eyes. For our narrator, the notable event of Jehoiakim's eleven-year reign was that Jerusalem switched from being a vassal of Egypt to one of Babylon.[93] In 605, Nebuchadnezzar defeated Egypt at Carchemish (cf. Jer 46:2). In this same year, Jehoiakim cut Jeremiah's scroll into ribbons and threw it into the fire (Jer 36). The next year brought the initial humiliation of Judah to Babylon when some of Jerusalem's crème de la crème (such as Daniel and his three friends) were deported. Three years later, Jehoiakim rebelled against Nebuchadnezzar by withholding tribute, likely inspired by Neco's rebuff of Nebuchadnezzar at the Egyptian border in 601.[94] "Strike while the iron's hot," Je-

---

90. "The verb [...] implies excessive force. In other contexts it is translated as 'drive' (Deut 15:2, 3; Isa 58:3) and 'oppress' (1 Sam 13:6; Exod 5:6). The participial form is translated as 'tyrant' (Isa 14:2; 60:17)," (Hobbs, 2 Kings, 342). Gray adds, "It is noteworthy that there was no longer anything in the treasury of palace or Temple on which to draw for the tribute, as in the case of Hezekiah's tribute to Sennacherib," (I & II Kings, 683).

91. As previously mentioned, "the people of the land" (v. 35) seems to be a technical phrase for the landed aristocracy of Judah (i.e., "the nobles"). Barnes thus notes that, in Jehoiakim taxing them for the indemnity, "there is a sense of bitter poetic justice, for those stalwarts seemed to have a consistently anti-Egyptian bias in their political actions," (1–2 Kings, 374; cf. Sweeney, I & II Kings, 452; Wray Beal, 1 & 2 Kings, 517).

92. Note the discussion of the discovery of Jehoiakim's palace (Y. Aharoni, "Beth-Haccherem," in Archaeology and Old Testament Study, ed. D. Winton Thomas [Oxford: Clarendon, 1967], 178–83).

93. Malamat notes six changes in Judah's allegiance to Egypt/Babylon in the last two decades of her existence ("Twilight," 123–45).

94. ANET 564; cf. Josephus, Antiquities 10.88. After forcing Nebuchadnezzar to with-

hoiakim thought. Remember that Jehoiakim had likely become king because of his pro-Egyptian policies; he probably saw Neco's "victory" over Nebuchadnezzar as evidence of an Egyptian comeback.

Following his "defeat" against Egypt, Nebuchadnezzar retreated to Babylon and spent the next few years putting out fires in other places and rebuilding his chariot forces.[95] But Judah was never far from his mind. It seems as if Nebuchadnezzar—whom Yahweh once called "my servant" (Jer 27:6)—paid marauding hordes of Chaldeans, Syrians, Moabites, and Ammonites to wreak havoc on Judah (v. 2; cf. Jer 35:11; 49:28–33; Zeph 2:8–10). Yet—and this is critical—in whatever way these raids materialized in the physical realm, "theologically, the author stressed that Yahweh Himself lay behind these events."[96] Note that this series of unfortunate events is particularly blamed on the wickedness and violence of Manasseh (vv. 3–4).

If we find ourselves wondering why Neco never came to the aid of Jehoiakim,[97] it's because he had been weakened significantly by his rebuff of Nebuchadnezzar in 601. Neco "also turned his interest to the sea. [...] Neco's maritime policy made Egypt a sea-power, but it did not strengthen Egypt's military position in Western Asia."[98] Meanwhile, Babylon had gradually established itself at the top of the totem pole. Nebuchadnezzar held an iron grip over Solomon's former territory—"from the Brook of Egypt to the river Euphrates" (v. 7; cf. 1 Kgs 4:21). "Egypt may have been able to repel an invasion at this point but was hardly in any position to help its small northern allies."[99] For too long, Jerusalem's kings had relied on the broken reed that was Egypt. But that trust had always been misplaced, and Jehoiakim could rely on Egypt no longer.

---

draw, Neco headed north and captured Gaza (Jer 47:1).

95. *ANET* 564.

96. Hubbard, *First and Second Kings*, 233.

97. "Other states held Egypt in similar regard, as revealed in an Aramaic letter discovered at Saqqara: The ruler of some city, apparently in Philistine, urgently appeals to Pharaoh for military assistance to repell [sic] the approaching Babylonians, reminding his suzerain of his treaty obligations," (Malamat, "Twilight," 128–29).

98. Gösta W. Ahlström, *The History of Ancient Palestine* (Minneapolis: Fortress, 1993), 783.

99. House, *1, 2 Kings*, 394. "Unquestionably, Jehoiakim saw in Egypt the hope of salvation for Judah, and it is known from an Aramaic letter from Saqqera (Memphis) that a ruler from Gaza, Ekron and Ashkelon thought likewise and approached Egypt for help against Babylon," (Jones, *1 and 2 Kings*, 2:634).

Nor could Judah rely on the Lord, for Yahweh had turned his back on his people. "Solomon had prayed that Yahweh would 'forgive' (1 Kgs 8:30, 34, 36, 39, 50), but now the message is *the LORD was not willing to forgive* (24:4)."[100] Jehoiakim was guilty of reversing all the good his father, Josiah, had accomplished. Rather than emulating Josiah, Jehoiakim followed the example of Manasseh. Jeremiah describes the king as a monstrous tyrant who robbed his subjects, resisted the prophets, and was guilty of violence and idolatry.[101]

What happened to Jehoiakim? The circumstances of his death are a bit murky (he was only thirty-six). No official burial notice is given as is done for previous kings. According to the history books, he died in December 598 as Nebuchadnezzar was about to capture Jerusalem. At one point, Nebuchadnezzar had him in chains (2 Chr 36:6), but this seems to have happened earlier in Jehoiakim's reign. The LXX of 2 Chronicles 36:8 claims he was buried in the garden of Uzza with Manasseh and Amon, but such a detail is missing from the Hebrew text, and the narrator of Kings says nothing about it.

Though there is no mention of this in the text as with previous royal slayings, pro-Babylonian conspirators possibly assassinated Jehoiakim. They likely did so in a last-ditch effort to placate Nebuchadnezzar on the eve of his wrath and unceremoniously dumped the corpse outside the city as they would a donkey (cf. Jer 22:19; 36:30–31).[102] Josephus claims that Nebuchadnezzar personally executed Jehoiakim and dumped his body at the base of the city walls.[103] Green posits this reconstruction of Jehoiakim's downfall:

> It seems plausible to theorize that when the siege of the city began, there was deep concern among the residents of Jerusalem in general and among the pro-Babylonian faction in particular. This concern and fear precipitated blame upon Jehoiakim for the political problems which were moving the city toward

---

100. Olley, *Message of Kings*, 361.

101. Jeremiah 8:4–12; 10:1–9; 11:1–17; 13:1–11; 17:21–23; 18:18–20; 19:3–5; 22:13–14, 17; 23:1–2, 9–40; 25:1–7; 26:1–24; 36:20–36.

102. Wray Beal believes, however, that Jeremiah's words "may be no more than a rhetorical denigration of a hated king," (*1 & 2 Kings*, 518).

103. Josephus, *Antiquities* 10.97.

destruction, and it could legitimately have been felt that if Je-hoiakim had remained a loyal vassal to Nebuchadrezzar, the Babylonian army would not then be investing the city. As this sort of sentiment deepened and spread among the residents of the city, the next step could easily have been an attempt to remedy the situation by eliminating the cause of it, namely, Jehoiakim himself. Under such circumstances, if the king was still alive when the Babylonians arrived, he could have died in the ensuing coup at the hands of the pro-Babylonian faction in the city as that faction attempted to save Jerusalem from de-struction. His body could, in that case, have been thrown out as a sop to appease Nebuchadrezzar and to induce the Baby-lonian king to change his mind about conquering the city.[104]

2 KINGS 24:8-20

Like his uncle, Jehoahaz, Jehoiachin[105] (with all the maturity of a college freshman) was scarcely able to transform the palace into a frat house before being exiled by a foreign monarch in favor of a more sympathetic family member. And like both his father and uncle, Jehoiachin was evil—Jeremiah affectionately re-membered him as "a leaky bucket, a rusted-out pail good for nothing" (Jer 22:28 Msg). He assumed the throne upon his father's death in December 598, but managed to get himself deposed and deported before the opening day of baseball season. In fact, his reign lasted exactly three months, ten days (2 Chr 36:9).

In December 598,[106] Nebuchadnezzar set out for Jerusalem, perhaps with the intent to punish Jehoiakim for his revolt. Discovering the old king to be dead and his son on the throne didn't change things much; the Babylonian monarch still brought a siege against the holy city. Hobbs notes that, since the siege took

---

104. Alberto R. Green, "The Fate of Jehoiakim," *AUSS* 20 (1982): 107–8.

105. *Jehoiachin* was likely his throne name; his given name was *Jeconiah* (1 Chr 3:16; Jer 24:1) or *Coniah* (Jer 22:24).

106. "Noting the event by the regnal year of the conquering king is unusual, but is an indi-cation of Babylon's authority in Judah at this time. This authority is also implied in that Jehoiachin is the subject of only one verb in vv. 10–17: he surrenders to Nebuchadnezzar. His one action is juxtaposed to Nebuchadnezzar's many actions (his servants 'went up', he 'arrived', 'took captive', 'brought out treasures', 'cut in pieces', 'exiled' Jerusalem and 'exiled' Jehoiachin, 'carried captive', 'brought captive', 'made Mattaniah king' and 'changed his name'). The juxtaposition shows Baby-lon has complete control over Judah and its monarchy," (Wray Beal, *1 & 2 Kings*, 519).

place in winter and with the harvest a few months off, food would have been quite scarce in a city Jerusalem's size.[107] Wishing to forestall the inevitable, Jehoiachin "gave himself up to the king of Babylon" (v. 12), fulfilling the word of the Lord spoken through Jeremiah (Jer 22:24–27). The surrender of Jerusalem occurred on March 16, 597.

What ensued was a wholesale deportation to Babylon[108] of everybody who was anybody in Judah: officials, soldiers, craftsmen, and smiths—"the rationale being, of course, that without soldiers or the help of smiths to forge new weapons, no further insurrection was possible."[109] Just as the Who's Who of the World had once come to marvel at the splendor of Solomon, so now the Who's Who of Jerusalem and Judah are scattered to the ends of the earth.[110] "None remained, except the poorest people of the land," sighs the narrator (v. 14). From a peak of about 250,000 during the reign of Hezekiah, Albright estimated that Judah's population had been cut in half after this deportation.[111] The deportation figures given (vv. 14, 16) are arguably rough estimates; Jeremiah claims that there were 3,023 refugees (Jer 52:28), likely including only adult men.[112] Nebuchadnezzar also emptied Solomon's Temple and the royal palace of their treasures[113] (v. 13;

---

107. Hobbs, 2 Kings, 351.

108. "The repeated phrase 'to Babylon' (vv. 15-16) hammered home the point that Judah, like Israel, was headed for exile," (Hubbard, First and Second Kings, 234).

109. Fritz, 1 & 2 Kings, 417. Lest we underestimate the lack of competent leaders in the land, Bright reminds us, "The nobles left to serve Zedekiah seem all to have been chauvinists of the most reckless sort, completely blind to the realities of the situation," (History, 328). As we will discover, their foolishness hastened the end of Judah.

110. Provan, 1 & 2 Kings, 278.

111. William Foxwell Albright, The Biblical Period from Abraham to Ezra (New York: Harper: 1963), 84.

112. Bright, History, 328, n. 52. Cogan believes the 3,023 in Jeremiah 52:28 was comprised only of deportees from the countryside (II Kings, 312). Malamat suggests that the numbers represent a deportation in two phases, the first just prior or on the event of Jerusalem's surrender, and included 3,023 people from the countryside. The second phase was of the inhabitants of Jerusalem and included the seven thousand, for a grand total of ten thousand ("Twilight," 133–35).

113. In the list of treasures taken from the Temple, no mention is made of the famed Ark of the Covenant—arguably the Temple's greatest treasure—that Solomon had placed in the Most Holy Place (1 Kgs 6:19). It seems to have already been missing during Jeremiah's ministry (Jer 3:16; cf. 2 Chr 35:3). Haran submits the intriguing theory that Manasseh was responsible

cf. Jer 27:19–22), bringing fulfillment to the word of Yahweh (20:17). "Stripped of everything but an existence that lacks integrity and dignity, Judah stumbles closer to its end."[114]

In Jehoiachin's place, Nebuchadnezzar installed Mattaniah, a third son of Josiah, as king and demonstrated his sovereignty over him by changing his name to *Zedekiah*.[115] Like his brother, Jehoiakim, Zedekiah's reign lasted eleven years. And like his brothers and predecessors, Zedekiah was an evil king in God's eyes.[116] It would be during his reign that a kingdom would be lost, thrust from God's presence into the dark despair of exile (v. 20). The end began with yet another revolt against Babylon.

2 KINGS 25:1-21

Much of what we know about Zedekiah's reign (597–586), one that began when he was barely old enough to drink, comes from the book of Jeremiah. He is portrayed there as a wishy-washy politician, paying lip service to Jeremiah in private, but rejecting the prophet in public[117] (e.g., Jer 38). Granted, hindsight is always 20/20, but it's as if someone wrote a book called *How to Make a Bad Situation Worse* and gave Zedekiah a complimentary copy. Zedekiah was torn between competing factions: pro-Egypt, pro-Babylon, and pro-independence. His military commanders were spoiling for a fight. The religious establishment

---

for the Ark's disappearance. "Thus when the fateful moment of final destruction arrived, eleven years after the exile of Jehoiachin, the Temple was already deprived at least of most of its inner accessories," (M. Haran, "The Disappearance of the Ark," *IEJ* 13 [1963]: 58).

114. House, *1, 2 Kings*, 395.

115. *ANET* 564. The change from *Mattaniah* ("gift of Yahweh") to *Zedekiah* ("Yahweh is righteous") may have been meant "to stress that Yahweh's act against Jerusalem was justified judicially rather than merely to emphasize Zedekiah's status as a vassal," (Wiseman, *1 and 2 Kings*, 331).

116. "This verse's judgment on Zedekiah is confirmed by the incidents from his reign found in Jer 27–39. From these stories Zedekiah emerges as a weak, indecisive figure, easily swayed by the weight of circumstance," (Hobbs, *2 Kings*, 354). In addition, the Chronicler accuses him of not listening to the word of the Lord through the prophets, breaking an oath made in the Lord's name, and allowing idolatry to flourish in the Temple (2 Chr 36:12–14).

117. "Zedekiah is portrayed as an indecisive, anxious king who could not facilitate good policy in an impossible situation. [...] Zedekiah is not afraid of the judgment of Yahweh or the treatment he may receive from Babylon; he is afraid rather of his own political constituency that would never accept such a policy of surrender," (Brueggemann, *1 & 2 Kings*, 587).

believed (falsely) that Yahweh would never allow his Temple to be destroyed.[118] Political enemies were clamoring for Jehoiachin to return from Babylon and re-assume his throne (Jer 28:1–4).[119]

If Nebuchadnezzar needed a valid reason to finish off Jerusalem and punish Zedekiah, the Judean ruler gave him plenty. In an echo of Ezekiel 17:15–21, Josephus records that Nebuchadnezzar called Zedekiah, upon his capture, "a wicked wretch, and covenant-breaker, and one that had forgotten his former words, when he promised to keep the country for him."[120] This is how Zedekiah's betrayal of the Babylonians unfolded:

The year 594 proved to be an unstable one in the geopolitics of the region.[121] Nebuchadnezzar faced revolts among his troops in Babylon, the aftermath of which might have included the Fiery Furnace narrative of Daniel 3. The year before, Elam had attacked Babylon, but was defeated (cf. Jer 49:34–39). In Egypt, Psammetik II (c. 594–589), son of Neco, ascended Egypt's throne. A few years later, perhaps out of an ambitious desire to counter Babylon's hegemony, he successfully attacked Nubia to the south and several Phoenician cities to the north, likely fueling regional hopes that Babylon, with Egypt's help, could be beaten back. In 592, Psammetik took a victory tour through Palestine to fan such hopes.[122] His son, Apries (c. 589–570), continued to foster these same prospects when he succeeded his father.

About this same time, an anti-Babylonian plot involving the strange bedfellows of Judah, Edom, Moab, Ammon, Tyre, and Sidon began to grow (Jer 27–28). To be sure, these anti-Babylonian feelings were inflamed by Egypt's re-

---

118. "The Zion theology proclaimed the inviolability of the city (Pss. 46; 48; 76). Surely the capture had been only an historical accident. In short, there were hopes, encouraged by prophetic announcements, that the whole bad dream would be reversed in the immediate future and Jehoiachin and the exiles would return," (Miller, *History*, 469).

119. "[Zedekiah's] position may have been somewhat compromised by the continued presence of his nephew Jehoiachin, who, though in captivity, was still held in esteem by his fellow exiles (note that the dates in Ezekiel are based on the years of Jehoiachin's exile)," (Cogan, *II Kings*, 322).

120. Josephus, *Antiquities* 10.138.

121. Moshe Greenberg, "Ezekiel 17 and the Policy of Psammetichus II," *JBL* 76 (1957): 304–9.

122. K. S. Freedy and D. B. Redford, "The Dates in Ezekiel in Relation to Biblical, Babylonian and Egyptian Sources," *JAOS* 90 (1970): 462–85.

vival. Zedekiah sent ambassadors to Egypt "that they might give him horses and a large army" (Ezek 17:15). One of the Lachish Letters mentions a Judean general named Coniah visiting Egypt,[123] presumably to negotiate Egypt's assistance in a potential revolt.

But in reality, the rebellion was doomed from the beginning. For one thing, and in what is an all-too-common theme in Kings to this point, Egypt never came through (cf. Ezek 17:17). Apries' "life was to be marked by a series of difficulties, ending in a coup d'état and death in battle during a vain attempt to regain his throne,"[124] (cf. Jer 44:30). But the bigger reason for the futility of this revolt was that it was not consistent with the will of the Lord (cf. Jer 21:1–10). He was intent on removing Judah from his presence because of the sins of Manasseh, and his word spoken through the prophets would soon come to pass.

T hough our narrator does not mention it, the Babylonians attacked other cities in Judah before laying siege to Jerusalem, Lachish and Azekah[125] among them (Jer 34:6–7; 44:2; Lam 2:2–5). Nebuchadnezzar's "grand strategy was to remove any military threat by systematically destroying the various fortress systems in Judah."[126] Finally, on the tenth day of the tenth month of Zedekiah's ninth year (i.e., January 587), the Babylonians showed up with their siege works (cf. Jer 32:24; 33:4; Ezek 4:2; 17:17) and began nailing the final nail in Judah's coffin. For eighteen months (cf. Jer 52:6), the holy city held out, aided by Hezekiah's tunnel, as well as intervention by Egypt (Jer 37:5). But Jerusalem could not last forever, and the loss of two harvests over these sixteen months would have taken their toll on Judah's food supply (cf. Jer 38:2–4).

In July 586, on the eve of her collapse, Zedekiah and his entourage escaped through a breach in the wall[127] (v. 4; cf. Jer 39:3) and made a mad dash toward

---

123. *COS* 3.42B.

124. Patterson, "1, 2 Kings," 949.

125. A piece of pottery unearthed at Lachish tells of the fall of Azekah to Nebuchadnezzar's army (*COS* 3.42C). More generally, the Lachish Letters "provide a brief, firsthand glimpse of the uneasy military situation in the Judean countryside," (Hubbard, *First and Second Kings*, 234).

126. Hobbs, *2 Kings*, 362.

127. Along the northern wall there has been discovered charred remains and numerous arrowheads "that seem to point to a battle which took place here during the capture of Jerusalem by the Babylonians," (N. Avigad, "Jerusalem, the Jewish Quarter of the Old City, 1975," *IEJ* 25

Jericho.[128] It's thought that Zedekiah was seeking asylum among his Transjordan allies, Ammon and Moab (Jer 27:3).[129] But the king was overtaken by Babylonian troops; like his brother, Jehoahaz, Zedekiah was hauled to Riblah before a king, but this time it was Nebuchadnezzar and not Neco. The Babylonian ruler poked Zedekiah's eyes out, but not before making sure the butchering of his sons was the last thing Zedekiah saw in this life. "The Hebrews had no belief at this time in a personal immortality. A man's hope for the future lay in his family. By this action Nebuchadnezzar intended to wipe out the family and memory of a rebellious vassal."[130] At that point, the last king of Judah was taken to Babylon in irons (cf. Ezek 12:12–14) and, at the ripe old age of thirty-two, rotted away in prison for the rest of his life (Jer 52:11). If he had only listened to the word of Yahweh through Jeremiah (34:1–3; 38:14–28), he would have saved himself and his city.[131] Also executed by Nebuchadnezzar at Riblah were priests, military leaders, city officials, and members of the aristocracy (vv. 18–20).[132]

In late summer, Nebuchadnezzar's top lieutenant, Nebuzaradan,[133] came to

---

[1975]: 261). "The wall was probably breached in the north of the city, although there is no evidence to substantiate this; it makes strategic sense to attack the city from this direction. The escape would have been made from the southern end of the city of David, at the confluence of the Kidron and Hinnom Valleys, and the continuation of the Kidron to the southeast would have provided access to the route to Jericho," (Hobbs, 2 Kings, 363).

128. The phrase "way of the Arabah" (v. 4 NASU) is another name for the road from Jerusalem to Jericho (Aharoni, Land of the Bible, 55). "The plains of Jericho are stretches of flat and dry ground east of Jericho. It was an open area [with little vegetation], which made it easy for the Babylonian troops to retrieve the fugitives," (Walton, Bible Background, 411). "By portraying the capture of Zedekiah and the end of Davidic rule in this man, [the narrator] brings Israel's history full circle from beginning to end at the city of Jericho," (Sweeney, I & II Kings, 467).

129. Hubbard, First and Second Kings, 235.

130. Robinson, Second Book, 243.

131. "Zedekiah provides yet another example of the folly of persistent rejection of the word of God," (Olley, Message of Kings, 366).

132. "Probably these executions were exemplary, certain leading men of the nationalist resistance party being selected from various sections of the people. The priests in those days of vassalage were the champions of nationalism," (Gray, I & II Kings, 700).

133. "The title Nebuzaradan bore was literally 'chief executioner,' that is, chief of the royal bodyguard responsible for executing sentences of death," (Hubbard, First and Second Kings, 235–36). But Wray Beal's quip that he is Babylon's "hatchet man" (1 & 2 Kings, 527) points to a larger role for Nebuzaradan.

Jerusalem and began dismantling the city.[134] Starting with the Temple and the palace, and continuing with every other house in Jerusalem, the Babylonians set fire to the holy city. The walls of the city were taken apart as if they were made of Lego bricks. It is indeed a sad scene to contemplate; it has been a long time coming, but tragedies don't have to be unexpected to be gut-wrenching.

Some 832 people were taken into exile (Jer 52:29), leaving only the poorest of the poor behind to farm the land. What remained in the Temple that was of value was also taken back to Babylon; the rest was destroyed. "Burning the temple and palace and the houses of the powerful removes the primary visual evidences of governmental power and the deity's patronage."[135] Describing this final looting of the house of the Lord (vv. 13–17) seems to have been important to the narrator, paralleling almost exactly the original listing of vessels, pillars, and implements (1 Kgs 7:15–51).[136] It's as if we are meant to feel in our soul a sense of loss, denigration, and hopelessness over the removal of each of the Temple's components. The glory of Yahweh was no longer in this place,[137] thus the glory of Solomon and Israel could not endure.[138]

---

134. "Conquest and looting were insufficient punishment for the capital city that had proven itself recalcitrant so many times; the city's destruction establishes that there were no plans to reconstitute Judah around a Babylonian provincial center in Jerusalem," (Cogan, *II Kings*, 323–24). Unger marvels, "Excavations at Jerusalem and in Palestine in general show how thorough was the damage and destruction wrought during the Chaldean invasions. Not a trace of the Solomonic temple nor of the palaces of the Davidic kings has remained. Diggings at Azeka, Beth-Shemesh and Kirjath-sepher and surface examinations elsewhere furnish mute evidence of the terrific desolation," (Merrill F. Unger, *Archaeology and the Old Testament* [Grand Rapids: Zondervan, 1954], 291). "The [Babylonian] destruction [...] obliterated the whole eastern quarter of Jerusalem, and the western slope was never again included within the town," (Kenyon, *Digging*, 171).

135. Wray Beal, *1 & 2 Kings*, 527.

136. Jones, *1 and 2 Kings*, 2:644; Wray Beal, *1 & 2 Kings*, 528.

137. "Perhaps because of deliverance in the days of Hezekiah, there was a tendency to think that the temple as the place of divine residence would be spared (Jer. 7:4). Such thinking is utterly errant; Ezekiel the priest observes the glory of God leave the temple toward the east (Ezek. 10:18–19). The name of God will not be compromised," (Konkel, *1 & 2 Kings*, 657).

138. "For covenant-minded readers the loss of the temple means much more than the destruction of a significant public building. To them the temple symbolizes God's presence in the midst of the chosen people, ongoing worship of Yahweh, the possibility of receiving forgiveness by the offering of sacrifice, and the opportunity to gather as a unified nation at festival time. Of course, the temple was rarely used properly, yet as long as it stood, the *hope* for the ideal exist-

have at times compared the destruction of Jerusalem for ancient Israel to 9/11 for Americans. But in reality, it was much worse. The loss of the Temple alone was devastating, something akin to losing the Statue of Liberty, the U.S. Capitol, and the National Cathedral all at once. Indeed, no greater symbol of Israel's heritage, identity, and future existed than Solomon's Temple. But the divergences between 9/11 and the collapse of Judah don't end there. Though that date was a national nightmare, arguably greater than Pearl Harbor (in terms of proximity) or JFK's assassination (in terms of immensity), 9/11 did not leave Americans dispossessed from their land. For a glimpse at what it must have been like for Judah, we need only look at the plight of modern refugees. Olley reminds us:

> Emotions involved in being away "from one's land" are felt by millions in the world today. The flood of refugees from strife-torn and often ravaged regions bears witness to the anguish, while even migrants who have moved voluntarily still look back to the "home" country. "Land" is a focus of identity and tradition, of personal and family memories, of rootedness and belonging—and when buildings have been razed and the land devastated the sense of loss is greater. The first generation of "exiles"—or refugees or migrants—may have little hope of return, but the place of ancestral land in identity continues in future generations. There can be a sense of a gap in one's life.[139]

The pain of the exiles—Judean refugees—is palpable elsewhere in Scripture. "By the waters of Babylon, there we sat down and wept, when we remembered Zion," lamented the psalmist (Ps 137:1), and Jeremiah's agony over the destruction of the holy city is enshrined in Lamentations. The exiles felt alienated from their countrymen, alienated from their heritage, alienated from their future, and—worst of all—alienated from God. And this is the image the divine narrator wishes to leave with us—that sin brings with it both individual and corporate consequences, the worst being alienation from the Lord who alone fosters community, hope, and a future on behalf of his people.

---

ed. Now what will happen to God's people?" (House, *1, 2 Kings*, 398–99; emphasis his).

139. Olley, *Message of Kings*, 368.

2 KINGS 25:22-30

Before drawing such a sad history to a close, the narrator saw fit to preserve a two-part appendix to the story. To administrate a land so traumatized by war and exile and poverty, Nebuchadnezzar appointed a pro-Babylon member of the bureaucracy, Gedaliah. His grandfather, Shaphan, had been Josiah's secretary (22:3, 8–12), and his father, Ahikam, had protected the prophet Jeremiah (Jer 26:24). A seal bearing the inscription "Gedaliah who is over the house" was discovered in the ruins of Lachish,[140] and the name of one of his lieutenants, Jaazaniah, has been found on an onyx seal at Mizpah dating to this period.[141]

Sadly, less than a year into his administration at Mizpah,[142] and despite Jeremiah's warnings, Gedaliah was assassinated by another lieutenant named Ishmael—the thirteenth ruler of Israel/Judah to be offed in Kings.[143] From Jeremiah, we learn that Ishmael was just the bullet, while the king of Ammon pulled the trigger (Jer 40:13–14). "A member of the royal family, Ishmael apparently opposed any accommodation to Babylon. He may even have hoped to reestablish the monarchy in Judah with himself as king."[144] In light of the circumstances, Gedaliah had taken his cue from Jeremiah's sermons and had encouraged a "let's make the best of a bad situation" spirit. But the locals quickly mistook his "live and let live" approach to be unpatriotic and a little too buddy-buddy with the Babylonian enemy.[145]

---

140. S. H. Hooke, "A Scarab and Sealing From Tell Duweir," *PEQ* 67 (1935): 195–97.

141. William F. Badé, "The Seal of Jaazaniah," *ZAW* 51 (1933): 150–56.

142. Mizpah was located eight miles north of Jerusalem on a small plain near Bethel (cf. 1 Kgs 15:22). In the past (e.g., Judg 20:1; 1 Sam 7:16), Mizpah had proven to be "an important center to which Israel could go in times of trouble," (Hobbs, *2 Kings*, 366). Malamat notes that the territory of Benjamin had likely surrendered to Nebuchadnezzar long before Jerusalem's destruction, and thus was a place to which Judean refugees fled. The site of Mizpah does not contain evidence of destruction during this period as do other sites in Palestine (A. Malamat, "The Last Wars of the Kingdom of Judah," *JNES* 9 [1950]: 226–27).

143. Josephus reports that Ishmael and his men feasted with Gedaliah until the latter was drunk, and then they slew him (*Antiquities* 10.168–69).

144. Hubbard, *First and Second Kings*, 237; cf. Barnes, *1–2 Kings*, 384.

145. "The murder is hardly an act of rebellion against the Babylonians; it is a vendetta against those who are viewed as collaborating with the Babylonians," (Konkel, *1 & 2 Kings*, 665). Josephus remembered Gedaliah as possessing "a gentle and righteous disposition" (*Antiquities* 10.155). An extended account of Gedaliah's assassination can be found in Jeremiah 40:7–41:18.

When the remaining citizens of Judah—the ones God had called "bad
figs" (Jer 24:3, 8–10)—heard the news of Gedaliah's murder, they panicked and
fled to Egypt,[146] taking a very reluctant Jeremiah with them (Jer 42:7–43:7).
Their fear was well-founded. In 582–581, the Babylonians retaliated by deporting another 745 citizens to Babylon and made Judah a province of Samaria (Jer
52:30). Israel is now without hope; she is "indeed cut off" (Ezek 37:11). And
with that sad note, Israel has in many ways now come full circle—"The epic saga
that began with the exodus from that land [i.e., Egypt] has turned into a horror
story of sin and judgment (21:15), and Israel now returns whence it came."[147]

A second, final postscript wraps up the book. In 561, Nebuchadnezzar's
son, Evil-merodach, pardoned Jehoiachin from prison[148] and honored
him with a royal stipend and a seat at the king's table[149] (cf. 2 Sam 9:7;
19:33; 1 Kgs 2:7). A clay tablet recovered from Babylon lists Jehoiachin, his wife,
and his five sons as receiving oil and barley rations from the king.[150] Other favors
included a residence and land enough to support Jehoiachin's family[151]—seven
sons were born to him during the Exile (1 Chr 3:17–18). Most significantly,
Jehoiachin was elevated above other exiled kings, those of Tyre, Gaza, Sidon, Ar-

146. "The exiles in Babylon viewed Gedaliah's murder as the death blow to national existence, and instituted fast days to mourn this loss, as well as the destruction of Jerusalem and the
Temple (cf. Zech 7:5; 8:19)," (Cogan, *II Kings*, 327). "The incident revealed two things. First, it confirmed that Judah was, in fact, finished as a nation. Second, it reiterated that hope for Judah's restoration must lie outside the land. That idea would have encouraged the book's exilic readers. Should
Yahweh ever restore Judah, they would play a key role," (Hubbard, *First and Second Kings*, 238).

147. Provan, *1 & 2 Kings*, 279.

148. "When a U.S. president leaves office, he sometimes pardons people of wrongdoings.
Middle Eastern kings did that when they came to power; it was a way of showing that the administration was new and of showing what its priorities and principles might be," (Goldingay, *1 and
2 Kings for Everyone*, 190).

149. "The change of clothes here may signify a change of status beyond that which any
inmate undergoes upon his release," (Jon D. Levenson, "The Last Four Verses in Kings," *JBL* 103
[1984]: 356).

150. *ANET* 308; cf. W. F. Albright, "King Joiachin in Exile," *BA* 5 (1942): 49–55.

151. D. J. Wiseman, *Nebuchadrezzar and Babylon* (Oxford: Oxford Univ. Press, 1985),
82–83.

vad, and Ashdod, just as Daniel and his three friends were elevated above their own colleagues (Dan 1:19–20; 2:48–49).

The book of Kings thus ends with a son of David still alive; though Jehoia-chin dies in Babylon, no concluding formula is ever given for him. It is noteworthy that the narrative does not end with a mutilated Zedekiah bereft of heirs; "Jehoia-chin lives, and his reappearance in the narrative is strikingly reminiscent of the reappearance of Joash after that earlier destruction of the 'whole royal family.'"[152]

Brueggemann eloquently reminds us, "Hope, elusive and emancipatory, is a refusal to accept an end, a refusal to give Nebuchadnezzar the final word, a refusal to think that our defeats have in them the defeat of holiness."[153] This last scene concerning Jehoiachin's release gave the exiles just such a hope—hope that their story, and Yahweh's, was not over. They had watched as the full fury of a holy God had been poured out upon them. But David had long ago celebrated that though the Lord's "anger lasts only a moment, [...] his favor lasts a lifetime; weeping may stay for the night, but rejoicing comes in the morning" (Ps 30:5 NIV). Indeed, God had sworn never to remove his love or the throne from the lineage of Jesse's son. The lights had gone out in Judah, but the Davidic lamp still burned (cf. Ezek 17:22–24).

The King of kings was planning a resurrection.

---

152. Provan, *1 & 2 Kings*, 280.

153. Brueggemann, *1 & 2 Kings*, 608.

TALKING POINTS

I n my adolescence, I remember the moral sins of President Clinton being
well publicized and widely denounced by religious conservatives. It was to
my shock, then, when in the 2016 campaign, the moral failings of President
Trump received a pass. Whereas in the 1990s it had been declared that "character counts" and a leader's morals can impact an entire nation, it seems we had
outgrown such a "foolish" notion in the new millennium. I was not a supporter
of Secretary Clinton in the 2016 election, and roughly for the same reasons, but
the ease with which Christian conservatives made their peace with President
Trump's sins was alarming to me. Konkel reminds us that "the effects of the sins
of one person can extend to many others. Other individuals are drawn into errant
ways, and many victims suffer the results of evil. This is particularly true when
transgressions are committed by persons in political power. Most often oppressive actions are exercised under the rubric of peace and liberty."[154] The sins of
Manasseh were unprecedented, and despite his repentance (whether temporary
or permanent), his sins made Judah's end a foregone conclusion. Will President
Trump's sins have a lingering impact on the country? As of this writing, it's too
early to tell. But do not be deceived: a leader's morals impact an entire nation.

S ometimes, God doesn't make sense. For every occasion when we suffer
because of our sin, there are many more when we suffer *in spite of our faithfulness*! As we read the account of Josiah's life, a king of unprecedented
righteousness and leader of impressive religious reform, we are left to marvel at
the brevity of his life and how quickly things unravel for Judah. Much of Kings is
predicated on the theology or worldview of Deuteronomy—obey and be blessed; rebel and be cursed. Surely, we think, Josiah's unprecedented righteousness
should have bought Judah more time.[155] But it did not. When we, like Josiah, face
our own "land of Megiddo"—Armageddon—the place where God doesn't make
sense, we must remember three important truths. *First, God is not a genie in a*

---

154. Konkel, *1 & 2 Kings*, 627.

155. "Does not repentance yield divine compassion? Does not turning again toward the
Lord reap forgiveness? The assurance of destruction for Judah here amid covenant renewal and
comprehensive expunging of all forms of apostasy puts the reader on edge. At the end of these chapters we are left to grapple with an enduring theological problem," (Hens-Piazza, *1–2 Kings*, 392).

lamp.[156] The faithful do not serve God only to be blessed (cf. Job 1:8); in fact, one could argue that the New Testament reverses this age-old expectation—Christians can expect to suffer if they are faithful (2 Thess 1:5; 2 Tim 3:12). The bigger point here, however, is that God will do what he wills, so our obedience does not come with a money-back guarantee. *Second, we must endure the consequences of sin.*[157] All suffering is due to sin, whether ours or others'. Sometimes suffering is due generally to living in a fallen world and nothing more. Thus, we wait for the redemption of all things (Rom 8:18–25). *Finally, however, we have the confidence that God sees, hears, and knows about our suffering.* I speak from personal experience when I say any tragedy can be endured when we allow God to sit with us in our suffering and grief. He will never forsake us, neither in this life, nor in the next (Matt 28:20).

One constant theme in the final chapters is God's absolute sovereignty over all things. From the perspective of an outsider, Judah collapsed before the Babylonian war machine because her military was inferior. Yet, "Israel's history is littered with battles fought under odds equally as unbalanced, yet which resulted in victory for the faithful Israelite force."[158] No, Judah went into exile because God was against her. But God's sovereignty and wrath are not the only parts of his character on vivid display here. There is also his patience and willingness to forgive. As bitter as his punishment was, we must also note that God delayed punishment for four hundred years following Solomon's

---

156. "In the view of the writer, there is a most serious lesson to be learned from the reign and reform of Josiah. Not even the deliberate imitation of David, so clear in the narrative of Josiah's reign, can restrain the hand of judgment. Yahweh acts again out of his freedom. If any hope is to be found in exile, it must be firmly anchored in this truth. The promise of deliverance and restoration must come from the same freedom to offer grace which is dependent upon nothing," (Hobbs, *2 Kings*, 343).

157. "That God allows the forces of evil and their consequences to hold sway in life may actually be an expression of divine compassion. It may be the only way to rupture this spiritual impasse, this shortsightedness. Judgment may save us from ourselves. Exile may be not only punishment for a wayward path in life, but an awakening to the prospect of return. It may be the only intervention left to the Lord to put us in touch once again with our need for God. If this is the cost, God may not be bent upon destroying a people or an individual, but rather uncompromisingly determined to win back human hearts," (Hens-Piazza, *1–2 Kings*, 393–94).

158. Hobbs, *2 Kings*, 356.

idolatry. And Kings does not leave us with Jerusalem in smoldering ruins, but with the image of a king restored. "If the narrative has shown the prophetic word of judgment to be sure, then the prophetic word of restoration and hope must equally be sure. The openness of the final verses of 1 – 2 Kings invites those in exile, and every reader afterwards, to dare to believe in such words, and in the audacious grace of the God of such words."[159]

When the narrator begins reckoning time by the reign of Nebuchadnezzar (24:12), it is arresting—this is the first time in Kings that the narrator dated an event in relation to a Gentile ruler. "Chronology is sovereignty," Leithart reminds us, "and Nebuchadnezzar's taking over for the kings of Judah is a sign of Judah's exile."[160] Indeed, in the closing scenes of Kings, Nebuchadnezzar appears unyieldingly sovereign. Perhaps that is why a tiny detail in the book's final act seems so thrilling—"And in the thirty-seventh year of the exile *of Jehoiachin king of Judah*, in the twelfth month, on the twenty-seventh day of the month, Evil-merodach king of Babylon..." (25:27; emphasis mine). Did you catch that? Whereas Nebuchadnezzar had once been the basis of Israel's timeline, he has now been unseated, and chronological reckoning is restored to as it had been before the Exile. The lamp of David is once again the standard. Likewise, it is no small thing that Christians reckon time by the advent of our Lord—*before Christ* and *anno Domini*. Chronology is sovereignty, and as long as we continue to use B.C. and A.D., we exiles will continue to hear the roar of the Lion of Judah.

---

159. Wray Beal, *1 & 2 Kings*, 531.

160. Leithart, *1 & 2 Kings*, 276.

EPILOGUE

The first book of the New Testament begins with the genealogy of Jesus Christ, affirming how he was "the son of David," (Matt 1:1). Very carefully, the apostolic evangelist traces our Lord's lineage from Abraham to Judah to David, and on through Hezekiah, Josiah, and the final kings of Judah. Scholars note that the genealogy is actually incomplete; Matthew intentionally leaves out various names (including the names of a few Judean monarchs known to Kings) in order to create three lists of fourteen names. In Hebrew, the consonants *d* and *w* held numerical values of four and six respectively. Those same consonants make up the name *David* in Hebrew, *dwd*, meaning the name *David* adds up to fourteen (four + six + four). By providing three (a significant biblical number) lists of fourteen names each, Matthew is pointing to Jesus' exclusive claim to the throne and lamp of David.[1]

But as we make our way through the Gospels, Jesus speaks less of thrones and more of crosses. This naturally confused the apostles, who no doubt signed on to be followers of this itinerant rabbi with visions of imperial cabinet positions dancing in their heads. Jesus entered Jerusalem triumphantly on the back of a donkey (Matt 21:1–11), much like Solomon had a thousand years prior. As soldiers had done for Jehu, the crowd spread their coats out before Christ, confident he too would overthrow a brutal, oppressive regime. The Jews hailed him as the "Son of David," but crucified their king less than a week later out of disillusionment and disappointment. Yet, as Christ was about to ascend into heaven, the apostles were still inquiring as to his plans to establish an earthly kingdom (Acts 1:6).

---

1. Leon Morris, *The Gospel according to Matthew* (Grand Rapids: Eerdmans, 1992), 23.

The early chapters of this book ended with Christological reflections, but the latter chapters did not. I did that on purpose; as I drew closer to the end of 2 Kings, it became apparent to me that the Holy Spirit was hammering one point home about Jesus more so than all the others. Though the human narrator may not have been aware of the point—the Old Testament writers often wrote of greater truth than they realized (1 Pet 1:10–12; 2 Pet 1:19)—we are intended to conclude that every king in Jerusalem, no matter how righteous, was wholly inadequate for what the people needed. Like kudzu on a hillside, the vines and branches of sin had spread too far; the tree of Israel needed to be cut down to the Stump of Jesse (Isa 11:1).

Kings opens with an impressive display of Solomon's wisdom and glory. Surely his is a kingdom we would love to inherit. But we saw that it was a house of cards, one that collapsed under the weight of selfishness and idolatry. After Solomon, wisdom disappears from Israel, "a sign that wisdom is not capable of preserving Israel from division and ultimately dissolution unless it comes as an incarnation of divine wisdom."[2] Likewise, the end of Kings introduces us to Josiah. His righteousness surpasses all those before or after him. Though he knows exile is inevitable, he nonetheless seeks to reform Judah and rededicate her to her God. Unlike all the other kings, he hears the Law and obeys it, for he has a "hearing heart" (2 Kgs 22:11, 18–19; 23:25). Yet, not even Josiah's obedience to the Law is enough. "Josiah points to Jesus largely because of his failure, by showing that the law is weak and by leaving Israel desperately hoping for a greater king to perform what the law cannot accomplish."[3]

The German philosopher Georg Hegel once quipped, "But what experience and history teach is this—that nations and governments have never learned anything from history or acted upon any lessons they might have drawn from it."[4] As a lifelong history buff, I realize Hegel's words ring true. Particularly, some of us can be slow to recognize that every king, president, and dictator is hopelessly flawed. Some of us expect perfection from our leaders, and we become disillu-

---

2. Leithart, *1 & 2 Kings*, 270.

3. Ibid. "It is a central mystery of the Book of Kings that Josiah's pious turning back to God will lead to no greater reward than does the repentance of Ahab but to a mere delay in judgment for a generation," (Nelson, *First and Second Kings*, 143).

4. Georg Wilhelm Friedrich Hegel, *Lectures on the Philosophy of World History*, trans. H. B. Nisbet (Cambridge: Cambridge Univ. Press, 1975), 21.

sioned when their sins are exposed. There is only One who has been tempted in every way, yet remained morally unscathed (Heb 4:15). He is the King of kings.

Others of us live under the delusion that a leader's weaknesses don't matter that much (and especially if said leader is of our political persuasion). We are willing to overlook certain revolting traits if the economy is strong, taxes are low, and our national defense is formidable. We are no better than the Israelites who came to Rehoboam at Shechem, petitioning not for the restoration of spiritual righteousness, but the alleviation of secular burdens. Too often, Christians' interest in politics concerns more of the here-and-now and less of the hereafter.

In the event that you aren't getting my point, let alone one of the major points of Kings, let me put it in bold italics. *Every earthly leader will one day disappoint you.* Political leaders. Church leaders. Business leaders. Good leaders. Bad leaders. Righteous leaders. Wicked leaders. Leaders who know the Word and live it; leaders who call it "Two" Corinthians and mistake communion bread for the contribution plate. All these leaders merit our respect, for they hold their positions by God's decree (Rom 13:1). But they should never be invested with our hope and trust. In the grand scheme of things, earthly leaders are severely limited by heaven's sovereignty concerning what they can do to the elect of God. Perhaps this is why Paul never railed much against the wickedness of Rome's emperors—they mattered little to the grander purposes of the gospel.

The ultimate message of Kings for the church of Christ can be summarized in these four statements:

1. *Our future is not determined by us, but by God's Word.* We cannot outwork or outwit the Word or will of the Lord; resistance is futile. It will surely come to pass, for it stands forever.

2. *Our future is never subject to fate, but to God's faithfulness.* Just as God's faithfulness to David was the key to Israel's hope, so a Son of David is the key to ours. Christ will never forsake us.

3. *Our future is not in institutions, but in God.* Though she lost her Temple, throne, and land, Israel never lost her God. As long as the church has a God, she has a future.

4. *Our future is secured by God, so the proper response is trust and obedience.* There is no other way to be happy in Jesus. The faithful are citizens of an unshakable kingdom.

Like ancient Israel, every earthly kingdom is doomed to eventual exile. When the archangel gives that much-anticipated trumpet blast, nations will be destroyed. Despots will be deposed. Rods of earthly iron will be snapped in two. Dogs and vultures will feast on the flesh of those who—like Jeroboam, Baasha, and Ahab—were deluded enough to stand against the King of kings (Rev 19:17–21). And as every other crown is ground to dust and every throne is resigned to gather cobwebs, the kingdom will become the Lord's. Even now, he reigns, but not every enemy has been placed under his feet (1 Cor 15:26)—and so we look forward to that day.

As we wait, Christians are to be about their Father's business. The pages of Kings are full of salt-of-the-earth people who made a difference. Some were in great positions of influence—Nathan, Elijah, Obadiah, and Elisha. Others were not—the unnamed Judean prophet who condemned Jeroboam's altar, the Shunnamite woman who showed hospitality, Naaman's slave girl who evangelized her master. But whether weak or powerful, they were each willing to be instruments in the hands of the Lord. They each were witnesses to the fact that not a single Word of God will fail, for it stands forever. They each, along with us, now await the consummation of all things, the time when we inherit a kingdom that will never pass away, one lit by a Lamp that will never be extinguished (Rev 21:3).

Lord, come quickly.

ABBREVIATIONS

ABD *The Anchor Bible Dictionary.* Ed. David Noel Freedman. 6 vols. New York: Doubleday, 1992.

ANET *Ancient Near Eastern Texts Relating to the Old Testament.* Ed. James B. Pritchard. 3rd ed. Princeton, NJ: Princeton Univ. Press, 1969.

AUSS *Andrews University Seminary Studies*

BA *Biblical Archaeologist*

BAR *Biblical Archaeology Review*

BASOR *Bulletin of the American Schools of Oriental Research*

Bib *Biblica*

BibSac *Bibliotheca Sacra*

BJRL *Bulletin of the John Rylands Library*

CBQ *Catholic Biblical Quarterly*

CEV Contemporary English Version

COS *The Context of Scripture.* Ed. William W. Hallo. 3 vols. Leiden: Brill, 1997–2003.

DDD *Dictionary of Deities and Demons in the Bible.* 2nd ed. Ed. Karel van der Toorn, Bob Becking, and Pieter W. Van der Horst. Grand Rapids: Eerdmans, 1999.

DOTHB *Dictionary of the Old Testament: Historical Books.* Eds. Bill T. Arnold and H. G. M. Williamson. Downers Grove, IL: InterVarsity Press, 2005.

ESV	English Standard Version
EvQ	*Evangelical Quarterly*
HALOT	*The Hebrew and Aramaic Lexicon of the Old Testament.* Ludwig Koehler, Walter Baumgartner. Trans. and ed. M. E. J. Richardson. 4 vols. Leiden: Brill, 1994–99.
HCSB	Holman Christian Standard Bible
IDB	*The Interpreter's Dictionary of the Bible.* Ed. George Arthur Buttrick. 4 vols. Nashville: Abingdon, 1962.
IEJ	*Israel Exploration Journal*
ISBE	*The International Standard Bible Encyclopedia.* Ed. G. W. Bromiley. 4 vols. Grand Rapids: Eerdmans, 1986.
JAOS	*Journal of the American Oriental Society*
JBL	*Journal of Biblical Literature*
JBQ	*Jewish Bible Quarterly*
JETS	*Journal of the Evangelical Theological Society*
JHS	*Journal of Hebrew Scriptures*
JJS	*Journal of Jewish Studies*
JNES	*Journal of Near Eastern Studies*
JQR	*Jewish Quarterly Review*
JRJ	*Journal of Reformed Judaism*
JSOT	*Journal for the Study of the Old Testament*
JSS	*Journal of Semitic Studies*
KJV	King James Version
LXX	Septuagint, the Greek translation of the Old Testament
Msg	The Message
NASU	New American Standard Bible — Updated Edition
NBD	*New Bible Dictionary.* 3rd ed. Ed. D. R. W. Wood. Downers Grove, IL: 1996.
NCV	New Century Version

NEAEHL	*The New Encyclopedia of Archaeological Excavations in the Holy Land.* Ed. Ephraim Stern. 4 vols. Jerusalem: Israel Exploration Society, 1993.
NIBD	*The New Interpreter's Bible Dictionary.* Ed. Katharine Doob Sakenfeld. Nashville: Abingdon, 2006–09.
NIDOTTE	*New International Dictionary of Old Testament Theology and Exegesis.* Ed. Willem A. VanGemeren. 5 vols. Grand Rapids: Zondervan, 1997.
NIV	New International Version
NJB	New Jerusalem Bible
NKJV	New King James Version
NLT	New Living Translation
NRSV	New Revised Standard Version
NT	New Testament
NUBD	*The New Unger's Bible Dictionary.* Ed. R. K. Harrison. Rev. ed. Chicago: Moody Press, 1988.
OT	Old Testament
PEQ	*Palestine Exploration Quarterly*
SJOT	*Scandinavian Journal of the Old Testament*
SJT	*Scottish Journal of Theology*
TynBul	*Tyndale Bulletin*
UF	*Ugarit-Forschungen*
VT	*Vetus Testamentum*
ZAW	*Zeitschrift für die alttestamentliche Wissenschaft*
ZDPV	*Zeitschrift des deutschen Palästina-Vereins*

ACKNOWLEDGMENTS

To all those who have sat with us in our grief. Words cannot express my gratitude.

To Kirk Brothers. Many years ago, you introduced me to Kings with the headline, "How to Lose a Kingdom in 400 Years." Good titles are long remembered. Thank you for blessing this book with your words.

To Jeff Jenkins. "My father, my father! The chariots of Israel and its horsemen!"

To Jesse Robertson. For the paper clips—and for so much more.

To Lindsay Ray for her exceptional talent and assistance in research.

To Kristy Hinson and Katie Gilchrist for making this drivel readable. You both are editors of the first rank.

To Josh Feit for, time and again, designing amazing covers for all the books published by Start2Finish.

To Shirley Eaton. Hittites around the world salute you.

To Audrey and Mikaela. I pray every day that God will make you a blessing in Israel. Your daddy loves you.

To my wonderful, amazing, long-suffering wife. Thank you for bearing so patiently with me during this project.

To the King of kings. Blessing and honor and glory and power forever and ever!

BIBLIOGRAPHY

Aharoni, Yohanan. *The Land of the Bible: A Historical Geography*. Trans. A. F. Rainey. London: Burns, 1967.

Alter, Robert. *Ancient Israel: The Former Prophets: Joshua, Judges, Samuel, and Kings*. New York: Norton, 2013.

Auld, A. Graeme. *I & II Kings*. Philadelphia: Westminster, 1986.

Barnes, William H. *1–2 Kings*. Carol Stream, IL: Tyndale, 2012.

Beek, M. A. "The Meaning of the Expression 'The Chariots and the Horsemen of Israel' (II Kings ii 12)," in *The Witness of Tradition: Papers Read at the Joint British-Dutch Old Testament Conference held at Woudschoten, 1970*. Leiden: Brill, 1972.

Bright, John. *A History of Israel*. 4th ed. Louisville: Westminster John Knox, 2000.

Brueggemann, Walter. *1 & 2 Kings*. Macon, GA: Smyth & Helwys, 2000.

Cogan, Mordechai. *I Kings*. New York: Doubleday, 2001.

—. *II Kings*. New Haven, CT: Yale Univ. Press, 2008.

Cogan, Morton. *Imperialism and Religion: Assyria, Judah and Israel in the Eighth and Seventh Centuries B.C.E.* Missoula, MT: Scholars, 1974.

Davis, Dale Ralph. *1 Kings*. Ross-shire, Scotland: Christian Focus, 2002.

—. *2 Kings*. Ross-shire, Scotland: Christian Focus, 2005.

DeVries, Simon J. *1 Kings*. 2nd ed. Nashville: Nelson, 2003.

de Vaux, Ronald. *Ancient Israel*. 2 vols. New York: McGraw-Hill, 1965.

Fretheim, Terence E. *First and Second Kings*. Louisville: Westminster John Knox, 1999.

Fritz, Volkmar. *1 & 2 Kings*. Trans. Anselm Hagedorn. Minneapolis: Fortress, 2003.

Ginzberg, Louis. *Legends of the Jews*. 2nd ed. Trans. Henrietta Szold and Paul Radin. Philadelphia: Jewish Publication Society, 2003.

Goldingay, John. *1 and 2 Kings for Everyone*. Louisville: Westminster John Knox, 2011.

Gray, John. *I & II Kings*. Philadelphia: Westminster, 1963.

Hagan, G. Michael. "First and Second Kings," in *A Complete Literary Guide to the Bible*. Eds. Leland Ryken and Tremper Longman III. Grand Rapids: Zondervan, 1993.

Hens-Piazza, Gina. *1–2 Kings*. Nashville: Abingdon, 2006.

Herzog, Chaim and Mordechai Gichon. *Battles of the Bible*. Toronto: Stoddart, 1997.

Hobbs, T. R. *2 Kings*. Waco: Word, 1985.

House, Paul R. *1, 2 Kings*. Nashville: Broadman, 1995.

Hubbard, Robert L., Jr. *First and Second Kings*. Chicago: Moody, 1991.

Inrig, Gary. *I & II Kings*. Nashville: Holman, 2003.

Jones, Gwilym H. *1 and 2 Kings*. 2 vols. Grand Rapids: Eerdmans, 1984.

Keil, C. F., and F. Delitzsch. *Biblical Commentary on the Old Testament*. Vol. 6. Grand Rapids: Eerdmans, 1950.

Kenyon, Kathleen M. *Digging up Jerusalem*. New York: Praeger, 1974.

King, Philip J. and Lawrence E. Stager. *Life in Biblical Israel*. Louisville: Westminster John Knox, 2001.

Kitchen, K. A. *The Third Immediate Period in Egypt (1100–650 B.C.)*. 2nd ed. Warminster, England: Aris, 1986.

Konkel, August H. *1 & 2 Kings*. Grand Rapids: Zondervan, 2006.

Leithart, Peter J. *1 & 2 Kings*. Grand Rapids: Brazos, 2006.

Maclaren, Alexander. *Expositions of Holy Scripture*. 32 vols. Grand Rapids: Baker, 1984.

Malamat, A. "The Twilight of Judah: In the Egyptian-Babylonian Maelstrom," in *Congress Volume: Edinburgh 1974*. Vol. 28. Leiden: Brill, 1975.

McKay, J. W. *Religion in Judah Under the Assyrians, 732–609 BC*. Naperville, IL: Allenson, 1973

Miller, J. Maxwell, and John H. Hayes. *A History of Ancient Israel and Judah*. 2nd ed. Louisville: Westminster John Knox, 2006.

Monson, John. "1 Kings," in *Zondervan Illustrated Bible Backgrounds Commentary*. Vol 3. Ed. John H. Walton. Grand Rapids: Zondervan, 2009.

—. "The Temple of Solomon: Heart of Jerusalem," in *Zion, City of Our God*. Eds. Richard S. Hess and Gordon J. Wenham. Grand Rapids: Eerdmans, 1999.

Montgomery, James A. *A Critical and Exegetical Commentary on the Books of Kings*. New York: Scribner's, 1951.

Nelson, Richard D. *First and Second Kings*. Louisville: John Knox, 1987.

Olley, John W. *The Message of Kings*. Downers Grove, IL: InterVarsity Press, 2011.

Patterson, Richard D. and Hermann J. Austel. "1, 2 Kings," in *The Expositor's Bible Commentary*. Rev. ed. Vol. 3. Eds. Tremper Longman III and David E. Garland. Grand Rapids: Zondervan, 2009.

Provan, Iain W. *1 & 2 Kings*. Peabody, MA: Hendrickson, 1995.

—. "2 Kings," in *Zondervan Illustrated Bible Backgrounds Commentary*. Vol 3. Ed. John H. Walton. Grand Rapids: Zondervan, 2009.

Provan, Iain, V. Philips Long, and Tremper Longman III. *A Biblical History of Israel*. Louisville: Westminster John Knox, 2003.

Robinson, J. *The First Book of Kings*. Cambridge: Cambridge Univ. Press, 1972.

—. *The Second Book of Kings*. Cambridge: Cambridge Univ. Press, 1976.

Sweeney, Marvin A. *I & II Kings*. Louisville: Westminster John Knox, 2007.

Thiele, Edwin R. *The Mysterious Numbers of the Hebrew Kings*. Rev. ed. Grand Rapids: Kregel, 1983.

Wallace, Ronald S. *Readings in 1 Kings*. Grand Rapids: Eerdmans, 1996.

Walsh, Jerome T. *1 Kings*. Collegeville, MN: Liturgical Press, 1996.

Walton, John H., Victor H. Matthews, and Mark W. Chavalas. *The IVP Bible Background Commentary: Old Testament*. Downers Grove, IL: InterVarsity Press, 2000.

Wiseman, Donald J. *1 and 2 Kings*. Downers Grove, IL: InterVarsity Press, 2008.

Wood, Leon. *A Survey of Israel's History*. Grand Rapids: Zondervan, 1970.

Wray Beal, Lissa M. *1 & 2 Kings*. Downers Grove, IL: InterVarsity Press, 2014.

Yadin, Yigael. *The Art of Warfare in Biblical Lands: In the Light of Archaeological Discovery*. London: Weidenfeld, 1963.

Zevit, Ziony. "1 Kings," in *The Jewish Study Bible*. Eds. Adele Berlin and Marc Zvi Brettler. Oxford: Oxford Univ. Press, 2004.

—. "2 Kings," in *The Jewish Study Bible*. Eds. Adele Berlin and Marc Zvi Brettler. Oxford: Oxford Univ. Press, 2004.

KINGS OF ISRAEL

Date	Name	Notes
930–909	Jeroboam I	introduced idolatry at Dan and Bethel
909–908	Nadab	assassinated by Baasha
908–886	Baasha	eliminated House of Jeroboam
886–885	Elah	assassinated by Zimri
885	Zimri	eliminated House of Baasha; reigned a week; committed suicide
885–874	Omri	moved capital to Samaria; subdued Moab
874–853	Ahab	most wicked of all Israel's kings
853–852	Ahaziah	son of Ahab; died of injuries
852–841	Jehoram	son of Ahab; assassinated by Jehu
841–814	Jehu	eliminated Baal and House of Ahab from Israel
814–798	Jehoahaz	wicked, but asked God for relief from Hazael
798–782	Jehoash	present at Elisha's deathbed; expanded Israel's territory
793–753	Jeroboam II	longest-reigning king of Israel; expanded Israel's territory
753	Zechariah	assassinated by Shallum
753	Shallum	reigned a month; assassinated by Menahem
752–742	Menahem	committed heinous war crimes; supported by Tiglath-pileser III
742–740	Pekahiah	assassinated by Pekah
752–732	Pekah	rival of Menahem; reigned from Gilead at first; assassinated by Hoshea
732–723	Hoshea	most righteous king of Israel, but still wicked

KINGS OF JUDAH

Date	Name	Notes
970–930	Solomon	started out righteous; built the Temple
930–913	Rehoboam	king responsible for Israel's division; wicked
913–910	Abijam	wicked
910–869	Asa	righteous, but did not eliminate the high places
872–848	Jehoshaphat	righteous, but had an alliance with House of Ahab
853–841	Joram	wicked, married to Athaliah, Ahab's daughter
841	Ahaziah	wicked, assassinated by Jehu
841–835	Athaliah	mother of Ahaziah; not considered legitimate ruler by narrator, reign of terror for six years
835–796	Joash	started out righteous; renovated the Temple; assassinated by his servants
796–767	Amaziah	righteous; defeated Edom; assassinated
792–740	Azariah	righteous; struck with leprosy
750–732	Jotham	righteous; rebuilt Judah's defenses
732–715	Ahaz	wicked; willingly subjected Judah to Assyria
715–686	Hezekiah	righteous; led significant religious reform
696–642	Manasseh	longest-reigning king, but also the most wicked
642–640	Amon	wicked; assassinated
640–609	Josiah	righteous; led most important religious reform; killed in battle by Pharaoh Neco
609	Jehoahaz	wicked; reigned 3 months; deposed by Neco
609–598	Jehoiakim	wicked; son of Josiah; assassinated(?)
598–597	Jehoiachin	wicked, son of Jehoiakim; honored in exile
597–586	Zedekiah	wicked; son of Josiah; died in Babylon

ὥσπερ ξένοι χαίρουσι πατρίδα βλέπειν
οὕτως καὶ τοῖς κάμνουσι βιβλίου τέλος

www.ingramcontent.com/pod-product-compliance
Lightning Source LLC
Chambersburg PA
CBHW051708020426
42333CB00014B/891